J. E. (Joseph Epiphane) Darras, Charles I. (Charles Ignatius) White,

M. J. (Martin John) Spalding

A General History Of The Catholic Church From The Commencement Of The Christian Era

Volume 2

J. E. (Joseph Epiphane) Darras, Charles I. (Charles Ignatius) White, M. J. (Martin John) Spalding

A General History Of The Catholic Church From The Commencement Of The Christian Era
Volume 2

ISBN/EAN: 9783742852595

Manufactured in Europe, USA, Canada, Australia, Japa

Cover: Foto ©Thomas Meinert / pixelio.de

Manufactured and distributed by brebook publishing software
(www.brebook.com)

J. E. (Joseph Epiphane) Darras, Charles I. (Charles Ignatius) White,

M. J. (Martin John) Spalding

A General History Of The Catholic Church From The

Commencement Of The Christian Era

A

GENERAL HISTORY

OF THE

CATHOLIC CHURCH:

FROM THE COMMENCEMENT OF THE CHRISTIAN ERA
UNTIL THE PRESENT TIME.

BY,
Joseph Épiphane
M. L'ABBE J. E. DARRAS.

FIRST AMERICAN FROM THE LAST FRENCH EDITION.

WITH AN

INTRODUCTION AND NOTES

Martin John
BY THE MOST REV. M. J. SPALDING, D. D.,

ARCHBISHOP OF BALTIMORE.

VOL. II.

NEW YORK:

P. O'SHEA, PUBLISHER,
27 BARCLAY STREET.
1868.

1872, Feb. 29.
Minot Fund.

CONTENTS.

THIRD PERIOD.

CHAPTER I.

CHAPTER II.

CHAPTER IV.

CHAPTER V.

CHAPTER VI.

CHAPTER VII.

CHAPTER VIII.

CHAPTER IX.

CHAPTER X.

CHAPTER XI.

CHAPTER XII.

FOURTH PERIOD.

CHAPTER I.

CHAPTER II.

CHAPTER V.

CHAPTER VI.

CHAPTER VII.

CHAPTER VIII.

GENERAL HISTORY OF THE CHURCH.

THIRD PERIOD.

From the Fall of the Western Empire (A. D. 476) to its Re-establishment under Charlemagne (A. D. 800).

CHAPTER I.

SUMMARY.

§ I. Pontificate of St. Simplicius (a. d. 476—483). *Second Period.*

1. General view of the third period of Church History.—2. Political division of the Western Empire.—3. Council of Arles.—4. Faustus, bishop of Reez. —5. Persecution of the Church of Africa by Hunneric.—6. Revolution in Constantinople. The Emperor Zeno exiled by Basiliscus.—7. Restoration of Zeno. Reaction in favor of orthodoxy against Eutychianism.—8. Acacius, Patriarch of Constantinople, embraces Eutychianism.—9. Zeno's *Henoticon* —10. Theological estimate of the *Henoticon.*—11. John Talaia, lawful Patriarch of Alexandria, is driven from his see, and flies to Rome.—12. Death of St. Simplicius. Various acts of this Pope's pontificate in the West.

§ II. Pontificate of St. Felix III. (a. d. March 8, 483—February 28, 492).

13. Election of St. Felix III. Odoacer, king of the Heruli, claims the right to confirm pontifical elections.—14. Council of Rome. Apostolic legates sent to the Emperor Zeno.—15. The legates weakly prove false to their mission. —16. Council of Rome. Condemnation of the legates.—17. Deposition of Acacius. Other legates are sent to Constantinople, who also apostatize, and are condemned by St. Felix III.—18. Acephali.—19. Council of Rome. Confirmation of the sentence against Acacius.—20. Death of Acacius. Euphemius, his successor.—21. St. Sabas. St. Theodosius the Cenobite.— 22. Gontamund in Africa. Council of Rome in favor of the Catholic bishops of Africa.—23. End of the rule of the Heruli. Theodoric the Great, king of the Ostrogoths, in Italy.—24. Death of St. Felix III.

§ I. Pontificate of St. Simplicius (a. d. 476—483). *Second Period.*

1. The third period of Ecclesiastical History opens at the moment when the extinction of the Western Empire made

Vol. II.—1

room for the appearance of new nations hitherto shut out from the pale of ancient civilization, and foreign to the intellectual, political, and religious impulse given to the age by Christianity. The Goths, Germans and Franks saw, in the Church, an independent society, which had neither shared the overthrow of the Roman Empire, nor been crushed by its fall. The influence of the Christian religion was, therefore, but increased by this great political event; and the bishops found themselves naturally at the head of the new world, which they controlled by the superiority of a hierarchy which had proved stronger than all other institutions—more lasting than the very empire. The various provinces of the West were parcelled out by barbarians whose very name was a terror to the Roman race everywhere oppressed as the weaker power. The Church interposed between the victor and the vanquished, to afford protection, mercy and peace; she was not unequal to the mission. The Pope and the bishops became the connecting link between the barbarian element and the old nationalities; and by opening the way for a fusion of the races, they became the fathers of modern civilization. This is the political achievement described in a single word by the infidel historian, Gibbon, when he compares it to the formation of the hive by the bees. As the Church went on scattering broadcast her blessings, grateful nations gradually clothed her with an almost unlimited power, even in temporal matters; and thus the Middle Ages show us the Papacy controlling kings and people, not by any usurpation of power, but by a necessary consequence, and as if by the very logic of events.

2. After the fall of the empire the West was politically divided as follows: the Arian Vandals held Africa; the Suevi and Visigoths were masters of Spain; the Franks and Burgundians had settled in Gaul, the Anglo-Saxons in Great Britain; the Heruli, and after them the Ostrogoths, ruled Italy. The East was still governed by the emperors of Constantinople; but court intrigues, domestic strife and weakened authority, the unfailing marks of an irretrievable decline, began to character-

ize this sad period, which has been branded with the name of
Lower Empire. Zeno, a weak and capricious prince, the tool
of men and the sport of events, though altogether unable to
uphold the rights of his crown, still tried to exercise, in spiritual
matters, an authority which he was powerless to shield from
contempt in the government of his states; and in the attempt
to bring about a general reconciliation of opinion, only made a
wider breach. The Persians, who held sway over Armenia and
the provinces of Upper Syria, still carried on against the Christians the system of persecution which had furnished so many
victims to the fury of Sapor II. Such was the situation of the
political and religious world in 476, at the second period of the
pontificate of St. Simplicius—a period made memorable by the
fall of the Roman Empire, which had just yielded under the
blows of Odoacer, the youthful barbarian who had received
the blessing of St. Severinus and had since become king of the
Heruli.

3. St. Simplicius had not quitted Rome during this season
of confusion. He kept his post at the Church's helm, and by
words and means succored the Christian communities suffering
under so many revolutions. The Franks were destined to lead
the way for the barbarous tribes in bending submissively to
the yoke of faith. Among its high prerogatives, this nation,
called to so noble a destiny, was to bear the title of *Eldest
Daughter* of the Church. The Gallic provinces which were
now under the rule of the Franks, boasted a generation of holy
bishops in the various sees. A council held at Arles (A. D.
476), against the Predestinarian heresy, was illustrated by such
names as St. Patiens of Lyons, St. Sidonius Apollinaris of Clermont, St. Euphronius of Autun, and St. Eutropius of Orange,
who were all present. This council had been rendered necessary by the error of Lucidius, a priest of the province of Arles,
who had been misled by the teachings of Pelagius. The council renewed the anathemas already pronounced against the
propositions of the sectary. "If any one saith," decreed the
council, "that the damned had not, during life, received from

God the means necessary for salvation, and that men are thus cast into eternal darkness by the divine foreknowledge, let him be anathema." " If any one saith that Jesus Christ did not die for all men, and that He does not desire that all should be saved, let him be anathema." These formulas give very nearly the text of the errors broached, in later times, by the Jansenists. The Council of Arles was spared the necessity of pronouncing a personal condemnation against Lucidius. He had swerved, indeed, for a moment; but the voice of Faustus of Rees recalled him to his duty. A private interview with that prelate had dispelled all his doubts, and let in the pure light of Catholic faith to illumine the intellect for a moment clouded by Pelagian sophistry. Lucidius acknowledged his fault in a letter to the council, in which the perfect sincerity of his confession is only equalled by the clearness and precision of his retractation. " Your condemnation," he writes to the Fathers, "is salvation to the faithful, and your judgment strikes but to heal. I know no better means of redeeming my past errors than humble acknowledgment; I offer this wholesome confession as my best defence." The noble expression, in its very humility, does him greater honor, if possible, than the most splendid triumph. This submission to the voice of authority is an old tradition in the Church of France.

4. Faustus himself had but lately given an example of the same kind. In a work on the nature of spirits, more commendable for purity of style than of doctrine, he had laid down the proposition that God alone is a spiritual Being in every sense of the term; and that angels and souls are substances of a higher order than bodies, but still belonging to the material world. This heterodox teaching met with a spirited refutation from Claudian, brother of St. Mamertus, bishop of Vienne Claudian had been brought up in solitude, and there he had gathered treasures of learning. He was familiar with the best classical models of profane antiquity and deeply versed in Scriptural knowledge : these mental acquirements were enhanced by the external qualities with which he had been also

endowed. He was consulted as an oracle of learning and holiness. St. Mamertus, his brother, had secured him to his church in Vienne, by the bonds of the priesthood, and intrusted him with a part of the episcopal care. He was well fitted by his earlier studies to explain the Catholic teaching on the nature of the soul. His well-ripened notions on the highest questions of philosophy were brilliantly displayed in his three books on the *Nature of the Soul;* in which he goes to the very principle of the question and overthrows the incorrect theories of Faustus of Reez. Both parties profited by the issue of the contest. Claudian bore his triumph with all meekness; Faustus humbly admitted his error without reservation. It may justly be advanced, as a partial palliation of the error of Faustus, that the Church had not as yet pronounced on this subject. Thus the heterodox tone of some of his writings did not hinder his popular canonization at Reez, where a church was placed under his invocation. St. Sidonius Apollinaris held him in the highest esteem and admiration: "Faustus," he says, "would seem to have wedded philosophy after having made it humble and Christian. He led it to his monastery, and set the philosophy of Plato to defend the Church of Jesus Christ. His eloquence has outrun that of his masters and is only surpassed by the holiness of his life." The episcopal See of Limoges was, at the same period, illustrated by the virtues of St. Ruritius. Though sprung from a noble and wealthy family, he had cast off his great wealth, the honors of the world and the marriage-tie which bound him to Heria, daughter of the patrician Ommacius, to serve God in solitude, poverty and continence. He was soon drawn from out his retreat to assume the high but fearful responsibility of the episcopate, which he had never sought or desired; and he now consecrated his ample means to building, in the neighborhood of Limoges, a church in honor of St. Augustine, whose illustrious name had been more deeply fixed in the hearts of the Gallic bishops by the Pelagian attempts to defame the memory of the Doctor of Grace. Meanwhile Perpetuus, bishop of Tours, had persuaded Paulinus of Perigueux,

a Christian poet, to write the life of St. Martin, in verse.
Pomerius, a native of Mauritania, driven to Gaul by the Vandal
persecution in Africa, was chosen on account of his surpassing
qualities to govern a monastery near Arles. The fruits of his
studious retirement appeared in a dialogue on the *Nature of the
Soul*, and a treatise on the *Institution of Virgins*, neither of
which has reached us. The only writings of Pomerius still
extant are the three books on the *Contemplative Life*, long
attributed to St. Prosper.

5. Whilst the provinces of Gaul were thus rejoiced to see
the faith so flourishing under the care of illustrious and holy
bishops, closely united to the See of Rome, the Church of
Africa groaned under the tyranny of the Vandals who strove
to implant Arianism there by force of arms. Genseric died on
the 25th of January, A. D. 477, after a reign of thirty-seven
years, and was succeeded by his eldest son Hunneric, who had
married the Princess Eudoxia, sister of Zeno, Emperor of the
East. The Catholics at first entertained great hopes that the
influence of the new queen would be favorable to them. The
Church of Carthage, now twenty-seven years deprived of its
bishop, had been unable to obtain from Genseric the liberty to
elect another. Zeno's intercession drew the desired permission
from Hunneric; but the Vandal shackled his favor with such
restrictions as almost to annul its effect. The edict allowing
the election, and publicly proclaimed by the royal notary
Vitaritus, was worded as follows: "At the prayer of the
Emperor Zeno and of the most noble Placidia, his sister, our
master permits you to elect a bishop of your own choice:
provided the bishops of our religion, at Constantinople and in
the other provinces of the East, are allowed to preach in their
churches in whatever language they wish, and to carry on
their manner of worship, as you are at liberty here and in
your other churches in Africa, to celebrate the Mass, to preach
and to conduct your own worship. If this be not executed, the
bishop who may be consecrated here and the other bishops
shall be sent among the Moors." This was giving with one

hand and taking back with the other. The bishops present at the publication of this insidious edict cried out that they refused the election granted on conditions they were not at liberty to accept, and which left a continual opening for the tyranny of persecutors. But the people of Carthage, so long deprived of a pastor, insisted upon the election being held in spite of the restrictive clause. The unanimous vote fell upon a holy priest of the city, named Eugenius. His humility and the charity and compassion he showed toward the poor, had recommended him to the suffrage of both clergy and people. The fruits of his administration did not disappoint the hopes entertained of him. His eloquent discourses and yet more eloquent works were the means of conversion and salvation to many souls. The Arian bishops thought to check the progress of his apostolic work by obtaining from Hunneric a decree forbidding him to admit into his church any Christian of the Vandal race. They thought thus to shut in the holy bishop's zeal within the circle of native Africans who had long been attached to Catholicity, and to hinder the conversion of the Arians to the true faith. Eugenius refused to obey the unjust order. "The house of God," he answered, "is open to all; no one can drive out those who enter it."

This was the signal for persecution. Guards were stationed by Hunneric at the church doors, who plucked out the eyes or the hair of the Vandals as they tried to enter. The Catholics who held offices, honors or employments at court were banished to the plains of Utica, and made to share the hard field-work of the slaves. The consecrated virgins were put to the most cruel torture; the most infamous means were used to make them give testimony against the honor of the Catholic bishops and clergy. A general decree of banishment was at length issued against all bishops, priests, deacons and the most faithful Catholics. They were exiled, to the number of four thousand nine hundred and seventy-six, to the Maurita-nian deserts. The people thronged the route by which the con-fessors passed; the valleys were filled, the hill-sides covered by the faithful, bearing tapers in their hands and begging the blessing of the holy martyrs for their little children. On a day appointed by Hunneric himself, the 1st of February, A. D. 484, a conference was held in Carthage between the Catholic and the Arian bishops. Since good faith had been the last of the motives that suggested this meeting, it only afforded the royal barbarian a new occasion of urging the persecution. The Catholics had chosen ten of their principal bishops to uphold the cause of the faith. They were not heard. The Catholic bishops laid before Hunneric and the Arian prelates a clear profession of faith, embodying the true teaching on the unity of substance and the Trinity of the divine persons; on the necessity of the term *consubstantial*, or ὁμοούσιος, the divinity of the Holy Ghost, and, in fine, on all the dogmas attacked by the Arians. The Vandal king answered by a decree closing all the Catholic churches and confiscating their property, and handed over all the orthodox bishops and clergy to the action of the judicial tribunals. All the bishops who had been present at the conference of Carthage were thrown on board some vessels bound for the Island of Corsica, where they were employed in cutting timber for the building of ships. The faithful who remained true to the last were rewarded with the most painful torments. Whole cities were depopulated, and the inhabitants dragged into exile when Hunneric's butchers had cut out their tongues to the very roots. St. Eugenius, bishop of Carthage, was banished to a solitude near Tripoli, and placed under the tyrannical charge of an Arian bishop who subjected him to a long imprisonment in a damp cave, where he hoped to see him yield to ill treatment; but God preserved the holy prelate's life. The Arian bishops themselves became persecutors and torturers. They went through the country with bands of armed soldiers, rebaptized all whom they could find on the highways, and everywhere multiplied the number of their victims. In the mean time a fearful disease, which may well be deemed a punishment from God, was slowly wasting Hunneric's body. He died in the most torturing agonies, at the close of the year 484. This event put an end to the persecution, and recalled a host of exiles to their homes. The historian of this struggle of the African Church against Arian Vandalism, Victor, bishop of Vita, has preserved the names and recorded the sufferings of the many martyrs who then shed their blood for the faith. The fact that he was an eye-witness of what he relates, that he shared the banishment and persecution, lends a thrilling interest to his narrative. It is a long martyrology compiled in a spirit of faith and charity by a martyr's pen. In this desolated Church, even when the very name of Catholic was a title to proscription, the persecuted faith did not want for apologists. With the uplifted sword of the executioner glittering over their heads they still wrote eloquent works which have reached our own day. Antoninus, bishop of Cyrtha, addressed to the confessors a *Justification* of their faith, encouraging them to suffer for God and the truth. The errors of the Arians and Donatists were refuted by Cerealis, bishop of Castela, in Mauritania Cæsariensis, the present Algeria; Victor, bishop of Cartenna, in the same province; and Asclepias, bishop in the territory of Bagai, in Numidia. But all these learned doctors were surpassed in religious polemics by Vigilius, bishop of Tapsa. His numerous controversial works are all written in the form of dialogues. The Catholic interlocutor is represented as St. Augustine or St. Athanasius, names so precious to the African Church, and which seem, by the very authority of genius, to consecrate the truths of faith against Arianism, Manicheism and Eutychianism. These heresies speak through their authors, whom Vigilius introduces with the very arguments in support of their errors that they had used to make them popular. The Bishop of Tapsa writes in a grave, simple, clear and natural style. His doctrine is sound and established with solid arguments and unanswerable proofs drawn from the Scriptures and the Fathers of the Church. The objections proposed by the heretics are answered with a wonderful ease and penetration. His *Dialogues* against Arius,

Sabellius and Photinus, and his five *Books against Eutyches,*
are particularly remarkable.

6. The works against Eutychianism were more immediately
useful, as the East was still a prey to its ravages. In the beginning of his reign, the Emperor Zeno had taken into familiar
favor an apostate monk called Peter *the Fuller,* from his original trade. Peter made open profession of Eutychianism,
admitting only one nature in Jesus Christ. He endeavored to
give easier entrance to the error by adding to the *Trisagion* of
the Greeks, the words: *Thou Who wast crucified for us, have
mercy on us ;* thus ascribing the Passion to the three Persons of
the Trinity, by the unity of nature which he held to subsist in
the Person of Jesus Christ. The apostate succeeded, through
the favor of Zeno, in seizing upon the Patriarchal See of Antioch. But the emperor was at length undeceived by the protestations of Gennadius, Patriarch of Constantinople and of
the other Catholic bishops,—and Peter the Fuller was banished to an oasis in the Theban desert. But the vicissitude
of the times was soon to recall him. Zeno held but with feeble
grasp the sceptre which he was too weak to defend against
external enemies or the intrigues of his own court, and it was
snatched from his hand by his brother-in-law, Basiliscus. The
imperial fugitive sought the shelter of a fortress in Cappadocia,
where he placed his life in the care of a few faithful soldiers,
leaving the usurper to enjoy his short and turbulent reign.
Basiliscus inaugurated his reign by recalling Timothy Ælurus,
who had spent twenty years of exile in the Tauric Chersonesus. The murderer of Proterius now appeared in Constantinople, strong in the power of a usurper. At his approach,
Timothy Solofaciolus, the Catholic Patriarch, withdrew to the
monastery near Canopus, where he had formerly followed the
solitary life. Peter the Fuller was at the same time recalled
to Antioch by the usurper's order. Here he exercised patriarchal authority, ordained bishops for the various sees of the
province, and used all his influence to spread the Eutychian
error. Basiliscus, however, by his unrestrained abuse of power

soon provoked an energetic resistance in the very heart of
Constantinople. This emperor of fortune, who seemed bent
on sowing trouble and confusion in the Eastern Church, published an edict enjoining all the bishops and clergy to anathematize the Council of Chalcedon, on pain of deposition. Acacius, bishop of Constantinople, openly refused to sign the
impious decree; and to warn the faithful of the danger which
threatened the faith, he laid aside his episcopal insignia, put
on mourning and spread a black veil over the altar and the
Patriarchal throne. Happy would it have been for him had
he preserved the same courageous attachment to the true faith!
The priests and the abbots of the neighboring monasteries
rallied around their bishop who wrote, in conjunction with
them, to tell the Pope, St. Simplicius, what the Church was
suffering in the East. The Roman Pontiff multiplied his
efforts and his zeal to meet the serious crisis. He simultaneously wrote a letter to Basiliscus, two to the Eastern Patriarchs and one to the priests and archimandrites of Constantinople (A. D. 476). He urges the emperor to follow in the
footsteps of Marcian whose memory was held in benediction
by the Church; to remove the apostate usurpers from the Sees
of Alexandria and Antioch, and to protect the Catholic faith
against the Eutychian heresy. The Pope sent with his own
letter, one of St. Leo his predecessor, containing an explicit
development of the mystery of the Incarnation. "The rule
of Catholic teaching," wrote the Pontiff, "is ever the same in
the successors of him to whom our Lord left the care of His
fold with the promise of his unfailing help, *even to the consummation of ages.*" In his letter to Acacius, Simplicius directs
him as legate at the court of Constantinople to use all his
influence to procure the banishment of Timothy Ælurus, and to
thwart the plan, then on foot in the East, for the meeting of
another council.

The final sentence against Eutychianism had been pronounced at Chalcedon, and nothing now remained but simply
to carry it into execution. The Pope encouraged the priests

and archimandrites of Constantinople to resist the attempts
of the heretics, and sent them a copy of his letter to the
emperor.

7. Acacius, strengthened by the support of the Sovereign
Pontiff, left nothing undone to carry out his instructions. He
had recourse to St. Daniel, the Stylite, whose holiness and
eminent virtue had the greatest power over the minds of the
people, and told him of the perilous position of the Church
and the faith. Basiliscus dreaded the effect of an accusation
coming from the column where the holy hermit preached so
eloquently to the multitude by the sanctity of his life; he
therefore sent some of the officers of his court to complain
to the saint of what he called the insolence of Acacius, whom
he accused of stirring up the people against him. Daniel sent
back the reply to the emperor, that his reign would soon be
cut short as a punishment for his impiety, and that the hand
of God was already raised in anger against him. Moved by
the urgent entreaties of Acacius, the holy old man thought
that he might follow the example of St. Anthony who had, on
a similar occasion, gone into Alexandria to defend the persecuted Church. He accordingly repaired to Constantinople,
where the people were so moved at his presence that Basiliscus thought it prudent to quit the capital to escape the effects
of the popular emotion. From the palace into which he had
withdrawn, in the suburbs of the city, he sent messengers to
Daniel, but the hermit refused to receive them. The usurper
then came in person, hoping to win him over by this mark of
deference. Daniel publicly upbraided him for his fault and
added : "You shall soon feel the hand of Him who crushes
the mighty." The prediction did not long await fulfilment.
Zeno, who was still an exile in Isauria, soon received professions of loyalty from some of the most powerful senators
whom the tyranny of Basiliscus had revolted. Relying upon
their support, he marched toward Constantinople at the head
of a constantly swelling army of Isaurians, Lycaonians and
mercenary adventurers. Basiliscus, as cringing and base in

adversity as he had been haughty and proud in the moment of power, hastened, at these tidings, to the Church of St. Sophia, where he officially retracted all that he had done in favor of Timothy Ælurus and Peter the Fuller. He anathemathized Nestorius and Eutyches and received the Council of Chalcedon which he had hitherto rejected. But it was too late. The Thracian troops he had sent with his palace-guards against Zeno, after a bloody engagement under the walls of Niçe, went over to that prince's standard and he entered Constantinople in triumph (A. D. 477). Basiliscus was banished to Cappadocia, where he died of starvation. Zeno's first care was to go with the empress, to visit the holy solitary, Daniel, to whose prayers he ascribed his return. He wrote to St. Simplicius, intimating his desire to crush the Eutychian heresy, to enforce the decrees of the Council of Chalcedon and to restore Solofaciolus to the See of Alexandria. He accordingly annulled all the decrees issued by Basiliscus to the detriment of the faith and of the Catholic bishops. Peter the Fuller was deposed and the See of Antioch given to Stephen, a true Catholic. Paul of Ephesus suffered the same fate. Timothy Solofaciolus was restored to the throne of Alexandria. The intruder Ælurus is said to have caused his own death. The heretical bishops elected, as his successor, Peter *Mongus*, or the Stutterer, archdeacon of Timothy Ælurus, hoping by this means to perpetuate the schism in the Church of Alexandria. But Zeno gave them no time to carry out their plans. Peter Mongus was by the emperor's order sent into exile. The energetic measures adopted by the emperor to uphold the Catholic faith in the principal Eastern sees, caused a violent reaction on the part of the heretics. St. Stephen, legitimate Patriarch of Antioch, who had succeeded the usurper Peter the Fuller, was killed in his own church in the heat of a popular tumult; his mangled body was dragged through the streets of the city, loaded with outrages and then thrown into the Orontes. Zeno dealt by the ringleaders of the sedition with the utmost severity, and would have made the rebellious city feel the further weight of his indignation, had they not sent a deputation of their chief citizens to solicit forgiveness. The emperor granted it. A new Patriarch, Stephen the Younger, was elected for Antioch and consecrated at Constantinople by Acacius. This consecration was not conformable to canonical rule; it should regularly have been performed at Antioch, by the assembled bishops of Syria. To secure the validation of the act the emperor and Acacius wrote to Pope Simplicius. They urged the great necessity in which they were placed to act thus and to overlook the canonical observance in order to establish quiet in Antioch. St. Simplicius received their explanation; and in a letter to the emperor, dated June 22, A. D. 479, he expressed himself as follows: "Since you have deemed it necessary for the peace of Antioch to consecrate a bishop for that see in Constantinople, still reserving to the assembly of the Eastern bishops the right of consecrating the bishop of Antioch for the future, the Apostle St. Peter receives your promise and your oath, provided that this exceptional case be not hereafter adduced as a precedent." The Sovereign Pontiff at the same time addressed the same explanation and caution to the bishop of Constantinople.

8. Peace was thus restored to the Eastern Churches. In justice to Zeno it should be stated that for the two years which followed his restoration, he left nothing untried to bring about this desirable result. But the uprightness of intention, for which we must give him credit, was supported neither by prudence, strength of mind nor connection of design; in a word, by none of the qualities which make a great prince. Guided by Acacius, he was not long in spoiling his own work and affixed his name to a too famous edict, the source of numberless divisions in the Church. The first troubles were occasioned by the death of Timothy Solofaciolus, Patriarch of Alexandria (A. D. 482). The bishops, clergy and monks of the city, elected, as his legitimate successor, John Talaïa, a zealous priest, whose talents and virtue had won the appreciation of Solofaciolus, by whom he was accordingly intrusted with the ad-

ministration of the temporal affairs of the Church. John Talaïa
immediately wrote to St. Simplicius to obtain letters of communion, and at the same time sent circulars to the bishops of
the great Eastern and Western sees to notify them of his election. By an unfortunate combination of circumstances Acacius of Constantinople only received Talaïa's letter after having already learned his election, though indirectly. This involuntary delay in the transmission of the Synodal letters was
enough to prejudice Acacius against John Talaïa. He determined to use all his influence with the emperor to procure the
nullification of Talaïa's election. Without troubling himself
to reconcile his past conduct with his new-born resentment, he
urged upon the emperor the reappointment to Alexandria of
the intruder Peter Mongus whose banishment he had so
strongly urged. He persuaded the emperor that the two factions, Catholic and Eutychian, would continue to disturb Alexandria until a bishop was elected equally acceptable to both
parties. "Peter Mongus," he said, "will perfectly fulfil this
condition. The Eutychians are devoted to him; the Catholics
can urge no reasonable objection against him when he has once
abjured his error." Peter Mongus was secretly informed of
the intrigue in his favor and had it seconded by all his friends
at court. He pledged himself to bring about a union of the
two parties, and Zeno, deceived by this skilful strategy, yielded
to the natural weakness of his character. He wrote to the
Pope, protesting the unworthiness of Talaïa, and asked for the
restoration of Peter Mongus to the See of Alexandria, as the
only means of pacification. Simplicius returned no direct
reply to this communication of the emperor. On the 15th of
July, A. D. 482, he wrote to Acacius expressing his surprise and
grief at having received no letter from him in connection with
Zeno's, in so important a matter. He adds: "The acts of a
very full and orthodox council held in Egypt, were lately sent
to this See, according to the usual custom. They informed
us, at once, of the death of our brother of holy memory, the
Bishop Timothy, and of the unanimous choice of the faithful

which had placed John in the vacant see. As he was believed
to be gifted with all the qualities that make a good bishop,
it seemed that there was nothing left but to thank God, to
rejoice that a Catholic bishop had, without difficulty, succeeded
the deceased prelate, and to give to his authority, by the confirmation of the Apostolic See, the *desired stability.* Yet I have
just received letters from the emperor, in which he represents
Talaia as unworthy of that exalted dignity. I have, therefore,
suspended the sentence of confirmation lest I be accused of
having acted too inconsiderately in a matter of so great moment." These words are remarkable, inasmuch as they go to
prove the right of the Pope on the confirmation of bishops.
1st. We find a council, and a full council, asking the Pope's
approval of an episcopal election carried on canonically and
without opposition. 2d. Though John had been consecrated
immediately after his election, still his authority, to be full,
entire, unshaken, needs to be *confirmed* by the approval of the
Holy See. St. Simplicius, in his letter to Acacius, formally
opposed the restoration of Peter Mongus to the Patriarchal See
of Alexandria. "This promise," says the Pope, "to embrace
the true faith, can only secure his return into Catholic communion, but not his elevation to the episcopal dignity." The
Sovereign Pontiff wrote to the emperor in the same strain. The
energy and earnestness he ever displayed in the cause of faith
and sound doctrine, seemed to grow in the soul of St. Simplicius in proportion as a long and painful illness wasted his body.
He renewed his appeals to Acacius, but his letters remained
unanswered.

9. Acacius was a court-bred bishop, wily, proud, as obstinate in his resentment as he was pliant and wavering in his
affections ; unprincipled, effeminate, inconsistent; in a word,
one of those degenerate Greeks who must stand at the foot of
the throne to hasten its downfall by their dark and secret intrigues. He made no account of the Pope's wishes, persisted
in urging on the emperor to pretended measures of conciliation,
and thus drew him into the performance of an action fraught

with the most disastrous results. Like all weak-minded princes, Zeno was easily led by those who would flatter his inclinations or his secret wishes. He solaced himself with the hope of settling religious disputes; and whilst proving himself utterly unable to maintain peace in his own court, he thought himself called to heal by a word dissensions which were altogether out of his province. The famous edict known as the *Henoticon*, Ἐνωτικον (*formula of union*), was published under the influence of these ideas. "We are entreated on all hands," says Zeno, in this edict, "to effect a union of the Churches and to remedy the fatal effects of their division. For a vast number of persons have thus been deprived of the benefits of baptism and communion. Blood has even been shed in the domestic strife. Who would not wish to see the end of such a state of things? We have, therefore, determined to make a solemn profession of our faith in the presence of the whole world. We proclaim that we have never held and never will hold any other profession or teaching, any faith or definition of faith than that of the three hundred and eighteen Fathers of Nice, confirmed by the hundred and fifty of Constantinople. Whoever holds any other is rejected from our communion; for this profession alone is the hope of our empire; in this profession alone all nations are baptized; it is the profession followed at Ephesus by the Fathers who deposed the impious Nestorius and his partisans. With them we also anathematize that heresiarch and condemn Eutyches. Their sentiments were opposed to those of the bishops assembled in those great councils. We admit, as a true exposition of faith, the twelve chapters of St. Cyril of Alexandria. We confess that our Lord Jesus Christ, God, only Son of God, Who became really incarnate, consubstantial to the Father, in His divinity; consubstantial to us, in His humanity; the same Who came down from Heaven to earth and was incarnate by the operation of the Holy Ghost in the womb of the Virgin Mary, Mother of God, is a single Son and not two. He is the same Son of God Who performed miracles and voluntarily suffered for us in the flesh.

We receive into our communion neither those who divide nor those who compound the two natures, nor yet those who admit only a simple appearance of incarnation. The holy Churches of God, throughout the world, the pontiffs who rule them, the whole extent of our empire, recognize no other faith. Join, then, in the expression of this unanimous faith. This edict brings no innovation into the various creeds; it aims only at uniting them. Whoever holds or has held a different belief from that which we have just expressed, whether at the present time or at any other, whether at Chalcedon or in any other council, we pronounce against him a solemn anathema, as we do against Nestorius and Eutyches." Such are the most important passages of the *Henoticon*.

·10. The spirit of Acacius, which inspired this instrument, is visible throughout. Confusion, incoherence, contradiction, abuse of power,—such are the most prominent features presented by the very first reading of the edict. The emperor asserts that all the Churches are with him in receiving no definition of faith other than that of Nice. He confounds two essentially distinct things. Doubtless the Nicene Creed was then, as now, the expression of Catholic faith; but it was not the only expression of this faith, since the bishops from all parts of the world met together at Chalcedon, had published a definition of faith, more detailed, more extensive, in some points, than that of Nice; and the Catholic world had adopted the profession of Chalcedon. The emperor sets out with the declaration that he follows only the Council of Nice, and in the space of a few lines he has recognized, as expressions of the true faith, the definition of the Council of Ephesus and the twelve chapters of St. Cyril. He is unwilling to receive the Council of Chalcedon, and yet he opposes Eutyches by a definition which is substantially that of Chalcedon. Could incoherence and contradiction be more glaring? What else can we behold in the prince who wields a dogmatic pen with the hand that should have been more fitly armed to drive back the barbarian invader from his bounds, than a usurper of the spiritual power, the leader of all the crowned heads who have tried to stretch the sceptre of their temporal power over the domain of conscience and of faith? Who was Zeno that he should say to the world: "This truth you shall believe; that error you must reject!" (A. D. 482).

11. Whilst the emperor, by his pretended *edict of union*, furnished fresh materials to the spirit of discord and dissension, Theodoric,* king of the Ostrogoths, of the royal line of the Amali, formerly Zeno's ally, turned his arms against him and besieged him in Constantinople. Hardly had the valor of his troops rescued him from this peril than the emperor saw his crown disputed by two pretenders: Marcian, son of Anthemius, emperor of the West, and Leontius, commander-in-chief of the Thracian troops. The Empress Verina, Zeno's mother-in-law, took part with the pretenders against her own son-in-law; she issued proclamations calling the citizens to arms and urging them to dethrone one whom she should have looked upon as her son. Zeno finally triumphed over his rivals rather by treason, however, than through skill or courage. The gravity of political events did not for a moment interfere with his religious cares. The *Henoticon* was published in all the cities of the empire and made a public law. An order was sent to Alexandria to banish John Talaïa from the Patriarchal throne and to give his place to Peter Mongus. The intruder now reappeared athirst for revenge. The orthodox bishops and priests of the Alexandrian province were maltreated and driven from their sees. The names of the Catholic Patriarchs, Proterius and Timothy Solofaciolus, were removed from the sacred diptychs and replaced by those of Dioscorus and Timothy Ælurus. Peter Mongus carried his resentment yet further: he caused the body of Timothy Solofaciolus, which had, according to the usual custom, been buried in the Cathedral of Alexandria, to be disinterred and thrown into a desert place without the city. Meanwhile the heretic had sent synodal letters to Pope Simplicius,

* The same who, under the title of Theodoric the Great, planted the Ostrogoth power in Italy.

begging him to confirm his authority; but the Pontiff was far from ratifying such a usurpation. Whilst the intruder thus harassed the Church of Alexandria, like the hireling who despoils the flock, John Talaïa, as another Athanasius, appealed to the Apostolic See. Here he found help and protection. St. Simplicius wrote a most energetic letter to Acacius of Constantinople, upbraiding him with having contemned the orders of the Holy See, brought about the restoration of Peter Mongus and caused the deposition of the rightful patriarch, John Talaïa, notwithstanding his innocence. Acacius replied that he did not deem Talaïa a legitimate Patriarch, and that he had thought himself justified in communicating with Peter Mongus since he had signed the *Henoticon*. Simplicius retorted that the *Henoticon* was of no force; that no one could be orthodox who rejected the ecumenical Council of Chalcedon: in fine, that Peter Mongus had been condemned as a heretic by the Holy See; that he could be freed from the condemnation only by the same authority.

12. Such was the embarrassed state of affairs in the East when St. Simplicius died (March 2, A. D. 483). The bearing of the Holy Pontiff, in the most trying circumstances, shows a charming combination of gentleness, condescension and firmness. That such commotion and trouble were not followed by a lasting peace was no fault of the Holy Pope. But the ever-growing pretensions of the bishops of Constantinople, the weakness of Zeno and the ambition of Acacius gave him no leisure to gather the fruits of his zeal and prudence. The firmness displayed in opposing the attempts of Eastern heretics was also shown in the case of certain Western bishops. The prelate of Ravenna had forcibly constrained the monk Gregory to accept the bishopric of Modena. The newly elected bishop complained to the Pope that he had been consecrated against his will. Simplicius most energetically remonstrated with the bishop of Ravenna, forbidding him to perform any such consecration for the future, on pain of losing his metropolitical right over the Churches of his province. Gaudentius, bishop of Auffinium,

had also seriously transgressed the canonical rules by conferring orders on unworthy subjects. Simplicius deprived the
unlawfully ordained subjects of the right to exercise ecclesiastical functions, forbade Gaudentius to confer orders for the
future, and assigned that duty to a bishop near Auffinium.
These proofs of apostolic rigor and energy do honor to the
character of the Holy Pontiff. They also bear witness to the
respect and submission then paid to the spiritual authority of
the Roman See; and though the preceding centuries afford
many instances of the same kind, yet it will not prove useless
to mention those we meet at every onward step in history;
for in spite of so many constant, authenticated facts, there are
still some minds that reject open evidence and treat the supremacy of the Roman Pontiffs as a thing of successive usurpation. St. Simplicius, jealous to preserve the direct action of
the Papacy in the Church, as the source of all power and jurisdiction, appointed, for the first time, a Primate for Spain, in
the person of the bishop of Seville. This was a purely personal prerogative which entailed upon that dignitary the care
of seeing to the observance of the canons throughout Spain,
under the direction of the Sovereign Pontiffs. The primacy
of the See of Seville lasted until the celebration of the Council
of Toledo, about A. D. 681. Though about the year 517, Pope
Hormisdas gave nearly equal powers to John, bishop of Tarragona, yet this pre-eminence of the bishop of Tarragona was
but temporary, and the See of Seville soon again resumed the
privilege of having for bishops the vicars or legates of the
Holy See. St. Simplicius divided the alms of the faithful into
four portions: the first for the bishop, the second for the clergy,
the other two for the uses of the Church, for pilgrims and the
poor. This order was afterward renewed in a positive manner by St. Gelasius I., by St. Gregory the Great, and by several other Pontiffs.

§ 2. ST. FELIX III.* (March 8, A. D. 483—February 28, 492).

13. The Holy See remained vacant but six days on the death of St. Simplicius. The clergy of the Roman Church assembled with the senate and people, in the basilica of St. Peter, to proceed to the election of a new Pope. During the preliminary proceedings the patrician Basil, præfect of the prætorium, in the name of Odoacer, king of the Heruli, protested that his master claimed the right of regulating the acts of the assembly and of confirming by his consent the election it might make. Such a claim was not received. The document was canonically examined only twenty years later, in a council at Rome, when it was decided that the election of the Roman Pontiffs was altogether foreign to the jurisdiction of the kings of Italy. Basil's communication failed in producing the effect looked for by Odoacer; and without regard to his claims the assembly elected Pope Felix III., a native of Rome and priest of the title of Fasciola.

14. The new Pontiff owed his first thoughts to the Eastern Church. John Talaïa was still in Italy, entreating the protection of the Holy See for his cause. Felix saw no possibility of his immediate restoration to Alexandria, and he conferred upon the exiled Patriarch the provisional government of the Roman Church in Campania; but Talaïa was not to revisit his Patriarchal See, and he spent the remainder of his life in his present charge. To secure the wise and prudent execution of the measures he proposed to take respecting the Emperor Zeno, the Pope called a council in Rome. John Talaïa laid

---

* This Pope is usually styled Felix III., in the *Catalogus of Sovereign Pontiffs*, and we have kept the title. We have seen that before the death of Pope Liberius a Pontiff, who assumed the title of Felix II., officiated at Rome, in the absence of the lawful Pope. Some authors have asserted that Felix could lawfully exercise his ministry as Liberius's legate and by his consent; that on the return of the latter, he retired into private life and deserved, by the practice of Christian virtues, the honors of canonization. As the name of Felix II. is inserted in the *Roman Martyrology*, we leave to his homonymes the titles of Felix III. and Felix IV., as a natural result, although we do not think that Felix II. could be lawful Pope during the lifetime of the Sovereign Pontiff who had never abdicated.

before it a juridical accusation against Acacius of Constantinople. He exposed all the intrigues of the wily prelate, enumerated his inconsistencies, and made him responsible for all the troubles then disturbing the East. The council made these charges the subject of a serious discussion. All the documents relating to the matter were examined, and it was decided to send legates to Zeno, to inform him of the election of the new Pope, and to urge him to pursue a course more worthy of a Catholic prince and one devoted, as he pretended to be, to the interests of the Church. The instructions given by Felix to his envoys were contained under four chief heads. They were : 1st, to hand to the emperor the letters relative to the promotion of the Sovereign Pontiff ; 2d, to claim the expulsion of Peter Mongus from Alexandria as a heretic ; 3d, to demand the support of the Council of Chalcedon as ecumenical ; 4th, to summon Acacius to defend himself, before the Holy See, against the charges brought forward by John Talaïa, and to anathematize Peter Mongus. If Acacius refused to give the required satisfaction, the legates were ordered not to communicate with him.

15. The mission was intrusted to the bishops Vitalis and Misenus, to whom the Pope afterward joined Felix, with the title of *defender* (or advocate) of the Roman Church. The letter to the emperor was a model of mildness and energy most happily blended. "Remember," said the Pontiff, "to what your enemies owed their fall and to what you are indebted for your restoration to the throne. They fell in the attempt to impugn the Council of Chalcedon, and you recovered your power by rejecting their errors. You are the only one who now bears the title of emperor : whilst you behold kingdoms falling into ruins about you, seek the favor of God for yourself. Beware of drawing down His wrath upon your empire." Such words were fraught with high and salutary teachings at a time when the Roman Empire in the West had lately crumbled to ruin and the only remaining power was the new kingdom of Constantinople, of recent origin, and whose long

agony already begun was to last through all the shameful
course of the *Lower Empire.* "It was you," added Felix,
"who banished Peter Mongus from Alexandria; you expelled
all who clung to his communion. Search the archives of your
palace for the letters you addressed to my predecessor at your
restoration. You then made professions of devotion to the
faith of Chalcedon; and now, by your order, the hireling, the
intruder so repeatedly condemned, Peter Mongus, is solemnly
reinstated in the See of Alexandria and the faith of Chalcedon
is condemned in your edict! How can you allow the flock of
Jesus Christ to be again harassed by the wolf you yourself
drove away? Has he not, for the last thirty years, stood
aloof from the Catholic Church and borne the title of teacher
of her enemies? As God rescued the empire from the heretical tyrant who had usurped your power,* it is for you now to
rescue the Church from the teachers of error and to bring
back the See of St. Mark to the communion of St. Peter."
The legates started for Constantinople furnished with these letters and with ample instructions of which we have given an
outline. In the course of the journey, Felix, defender of the
Roman Church, fell ill, and his two companions, Vitalis and
Misenus, pushed on to Abydos on the Dardanelles. Zeno and
Acacius had been notified of the arrival of the legates. It was
of vital importance to the Bishop of Constantinople that an embassy mainly directed against his ambitious views and claims
should fail at the outset. He convinced the emperor of the
fatal effects that would ensue from the protestations of the Holy
See were they heard throughout the East. Zeno proved his
appreciation of the prelates' secret suggestions by ordering the
arrest of the legates. Their letters and papers were taken
from them and they were cast into a dungeon. Some months
of rigorous confinement were followed by insidious overtures
from the imperial court. Zeno pressed Vitalis and Misenus to
communicate with Acacius and Peter Mongus, at first by caresses, gifts and prayers, and, when gentle means failed, by

* Basiliscus.

throats and ill treatment. He always promised to refer the whole matter, in the end, to the Pope's decision. Vitalis and Misenus were weak enough to yield, and promised to communicate with Acacius and the deputies of Peter Mongus, whereupon they were released from durance and solemnly celebrated the Holy Sacrifice in the presence of the heretics. The name of Peter Mongus was recited aloud in the public prayers. In vain did the Catholics of Constantinople protest against the disgraceful conduct of the legates; Vitalis and Misenus still continued to communicate with the heretics, and at their departure they received letters from Acacius for Felix III. The third legate, Felix, the defender of the Roman Church, only reached Constantinople after the shameful defection of his two colleagues. Their base example, however, in nowise lessened his courage. Neither captivity nor the emperor's promises nor threats could bend his constancy; and his noble and generous bearing, worthy of a representative of the Holy See, only served to show in stronger relief the dastardliness of Vitalis and Misenus.

16. The two bishops were to reap the fruit of their faithlessness at Rome. Simeon, a monk of Constantinople, was dispatched by Cyril, archimandrite of the monasteries of that city, to anticipate the returning legates and communicate to the Pope the sad intelligence of their fall. A council of sixty bishops was convened by the Pope, in the basilica of St. Peter (A. D. 484), and charged to inquire into the conduct of the legates. They were confronted with Simeon and the other monks he had brought with him. They were convicted of having communicated with Acacius and Peter Mongus in spite of the express order of the Pope. They urged in their defence the violent treatment they had undergone at the hands of the emperor and of the Bishop of Constantinople. Such a plea cannot be admitted in the bosom of the Catholic Church, whose annals abound with examples of generous devotion on the part of hosts of Christians who have confessed the truth at the price of their blood. Vitalis and Misenus were deposed from the

episcopacy and cut off from the communion of the Church. Vitalis died suddenly without having been reconciled; the sincere repentance of Misenus obtained his restoration to the communion of the faithful, in a subsequent council, under Pope St. Gelasius (A. D. 495). After the deposition of the legates, the Fathers of the council pronounced the solemn condemnation of Peter Mongus, founded on the former anathemas pronounced against him and his consecration by heretics.

17. The Pope still forbore to deal harshly with Acacius, though late events could not leave him in ignorance of the prelate's dishonesty and double-dealing. There is always in the Sovereign Pontiffs the father's heart withholding the judge's arm. Felix III. now made a last appeal to the misguided soul, hoping to move it by so marked a proof of condescension and mercy. "You have sinned," said the Shepherd of shepherds, to his wandering sheep: "go no further in your wayward course, but ask forgiveness for the past." The bishop's heart was too full of its own ambitious schemes to admit the mild appeal of authority. Without deigning even a reply, Acacius continued in communion with Peter Mongus, and used all his power to bring about the execution of the *Henoticon* in the East. So much obstinacy drove the Holy See to the necessity of using sterner measures. In the month of July, A. D. 484, the Pope convoked sixty-seven bishops at Rome, and read to them an act of deposition against Acacius of Constantinople. "You have," said the Pontiff to the unworthy bishop, "you have countenanced the heretical opponents of the Council of Chalcedon; you have supported an intruder in the Patriarchal See of Alexandria; you have laid violent hands upon peaceful ambassadors of the Holy See; you have refused to obey the holy canons which require you to answer before us the juridical charges brought to our tribunal by our brother and colleague in the episcopate, John, Patriarch of Alexandria; remain then, hereafter, associated with the heretics whose interest you so readily embrace; and know that by the present sentence you are deprived of your priestly dignity and of Cath-

olic communion; that you are condemned by the judgment of
the Holy Ghost and the authority of the Apostolic See." The
mission of bearing this judgment to Constantinople was intrusted to a cleric named Tutus, on whom the Pope bestowed
the title of defender of the Church. He also bore two letters,
one for the emperor, the other for the clergy and people of Constantinople. The Pope complained to Zeno of the unworthy
manner in which his legates had been treated. "This violence, however," he adds, "has not been deemed a valid excuse for their conduct; they have been deposed. I leave it to
you to decide which of the two communions you should choose,
that of St. Peter the Apostle or that of Peter Mongus."

He then notifies the emperor of the sentence pronounced
against Acacius, and begs him not to oppose its execution. The
letter addressed to the clergy and faithful of Constantinople
was intended by the Pontiff to retrieve, to a certain extent, the
public scandal given by the legates Vitalis and Misenus, by
making known their condemnation in the Roman Council. Tutus, the bearer of these dispatches, succeeded in baffling the
watchful guards who kept the Dardanelles to cut off all communication with the Pope; he reached Constantinople in safety,
and took up his abode in a monastery of *Acœmetes.** Acacius
obstinately refused to receive the letter addressed to him by
the Pope. That he might not plead ignorance of a sentence
which excommunicated him, one of the monks was daring
enough to fasten the decree to his pontifical mantle, as he was
entering the basilica, on a Sunday, to celebrate the divine
office. This bold deed drew upon the monks all the vengeance
of Acacius. Some of the religious were murdered by his
agents: they thus proved, at the cost of their lives, their unshaken devotion to the faith of the Church and their submission to the authority of Rome. Yet Tutus, whose bearing as
legate had been thus far unimpeachable, by an unaccountable

---

* This name was frequently given to the monks of Syria and Constantinople—ἀ κοιμάω
(*to be sleepless*). They were so called because, in their monasteries, the religious exercises
continued day and night, without interruption.

weakness allowed himself to be won over by an agent of Acacius. He accepted a considerable sum of money offered him
on condition of his communicating with the heretics; and a
few months later the heart of the Pope was filled with grief
by the intelligence that his legate had sold honor, conscience
and the dignity of the Roman Church, which he had been
commissioned to represent. The archimandrites were deeply
grieved at this scandal which reopened a wound but partly
healed; and they hastened to acquaint the Pope with the sad
event. On his return to Rome, Tutus was juridically examined before a council and convicted on his own testimony; he
was immediately deprived of his title of defender of the
Church and excommunicated. This sentence was at once
made known to the orthodox clergy and faithful of Constantinople, lest they should be led to imagine that Rome could look
with indulgent eye upon the weakness and pusillanimity of
such legates as Vitalis, Misenus and Tutus, or yield to a feeling of mercy which, in such a case, would be but connivance.
The zealous efforts of St. Felix III. were destined to fail before the wily schemes of Acacius. That prelate, excommunicated by the authority of the Holy See, rejected by the whole
Catholic portion of his flock, in open communion with notorious and condemned heretics, and deposed from the episcopal
dignity by a council, did not for a moment entertain the
thought of submitting. He continued to offer up the Holy
Sacrifice, erased from the sacred diptychs the name of Pope
Felix III., and strong in the imperial favor, entered upon a
system of open hostility against the Catholics. The rightful
Patriarch of Antioch, the virtuous bishop Calendion, who had
shown himself an intrepid defender of injured innocence by
taking up the cause of John Talaïa, was driven from his see
by the same Acacius who, eight years before, had conferred
upon him the episcopal consecration. Peter the Fuller, who
had been so long a forgotten exile, found himself a second time
intruded into the See of Antioch, in the midst of general indignation. The principal cities of the East were all deprived of

their lawful pastors.   Nestor, bishop of Tarsis, Cyrus of Hierapolis, John of Cyra, Romanus of Chalcis, Eusebius of Samo-
sata, Julian of Mopsuesta, Paul of Constantina, Manus of
Himeria, and Andrew of Theodosiopolis, were all banished for
their loyalty to the true faith and to the authority of the Holy
See (A. D. 484).

18. The ambition of Acacius had thus opened a schism
between the Church of Constantinople and the Church of
Rome, the centre of unity, the source of authority and deposi-
tory of the faith.   This unfortunate separation was to last
until A. D. 519, when, in the pontificate of St. Hormisdas, the
two Churches once more met in common communion.   Zeno's
Henoticon was the first cause of all the persecutions directed
against the Catholics.   Their steady refusal to sign a formula
of faith composed by an emperor, supported by arms, condemned by the Holy See, were treated as obstinacy, as insincerity, and as an insolence to the imperial majesty.   The so-
called *edict of union* not only carried trouble into the ranks of
the faithful, but the very heretics found in it a fruitful source
of dissension.   The majority of them did not think it clearly
enough in their favor.   They were indignant that Peter Mongus at Alexandria, and Peter the Fuller at Antioch, should
have agreed to sign it.   In this concession the heretics saw
only a pretext under which those prelates would abandon
their leaders to form a new faction of Eutychians; these were
called *Acephali* (without a head), to express their separation
from those who had long led them on in the way of error.   It
is not unworthy of remark that such disorder should have been
brought about by a prince who was by no means wanting in
uprightness of intention.   The pages of history teem with
narratives of disasters unwittingly brought on by irresolute
and wavering characters; and it might be well worth while to
study out the question, whether the greatest curse that God,
in His wrath, can hurl down upon a guilty people, be not to
give them a sovereign who is such but in name.

19. St. Felix III. was not insensible to the complaints

which daily reached him from all the Catholics in the East,
victims of Acacius's tyranny. In A. D. 485 another council
was called at Rome once more to discuss this sad question.
The anathemas already pronounced against Peter Mongus,
Peter the Fuller and Acacius, were renewed. A synodal
letter to all the orthodox priests and abbots of Constantinople
and Bithynia, informed the East of the sentence pronounced
against these relapsed heretics. In the preceding year the
partisans of Acacius had tried to take exception to the validity of his deposition, on the ground that the act was signed by
the Pope alone. The fathers of the council give the reason in
their synodal letter. The words deserve to be quoted :
" Whenever the pontiffs of the Lord meet together in Italy
to treat the cause and interests of the Church, it is a rule that
the successor of St. Peter in the Apostolic See, in the name
of the pontiffs of all Italy, decide and pronounce without
appeal, since he is charged with the care of all the churches.
He is their head ; to him our Lord has said, in the person of
the Prince of the Apostles : ' Thou art Peter ; and upon this
rock I will build my Church, and the gates of hell shall not
prevail against it.' Obedient to these words, three hundred
and eighteen Fathers of Nice acknowledged the right of the
Church of Rome to confirm and exercise jurisdiction over all
the others. Through the grace of Jesus Christ the succession
of our pontiffs has kept these two prerogatives down to our
own time. In the present case, the judgment pronounced upon
Acacius, by the Council at St. Peter's, was confirmed by the
Holy Father, Felix, our head, who communicated it to the
East through Tutus, defender of the Church." Felix added to
the council's dispatch a long and eloquent rescript addressed
to the faithful of the East, reviewing the whole series of sad
events which had darkened the last ten years of the Church of
Constantinople. He refuted all the arguments brought forward in defence of Acacius's conduct. His condemnation was
plainly proved to be regular and canonical; and the Pope
demanded that the lawful sentence should be immediately put

into execution. These energetic measures, proceeding from the centre of unity, hardly found entrance into the East. Zeno, still bound by the wiles of Acacius, had forbidden all communication between Rome and his states. Yet in spite of the strict watch he kept upon his boundaries, especially at the Dardanelles, justice and truth, ever slow, but equally sure in their progress, were breaking upon the universal mind. The very violence of the triumphant Eutychians, their persecutions, injustice and cruelty toward the Catholics stirred up a feeling of contempt and indignation in every honest heart. Such was the outcry against the intruder Peter the Fuller in the See of Antioch, that Acacius himself, who had been chiefly instrumental in bringing about the usurpation, was forced to break off all open relations with him. Still this did not hinder Peter from expelling, according to the impulse of his madness, the Catholic bishops of the province of Antioch, and from giving their sees to the most unworthy subjects. Thus he conferred episcopal consecration upon a Persian slave driven from his own country on account of his crimes, and who had never been baptized. The bishop thus unlawfully set up by an intruded Patriarch, was called Xenaias; he was placed in the See of Hierapolis, after the expulsion of Cyrus, the rightful prelate. When Peter the Fuller was blamed for a consecration so contrary to the first elements of the plainest theology, he answered: "The grace of the episcopate supplies the want of the baptismal." No further evidence was needed of the ignorance of the wretched heretic. Xenaias was not more learned. He spent the whole time of his usurped episcopacy in overturning the statues of the saints, which he called idolatrous images; he thus made himself a worthy forerunner of the stupid ferocity of the Iconoclasts.

20. Egypt was no better off under the despotic rule of Peter Mongus. By the help of a few Eutychian bishops and abbots, Peter held a kind of permanent cabal: every day he renewed his anathemas against the Council of Chalcedon and the august memory of St. Leo the Great. Every cleric and

monk who did not receive the writings of Dioscorus and Timothy
Ælurus, was sent into exile. This persecution was carried to such
a pitch, that the archimandrite Nephalius resolved to undertake
the journey to Constantinople to lay the complaint of the desolate
Church at the feet of the emperor. Zeno had restored Peter
Mongus with the sole view of quieting Alexandria. It was visible
to him that the men of his choice were not more fit than his
decrees to carry out his purpose. He positively ordered the
Patriarch to cease his persecution, and to recall the monks he
had banished. The three apostates, Acacius, Peter the Fuller,
and Peter Mongus, occupying respectively the Sees of Constantinople, Antioch and Alexandria; making free use of all the
influence they possessed at court; leagued in the same views
of independence of the Holy See, and the same attachment for
heresy, must have looked upon their triumph as certain and deemed Eutychianism forever rooted in the East. But God was about
to put to confusion their proud conceits and ambitious projects.
Peter the Fuller was stricken down, the first, in A. D. 488;
in the next year, 489, Acacius followed him to the grave; and
the year 490 brought the final summons also to Peter Mongus,
the usurper of Alexandria, the hoary persecutor who disgraced
the throne of a Cyril and an Athanasius. Peter the Fuller
and Peter Mongus were succeeded by heretics. But after
the short reign of Fravitas, who held the patriarchal throne
but a few months, the See of Constantinople was filled by a
pious and holy priest named Euphemius. As his orthodoxy
had been proved, St. Felix admitted him to *Catholic communion;*
but he refused him *episcopal communion* because Euphemius,
out of regard for Zeno, refused to efface the name of Acacius
from the sacred diptychs. The conduct of St. Felix, on this
occasion, in granting the first and refusing the second communion to Euphemius, clearly shows the distinction between
the two: the first regarding faith, and granted to all the faithful; the second, the episcopal communion, properly so called,
and solicited from the Holy See, by bishops elect, as a necessary
confirmation of their election. The death of Acacius, and

the election of his two successors had naturally reopened
negotiations between the Holy See and the court of Constantinople. The Sovereign Pontiff seized the occasion to make a
last effort and to recall Zeno again to Catholic sentiments
and conduct. The Pope's letter is the outpouring of a most
sincerely affectionate heart: "It is with abundant tears,
venerable emperor," says the Pontiff, "that I write these lines,
prostrate at the feet of your piety. How could I find any
trouble in humbling myself before the powers of the empire,
when the Apostle says of himself that he made himself the
outcast and reproach of all men? I entreat you, well-beloved
son, not to reject my paternal entreaties, not to despise my
words; for unworthy as I am, it is the Apostle St. Peter who
entreats you by my voice, and through him, our Lord Jesus
Christ Himself, who does not wish to see His Church torn to
pieces. The old and the new Rome* must be united in one
faith, that faith which, according to St. Paul, is preached
throughout the world; so that the two cities may have but
one faith, as they bear the same name. My entreaties will
ever continue to present themselves before your throne as
long as the traces of these fatal divisions last." The tender,
dignified, lofty tone of these words, shows the heart that bears
the charge of all the Churches. We must notice here the
title of *son*, given by the Pope to Zeno. This is the first
instance we find in history of a form since consecrated by
custom. The superscription was thus worded: "*Gloriosissimo
et serenissimo filio Zenoni Augusto, Felix, episcopus, in Domino
salutem.*" Zeno's was not a mind to understand the mission of
a Christian emperor and the immense authority which would
accrue to kings and princes from a concord of the spiritual
and temporal powers. His last years were given up to infamous pleasures and ceaseless orgies. Inebriety and voluptuousness had made him cruel; his sceptre had fallen into the hands
of his eunuchs who now ruled in his name; and the evils which

---

* The Pope calls Constantinople the new Rome, as it had, in fact, succeeded to the
imperial power of the old.

wrung tears from the eyes of Jeremiah were now renewed in
the East. The words of Holy Writ were verified in them
now : " *Servi dominati sunt nostri.*" *

The death of Zeno, which occurred A. D. 491, was naturally looked upon as a release. The modern Greeks have surrounded his death with the most shocking details. They pretend that the Empress Ariadne, his wife, had him buried alive
during a lethargy caused by intoxication. The account has
not been adopted by reliable historians. However this may
be, the memory of Zeno will ever remain charged with all the
dissensions, strifes and persecutions which distracted the
Church during his reign, and which he could so easily have
checked by a simple and true submission to the orthodox faith
with all the Catholics.

21. Whilst the East was torn by hostile factions, under
the influence of Eutychianism, the deserts about Jerusalem
bloomed with the most charming virtues of solitude. St. Sabas,
whose earliest infancy had been prevented by the graces of
the Holy Ghost, had entered a monastery near Cæsarea (Cappadocia) at the age of eight years. His progress in religious
humility, patience, gentleness and obedience corresponded with
his early promise. A natural attraction toward the spot hallowed by the Saviour's sufferings drew him to Palestine, where
he fixed his abode in a natural grotto on the bank of the brook
Cedron (A. D. 478). Here he spent many solitary years, ever
absorbed, as he wove his mats, in the contemplation of divine
things. The example of Christian solitude is seldom fruitless.
The silence and seclusion of the desert supply so many wants
in the human heart! In the year 491 the Abbot Sabas saw
himself surrounded by more than a hundred and fifty disciples
who lived in *lauras* or private monasteries under the general
direction. The noise and tumult of the world were lost at the
foot of the mountain inhabited by these holy religious. The
names of Peter Mongus and Peter the Fuller were only uttered
as those of the Church's enemies. One of the Armenian

* Lament. Jerem. cap. 5, v. 8.

monks·wished to sing the Trisagion, with the addition of Peter the Fuller : *crucified for us ;* but St. Sabas enjoined a strict adherence to ancient usage and Apostolic tradition, against which neither heresy nor schism can prescribe. Another monastery had been established at the foot of the mountain, near the lauras, under the government of St. Theodosius, a fellow-countryman of St. Sabas. This establishment was to the first a kind of novitiate. Young men were here formed to the austere practices of the religious life and trained, at the same time, to works of charity ; for the monastery had, under its dependence, four infirmaries or hospitals for the sick poor and a lodging for travellers and pilgrims who were brought in great numbers to the neighborhood of the holy places. Four churches supplied the religious wants of the monks of different nationalities. The preaching and recitation of the divine office were held separately ; but all assisted at the same sacrifice and communicated together. Contemporary historians compare the monastery of the abbot Theodosius to a great city, where all the arts necessary to life were practised. Happy production of Christian faith ! Holy communities where obedience was the joy of subjects, humility the crown of inferiors ; where virtue, talent and merit found a deeper seclusion in proportion as their lustre was greater—how little do you resemble those monstrous aggregations of men, the dream of a fruitless philosophy, where equality was to be founded and supported on motives of interest, subordination established without religious principles, devotedness inspired without faith !

22. Africa enjoyed a few moments of quiet under Hunneric's successor, Gundamund. St. Eugenius, the courageous bishop of Carthage, had been recalled in the year 487 ; but the other Catholic prelates were not restored to their flocks until A. D. 494. St. Felix III. was deeply moved by the situation of the faithful in Africa, deprived of their lawful pastors, and forced to depend upon the secretly-administered instructions and spiritual succors of a few zealous priests who had succeeded in eluding the vigilance of the persecutors. He accord

ingly called a council of the Italian bishops to provide means
for their relief (A. D. 487). Four African bishops, Victor, Donatus, Rusticus and Pardalius were present at the council.
Particular attention was given to the question of public penance
The great number of defections caused by the Vandal persecution called for a decisive regulation of this question. Many
weak and timid Catholics had purchased exemption from the
persecution by allowing themselves to be rebaptized by the
Arians. They now asked to be received back into communion.
The canons of the Council of Rome require a consideration of the
penitent's dispositions and contrition, and an inquiry into the
amount of violence inflicted; so that one who yielded without a
blow be more severely punished than he who offered a long and
steady opposition. Then passing over to particular cases, the
Fathers prescribe a life-long penance for rebaptized bishops,
priests and deacons. They are only to receive lay communion,
and that *in extremis*. The inferior clergy, monks, religious and
seculars, who show a sincere sorrow for their fall, are to be
treated in the manner prescribed by the Council of Nice; that
is, they are to pass three years in the ranks of the *catechumens*,
seven among the *prostrati*, and two *inter consistentes*—that is,
among the lay faithful who were present at the prayers. If they
have only fallen after undergoing cruel torture, they may be
admitted to communion after three years of penance. Bishops
and priests were also forbidden to receive into their cities any
penitents from another Church without a written testimony from
their rightful bishop, stating the motive of their penance, the
length of time already fulfilled and that yet to be made up.
The council adds that, should any unforeseen difficulties occur
in the application of these canons, the solution shall be asked
from the Holy See.

23. Meanwhile an important political revolution was preparing in Italy where Odoacer had established the power of the
Heruli, which, however, he himself was to survive. The emperors of the East, after the death of Romulus Augustulus, still
claimed the right of sovereignty over Italy. The rank of pa-

trician was bestowed by Zeno upon Odoacer, and Rome, thanks
to this forced investiture, could still imagine herself governed
by an imperial lieutenant. Odoacer, who was as prudent as he
was skilful, had not sought to contradict these claims which
were still in keeping with the popular feeling. He had availed
himself of the peace which his friendly relations with the Byzantine court secured him from the East, to subdue the Rugi
of Noricum (now Bavaria), and to give permanence to his late
conquests. As the power of the Heruli spread in the West,
its progress was paralleled in the East by that of the warlike,
haughty and restless Ostrogoths, at the very gates of Constantinople. Their king was Theodoric, of the royal line of the
Amali. He was gifted with the high accomplishments which
form great men : brought up, from the age of seven years, at
the court of Constantinople, he had early made himself familiar
with the political and military establishment of the Greeks,
and had appropriated the refinement of his teachers without
adopting their vices or imitating their effeminacy. On his return among his fellow-countrymen he illustrated his youth by
victories won over the Sarmatians, and soon his deeds made
even Byzantium tremble. Theodoric's character was aspiring.
Yet he was led on to feats of arms less by ambition or love of
adventure than by the unquiet nature of his subjects. They
had received the territories of Dacia and Mœsia ; but the sickle
and the pruning-hook seemed heavier on their hands than the
sword or spear in combat ; and their king was forced to yield
to their warlike instincts. Whatever fear or affection could
bestow was profusely lavished by Zeno on the king of the
Ostrogoths (A. D. 478)—military adoption, the rank of patrician and consul, a triumph, an equestrian statue. But if the
imperial bounty moved the heart of the king it could not cool
the ardor of the Ostrogoths for military exploits. To reconcile
his debt of gratitude with the necessities of his position, Theodoric solicited the grant of the kingdom of Italy, reserving the
right of establishing it by force. "Italy," he said, "belonged
to your predecessor : it is the cradle of your empire. Why

will you give it up to the Turci and Heruli? Let me conq-
it: should I succeed, you will share the honor; if I fail, you
will gain the yearly allowance you have engaged to pay us."
Zeno was but too well pleased to rid himself of his undesira-
ble neighbors by granting them territory over which he really
had no control, and readily entered into the agreement proposed by Theodoric. The Ostrogoths, with their families and
flocks, set out by way of the Julian Alps (A. D. 489).   Twice,
at Verona and at Milan, did Theodoric defeat Odoacer's Ital
ian troops who fought but tamely for their barbarian master.
The king of the Heruli knocked in vain for shelter at the
gates of Rome; they were barred against him. He saw no
resource left but to shut himself up in Ravenna, a city built in
the midst of a marsh, carefully fortified and defended by a
garrison of twenty thousand men; here he sustained a siege
of three years, during which Theodoric subdued the whole of
Italy.   At length, destitute of provisions, the unfortunate
monarch was forced to capitulate (A. D. 493) to his rival, who,
on suspicion of treachery, stabbed him in the midst of a solemn
banquet. The power of the Heruli was thus supplanted in
the ancient capital of the Roman world by that of the Ostrogoths. The military movements necessarily attendant upon
these struggles could not but prove disastrous to the inhabitants of city and country. The people of the districts thus
devastated had no other resource than to appeal to their
bishops. Hitherto these pastors had wielded in the defence
of their flocks none but spiritual weapons, had provided no
shelter for them other than the churches. They now began
to build castles and fortresses to protect their people from open
violence. Honoratus, bishop of Novara, set the example.
Gundebald, king of the Burgundians, on the plea of helping
his ally Odoacer, had marched his troops into Liguria. Their
route was marked by pillage, devastation, ruin. Honoratus
succeeded in saving his episcopal city from the fury of these
barbarians. The charity of the bishops was ever the same;
but new evils drove it to seek new remedies; now the new

evil was the want of an armed protection to shield the oppressed people. We shall yet see the force of circumstances obliging the Pope, St. Gregory the Great, to take upon himself the defence of Rome, and to require the bishops to do the same for their respective dioceses.

24. A few months before the close of the struggle between Theodoric and Odoacer, St. Felix III. had been called away from the scene of blood and strife (February 25, A. D. 492). Through eight years of administration, whilst the East was disturbed by heresies and the West flowed with the blood of the contending Ostrogoths and Heruli, the energetic yet withal prudent and moderate character of this pious Pontiff succeeded in maintaining the authority of the Holy See and insuring respect for it, in spite of the defections, the intrigues and the passions of men.

CHAPTER II.

SUMMARY.

§ I. Pontificate of St. Gelasius I. (March 2, a. d. 492—Nov. 19, 496).

1. The Holy See was but five days vacant. St. Gelasius I. was elected Pope on the 2d of March, a. d. 492. His promo-

tion was almost simultaneous with the elevation of the emperor
Anastasius to the throne of the East. The reign of the new
emperor was destined to be as inglorious as that which had preceded it. Anastasius was at best but an indifferent prince,
without settled character or fixed principles, and so inconsistent
that it is impossible to hold up any one of his virtues for admiration without discovering the contrary vice to censure. It was
his maxim that *a prince may lie or even perjure himself—for
political purposes;* this execrable doctrine he had borrowed
from his mother's Manichean teaching. Ignorant of the first
principle of gratitude, he forgot the benefactor as soon as he
had obtained the favor. Once, when wrecked upon the coast
near Alexandria, he had been sheltered and most tenderly and
disinterestedly cared for by John Talaïa; nothing then fore-
shadowed the high destiny of Anastasius. When John Talaïa
was forced to fly to Italy, an exile and a fugitive, he thought
himself warranted to rely upon the protection of Anastasius,
and turned toward Constantinople; he was met, halfway, by
an order from the emperor enjoining him to leave the imperial
territory at once on pain of being treated as a rebel and a
fomenter of sedition. Thus did Anastasius requite the debt of
gratitude. The Eastern Church had but little to hope from the
reign of such a ruler.

2. Peace seemed to smile with more favorable promise
upon the West, where Theodoric had just won himself a throne.
This monarch managed to secure an ascendency over nearly
all the barbarian kings, by ties of family or protection. He
gave his daughter Theodegotha to the king of the Visigoths,
Alaric II. The name of Clovis, the young king of the Franks,
was winning a wide celebrity. Theodoric sought and obtained
for himself the hand of that monarch's sister. The contemporary
rulers placed such implicit confidence in the judgment of the
king of the Ostrogoths, that they often made him the umpire
of their difficulties. He spoke to them as a father to his children. "You have received tokens of my good-will," he writes
to them; "you are youthful and brave, but you need advice.

Your disorders afflict me, and I cannot look with indifference on
your subjection to your passions." Sicily, the Alps, Rhetia
and Geneva readily put themselves under the rule of a sovereign whose chief aim was the good of his subjects. " Let
others," he wrote to one of his generals, "make war to plunder
or to destroy; our aim must be so to overcome, by the help of
God, that the conquered may regret that they were not sooner
brought under our power." Though like the rest of his nation,
an Arian, Theodoric respected the Catholic bishops. During the
first year of his rule in Italy, he had made a law declaring all
the Italians who had taken up arms for Odoacer and the Heruli,
unqualified to make a will or to dispose of their goods. Such
an edict was a source of general consternation, for Italy could
count the disqualified by the number of its inhabitants. The
grief-stricken people had recourse to their usual refuge, St.
Epiphanius of Pavia, and begged the illustrious prelate to intercede in their behalf with Theodoric. Epiphanius associated
to his mission Lawrence, bishop of Milan; and together they
set out for Ravenna, where the king of the Ostrogoths was then
holding his court. He granted their request, and revoked his
decree; then calling St. Epiphanius aside, he thus addressed
him : "Glorious Pontiff, your great merit leads me to intrust
you with an affair of the highest importance. You behold Italy
now but a vast desert and its most fertile fields untilled for
want of workmen. The wretched inhabitants are disheartened
and the country wasted by the repeated inroads and ravages
of the Burgundians. Take upon yourself, then, with the help
of God, to go and sue for peace from their king, Gundebald.
He holds you in filial reverence and has long wished to see
you. Undertake the mission I propose; your very presence
will pay the ransom that is to free Italy." Epiphanius agreed
to act as mediator between the two kings. In the month of
March, A. D. 494, accompanied by St. Victor, bishop of Turin,
he crossed the Alps still covered with snow and ice. The
Pope had given St. Epiphanius letters for Rusticius, bishop of
Lyons, which city Gundebald had made his capital. Gelasius

expressed his gratitude for the provisions and money sent by
the holy bishop of Lyons for the relief of the suffering Italians
during the contest between the Ostrogoths and the Heruli. He
also entreated him to use his influence with Gundebald to further the success of the embassy. Finally St. Epiphanius was
charged to sound the Gallic bishops relative to the religious
questions agitated in the East. Rusticius having been notified
of the approach of the two prelates, went out to meet them beyond the Rhone and accompanied them into his episcopal city.
Whatever apprehensions might have been felt for the success
of this mission on account of the haughtiness and insincerity
of Gundebald, they speedily vanished under the influence of
the virtues of St. Epiphanius. " Great prince," said the illustrious bishop to the king of the Burgundians, " it is through love
for you that I have undertaken so arduous a journey; I have
dared the risk of death to bring you the price of eternal life.
Chosen by God to be the mediator between two great kings, I
shall have the happiness to see the accomplishment of the merciful designs of which I come to speak to you. King Theodoric desires peace; he intends to ransom the prisoners; return
them unransomed. Believe me, no one wins more in the trial
of generosity than he who receives nothing. Give back, great
prince, give back to their homes so many wretched exiles;
restore them to your glory!" Gundebald was moved by the
grace of persuasion which flowed from the lips of the holy
bishop. The prisoners were released. Six thousand captives went on their way to Italy, blessing the name of their
deliverer, St. Epiphanius. The mission of the two bishops had
proved a complete success. In obedience to the orders of the
Sovereign Pontiff, St. Epiphanius questioned the Gallic bishops, who protested that during the religious disputes in the
East they had always sided with the Holy See against the
claims of the Bishops of Constantinople.

3. St. Gelasius had no sooner been raised to the chair of St.
Peter than his first glance, as Pontiff and Father, was directed
toward the East. He had written to the Emperor Anastasius

to notify him of his election. Euphemius, Bishop of Constantinople, had expected a like communication from the Pope; but
Gelasius abstained from this attention, since Euphemius was not
admitted to the episcopal communion of Rome. The Patriarch
took this occasion to write two letters to the Pope, assuring him
of his attachment to the Catholic faith and of his earnest wish
to see peace and union existing between the Roman and Greek
Churches. He excused himself for not effacing from the diptychs * the names of Acacius and Peter Mongus, on the ground
that the people of Constantinople did not leave him at liberty
to do so (A. D. 493). St. Gelasius answered the letters of Euphemius with Apostolic firmness. "Can I allow," wrote the
Sovereign Pontiff, "mention to be made during the Holy Sacrifice, of the names of formally excommunicated heretics and
of their successors? This is not showing the wise condescension which stoops to raise a fallen brother; this would be but
an act of rash blindness, which throws itself into the abyss.
Acacius has been convicted of leaguing with the Eutychian heresy and of communicating with its abettors. You may not,
then, imagine yourself true to the Catholic faith whilst his
name remains in your diptychs. Do not allege that you are
forced, in spite of yourself, to act as you do; such words should
never pass a bishop's lips when the triumph of truth is concerned; for, as minister of Jesus Christ, he has pledged his life
to its defence. My brother, Euphemius, we shall both appear
before the judgment-seat of Jesus Christ. At that bar vain
are all empty discussions, delays and evasions. On that awful
day will it be known whether I am bitter and harsh, as you
complain, or whether you cast aside the wholesome remedy;
you who seek to draw the physician into the same disorder
with yourself rather than seek health by his ministry." It is
a labor of love to transcribe such words. It is glorious to
meet in the Holy See that traditional loftiness of sentiment,

---

* We have already had occasion to explain the meaning of this word. The *diptychs*
formed a double catalogue of the deceased and living bishops admitted to the communion
of the Church, and commemorated in the Holy Sacrifice.

that firm and noble bearing, which the Sovereign Pontiffs seem to transmit as a lasting heritage. The emperor Anastasius had no idea of renewing the ancient union between Rome and Constantinople. The ambassadors whom he had sent to Italy to congratulate Theodoric on the success of his undertaking (A. D. 493) were under positive orders not to see the Pope, or on any pretext whatever to hold communication with him. St. Gelasius followed a directly opposite course. He availed himself of the opportunity offered by the departure of an embassy sent by Theodoric to Constantinople, to address a detailed circular to all the bishops of the East. In this letter he reviewed and confuted all the arguments brought forward by the partisans of Acacius and Peter Mongus. He dwelt particularly upon the obedience due to the authority of the Roman Church. " By what reasoning or on what grounds can the obligation stand," writes the Pope, " of deferring to other sees, if the ancient respect due to the See of St. Peter is cast off ?—to that first See, to which every sacerdotal dignity has always looked for strength and confirmation ; whose supreme prerogative was proclaimed by the unanimous and invincible judgment of the three hundred and eighteen Fathers of Nice, recalling these words of our Lord : ' Thou art Peter, and upon this rock I will build my Church ;' ' but I have prayed for thee, that thy faith fail not ;' ' feed my lambs, feed my sheep.' " From these words it is evident that the Sovereign Pontiffs esteemed their authority as the highest and holiest on earth. To deny or to contemn it was to sap the very foundations of the spiritual power and give up the Church to anarchy. The Greeks of the Lower Empire, passionately given to theological quibbles, were far below the comprehension of such language. They called up a thousand pretexts to evade the Pope's reasons.

4. This afforded Gelasius a fresh opportunity to give to Theodoric's ambassadors special instructions for combating heresy. " I can plainly see," he says, " that the Greeks have no other end in view than the overthrow of the Catholic faith. They repeatedly threaten to withdraw from the Church of

Rome. It seems to me that this threat has long ago been executed. They have the effrontery to quote canons against us, whilst they unceasingly violate them to satisfy their wicked ambition. By what canon, for instance, did they expel John of Alexandria from his Patriarchal See, without the shadow of conviction against him? By what canon was the Patriarch of Antioch proscribed that his see might be given to an intruder? By what tradition do they dare to call to judgment the Apostolic See itself? And yet all these outrages come from the bishops of Constantinople, to whom the canons grant none of the prerogatives of the great Sees! When there is question of a judgment in matters of religion the supreme authority is vested by the canons in the Apostolic See.' No temporal sovereign, whatever his power, can arrogate to himself this right without, by the fact, becoming a persecutor." This prudent firmness of the Sovereign Pontiff won the adherence of the bishops of Dardania, who wrote to him to profess their devotion to the Holy See and to the Catholic faith. The noble example was followed by the Province of Thessalonica (A. D. 494). Anastasius, with a display of the most whimsical inconsistency, complained that the Pope did not write to him directly; and yet he had expressly forbidden his ambassadors to hold any communication with the Pope. Gelasius learned this from the deputies of Theodoric, on their return from Constantinople. He at once took measures to remove the new pretext for a misunderstanding, by writing to the emperor in a strain of surpassing mildness and affection : " I entreat your piety," he wrote, " not to interpret as arrogance my fidelity to a duty of which I must one day give an account to Almighty God. Let it not be said that a Roman emperor has turned away from the truth when it sought him. As you well know, august prince, the world is governed by two principles—the sacred authority of the Pontiffs and the royal power. Now although you sway the temporal destinies of the human race, you are still subject, in the spiritual order, to the ministers of religion; just as in the public administration the pontiffs of religion obey your laws because they know that the empire has been given to you by a disposition of Divine Providence." In complaining of the Pope's silence toward him, Anastasius was far from seeking to open the way for a reconciliation. When putting on the imperial purple the emperor had yielded to the urgent entreaties of Euphemius and sworn upon the Holy Gospels to follow henceforth the Catholic faith. But this was nothing more than a sacrilegious farce. No sooner was he fairly seated upon the throne than he threw off the mask and appeared in his true character—a bitter heretic and persecutor of the faithful. Euphemius was the first victim of his resentment. His hatred was increased by the remembrance of the oath pressed upon him at his accession, and by the opposition which his wicked projects ever met in the mildness of the holy prelate. The failure of an attempt to murder the bishop, made by some assassins in the pay of the emperor, put a climax to his thirst for vengeance. He called a council of bishops whom he had previously won to his interest by favors and bribes. They declared Euphemius unworthy of the episcopal dignity and deposed him. The emperor at once confirmed the sentence, in spite of the sensation caused by it throughout the city and the imminent danger of a sedition. Euphemius was banished to Ancyra (A. D. 495), where he died twenty years later. He was succeeded by Macedonius, librarian and treasurer of the Church of Constantinople, and, in this capacity, depositary of the act of adherence to the Catholic faith, which had been signed by Anastasius. On taking possession of his see the new bishop signed the *Henoticon*, as the only true profession of faith, and Anastasius took back his written abjuration of Eutychianism, to destroy this public monument of the imperial perjury.

5. Such were the phases presented by the Eastern schism during the pontificate of St. Gelasius. The close attention given by the Pope to their development did not lessen his care of the other Churches. The Pelagian heresy gave signs of returning life in some Churches of Dalmatia and Picenum

(the Marches of Ancona). The Sovereign Pontiff wrote to the bishops of these places, reminding them of the anathemas already pronounced against this heresy by his predecessors Innocent I., Zosimus, Boniface I., Celestin I., Sixtus III. and Leo the Great. The apostle of error in Picenum was an old man named Seneca, who openly denied the dogma of original sin and its natural consequence, concupiscence. He permitted an unlimited obedience to the movements of free-will, and thus justified the most shameful excesses. St. Gelasius wished to hold a personal conference with Seneca; but the rude and ignorant pretender stubbornly persisted in his error: every effort to enlighten his understanding or to touch his heart proved equally fruitless. The Pope was obliged to warn the bishops of Picenum against his obstinacy, by bringing out before them all the venom which lay secreted in the doctrine of Pelagius (A. D. 493). In the following year (A. D. 494) Gelasius presided over a council of seventy-six bishops, held at Rome, which regulated several questions of general interest to the Church. Here the list of canonical books of the Old and New Testament was fixed. It is similar to the one subsequently published by the Council of Trent.* The council also established the primacy and the supremacy of the Church of Rome, by the words of our Lord Himself. The second rank is given to the Church of Alexandria and the third to Antioch. Nothing is said of Jerusalem; doubtless because that unhappy city had so far fallen from its former political greatness and influence that the purely nominal prerogatives of its bishops were now contested by no one, simply because they could no longer give umbrage. The number of ecumenical or general councils, whose decrees were to be deemed the standard of faith and morals, was fixed at four: Nice (A. D. 325), Constantinople (A. D. 381), Ephesus (A. D. 431), and Chalcedon (A. D. 451).

---

* There is, indeed, a slight difference between the two canons, but limited to the form. The catalogue of Gelasius mentions but one book of the Machabees, whereas the Council of Trent numbers two. This difference is due to the fact that in the earlier editions of the Bible both books of the Machabees are generally found in one.

The most interesting result of the Council of Rome was the catalogue of lawful and of forbidden books. This is the first decree of the kind issued by a council; and it is also the first trace we meet in ecclesiastical history of an institution afterward extending by degrees, and now known as the *Congregation of the Index*, which is charged by the Sovereign Pontiff to examine new works, as they appear, and to censure those which are blameworthy. The Council of Rome names the Fathers whose authority is admitted by the Church: St. Cyprian, St. Gregory Nazianzen, St. Basil of Cæsarea, St. Athanasius, St. Cyril of Alexandria, St. John Chrysostom, St. Hilary of Poitiers, St. Ambrose, St. Augustine, St. Jerome, St. Prosper, St. Leo the Great. It is allowed to read the works of Rufinus and of Origen, provided the care and reserve prescribed by St. Jerome be observed. Then follows a prohibition to read heretical and apocryphal works; amongst others, the Acts of the Council of Rimini convoked by the emperor Constantius; the *Travels of St. Peter*, under the name of St. Clement; the Acts of St. Andrew, of St. Thomas, of St. Peter and of St. Philip; the Gospels of St. Thaddeus, of St. Mathias, of St. Peter, of St. James, of St. Barnabas, of St. Thomas, of St. Bartholomew and of St. Andrew. To the heretical and apocryphal works the council adds some books written by Catholics, but in some points a little at variance with orthodox teaching; such are some of the writings of Lactantius, Arnobius, Clement of Alexandria, Cassian and others.

6. St. Gelasius, in the course of the same year, gave to the Italian bishops several particular regulations on points of discipline or of canon law. The reins of discipline had been sadly relaxed in Italy by the disastrous consequences of the late war. The Pope renewed the old canons relating to ordination and the choice of subjects, but shortened the intervals hitherto observed in the gradation of orders. Thus the candidate is first to be made *lector, notary* or *defender*, for these three offices seem to have been conferred by the first ordination; three months later he may be made *acolyte ;* six months

must elapse before he can be ordained *subdeacon*, if he have
reached the canonical age; he may be promoted to the office
of *deacon* in the ninth month, and at the close of the year be
ordained *priest*. This rule applied to monks who were to be
raised to the priesthood. For seculars the period was longer;
they could only be ordained priests after eighteen months spent
in the various degrees of the ministry. Other canons concern
the qualities necessary for the candidates. They must be *sufficiently instructed, even in human learning*; they must be *entirely
free from physical deformity* or *serious bodily defect*; they must
never have incurred any suspicion of crime; they must not be
fugitive clerics, that is, having quitted their diocese without
the bishop's leave. St. Gelasius decreed that all those should
be expelled from the body of the clergy who had been convicted of buying their ordination for money; for simony is as
great a sin in the giver as in the receiver. He forbids women
to serve the altar, thus usurping the functions which belong
only to men. He confirms the prescription of St. Simplicius
relative to the division of ecclesiastical revenues into four portions: the first for the bishop; the second for the clergy;
the third for the poor; the fourth for the maintenance of the
churches, sacred vessels, &c. The seasons fixed for ordinations are the ember days of the fourth, the seventh and the
tenth months, and the beginning of Lent. This is still the
rule of the Church. Solemn baptism is only to be conferred
at Easter and Pentecost. Virgins consecrated to God are to
receive the veil only on the Epiphany, at Easter, and on the
feasts of the apostles; except in case of a dangerous illness,
when this consolation may be granted them before death.
Priests shall not raise themselves above their proper rank.
They have power neither to bless the chrism nor to confirm,
nor are they empowered to ordain. These various regulations
are dated March 11 (A. D. 494).

7. In the following year St. Gelasius convoked a council of
forty-five bishops, at Rome. Misenus, one of the legates who
had betrayed the cause of the Church, at Constantinople, in

A. D. 483, under the pontificate of St. Felix III., begged to be
restored. The Pope granted his petition after having made
him pronounce the anathema against Eutyches, Peter Mongus,
Peter the Fuller and Acacius.   Not content with providing,
by these repeated councils, for the discipline and doctrine of
the Church, St. Gelasius kept a watchful eye on the regularity
and grandeur of the liturgy. He composed hymns, like St.
Ambrose, with prefaces and prayers for the Holy Sacrifice and
the administration of the sacraments.   The *Sacramentary*
which bears his name and which there is every reason to
believe authentic, is divided into three books, the first of
which is called *The Course of the Year;* the second *The Feasts of
the Saints;* the third *The Sundays of the Year.* It contains
the masses for the whole year and the formulas for all the
sacraments.   This precious monument of the early liturgy
establishes the existence, at the end of the fifth century, of
most of the usages now observed in the Church of Rome.
The name of St. Gelasius is also connected with the abolition
of an idolatrous ceremony which had outlived the fall of
paganism and had withstood the efforts of all the Sovereign
Pontiffs his predecessors.   Christian Rome saw the yearly
renewal in her midst of the disorders attending the *Lupercalia,*
when young men ran through the streets in a state of obscene
indecency and gave themselves up to the worst excesses of
unbridled license.   The peculiar characteristic of all abuses is
that they become so deeply rooted in the habits of the people
that it is next to impossible to overcome them; and the task
is always the harder in proportion as they are more unreason-
able and absurd.   By his efforts against the *Lupercalia,* the
Holy Pontiff made many enemies even among enlightened
men.   Their recriminations found an organ in the senator
Andromachus who wrote a treatise to uphold this untenable
cause.   He attributed the plague then raging in Rome to the
suppression of this festival, *which had,* said he, *irritated the
tutelary genii of the empire.* Gelasius met these arguments in
a spirited and eloquent work.   " Were not sacrifices offered to

the god Februarius," said the Pontiff, "were not the Lupercalia celebrated when the Gauls took Rome? In the time of
the invasions, when Alaric sacked this city, why did not Castor
and Pollux, whom the heathens continued to worship, give
favorable winds and sea, to supply Rome with grain in plenty?
Tell me, you who are neither Christians nor heathens; you
who defend the Lupercalia and indecent songs worthy of a
religion whose very rite is a disgrace; what good can come of
a superstition that causes such a corruption of morals? But,
you will say, the Lupercalia have been tolerated since the
establishment of Christianity. Are you not aware that it is
impossible to heal all moral evils at once, just as no physician
can at once restore a shattered constitution to perfect health?
The most serious evils must be first attacked that, in the end,
all may be met. For my part, in exercising my authority, I
obey the voice of conscience; I proclaim to the Christians that
such practices are vicious and fatal; I forbid them henceforth
to take any part in them. Had my predecessors thought the
season well timed they would have acted as I have done.
But of my own actions and not of theirs must I give an account,
when I shall stand before our common Judge." The zeal of
the learned Pontiff was ever renewed to secure the triumph of
justice and truth; and yet in the midst of so many weighty
and harassing occupations he still found time to write valuable works against the Nestorian and Eutychian errors.

8. In a treatise on the *Anathema*, which was interrupted by
death, he proves the ecumenical character of the Council of
Chalcedon and the obligation binding on every Catholic to
submit to its decisions. He then proposes this objection:
"If the Council of Chalcedon be received, it must be received
in full, and thus we must admit the prerogative of second
rank granted by its twenty-eighth canon, to the Bishop of Constantinople." Gelasius answers it himself: "The whole
Church readily receives what the council ordains with the
approbation of the Apostolic See. But the decision passed in
opposition to the orders of the Roman See and at once con-

tradicted by the legates of the Sovereign Pontiff, was never
approved or ratified by the Pope, notwithstanding all the
solicitations of the emperor Marcian. Even Anatolius, then
Bishop of Constantinople, declared that the validity of the
canon depended upon the approval of the Roman Pontiff;
but the Roman Pontiff, far from confirming, has ever
steadily opposed it. The twenty-eighth canon of the Council
of Chalcedon is therefore null and void." The manner in
which the Pope treats the division of the temporal and spiritual authority is equally remarkable : " Before the coming
of Jesus Christ," he says, "it was not impossible for the
priestly and the royal authority to meet in the same person,
as we find in the case of Melchisedech. But since the advent
of Him Who is truly both King and Pontiff, the king no longer
bears the name of pontiff, nor does the Pontiff claim the royal
dignity. God has spared human weakness by dividing the
duties of the two powers; that the Christian emperor may
submit to the spiritual authority of the Pontiff, and the Pontiff
obey the emperor's ordinance in temporal matters." This
definition of the two powers clearly shows that no bishop can
be bound or released, in spiritual concerns, by any secular
power; that therefore Peter Mongus, when under ecclesiastical censure, could not be lawfully absolved or reinstated by an
imperial decree of Zeno. This is the precise bearing of the
Pope's argument. It has been attempted to stretch the application of these words, and modern innovators claim to prove
them an indirect condemnation of the temporal sovereignty
now vested in the Holy See, as the times and the wants of
society have consecrated it in our midst. St. Gelasius referred
only to the special attributes of each individual power, neither
of which may encroach upon the other's demesne. He by no
means intended to convey that the Pope, as spiritual sovereign,
was, by that very title, incapable of holding, as temporal
king, a territory which should secure his personal independence,
in so far as it tends to promote peace and quiet among all nations.

9. The life of this holy Pope was as worthy of admiration

as his erudition. The lofty dignity with which he had been
invested was, in his eyes, a servitude rather than a claim to
power. His time was given to prayer and meditation on the
Holy Scriptures. His mind, rich in ecclesiastical learning,
displays itself in his immense correspondence and the works
we have quoted. His happiness was to be amongst the servants of God and to speak with them on spiritual subjects.
He practised the mortifications and fasts of the most austere
anchorets; though himself a model of poverty, he yet fed
those poorer than himself. The least neglect of a Pontiff he
looked upon as a great evil to souls. The greatest prudence,
moderation and patience marked his conduct in the midst of
the intricate negotiations that beset his pontificate. Such is
the portrait of this holy Pontiff, left us from the testimony of
eye-witnesses, by Dionysius the Little, who wrote his life.
St. Gelasius died on the 21st of November, A. D. 496, having
ruled the Church of God for four years. He had established,
as an obligatory custom, that all the faithful should receive
the Holy Eucharist under both forms. This ordinance was
chiefly intended to combat the doctrine of the Manicheans of
the day, who held wine in abhorrence, asserting it to be the
gall of the prince of darkness, and a creature of the devil. Such
were their own words. The custom of receiving under both
kinds was observed until the twelfth century, when it began
to fall into disuse, and was finally abolished by the Council of
Constance, in A. D. 1416. The Council of Trent, however,
granted this privilege to the kings of France on the day of
their coronation, and to the deacons and sub-deacons of certain
churches on Sundays and high festivals.

§ II. Pontificate of St. Anastasius II. (Nov. 28, A. D. 496—
Nov. 16, 498).

10. After an interregnum of seven days Anastasius, a
native of Rome, was raised to the Chair of St. Peter (November 28, A. D. 496). The Church of God, long wrung with grief—

in the East, by the Greek schism; in Africa, Italy, Spain and Gaul, by the inroads of barbarians, carrying along with them Arianism or idolatry—was now raised up by two subjects of great consolation. One was the heroic perseverance of the first Christian nation of the East, the Armenians; the other, the conversion of the first Christian nation of the West, the Franks. The Persian monarchs had long followed a system of open and bloody persecution to destroy Catholicity in Armenia. But there, as in the Roman Empire, the blood of martyrs had proved the fruitful seed of new conversions. Toward the year 480, Nestorianism began to make its appearance in Armenia, brought from Mesopotamia by the youths who had gone to acquire letters and science in the schools of Edessa. One of the most energetic fomenters of the error was a certain Barsumas, a man of pliant, ingenious and enterprising disposition. He had, by means of intrigues, raised himself to the bishopric of Nisibis. In order to ingratiate himself into the favor of Perozes, king of Persia, Barsumas suggested to him to change the aim of the persecutions hitherto inflicted upon the Armenian Christians; to oblige them now to embrace the doctrines of Nestorius instead of those of Zoroaster. With a view to draw into open error a number of questionable and staggering vocations, Barsumas drew a decree from a false council assembled by him, allowing all the clergy and bishops, and even Patriarchs, to marry; he began by setting the example himself. The metropolitan of Seleucia excommunicated Barsumas, who sent the decree to the king of Persia; the monarch ordered the metropolitan to be suspended to a beam by the annular finger and in that position scourged to death. To complete his satisfaction, Barsumas obtained permission to persecute the Catholics. Upward of seven thousand seven hundred of them were immolated to the heretic's thirst for revenge. Christopher, Patriarch of Armenia, on learning the progress of heresy and the disasters caused by the fury of a wretched apostate, at once issued a circular to all the countries in his jurisdiction, to prepare them to meet the

Nestorian plague. So firm was their devotion to the true faith that Barsumas was forced to back his preaching by the more tangible argument of a Persian army. But the Armenians putting their trust in the intercession of the glorious martyrs who, for two centuries past, had given their blood for the faith of their fathers, rose up, as one man, protesting that they would rather perish in one day on the field of battle than live to see the continual humiliations endured by the Church under the Persian yoke. They conquered and cut to pieces the army of Perozes (A. D. 481). In the spring of the following year (482) a renewed attempt of the Persian king gave to the Armenians a like triumph.

11. The hero of these combats, the Machabee of Armenia, was the general Vahan, the descendant of a Chinese imperial family which had taken refuge in this country. Vahan followed up his success with untiring energy; he was never cast down by reverses; and the triumphs which raised the courage of his troops never betrayed him into the rash imprudence of presumptuous confidence. Until the death of Perozes, in A. D. 484, he met the combined efforts of the whole of Persia. The successors of the persecuting monarch were terrified at the gigantic proportions of a struggle in which a whole people had sworn to die rather than deny their faith; they accordingly proposed to Vahan the most honorable terms of peace. The right of Armenia to retain its faith was recognized. All the pagan temples were destroyed. The Persians pledged themselves to make no further efforts amongst the Armenians to gain proselytes to the idolatry of Zoroaster. The treaty of peace was drawn up on these terms, and Vahan signed it on behalf of his countrymen who solemnly bestowed upon him the rank of governor-general of Armenia. On the hero's return to Dovin, the capital of Armenia, he was met by the venerable Patriarch John Mutakouni, followed by his clergy in solemn procession bearing the relics of St. Gregory the Illuminator; the procession was swelled by the people of the city and of the neighboring country and by the army with

which he had won his country's freedom. The whole multitude proceeded to the cathedral of Dovin, to make a solemn return of thanksgiving to God. Even here, notwithstanding the majesty of the holy place, the people were unable to contain their feelings, and broke out into long and loud acclamations of indescribable enthusiasm : the object of all this manifestation of feeling, whose heroism was equalled but by his modesty, could command a moment of silence only to depose upon the altar of the God of armies the sword which had won such renown in His cause.

12. Whilst Armenia was thus gloriously asserting her right to remain Christian, the nation of the Franks, one day to be known as the *eldest daughter of the Church*, was entering the true fold. Gregory of Tours, the early historian of this glorious race, speaks in very modest terms of the first steps of the Franks in Gaul: "It is supposed," says the historian, "that Clodion, a man of authority and distinction in his nation, was at that time king of the Franks; they held their residence at Dispargum, on the frontier of the Thuringian territory of Maestricht. The Romans held possession of the country stretching southward to the Loire; beyond the Loire were the Goths. The Burgundians, who also professed Arianism, lived beyond the river Rhone which flows by the city of Lyons. Clodion sent spies into the city of Cambray and received from them a report of the state of the surrounding country; he subsequently defeated the Romans and took possession of the country. After a short stay here he extended his conquests as far as the river Somme. Some writers assert that king Meroveus, father of Childeric, was of the race of Clodion." Clovis (A. D. 481), the son of Childeric, was in command only of the small tribe of the Franks of Tournay when he defeated the Roman patrician Syagrius at Soissons (A. D. 486). Clovis, who was as skilful a politician as he was an intrepid warrior, though still a heathen, made every effort to win the favor of the Catholic clergy for his cause, as he held their holy mission and salutary influence in the highest veneration. He avoided

in his march the great cities which had already submitted to
him. This was the only means of saving from plunder the
convents and basilicas which the piety of the faithful had im-
mensely enriched. Yet one of the churches of Rheims, of
which city St. Remigius, the most illustrious of the Gallic prelates, was then bishop, could not escape the rapacity of a band
of marauding Franks. Amongst the articles which formed
their booty was a sacred vessel of unusual size and beauty.
St. Remigius was informed of the fact and sent to Clovis to
claim the prize. Delighted at the prospect of serving the
bishop, the king said to the deputies: "Come with me to Soissons, and if the stolen vessel be found among the plunder you
shall have it." The precious article was soon found amid the
spoils heaped up under a tent in the public square. "My brave
comrades," said Clovis to the Franks who pressed around their
leader, "you will not take it amiss that I restore this vessel to
those who claim it." The officers and soldiers exclaimed, in
reply: "What! cannot you take it without asking for it? Are
you not master, and is not ours also yours?" "Not so,"
answered a rude and jealous soldier; "you shall have this cup
only when it is yours by lot." And with a blow of his battle-
axe, he shivered the costly object of dispute. Clovis silently
gathered up the fragments and gave them to the messengers
of St. Remigius.[*] A year had passed away since this event;
the king was one day reviewing the Franks in a *field of Mars*
(a yearly gathering of the warriors), when he recognized the
soldier whose rude audacity had appealed to the right of division: "Your arms," said the king to him, "are in the worst
condition of any that I have seen in the army; your mace,
your sword and your battle-axe all show your slovenly carelessness." Then snatching away his axe, Clovis threw it upon
the ground. The soldier stooped to pick it up, but the king,

---

[*] Such is the account of contemporary writers. Some modern authors, in their zeal to
show that perfect equality existed between the chief and his subjects, have distorted the
account, and in order to press their own view upon the reader, have passed over the chief
incident, that is, the restoration of the vessel, although in fragments, to the deputies of St
Remigius.

suddenly lifting up his own, clove in two the trooper's skull.
"So," he exclaimed, "you did to the cup at Soissons!" This
bloody execution performed by the hand of the king himself
seems repugnant to our day and custom : then it was deemed
but severe, and was more powerful than laws to teach the victors that they should spare the vanquished. St. Remigius
entertained a strong hope of implanting the true faith in the
heart of a prince whose power kept pace with his renown, and
who was evidently destined to rule the whole of Gaul.

He deemed that this could be best brought about by giving
to Clovis a Christian wife. He therefore effected for him an
alliance with a princess as distinguished for virtue as for nobility of birth—one whose memory, perpetuated by the Church
in the calendar of the saints, is imperishably dear to every
French heart. Clotilda was the niece of Gundebald, king of
the Burgundians. Brought up in an Arian court under the
eye of an uncle who had murdered her father and mother to
gain possession of their wealth, she was still a Catholic, and
the holiness of her life corresponded to the purity of her faith.
As queen of the Franks, her virtue and her charms won her
husband's heart; she made use of his perfect confidence in her
only to draw him gradually out of the darkness of heathenism.
He seemed already on the point of yielding to her wishes, when
an unfortunate event turned him suddenly back. Their first-
born son, baptized under the name of Ingomar, died whilst yet
in his baptismal robe. Clovis harshly reproached Clotilda, and
said : "Had the child been consecrated to my gods, he had not
died." He was, however, appeased and allowed his second
son to be carried to the baptismal font and baptized under the
name of Clodomir. The illness of his child threw Clotilda
into a state of harrowing anguish. Clovis already accused her
of causing the death of both children. Clodomir however
recovered ; but Clovis was still distrustful. It was necessary
that a conversion, fraught with consequences so important,
should be effected in such a manner as to convince the world
that it was the work of Heaven—of the power of the Most High.

13. Several bodies of Suevi or Alemanni crossed the Rhine at Cologne, A. D. 496, and invaded the dominions of Sigebert, chief of the Ripuarii. Clovis armed his Franks and hastened toward the Rhine, to the help of Sigebert. The two armies met near Tolbiac (the present Tulpick in the duchy of Juliers). Both nations were equally brave, equally jealous of their glory and their freedom; the shock of battle was fearful. Sigebert was wounded and his troops thrown into a state of disorder; the panic was rapidly spreading along the ranks, when Clovis, seeing the desperate state of his cause, cried aloud: "God, whom Clotilda worships, I have no refuge but Thee. Come to my help, and I will believe in Thee, I will be baptized in Thy name." This vow, uttered in a loud voice, rallied his scattered warriors about him. Clovis himself felt a new courage within his bosom, and cheering on his Franks, rushed with headlong daring upon the enemy. The consternation and terror the Burgundians had caused, now returned to their own ranks; and their king remained upon the field amid the flower of his army (A. D. 496). On his return to his own domain after this victory, Clovis put himself under the direction of St. Remigius and of St. Vedastus, a holy priest from the neighborhood of Toul. One day the holy bishop of Rheims was reading to him the Passion of Jesus Christ; Clovis, filled with the honest indignation of a soldier whose soul is wrapt up in arms, exclaimed: "Oh! that I had been there with my Franks!" On another occasion he said to St. Remigius: "I would willingly go on listening to you, but I foresee an obstacle; my people will not give up their present belief; but I will go and speak to them as you advise." A general assembly of the chiefs was accordingly called; but the king had hardly begun to speak when the Salians exclaimed: "We forsake mortal gods; we wish for no other than the Immortal God of Remigius." The bishop joyfully made preparations for the baptism of the king and the Franks, and, assisted by St. Vedastus, continued to instruct and to prepare them according to the canons, by some days of fasting, penance and prayer.

The baptismal fonts of St. Martin's, the great church of Rheims, were magnificently adorned; the nave was decorated with white hangings; the same emblematic color also appeared in the dress of Clovis and the other catechumens chosen from among the flower of the Salians. On Christmas night (A. D. 496) all the streets were tapestried from the king's palace to the basilica; the church blazed with a thousand fires shed from richly perfumed tapers. The procession moved on towards the basilica, preceded by the cross and the book of Gospels borne in state. St. Remigius led the king by the hand; they were followed by Queen Clotilda, and the two princesses Albofleda and Lantilda, sisters of Clovis. Upward of three thousand officers and nobles of the court, all dressed in white ornaments, were going to receive baptism with their king. Clovis, struck by the splendor of this august night, asked the holy bishop: " Father, is this the Kingdom of Christ, into which you promised to lead me?" " No," answered St. Remigius, "it is but the opening of the path that leads to it." Standing before the font the king begged the grace of regeneration in this saving water. The bishop addressed him: " Bow down your neck in meekness, great Sicambrian prince; adore what you have hitherto burnt, and burn what you have hitherto adored." Then, having made him profess his belief in the Holy Trinity, he baptized him and anointed him with holy chrism. The three thousand officers and soldiers who accompanied him, besides a great number of women and children, were then baptized by the attendant bishops and other clergy. Albofleda received baptism; and Lantilda, who was already a Christian, but had fallen into Arianism, was reconciled to the Church and received the unction of holy chrism. Clovis, unwilling to see the rejoicings of so happy a night marred by the tears of the unfortunate, ordered the release of all captives and made costly offerings to the churches. That Christmas night which lighted the birth of the Franks to the true faith, has always been dear to France as a family festival. " Noël!" was ever the cheer and the battle-cry of our fathers.

14. If we have seemed to dwell upon this event with some complacency, it is because of a natural sentiment which must be readily understood. Besides, at the time of its occurrence it was hailed with joy by the whole Catholic world. Pope Anastasius II. was particularly rejoiced at this conversion, as he hoped to find in Clovis a powerful champion of the Church. He was then, in fact, the only truly Catholic sovereign. The emperor Anastasius, in the East, was given up to Eutychianism; Theodoric, in Italy; Alaric II., king of the Visigoths, in Spain and Aquitania; Gundebald, king of the Burgundians, in Gaul; Thrasimund, king of the Vandals, in Africa, were all Arians. The Pope wrote to Clovis in these words : " We congratulate you, most glorious son, that your conversion to the Christian faith is simultaneous with our promotion to the pontificate. Can the Chair of St. Peter be insensible to a feeling of joy that the nations are now gathering under its shadow, when it sees the net which the fisher of men has been ordered to cast into the sea of the world, filling up through the flow of ages ? We have been moved to impart to your Highness some of the joy we feel, that knowing your father's heart, you may increase in good works; that you may perfect our consolation and be our crown; and that your Mother, the Church, may rejoice in the progress of so great a king whom she has borne to God. Glorious and illustrious son, be then your Mother's consolation; show yourself in her defence an unshaken pillar; for in these days the charity of many has grown cold, and the bark of Peter is beaten by a furious storm. Yet we hope against all hope ; and we bless the Lord that he has drawn you out of darkness, to give to the Church, in so powerful a prince, a protector able to defend her against all her enemies. May Almighty God ever shower down His heavenly blessings upon your person and kingdom! May He give charge to His angels to keep you in all your ways, and ever crown your arms with victory." St. Avitus, Bishop of Vienne, although a subject of Gundebald, also writes to congratulate Clovis on his conversion. " It is not," he writes, " without a mystery of grace

that the light of faith dawned upon your nation on the very
day of the Saviour's birth. It was fitting that you should be
regenerated in the waters of baptism on the day that brought
down the Lord of heaven and earth for the salvation of the
world! Oh, how full of consolation for the Church was that
hallowed night! What a sight to behold that head dreaded
by nations, humbly bowed before the servants of the Lord; to
see those tresses which have grown under the helmet of war,
now crowned by the holy unction with the helmet of salvation; to see the warrior put off for a time his breast-plate, to
wear the white robe of the neophyte! Doubt not, most illustrious of monarchs, the unpretending purity of this new habit
will give new power to your arms; and what your good fortune has hitherto done for you, your piety will but do better
still. The world resounds with your triumphs. Though of
another country, your glory moves us also. Every time that
you engage in battle the victory is equally ours." The hopes
expressed by St. Anastasius II. and St. Avitus of Vienne
were not deceived. From the days of Charles Martel to our
own the Church has ever safely leaned upon the sword of
France. St. Avitus, whose noble address to Clovis we have
just quoted, was grandson of the emperor Avitus, and son of
the senator Hesychius who had, after his marriage, been
raised to the See of Vienne, on the death of St. Mammertus.
St. Avitus succeeded his father in A. D. 490. His elder brother, Apollinaris, also became bishop of Vienne. To the lustre
of noble birth, Avitus joined the brighter glory of virtue and
talents. He is particularly distinguished as a Christian poet.
Six remarkable poems of his are still extant: 1st, on the creation; 2d, on the fall of man; 3d, on the expulsion of our first
parents from the Garden of Eden; 4th, on the deluge; 5th,
on the passage of the Red Sea; 6th, on virginity. The first
three together form a complete epopee, and might be styled
Paradise Lost. These works show a true poetic genius, and
deserve a wider reputation, at least in Christian schools.

15. From such a page it is painful to turn again toward

the East, still a prey to lamentable dissensions. Pope Anastasius II. had availed himself of the occasion offered by Theodoric's embassy to Constantinople, to send to the East two
legates, the bishops Cresconius and Germanus. Their mission
was to make new efforts to obtain from the emperor Anastasius
the removal from the diptychs of the names of Acacius and
Peter Mongus; they were also to demand the recognition of
the Council of Chalcedon, and consequently the extinction of
the schism. The arrival of the Pope's legates in the East
caused a deep sensation. Two priests of the Church of Alexandria were sent to Constantinople to work together for the
reconciliation of the See of St. Mark with the Apostolic See.
The legates were charged to lay before the Pope the profession of faith of the Alexandrian clergy. Even Macedonius,
Patriarch of Jerusalem, seemed disposed to do his share in
bringing about a lasting reconciliation. He wished to send to
the Roman Pontiff synodal letters stating the grounds of
future negotiations. But all these brightening hopes were
crushed by the unbending obstinacy of the emperor Anastasius,
who opposed the desire of Macedonius and forbade him, on
pain of exile, to hold any communication with the Holy See;
" not wishing," he said, " to hear of any accommodation, unless
the Pope consented to sign the *Henoticon.*" Some historians
assert that it was his aim to insnare the Sovereign Pontiff and
to bring him, by insidious wiles and promises, to betray the
cause of God and of truth. He little knew the unfailing
firmness of the Chair of Peter, against which the gates of hell
shall never prevail. Still less was he acquainted with the
noble character of St. Anastasius II., its occupant. When the
legates returned to Rome, the pious Pontiff was no more; he
had gone to his reward on the 16th of November, A. D. 498.
His reign had been short; but it had sufficed to prove his
apostolic zeal for the progress of the faith; wisdom and prudence characterized all his decisions. Having been consulted
by the Catholics of Constantinople concerning the baptism
administered by Acacius and his partisans, the Pope answered

that the sacraments of Baptism and Orders conferred by a bishop who was excommunicated and suspended from ecclesiastical functions, were still valid, and that those who had received the sacraments from them were not to be disturbed on that account.

§ III. PONTIFICATE OF ST. SYMMACHUS (Nov. 22, A. D. 498— July 19, 514).

16. On the 22d of November, A. D. 498, the deacon Symmachus was chosen to succeed St. Anastasius II. Meanwhile the senator Festus, an agent of the Eastern emperor, had been sent to Rome, with secret instructions to gain the approval of the Holy See for the *Henoticon*. During the pontifical election he bribed some clerics to elect the arch-priest Lawrence, who was in communication with Anastasius. The two newly-elected candidates were consecrated on the same day—Symmachus in the basilica of Constantine; Lawrence in that of St. Mary Major. Thus this pretended *edict of union*, which had already separated the East and the West, now threatened, by miserable intrigues, to rend the Roman Church itself. The schism brought from Constantinople to Rome bid fair to cause a civil strife. An instant remedy was needed; the most regular, and in fact the only canonical mode of action, would have been to call a council of the Italian bishops; but the convocation would have taken several months. The city had in the mean time become the scene of bloody tumults. The urgency of the case therefore drove them to seek another remedy; it was agreed that Symmachus and Lawrence should go to Ravenna and abide by the decision of King Theodoric. This monarch, though an Arian, had on numberless occasions proved his high esteem for the Church; besides, his prime minister, Cassiodorus, was a fervent Catholic. The famous regulations he had just published in his master's name, his reputation for virtue, justice and wisdom had established his renown in Italy, and made him the model of great ministers. These considera-

tions doubtless led the Roman clergy to submit a purely ecclesiastical case to the court of Ravenna. The wisdom of the act was proved by the issue. At the instigation of Cassiodorus, Theodoric decided that the pontifical authority resided in him who had been first elected and by the greater number of suffrages. These two conditions met in the election of Symmachus, who was at once recognized as Sovereign Pontiff and entered upon the immediate discharge of his duties. His first act of authority was the convocation of a council in the basilica of St. Peter (March 1, A. D. 499), to regulate the manner of pontifical elections, and thus to preclude the recurrence of the canvassing and factions which had marked his consecration. The council numbered seventy-two bishops, sixty-seven priests, and five deacons. Three canons were drawn up relative to the election of the Sovereign Pontiffs. The first ordained that *if any priest, deacon or cleric, during the lifetime of the Pope, and without his participation, is convicted of having given or promised his suffrage for the pontificate to any aspirant, whether in writing or by a verbal promise, he shall be deposed from all ecclesiastical functions.* The second prescribes *that if the Pope dies suddenly without being able to provide for the election of his successor, he shall be consecrated who has received the suffrages of all the clergy; if there be a division, the majority shall carry the election.* The third decrees that *any one who has any knowledge, in whatever manner acquired, of culpable intrigues, shall make them known;* promising even to accomplices who may make such revelation, the pardon of the crime in which they shared; thus leaving to the authors of these shameful dealings no hope of concealment, and hence of impunity. These decrees were subscribed by all the bishops, priests and deacons in the assembly. Among the signatures appears the name of the arch-priest Lawrence, of the title of St. Praxedes, the same who had been elected antipope.

17. This ambitious priest had promised Festus that in case he were placed upon the papal throne he would conform to the wishes of Anastasius, and sign the *Henoticon.* When the elec-

tion of Symmachus had been confirmed by the decision of Theodoric, Lawrence seemed to repent of his conduct; he shared the labors of the council, and Symmachus bestowed on him the dignity of bishop of Nocera. The schism seemed to be at an end. But Festus felt the necessity of pleasing the emperor, and not finding Symmachus as yielding as he would have wished, he rekindled the flame of discord. In the year 500 he called Lawrence to Rome and they hired false witnesses to convict Symmachus of adultery and of embezzlement in the administration of Church property. These complaints were brought to Theodoric. The king of the Ostrogoths charged Peter, bishop of Altinum, to go to Rome and examine on the spot the grounds of the accusation. Peter, forgetting the impartiality due to the nature of his mission and the consideration he owed to St. Symmachus, at once sided with the antipope and his partisans. Symmachus saw himself beset with snares and dangers, exposed to the insults of a faction paid in Byzantine gold, and forced to shut himself up as a prisoner in the basilica of St. Peter. In this extremity the Catholics of Rome had recourse to Theodoric, and begged him to call a council of Italian bishops from all the provinces. Theodoric accordingly sent letters of convocation to the bishops of Emilia, Liguria, and Venetia. But these prelates gave a noble proof of loyalty and devotion to the Holy See. To the king's summons they returned the answer that the convocation of councils belongs only to the Pope; that the Sovereign Pontiff derives this prerogative from the primacy of the Chair of St. Peter, on which he is seated; that the canon law, in this particular, is most explicit; and that it was an unheard-of occurrence in the history of the Church that the Pope should be subject to the judgment of his inferiors. To remove this objection, Theodoric begged Symmachus to write in person to the bishops to attend the council. In obedience to this canonical call one hundred and fifteen bishops met at Rome in the month of July, A. D. 501. As soon as they had assembled in the *Julian basilica*, Symmachus entered the church, and having expressed his gratitude to Theodoric for the convocation of the council, declared that he had himself desired it, and, *in the presence of all the fathers, gave them authority to judge the case.* These are the words used in the acts of the council. But the city continued to present a scene of unabated tumult; the sedition excited by Festus and the antipope Lawrence grew daily more violent. A troop of furious rioters even dared to attack the Pope as he was on his way to the council, and severely wounded several priests who accompanied him. When Theodoric heard of these disorders he sent some of his officers to repress them, with orders to use the sternest measures against the guilty parties. He also wrote to the Fathers of the council at the same time; his letter shows the exalted sentiments and noble mind of his able minister Cassiodorus. "Had it fallen within the sphere of my powers," wrote the king, "to take personal cognizance of this matter, I could, by the help of divine grace, have brought it to a satisfactory close. But it is the cause of God and of His ministers; hence I called upon you to discuss it; for I did not deem it my province to decide in ecclesiastical matters. Pronounce your judgment, then, according to the dictates of your conscience, and thus restore peace to the senate, the clergy and the people of Rome." After mature deliberation and a thorough investigation of the charges, the council was convinced that Symmachus had been lawfully and canonically elected and that he was perfectly innocent of the crimes imputed to him. They then held a closing session, commonly called *Synodus Palmaris*, perhaps from the name of the church in which the bishops met. Here the authority of Symmachus was solemnly recognized, his innocence proclaimed, and his communion identified with that of the Church. "Those clerics who have separated themselves from him and taken part in the schism," says the decree, "must make satisfaction to him and obtain his pardon before they can be reinstated. Whoever, after this decision, ventures to exercise the functions of the holy ministry without being in communion with Symmachus, shall be canonically punished as a schismatic."

18. The questions arising out of the election of St. Symmachus had recalled the protestation presented at the death of St. Simplicius by the patrician Basil in the name of Odoacer, king of the Heruli. It will be remembered that the barbarian claimed the right to confirm or to annul the election of the Roman Pontiffs. This document had never been juridically examined. A council held in Rome (A. D. 502), by Pope St. Symmachus, thus decides its value: "Such a document could never bind a Roman Pontiff, since no one has the right to make laws in the Church without the Pope's consent. If the canons and the traditions of the holy fathers nullify whatever the bishops of a province may do without the metropolitan's approval, how much less value should be attached to any decisions of laymen in ecclesiastical matters, without the concurrence of the Sovereign Pontiff, who holds, together with the prerogative of St. Peter, the primacy of the priesthood in the whole Catholic world; and whose consent is indispensable to the legal force of even decrees of the councils?" Thus the unanimous judgment of the fathers rejected the patrician Basil's protestation as opposed to the canons, as irregular and of no effect. In the following year (503) Symmachus convoked another council at Rome, near the venerated tomb of the Prince of the Apostles, which was even then called the *Confession of St. Peter*. The discussions of this council again turned upon the authority and prerogatives of the Apostolic See, against which the schismatics raised many objections. They were set forth in a treatise called *Against the Synod of the Irregular Absolution;* for so they called the synod in which the innocence of Symmachus had been proclaimed. "By asserting," said they, "that the Pope, as supreme judge, can himself be judged by no one, is he not left free to commit any crime with impunity? If it be true that the Pope can never be subjected to the judgment of his inferiors, why did Symmachus submit to the decision of the council assembled at Rome by Theodoric? How could this Pope refuse to admit the authority of Peter, bishop of Altinum, sent by the king to take cognizance of the difficulty, when he himself sends to

other Churches legates and bishops to settle all disputes and provide for the maintenance of ecclesiastical discipline?" St. Ennodius, then but a deacon, and subsequently bishop of Pavia, undertook to refute these objections in a sound and eloquent treatise. "St. Peter," he said, "has transmitted to his successors a lasting gift of merit, together with the heritage of his innocence. Should any one of them prove personally less worthy of the lofty position, his defect would be supplied by the merits of so illustrious a predecessor. Jesus Christ, upon Whom the Church ever rests, has a care that its foundation, that is, the Pope, its visible head, shall never fail. Pope Symmachus consented, through humility, to submit to a judgment which could by no means oblige him. He was forced to it by the violence of the schismatics." This treatise of Ennodius was solemnly approved by the council which adopted its teaching and formally recognized its authority. The Fathers wished now to condemn personally those who had unjustly accused Symmachus. But the merciful Pontiff declared that he freely forgave them all the evil they had sought to do him. The council then only renewed the ancient canons which forbade the faithful to accuse their pastor, except in the case of his teaching errors against the faith. It was also forbidden to deprive an accused bishop of his property or to expel him from his see, until a formal sentence had been pronounced against him. These various statutes were confirmed on pain of deposition in the case of clerics, and of excommunication for monks and laymen; they are all threatened with an anathema if they fail to amend.

19. The acts of these councils are a fair index of the light in which the Catholics then viewed the authority and prerogatives of the Roman Pontiff. This testimony is not a little strengthened by the sensation to which the event gave rise in Gaul. When it became known that a council of Italian bishops had undertaken to sit in judgment upon the Pope, all the Gallic bishops were alarmed at it, and charged St. Avitus, bishop of Vienne, to draw up a protest in their name. He addressed

his letter to Faustus and Symmachus, two patricians of consular rank. "We were in a state of great alarm," he writes,
"concerning the Roman schism ; for we felt that the episcopacy of which we are members is seriously threatened when
its head is thus attacked. In the height of our agitation, we
received the decree of the Council of Rome in the matter of
Pope Symmachus. It is not easy to understand on what principle a superior can be judged by his inferiors. We are directed by the Apostle not to hear an accusation against a simple
priest ; how much less, then, against the Prince of the Universal Church! The council plainly discovers this in its decree,
by taking exception, in a certain measure, to its own compe-
tency in a case it had almost rashly undertaken to discuss.
In my twofold character, then, of bishop and Roman senator,
I beseech you to use the power God has given you in behalf
of religion, and show that you bear as true a love to the Chair
of St. Peter, in the Roman Church, as you do to Rome as the
capital of the world. If the other prelates be found defective
in some point, they can be reformed ; but if the Pope be im-
peached, it is no longer a single bishop, but the whole hierarchy is imperilled. You are aware of the wild storms of heresy
through which we now strive to steer the bark of faith ; if you
share our fear of these storms, you should strive with us to
defend your pilot. When senseless sailors revolt against him
who holds the tiller, does prudence recommend compliance with
their madness by exposing them to danger as a punishment?
It behooves not the flock to call its Pastor to account. That
power belongs to God." This splendid effort does even less
honor to Pope Symmachus than to the Gallic bishops, in whose
name it was written. It is the noblest monument of the Gallic
Church (A. D. 503).

20. The Church was making marvellous strides in Gaul,
owing to the zeal of the holy bishops who filled its sees. Gaul
was divided into three dominations : that of Clovis, in the
north ; of Gundebald, in Burgundy ; and of Alaric II., king of
the Visigoths, in the south. Clovis aimed at establishing the

Frankish monarchy on a basis of unity. His conversion to Christianity could not blot out from his ardent, ambitious nature every vestige of barbarism. The unaffected, simple narrative of Gregory of Tours, by the traits of craftiness and cruelty it records, shows what a herculean task it must have proved to the Church, thoroughly to humanize, to civilize, to Christianize the inborn barbarism of this nation. It is easily understood that such a work demanded ages to reach even a relative perfection. Clovis had, at least, recognized the true principle of all civilization—the Christian faith. He had adopted its living rule, the Catholic Church. The completion of the work was a matter of time. St. Remigius, not content with having won over the Franks to the faith, was striving to draw into the true fold the Arian faction of the Burgundians. In the year 501, he succeeded in assembling at Lyons, Gundebald's capital city, the most illustrious Gallic bishops. Among the prelates were St. Eonius of Arles, Honoratus of Marseilles, St. Avitus of Vienne, St. Apollinaris of Valence, his brother, and several others. The bishops in a body called upon Gundebald at his country-seat of Sarbiniacum.[*] Hostilities had already begun between Clovis and the Burgundian king. Gundebald complained of it to the bishops. " If your faith be the true one," he said to them, " why do you not hinder the king of the Franks from declaring war against me, and joining my enemies to ruin me? The true faith does not countenance the lust of another's possessions nor a thirst for blood." Avitus, in the name of his colleagues, modestly replied : " We know not why the king of the Franks has undertaken the war of which you complain ; but we know that the Scriptures tell us of nations destroyed for having forsaken the law of God. Do you, then, with your people, return to the way of the truth, and God will give you peace." " What !" said Gundebald, " do you pretend to say that I am in the path of error because I do not adore three Gods ?" " Great king," returned Avitus, " we do not adore three Gods. If you would learn the solid

* Sarvigny.

grounds of our faith, order your bishops to confer with us in your presence, and we will give a full explanation of our faith in the Trinity." Gundebald agreed. The first day of September was fixed for the conference. St. Avitus was chosen to speak for the Catholics; an Arian bishop, Boniface, was his opponent. The discussion began. St. Avitus clearly proved that the Catholics by no means adore three Gods; that they rest their belief upon the Scripture and tradition, and there learn their doctrine of one God in three Persons, coequal, coeternal, consubstantial in all things. A general and deep impression was visibly produced by the natural eloquence, grace and conviction which marked the discourse of the bishop of Vienne. Boniface found no better reply to the learned arguments of the Catholic bishop than insult and calumny. He carried his rage to such an excess that Gundebald himself, unable to endure it longer, broke off the conference. He was shaken; from this time the veneration he had ever shown St. Avitus was increased, and he held repeated and long conferences with the holy bishop. One day St. Avitus was urging him to declare himself decidedly for the faith. Gundebald, unable longer to withstand the evidence of the truth, begged the bishop to reconcile him privately by the unction of holy chrism. He was unwilling to give to the step an official and public character, lest his Arian subjects should seize the occasion to revolt against him. "If you really believe," said St. Avitus, "why do you fear to confess your faith? You are a king, and you fear your subjects. You are the chief of the people, and not the people yours. When you go to battle, you march first, and your soldiers follow you. Do the same in the way of truth; show it to your subjects by entering the first upon it." Gundebald lacked courage to follow this noble advice. Human motives bound him to a cause which now commanded neither his sympathy nor his conviction. Though the pages of history reproach Gundebald with acts of cruelty which speak a barbarous origin and manners, yet they also record his efforts to infuse into the hearts of his people the elements of Christianity and civilization. The code of laws which he published, A. D. 502, *in the name of God*, is perhaps not altogether blameless; but considering the state of the Burgundians, and the period of its appearance, it was certainly a step forward.

21. Alaric II. followed the example set by Gundebald, and gave a code of laws to the Visigoths under his jurisdiction. It was almost a complete reproduction of the *Theodosian Code*. Whatever changes or additions he deemed it necessary to make had all been considered and approved by the Catholic bishops of his kingdom. This Arian monarch further showed his regard for the orthodox prelates, by allowing them to hold a council at Agde, in Languedoc. They met to the number of thirty-five, including the deputies of ten who were unable to attend in person (A. D. 506). The council published numerous and important canons and regulations of discipline. It forbids bishops to alienate ecclesiastical property; but they are allowed to free any slaves attached to Church lands. This distinction clearly proves the aim of the bishops and councils to bring about gradually, by gentle means and without coercion, the extinction of slavery in Christian society. Laymen who do not communicate at Christmas, Easter, and Pentecost, are not to be deemed Catholics. Should any one wish to have a private oratory on his estate, he may have the Holy Sacrifice offered in it for his family's convenience; but on the festivals of Easter, Christmas, the Eiphany, the Ascension, Pentecost and other greater solemnities, when Mass is to be celebrated in the parish churches, it cannot be offered in private oratories without special leave of the bishop. We may here remark that the word *Mass* was already used, in speaking of the Sacred Mysteries, at the beginning of the sixth century. It arose from an old Roman custom of dismissing any assembly whatever with the sacramental formula: *Ite, missa est*. In a letter to Gundebald, St. Avitus calls attention to the fact that this expression was consecrated by general usage; that it was used in the palace, after a public reception or ceremony; in the prætorium,

after the passing of sentence; and in the church, after the celebration of the Holy Sacrifice. The council also renewed the prohibition to clerics and monks of travelling without leave and letters from their bishop or abbot. Finally, the forty-second canon bears upon an abuse of which we have already heard, though in a different form. Most of the preceding councils had condemned the arts of magic and all kinds of divination, as so many relics of idolatry; but man's natural love of the marvellous, his ceaseless anxiety to sound the secret depths of futurity, revived the practice of divination, but covered it with the cloak of Christianity. The superstitious practice before mentioned, as *the lot of the saints*, had received various modifications of form. It consisted in opening at random a copy of the Scriptures. The first words that occurred on the opened page were esteemed a presage of the future. The book was sometimes previously laid upon the altar, thus to receive a kind of preparatory blessing. This abuse long prevailed in spite of the watchful energy of pastors and the prohibitions of councils. The canons of Agde were subscribed by the most distinguished bishops of Southern Gaul, who were present : St. Cesarius of Arles, St. Quintian of Rhodez, St. Galactorius of Béarn or of Lescar, St. Glycerius or Lizier of Conserans.

22. The most illustrious of all these names is that of St. Cesarius, who had succeeded St. Eonius in the metropolitan see of Arles (A. D. 502). The earliest years of St. Cesarius had shown proofs of his wonderful disposition to virtue and piety. At the age of seven years he was known to have disposed of his own garments to clothe the poor. When he had reached his eighteenth year he left his father's roof and presented himself to St. Sylvester, bishop of Châlons-sur-Saône, his birth-place; throwing himself upon his knees before him, he begged the holy prelate to confer on him the clerical tonsure, and to receive him into the service of the Church. The bishop was unable to refuse a request so earnestly proffered After spending two or three years at Châlons, Cesarius repaired to

Lerins, the nursery of saints. Here he was soon looked up to as the model of the religious. The esteem in which he was held appeared at the death of St. Eonius, metropolitan of Arles, when the unanimous voice of the clergy and people called for Cesarius to fill the vacant see. On learning his election the humble religious hid himself in some deserted tombs, seeking in the abodes of the dead a shelter from the honors conferred on him by the living. It was found necessary to draw him out by force, that this light, which was to illumine the house of the Lord, might be placed upon the candlestick. Cesarius was but thirty-three years of age. Several holy foundations marked the opening of his administration. He ordered that all the clergy should daily recite the office of Tierce, Sexte and None, with the proper hymns, in the Church of St. Stephen.* His charity founded a hospital for the reception of the indigent sick, who were most carefully provided for. The divine office was recited here, as in the Cathedral Church; but in a low voice, so as not to disturb the patients. No misery was long unknown and none ever unheeded by the merciful heart of the holy bishop. He established a charitable foundation for the ransom of captives; and the thought that some poor wretch might be near him, suffering from want, gave him no moment of rest. He daily sent out his attendants through the streets of the city to gather together all the poor and needy, whom he loved and relieved as the suffering members of Jesus Christ. St. Cesarius founded a monastery of nuns, which he placed under the direction of his sister, St. Cesaria. He gave them a rule of strict enclosure. They never went out, and nobody was admitted into the monastery, neither men nor women; even the church was closed to all except the priests or bishops who came to offer up the prayers and the Holy Sacrifice. The life of these religious was a continued series of prayer, pious duties and mortification. Their

---

* Here is the practice, which subsequently became obligatory in every cathedral, of reciting the canonical office.

poverty was of the strictest character. Many communities of nuns have since adopted the rule of St. Cesarius.

23. Clovis was meanwhile advancing toward the apparent realization of his great plan; he was gradually subduing the whole of Gaul. He had been lately raised from a serious illness in a miraculous way: St. Severinus, abbot of the monastery of Agaune, in Le Valais, had suddenly removed the disease by spreading his mantle over the illustrious patient. Clovis knew no better means of showing his gratitude to God than by overthrowing the Arian power of the Visigoths in Southern Gaul; and he therefore set out upon the expedition. St. Remigius, on this occasion, gave him a counsel equally worthy of the prelate who offered, and of the prince who received it. "Choose," said the bishop, "such counsellors as may add a new lustre to your glory. Make yourself accessible to all; let no one leave your presence with a heavy heart. If you wish to reign with glory, be agreeable with young men, but treat of business only with the aged." Alaric II., long aware of the designs of Clovis, showed the sternest rigor toward all whom he suspected of desiring the rule of the Frank. St. Cesarius of Arles became an object of suspicion, from the mere fact that his birth-place, Châlons-sur-Saône, was under Frankish domination; as this might lead him to favor their design, he was exiled to Bordeaux. Alaric was soon, however, convinced of the injustice of his suspicion, and sent back the holy bishop to his flock. But this ill-timed severity had only embittered the feelings of all against an Arian king. Every thing thus favored the aims of Clovis. In the course of his march, the Frankish king seized every opportunity of showing his reverence for religion; this rallied to his standard the whole body of Catholic Gauls. On his way through 'he province of Tours he wished to give a proof of his veneration for St. Martin, who then held the highest rank in the popular veneration. Clovis issued an order to his whole army, forbidding them, under the severest penalties, to touch any thing but grass and water, throughout the whole extent of the province. A

soldier having found some hay, forcibly took it from a poor
peasant, saying that it was but grass. On being notified of the
act the king immediately ordered the execution of the soldier.
"How can we hope for victory," said he, "if we offend St.
Martin?" At the same time he sent rich presents to the
saint's tomb. Here, again, we may be allowed to make the
same remark that was suggested by the analogous execution of
the soldier of Soissons. Looking upon this deed in the light
of the present day, it might perhaps become a fruitful theme
for criticism; but it is the height of injustice to measure the
habits, convictions and morals of one age, by the rule of the
habits, convictions and morals of a totally different one. At
the date of which we are now treating, a period of transition
from Roman to modern civilization, the barbarian element was
uppermost; it was represented by the conqueror; and victory,
like power, always wields a paramount influence. Clovis aimed
at fixing his system of government in the affections of the
Gauls, the conquered race; and his surest means of success
was to countenance, when the occasion called for them, just
such executions, which were quite lawful according to the barbarian legislation, and which shielded the conquered from the
excesses of the conquerors.

24. Alaric, after remaining long shut up within the walls of
Poitiers, at length came forth and offered battle to Clovis in the
plains of Vouillé, where he lost both crown and life. Clovis
marched on to Languedoc, and would have passed even farther,
had not Theodoric the Great, king of the Ostrogoths in Italy,
and father-in-law of Alaric II., thrown a large army into Provence and Spain, and thus saved what was left to his youthful
grandson (A. D. 507). The evils ever attending an armed invasion were, in this case, retrieved by two benefits of vast importance: the establishment of territorial unity, and for the Church
an unlimited right of asylum and protection. At a time when
all manner of authority was called in question and force was
always the *ultimatum* of governments, it was a great deal to
recognize the inviolability of the Church which undertook the

guardianship and the defence of the vanquished. The battle of Vouillé had completed the work of Clovis. He entered with energy upon the task he had undertaken, and regulated the administration of the new provinces he had just subdued. By the advice of St. Remigius he convoked a council at Orleans (A. D. 511), with a view to the restoration of discipline, sadly relaxed in the midst of so many military movements. The council solemnly confirmed the right of asylum granted to the churches and to the dwellings of bishops. "He who has taken refuge there," says the decree, "cannot be withdrawn until the pursuer swears upon the Holy Gospels that no harm shall be done him." Here we have another evidence of the Church's constant care for the weak and oppressed; preferring to throw her protecting mantle over some unworthy of her interest, rather than risk the loss of innocence by means of passion and brute force. Another canon of the Council of Orleans forbids the admission of laymen to Holy Orders, without the consent of the crown officers in the king's name. This decree has been a fruitful source of discussion amongst jurists, who claim that the civil power has, from time immemorial, enjoyed the right, in France, of intervening in the administration of spiritual and purely ecclesiastical matters. The men of law to whom we refer have done the Council of Orleans the undeserved honor of making it a party to such an opinion. The motive for this decree is most simple and natural; it has not the slightest relation with the theories since started and persistently thrust forward by a certain modern school. Laymen, of free estate, owed military service to the king. The clerical state, by royal exemption, was free from military obligation. But every privilege bears the onerous condition of gratitude. It was just that the king should know who enjoyed his exemption; hence laymen were not admitted to Holy Orders without his consent. The fifth canon directed that the revenue of domains held by the Church, through the royal bounty, should be applied to repairing sacred edifices, to the support of the priests and the poor, and to the ransom of captives. The twenty-seventh orders that the rogation days shall be observed in all the Gallic churches, and that, during these three days, slaves shall be exempt from the usual labor. We have recorded the origin of this institution, at Vienna, under the government of St. Mammertus (A. D. 474). The Council of Orleans renewed the censures pronounced at Agde against divination and the *lot of the saints*. The remaining decrees relate to clerical and monastic discipline, and offer nothing of importance. All these decrees were sent by the bishops *to their lord, the most glorious king Clovis, son of the Catholic Church.* "If," said they, "you deem these decrees worthy of your approval, the agreement of so great a prince, with so many assembled bishops, must secure their observance."

25. The king of the Franks ratified all the canons of the Council of Orleans, and ranked them among the decrees binding throughout the whole extent of his empire. He closed his royal career by bestowing splendid endowments on churches and monasteries. The deed is still extant which transfers the estate of Mici to the Church of Verdun, in the person of the priest St. Euspicius and of Maximin, his nephew. In pursuance of the advice given him by St. Genevieve, who was still living, Clovis had, before setting out on his expedition against Alaric II., laid the corner-stone of a church in Paris, dedicated to Saints Peter and Paul; this he hoped would draw down the blessing of God upon his arms. St. Genevieve died shortly afterward at an extreme old age, and was buried in the church of which became suggested the erection (A. D. 512). This sepulchre became renowned by the many miracles·which God granted to the intercession of the lowly shepherdess of Nanterre, now become the patroness of Paris and of France. The basilica which entombed these precious relics was afterward known by her name, which it has again gloriously regained after twice losing it during the vicissitudes of our political revolutions. The death of Clovis had preceded that of St. Genevieve by a year (A. D. 511). He left to France a monarchy founded on a solid basis; he even left it a name

destined to be illustrated in a long line of kings. (*Clovis* is the Latinized translation of the real Frankish name *Klodwig*, whence the French name Louis.)

26. Not wishing to break off the connection of the history of the Gallic Church during the pontificate of St. Symmachus, upon which we had entered, we have necessarily anticipated the chronological pace of events, and overlooked other portions of the Christian world. Africa, which had begun to taste the sweets of peace for a while under the reign of Gundamund, saw a revival of the persecution against the Catholics, by his brother and successor, Thrasimund (A. D. 496). The new king of the Vandals no longer followed the old system of persecution by open violence, barbarous torture and bloody executions. Gundamund hoped to seduce the Catholics by promises of posts of honor and dignity, by money or by favors. Still he again banished St. Eugenius, bishop of Carthage, who died in the year 505, at Albi, in the Gallic territory under the rule of the Arian Visigoths. He also threatened with the severest penalties those who should consecrate bishops for the vacant sees, hoping thus to break the perpetuity of ecclesiastical government, by interrupting the succession in the episcopate. The African clergy, with one accord, determined to resist this despotic law. All the Christian communities were, as before, provided with pastors. The Church of Africa, so rich in great names and illustrious saints, seemed to feel the approach of a long lethargy, and to redeem itself, by anticipation, with all the life and fruitfulness of its youth. The reputation for holiness acquired by Fulgentius, a youth of an illustrious Carthaginian family, already filled the world and was the admiration even of Rome, whither he had been driven by persecution, in the beginning of Theodoric's reign (A. D. 500). Fulgentius devoted himself with ardor to the study of St. Augustine's works, in which he had found the motives of his conversion. He is deemed the best interpreter of the illustrious doctor's writings on Grace and the Incarnation　The letters in which St. Fulgentius explains

those sublime doctrines are precious for their theological purity and elegant style. Cassian's work on *The Monasteries of
Thebais* gave birth, in the ardent nature of the young African,
to a great love of solitude; he accordingly determined to bury
his growing fame and the bright promise of his virtue and talent in one of those holy retreats. But the day of the An-
thonies and Athanasiuses had passed away. The Theban solitude, once the refuge of genius and persecuted sanctity, was
now open to the Eutychian heresy and the schism of Peter
Mongus. The bishop of Syracuse, to whom St. Fulgentius
had made known his intention, deterred him from it on that
account; he then returned to his own country, just as Thrasimund had issued his prohibition against the consecration of
new bishops. The election of St. Fulgentius to the vacant See
of Ruspa was one of the first and most glorious violations of
the late decree (A. D. 508). The new bishop did not change
his manner of life in the dignity just conferred upon him.
The first work of his episcopate was the erection of a monastery in the town of Ruspa, where he lived among the
brothers, sharing their coarse dress, their prayers and austerities; undistinguished from the rest save by a peculiar degree
of humility, gentleness, patience and mortification. Hardly
had two years elapsed since his promotion to the episcopacy
when Thrasimund's satellites seized him and sent him, by the
king's order, to Sardinia, with sixty bishops of the province
of Byzacium. The confessors of Jesus Christ bore with
them into exile the body of St. Augustine, which remained
for two hundred years at Cagliari; as if the bones of the doctor of grace would abandon their country when it forsook the
teachings of grace and the way of truth.

27. The Pope St. Symmachus, in his charity and pastoral
care, sent yearly supplies of money and clothing to these holy
exiles. King Theodoric also wished to share in this work of
charity. Symmachus, whose heart was enlarged by the increase of misery, every year devoted a considerable sum to
ransoming captives. He poured out the tenderness and pater-

nal solicitude of his heart in consolatory letters to the African bishops; and his tender charity was only equalled by his
zeal in maintaining the rights of the Church. In the year
504 he had held a council at Rome, whose decrees are full of
a truly apostolic energy. They are especially directed against
the usurpation of ecclesiastical estates by the Arian princes.
"It is a sacrilege," says the Pope, "of which God reserves
the punishment to Himself, that the rulers of a country
should take from the Church what the faithful have bestowed
for the remission of their sins and the good of their souls.
Let him then be anathema who unjustly withholds or dis-
honestly disputes the title to ecclesiastical property! Every
such act then, even though ordered by the king, is tainted
with injustice and is null and void." When these energetic
decrees were read, the Fathers of the council adopted them
by acclamation. This firm and decided tone in the sixth
century, under an Arian king, is worthy of remark. It is Theodoric's highest panegyric that not only he never took offence
at these decrees of the Catholic bishops, but shaped his conduct by them in every point. The Church of Narbonne had
been unjustly despoiled; Theodoric immediately wrote to
Duke Ibas, the general who was in command of the Roman
province in Gaul, to restore all that had been taken. He did
the same for the Church of Milan, when the bishop Eustor-
gius had been deprived of the territorial property held by his
see in Sicily. "It is our will," said this great king, "that
nobody suffer any injustice; for the sovereign's glory is the
security of his subjects." "Strive to make yourself as illustrious in peace as you are already renowned in war," wrote
Theodoric to Ibas, "by vigorously crushing every attempt at
oppression." Theodoric's religious reverence had suffered a
momentary violence from the calumnies uttered against St.
Cesarius of Arles. His unprincipled accusers charged the
holy prelate with taking part in some political plots against
the Roman sovereignty. Theodoric governed Provence and
Spain in the name and as guardian of his grandson Amalaric;

he summoned St. Cesarius to Ravenna. The monarch's heart
was touched by the majesty of the venerable prelate. "May
God punish those who have unjustly accused this holy man,"
said Theodoric; "his angelic countenance so plainly bears the
impress of innocence and virtue, that suspicion of him would
be a crime."

28. St. Cesarius availed himself of his journey into Italy
to repair to Rome, where he consulted St. Symmachus on
several points of discipline and canon law; and especially on the
treatment of those who withhold Church property. He also
settled a question agitated since the time of St. Leo the Great,
between the two metropolitan Sees of Arles and Vienne, and
especially kept alive by political revolutions. Several decisions
had been successively obtained by the bishops of the two sees,
but only to the greater intricacy of the question. After mature
deliberation, St. Symmachus simply confirmed the decree of St.
Leo the Great, and annulled all those since rendered. This
regulation, which we mentioned in its proper season, restricted
the jurisdiction of the See of Vienne to the four episcopal
churches of Valence, Tarentaise, Geneva, and Grenoble, and
ordered that all the remaining churches of the province should
be subject to Arles (A. D. 513). Symmachus took pleasure in
heaping every possible honor and dignity upon the illustrious
bishop of Arles. He conferred upon him the *pallium*, a kind
of mantle usually worn by the Roman Pontiffs, and which they
granted to the bishops whom they wished especially to honor;
the *pallium* has since become the distinctive mark of the archbishops. The Pope also constituted St. Cesarius legate of the
Holy See in Gaul and Spain; and charged him, in this character, to look to the welfare of the Church in those two provinces.
The Gallic provinces now offered another subject of sweet consolation to the heart of the Sovereign Pontiff. Prince Sigismund,
son of Gundebald, king of the Burgundians, had just made a public abjuration of Arianism into the hands of the great St. Avitus.
Sigismund, after his reconciliation to the Catholic Church, came
to Rome, where he was honorably received by Symmachus

The conversion of his son seemed to give no offence to Gundebald, for, in the course of the following year, Sigismund was called upon to share his father's power; he fixed his capital in Geneva. This city was, even at that early date, an asylum for the heretics driven from all parts of Christendom. The young prince gave his undivided attention and energy to re-establish the true faith here in all its purity; he rebuilt and enlarged the monastery of Agaune, in honor of the holy martyrs of the Theban Legion; and, in all his undertakings, was guided by the counsels of St. Maximus, bishop of Geneva.

29. Thus strong in the union which reigned between the Pope and the bishops, the Western Church steadily pursued its course of peaceful conquest. But the East was not so bleak. Anastasius's attention had been for a moment called away from his anti-Catholic projects, by a three years' war with the Persians; but in the year 505 he resumed the hostile attitude he had taken toward the Church in the beginning of his reign. Seconded by the intrigues of Xenaias, monophysite bishop of Hierapolis, whom he had called for this end to Constantinople, and by the artifice of the monk Severus, late secretary to Peter Mongus, he soon succeeded in bringing up a formidable array to the support of Eutychianism. The Patriarch Macedonius, by his resistance to the emperor's impious orders, proved himself full worthy of his high position. The people, who were so easily aroused by all dogmatical disputes, were divided into two formidable parties, and their fierce encounters often stained the streets with blood. But Macedonius remained unshaken. Anastasius hired a wretch named Ascholius to murder him; but the assassin missed his stroke and was discovered. Macedonius revenged himself on the intended murderer, by taking him under his protection and bestowing a yearly pension upon him; but this magnanimous conduct failed to move the emperor. He caused an offer of two thousand pounds of gold to be made to Macedonius, and to the other Eastern bishops, on condition of their condemning the decrees of the Council of Chalcedon. To this proposition the patriarch answered, that such a step

could not be taken without an ecumenical council presided over
by the Pope. In his irritation at this reply, the emperor deprived
the Patriarchal Church of the right of asylum and transferred the
prerogative to the heretical churches. Macedonius stood his
ground and anathematized all who dared to speak against the
Council of Chalcedon. The public mind in Constantinople
daily grew in bitterness. During a rising of the heretics,
secretly excited by Anastasius, the Catholics ran through the
streets and public places, crying out: "Christians! now is the
day of martyrdom! Let us not forsake our father!" The
cowardly emperor, the willing cause of all this disorder, was so
thoroughly frightened at the proportions assumed by the sedition, that he actually ordered vessels to be prepared for his
flight. On the following night he sent for the Patriarch Macedonius, treacherously assured him that he wished to embrace
the Catholic faith, and accordingly handed him a captious profession of faith, in which he received the first two councils, of
Nice and Constantinople, without alluding to those of Ephesus and
Chalcedon. Macedonius, fully trusting a recantation which he
deemed sincere, did not perceive the deceit; he received the
declaration of Anastasius and imprudently signed it himself.
This was signing Zeno's *Henoticon*. His eyes were opened to
his mistake by the Catholic religious of the monastery of St.
Delmacius. The Patriarch immediately issued an unequivocal
retractation, in which he pronounced all to be heretics who did
not receive the Council of Chalcedon.

30. To this bold protest the emperor replied by banishing
Macedonius to the very place in which his predecessor, Euphemius, was closing his term of exile (A. D. 510). The Council
of Chalcedon was the terror of the Monophysites,* or Eutychians. The acts of this council were kept in the archives of the
Church of Constantinople. Some days before the banishment
of Macedonius, Anastasius had sent for the acts, as if for the
purpose of consulting them. The Patriarch, well aware of the
emperor's intentions respecting the sacred deposit, sealed the

* μόνος, single; φύσις nature.

papers with his ring, and laid them upon the altar, thus placing
them under the immediate protection of God Himself.   But
the emperor's impiety braved even the holiness of the altar;
he seized the acts, tore them to pieces, and threw the fragments into the fire.   Macedonius was replaced on the throne
of Constantinople by Timothy, a priest of notoriously loose
morals, whose vices alone could have recommended him to
the emperor's choice.   Most of the orthodox ecclesiastics were
thrown into prison; some escaped persecution by flight.   A
council composed of courtier-bishops, bought in advance by the
emperor's gold, confirmed the condemnation of Macedonius,
and deposed him without a hearing; thus constituting themselves accusers, witnesses and judges in a case diametrically
opposed, in every point, to justice, right and truth.   While
thus rending the East, Anastasius strove to inflame the West
by a manifesto, or rather a slanderous libel against the Pope,
St. Symmachus, whom he accused of forsaking the true faith
to take up the error of the Manicheans, and of having been
elected in opposition to the canonical rules.   The Sovereign
Pontiff seeing his honor and faith thus called in question,
replied with dignified energy.   "I cannot," he writes to the
emperor, "pass over your insults; they are too much to my
honor, too much to your guilt before God.   You say that I
have gone over to Manicheism.   All Rome will bear witness
the purity of my faith; and if the test be forced to an issue,
her archives can furnish the proofs.   If I have fallen away in
the least degree from the Catholic doctrine which I received
from the Chair of the Blessed Apostle St. Peter, let the world
rise up against me and put me to confusion.   But insults prove
nothing; calumnies are not reasons.   I know not on what
grounds you can accuse me of not being canonically elected.
God has judged.   Who are you that dare to oppose His sovereign judgment?   You are charged with using the arms of your
soldiers to force the Catholics of Constantinople into the Eutychian heresy.   Prince, remember the lot of all the emperors
who persecuted the Catholic faith; they nearly all made a

wretched end. Now it is a persecution to grant freedom to
all heresies and to refuse it only to the orthodox communion.
If you deem it an error, you should at least tolerate it with
the other errors; if you believe it to be true, you should embrace, and not persecute it."

31. The deposition of Macedonius by the false Council of
Constantinople was openly condemned by Flavian, patriarch
of Antioch, and by Elias of Jerusalem. They had not, indeed,
always shown a sufficiently clear understanding of the orthodox doctrine, or at least sufficient spirit to make a plain profession of it. Their opposition was exceedingly irritating to
the emperor, who called a council at Sidon (A. D. 511) to force
them to an explanation, and to a rejection of the Council of
Chalcedon. Flavian and Elias made their profession of faith
in a style by no means satisfactory to the leaders of the schismatical faction. Anastasius was on the point of banishing them
both; but the Patriarch of Jerusalem had foreseen the storm,
and had sent to Constantinople the man who could best avert
it. This was the holy abbot Sabas. The saintly hermit consented to quit his retreat, in imitation of the patriarchs of the
desert, who, in like junctures, had gone to oppose the progress
of heresy in the capital of the East. He appeared in the imperial palace in his poor hermit's dress, asking nothing for his
monastery or for himself; seeking neither the favor nor the
admiration of men. At his approach Anastasius was irresistibly
moved to a feeling of respectful veneration. The guards,
taking the aged hermit for a beggar, had at first rudely driven
him back from the palace gates. The emperor ordered him to
be admitted. In the words of a contemporary historian, "he
deemed him an angel in mortal guise." "I am come," said
Sabas, "to entreat your piety, in the name of the holy city of
Jerusalem and of our holy Archbishop, to give peace to the
Church, and not to trouble the episcopate and the priesthood,
that we may in peace pray day and night for your highness."
Touched by the old man's holy simplicity, Anastasius granted
his request and sent him back to his monastery loaded with

gifts. This was, however, but a passing concession wrung from a proud soul by the sight of exalted holiness. But Anastasius was not changed. All the supporters of Macedonius he esteemed as enemies. In this extremity the Eastern bishops had recourse to the Sovereign Pontiff, and appealed to him by a letter worthy of notice.* "Hasten," they write, "to the help of the East, whence our Lord sent forth two great lights, Peter and Paul, to illumine the whole earth. If your predecessor, the great Pope Leo, did not deem it unworthy of him to go before the fierce barbarian Attila to ward off threatened bondage from multitudes of his children, how much more should your Holiness snatch from an equally disastrous slavery thousands of souls already groaning under its weight or daily falling into it, and show us more plainly the true path of faith between the deceitful and crooked ways of Eutyches and Nestorius? Some falsely think that between these two heresies it is impossible to find a road leading to salvation, and that they must of necessity follow one or the other error. Hasten, therefore, by the help of God, to our relief. As between Arius, who divided the divine nature, and Sabellius, who confounded the Persons, the holy Fathers draw the line of Catholic belief by establishing the Unity of substance and Trinity of Persons; we beseech you, now, between Eutyches who confounds, and Nestorius who divides the natures, to show us the true orthodox teaching, that which has been handed down to us by St. Leo and by the disciples of the Fathers of Chalcedon, concerning the two natures, divine and human, united in the same person of Jesus Christ, our Saviour and our God." In such a strain as this, even in the first years of the sixth century, after two ecumenical councils called upon this very question, did the whole Eastern Church appeal to the Pope to show the way of truth: fourteen centuries ago the whole Eastern Church thus sponta-

* This precious ecclesiastical monument of the sixth century is well worth study and meditation even in our day. Fleury vouchsafes it no further notice in his history than the mere statement that it is very long. Berault Bercastel does not even give it passing mention. The original text is found in every collection of the councils.— Vid. ROHRBACHER. Universal History of the Catholic Church, t. VIII., p. 569, 2d ed.

neously proclaimed that, under God, its only hope was in the Sovereign Pontiff.

32. On the 8th of October, A. D. 512, St. Symmachus addressed to the Eastern Catholics a letter which seems to meet their prayer. He insists upon the necessity of an invariable submission to the Council of Chalcedon. But St. Symmachus did not enjoy the consolation of seeing the reunion of the two Churches, the subject of all his prayers. He died on the 19th of July, A. D. 514, after a pontificate of fifteen years, every step of which had been imbittered by a new strife. The Holy Pontiff had proved himself worthy to do battle for the Lord; his courage, zeal, watchfulness and charity were always equal to the trying events that called for their exertion.

CHAPTER III.

SUMMARY.

§ I. Pontificate of St. Hormisdas (July 26, a. d. 514—August 6, 523).

1. Election of St. Hormisdas. Revolt at Constantinople against the Emperor Anastasius.—2. Mission of St. Ennodius to the East.—3. Eutychian persecution in Illyria and Epirus.—4. Death of Anastasius.—5. Justin the Elder ascends the throne of the East.—6. End of the Eutychian schism in Constantinople.—7. Theological Proposition of the Scythian Monks: *Unus de Trinitate passus est.*—8. Homerites. Martyrdom of King St. Arethas.—9. St. James the Doctor, Bishop of Batnae or Sarug. St. Isaac, Bishop of Nineveh.—10. Country of the Angles, *Isle of Saints.*—11. Saints of Scotland and Ireland.—12. Death of St. Hormisdas.

§ II. Pontificate of St. John I. (August 18, a. d. 523—May 27, 526).

13. Arian Reaction on the part of Theodoric the Great. Journey of St. John I. to Constantinople.—14. Boetius put to Death by Theodoric the Great. Symmachus.—15. Imprisonment and death of St. John I. Death of Theodoric the Great.—16. Councils of Arles, Valence, and Lerida.

§ III. Pontificate of St. Felix IV. (July 12, a. d. 526—October 12, 529).

17. Promotion of St. Felix IV. Justinian and Theodora.—18. Justinian's Legislation.—19. Conversion of the Heruli settled on the banks of the Danube, and of Gordas, King of the Huns.—20. Athalaric, king of the Italian Ostrogoths.—21. Death of St. Felix IV.

§ IV. Pontificate of St. Boniface II. (Oct. 16, a. d. 520—Dec., 531).

22. Election and first acts of St. Boniface II.—23. Councils of Rome, Orange, Vaison, and Toledo.—24. St. Benedict.—25. Visit of Totila, King of the Ostrogoths, to St. Benedict.—26. Death of St. Boniface II.

§ V. Pontificate of St. John II. (January 22, a. d. 532—April 26, 535).

27. Athalaric claims a tribute for the election of the Sovereign Pontiff.—28. New investigation of the Proposition: *Unus de Trinitate passus est.*—29.

Sedition of the *Greens* and *Blues* in Constantinople.—30. Belisarius puts an end to the Vandal rule in Africa. Pharas.—31. Holy personages in Gaul.—32. Murder of the son of Clodomir.—33. Suppression of the Order of Deaconesses. Council of Orleans.—34. St. Medard of Noyon, St. Radegundes, St. Marcou, St. Evroul, &c.—35. Deposition of Contumeliosus, Bishop of Reez. Death of St. John II.

§ VI. Pontificate of St. Agapetus (May 4, A. D. 535—April 22, 536).

36. Election of St. Agapetus. Adoption of the *Christian Era*, first used by Dionysius the Little, about the year 535.—37. Letter of Justinian to St. Agapetus. Reply of the Pope.—38. Council of Carthage.—39. Belisarius attacks Theodatus, King of the Goths, in Italy.—40. Journey of St. Agapetus to Constantinople. Death of the Pope.

§I. Pontificate of St. Hormisdas (July 26, A.D. 514—August 6, 523).

1. St. Hormisdas succeeded St. Symmachus on the 26th of July, A. D. 514. Constantinople was at this time the scene of a revolution which had well-nigh proved fatal to Anastasius. The emperor, in his strange mania for changing every thing, one day made known his intention of reforming the Gospels, as he thought their style too simple. He wished also to change the Liturgy, and especially to oblige the clergy and faithful to sing the Trisagion with the heretical additions made to it by Peter the Fuller. The Catholics opposed these sacrilegious innovations. The new patriarch, Timothy, on the other hand, encouraged them with all his influence. He pitched upon the occasion of a solemn procession, when the streets of Constantinople were full of people, to inaugurate the impious chant required by the emperor; but the mass of the people indignantly rushed to arms. The sedition was fearful, and ten thousand persons are calculated to have lost their lives in it. Vitalian, one of the emperor's generals, thought this a fitting opportunity to satisfy some resentful feelings he entertained toward his imperial master. Placing himself at the head of the rebels, he found himself in less than two months master of Thrace, Mœsia and part of Illyria. The month of June, A. D.

514, saw him at the gates of Constantinople. The Catholics
hailed him most enthusiastically, and were for proclaiming him
emperor. Anastasius, trembling with terror in his palace,
capitulated. Without his diadem, and in the posture of a suppliant, he appeared before the people in the circus, promised
to recall the exiled bishops, to enter into the fold of the true
Church and to become its protector. These new protestations
were indeed but new untruths; but they served to appease the
popular tumult. The people, the army, and the senate maintained Anastasius upon the throne, and Vitalian was obliged
to content himself with the title of Governor of Thrace. To
give some show of fulfilment of the promises wrung from him
by abject terror, Anastasius wrote to Pope Hormisdas a letter
full of feigned reverence, in which he strives to justify his
long silence toward the Sovereign Pontiffs; the emperor begs
Hormisdas to send legates to a council convoked at Heraclea,
to treat of the reunion of the two Churches and the extinction
of the Eastern schism. This dispatch was speedily followed
by a second renewing the same protestations and the same
requests (A. D. 515).

2. Hormisdas joyfully seized this occasion of extinguishing a heresy which had so long desolated the Church. He sent
to Constantinople, as legates, St. Ennodius, the successor of St.
Epiphanius in the See of Pavia; another bishop named Fortunatus; Venantius, a priest; the deacon Vitalis, and a notary,
Hilarius. They received written and minutely detailed instructions. This memorial, the oldest of its kind now extant, is a
true model of urbanity, of prudence, and of Christian and pontifical diplomacy. The only admissible basis for a serious
arrangement was the formal and distinct recognition of the
Council of Chalcedon, and of the letters of St. Leo the Great
against Nestorius, Eutyches, Dioscorus, and their adherents;
a solemn abjuration of the Eutychian and Monophysite heresies was also required. The Pope likewise sent by his legates a letter for the emperor, laying down the same terms for
the reunion of the two Churches, and offering to assist in per-

son at the council, to close this important matter. Such a proposal was without precedent in the history of the Sovereign
Pontiffs. Anastasius had not dreamed of entering into serious
negotiations with the Holy See; he had only aimed at gaining
time to deceive everybody. The legates were sent back with
letters to the Pope, in which Anastasius distinctly condemned
the doctrine of Eutyches, and expressed himself surprised that
the Pope should have suspected him of holding heterodox
views respecting the Council of Chalcedon, *whose decrees*, he
said, *he had always respected and upheld* (A. D. 516). Whilst he
thus lied to his conscience, the emperor was sending into exile
the Catholic bishops of Nicopolis, Lignis, Naissus, and Pauli-
tale, for refusing to embrace Eutychianism. Dorotheus, metropolitan of Thessalonica, pressed by threats and intimidations,
weakly consented to communicate with Timothy, the unworthy
Patriarch of Constantinople. The apostasy of Dorotheus however gave to his suffragans, the Illyrian bishops, occasion to
show a noble example of firmness and courage. They met in
council under the presidency of John, bishop of Nicopolis, and
successor to Alcyso, who had been banished by Anastasius,
and had died in exile. They proclaimed that they no longer
held communion with their metropolitan since his fall, and that
they owned no other communion than that of the Roman
Church. They sent the reports of their sessions and their decrees to Pope Hormisdas for confirmation.

3. The holy Pope was much consoled by these proofs of
faithful devotion to the cause of God. In reply he congratulated the bishops of Illyria and Epirus, and urged them to pronounce an anathema against Eutyches and his partisans, which
they had omitted to do in the canons of their council (A. D.
516). Yet the apostate metropolitan Dorotheus did not wince
under such a reproach. Backed by the armed force placed at
his disposal by the emperor Anastasius, he exacted enormous
tributes from the Churches of Illyria, and daily found new
modes of oppression. The persecuted bishops again appealed
to the Sovereign Pontiff, who determined to send a second

embassy to Constantinople, to obtain from the emperor a cessation of these acts of violence. But Anastasius, now freed from the fear of Vitalian's arms, took no pains to hide his real designs. He turned away the legates with insults, and committed them to one of his ships, under a guard who were ordered to allow them no communication with any city of the empire (A. D. 517). The courageous ambassadors, however, found means to secure the delivery of some of the protests addressed by the Pope to the Eastern Churches. The emperor, on becoming aware of the fact, took the opportunity of writing to St. Hormisdas in a strain of reproach and insult. "We can bear," he wrote, "to be insulted and even despised, but not commanded." As though in matters of faith the emperor were not as much bound by the laws of the Church as the least of the faithful.

4. The monk Severus, by his zeal in persecuting the Catholics, had won the favor of the heretical emperor, who raised him to the Patriarchal See of Antioch. Severus did not lose the opportunity afforded by his new dignity to redouble his persecution. In A. D. 517 he had led an armed force against the monasteries around Jerusalem, and put three hundred and fifty religious to the sword. The archimandrites begged the Pope to use his influence in their behalf with the court of Constantinople; but we know how little hope St. Hormisdas could have of moving an emperor like Anastasius, especially since he had taken Severus under his special protection. Elias, Patriarch of Jerusalem, for refusing to communicate with the apostate, was banished, and his See given to John, who had promised to receive the communion of Severus. But hardly had this disgraceful weakness placed him upon a throne that was not his, when John proved himself quite another man. Moved by the words of St. Sabas, at the risk of his life he gathered the people into the great basilica of Jerusalem, and there, in the very face of the imperial officers, amid the joyful acclamations of all the Catholics, he uttered a solemn anathema against Eutyches and all heretics who did not receive the Coun-

cil of Chalcedon. This unlooked-for event drove the emperor
to fury; but time was denied him for revenge. Heaven had not
withheld its warnings. During the preceding year, Timothy
of Constantinople, his creature and accomplice, had died impenitent; and was closely followed to the grave by John Nice-
otis, Eutychian Patriarch of Alexandria, whose death had
given rise to serious disorders in Egypt. The barbarians profited by these religious troubles to make their inroads upon the
empire. The cavalry of the Gethæ or Goths crossed the Danube, plundered Macedonia and entered Thessaly, on one side,
as far as Thermopylæ, no longer defended by the shade of
Leonidas; on the other, to the frontiers of Epirus. The invaders dragged at their horses' heels a long train of captives.
The ravages of the barbarians were closely followed by the
most fearful earthquake recorded in history (A. D. 518); the
twenty-four cities of Dardania were utterly destroyed. At
length, Anastasius, who had refused to heed so many warnings of the divine anger, was found in a retired chamber of
his palace, struck dead by lightning during a storm (A. D. 518).
Thus perished, at the age of eighty-eight years, Anastasius, to
whom historians have given the name of *Silentiary*, as before
his elevation to the throne, he was employed as usher in the
palace, and was charged to maintain order and *silence* in the
imperial residence. His reign forms one of the most disgraceful passages in the annals of the Lower Empire.

5. It was reserved to the next emperor, hand in hand with
John, who had succeeded the intruder Timothy in the See of
Constantinople, to restore peace to the Church and extinguish
schism in the East. God seemed to have led this prince by
the hand through extraordinary vicissitudes, to raise him up to
this high destiny. In the year A. D. 470, a shepherd-boy of
the village of Bederiana in Thrace entered the gates of Constantinople on foot: it was Justin. Whilst keeping his father's
flocks in a distant part of his native province, the scene of so
many battles, he felt within him a growing thirst for glory and
arms. He accordingly set out for the capital to seek service

in the imperial legions. The emperor Leo, his fellow-countr_man, admitted him among his guards. The young herdsman was a Catholic—stanch, loyal, and generous. He distinguished himself in the wars against the Persians and Isaurians, who harassed the empire for six years after the death of Zeno. Leo the Thracian made him military tribune and then general; Anastasius granted him the title of senator. At the time of the latter emperor's death, the former shepherd of Bederiana added to all these dignities that of captain of the guards. The eunuch Mantius, great chamberlain to Anastasius, was intriguing to put the sceptre into the hands of one of his friends; to this end he had intrusted the captain of the guards with large sums of money to distribute among the soldiers. Justin divided the money, but in his own name, and announced himself as a candidate for the empire. Fifty years of good and loyal service in the army had won him the affection of all the soldiers; they proclaimed him emperor the day after Anastasius' death, and the Thracian shepherd was now emperor, under the name of Justin the Elder. The new emperor had never consented to learn either to read or to write; the letters composing his name were engraved on a wooden tablet, and he thus signed the acts of his government. But he had the wisdom to surround himself with prudent and honest advisers. The upright and able Proclus, his minister and friend, managed his public concerns with great care; and it was soon shown that a right intention and honorable views make a better sovereign than the spirit of double-dealing and deceit, which had so long disturbed the East under Anastasius the Silentiary.

6. On the Sunday following the election of the emperor Justin (June 15, A. D. 518), when the Patriarch John had entered the basilica of Constantinople with his clergy, the people broke out into a unanimous cry: "Long live the emperor! long live the empress! long live the Patriarch! Why are we excommunicated? You are orthodox; what do you fear? Away with Severus the Manichean! Proclaim the Council of Chalcedon! The emperor too is orthodox. Long life to the

new Constantine! Long life to the new Helena!" It is impossible to repress a feeling of joy at the sight of a whole people thus calling for the faith of its fathers. The echo of such
an outburst comes down through successive ages to the Catholic heart, like a cry of victory. The Patriarch, yielding to the
wishes of the multitude, appeared in the pulpit and made the
following announcement: "We make known to your charity
that to-morrow we shall solemnize the memory of our holy
fathers of Chalcedon who drew up the profession of the true
faith." These words were followed by enthusiastic applause.
On the next day the ceremony of reconciliation was duly performed. The name of St. Leo the Great was restored to the
diptychs; and those of the heretics who had so long desolated
the Church were blotted out. These spontaneous measures,
dictated by a holy enthusiasm, were ratified four days later
(June 20, A. D. 518) by a council of forty bishops then convoked in Constantinople. Orders were sent to all the cities of
the empire requiring the recognition of the Council of Chalcedon; and they were everywhere obeyed amid the joyful acclamations of the people. The great Churches of Antioch,
Jerusalem, Tyr, Ptolemais, and Alexandria sent letters of
thanksgiving to Constantinople for so happy a change. Anastasius had hardly been dead one month, and all the East was
once more Catholic. Justin sent a request to Hormisdas that
he would consummate the reconciliation of the two Churches
by an act of his apostolic authority. He urged the Pope to
send legates to Constantinople to perfect this great work. The
glorious mission was intrusted by Hormisdas to Germanus,
bishop of Capua, another bishop named John, the priest Blan-
dus, and the deacons Felix and Dioscorus. The passage of
the legates on their way to the East was like a triumphal
march. The bishops and magistrates of the several cities on
their route came forth accompanied by the troops and people
to give them solemn escort. The clergy readily signed the
profession of faith and communion drawn up by the Sovereign
Pontiff and intrusted by him to the legates. At length, on

the 28th of March, A. D. 519, the act of reunion, penned by the Patriarch of Constantinople, was publicly read in the basilica of the Eastern capital. It was thus worded : "We receive all the decrees of the four ecumenical Councils of Nice, Constantinople, Ephesus, and Chalcedon. We anathematize all heretics, especially Nestorius, former Bishop of Constantinople and condemned in the Council of Ephesus by the blessed Pope St. Celestin. We anathematize Eutyches and Dioscorus, bishops of Alexandria, who were condemned by the holy Council of Chalcedon. We include in the same condemnation the parricide Timothy, called Ælurus, and his disciple Peter Mongus of Alexandria. We also anathematize Acacius, once bishop of Constantinople, their accomplice and partisan. By following in all things the authority of the Apostolic See we hope to remain unshaken in our devotion to the communion of the Chair of St. Peter, the true and solid foundation of the Church; the centre of unity, and source of authority." When the Patriarch, in the presence of all the faithful, signed this profession, the pledge of peace after so much strife, tears flowed from every eye, and the arches of the basilica rang with the enthusiastic outburst that hailed Pope Hormisdas and the emperor Justin. The legates sent to Rome two copies of the formula, subscribed by the Patriarch, one in Greek, another in Latin. The names of Acacius, Zeno and Anastasius were erased from the diptychs. Thus ended (A. D. 519) the Eutychian schism of Constantinople, which had lasted thirty-five years, since the condemnation of Acacius.

7. The whole Catholic world was overjoyed at the tidings of this event. St. Hormisdas was more touched by it in proportion as he had done more toward its completion. Still the formula of reunion did not meet with the same ready acknowledgment in all the Eastern Churches. Dorotheus, the excommunicated Patriarch of Thessalonica, refused to sign it. The legate sent to present it to him even ran great personal risk. The emperor Justin showed great irritation at this resistance. The Sovereign Pontiff counselled moderation, and wrote to his

deputies at the court of Constantinople: "You must so manage that no one embrace the Catholic faith without knowing
the motives that lead him to take the step; let no one complain that the prince has forced upon him a truth of which he
is not convinced. Since the Bishop of Thessalonica has proved
unwilling to receive your instruction, ask the emperor to send
him to Rome, that he may confer with us and find a solution
to his difficulties. If he reject instruction, he will prove his
bad faith by resisting the orders of God and of his prince."
The Sovereign Pontiff's indulgence was crowned with success.
In a few months Dorotheus submitted. St. Hormisdas empowered the Patriarch of Constantinople to end the matter;
and submitted to his judgment a question which had arisen
between some Scythian monks and the legates. The monks
wished to insert in their profession the proposition, *One of the
Trinity suffered.* These words were susceptible of an orthodox
interpretation; but the Catholics wished to substitute this
form: *One of the Persons of the Trinity suffered,* as more clearly
expressing the distinction of Persons in the unity of substance.
The prudence of the Church of Rome was by no means partial
to a discussion which depended chiefly on words, and the Pope
speaks thus of the Scythian monks who afterward went to
Rome on account of this question: "We strove to heal them
by our patience; but they are too much accustomed to disputes, too fond of novelty, and too deeply fixed in their own
views. They treat as heretics all who hold an opinion other
than their own. Practised in slander, they spread trouble and
sedition everywhere on their path; we could restrain them
neither by warnings, nor by gentleness, nor by authority." St.
Hormisdas contented himself with blaming their stubbornness,
without condemning the proposition, which was afterward
received by John II.

8. These memorable events took place in the year 520.
Whilst the Eastern Church was thus again born to Catholicity
under Justin, the faith was making new conquests in Colchis.
The king of the Lazi, who had heretofore been a vassal and

tributary of Persia, recognized the sovereignty of the Greek
emperor, and became a Christian. Zathus—for so the king
was called—was received as a son by Justin, and espoused the
princess Valeriana, who bestowed as a dowry upon her new
kingdom the faith of Jesus Christ (A. D. 522). The Gospel had
also made its way into Yemen (Arabia Felix). Here the faithful began to feel the persecutions which multiplied martyrs to
a fearful extent in other lands. In the year 523, the Jewish
leader Dunaan was placed by his coreligionists upon the throne
of the *Homerites*, as the Greeks called those tribes by a corruption of the Eastern name *Hamiar*, which really belonged to
them. The new monarch distinguished himself by his cruelty toward the Christians. Two hundred and eighty priests
were murdered; all the Ethiopians in the land suspected of
favoring the Catholic faith were massacred. Dunaan had issued
orders to destroy all the churches and to build synagogues in
their stead. In his Jewish zeal for proselytism he undertook
a formidable expedition against Nadiran, a city of some importance in the northern part of Yemen, and wholly peopled by
Christians. The city was defended with undaunted courage.
Unable to overcome by open force, Dunaan resorted to an infamous stratagem. He sent heralds to the besieged, promising
to spare their lives, to leave them in undisturbed enjoyment
of their wealth and the free exercise of their religion, on condition of their opening their gates to him. His lying promises were believed; but his first act on entering the city was
to give up the houses to plunder and to burn the church, with
the priests and people who had sought shelter within its walls.
Those of the inhabitants who refused to deny their faith were
put to death, without distinction of age or sex. Large fires
were lighted in deep pits, and these generous victims of their
fidelity to the name of Jesus Christ were thrown into them in
one promiscuous heap. The martyrdom of Arethas, the conquered king of Nadiran, was attended by circumstances which
well proved his heroic courage. This prince, who showed himself worthy to change the earthly diadem he had just lost for a

heavenly crown, was then ninety-five years old. Dunaan summoned him into his presence, and, insulting his misfortune, said to him: "See to what end your trust in Christ has brought you! Disown that name, the cause of your misfortune, and think of your old age." "It belongs only to impostors, and not to kings," answered Arethas, "to violate the most solemn oaths, as you have done in the case of this unhappy city. Kings—of whom I have met many in my long career—keep their word; they abhor double-dealing and treachery. For my part, I shall never betray the duty I have promised to Christ, my God. I shall never become an apostate Jew like yourself." Then turning to the captive Christians who stood about him, "Brethren," he said, "did you hear my words to this Jew?" "Yes, father." "Have I spoken the truth or not?" "The truth," they replied. "If it be true, and if there stand amongst you some base and coward Christian ready to forswear his God, let him speak, nor longer let his presence contaminate the assembly of the saints." With one voice they uttered their resolve to die for Christ. Dunaan, in anger, ordered them all to be executed on the sea-shore. Arethas first received the fatal blow. His subjects, now become his fellows in glory, were dispatched after him, and as their heads were struck off their bodies were cast into the sea. A little child four years of age was led along by his mother, who was going to execution; the tyrant questioned him: "Would you rather live with me than die with your mother?" "I will not deny Jesus," answered the child; "I would rather die with my mother." "See," said Dunaan to his officers, "the perversity of that race which Christ has misled even from early infancy." Yet he was ashamed to order the execution of the young and brave confessor; he accordingly gave him in charge to one of his officers to be carefully brought up, reserving the right to take him back at the age of fifteen years, when he should be pardoned if he renounced his faith, but put to death if he persevered in the generous constancy of which he had just given such noble proofs. The persecutor of the Christians was not to see the period fixed in this delay of his revenge. In the following year (524), Elisbaan, king of Ethiopia, encouraged by the favor of the emperor Justin, attacked the Jewish tyrant, defeated his army in a bloody battle, and put him to death, together with all his kindred; the conqueror then reopened all the Catholic churches, and restored to the Homerites the free exercise of a religion which they had gloriously confessed under the executioner's sword.

9. Armenia was at this time the home of wonderful holiness and learning. St. James, called the *Doctor*, bishop of Batnæ or Sarug, devoted a life of seventy-two years to the defence of the Catholic faith against the errors of Nestorius and of Eutyches, and to the practice of the most exemplary virtue. He died in the year 522, rich in glory and merit. His numerous works are written in the Syriac tongue, and are remarkable for their sound doctrine and flowing elegance of style, rich in images and poetical figures. One of his contemporaries, but one who outlived him by many years, was St. Isaac, bishop of Nineveh, who had taken up the monastic life at a very early age. On the day of his consecration two pleaders came before him; for the bishops of that period were expected to regulate not only the spiritual concerns of their flocks, but all disputes of whatever nature that might arise amongst Christians. One of the parties claimed the payment of a debt; the other admitted the claim, but begged a delay. The creditor urged the argument: "If you do not pay me, I shall sue you." "The Gospel," said St. Isaac, "directs us not to claim what has been taken from us, and much more to grant a respite to him who asks it." "I have nothing to do with the Bible," answered the creditor; "that is not the question." Isaac thought within himself: "If these people do not heed the Gospel, to what end am I come here?" And reflecting upon the fearful responsibility of the pastoral charge, he resigned his dignity, and retired to the desert of Scete, in Egypt. He wrote four books on the *Monastic Institute*, and was esteemed the model and teacher of the religious who peopled that solitude.

The city of Nineveh was honored in the same century by a
pious and elegant writer named John Sabbas, who has left us
several treatises on mysticism, the fruit of a life spent in the
contemplation of heavenly things.

10. Whilst the true faith shone so brightly in the East, the
far-off Western Islands of Great Britain and Ireland had won
the distinctive title of *Isles of Saints*. This glorious name, bequeathed to England by the Christians of the sixth century,
but since so long forgotten, may once again belong to it, if the
promise of so many late conversions be not too soon blighted.
St. David, archbishop and patron of Wales, after having spent
some years in solitude in the Isle of Wight, which he edified by
his many virtues, built and dedicated a chapel at Glastonbury,
and founded twelve monasteries, the chief of which was in the
Vale of Ross, near Menevia, now called St. David's. He was
present at a council held in A. D. 519, at Brevy, in Cardigan-
shire, where he eloquently attacked and confuted the Semi-
Pelagian heresy threatening to spring forth again in Britain.
He was then appointed as successor to St. Dubritius in the
episcopal see of Caerleon, which he transferred to Menevia.
St. David spoke with great force and energy; but his example was more powerful than his eloquence, and he has in all
succeeding ages been the glory of the Welsh Church. The rule
which he gave to his monasteries made him the spiritual father
of many saints, both English and Irish (A. D. 470–544). St.
David's predecessor, St. Dubritius, had opened a celebrated
school at Warwick, where he remained seven years, explaining
the Sacred Writings. The holy teacher's reputation brought
him many scholars from all parts of Great Britain. He at one
time explained the sacred word to a thousand disciples. In
A. D. 446, he was consecrated by St. Germanus of Auxerre
bishop of Llandaff, and subsequently became archbishop of Caerleon. This dignity he resigned to St. David (A. D. 519), and
retired to the solitude of a monastery at Bardsley, where he
died soon after. St. Thelian, his disciple, made a pilgrimage to
Jerusalem in the year 500. On his return, he was raised to

the See of Llandaff, to succeed St. Dubritius, who had been removed to Caerleon. He made his Church illustrious by his learning, piety and zeal, and by the great care with which he chose his clergy from among enlightened and virtuous men. So great was his influence, that his decision, in any question whatever, was always received without appeal. He displayed the most heroic charity during the prevalence of a contagious disease in the province of Wales, and died A. D. 580, in the retreat of Bardsley, whither he had withdrawn to make ready for his passage to eternity. At about the same time (A. D. 516), St. Daniel, another Welsh bishop, founded the celebrated monastery of Bangor, near the arm of the sea that separates Anglesey from Wales. The same fruitful country was at this time in admiration of the holy abbot Cadoc, son of a prince who ruled the southern portion of the province. Cadoc had succeeded his father in the government of his state, but soon gave up the royal dignity to embrace a monastic life. He established a monastery at Lan-Carvon, three miles from Cowbridge. This retreat became a nursery for illustrious and holy men. St. Iltutus, St. Gildas the Albanian, St. Sampson, and St. Magloire here learned the lessons of holiness and virtue which afterward illustrated their native land.

11. Scotland and Ireland by no means yielded to England in the great religious movement so evident in Great Britain. St. Kentigern, of royal blood among the Picts (A. D. 516–601), spread the Gospel throughout his native land, and founded the bishopric of Glasgow in a solitary place, soon peopled by the throngs which his presence and teachings drew thither, and thus gave rise to the present city of that name. Kentigern sent missionaries to preach the faith in the Orkney Islands, in Norway and Iceland. Catholic Ireland could also count with pride her glorious generation of saints: the most remarkable names of the century are those of St. Columban, of the illustrious house of Neil, and founder of the great monastery of Dair-Magh, now called Durrow (A. D. 429–570); St. Finian, bishop of Clonard, one of the most illustrious Irish

bishops, next to St. Patrick (A. D. 500–552); St. Tigernach, bishop of Clones, in the county of Monaghan (A. D. 490–550); St. Albœus, archbishop of Munster, founder of a monastery in the Isle of Arran, to which he left a most admirable rule (A. D. 460–525); and St. Bridget, virgin, abbess, and patroness of Ireland. Whilst still in early years she received the veil at the hands of St. Mel, nephew and disciple of St. Patrick. She built herself a cell in the hollow of a large oak, hence called Kill-dara, or cell of the oak. Being joined soon after by a number of her own sex, St. Bridget formed them into a religious community, which soon branched out into several other convents throughout Ireland (A. D. 470–523).

12. The glorious pontificate of St. Hormisdas was now fast drawing to a close (A. D. 523). The question of grace had once more arisen in the Church of Africa, so cruelly decimated by King Thrasimund. Possessor, an African bishop, consulted the Pope on the writings of Faustus, bishop of Reez, which we had occasion to mention in speaking of the Church of Gaul. Hormisdas referred him to St. Augustine's works on the subject. The Pope at this time bestowed the rank of primate of Spain upon the bishop of Tarragona, yet confirming the same dignity granted by St. Simplicius to the bishop of Seville, for the provinces of Andalusia and Portugal. In a decretal addressed to all the Spanish bishops, Hormisdas forbade the ordination of priests *per saltum*, that is, without observing the intervals prescribed by the canons. Orders could not be conferred upon public penitents. Strict inquiry must be made into the honesty and learning of the candidate. Lastly, the Pope required that provincial synods should be held at least once a year, since they were the best means of preserving discipline. The Sovereign Pontiffs always strove to call attention to this fact. Councils are the great assizes of the Church. They discuss the laws which guide her, publish rules of discipline, and take measures for the common welfare; here disputed points are settled, conflicts of opinion decided, the objections of innovators and heretics answered. The Church

has ever set the greatest value upon the freedom of these solemn assemblies, where, by the help of the Holy Ghost, all the wants of the faithful are supplied.   St. Hormisdas died on the 6th of August, A. D. 523, after a pontificate of nine years.   He had spent, in ornamenting the churches of the city, five hundred and seventy-one pounds of silver, collected from the charity of the faithful; this was a large sum at that time.   St. Hormisdas may well be held up as an example of moderation and firmness, two most important qualities for one who governs men.

§ II. PONTIFICATE OF St. JOHN I. (Aug. 13, A D. 523—May 27, 526).

13. St. John I. was chosen to succeed St. Hormisdas on the 13th of August, A. D. 523.   His accession to the Sovereign Pontificate is marked by a new phase in the history of Theodoric, king of the Ostrogoths.   This great king had heretofore shown himself worthy of his high destiny; and the first part of his life could be fitly urged as a model of wise, dignified and prudent administration.   But this period seems to have brought out the inborn barbarism of his nature in all its intensity. This outburst of violence which was soon to degenerate into cruelty, was first caused by the energy with which Justin sustained the cause of Catholicity in the East.   The emperor, wishing to strike a decisive blow at Arianism, disqualified all Arians for any trust either military or civil.   Theodoric had always professed Arianism, even whilst paying the homage we have recorded to the virtue and learning of the Catholic bishops.   Justin's decree aroused the sectarian spirit which had till then so quietly slumbered in the breast of Theodoric; the Ostrogoth declared that if the emperor's edicts were carried out, he should retaliate most fearfully upon the Italian Catholics.   His minister, Cassiodorus, was unwilling to follow his master into the way of violent reaction he was preparing.   He quitted the court, and the spirit of wisdom which had hitherto regulated the administration left with him.   Theodoric summoned the Pope to Ravenna.   " Go to Constantinople," said

the king to him, "and require the Emperor Justin to allow the
Arians who have been forcibly converted to return to Arianism." "Do with me what you will," answered the courageous
Pontiff, "I am in your hands; but such a proposal I cannot
make, as it would be an apostasy." Theodoric still insisted
upon his going to Constantinople to assure the Emperor Justin
that if he proscribed Arianism in the East, Catholicity should
pay the penalty in the West. The Pope yielded, and set out
for Constantinople, accompanied by five Italian bishops—Eccle-
sius of Ravenna, Eusebius of Fano, Sapinus of Capua, and two
others, whose names are lost to us. This was the first time
that the head of Christendom, the Roman Pontiff, had undertaken such a journey. The tidings of his approach caused a
lively emotion in Constantinople and throughout the East.
The Pope was met at the distance of twelve miles from the
city by a countless throng of the faithful. The Emperor Justin bowed in humble reverence before him, and entreated the
favor of receiving the crown from his hand; Justin was the
first emperor crowned by a Pope. The Patriarch Epiphanius,
who had succeeded John in the See of Constantinople, begged
the Pontiff to officiate at the solemn service in the great basilica
on the festival of Easter, A. D. 525. The Pope yielded to his
earnest wishes, and afterward communicated with all the
Eastern bishops, only excepting Timothy, patriarch of Alexandria, who still refused to receive the Council of Chalcedon.
When St. John I. had received all the marks of respect and
reverence due to his dignity, he entered upon the business that
had brought him to Constantinople. He represented to Justin
the evils which threatened Italy, and without in the least giving way to error, said that all possible freedom for repentance
should be granted to every conscience. The emperor yielded
to his reasoning, and the Arians were left in peace. This duty
fulfilled, the Pope set out on his return, loaded with rich presents by Justin; * but instead of the honors which had met him

* Justin presented the Pope with a gold paten enriched with jewels, and of twenty
pounds weight, a gold chalice weighing five pounds, five silver vessels, and fifteen palls

in the East, a cruel and cheerless prison awaited him in the West (A. D. 525).

14. During the Pontiff's absence, Theodoric had put to death, on unjust suspicion, the most learned and virtuous of the Romans, the illustrious senator Boetius. This distinguished man knew how to lighten the cares and toil attending the highest civil offices by the relaxation of philosophical and literary pursuits. He was a fervent Christian of deep conviction; was honored with the friendship of the Popes St. Symmachus, St. Hormisdas, and St. John I., with all of whom he was contemporary; and under their protection and guidance he undertook to reconcile reason with faith, philosophy and the religion of Christ, and to prove that the one is but the porch that leads to the other. Boetius devoted the labors of a lifetime to this idea, which Christian philosophers have followed up from age to age, and to which we owe the best efforts of the brightest genius. Amongst other works which he wrote in support of this theory we still have his *Introduction to the Philosophy of Aristotle;* the *Interpretation of Aristotle;* and the translations of the same philosopher's *Analytics, Topics,* and *Sophisms.* To Boetius is due the first application in the study of theology of the system now known as the *scholastic,* which embraces these two incalculable advantages—order in the whole, and precision in details. Upon such a man did Theodoric vent the barbarian fury which revived in his breast as life and strength decayed. Boetius was thrown into prison on the charge of holding secret correspondence with the court of Constantinople in the view to bring back Italy to the imperial rule. In the solitude and darkness of his dungeon he wrote his masterpiece, *The Consolation of Philosophy.* The Christian Socrates held high converse in his captivity, not with a *familiar demon,* as did the Grecian philosopher, but with uncreated Wisdom, the

of cloth of gold. On his return, John sent these gifts to the churches of St. Peter, St. Paul, St. Mary Major, and St. Lawrence. This beautiful precedent has always been followed by his successors, who invariably present to churches or public institutions the gifts which are made to them in person.

Word of God. This noble work, divided into five books of mingled prose and verse, reflects a truly wonderful clearness of mind and serenity of soul; it treats of the mystery of Providence with noble elevation. The illustrious and blameless prisoner proves to his own consolation that the prosperity of the wicked is more deserving of pity than of envy, and that persecuted virtue claims the respect of the world. The same high dignity of thought and feeling is brought to the solution of questions concerning the foreknowledge of God and free-will. Whilst Boetius thus improved his captive hours in the stronghold of Calventianum, midway between Pavia and Milan, Theodoric's mind was busy in contriving a form of punishment that should multiply the horrors of death for his prisoner. Boetius was put to the torture; a strong cord was fastened round his head and forcibly tightened until his eyes burst from their sockets; and as he still denied the imaginary crime laid to his charge, he was stretched upon a beam and beaten with clubs by two executioners, upon every part of his body, from the neck down to the feet; and being still alive, he was beheaded, or rather his head was split open with an axe (October 23, A. D. 526). Symmachus, his father-in-law, like him, deeply versed in both sacred and profane learning, and like him also, the friend and adviser of Popes, met with the same fate in the following year.

15. Both these executions had taken place when St. John I. had returned to Italy. He reached Ravenna only to be thrown into a dungeon by order of Theodoric, who was *displeased*, as he said, *with the issue of the embassy to Constantinople*. The Pope sank under the weight of his imprisonment (May 27, A. D. 526). Theodoric outlived his august victim but three months. The avenging hand of God seemed to weigh heavily upon the tyrant; he fell into a deep melancholy and became a prey to the most gloomy forebodings. One day when the head of a large fish was served on the royal table, he suddenly exclaimed that he saw in the dish the head of Symmachus, as though recently cut off, glaring revengefully and fiercely

gnashing its teeth at him. The terrified monarch, trembling
with horror, hastily rose from table. He died a few days after,
lamenting his crime, in the thirtieth year of his reign (A. D.
526). The Ostrogoth power which he had established in Italy
was doomed to a speedy fall; and eight years later saw the
Italian peninsula under the sceptre of the Eastern emperors
(A. D. 534). During the short pontificate of John I., the death
of Thrasimund, and consequent accession of Hilderic to the
throne, had restored peace to the African Church. Hilderic,
who had received Christian training at the court of Constantinople, inaugurated his reign by recalling the bishops banished
to Cagliari by his predecessor. All these holy confessors were
met on their return by the joyful acclamations of their spiritual
children. The return of St. Fulgentius bore all the appearance
of a triumph. He landed at Carthage amid an immense throng
of the faithful, bearing palm branches and lighted tapers to escort him to his church (A. D. 524). For a moment the African
Church seemed about to live again the halcyon days of its glory.
Hilderic strove to raise it from its ruins. The bishops met in
councils to supply the spiritual repairs necessitated by so long
a storm. The Council of Junque, held in A. D. 524, and that
of Carthage, in 525, drew up rules of discipline in accordance
with the wants of the people. The faith of Nice was solemnly
declared to be that of the whole of Africa; and Vandal Arianism seemed forever crushed. But Hilderic's reign was short;
he was dethroned and murdered by Gelimer, and was thus hindered from giving a lasting firmness to the noble work he had
so promisingly begun.

16. Three councils had been held in A. D. 524, at Arles, Valence, and Lerida, cities within the dominions of Theodoric.
The Council of Arles, under St. Cesarius, published but four
canons, which renew ordinances already established, to the
effect that nobody shall be ordained deacon before the age of
twenty-five years; priest or bishop, before thirty, and forbid the
conferring of orders upon unsettled clerics, persons twice married, or who have been public penitents. Of the sixteen canons

of Lerida, the following are worthy of mention : The ministers
of the altar, whose hands distribute the blood of Jesus Christ,
may not shed human blood under any pretext whatever, not
even to defend a besieged city.   Seven years of public penance
are prescribed for any one, man or woman, who causes the death
of a child conceived or born of adultery.   Bishops are forbidden to touch the donations made to monasteries.   Incestuous
persons incur excommunication, and all ordinary intercourse with
them is prohibited.   The bishop is left free to reinstate, after
whatever delay seems proper to him, a cleric who may have
fallen into the crime of fornication, in proportion as the culprit
shows more or less exactness in the discharge of the penance
laid upon him.   It is forbidden to violate the sacredness of the
church to draw thence a slave who has come for refuge.   The
Council of Valence was almost entirely taken up with regulations concerning the vacancy of episcopal sees at the death of
the incumbent.   If clerics take this opportunity to turn something to their advantage, either from the property of the deceased bishop or of the Church, they shall be compelled by
the metropolitan or the suffragans of the province, to make
restitution.   The nearest bishop shall come to perform the
funeral obsequies, and take charge of the vacant see until the
consecration of a successor.   He shall also draw up an inven-
tory of the late bishop's property, and of that of the Church,
to be sent to the metropolitan.   The heirs of the deceased prelate shall arrange with the metropolitan about the division of
his inheritance.   We must also call attention to the canon which
orders that the Gospel shall be read at Mass, before the offertory and dismissal of the catechumens, in order that the precepts of the Lord and the bishop's instructions may be heard
not only by the faithful, but by the catechumens, penitents and
all who were not admitted to the sacrifice itself, that this means
of conversion or of edification may not be lost to them.   Thus
did the Church regulate her authority and discipline under the
wholesome influence of her councils.

§ 3. PONTIFICATE OF ST. FELIX IV. (July 12, A. D. 526—October 12, 529).

17. St. Felix IV. was elected Pope on the 12th of July, A. D. 526. The king of the Goths, who had caused the death of St. John I. in a dungeon, had sought to influence the election of the new Pontiff; but such was the harmony of action on the part of the Roman clergy and people that Theodoric's efforts proved utterly fruitless. In the year following the accession of Pope Felix IV., Justin had his nephew Justinian crowned as Augustus, and died himself a few months later, closing his prosperous reign by the choice of a successor able to carry on his work. Justinian would have been an accomplished prince had he not marred his fame by an unworthy union. In spite of the remonstrances of Justin and of the whole court, he married a vile courtesan named Theodora, for whom he had conceived an unbridled passion. As soon he had ascended the throne, Justinian publicly shared his power with the object of his shameful affection. Theodora had the full disposal of the army, the senate, the magistracy, and the finances. Generals, senators, and even governors of provinces were at her feet. In the prologue to one of his laws, Justinian announces that he has consulted the *most honorable spouse given him by Heaven!* But all his efforts have not been able to redeem in the eyes of posterity the name of the crowned courtesan. Could Justinian's fame be withdrawn from the blighting shadow which he took pleasure in attaching to his history, few princes would present such a combination of good qualities. He was of majestic figure; a countenance full of graceful dignity and singularly expressive revealed the noble soul within. He spoke and wrote with ease and elegance; he was familiar with jurisprudence, architecture, music and even theology, and his piety was remarkable. As soon as he had become emperor he presented to the churches all the property he had before held. Unfortunately, and as if by studied contrast, Theodora pos-

sessed the vices exactly contrary to the emperor's virtues. Justinian was a Catholic; Theodora had openly embraced Eutychianism. The emperor was kind, affable, accessible to all who came to seek favors or redress; his empress was a proud, haughty woman, and treated the most illustrious personages with overbearing disdain. He was disinterested; she sold offices of civil trust. He was mild and merciful; she was cruel and bloodthirsty. Justinian's first care, on receiving the imperial sceptre, was to repair the ruin caused by a fearful earthquake (A. D. 525), which had overthrown most of the cities of Syria. Antioch, Daphnæ, and Seleucia, were now but shapeless heaps of ruins. The shock lasted six days with fearful violence, and during six months was several times repeated, though less violently; and it was only after a lapse of eighteen months (A. D. 527) that the soil was so far restored to firmness as to allow the erection of buildings. Justinian took this occasion to rebuild the ancient city of Palmyra, originally raised by Solomon under the name of Cadmor, and destroyed by Nabuchodonosor on his way to besiege Jerusalem. The emperor restored it with truly royal splendor; the gigantic remains, which might seem to have been the work of another race of men, still excite the wonder of modern travellers.

18. But Justinian's best claim to the remembrance of posterity is undoubtedly his code of laws, which constitutes *the body of the Roman law*, the basis of our present system of jurisprudence. He had long been contemplating a thorough readjustment of the statutes, and put it in execution in the very first year of his reign. "In order to put an end to the length of lawsuits," said the emperor, in his decree of A. D. 528, "and to do away with the great number of perplexing constitutions found in the Gregorian, Hermogenian and Theodosian codes, published by Theodoric, by his successors or by ourself, we design to condense them all within the compass of one code bearing our glorious name." This code, known as the *Justinian Code*, was completed within the year. It contains a collection of all the imperial constitutions from the time of

Adrian until the year 534. In the year 529 Justinian ordered the systematic arrangement of the *Digest* or *Pandects*, an immense collection, in which the system of civil law was established from two thousand treatises on jurisprudence. This great work was completed in three years by Tribonian and sixteen assistants furnished him by Justinian. The materials were scattered among the multiplied writings of men of law. This separation showed the necessity of gathering all the principles of law into one body, and hence the origin of the *Institutes* published by Justinian in A. D. 533, and even now studied in our modern schools. Finally the *Novellæ*, a collection of the edicts issued by the emperor, from A. D. 534 till 565, completed the list of these great works. In this legislation the stern character of the old Roman law yields to the influence of Christian principles. The question of slaves is treated with a hitherto unknown mildness. Paternal authority loses the last traces of the pitiless severity which characterized it in the days of ancient Rome, and puts on an aspect more conformable to nature. An eminent civilian* asks himself how, in an age when the general tendency was downward, Justinian could have risen so high. "This is a truly original creation of Justinian," he says; "but it is not the chance discovery of a genius above the level of his age; it is a Christian work prepared by the ceaseless Christian toil of two hundred years, and brought to maturity at a time when Christianity was every thing."

19. Whilst Justinian by these new enterprises thus fixed the conquests of the Christian spirit over the manners and legislation of the empire, the Gospel was also making new progress amongst barbarous nations. In A. D. 528, Gretes, king of the Heruli, who had been settled by Anastasius on the banks of the Danube, came to Constantinople to offer his services to Justinian. The bond of alliance between them was much strengthened by the baptism of the king with twelve of his relatives and his whole court, on the Epiphany. The emperor

* M. Troplong.

acted as sponsor to the king, and loaded him with gifts. The remainder of the nation soon followed the king's example, and embraced Christianity. During the same year, the Tzanians, a half-savage tribe of Mount Taurus, also became Christians, and enlisting in the Roman armies, thenceforth did their duty with as much courage as fidelity. Gordas, king of the Huns inhabiting the Tauric Chersonese, also entered the true fold; he was baptized in Constantinople, and had the emperor for godfather. Justinian's reputation drew illustrious foreigners from all quarters, who disputed the honor of serving him. Among these persons of rank was the eunuch Narses, whose name afterward became so celebrated; Justinian received him with great consideration, and bestowed upon him the highest dignities.

20. Meanwhile, Athalaric, successor of Theodoric on the Gothic throne of Italy, published a law confirming the rights of the Roman clergy. It read as follows : " Should any one wish to bring a suit against a cleric of the Church of Rome, he shall first make application to the Pope, who will decide the case himself or by deputy. Should the complainant fail to obtain satisfaction, he may apply to the civil power, when he has proved the denial of justice on the part of the ecclesiastical tribunal ; but any one coming before us, without having previously applied to the Holy See, shall forfeit his bond and pay ten pounds in gold, to be distributed to the poor by the hands of the Pope." The same law also confirmed the exemption from secular tribunals, in favor of clerics, which had already become customary. Nothing short of the deep confusion into which the public mind was plunged by the great philosophical and social revolution of the last century could have suggested the thought of suppressing ecclesiastical jurisdiction in the midst of Catholic nations. Clerics, whatever may be their fault, are first of all accountable to their bishop, the ordinary ; they have given up all the benefits of civil life, to place themselves at the service of every want, of every misery. Should they ever be so unhappy as to betray their holy voca-

tion, it belongs to the bishop to examine the grievousness of their fault, before giving them up, should such a necessity arise, to the secular arm.

21. The care of St. Felix IV. for the interests of the faith reached every part of the Catholic world. Semi-Pelagianism was reviving in Southern Gaul, notwithstanding the zeal of the pious bishops of that province. St. Cesarius of Arles applied to the Pope for advice and for a rule of conduct in opposing the progress of error. St. Felix knew no better means of guarding the faithful from being misled by the heresy than to send to St. Cesarius extracts from the most convincing passages in St. Augustine's works on grace and free-will, as a precise expression of the apostolic tradition and teaching. A council of the bishops of Southern Gaul, held on the 3d of July, A. D. 529, at Orange, on the occasion of the dedication of a church in that city, subscribed to these decisions of Felix IV. "We have learned," said the Fathers, "that errors opposed to the Catholic teaching on grace and free-will have been spread amongst the faithful; hence we have judged it expedient to publish the articles drawn from the writings of the Fathers of the Church, and sent to us by the Holy See for that purpose." The council then established the dogma of original sin, the gratuitousness of grace and faith, and the agreement of free-will with preventing grace in man. St. Felix IV. died in the course of the same year (October 12, A. D. 529), after a pontificate of three years and some months. "Felix was endeared to all," says an ancient author, "by his modest simplicity, his kindly disposition and unfailing charity toward the poor."

§ 4. PONTIFICATE OF ST. BONIFACE II. (October 15, A. D. 529—December, 531).

22. Each new vacancy of the Holy See brought out more clearly the growing tendency on the part of the kings of Italy to control the election of the Sovereign Pontiffs. We saw

Theodoric's attempt to rule the election of St. Felix IV.; and even Athalaric, with all his show of good-will toward the Church of Rome, yet wished to lay the weight of his influence upon its clergy and faithful in the choice of a Pontiff. This usurping bent on the part of the Ostrogoth kings was a pernicious example for the freedom of the Roman Church. When the emperors of Constantinople, and after them, the German emperors, had become masters of Rome, they followed the same line of policy, and sought the right, if not to appoint the Pope, at least to confirm his election. It was only after long and steady struggles that the Church won back the freedom she had enjoyed even under pagan emperors. The death of Felix IV. gave greater prominence to the evil of this secular interference. The election of a successor resulted in the promotion of Boniface II., son of Sigisvult, of the Gothic race (October 15, A. D. 529). But Athalaric's influence had, in the mean time, contrived the factious election of an antipope named Dioscorus. The schism was happily but short; Dioscorus died twenty-nine days after his intrusion (November 12, A. D. 529). The desire to prevent the recurrence of such scandalous contentions led Boniface into the adoption of a measure more zealous than prudent. He issued a decree by which he appointed his own successor, in the person of the deacon Vigilius. Such a step was in direct opposition to the tradition of the Church and to the numerous canons which forbid the Pope, during his lifetime, to bequeath his dignity as an inheritance. Whilst the pontifical election was thus withdrawn from the influence of secular usurpation, it was equally taken from the Church. The innovation might therefore lead to the most fatal results; the elective monarchy of the Church was made a kind of hereditary power, which an unscrupulous holder might transmit in a single family, to the detriment of the interests of religion and faith. Time and reflection changed the Pontiff's views. In a council held at Rome during the year following, the Pope recalled his decree and declared it annulled. As a stronger proof of the sincerity of his conviction, he threw it with his own hands into the flames, in presence of the assembled bishops (A. D. 530). This courageous reparation of a too hasty step in a point of discipline, does honor to the memory of St. Boniface II.

23. During the remainder of his peaceful reign, Boniface, following the custom of the Roman Pontiffs, assembled a council each year in Rome, to look to the spiritual wants of Christendom. The council of A. D. 531 took cognizance of an appeal of Stephen of Larissa, metropolitan of Thessaly, the regularity of whose election was questioned by Epiphanius, Patriarch of Constantinople, on the ground that it had been carried on without his agreement or approval. Since the surreptitious decree of the Council of Chalcedon, the Bishops of Constantinople had not ceased to claim for their See the right of jurisdiction over all the metropolitans of the East. The countless troubles brought upon the Church by these ambitious claims are but too well known. Stephen had been raised to the See of Larissa, in the presence of all the bishops of the province, with the unanimous consent of all the clergy and of the people of the city. Still, Epiphanius thought himself none the less empowered to suspend him from his episcopal functions, and to declare his consecration null and simoniacal. From this unjust sentence the metropolitan of Larissa appealed to the judgment of the Holy See. The decision must have been favorable, though history has not preserved the form in which it was given. During the same year St. Boniface confirmed the decrees of the Council of Orange, which had been laid before him by St. Cesarius of Arles. "You acquaint us," said the Sovereign Pontiff, "that certain Gallic bishops attribute to nature and not to grace the first act of faith by which we believe in Jesus Christ; and you ask us to ratify by the authority of the Apostolic See the profession which you have drawn up against them, holding, according to Catholic doctrine, that faith in Jesus Christ, the very groundwork of Christian life, is inspired by the preventing grace of God. This truth has been clearly enough established by many

fathers, and especially by the great St. Augustine of happy memory. We therefore approve the decision of your council, which agrees, in every point, with Catholic tradition." Such was the authority given by the approval of the Holy See to the acts of the second Council of Orange, that its decisions have become rules of faith which no one may contradict without, by the fact, declaring himself a heretic.

The attention of the bishops was now called to the perpetuity of the Catholic priesthood, and the means of securing it in the various Churches. The Councils of Vaison (A. D. 529) and Toledo (A. D. 531) gave particular care to this question. The first urges ecclesiastics to give their personal care and efforts to the instruction of youths in sacred learning; thus to prepare themselves fit successors. In this wholesome caution we see the dawning idea of ecclesiastical seminaries. The Council of Toledo presents it in a more advanced stage. Its first canon decrees that "young candidates for holy orders shall first be tonsured and placed in the rank of lectors, to be instructed in a house attached to the church, and under the eyes of the bishop. If they freely promise to observe continence, they may be ordained sub-deacons at the age of twenty years. At the age of twenty-five, if their conduct has been irreproachable, they may become deacons. When once ordained priests, they are not at libery to quit the church which has thus trained them, without their bishop's leave." The regulations for episcopal elections also demanded an equal amount of care and attention. Those who had some influence in the elections abused it to wring promises from the candidates, to fulfil which they were afterward obliged to draw upon the property of the Church. To such an extent was this abuse sometimes carried, that even the sacred vessels had been offered for sale in order to meet the promised payments. Boniface II. renewed the decrees against such scandalous simony, and brought them to the notice of all the bishops throughout the Catholic world.

24. Whilst the Pope and the councils thus worked together

to uphold the rules of ecclesiastical discipline, God raised up
a man destined to become the patriarch of the monastic life in
the West; we allude to St. Benedict.* It is true that many
monasteries had been established in Italy, before his day,
under the twofold influence of St. Ambrose and St. Jerome.
The same pious foundations were multiplied in Africa, under
the patronage of St. Augustine; in Northern Gaul, by St. Martin of Tours; and in the South, by Cassian. But these numerous
monasteries were not under the same rule; each had its peculiar observances, somewhat arbitrarily determined. In the confusion attending the barbarian invasions this variety and inconsistency in the rules might give rise to great disorders, and
even to the ruin of monastic institutions in the West. St.
Benedict undertook to make them lasting by union. An Italian
by birth, it was in Italy that he carried out the great work for
which Divine Providence had chosen him. Though nursed in
the lap of luxury, he early cast aside all temporal advantages
and retired into a solitary cave amid the Apennines, about
forty miles from Rome. But in spite of the great care he took
to keep himself hidden from the gaze of men, the lustre of his
holiness soon made him known, and his desert was speedily
peopled by fervent disciples, the most illustrious of whom were
St. Placidius and St. Maurus. Twelve monasteries soon bore
witness to the zealous industry of these holy workmen. Prayer,
manual labor, and works of charity made up their daily life,
and the solitude of Subiacum became the dwelling-place of
angels. Yet St. Benedict's humility and love of retirement drew
him from this blest abode to the summit of an untenanted
mountain overlooking the little town of Cassino, in ancient
Samnium. His reputation followed him here and a monastery
arose over the site of a former temple of Apollo, and the community of religious multiplied to such an extent that it soon
resembled a great city peopled by several thousand inhabitants.
The necessity of subjecting so many different beings to one
fixed rule, first suggested to St. Benedict the idea of conden-

* In Latin *Benedictus*, Blest.

sing into one code of laws all that concerns the monastic life
A continued and deep study of *Cassian's Conferences*, of the
Lives of the Fathers of the Desert, and of the *Rules of St. Basil*,
but above all, personal experience joined to exalted virtue, had
been long preparing him for this great work; and his rule has
since been adopted by all the Western monasteries, just as St.
Basil's had been by all the Eastern. St. Benedict admits candidates to the monastic life only after long and serious trial.
The practice of the evangelical counsels was realized by the
monks worthy of their vocation, in the three vows of perfect
continence, voluntary poverty, and religious obedience. The
abbot's authority is as ample and complete as possible, but it
must be exercised as a father's power and according to the
words of Jesus Christ; the highest in the monastery is but the
servant of his brethren. The rule determines the various
duties and offices in the monastery. The time and length of
exercises of piety and common prayers, the kind of mortification allowed to each person, are fixed with careful exactness.
The regulation for meals and clothing are equally precise. The
habit appointed by St. Benedict for his disciples was adopted
because of its convenience, and remained common among all
the learned professions of Europe until about the fifteenth century. It consisted of a white woollen tunic, a hood or cape
which covered the shoulders and formed in its upper part a
cowl that covered the head. The rule prescribed various penances, graduated according to the degree of guilt. The most
serious penalty was excommunication, which cut off a religious
from all intercourse with his brethren until he had atoned for his
fault or repaired the scandal given to the community. The incorrigible were expelled from the monastery. But the natural mildness of the holy founder left full room for repentance, and allowed
the religious thus expelled to be received back as often as three
times, if they seemed to have returned to better sentiments. We
have here given but an inadequate view of the spirit which ani
mates this rule of St. Benedict, a rule which has won the admiration of the greatest minds. St. Gregory the Great looked

upon it as a master-piece of prudence. Cosmo de Medicis made
it his deep and assiduous study. "I find in it," he said, "the
wisest laws for the government of states, and a deep knowledge
of the human heart." The order of St. Benedict soon spread
throughout the West. By turns, writers, preachers, historians
and husbandmen, these religious undertook the task of civilizing
the barbarous tribes, of saving from shipwreck the existing
models of Greek and Latin literature, of gradually bringing the
land under cultivation, and the warlike hordes of the North to a
more peaceful manner of life. Modern society has reaped the
fruit of their devoted labors, but public gratitude has not
always been proportioned to the services rendered. How often
has not undeserved calumny assailed these humble benefactors
of humanity, who buried their youth, nay even their whole life,
in the solitude of the cloister, to give to an admiring posterity the master-pieces of the ancients ; or who spread abroad
in agricultural colonies, over every part of the country, teaching
the barbarous tribes to till and fertilize the marshes and barren
moors of old Europe, and to draw from the always fruitful soil
the subsistence for which they had too long depended upon the
chances of war, plunder, or bloodshed! Thus we can see how St.
Benedict's influence reaches even to our own day. By a privilege
of wonderful fruitfulness, his order has had the glory of giving
to the Church thirty-five popes, two hundred cardinals, eleven
hundred and sixty-four archbishops, five thousand five hundred
and twelve bishops, and fifty-five thousand four hundred and
sixty religious publicly venerated for holiness of life.

25. The father of this illustrious generation lived in the
lowliest humility and the practice of the most austere mortifications. The miracles which God was pleased to work
through his intercession excited universal wonder; he alone
seemed blind to his own virtue and merit. His life was not,
however, free from trials; some monks whose irregularity he
had tried to correct, one day mingled poison with the water
he drank ; but when the saint made the sign of the cross over
the goblet, as was his wont, it broke of itself. Acquainted by

divine inspiration with the intended crime, he simply said to the authors of the deed: "May Almighty God have mercy upon you, my brothers; why did you seek to treat me thus? Did I not tell you that your life and mine could not agree? Go and seek a superior to your taste; you will have me no longer." And he quitted the monastery. The same failure attended another attempt of the same kind, made by a priest jealous of the saint's virtue and reputation. St. Benedict had received as an alms from this priest, a poisoned loaf of bread; he ordered it to be laid aside, and forbade his disciples to speak of the matter, out of regard for the reputation of the unworthy priest. St. Benedict's fame was known even amongst barbarous nations. Totila, king of the Ostrogoths, whom we shall yet have occasion to mention, wished to visit in person the illustrious religious. The very sight of Benedict inspired him with a respect so deep and reverent that he threw himself upon his knees, not daring to approach near to him. Benedict repeatedly bade him rise; but the formidable conqueror persisted in keeping this humble posture. Then the servant of Jesus Christ drawing near to the Gothic king, said to him: "You have already done much mischief and still continue your blighting course; cease now your iniquities. You will take Rome, you will cross the sea, but you shall die in the tenth year of your reign." The saint's prophecy was fulfilled, for the name of Totila was inscribed in the list of Rome's barbarian conquerors. Benedict, however, did not live to see this invasion (A. D. 546); he died (A. D. 543) three years before, full of days and merit, leaving a spiritual posterity whose glory it is to follow in his footsteps.

26. We have given place to this brief sketch of St. Benedict's labors, under the pontificate of St. Boniface II., because it was during this period that the foundation of the monastery of Monte Cassino actually occurred; but St. Boniface filled the Pontifical Chair only two years. He died in December, (A. D. 531), and was buried in the basilica of St. Peter.

† § V. PONTIFICATE OF ST. JOHN II. (January 22, A. D. 532—April 27, 535).

27. St. John II., who was surnamed Mercury on account of his eloquence, was consecrated on the 22d of January (A. D. 532). It was the misfortune of the times that the election of the Sovereign Pontiff in great measure depended upon the temporal rulers; and thus ambitious men used every means to raise themselves to this high dignity. During the vacancy of the See, several candidates had been guilty of simoniacal proceedings, and the sacred vessels had even been publicly put up for sale. The new Pontiff's first care was, therefore, to renew the decrees of his predecessor, St. Boniface, against simony. Athalaric, who still reigned in Italy, confirmed the Pope's decree by his royal sanction, and even had it engraved on a marble tablet set at the entrance of the pavement of St. Peter's. Yet, by an inexplicable contradiction, the king allowed his officers to lay the exorbitant tax of three thousand ases in gold on the Pope's letters of confirmation. The tax for metropolitans was fixed at two thousand; that for simple bishops, at five hundred. The result of this iniquitous exaction was appropriated to the poor of Ravenna, where the Gothic kings held their court. Nothing was thus wanting to fill the measure of usurpation. Temporal sovereigns claimed the right to confirm pontifical elections, and required of the Pontiff elect the payment of a kind of right of investiture. Such an abuse of power cannot find palliation even in the appropriation made of the extorted gain. Circumstances made it necessary to bow to the law of the conqueror, in order to avoid greater evils; but the conquerors here were barbarians, and their laws were dictated by the pride of armed domination and the harshness of native character. The Church struggled patiently against these pretentious abuses. She ever protested against violence; and if it be attempted to establish these facts as precedents on which to carry out the historical system which

aims at subjecting the spiritual power of the Pope to the civil
authority of princes, it can easily be proved that the acts of
the Gothic kings constitute no precedent, since they were in
direct opposition to every canon law, and rested upon no other
right than that of the stronger. Moreover, it would be a serious mistake to think that such hostile sentiments marked all
Athalaric's policy toward the Popes. Cassiodorus, whom he
had just made præfect of the Prætorium, was at this time
writing to Pope John II., asking the help of his prayers and
wise counsels. "If I have become judge of the palace," wrote
the virtuous minister, "I have not ceased to be your disciple,
for we can govern with prudence and justice only when we
follow your advice. The See of Peter, the admiration of the
world, should grant a special protection to those who are most
closely bound to it; as rulers of Italy, we feel privileged to
claim from it a larger share of benevolence." The king who
chose a minister capable of conceiving and expressing such
sentiments toward the Holy See, could hardly be its real
enemy.

28. The time of St. John's promotion to the Apostolic See
witnessed Justinian's continued care to bear out in the East
the policy of his predecessor Justin, by working great reforms
in behalf of the Catholic faith. His great aim was to win the
barbarians to the true fold, and to crush the ever-renewed
attempts of Eutychianism. To strengthen his efforts by the
Pope's co-operation, he sent to Rome Hypatius, archbishop of
Ephesus, and Demetrius, bishop of Philippi. These deputies
were charged to lay before John II. some propositions tainted
with heresy, and yet obstinately upheld by the Acæmetes of
Constantinople. These monks maintained that the Blessed
Virgin is not really and properly the mother of God, and that
it cannot be said that *one of the Trinity suffered ; unus de Trinitate passus est.* It will be remembered that this proposition
was adopted in the time of Pope Hormisdas, by some Scythian
monks, who wished to lay it down as an article of faith, and
that the discussion to which it then gave rise had not yet been

settled. St. Hormisdas had severely censured the untimely zeal and turbulence of the monks who raised dangerous disputes on the proposition, but he had refrained from giving a decisive judgment on the question. The obstinacy of the Scythian monks drove the Acœmetes into the opposite error. They asserted that Jesus Christ was not *one of the Trinity*, because otherwise he could not have suffered the torments of the Passion. This was open heresy. John II. left no means untried to bring back the Acœmetes to a sounder doctrine; but failing in all his efforts, he was forced to declare them excluded from his communion and that of the whole Catholic Church. As soon as he had formally passed this sentence, he wrote to acquaint Justinian with it. In answer to their expressed desire, the Pope made known the contents of the letter to the Roman senators. It was in substance as follows: "The emperor has made known to us that three questions have lately arisen in the East, viz.: Can Jesus Christ be called *one of the Trinity;* did He really suffer in the flesh, the Divinity remaining impassible? can the blessed Virgin really and properly be called *Mother of God?* We have given an affirmative answer to these three questions, and have approved the belief of the emperor, which agrees in every point with the Sacred Writings, the Fathers and Catholic Tradition." St. John quotes the authorities upon which his doctrine rests, and shows that in opposing it, the Acœmetes have clearly fallen into the error of Nestorius, and have, therefore, brought upon themselves the same excommunication. Justinian gave a place to the Pope's answer, amongst the laws of the empire, in the second edition of his *Code*, published in the year 534.

29. In spite of the opposition on the part of the inhabitants of Constantinople, in spite of the seditions raised by heretics in various parts of the East, Justinian kept steadily in view the restoration of Catholic unity. In the year 532 he was nearly torn from his throne by a contest between the *Greens* and *Blues*, so called after the two factions of the circus, and which was only quelled by the energy of Belisarius. Thirty thou-

saud persons were massacred in the circus, and thus, with their blood, atoned for the rebellion. In Palestine, the Samaritans of the country districts, jealous of the open favor shown to the Christians by Justinian, rose up in arms, to the number of forty thousand, seized upon ancient Samaria (Neopolis), and there made fearful carnage, murdered the bishop, tore the priests in pieces, and wasted the neighboring country. A chief of banditti, named Julian, put himself at their head, and carried death and plunder to all the neighboring country. The imperial troops only overcame these rebels after a long and bloody struggle, which ended in Julian's remaining on the field with twenty thousand of his followers; the rest were taken prisoners and sold as slaves in Persia and Ethiopia. The tidings of the revolt and of the victory which had crushed it, reached Constantinople together. Justinian, nevertheless, determined to make the cities of Palestine pay dearly for their rebellion. The terrified inhabitants sought to ward off the threatened blow by means of the wonder of the desert, St. Sabas, now ninety-three years of age, whom they deputed for that end to the court of Constantinople. The emperor, on learning his approach, sent Epiphanius, patriarch of Constantinople, on board of an imperial galley, to meet and conduct to his presence the holy hermit, whom he looked upon as an angel of peace (A. D. 531). His intercession saved the guilty. "Father," said the emperor to him, "you have founded several monasteries in the solitudes of Palestine; ask me for some revenues which may secure the subsistence of your monks." "They do not need the gifts of your bounty," replied the saint; "their inheritance, both in this life and in the next, is the God who fed Israel in the desert and for forty years sent down the daily manna from heaven. It is enough for us, prince, that you relieve the faithful in Palestine of the expenses of the late war, and that you protect us from the Saracen invasions." The emperor was moved by this disinterestedness, and granted the requests; and Sabas went back to die among his beloved disciples (December 5, A. D. 531), ending his long career as he had always filled it, in the actual exercise of charity. The patriarchal Church of Alexandria was still torn by heretical factions striving for sovereignty. The people were eagerly disputing the point whether the body of Jesus Christ was corruptible or not. The Eutychian monks ever kept these subtle questions before the public mind. "If the body of Jesus Christ was not corruptible," said one faction,* "we must deny the reality of his Passion, and attribute to him an ideal and imaginary body, as the Manicheans do." The others answered: "The body of Jesus Christ was always incorruptible; for if we say it was corruptible, we must admit a distinction between the body of Jesus Christ and the Word of God." There was but one logical means by which to clear this alternative; it was simply and purely to follow the Church in acknowledging two natures in Jesus Christ. But heresy never dreams of coming to terms; the two factions began a strife which threatened to grow into a civil war. The emperor called to Constantinople several bishops, whom he commissioned to examine the question and to draw from the disputants an admission of the orthodox solution. Success crowned his efforts.

30. While the emperor enjoyed the happiness of winning triumphs for the truth in these bloodless contests, the victorious arms of his youthful but already illustrious general, Belisarius, had at length freed Africa from the galling yoke of Vandal oppression. The Roman army, composed of sixteen thousand men, landed without opposition on the coast of Carthage. The cause of this hostile movement was the late usurpation of Gelimer, who had dethroned his relative, Hilderic, for the purpose of reigning in his stead. Justinian, who had long been in friendly relations with the rightful king, took up arms in his defence. On receiving the first tidings of the landing of Roman troops, whom the people hailed as liberators, Gelimer murdered Hilderic, hitherto kept in close confinement. This cruel deed but hastened the hour of his own ruin. No hand would raise a sword in defence of the tyrant. Deserted by his troops, he

---

* They were hence called *Corrupticola.*

fled with his family, and sought shelter on a bleak and lonely
mountain on the extreme frontier of Numidia. Belisarius
ordered his lieutenant Pharas to pursue the fugitive. Pharas,
respecting the misfortune of a fallen foe, sent him a most considerate letter, urging him to submit, and promising him, on
that condition, his life and an honorable subsistence. Gelimer
thanked him for his advice, and in conclusion asked the lieu
tenant *to send him a loaf of bread, a sponge, and a lyre: a loaf*
of bread, because he had been in want of it for three months; a
sponge to wipe away his tears; and a lyre to sing his misfortunes.
Such misery would have awakened still deeper compassion had
it not been the punishment of base treachery and of barbarous
cruelty. Meanwhile, Gelimer daily beheld some member of
his family fall by his side, a prey to the pangs of hunger. His
courage began to fail him. As he was one day wandering
among the solitary mountain paths, he chanced to come upon
his nephew, who was contending with a Moorish peasant for a
piece of half-baked dough. The sight utterly unnerved him.
He surrendered to Belisarius, who made his triumphal entry
into Constantinople, preceded by Gelimer walking before the
conqueror's car, clad in purple and surrounded by his relatives
and the officers of his court. When the captive king entered
the circus, where he was awaited by the emperor and an immense throng of people, not a sigh, not a tear escaped him; he
only uttered the exclamation: "Vanity of vanities! All is
vanity!" (A. D. 534). It was not long before the fate of Belisarius verified once more the words of Ecclesiastes. But the
conquest of Africa by the imperial army gave back that country to the Catholic faith. Justinian raised up the ruined
churches and built new ones; the bishops publicly resumed
the exercise of their holy ministry, and strove to remove the
traces of ruin which a century of violence and persecution had
heaped up in all parts of the land. The triumph of Belisarius
was a fatal blow to Arianism in Africa.

31. This heresy met the same fate in Spain and in Septimania, where it had been implanted by the Visigoths. Childe-

bert, king of Paris, one of the four sons of Clovis, and conqueror of Amalaric, king of the Visigoths in Spain, turned his triumph to the advantage of the true faith. Under the rule of this king and his brothers Gaul continued to furnish the Church with generations of saints. St. Remigius, of memory ever dear to the heart of the Franks whom he converted to the faith, left the metropolitan see of Rheims to St. Romanus, abbot of Mantenay, near Troyes (January 13th, A. D. 533). The apostle of the Franks had founded a monastery, which became a fruitful nursery of illustrious and saintly men, the most renowned of whom was St. Thierry, patron of Austrasia. He had been brought up by his father in the mountains of Vosges and Ardennes, in the midst of a band of robbers, who availed themselves of the disordered times to ravage the neighboring country. But blessed, in early infancy, by divine grace, he became a model of virtue, even in that atmosphere of crime. He was forced to enter the marriage state against his will and inclination; but he soon persuaded his wife to enter the cloister, and he himself retired to the monastery of Rheims, under the direction of St. Remigius. He outlived the holy archbishop, his predecessor, but a few months, and died on the 1st of July, A. D. 533. Meanwhile Childebert had erected the abbey of Celle, in Berry, and placed it under the direction of St. Eusicius, who was succeeded in the government of the monastery by his disciple St. Leonard. Christianity, which they had so lately embraced, had not yet had time to sink deeply into the habits and manners of the Franks, nor to soften their barbarian rudeness. The bishops called by God to govern them needed an apostolic firmness and energy. But the episcopacy was equal to the great task. At Clermont, in Auvergne, St. Quentin publicly excommunicated Hortensius, a lieutenant of King Thierry, for unjustly holding in captivity some innocent persons on whose property he had cast a covetous eye. The intrepid bishop, whose weight of years deprived him of the use of his feet, had himself carried by his clergy to the public square before the palace of Hortensius, and shaking off the dust from his shoes against the palace walls, he exclaimed: "Cursed be this dwelling! may it become deserted, and none remain to dwell within its walls!" The imprecation is borrowed from the Psalms of David; and it was not slow of fulfilment. An unknown form of disease came upon all the inhabitants of the palace. Hortensius was terrified, and at once released the prisoners, begging the saint to intercede with God to withhold His avenging hand. Quentin was moved by these signs of repentance; he prayed for Hortensius, and the scourge passed away. The firmness shown by the holy bishop in regard of the powerful was equalled by his gentle and tender charity toward the poor. He was succeeded by St. Gal, who inherited both his dignity and his saintly virtue (A. D. 532). The see of Treves was at the same time illustrated by St. Nicetius or Nizier, whose fearless discharge of the episcopal duties won him the title of the Ambrose of Gaul. King Thierry's officers sought him out in his monastic retreat, to make him bishop. Night having overtaken the party on their return to the king, the officers pitched their tents and left their horses to roam at will amid fields crowned with the ripening harvest. At this sight Nicetius exclaimed: "Withdraw your horses at once from the harvest of the poor, otherwise I shall cut you off from my communion." "What!" replied the lords, "you are not yet a bishop, and you already threaten excommunication!" "It is indeed the king," returned the saint, "who has taken me from my monastery to raise me to the episcopal dignity, but if needs be I shall dare to oppose the king himself for the defence of the right or the support of the weak!" He then hastened to drive the horses from the harvest-field. Such conduct promised a generous and independent spirit to the Church; and the episcopate of Nicetius fully carried out the bright promise. After Thierry's death (A. D. 534), Theodebert, his son and successor, by nature generous and capable of noble views, yet given up to unbridled passions, shocked his kingdom by the example of an adulterous alliance. The monarch one day entered the church whilst Nicetius was officiating. The bishop, turning with dignity toward Theodebert, ordered him no longer to desecrate the holiness of the august Mysteries by his presence, notifying him, at the same time, that if he staid longer in defiance of this warning, the sacrifice should be interrupted. Theodebert withdrew; and afterward, yielding to the fatherly warnings of Nicetius, put an end to his disorderly manner of life.

32. The fierce and barbarous instincts which even yet ruled the Frankish monarchs had just been displayed in a fearful manner. Clodomir, one of the sons of Clovis, and king of Orleans, had died, leaving three infant children: Theobald, Gonthaire, and Clodoald. Childebert and Clotaire, their uncles, despoiled them of their paternal inheritance, leaving the unfortunate princes with no other resource than the affection of their grandmother, St. Clotilda, who had them brought up under her own care at Paris, where she then resided. "Childebert," says St. Gregory of Tours, "seeing that his mother bestowed her affection on the sons of Clodomir, became jealous; and fearing that through her influence they might one day recover their states, he sent a secret message to his brother Clotaire, in these words : 'Our mother has taken charge of our nephews, and proposes to give them back the throne. Come to Paris, that we may decide upon our best course.' Clotaire readily answered the summons. Childebert had already spread the report that the two kings had agreed to restore the kingdom to their nephews. They accordingly sent word to St. Clotilda : 'Send us the children that we may raise them to the throne.' The queen was well pleased, and did not suspect the treacherous plot. She sent the young princes, saying to them : 'I shall not feel that I have lost my son Clodomir when I see you wearing his crown.' As soon as Childebert and Clotaire found the young princes actually in their power, they sent to the queen Arcadius, an Arvernian * senator, with a pair of scissors and a naked sword. 'Illustrious queen,' said the messenger, 'our lords, your sons, await your pleasure concerning the disposition to be made of your grand-

* Of Auvergne.

sons. Order that they live shorn of their locks (long hair was
then the distinctive mark of royalty), or that they die.' Overwhelmed with grief and terror at the words of the senator and
the sight of the instruments he bore in his hands, Clotilda gave
full vent to her grief, and uttered the imprudent exclamation :
' I would rather see them dead, if they are not to hold the
throne which belongs to them.' Arcadius, without awaiting
any further answer, came back to his masters and gave the
account of his mission. Clotaire immediately seized Theobald,
the eldest of the children, who was but ten years old, and
stabbed him under the arm-pit, stretching him lifeless at his
feet. At this sight, Gonthaire, who was but seven years
of age, threw himself at Childebert's feet, and, clinging to his
knees, exclaimed in terror : ' Help me, father ! let me not be
murdered like Theobald !' Childebert was touched by the
tears and cries of the helpless child, and, turning to Clotaire,
begged that the innocent victim might be spared. But the
murderer, carried away by a savage fierceness, exclaimed : ' It
was you who urged me to the deed, and do you now recoil ?
Hinder me not, or you die in his stead !' Then seizing the
child, he buried in his heart the dagger still reeking with his
brother's blood. During this fearful tragedy, some of the palace officials had succeeded in withdrawing Clodoald, the youngest of the three, from the fury of his uncles. When grown up,
he cast off his rights to an earthly kingdom, and devoted to God
a life which God had almost miraculously saved." He was ordained priest and founded a monastery at *Nuventium* (Nogent,
two leagues from Paris). This place afterward took his name,
and was called *St. Cloud*, the modern French name for St. Clodoald. The monastery has since become a collegiate church.
and the village of Nogent was made the royal residence of St.
Cloud, which name thus recalls at once all the most barbarous
features of worldly policy and the sweet and true consolation
which religion only can afford to the deepest misery (A. D.
532).

  33. From this bloody picture of two princes murdered in

open day, in the midst of the royal palace, and by the hand of an uncle, we may form some idea of the rugged field which Christianity was called to till in these Frankish natures. To give more unity to the efforts of their zeal, the Gallic bishops felt the necessity of holding councils. That of Orleans, the second held in that city (June 23d, A. D. 533), counted twenty-six bishops, many of whom the Church ranks amongst her saints. Chief among them were St. Flavius, or, as he is commonly called, *St. Flieu*, of Rouen; St. Leo of Sens, St. Julian of Vienne, St. Lo of Coutances, St. Eleutherius of Auxerre, St. Innocent of Le Mans, St. Agrippinus of Autun, and St. Gal of Clermont in Auvergne. This illustrious assembly drew up rules of discipline to secure the freedom of elections against the inroads of the temporal power, and the shameful abuses of simony. One of the most noteworthy canons is that which forbids the order of deaconess to be henceforth conferred upon any woman whatever. The necessity for this order had existed only as long as it was necessary to baptize women lately converted to the faith. As Christianity gradually pervaded society, the baptism of adults had become a thing of rare occurrence, and the deaconesses were no longer called upon to discharge their office.

34. One of the most celebrated prelates of this day was St. Medard, sprung from a noble Frankish family of Salency, and consecrated bishop of Noyon by St. Remigius (A. D. 530). No higher testimony could have been borne to his merit than the suspension of the ordinary rules of discipline, which was granted in his favor. At the death of St. Eleutherius, bishop of Tournay, the unanimous voice of clergy and laity called St. Medard to govern that church, together with his own diocese of Noyon. The two sees remained thus joined for more than six hundred years. The name of St. Medard is linked with that of St. Radegundes, wife of King Clotaire, to whom the bishop of Soissons gave the veil even whilst her husband was still living. This fact of a queen being admitted into a religious order before her husband's death, gave rise to a theological dis-

cussion which has not as yet found a satisfactory solution. The law of the Church, relative to marriage, does not allow either of the parties to enter the religious state whilst the other still lives, unless they agree, by common consent, to forsake the world. But Clotaire was by no means thus disposed. His dissolute life has furnished a scandalous page in history. As lawful spouse, therefore, St. Radegundes could not regularly take the veil. But were the canonical rules on the subject as clear and explicit then as they are now? Were they known to the Frankish bishops? Such are some of the questions which naturally spring from this particular fact of history. Be this as it may, the world now saw three members of the royal dynasty of the Franks bid farewell to every earthly allurement, to spend a life of solitude in the practice of holy contemplation and good works. They were: St. Clotilda, St. Radegundes, and St. Clodoald or St. Cloud. Their example by degrees affected the public manners. A host of saintly religious were training others in the monasteries now springing up in all parts of the country, many of which gave rise to populous cities. Ebredulfus, commonly called St. Evroul, a lord of Childebert's court, answering the call of divine grace, divided his property among the poor; and having thus reduced himself to want, retired into the forest of Ouche, in the diocese of Lisieux, where he converted several robbers, who became his disciples. Their number grew so rapidly that he soon found his cell surrounded by fifteen hundred others, not to mention thirteen monasteries founded by him in the neighboring provinces. Many religious institutions likewise owe their existence to St. Marculfus or Marcoul, who planted them even in Neustria and Great Britain. St. Fridolinus meanwhile dotted Austrasia with these holy settlements. St. Pourçain, in Auvergne, St. Carilephus or Calais, in Maine, St. Junian and St. Leonard, in Limousin, were all simultaneously engaged in founding abbeys which inherited their names, and around which arose the cities of St. Leonard, St. Junian, Calais, and St. Pourçain. In Burgundy, St. Seine (Sequanus) raised a monastery in the Segustrian forest, situated in the diocese of Langres, near the source of the Seine.

35. The flourishing state of the Gallic Church which brought up saints in every rank of society, was only disturbed by the scandalous conduct of Contumeliosus, bishop of Reez. This prelate, truly unworthy of his high and holy calling, was charged with several crimes, which proved to be but too justly imputed to him. St. Cesarius of Arles, and the other bishops of the province, examined the charges and sent a report to Pope John II. (A. D. 534). The Sovereign Pontiff pronounced his solemn judgment in the lamentable case; Contumeliosus was deposed from his bishopric and confined in a monastery to do penance for his crimes. John II. at the same time enjoined St. Cesarius to appoint a provisional bishop to administer the diocese of Reez until the death of the titulary. Contumeliosus appealed from this decision; but in the mean time John II. had died (April 26th, A. D. 534). His successor, St. Agapetus, re-examined the case, and simply confirmed the first sentence.

§ 6. PONTIFICATE OF ST. AGAPETUS (May 4, A. D. 535--April 25, 536).

36. The accession of St. Agapetus to the Sovereign Pontificate is marked by an event of vast importance in chronology : the adoption of the Christian era in both private and public acts. The years had hitherto been reckoned according to the consular annals. The fall of the Western Empire had complicated the system with new difficulties. A priest of the Roman Church, no less illustrious for science than for virtue, Dionysius the Little, undertook this useful reform. He had been appointed to carry out the cycle of St. Cyril, which ended in A. D. 531. Whilst engaged in this work, he conceived the idea of making the starting-point of modern history coincide exactly with the year of our Lord's Incarnation ; and on this basis he computed a paschal cycle which he carried out to the year 627. Dionysius the Little did not limit his labors to the discharge of

this duty. He gathered into one huge collection the canons of all the Eastern and Western councils. This work, which showed the most consummate care and intelligence, was hailed by the enthusiastic applause of the whole Catholic world. The illustrious scholar subsequently completed it by the addition of all the decretals of the Popes since St. Sericius. This last work contains a few omissions, owing doubtless to the impossibility of procuring some rare and little known documents. Such as it is, however, it has been of great use and service to the Church, though not publicly authorized by her. Dionysius spent the first half of the sixth century in these great works, and died in the odor of sanctity about the year 540.

37. On learning the election of St. Agapetus, Justinian sent him his profession of faith, requesting, at the same time, that the converted Arians might be allowed to retain their ecclesiastical dignities. Justinian also asked the Pope to admit to his communion Achilles, consecrated bishop of Larissa, in the place of Stephen, by Epiphanius of Constantinople; and finally, he begged that the vicariate of Illyria might be transferred from the see of Larissa to that of Justiniana.* The Pope, in reply, approved Justinian's profession of faith; "not," he said, "that we admit the right of laymen to preach; but we praise your zeal in upholding the Catholic doctrine by your authority." In respect to the converted Arians, he calls the emperor's attention to the fact that the canons forbid that reconciled heretics shall be considered in orders; and promises that the matter of Achilles, named bishop of Larissa, shall be submitted to the careful examination of the legates whom he proposes soon to send to the East. "You excuse our brother and fellow-bishop Epiphanius," says the Pope, "for having consecrated him, as he did it by your order. But he should himself have made known to you the prerogatives of the Apostolic See, knowing, as he does, how ready you always are to assert its

---

* This was a new city which Justinian was building in Dardania, near his native village. He called it *Justiniana Prima*, to distinguish it from the other cities to which he had granted his name. It was made the capital of Illyria.

rights." The Pope provisionally admitted Achilles to his communion; as to the vicariate of Illyria, the legates would acquaint Justinian with the Pope's decision on the subject. This letter, dated October 15th, A. D. 535, was soon followed to Constantinople by five apostolic legates: Sabinus, bishop of Canossa, Epiphanius of Eclanum, Asterius of Falerno, Rusticus of Festula, and Leo of Nola.

38. Simultaneously with Justinian's letter, St. Agapetus had received the acts of a council held by two hundred and seventeen bishops at Carthage, under the presidency of Reparatus, bishop of that metropolis. It was their wish to devote the first-fruits of their freedom to the restoration of discipline, which had suffered so severely during the Vandal persecution. When this august assemblage met for the first time in the great basilica of Carthage, the thought of past sufferings, the joy of a deliverance so unlooked for, drew tears from the venerable bishops who composed it; and St. Augustine's solemn anthem of thanksgiving went up from every heart and from every tongue in this assemblage of his fellow-countrymen.* The canons of the Nicene Council were then read, as they established the Catholic faith against the errors of Arius; the question was proposed what should be the treatment of the Arian bishops returning to the truth. The council was of opinion that they should be admitted only to lay-communion; before deciding the point, however, it was determined to ask the judgment of the Apostolic See in the matter. The council moreover asked the Sovereign Pontiff if it were allowed to confer orders on those who had been baptized by Arians; and as several African bishops had gone, during the Vandal persecution, to Italy and Sicily, the council begs the Pope not to receive into his communion such as could not prove by letters from the bishops of Africa that they had been sent for the good of the churches. St. Agapetus returned a detailed answer to each question. The Arian bishops were not to be reinstated;

---

* The *Te Deum* is attributed to the joint composition of Sts. Ambrose and Augustine.

but a sufficient revenue should be assigned them from the
Church property for their support. Converts from Arianism
were not to be raised to Holy Orders, lest the Catholic priesthood should be infected with the errors of that sect. Finally,
he approves the precaution recommended by the council respecting the clerics who had quitted Africa during the persecution, and urges the necessity of using every possible means
to check vagrancy among clerics.

39. The distinguished success of Belisarius in the subjugation of Africa, led Justinian to send him into Italy for the purpose of crushing the Gothic domination there, and of giving
back the cradle of the empire to the rule of the emperors. This
movement found a plausible pretext in the cruelty of Theodatus who had lately caused the death of his benefactress, Ama-
lasontha (A. D. 534). The imperial fleet, under Belisarius, cast
anchor on the coast of Sicily; and Theodatus, terrified by the
prestige of Justinian's arms, appealed to Pope St. Agapetus and
the Roman senate. He declared that if they did not dissuade
Justinian from this design, he would put to death all the senators
with their families. The pen which sent to Rome this language
worthy of a tyrant, was at the same time engaged in tracing a
most abject letter to Constantinople, offering to yield the throne
to Justinian in consideration of a life-pension of twelve hundred
pounds of gold. "I would rather," he writes to Justinian,
"live as a peaceful husbandman, than thus hedged about with
the cares and perils of royalty." These philosophical reveries,
however, would not have hindered him from carrying out his
threat against the senate, had not the Pope, St. Agapetus, undertaken to negotiate in person with the emperor Justinian.
He prepared to start, but so strict was his observance of poverty that he had not the means necessary to defray his travelling expenses; he was accordingly forced to borrow the funds
from the officers of the king on whose behalf he undertook the
distant mission. Theodatus had not the generosity to furnish
the necessary sum; and he even required as surety for the

borrowed money, that all the sacred vessels of St. Peter's should be left in the hands of his officers.

40. St. Agapetus reached Constantinople on the 2d of February, A. D. 536. He was met at his approach by the five legates whom he had sent to the East. Epiphanius, Patriarch of Constantinople, had died the year before. The empress Theodora's influence with Justinian had bestowed the See upon Anthimus, the Eutychian bishop of Trebizond. St. Agapetus refused to communicate with him, in spite of the prayers and threats of the empress; he even overcame her influence in the emperor's mind. Anthimus, though deposed, preferred the loss of his See to signing a Catholic profession of faith. The Pope presided in the council which pronounced his condemnation. The political question which had brought the Sovereign Pontiff to the East, neither did nor could receive a solution favorable to the views of Theodatus. The conquest of Italy was a settled purpose with Justinian; all the preparations for it had been made. Agapetus lost no time in useless negotiations, but gave his attention to the various wants of the Eastern Church. The Church of Aléxandria sought his intervention to put a stop to the machinations of the Eutychian heretics who still continued to teach their errors in that city. St. Agapetus, in conjunction with the emperor, designed to call a council to remedy all disorders and abuses; but his intention was thwarted by death, which struck down the Holy Pontiff in a strange land (April 17, A. D. 536). "It was a festive day for him," says an eye-witness, "but a season of deep mourning for us. Never were such obsequies celebrated for Pope or emperor. Not all the public squares, nor the porticos, nor the house-tops could contain the vast crowds that thronged around the funeral car. Constantinople now saw all her subjects within her city walls." The remains of St. Agapetus, thus surrounded by marks of reverent honor, were brought from Constantinople to Rome, where they were laid with those of his predecessors in the basilica of St. Peter.

CHAPTER IV.

§ I. Pontificate of St. Sylverius (June 8, A. D. 536—July 20, 538).

1. Election of St. Sylverius forced by Theodatus, king of the Ostrogoths.—2. Theodora's intrigues to contrive the election of a Eutychian Pope.—3. Successes of Belisarius in Italy.—4. Theodora induces Belisarius to banish St. Sylverius to Patara. Justinian orders the Pope to be restored.—5. Martyrdom of St. Sylverius.

§ II. Pontificate of Vigilius (July 20, A. D. 538—January 10, 555).

6. First proofs of Apostolic energy on the part of Pope Vigilius.—7. Disgrace and death of Belisarius.—8. Totila's mildness toward the Neapolitans.— Siege and capture of Rome by Totila.—9. Ravages of Chosroes in the East. —10. Justinian's Decree of Proscription against the *Three Chapters.*—11. Pope Vigilius visits Constantinople. *Judicatum* issued against the *Three Chapters.*—12. Letter of Vigilius to Aurelius, bishop of Arles, on this subject. The Pope's firmness. He is outraged in the Church of St. Peter at Constantinople.—13. Fifth General Council held at Constantinople.—14. Death of Pope Vigilius.

§ III. Pontificate of Pelagius I. (April 16, A. D. 555—March 2, 559).

15. Troubles attending the election of Pelagius I.—16. Charity and prudence of Pelagius.—17. The Tuscan bishops refuse to receive the condemnation of the *Three Chapters.* Religious spirit in Gaul.—18. Death of Pelagius I.

§ IV. Pontificate of John III. (March, A. D. 559—July 23, 572).

19. Phantasiasts in Constantinople.—20. Death of Justinian. Accession of Justinian the Younger.—21. Narses invites Alboin, king of the Lombards, to Italy.—22. Death of John III.

§ V. Pontificate of Benedict I. (May 16, A. D. 573—July 31, 577).

23. Vacancy of the Roman See.—Religious and political View of the Christian World.—24. Benedict I. The Deacon St. Gregory and the Angles. Death of Benedict I.

§ 1. PONTIFICATE OF ST. SYLVERIUS (June 8, A. D. 536—July 20, 538).

1. As soon as Rome was made acquainted with the death of St. Agapetus, Theodatus, fearing the possible election of a Pope less favorable to his interest than to that of the Greeks, on his own authority contrived the consecration of the deacon Sylverius, without allowing the least right of suffrage. He even threatened with death any cleric who dared to oppose his tyrannical orders. The Roman clergy, thus forced into compliance, preferred freely to ratify an election which Theodatus would have imposed by force of arms, had it been resisted. Thus was St. Sylverius raised to the Sovereign Pontificate on the 8th of June, A. D. 536. Whatever may have been the hopes entertained by Theodatus, the bearing of the new Pope completely defeated them. St. Sylverius proved himself a worthy successor to so many noble Pontiffs who had upheld the independence of the Holy See at the risk of life itself. He too could be a martyr.

2. Belisarius, in his Italian expedition, was charged with two missions : His public and official duty was to make way for the Grecian rule by uprooting that of the Ostrogoths. This was the end which Justinian aimed at obtaining by his general's arms. The other was private and personal, and emanated from Theodora. The crafty woman deemed this a favorable opportunity to place upon the Chair of St. Peter a Pope unprincipled enough to admit the Eutychians to his communion. She thought to have found a willing instrument of all her wishes in the Roman deacon Vigilius, who had long resided

in Constantinople as envoy of the Popes, and whom Boniface
II. had wished to name as his successor. The empress offered
him seven hundred pounds in gold and a secret order to Belisarius, by which the general was to contrive his election to
the Papacy; she required of him, in return, to reject the Council of Chalcedon, and to receive to his communion Anthimus,
Patriarch of Constantinople, deposed by St. Agapetus. Vigilius was weak or ambitious enough to agree to such terms, and
went to Rome with the intention of fulfilling them; but none
of these things was to be accomplished. Vigilius the deacon
had contracted engagements which Vigilius the Pope afterward spurned with indignation—a striking example of the
ever-watchful care exercised over the Church by Divine Providence, which will never suffer the gates of hell to prevail
against the indefectible Chair of Peter. When Vigilius reached
the Eternal City the election of Sylverius was an accomplished
fact. The aspiring deacon contented himself with delivering
Theodora's order to Belisarius, and set out on his return to
Constantinople.

3. Since his arrival in Sicily, Belisarius numbered his steps by
victories. The whole island obeyed his laws. He then crossed
the strait, passed up through Italy, and halted before Naples.
Hitherto Belisarius had stood before the admiring world a
great captain, as merciful to the conquered as he was formidable to his enemies; but now his character seemed to deny
itself. Enslaved by the influence of the courtesan Antonina, a
former associate of Theodora, and whom he had been so weak
as to marry, he became cruel to flatter the bloodthirsty disposition of this unnatural woman. Naples flowed with the
blood of its wretched inhabitants who were butchered without
distinction of age or sex; priests were slain at the foot of the
altar, and the city was left a desolate, deserted heap of ruins.
Leaving this scene of carnage behind him, Belisarius appeared
before the walls of Rome. To spare the Eternal City a like
fate, Sylverius persuaded the inhabitants to prevent the vengeance of an angered conqueror, by opening their gates to the

imperial army. Meanwhile Theodatus, whose base and dastardly character had roused the hatred of his subjects against him, had been put to death, and Vitiges succeeded to the difficult task of beating back the Greek invader. The Italians, left to their own resources, amid the ceaseless din and strife of hostile arms, knew not to which leader they could look for protection; and as if to fill the measure of desolation for this fair land, once queen of the world, but now the spoil of every barbarous tribe, the Franks, under Theodebert, king of Austrasia, suddenly fell upon the northern provinces and devoted them to fire and sword. Whilst these events crowded upon each other with a rapidity that scarce allows the historian to seize them all in their fulness, Belisarius was marching into Rome, where the Pope received him as a deliverer. Availing himself of the credit which this favor had won for him with the Greek general, the Sovereign Pontiff made every effort to obtain some compensative measures for the unfortunate city of Naples. Belisarius granted immunities to such of the inhabitants of the surrounding country as would repeople it, and all traces of the invasion by degrees disappeared.

4. But under all this seeming benevolence, Belisarius, the tool of his wife, Antonina, to whom the empress secretly conveyed her wishes, meditated a sacrilegious attempt upon the person of the Sovereign Pontiff. The holy Pope had lately answered a request of the imperial courtesan that he would recall Anthimus to the See of Constantinople, by a letter full of apostolic firmness and vigor. "Never," he wrote, "can I be guilty of such a crime. I know that this sad case may cost me my life; but I cannot prove false to my conscience in communicating with a heretic justly condemned by my predecessor." St. Sylverius was not mistaken. His firmness won him the martyr's palm; and Belisarius, by laying sacrilegious hands upon the Lord's anointed, brought down upon his future career the blight of divine vengeance.

It was with reluctance, however, that he yielded to the wish of the empress. On receiving the final order to seize the Pon-

tiff, he exclaimed : "I must do as I am ordered; they who
seek the life of Sylverius shall answer for it at the last day,
not I." He sent for the Sovereign Pontiff and urged him to
yield to Theodora's request. Sylverius refused; and on leaving the general, took refuge in the church of St. Mary, to ·
escape the violence which he apprehended. He was again
summoned by Belisarius, and this time was held a prisoner in
the palace; false witnesses were heard, who deposed that he
had taken part in some intrigues tending to place the city in
the power of Vitiges, king of the Goths. On such calumnies
as these Sylverius was condemned and stripped of the pallium
and other pontifical ornaments in the very apartment of Belisarius. He was clothed in the dress of a monk, and the report
was spread that he had been juridically deposed. Sylverius
was then exiled to Patara, in Lycia (A. D. 537). The bishop
of that city, moved by a respectful compassion for the misfortunes of the venerable Pontiff, hastened to Constantinople and
boldly upbraided the emperor with the outrages heaped upon
the Head of the Church. Justinian was, or at least feigned
to be, ignorant of the atrocity of the case, and ordered that
Sylverius should be sent back to Rome with all the honor due
to his high rank. Theodora tried in vain to thwart the design
of her imperial consort; for once Justinian stood firm in his
praiseworthy resolution, and Sylverius was brought back to
Rome.

5. Meantime, the deacon Vigilius, whom the advice of Belisarius had recalled to Rome, assembled a council of the clergy,
and, whether by threats or by bribes, secured his election to
the pontifical throne, as if the deposition of Sylverius were
really juridical (November 22, A. D. 537). Belisarius had been
a party to this usurpation. Vigilius, hearing of the Pope's
return, took measures with Justinian's general. They agreed
to carry out the secret orders of Theodora, fully assured that
her influence would secure their pardon from the emperor.
They accordingly caused Sylverius to be seized on the way,
and taken to the island of Palmaria, where the holy Pontiff

soon died of ill-usage and hunger, on the 20th of July, A. D. 538. The Church honors his memory as that of a martyr. Procopius gives a different account of his death. He says that the Pope was murdered, at the instigation of Antonina, by a soldier named Eugenius.

§ II. PONTIFICATE OF VIGILIUS (July 20, A. D. 538—Jan. 10, 555).

6. The coercion exercised by the temporal powers over the Papal elections finds, perhaps, no more conspicuous proofs than the regular accession of Vigilius to the Chair of Peter, which he had held as antipope during the life of the rightful Pontiff. Under different circumstances the clergy, secure in the right of free suffrage, would have chosen another Pope; but under the weapons of a victorious general backed by the imperial army, it became a matter of necessity to yield and to accept whatever irregularity might exist in such a succession. Vigilius, therefore, on the death of St. Sylverius, took his place in the list of Sovereign Pontiffs, and it does not appear that any protest was entered against his accession. Moreover, on taking possession of the heritage of St. Peter, he seems to have been endowed with a new spirit of apostolic vigor; and the Pope nobly redeemed the errors and failings of the deacon. Two letters which he addressed severally to Justinian and to Mennas, the legitimate patriarch of Constantinople, bear splendid witness to his orthodoxy. He declares his faith to be the same as that of his predecessors Celestin, Leo, Hormisdas, John, and Agapetus. Like them, too, he receives the four ecumenical councils and the letter of St. Leo the Great; and with them he anathematizes the partisans of Eutyches, but especially the intruder Anthimus, who persisted in braving the canonical rules by unlawfully holding the See of Constantinople (September 17, A. D. 540). In spite of this clear and positive profession of faith, some writers have not hesitated to pronounce the belief of Vigilius doubtful. Liberatus, a Carthaginian deacon, and Victor, bishop of Tunnona, both contemporary authors, quote a

letter purporting to have been addressed by him, in the beginning of his pontificate, to Anthimus, admitting the heretic to
his communion. Modern critics all agree in pronouncing this
letter apocryphal, as it bears witness against itself. The very
superscription would throw a doubt upon its authenticity ; it is
thus worded : *"Vigilius to his lords and christs."* The whole
history of the Roman chancery cries out against such a formula, never used by a Pope in addressing bishops. And
besides how can Vigilius be suspected of such a flagrant self-
contradiction ? Had he wished to admit the heretic Anthimus,
he would naturally have made capital of it with the empress
Theodora, whose wish it was ; whereas, on the contrary, he
answered Theodora's request by a plain and positive refusal.
Besides, the history of Vigilius's pontificate shows him assailed
with the most bitter and varied charges and recriminations in
the controversy on the *Three Chapters ;* yet to none of his enemies did the idea occur of holding up to him so fatal a document. These few brief arguments sufficiently prove that the
faith of Vigilius, as Sovereign Pontiff, remained unshaken in
spite of that Pope's unfortunate antecedents.

7. The disastrous period when an antipope became legitimate by the death of a holy Pontiff, to which he had contributed, offered no consoling offset in a political point of view.
War was perpetuating itself in Italy. Belisarius had gone to
receive the honor of a triumph at Constantinople. Vitiges, in
chains, walked before his chariot, as Gelimer had done before
him. The victorious general laid at Justinian's feet the treasures of the Gothic monarchy. He was repaid with injustice
and humiliations. God now visited upon Belisarius the outrages which St. Sylverius had received at his hands. The
conqueror, at the height of fortune and worldly prosperity, was
accused of conspiring against his sovereign, and of aiming at
the throne. The great captain was called to stand in judgment
before his imperial master, who questioned him on his alleged
conspiracy. The offended hero made no answer to the emperor's inquiries, and only said, as he left the hall : " Prince,

to the calumnies of my cowardly accusers I oppose but my character and my services of forty years in your armies. Judge me ; punish your general if you think him guilty." His property was confiscated and he was himself imprisoned. Justinian subsequently discovered the hero's innocence and sought to repair the wrong he had done him; but the injustice and foul ingratitude of those who owed him so much had broken that great spirit. Belisarius died at Constantinople of a broken heart (A. D. 565). He went to his grave without show or parade; his veterans alone wept over him. From his far-off exile, Gelimer, too, gave a tear to his memory.* The eunuch Narses succeeded in Italy to the rank, but not to the genius and loyalty of Belisarius. The Goths were rising on all sides.

8. In the year 541, Totila ascended the Gothic throne of Italy and was successively winning back all the victories òf Belisarius. The royal barbarian opened his military career by acts of unexampled cruelty; wasted fields, plundered cities, butchered inhabitants—all the horrors of war, heightened by the fierce disposition of his soldiers, had made his name one of terror. But from the time of his interview with St. Benedict, which we mentioned in speaking of the holy abbot, Totila's manner had suddenly lost its natural fierceness. Naples was the first to feel the happy effect of this unwonted mildness. The unhappy city had hardly yet been able to cover the traces of Belisarius's passage, when Totila appeared before its gates. After several months of a famine which recalled the most fearful scenes of the past, the inhabitants surrendered at discretion. The conqueror promised to treat them mercifully, and he kept his word. Seeing that the soldiers of the

---

* That Belisarius was deprived of his eyes and reduced to beggary is an idle fiction. Yet the fable has gained the footing of truth in the popular mind, and held full sway in the imagination of sculptors and poets. But history is never at liberty to tamper with the truth. Not a single contemporary author says a word about Belisarius as a needy beggar. The origin of this tale is traceable to John Tzetzes, a writer of small note in the twelfth century. He probably confounded the disgrace of John of Cappadocia, præfect of the prætorium, with that of Belisarius.—(M. Baptistin POUJOULAT, *Histoire de l'Empire Ottoman*, t. iv., p. 182.)

garrison were reduced by hunger, he feared that they might cause their own death by too eagerly partaking of the food he intended to distribute among them. He accordingly stationed guards at the gates, and gave a slight ration to each Neapolitan soldier; this supply was gradually increased until all danger had passed. To all who did not wish to enlist in his ranks, he furnished means of travel to the abode of their choice. Totila next laid siege to Rome. Vigilius gave notice of the fact to the emperor Justinian who was not in a state to offer any opposition. The siege was pressed with desperate fury. The famine had reached a fearful pitch. One day, five little children surrounded their father, crying for bread. " Follow me," said the wretched father. He led them to a bridge on the Tiber, and there, muffling up his face in his cloak, threw himself into the stream. The people, who had witnessed this act of despair, surrounded the generals and forced them, at length, to open the gates to Totila. The Goth agreed to spare the city until the return of the deacon Pelagius whom he had sent as ambassador to Constantinople, to offer peace to Justinian. The emperor would listen to no terms. Totila then determined to make the spot on which Rome stood but one vast pasture-land. He accordingly scattered the inhabitants throughout Campania, and began to tear down the palaces and walls. General consternation prevailed. The destruction of Rome would have been, in some sort, the signal of the world's dissolution. Throngs of terrified people poured in from all quarters upon St. Benedict, to consult him in the danger which threatened them. " Be assured," said the saint, " that Rome shall not be destroyed by the nations; but it shall be beaten by storms, and wither like a tree which decays at the root." * And in truth Totila gave up his design. He then passed over to Sicily, Sardinia and Corsica, which he successively devastated, and died in A. D. 552, in the battle known by the name of *Busta Gallorum,* near Tagina (now Lentagio, in the Apennines), where Narses defeated the Gothic forces.

* This prediction of St. Benedict is quoted by Pope St. Gregory the Great.

9. War had also carried its ravages into the East. Chosroes, king of Persia, for twenty years desolated the cities of Syria. In the year 540, he besieged and took Antioch, the capital of the East, sacked and destroyed it, and led away the inhabitants into bondage. The Eastern Christians multiplied their alms to ransom so many wretched captives from the king of Persia and give them back to their country. The collection was large enough to have ransomed all the prisoners; yet not one was redeemed. A Greek, an imperial commander, seized and appropriated the whole sum to his own use. Earthquakes, plague and famine added their destroying power to that of war. All evils seemed to have leagued together to hasten the downfall of the principal Eastern cities, once so wealthy and flourishing.

10. Religious dissensions, too, lent their discordant note to the general din. The works of Origen, which had been so fruitful of discussions in their earliest days, became anew the ground of lively and animated debate. Justinian, who plumed himself upon the extent of his theological learning, came upon the ground of debate with an edict condemning the errors attributed to Origen, relative to the six points already mentioned: the Trinity, creation, the pre-existence of souls, the animation of the heavenly bodies, the resurrection of the body, the eternal torments of the reprobate. As the supporters of Origen did not deem Justinian a competent authority in such matters, the imperial decree only complicated the dispute.* This want of success, however, failed to cure the emperor of his theological mania. In A. D. 546, he issued a new edict enjoining all bishops to condemn the *Three Chapters*. These *Three Chapters*, assailed with unexampled obstinacy by the Eutychians, were *A Profession of Faith, by Theodore, bishop of Mopsuesta; a work by Theodoret, bishop of Cyrrhus, on the twelve chapters of St. Cyril; and a letter written by Ibas, bishop of Edessa, to a Persian here-*

---

* The erroneous doctrines borrowed by heretics from Origen's works received a final condemnation in the fifth General Council at Constantinople (A. D. 553), since which time they have ceased to trouble the Church.

tic named Maris. The Council of Chalcedon had examined these three works, and, without passing any positive judgment on their theological soundness, had refrained from a condemnation. The Eutychians dared not openly attack the Council of Chalcedon, but they hoped to gain the same end by enticing Justinian into a condemnation of the *Three Chapters.* Justinian fell into the snare and published a new edict which he called the *Imperial Profession of Faith against the Three Chapters*, and addressed to the whole Catholic world (A. D. 546). It closed with the three following anathemas : " If any one defends Theodore of Mopsuesta, let him be anathema ! If any one defends the writings of Theodoret, let him be anathema ! If any one defends the impious letter of the bishop Ibas to the Persian Maris, let him be anathema !" Most of the Catholic bishops of the East were forced to sign Justinian's theological edict ; but all the emperor's endeavors to win Vigilius to his cause met with a courageous resistance from the Pontiff. " Is not the condemnation of the *Three Chapters,*" said Vigilius, " an indirect attack upon the Council of Chalcedon, which withheld its censure ?" He then expressed his wish that the *Three Chapters* should be canonically examined that they might then, if proper, be lawfully condemned. Justinian treated the subject with an ardor which degenerated into passion. He had obliged Mennas, Patriarch of Constantinople, to head the signatures to the Imperial Profession of Faith. Stephen, deacon and legate of the Roman Church, sharply upbraided Mennas for his weakness, and declared him cut off from his communion. Meanwhile Justinian was using all his influence to bring the Pope to Constantinople, that he might settle the dispute on the very spot where it arose.

11. Vigilius consented and entered the Eastern capital in the month of February, A. D. 547. His first act was to ratify the sentence pronounced against the Patriarch Mennas and to publish a decree of excommunication against the Eutychians and their adherents. The Pope then proceeded to a canonical examination of the *Three Chapters.* in a council of seventy bish-

ops, held at Constantinople. The examination revealed several serious errors in the disputed works; and after mature deliberation, Vigilius condemned the *Three Chapters* in a sentence which he styled *Judicatum* (judgment), saving, however, the authority of the Council of Chalcedon. But there were on both sides minds influenced by the spirit of contention. The opponents of the *Three Chapters* called for a clear and positive condemnation, without any restriction or reserve. Their supporters, on the other hand, were naturally much irritated. The latter party was very numerous and counted in its ranks the bishops of Africa, Algeria, and Dalmatia. Two deacons hitherto attached to the person of the Sovereign Pontiff, and who had accompanied him to the East, now deserted him, and spread the report in the provinces that Vigilius had abandoned the Council of Chalcedon.

12. Aurelius, bishop of Arles, who had been appointed by Vigilius legate of the Holy See, on receiving this notice wrote to the Pope to obtain reliable information on the subject. Vigilius replied that he had done nothing against the decrees of his predecessors nor against the four councils. "In your position, then," he added, "as vicar of the Holy See, warn all the bishops to give no heed to the false letters or reports that may reach them; let them be assured that we hold to the faith of our fathers. As soon as the emperor has dismissed us, we shall send you some one to give you a full account of our whole conduct; this we have hitherto been unable to do, both on account of the obstructions to travel in the winter season, and the state of Italy wasted by war." Vigilius at the same time wrote to Valentinian, bishop of Scythia, energetically refuting the slanderous charges brought against him. Thus the Pope's *Judicatum* did not produce the effect that might have been looked for. The Western Catholics thought the honor of the Council of Chalcedon compromised, and felt great mistrust; the Eutychians, on the other hand, urged Vigilius to a plain and positive condemnation of the *Three Chapters*, without reference to the Council of Chalcedon. The Pope

thought that this stormy debate would be most promptly and
decisively settled by calling an ecumenical council whose authority, admitted on all hands, would do away with all possibility of recrimination.   "Let the Latin bishops," said the Pope
to Justinian, "who see a stumbling-block in the condemnation
of the *Three Chapters*, come to the council; or at least leave
them free to give their opinion, and cease this division in the
Church of God."   But the Eutychians used all their influence
to thwart a measure which must prove so ruinous to their
hopes.   Theodore of Cæsarea, their leader, in contempt of the
Pope's orders, removed the names of the Catholic bishops from
the diptychs, and substituted in their places those of the intruded heretics.   After this open outrage, Vigilius declared that
he would no longer hold communion with the Orientals, and
refused thenceforth to admit them to his presence.   This apostolic firmness so enraged the emperor that the Pope was driven
to seek shelter in the church of St. Peter.   Justinian determined to take him by force, and sent a prætor to surround the
basilica with a troop of soldiery.   Constantinople now gave to
the world a spectacle of savage fury which the barbarian conquerors had spared downtrodden Rome.   The prætor ordered
the troops to enter the church with drawn swords; at their
approach the Pope took refuge under the altar and clung to
the columns which supported it.   The prætor caused the deacons and other clerics to be dragged by the hair from around
the altar.   Then, in their desire to tear away the Pontiff himself, his minions seized Vigilius, some by the beard, others by
the hair : "Know," exclaimed the Pope, "*that though you hold
us captive, yet you cannot hold St. Peter.*"   As he did not yield
to their violence, some of the pillars to which he clung were
broken.   At the sight of such unparalleled brutality cries of
indignation burst from the people and even from some of the
soldiers, when the prætor, fearing a sedition, thought it prudent
to withdraw his force (A. D. 551).   For the sake of Justinian's
reputation it is to be regretted that such acts cannot be attributed to the influence of Theodora; but she had died two years

before, still under the excommunication pronounced by Vigilius
against the Eutychians.   The emperor tried to win by craft
what he could not extort by violence, but Vigilius was on his
guard.   He succeeded in thwarting all the attempts made
against him, and feeling unsafe in the basilica of St. Peter, and
even in Constantinople itself, he left the city and took refuge
in the church of St. Euphemia, at Chalcedon.   Thus, after a
sojourn of seven years in the East, the Pope found himself
obliged to contend for liberty and life against the emperor.
Justinian's obstinacy was at length overcome by this steady
resistance.   He made the offer himself to assemble the ecumenical council for which the Catholics had been so long calling.

13. This council, the fifth ecumenical, was opened at Constantinople on the 4th day of May, A. D. 553.   One hundred
and sixty-five bishops were present; the East was represented
by a considerable majority.   The Pope was justly solicitous
lest the Western bishops should not think themselves sufficiently represented in a general council.   But this numerical
disadvantage of the Western bishops was no new feature in the
history of the Church; hence it was passed over.   In the eighth
session, or *Conference*, the *Three Chapters* were condemned in
nearly the same terms used by Pope Vigilius in his *Judicatum*.
With a prudence worthy of the Supreme Head of the Church,
the Pope would not promulgate this final judgment until full
time had been allowed for truth to make its way into all
minds.   Many Western Catholics deemed it rash to condemn
those whom the Council of Chalcedon had refused to anathematize, on the principle that the Church does not anathematize
the dead.   But as soon as heretics revived the errors of these
departed authors to harass the consciences of the faithful, the
reserve maintained by the Council of Chalcedon, far from showing propriety, was even dangerous ; and it became a matter of
urgent necessity to pronounce judgment.   These reasons gradually gained ground in the public mind, and some months after
the Council of Constantinople, Vigilius announced to the Catholic world that the *Three Chapters* had been regularly con-

demned (December 8, A. D. 553). Some historians affect to view this reserve and prudence on the part of the Pope as a serious mistake in a question of dogma. Vigilius had indeed protested, at the opening of the council, against the emperor's want of honesty in not awaiting the arrival of the Latin bishops. He clearly and energetically showed that such a proceeding was utterly wanting in justice, dignity and respect for the Church. This protest served only to irritate Justinian; and the Pope was sent into exile. It was mournful to see the Head of Christendom thus exposed to the pursuits of the Greek Church, defenceless, bereft of counsel and consolation, open to the attacks of all parties. In this critical juncture Vigilius hurries nothing, prejudges nothing; awaiting the moment when a calm shall come over the minds of all, he then ratifies, by his pontifical decision, the sentence of the very council whose deliberations he would have delayed until the coming of the Western bishops. Thus the council became ecumenical; its decisions and laws bind the whole Church. The succeeding Pontiffs confirmed the sentence pronounced against the *Three Chapters*, and the truth thus breaks through the clouds which had so long hidden it from sight. The debate on the *Three Chapters* had been so long and so intricate, only because the question concerning their authors was involved in that of the works themselves. Passion was rife on both sides for or against the memory of holy men who might have erred in good faith but whose life was beyond imputation. According as a point of view was taken in respect to the authors or to their doctrines, it was at once possible to absolve and to condemn. The Pope gave his whole attention to the single end of separating two questions so really distinct. He succeeded, but at the cost of personal peace and tranquillity, which must remain a glory to his memory, not a reproach.

14. Having settled all the claims which called him to the East, Vigilius obtained the emperor's leave to return to Italy. He had been absent eight years, and even now he was not to look upon Rome again. His sickly state forced him to stop at

Syracuse, where he died on the 10th of January, A. D. 555, after a pontificate of sixteen years. His remains were carried to Rome and deposited in the church of St. Marcellus, on the Salarian way. The dark shade thrown upon this pontificate by religious strifes and political revolutions is occasionally relieved by the light of literary efforts. Vigilius, true to the constant tradition of the Holy See, fostered the intellectual growth. This patronage encouraged Arator to present him with a hexameter poem, in two books, on the Acts of the Apostles. The poet enjoyed a high reputation in Rome. Formerly captain of the guards and intendent of the imperial estate, he had resigned his high position to enter sacred orders, and was now sub-deacon in the Roman Church. The Pope, after hearing the poem read, directed Surgentius, chief of the guards, to deposit it in the archives of the Church. He caused it to be publicly read in his presence in the church of St. Peter *ad vincula*. The poet read his own verses, surrounded by the nobility, clergy, and people. So eager were the hearers to have some passages repeated, that four readings were found necessary to complete the recitation. This fact proves that the mass of the people were not yet dead to literary beauty and excellence. But this taste soon disappeared under the heavy gloom which barbarian invasion left in its track. During the pontificate of Vigilius, the Gauls still stood before the world stanch adherents to the faith. The incendiary disputes so much agitated in the East did not trouble their peace. At this period St. Maurus, a disciple of St. Benedict, was laying the foundation of a monastery at Glanfeuil, in the diocese of Angers (A. D. 542); and St. Aurelian, bishop of Arles and vicar of the Holy See, seconded by the liberality of King Childebert, established, in his episcopal city, a monastery for men and a community of women. He placed them both under a rule of great austerity and strict enclosure (A. D. 547). The fifth Council of Orleans (A. D. 549), held by fifty bishops, recalled the canons relative to episcopal nominations. The second Council of Paris (A. D. 551), composed of twenty-seven prelates, deposed Saffarac, bishop of that city, and published several canons of discipline.

§ III. PONTIFICATE OF PELAGIUS I. (April 16, A. D. 555—March 2, 559).

15. The question of the *Three Chapters*, which had disturbed the pontificate of Vigilius, was destined to trouble the election of his successor. It was still feared in the West that the decision of the fifth General Council of Constantinople might weaken the authority of that of Chalcedon. Pelagius, who was elected Pope on the 16th day of April, A. D. 555, had, as deacon of the Roman Church, held to the condemnation of the *Three Chapters*. This was enough to bring upon him the most atrocious slanders. He was accused of hastening the death of Vigilius by ill usage, whereas the very contrary was the truth; the consolations and care of Pelagius had soothed the last moments of the dying Pontiff. Yet these idle reports had been spread amongst the Roman people and threatened, for a while, to enkindle the flames of sedition. So hostile was the public mind to Pelagius, that only two bishops—John of Perugia and Bonus of Ferentino—found sufficient resolution to consecrate him. The most illustrious and noble members of the clergy and senate refused his communion. The patrician Narses, the emperor's commander in Italy, advised him to dispel these odious suspicions by a public demonstration. Pelagius followed the advice, and ordered a general procession. On reaching the basilica of St. Peter he ascended the pulpit, and holding the book of Gospels and the crucifix above his head, made oath that he had done no hurt to his predecessor. Those who had hitherto entertained doubts, now threw them all aside and joined his communion. Pelagius, availing himself of these good dispositions, urged all those present to join him in banishing simony from ecclesiastical ordinations in every degree of the hierarchy. He gave the superintendence of Church property to his secretary. Valentine, a man fearing God, who secured the restoration of

all the gold and silver vessels and precious veils taken from the churches.

16. Pelagius had done good service for the Romans, even before his promotion to the Sovereign Pontificate. During Totila's invasion, in the general famine, the pious deacon had exhausted all the resources of his ingenious charity to relieve the wretched sufferers perishing for want of bread. He had several times been sent as ambassador to the formidable king of the Goths, whose fierceness had yielded to the deputy's forcible and winning eloquence. Rome was not unmindful of so many benefits, and the Pope was soon without an enemy. Still a number of Italians refused to admit the decrees of the fifth Council of Constantinople, though confirmed by Pope Vigilius. A schism was evidently on the point of breaking out. Pelagius took advantage of Justinian's favorable dispositions to crush these rising troubles at their birth. With this view he wrote to Narses, the emperor's lieutenant in Italy : "It is not persecution," he said, "to repress crime and help to the salvation of souls. Persecution consists in forcing men to do evil ; otherwise, it would be necessary to abolish every human and divine law which punishes crime. But schism is an evil; Scripture and the holy canons teach us that it should be put down, even by the secular power." These words of Pope Pelagius have been taxed with excessive and blind intolerance. "It is easy," says a modern historian,* "to meet these charges by making the necessary allowances for time and circumstances ; by taking into account the difficulties which beset the exercise of the spiritual authority on all sides. Without this energy which refuses to compound with error, it is impossible to establish a lasting power, especially a power intended to control the intellect."

17. Pelagius devoted the whole of his pontificate of three years to root out the last traces of religious dissensions. Encouraged by the Pope's exhortations, Narses exerted all his zeal

---

* *Histoire des Papes*, by the Count de Beaufort, t. L. n. 500

to spread in the Peninsula the doctrines of the fifth General
Council. Some bishops, more vehement than the rest in their
support of the *Three Chapters*, excommunicated the patrician.
The Pope immediately wrote to him, approving his conduct,
and assuring him that such an excommunication was null. The
Tuscan bishops showed a particular degree of obstinacy in rejecting the condemnation of the *Three Chapters*, and wrote to
the Pope, with a view to justify their schism. Pelagius replied
in a strain of tender and fatherly affection : " How can you per-
suade yourselves that you are not separated from the communion of the whole world by breaking with us, since; in spite of
our unworthiness, the authority of the Apostolic See is now
vested in our person? Our faith is that of Nice, explained
and confirmed by the Councils of Constantinople, Ephesus and
Chalcedon. If, after this declaration, any one of you still enter-
tains a doubt, let him come to receive the definition of the doctrine from our own lips, that thus knowing the truth, he may
join in communion with the Universal Church " (A. D. 556). In
a letter to King Childebert, Pelagius repeated the declaration
in terms even more explicit. He exhorts the king to quiet
the fears of such of his subjects as might imagine that the condemnation of the *Three Chapters* could prejudice the Council
of Chalcedon (A. D. 557). The Latin Church, less fiercely
tossed by the storms of religious disputes which were so disastrous in the East, was intent upon keeping inviolate the
respect due to tradition, the sacred deposit of the ecclesiastical
constitutions. Had the East but possessed a little more of the
same conservative spirit, the world would probably not have
been scandalized by the lamentable defection which still lasts
Gaul was at this period the greatest source of consolation to the
Sovereign Pontiff. At Soissons, the abbey of St. Medard was
growing up under the auspices of King Clotaire (A. D. 557).
The third Council of Paris (A. D. 557) by its prudent regulations secured the freedom of episcopal elections and the immu-
nity of Church property from all attacks on the part of temporal powers. On the 23d of December, A. D. 558, St. Germanus,

bishop of Paris, dedicated the church of St. Vincent, now known as Saint-Germain-des-Prés. As an offset to the repeated dissensions caused by territorial feuds between princes, the Church of Gaul presented a splendid array of virtue and holiness. St. Samson, bishop of Dol, St. Malo, St. Magloire of Aleth, illustrated Brittany or *Armorica*, which their preaching had won to the true faith. St. Pretextatus, bishop of Rouen, St. Leontius of Bordeaux, St. Euphronius of Tours, St. Paternus of Avranches, and St. Chaletric of Chartres attached to their episcopate the glory of the most exalted sanctity.

18. Meanwhile, Pelagius had ended his days at Rome on the 2d of March, A. D. 559. His death left the church of the Twelve Apostles, which he was erecting, in an unfinished state. This church now bears the title of Sts. Philip and James.

§ IV. PONTIFICATE OF JOHN III. (March, A. D. 559—July 13, 572).

19. On taking his seat in the Chair of St. Peter (March, A. D. 559), John III. at once proceeded to ratify the condemnation of the *Three Chapters*, as his two predecessors had done before. But in the East this discussion had given way to the new error of the *Phantasiasts*, or *Incorrupticolæ*, whose warmest abettor was no other than the emperor Justinian himself. These heretics taught that the body which Christ assumed in the womb of the Blessed Virgin was capable of no alteration or change, and was not even subject to the natural and innocent sensations of hunger and thirst, so that even before His death He ate without necessity, as He did after His resurrection; whence it would follow that the sufferings of His passion and death were not real. The heretics styled the Catholics *Corrupticolæ*, worshippers of corruption. The emperor sought to make this belief binding by means of a decree which he required the bishops to sign; but they near-

ly all refused. St. Eutychius, Patriarch of Constantinople,
displayed the most heroic courage. By order of Justinian
he was arrested and banished without even the form of trial
or examination, and his See given to John the Scholastic.
The error of the Incorrupticolæ would probably have renewed
the religious strife in the East; but on the 14th of November,
A. D. 566, Justinian was removed from the scene in the fortieth
year of his reign and the eighty-fourth of his life. The close
of his long career had sadly belied its opening promise. His
passion for religious discussions multiplied and fomented them,
to the great detriment of the Church. He neglected all business of state to mingle in affairs which should have been left
to competent minds. The historian Procopius thus speaks of
him : " He is always unattended by guards, spends long night-
ly vigils in discussing theological questions with the bishops,
or poring with unquenchable curiosity over the works of the
Fathers." History will ever justly reproach this emperor, so
gifted in many other respects, with sacrificing to a mere war
of words the highest duties of the sovereign in the midst of a
passionate and fickle people. This was the root of all the disorders which devastated the Lower Empire. So true is it, that
men, though gifted with superior talents and the highest qualities, must needs bow under the influence of the age, which
weighs them down in spite of themselves. Justinian was succeeded by his nephew Justin the Younger, whose accession
put an end to the persecutions brought upon the Catholics by
the error of the Incorrupticolæ. The Patriarch Eutychius
was recalled to Constantinople. But weak and wavering in
character, Justin had not the energy to hold the reins of government. Giving himself up to the most extravagant disorders, ending at length in an almost total insanity, he left the
charge of the government in the hands of Sophia, niece of Theodora. This was the signal for errors and consequent misfor
tunes. Divorce, which had been abolished by Justinian's code,
was re-established; a sacrilegious traffic in ecclesiastical dignities was publicly opened; private fortunes were confiscated to

satisfy the greedy courtiers. Sophia heeded neither services nor talents, and Italy soon fell victim to her baneful
policy.

20. Under the eunuch Narses, who had succeeded Belisarius
in command, this province was beginning to taste the sweets
of peace. His renown and wealth soon brought him into disgrace with the empress. She sent him a distaff and spindle,
with this ironical order, fit only for a common eunuch : " Come
at once to Constantinople. I have appointed you to superin-
tend the work of my maids. It belongs to men to handle
warlike weapons and command their fellows." Narses read the
insulting order, and casting upon the bearer a look of indignant anger, exclaimed : " Go tell your mistress that I will spin
her such a thread as she shall not easily unravel !" He immediately wrote to Alboin, king of the Lombards, to leave the
poor soil of Pannonia for the rich and fertile fields of Italy.
The royal barbarian could hardly have hoped for so favorable
a message. Long had he awaited an opportunity, only withheld by the presence of the imperial army. This barrier being
now removed, he entered Italy on the 2d of April, A. D. 568,
with his whole nation—his warriors, their aged parents, their
wives and children. Milan and Pavia submitted ; the northern provinces followed their example, and four years later
the Roman sway was confined to the two cities of Rome and
Ravenna, with a few seaport towns, all under the government
of an *exarch* appointed by the emperor at Constantinople.
Such was the web which Narses had left to the empress instead
of a distaff. He did not witness the result of his faithlessness,
as he died at the very time of Alboin's entrance into Italy.
The Lombard domination thus enthroning itself in this unhappy
land, inaugurated its sway by acts of barbarous atrocity. One
instance will suffice to show the spirit of the barbarian conquerors. Alboin had slain Cunimund, king of the Gepidæ, in
battle ; the skull of the fallen warrior, incased in gold, served
as a drinking-bowl at all the victor's banquets. He had also
married Rosamond, daughter of the unfortunate Cunimund. In

the month of March, A. D. 573, he feasted his companions in
arms with a splendid banquet; after draining many full
draughts from the execrable cup, he ordered it to be filled and
presented to the queen, bidding her rejoice with her father.
But a few days later Rosamond caused Alboin to be assassinated before her own eyes, and thus avenged her father's memory. Clepho next ascended the Lombard throne, and with him
avarice and cruelty shared the royal sway.

21. The new masters of Italy were Arians. The ravages
which they inflicted upon their newly-conquered territory were
doubly severe, as they partook of the spirit of religious persecution. The inhabitants, driven from their homes, stripped of
their possessions, wandered about the country without food or
clothing. The empress Sophia, the first cause of all this misery, made no effort to relieve it. Pope John III. multiplied
the resources of his charity to meet so much suffering. Rome
had not yet felt the yoke of the new conquerors; but the
Lombards were preparing to lay siege to it when the Sovereign
Pontiff died, July 13, A. D. 572. The fourteen years of his
reign had been cruelly imbittered by the religious dissensions
which disgraced the East, and the Lombard invasion so fraught
with misery to the West. Only in Spain and Gaul did the
Church enjoy a peaceful course of conquest. The Councils of
Braga and Lugo, in Galicia, had been followed by the conversion of the Suevi who held that province, and who passed from
Arianism into the bosom of the Catholic Church (A. D. 560).
Their king, Theodomir, had a son who lay dangerously ill.
Seeing him in the last extremity, the afflicted father asked
some of his followers : " Pray tell me, of what religion is this
Martin of Tours who works so many miracles in Gaul?" They
told him that he was a Catholic bishop. The king then sent
them to call upon the saint, promising, in case his son recovered, to become himself a Catholic. The prince was restored
and the king abjured Arianism. St. Martin of Pannonia, who
was then preaching the Gospel in that country, induced the
people to follow their monarch's example. His preaching was

efficacious, and the whole nation showed a most consoling ardor and zeal in its attachment to the true faith.

§ V. Pontificate of Benedict I. (May 16, a. d 573—July 31, 577).

22. After the death of John III. the Holy See remained vacant ten months. The terror and consternation inspired by the Lombards, who pushed their inroads to the very gates of Rome, had prevented the meeting of the clergy and people to elect a Sovereign Pontiff. The barbarians had plundered and destroyed the monastery of Monte Cassino, famine and war were fast converting Italy into a desert. Justin II., emperor of the East, sunk in luxurious license, allowed the Persian monarch Chosroes to overrun and waste the provinces of Syria. The provinces of Gaul, shared between Chilperic I., Sigebert, and Gontran, were deluged with blood by the deadly strife between Fredegonda and Brunehault. In Spain, the Catholics were subjected to a severe persecution by Leovigild, Arian king of the Visigoths, whose son Hermenegild had been converted to the true faith by St. Leander, bishop of Seville. Before his conversion, Hermenegild had shared his father's power; but Leovigild's treatment of the converted prince showed him to be equally regardless of the royal dignity and of the claims of natural affection. He pursued the prince, sword in hand, seized and kept him in close confinement, and at last ordered him to be beheaded (April 13, a. d. 586). St. Leander, the fearless bishop of Seville, who had, at the risk of his life, instructed Hermenegild in the truths of the faith, was proscribed, and devoted the days of his exile to the establishment of monasteries and to the increase of the religious life in Spain. The anger of Leovigild reached all the Catholics in his states. Many were banished and despoiled of all their property; others were imprisoned and put to death by hunger and various other torments. But God had merciful designs upon this suffering people. At the death of Leovigild, his son Recarede, brother of

Hermenegild, embraced the Catholic faith; and by force of reasoning rather than by the exercise of authority, led the Arian bishops to follow his example (A. D. 587).

23. Such was the situation of the world when Benedict I., or Bonosus, was elected to succeed Pope John III. (May 16, A. D. 573). His short pontificate was taken up by the care of the Italian difficulties which followed in the train of the Lombard invasion, and by the exercise of a tender and paternal charity during the grievous famine which decimated the population of the Peninsula. The glory of this pontificate was the choice made of the monk Gregory to fill the office of archdeacon of the Roman Church. Gregory had resigned the prætorian dignity to answer a supernatural call to the religious life. He was destined to give the onward impulse to the age, and to illustrate the Apostolic See under the name of Gregory the Great. Gregory happened one day to walk through the market-place of Rome, when his attention was arrested by the remarkable beauty and symmetry of some slaves exposed for sale. He asked what countrymen they were, and was told they belonged to the nation of the *Angles.* "They are not *Angles,* but *Angels,*" * he replied. "Alas! that such a people should still remain buried in the darkness of heathenism!" Gregory hastened to throw himself at Benedict's feet, begging the Pope to send him with some missionaries to preach the Gospel in Great Britain. Benedict, touched by this noble spirit of devotedness, granted his request. But the Roman people loved Gregory too well to part with him now, and they came to the Sovereign Pontiff, in the greatest consternation, begging that he might be recalled. Couriers were at once dispatched to bring back the apostle; Providence had designed Rome as the scene of his sublime mission. Benedict I. died on the 31st of July, A. D. 577, whilst the Lombards held Rome in a state of the closest siege.

---

* Non *Angli,* sed *Angeli.*

§ VI. Pontificate of Pelagius II. (November 30, A. D. 577– February 8, 590).

24. The choice of the Pontiff who was to succeed Benedict I. on the Chair of St. Peter was not this time submitted to the ratification of the Eastern emperor. The Lombards had cut off all communication between Rome and Constantinople. A monk named Pelagius was elected Pope, on the 30th of November, A. D. 577. The exarch who commanded in Italy in the emperor's name, was powerless to avert the storm that threatened the Eternal City. The deacon Gregory had ·been sent, as apocrisiarius or legate of the Holy See, to Constantinople, in the hope that Justin II. might be moved to send help to Italy; but the war against Chosroes had drained the imperial resources, and the ruinous administration of the empress Sophia left no hope of a favorable issue for the embassy. By the death of Justin II., which occurred A. D. 578, the empire came into the hands of his general Tiberius. This valiant, enlightened, and virtuous prince changed the odious name of Tiberius into the cherished and popular one of Constantine. He swayed the imperial sceptre with steady hand. With a view to satisfying the requests of the deacon Gregory, and to make a diversion in favor of Italy, still wasted by the Lombards, the emperor sent ambassadors to Childebert, king of Austrasia, with the offer of a considerable sum of money, on condition of his attacking the Lombards on one side whilst the imperial troops pressed them on the other. Childebert successively sent two armies into Italy, but they were both destroyed by reverses and pestilence. Tiberius was planning a formidable expedition against the Lombards, when he was stricken down by death, after a reign too short for the happiness of his subjects (A. D. 582). He left his sceptre to one no less brave and virtuous than himself, Count Mauritius, who had distinguished himself by several splendid achievements in the war against the Persians. Meanwhile, Pope Pelagius II. found himself left alone

in the midst of these ceaseless political revolutions, to uphold
the independence of Rome; he accordingly made arrangements
with Smaragdus, exarch of Ravenna, to come to terms with
the Lombards. The barbarians agreed to respect the territory
of the exarchate, which still belonged to the Eastern emperors. Rome was released, and Italy tasted some moments
of peace and quiet.

25. Seeing his efforts thus happily crowned with success,
Pelagius recalled the legate Gregory to make his genius avail-
able in the government of the Church. He directed him to
write, in his name, to the bishops of Istria, who refused to
receive the fifth general council and its decision in the case of
the *Three Chapters.* Gregory's three letters, which are still
extant, are models of wise and temperate reasoning and of
apostolic dignity. The bishops to whom they were addressed,
however, showed more obstinacy than good faith; but the exarch Smaragdus, fearing lest religious dissensions might add to
the misery of the country, already devastated by political
strife, summoned them to Ravenna, where several public conferences with orthodox doctors soon brought them back to
unity.

26. The province of Gaul now reflected the full splendor
of the talent and virtue which shone in St. Gregory, bishop of
Tours, whose name is linked with every event in French history during the latter half of the sixth century (A. D. 539–595).
He was a native of Auvergne, and was elected bishop of Tours
A. D. 577. The reputation he enjoyed in Gaul secured him an
important political influence during his whole life. He defended St. Pretextatus, bishop of Rouen, against the charges of Fredegonda, and the youthful Meroveus, who sought shelter at
the tomb of St. Martin from the persecution of Chilperic.
He was himself accused of high treason, by the implacable
Fredegonda; he appeared before the Council of Braine, held
A. D. 580, and cleared himself, under oath, of the slanderous
charges brought against him by hireling witnesses. The stormy
period through which St. Gregory passed has been chronicled

by him in a work called *Historia Francorum*, one of the most precious monuments in our annals. This work reviews a period of a hundred and seventy-four years, from A. D. 417 to A. D. 591. Gregory of Tours possessed the qualities most desirable in a historian : good faith, fairness, and the quiet courage that tells the faults as well as the virtues of princes. His style, as he acknowledges himself, aims neither at purity nor effect; but that is due to the age, in which the barbarian inroads and the din of civil strife had brought a decay in the study of pure and classic Latinity. But the unaffected plainness, the graphic simplicity of the first Gallic chronicler, gives us a good view of the spirit and manners of his age ; an age of transition, in which the most distinct races, Franks, Burgundians, Gauls, and Romans, met upon the same ground, and by their mingling prepared the future unity of the French monarchy. The work of law-giving, of civilizing, in a society composed of so many heterogeneous elements, naturally devolved upon the bishops, who were allied to all, and whose voice alone rose with controlling influence above the din of arms and the outburst of still savage passions.

27. Councils were therefore frequent. Here, so to speak, was framed the constitution of the infant nation. The Councils of Châlons-sur-Saône (A. D. 579), of Macon (A. D. 581–585), and of Lyons (A. D. 583), were busied in discussing questions at once of social interest and of religious discipline. At Lyons, the bishops issued regulations full of tender charity in behalf of lepers. Leprosy was making many victims, and threatened to become a lasting contagion, which disappeared only before the beneficent power of modern discovery and improved habits of cleanliness. The unfortunate sufferers, shunned by their fellow-men, viewed by all with superstitious dread, wandered about the open country naked and starving. The fathers of the third Council of Lyons (A. D. 583) direct that the lepers of each city shall thenceforth be fed and supported by the bishop, at the expense of the Church. An isolated abode was to be assigned them, that they might be no

longer doomed to wander abroad, nor yet bring terror with
them into frequented places.   This wise and beneficial measure
was afterwards generalized under the Church's influence;
particular rites were set down in the rituals, for the solemn
conveyance of the patients into the cells prepared for them;
a noble spirit of zealous charity gave rise to several religious
communities devoted to the service of these wretched outcasts.
St. Gregory of Tours, the moving spirit of councils, the adviser
of kings, the champion of the down-trodden, bearing an active
part in the events he records, still found time to compose works
destined to foster the piety of the faithful: such are the works
on the Glory of Martyrs, on the Glory of Confessors; the
Miracles of St. Julian, bishop of Brioude; the Miracles of St.
Martin, and a book of Lives of the Fathers.   The faithful
found them a well-stocked treasure-house of doctrine and of
examples of every virtue; which teaching and example were
ever kept before them by the churches dedicated to the saints,
by the various festivals, hymns, processions and pilgrimages
appointed in their honor, and by the accounts of their miracles;
thus works of this nature soon became the only literature of
Christian nations.

28. Another prelate of this age, an Italian by birth, but
the friend and contemporary of St. Gregory of Tours, likewise
devoted the leisure moments of his episcopate to the cultivation of learning.   Fortunatus, bishop of Poitiers (A. D. 530–
609), had been almoner of the monastery, in that city, under
the direction of St. Radegundes, from which charge he passed
to its episcopal throne.   He has left eleven books, both in prose
and poetry, dedicated to St. Gregory of Tours; they form
a collection of miscellaneous treatises on various subjects
Amongst others, we here find the hymn *Vexilla Regis*.*   Be

---

* St. Fortunatus quotes, in this hymn, the words of David: *Regnavit a ligno Deus*.
Hence it may be inferred that the words *a ligno*, which we do not find in the 95th Psalm
in the Vulgate, were then contained in the Gallican Psalter.   The *Vexilla Regis* was composed on the occasion of the reception, at the monastery of Poitiers, of a piece of the
true cross, sent by the Emperor Justin II. to St. Radegundes (A. D. 570).

fore his promotion to the episcopacy, he had written the lives of St. Germanus of Paris, of St. Albinus or Aubin of Angers, of St. Paternus of Avranches, of St. Amant of Rhodez, of St. Remigius of Rheims, of St. Medard of Noyon, of St. Martin of Tours, and of St. Radegundes, whose secretary and friend he had been. Thus did he devote to the illustrious saints of Gaul a talent destined to become a new glory to the land of his adoption, which he benefited as largely by his virtue as by his writings. The Gallic Churches enjoyed the high privilege of having most of their sees filled by saints, and the sixth century proved itself worthy to receive the glorious heritage of virtue left by its predecessors. St. Ageric of Verdun, St. Felix of Nantes, St. Avitus of Clermont, St. Siagrius of Autun, St. Leontius of Bordeaux, St. Bertichram of Le Mans and St. Dumnole his successor, St. Felix of Bourges, St. Dalmatius of Rhodez, St. Aunaire of Auxerre, St. Maurelius of Cahors, St. Elaphius of Châlons-sur-Marne, St. Evencius of Vienne, St. Ferreolus of Limoges, St. Veranus of Cavaillon, all contemporary with St. Fortunatus and St. Gregory of Tours, counterbalanced by their virtue and learning the vices and disorders of an age whose political destinies were swayed by the animosities of Fredegonda.

29. But the admirable harmony of devoted zeal in the Gallic episcopacy was now marred by a public scandal. Two brothers, Sagittarius and Salonius, bishops respectively of Gap and Embrun, gave up the care of souls and the discharge of their pastoral ministry, to share in the tumultuous disorders of civil war. Having gathered a band of armed men, they wasted all the neighboring region by their depredations. The brothers themselves, utterly regardless of their sacred character, often appeared at the head of the armies, and changed their peaceful mission for the bloody part of the warrior. They were first deposed in A. D. 567, by a council held at Lyons, but, by means of favorable letters obtained from Pope John III., were restored to their sees. But as their disorderly life and manners were only aggravated by impunity, Gontran king of Burgundy,

adopted measures of severity toward them.   The Council of
Châlons-sur-Saône (A. D. 579) renewed the condemnation pronounced against them by the Council of Lyons, and handed
them over to secular justice.

30. The East, never free from religious dissensions, had
meanwhile seen the beginning of fresh troubles, in the claims
of the Patriarchs of Constantinople.   In a council held in that
city in June, A. D. 589, to hear the charges brought against
Gregory, Patriarch of Antioch, by Asterius, count of the East,
John the Faster, Patriarch of Constantinople, who presided,
usurped the title of *Ecumenical* Bishop.   Pelagius II., on hearing of this arrogant claim, at once wrote to Constantinople; by
virtue of his apostolic authority he annulled the acts of the
council and forbade his legate, St. Gregory, to communicate
with John the Faster.   The pontifical rescript energetically
reviewed all that the Popes Julius, Celestin, Innocent and
Leo had taught regarding the Pope's authority, the necessity
of referring important cases to his judgment, and of pronouncing no final decision without his knowledge and approval (A. D.
590).   Whilst Pelagius was thus engaged in upholding the
rights of the Roman See, Italy was suffering under two fearful
scourges, famine and plague; Rome was literally decimated.
An overflow of the Tiber added the horrors of inundation to
the multiplied miseries of disease and hunger.   The victims
fell by thousands; Pelagius sank amongst the first (February
8, A. D. 590), having governed the Church eleven years and
ten months.   He had turned his dwelling into a hospital for
indigent old men, and death struck down the shepherd in the
midst of the labors which his ardent charity multiplied in
behalf of his flock.

CHAPTER V.

§ I. Pontificate of St. Gregory I. the Great (September 3, A. D. 590—March 12, A. D. 604).

§ I. PONTIFICATE OF ST. GREGORY I. THE GREAT (September 3, A. D. 590—March 12, 604).

1. AT a time when the Church was beset on all sides with dangers and difficulties, threatened in the East by the proud claims of the Patriarch of Constantinople, and in the West by the Lombard invasion; when Rome was bowed beneath the threefold weight of the barbarian's sword, the horrors of the plague, and the pangs of hunger; God raised up, for the universal good, a Pontiff whose great soul was equal to his sublime mission. Gregory the deacon had already won the admiration and esteem of the world by his bearing as legate of Pelagius II., at Constantinople. The emperor Mauritius then learned to respect and love him. When recalled to Rome, he had been the Pope's adviser in every affair of importance. His lofty stature, the noble mildness of his countenance, the massive forehead deeply marked by study and genius, all compelled respectful reverence. The Roman clergy, senate and people, with one voice called for Gregory to take the See left vacant by Pelagius II. (September 3, A. D. 590). The saint endeavored to escape, by flight, the honor tendered by the voice of a whole people. His retreat is made known by a dove; and the multitude bear him back to Rome in triumph. But his humility will not yet be overcome. The pontifical elections were still liable to the sanction of the Eastern emperor. Gregory relied upon the esteem and friendship shown him, while in the East, by the emperor Mauritius, to escape the honor thus pressed upon him; but Mauritius was not prepared to see things in the same light as the saint in his admirable modesty. He joyfully received the tidings of Gregory's promotion, and

gave immediate orders for his installation. The earnestness with which the holy deacon had shunned the burden of the pontificate was fully equalled by his zeal in the discharge of its duties. His whole career, made so illustrious by prodigious activity, unbounded devotedness, and a mind which soared above the level of his age, has been magnificently reviewed by Bossuet, whose words we quote : " Whilst Italy was steeped in misfortune and Rome was decaying under a fearful plague, St. Gregory the Great was raised to the Chair of St. Peter, in spite of his most earnest opposition. The great Pope appeases the plague by his prayers ; at once teaches emperors and secures to them due respect and obedience ; consoles and strengthens Africa ; encourages in Spain the Visigoths, converted from Arianism, and Recarede the Catholic, who has just come into the true fold ; converts England ; restores discipline in France, whose ever-orthodox kings he raises above all the monarchs of the earth ; conciliates the Lombards ; saves Rome and Italy, which the emperors were unable to help ; crushes the growing pride of the Patriarchs of Constantinople ; enlightens the whole Church by his learning ; rules the East and the West with equal vigor and humility, and gives to the world a perfect model of ecclesiastical government.

2. St. Gregory the Great was gifted with the highest order of eloquence. This talent he used with heroic self-sacrifice, even in the first days of his pontificate. The people, sinking under a scourge that carried off as many as eighty victims in an hour, thronged around the Holy Pontiff to catch from his lips the religious consolation his aching heart could give ; the only comfort of any worth in such an hour. St. Gregory seemed endowed with ubiquity to meet these pressing calls upon his exhaustless charity. His inspired strains raised his hearers above the thought of present suffering ; and even the relentless hand of death which was busy around him whilst he spoke, but gave more solemn sanction to his words. The fear of God's judgments enkindled new fervor in every heart. Day and night Gregory exhorted the dying, comforted the living, and sent up

burning petitions to the throne of divine mercy for his desolate flock. Heaven was at length moved, and the plague ceased.[*] St. Gregory gave his first thoughts to the reform of the pontifical court around him. The domain of St. Peter was extensive : in Sicily, in the cities of Syracuse and Palermo; in Calabria, in Apulia, in the Samnite territory, in Campania, Tuscany, and the country of the Sabines; in the cities of Norcia, Carseoli, and Ravenna; in Dalmatia, Istria and· Illyria; in Sardinia, Corsica, Liguria, and the Cottian Alps. Each district was placed under a distinct governor, called *defender* or *rector*. He was always one of the higher clergy of the Roman Church. The officers depending upon the Pope thus formed, even at that period, quite a numerous court. St. Gregory made it an object to choose them from among the most distinguished Italians. The instructions he gave them were worthy of his noble heart. He wished ecclesiastical revenues to be applied to the relief of every kind of misery and misfortune. In spite of the growing expenditure entailed upon the pontifical exchequer by this liberality, the great Pope still found means to encourage literature, science, and art. His palace became their centre. "There was no one employed in the pontifical palace," says Andres,[†] "who had not received a refined education, and whose sentiments, language, and instruction were not in keeping with the majesty of the pontifical throne."

3. The Pope himself was remarkable for profound and varied learning and eloquence above his age. Shortly after his promotion he wrote a beautiful treatise called *The Pastoral*, in answer to those who blamed him for his attempt to escape the burden of the pontificate by flight. This important work is divided into four parts; the first treats of vocation, of which

---

[*] After the disappearance of the plague, the anthem *Regina Cœli* was introduced into the Church service, to thank the Blessed Virgin, whose intercession was believed to have stayed the disease. Contemporary authors say that as the plague began to abate its violence, an angel was seen sheathing his sword upon the stately pile of Adrian. The edifice has since been called the castle of St. Angelo; a marble statue of an angel was raised upon it, but Benedict XIV. substituted one of bronze in its stead, which still remains.

[†] *De l'Origine, des Progrès, et de l'État de Toute Littérature*, t. i., ch. vii., p. 94.

he shows the necessity and examines the marks. In the second book, St. Gregory shows how the pastor, lawfully called to the post, should acquit himself of the charge which was not of his own seeking; how earnestly he should give himself to prayer, to teaching, to the relief of his neighbor, and what must be his humility, zeal, and discretion. In the third, he points out the instructions which a pastor should give, suiting himself to the various persons he is to know and teach; on this subject the holy doctor goes into most minute details. Finally, in the fourth part, St. Gregory shows, in a few words, how necessary it is for a pastor to search into his own conduct, in order to teach himself and to preserve recollection and humility. Such was the esteem in which *The Pastoral* was then held, that the emperor Mauritius wished to have a copy of it, and St. Anastasius, Patriarch of Antioch, translated it into Greek, for the use of the Eastern Churches.*

4. St. Gregory moreover practised what he taught. His care was not limited to Italy or to Rome. Having brought about a peace between the exarch of Ravenna and Agilulph, king of the Lombards, by means of Theodelinda, Agilulph's pious queen, he wrote to Recarede the Catholic, king of the Visigoths in Spain, to congratulate him on his adherence to the orthodox faith. "I cannot find words, my dear son," wrote the Pontiff, "to express the joy I feel at the tidings I hear of you. When we see that by a new miracle, in our own day, your highness has brought over the whole Gothic nation from the Arian heresy to the holiness of the faith, we cannot help exclaiming with the prophet, 'This change is the work of the right hand of the Most High!'" St. Gregory had in the mean time been striving to shield the African Churches from the fury of the Donatists, who were awaking to a new paroxysm of rage. We have forty letters on this subject, written by the saint in the course of two years. The patrician Gennadius, exarch or governor of Africa, zealously seconded the Pontiff's

---

* M. l'Abbé RECEVEUR: *Histoire de l'Eglise.*

endeavors. The Holy See possessed within the jurisdiction
of Gennadius a considerable domain, formerly presented by the
emperors of Constantinople, but lately devastated by war.
Gennadius repaired the damages at his own expense. Gregory
affectionately thanked him for this mark of generosity, and
begged him to crown his good work by defending the interests
of the faith against the attacks of the Donatists, who were dri-
ving bishops and priests from the churches, forcibly rebaptizing
Catholic children, plundering the dwellings of the faithful, and
giving themselves up unrestrainedly to every kind of disorder.
The exarch complied with the Holy Pontiff's wishes, and used
his power in behalf of the Catholics. One of the most baleful
influences that weakened the energy of the African Church
was the want of unity in the hierarchy. The primacy, instead
of being fixed in some one chief see, passed to the senior
bishop by ordination in the province; thus the centre or metropolis of the ecclesiastical province was always subject to
change, and the reins of primatial power often passed into the
hands of old men weakened by age and infirmity. To remedy
this crying evil, St. Gregory enjoined the provincial councils
henceforth to choose their primate from among the most able
bishops, and to see that he no longer dwelt in a village or hamlet, as was too often the case, but in a city of importance, that
he might thus be in a position more effectually to oppose the
Donatists. Sardinia and Corsica were subject to the governor
or exarch of Africa; but the distance of that officer from his
jurisdiction left the two islands to his subalterns who only
viewed their charge as a means of enriching themselves at the
expense of the wretched inhabitants. The civil magistrates
and imperial judges gave much more reasonable grounds of fear
to the poor islanders than the very barbarians. St. Gregory
was moved by their sufferings, and became their temporal as
well as spiritual saviour. His first step was to send to the two
islands zealous and charitable bishops, who watched the interests of their people with paternal care. He next wrote to the
court of Constantinople, to make known the crying abuses per-

petrated under cover of the imperial authority. His letters at
the same time reminded Gennadius of his duty toward his
subordinates, and stimulated the zeal of Januarius, metropolitan of Cagliari. Success crowned the holy Pontiff's zeal.
Orders reached Sardinia and Corsica which insured a more
humane mode of government.

5. But now the emperor Mauritius began to treat St.
Gregory's communications somewhat coldly. He felt secretly
irritated at the peace concluded by the Pope with the Lombards, and spoke of the Pontiff as a *simple man who had allowed himself to be caught by the empty promises of the barbarians*.
Gregory wrote to him on the subject in an admirable tone of
personal modesty and apostolic dignity. He closed his letter
with a warning to which the course of events afterward gave
a most fearful sanction. "Remove," said the Pope, "remove
from your soul, from your empire, and from your children, tho
crushing weight of the wrongs which are committed in the
provinces." We shall yet see the emperor Mauritius, as a penalty for his disregard of this warning, lose at once empire, children, and life. In the midst of the official duties which engaged his attention, and of a correspondence sufficient to
consume all his time, St. Gregory still found hours to devote
to study. In these moments he composed his Dialogues. He
thus tells us himself what suggested this work to him: "Feeling weighed down, one day, by the cares of business, I withdrew to a solitary spot to meditate more freely. As I sat
down in mournful silence by my deacon Peter, the friend of my
youth and partner of my studies, noticing my sadness, he asked
me if I had met with some new trouble. I answered him,
'Mine is a grief old and long-worn by usage and habit, but
made new by daily addition. I remember well how in the
monastery my soul soared high above perishable things; only
occupied with heavenly thoughts, it escaped from this bodily
prison by contemplation, looking upon death as the entrance
into life and the reward of its labors. Now, to the care of
souls I must join that of secular business; and after suffering

outward distractions at the call of charity, I always return home to myself weaker than before. The weight of my sufferings is increased by the thought of what I have lost; but even that thought is fading away, for in proportion as the soul descends, it loses even the remembrance of the good works it once performed. To crown my grief, I often compare my life to that of those holy men who have entirely forsaken the world, and their lofty flight but shows me more clearly my fearful fall.' 'I know not,' said Peter, 'whom you mean; I know no saints of such exalted virtue in Italy.' 'Time would fail me,' I replied, 'were I to attempt the recital of what in that regard I have both seen myself and learned from witnesses of known honesty and truthfulness.'" As Peter urged him to tell what he knew, St. Gregory consented, and this was the origin of the Dialogues. This work is divided into four books, the second of which is wholly devoted to the history of St. Benedict; the first and third mention many holy bishops, abbots, and monks of Italy; the fourth establishes the immortality of the soul. The critics of the eighteenth century tax St. Gregory with a childish credulity in the relation of miracles. The life of a saint is a supernatural life, and must needs present some deeds of a higher order than the facts of ordinary biographies; and the Gospel promise is fulfilled at every step of Church history: "Faith moves mountains." By bringing down the lives of the saints to the level of an every-day life, which is the great tendency since the rule of Protestantism in Europe, the true spirit of faith is ignored, and historical truth is quite as much slighted, as in too lightly receiving the legends handed down from age to age by popular tradition.

6. Whilst St. Gregory was thus recording the wonders of holiness that shone on past ages, the world was edified by an equally exalted saintliness in St. John Climacus and St. Theodore of Siceon. St. John Climacus, so called from the title of his principal work on the contemplative life, the Κλίμαξ, or *The Ladder*, was abbot of the monastery of Mount Sinai. At the age of sixteen years he forsook the world, where his birth and tal-

ents entitled him to a distinguished position, and embraced the life of an anchorite. He spent forty years in a solitude at the foot of Mount Sinai, communing only with heaven. The water that flowed from the rock, and the fruit of some date-trees near his cell, served him to sustain life. At the age of seventy-five years he was entreated to take the direction of the monastery of Mount Sinai. His long experience in the spiritual life made him the oracle of all the Eastern communities. At the earnest request of John, abbot of Raithu, a monastery near the Red Sea, he wrote his *Ladder of Religious Perfection*. Following the example of St. Gregory Nazianzen and St. John Chrysostom, he applies the mysterious ladder of Jacob to the different degrees of Christian and religious virtue. The scope of the work takes in every step of the interior life, from the first quitting the world to the most sublime contemplation and perfect peace of soul. The *Ladder of Religious Perfection* is followed by the *Letter to the Pastor*, a treatise on the guidance of souls, in which the pious solitary draws up rules of government for the superiors of monasteries, and reminds them of the duties of their state and the dispositions necessary to discharge them well. The reputation of St. John Climacus had crossed the sea. St. Gregory the Great, oppressed by the cares inseparable from a solicitude embracing all the Churches, wrote to the holy abbot, recommending himself to his prayers, and at the same time sent him fifteen beds for his hospital for the use of pilgrims, near Mount Sinai. St. John Climacus died A. D. 605, full of days and of merits. St. Theodore the Siceonite, so called from the hamlet of Siceon, his birthplace, situated about two miles from Anastasiopolis, withdrew, at the age of fourteen years, into a cell underground, where his only food was a little bread begged from the passers-by. A great desire to see the spot hallowed by the life and death of our Lord, led him to make three pilgrimages to Jerusalem. He availed himself of these distant journeys to open relations with the most celebrated monasteries of the East. On his return he was elected bishop of Anastasiopolis. The emperor had long been acquainted with St. Theodore's reputation. In the year A.D. 582, whilst yet but a general of the emperor Tiberius, Count Mauritius, returning triumphant from an expedition against the Persians, paid a visit to the saint in his Galatian cell. The victorious chief threw himself at the feet of the humble solitary, begging his prayers for his happy return to Tiberius. The saint, after recollecting himself a while in prayer, replied : " My son, you will soon be raised to the imperial throne ; I entreat you then to be mindful of the poor." As Mauritius seemed to doubt the prediction, the saint took him aside and convinced him of its truth, which time confirmed. Mauritius, in gratitude to the holy abbot, sent to his monastery six hundred bushels of wheat for the poor, with an order for the yearly renewal of the same donation. St. Theodore did not long hold the episcopal office bestowed upon him by the people of Anastasiopolis. He entreated, as a favor, the permission to return to his loved retreat, to end in solitude and prayer a life wholly devoted to contemplation. His wish was granted, and his happy death occurred in the opening of the seventh century.

7. The emperor Mauritius had lately issued a decree which called forth a stricture from St. Gregory. The decree forbade any officer, civil or military, actually in service, to embrace the clerical or the monastic life. St. Gregory modified the first clause, and made it unlawful for public officials to enter the religious state until their accounts had been settled ; but the clause relative to military men he wholly rejected, as contrary to the law of God and the good of souls. " Hear," said the Pope, " the words which Jesus Christ addresses to you by my lips : When you were but secretary, I made you captain of the guards, then Cæsar, and lastly emperor, and the father of an emperor.* I have placed my ministers under your authority, and you withdraw your soldiers from my service. . . . Tell me, my lord, what answer will you make to these words of your God when you stand in judgment before His awful tribunal ?"

---

* Mauritius had called his eldest son, Theodosius, to share the imperial power.

St. Gregory was especially interested in the soldiers, as their term of service among the Romans lasted twenty years at least. The Pope annulled as much of the decree as opposed the true spirit of the Church, and sent it thus modified to the metropolitans of the East and West.

8. In spite of all the efforts of St. Gregory's predecessor, John the Faster, Patriarch of Constantinople, secretly backed by Mauritius, still aimed at obtruding his arrogant claims upon the Eastern Churches. John took to himself the title of *Ecumenical Patriarch*, thus claiming a supremacy which belongs only to the See of St. Peter. St. Gregory's nuncio at Constantinople was instructed to arrange this matter. The Pontiff himself wrote to the ambitious patriarch, exhorting him to show more humility. "The popes themselves," wrote St. Gregory, " refused this title when offered by the council of Chalcedon; they glory in being styled the servants of the servants of God, though the guidance and the primacy of the Church were given to St. Peter, whose lawful successors they are." To lay yet greater stress upon the principle of the Roman sovereignty, the life and salvation of the Church, St. Gregory, in a council held at Rome, solemnly reinstated a priest of Chalcedon, unjustly condemned by the Patriarch of Constantinople. But John still persisted in his unjust and arrogant claim. Notwithstanding St. Gregory's energy, the question was only settled under the emperor Phocas, who gave ample satisfaction to Pope Boniface III.

9. In an age which knew no higher law than force of arms, promotions to the episcopate were not always unattended by violence. Maximus, bishop of Salona, had taken possession of his see by armed force. The Pope wrote to the intruder, suspending him from all episcopal functions. Maximus publicly tore the pontifical letter into pieces. Gregory was keenly alive to the outrage thus put upon the Holy See in his person. "I am ready to die," he wrote to his nuncio, " rather than see the Chair of St. Peter dishonored in my day." He then summoned Maximus to come and account for his conduct

at Rome. The culprit sought, by various schemes, to avoid the issue, and at length asked the Pope to send an agent to Salona to examine the difficulty. He was supported both by the emperor and the exarch. Obstacles only increased the holy Pontiff's energy. He commissioned Marinianus, bishop of Ravenna, to inquire into the facts connected with the promotion of Maximus. The bishop of Salona submitted to all that was required of him, and this act of humility secured his restoration. The peace concluded by St. Gregory the Great with the Lombards was but short-lived. Romanus, exarch of Ravenna, having seized upon Perugia, in contempt of the treaties to which he had sworn, Agilulph, king of the Lombards, irritated by this breach of faith, retook the city and then laid siege to Rome which was deficient in troops and in supplies. The Pope thus describes the condition of Rome and Italy : "We are met on all sides by sights and sounds of mourning and woe. Ruined cities, dismantled strongholds, wasted fields, have changed our once fertile land into a vast solitude ; and the wretched remains of the human race are incessantly scourged by the hand of God. Some are led away into bondage and fearfully mutilated ; others are put to death. Even Rome herself, once mistress of the world, how fallen now ! overwhelmed with sorrow, forsaken by her children, outraged by her enemies, buried in her own ruins ! Where is her senate, where are her people ? The very dwellings fall, the walls crumble. Why is the song of joy and triumph hushed ? Her princes and warriors once pressed the earth with conquering tread, the provinces poured into her walls the flower of their youth in search of glory and fortune. Now, a desolate and ruined city, she is slighted and shunned, and hardly does she remember her departed splendor." Grieved at such a state of things, St. Gregory again secured a peace. Agilulph did not include the Pope in his hatred toward the exarch. He agreed to treat on quite moderate terms, and in case they were not accepted, he offered peace separately to the Romans. St. Gregory wrote to the exarch, dwelling with particular force upon the fact that a partial treaty would be the ruin of Italy. Peace was concluded but three years later (A. D. 598), and then it was Callimachus, the successor of Romanus, who treated with Agilulph. The Pope refused to sign the agreement. Foreseeing that it would soon be violated, he preferred to keep his position as mediator in the contingency of a misunderstanding between the exarch of Ravenna and the Lombard king.

10. Gregory the Pope had not lost sight of the English nation which, as deacon, he had so longed to evangelize. He directed the priest Candidus, his nuncio in Gaul, to buy some young English slaves of from seventeen to twenty years of age, and to send them to Rome. It was his design to have them trained in the monasteries there, that they might be prepared to labor afterward for the conversion of their native land. When they had been sufficiently well grounded in the truths of the faith, the Pope sent them to England under the direction of St. Augustine, prior of the monastery of St. Andrew at Rome, with several religious upon whose virtue and prudence he could rely. To insure the success of an apostolic expedition designed to win a kingdom to the faith, St. Gregory furnished the missionaries with several letters for the princes and bishops of Gaul (A. D. 596). The Pontiff's name was a most powerful safeguard. St. Augustine and his companions happily reached the English coast, and first set foot upon the Isle of Thanet. The Angles and Saxons, both tribes of the German race, had for a century and a half held Great Britain, which has since been named after them *Anglia*, England. Their government was a *heptarchy*, or national federation, one of the kings of which was sovereign. The then reigning prince was Ethelbert, king of Kent and husband of Bertha, daughter of Charibert, king of Paris. The Frankish princess was a Christian, and had only consented to this union with the Saxon on the condition of being allowed the free exercise of her religion while living among a barbarous people. To this end she had brought with her a bishop named Luid-

hard. Here were two powerful auxiliaries for St. Gregory's missionaries. The joint efforts of the queen and the bishop prevailed upon Ethelbert to grant them an interview. The meeting took place on the Isle of Thanet in the open air. St. Augustine and his companions approached the appointed place in the slow and solemn pomp of a religious procession; before them was borne a silver cross and a banner displaying the august image of the Saviour. The king bade them sit down, and they began to preach the truths of the Gospel. Ethelbert listened with attention to doctrines to him so new and strange. His answer was full of wisdom and prudence. "Your words and promises," said the king, "are very fair; but as they are both new and uncertain I cannot at once receive them, nor so abruptly forsake the ancient belief of the Angles. Yet since you have taken the trouble to cross the seas in order to bring us what you esteem a better teaching, we are willing to treat you well and to grant you whatever may be needful for your support." He accordingly allowed them to settle in Duroverne (now Canterbury), his capital. The missionaries, as was their wont, entered the city in solemn procession, and thus formally placed under the dominion of the Church the land which was to continue true to Catholic teaching until the unbridled lust of a cruel tyrant would draw it into the ways of error and infidelity. The prejudices of the idolaters gave way before the holiness, zeal, and austerity of these apostles. Ethelbert himself, won by the pure and sublime morality of their life and teaching, professed himself a Christian; and so powerful was his example, that ten thousand Saxons followed their king to the waters of baptism.

11. To give form and permanence to the Church, St. Gregory raised St. Augustine to the episcopal dignity, directing him to go to Arles, and there receive consecration from the bishop Vigilius, apostolic vicar for Gaul. His after ministry in England was crowned with the most cheering success. On Christmas Day, A. D. 597, he baptized upward of two thousand pagans. These happy tidings filled the Pontiff's heart with

joy. He wrote a letter of congratulation to Ethelbert and Bertha, which was an outpouring of the emotions of his soul. He thanks the queen, in particular, for the protection she had extended to the pious missionaries. To Ethelbert he holds up the example of Constantine the Great, as most fit to raise his course of action to the level of his high vocation (a. d. 601). The Saxon prince proved worthy of the hope which the Pontiff rested upon him, and has since been ranked among the saints. St. Gregory had, in the mean time, sent fresh workmen to England, to reap the rich harvest now ripe for the Master's garner. "Who can describe," he wrote to St. Augustine, "what joy filled every faithful heart when we learned here that, by the grace of God and your endeavor, the English nation, drawn from the darkness of error, enlightened by the true faith, now tramples her idols under foot, offers to the Almighty the obedience of pure hearts and sincerely bows to His divine teaching?" Another letter regulates the establishment of bishoprics in England. "We allow you the use of the *pallium*," says the Pope, "but only for the celebration of Holy Mass. You will consecrate twelve bishops, who shall be subject to you. Henceforth the bishop of London shall be metropolitan, and receive the pallium from the Holy See. Appoint a man of zeal and charity to the see of York. Should that city and the neighboring country receive the word of God, he shall also consecrate twelve bishops, who must depend upon him as their metropolitan. We intend likewise to bestow the pallium upon him, but we wish him to be subject to your direction as long as you live. After your death, he shall remain the superior of the bishops he has consecrated, and no longer depend in any thing upon the bishop of London, your successor. The right of precedence between the bishops of London and York will be regulated by their consecration. We desire, moreover, that all the bishops in England be subject to you during your lifetime." In other more minute instructions, St. Gregory fixes a number of doubtful points of discipline submitted to him by St. Augustine. Among other directions, he advises them not to

destroy the temples, but only the idols of the false gods, and
to consecrate to the worship of the true God the buildings
still fit for use, " in order," as he wisely said, " that the people,
seeing you respect the monuments to which they are accustomed, may more readily come to them."

12. The great Pontiff who had just bestowed upon England
the boon of civilization was not careless of the Christian training of France.   In the year 595 he had written to King Childebert and Queen Brunehault.   His words are worthy of record.
" Your kingdom," writes the Pontiff, " is as much exalted
above other realms, as the kingly state is higher than the common condition of men.   To be a king is not a favor peculiar to
yourself, for there are others who wear the crown as well; but
to be a Catholic king, what so many others have not deserved to
be, is a special privilege; for in the midst of heathen nations
the light of your faith shines like the flame of a great torch in
the shades of a dark night."   While thus praising the piety
of princes, the Pope did not hesitate to point out the abuses
which had crept into some churches. · He wrote as follows to
four of the principal bishops of Gaul: " I learn that within
your jurisdiction holy orders are simoniacally conferred.   This
is seeking the empty name of priesthood without its sacred
character; the consequence is, that without any question of
moral worth, they only are ordained who buy the privilege,
thus showing themselves the most unworthy subjects.   If we
ought to seek for the service of the holy altars those whose
humility holds them farthest back, we should, on the same
principle, reject those who seek to thrust themselves too
readily forward.   On the death of a bishop there are ambitious
men who forthwith appear with shaven locks, and laymen
suddenly become pastors of the people. . What good can the
flock expect from those who dare to take the master's part
before they have learned as disciples?"   As a check to these
disorders the Pope recommended to the Gallic bishops to hold
a council, and appointed as presiding prelate Siagrius, bishop
of Autun, who enjoyed a high reputation for merit, and pos-

sessed the full confidence of the Frankish monarchs. The ceaseless strife to which the country was doomed delayed for some years the execution of the Pope's orders. St. Gregory still urged the matter (A. D. 600). He wrote on the subject to Queen Brunehault and to Kings Theodobert, Theodoric, and Clotaire : "Be mindful of the interests of God," he wrote to Brunehault, "and he will be careful of yours. Use your endeavors to assemble a council for the removal of simony, as we have recommended to you. Sacrifice to God this domestic enemy, that you may be enabled to overcome your foreign foes." Another letter is written in a yet more earnest tone: "As it is written that the glory of a nation is its justice, and sin is the curse of a people, no kingdom can firmly stand unless its rulers strive to root out the evils which they know. There are priests in your realm who lead a scandalous life; we say it with grief, for bad priests are the people's ruin. Look, therefore, to your own salvation and to the good of your subjects, by taking the steps necessary to remedy such disorders." In accordance with the Pope's desire, a council was held A. D. 602, and proceeded to draw up the rules so necessary for the Church of Gaul.

13. The powerful influence of the Sovereign Pontiff called together other councils in various parts of the Catholic world : at Seville, A. D. 590; at Saragossa, A. D. 592; at Toledo, A D. 597; and at Huesca, A. D. 598. These episcopal assemblies were chiefly engaged in discussing questions of religious and clerical discipline. St. Gregory personally presided over three councils in Rome. In the first of these councils, held A. D. 595, he renewed the canon against receiving any thing for ordinations, the pallium or letters of installation, on what pretext soever. He allowed monasteries to receive all persons of a servile condition, independently of opposition on the part of their masters, thus carrying out the end which his predecessors kept always in view—the gradual abolition of slavery, that unfortunate result of pagan civilization and disgraceful mark of man's degeneracy. In the second council, held in the year 600, he fixed the degrees of kindred

within which marriage is forbidden. In the third, which met A. D. 601, he forbade that the bishop should take any thing from the property, lands or revenue of a monastery, and laid down rules calculated to secure the freedom of abbatial elections. The ever-increasing number of religious communities made these laws a matter of necessity in the West. In the general impulse which drew numbers of chosen souls into the solitude of the cloister, Gaul was particularly conspicuous for fervor. St. Columban, a native of Ireland, had lately founded the celebrated abbey of Luxeuil, in the barren and rocky mountain district of Vosges; here six hundred religious followed him in the path of religious perfection (A. D. 590). He gave them a rule eminently marked by prudence, gentleness and firmness. The zeal, modesty and piety of the holy abbot seemed to communicate itself to all his brethren.

14. Yet St. Columban's arrival at Luxeuil had brought a passing trouble into the Church of Gaul. By a national computation, the saint and his companions thought it their duty to celebrate the festival of Easter on the fourteenth day of the moon, when it fell upon a Sunday. This system differed both from that of the Quartodecimani, who always observed the fourteenth day of the moon, and from that of the Church, which only celebrates the festival on the Sunday following the fourteenth day. The Gallic bishops did not think it proper to countenance, in foreign monks, an innovation which their reputation might make more dangerous. The consequence was a spirited debate, carried on with tenacity on the part of St. Columban; it is probable, however, that he at length adopted the general observance, as we find no further traces of the dispute in history.

15. In A. D. 602, Brunehault and her grandson Theodoric, king of Burgundy, sent a solemn embassy to Rome, to beg from the Apostolic See the confirmation of certain institutions founded by the queen. Particular mention was made of a hospital built at Autun, in honor of St. Andochius, to which were attached two monasteries, one for men, the other

for women. In an age when nothing was fixed, when kings no longer respected one another, and the people hardly showed respect to the king, Brunehault and Theodoric felt the need of securing the future stability of this foundation. St. Gregory granted their request. He declared all property bestowed upon the hospital of Autun to be inviolable. "Should any king, bishop, judge, or other secular person acquainted with the tenor of this decree, dare to infringe upon the rights herein contained, he shall be debarred from the dignity of his rank and honor, and make himself answerable to the tribunal of God. And if he refuse to give back what he has wrongfully seized, or to atone for his fault by a worthy penance, he shall be cut off from the communion of the body and blood of our Lord Jesus Christ, and incur the eternal anger of the Most High!" A certain school of historians, unfriendly to the pontifical power, has endeavored to distort this sanction into an abuse of jurisdiction. To form a right judgment in such cases, we must go back, in mind, to the date of their occurrence, and know what spirit ruled the times.* It is of little moment to know whether the popes have power over the temporal domain of kings. But it is important to know that the public spirit of the age granted them that power. No better proof of this fact can be needed than the request of the sovereigns themselves, that the Pope would give the sanction in question. "We hasten," says St. Gregory, in his bull, " to give the sanction you request." Besides, it was a blessing for prince and people that some such authority should be acknowledged in a society which so often disregarded every other power. Moreover, in a nation constituted on Christian principles, an excommunication naturally produced all the effects of a declen-

---

* The whole of this very intricate question has been thoroughly treated in the work entitled *Pouvoir du Pape au Moyen Age*, recently published by M. ——, director of the seminary of St. Sulpice. The author proves, according to Fénélon, that there existed in the Middle Ages a *public right* which placed nations and kings under the defence of the Holy See. If the public mind has changed on this subject in Europe, it does not furnish sufficient ground for attacking the Sovereign Pontiffs, who were guided by the principles established in their day.

sion from power. The excommunicated person was in fact cut off from all intercourse with the Christian community; but a king whose every relation with his subjects is interrupted ceases to be a king. So that the great question raised upon the power of the pope over the temporal domain of kings becomes an empty war of words. So long as the authority of the Sovereign Pontiffs was, in the natural order of things, looked upon as the general tribunal of the Christian world, the popes held an acknowledged sway even over temporal dominion, and we shall yet meet with its public and open exercise. When the spirit of religion which had warmed the hearts of European nations felt the chilling influence of Protestantism, the popes ceased to exercise a power which they had wielded only for the good of society, and which society now called in question. When Louis XIV. raised the debate on the rights of the Sovereign Pontiff, in the assemblies of the Gallican Church, he well knew that no pope could shake his throne. It remained to be seen whether the world gained in stability in proportion as the popes lost their controlling influence ; the history of the last century and of ours bears striking witness to the truth.

16. Weighed down as he was by multiplied political cares, St. Gregory did not forget the details of rite and ceremonial in the sacred worship. He collected into a single volume the prayers to be said by the priest at mass and in administering the sacraments. This collection is known as the *Sacramentary of St. Gregory*. All that was to be chanted, he caused to be collected into a separate volume called the *Antiphonary*. He himself set the chants to music, and wished them to be used throughout the Latin Church. He founded a school of chanters, in Rome, and bestowed upon it some landed property and two houses ; he even presided there in person, and did not deem it unworthy of him to teach little children ; he also sent scholars from this institution to France and England. The chanters sent by Adrian to Charlemagne, two centuries later, came from this Gregorian school. The zeal of the Holy Pope for the good of the Church was always controlled by a sense

of justice and conciliation which led him to respect every claim. A cenobite, named Probus, whose merit St. Gregory could appreciate, was drawn from his solitude and placed over the monastery of St. Andrew. But as monks could hold no personal property, and their estate must fall to the monastery, Probus was no longer able to make a will. Yet he had a son who was poor, and whom he did not wish to wrong of his heritage; he wrote to the Pope and made known his case. "When I quitted the world, I allowed several years to pass by without settling my estate, knowing that in due course of law my son would inherit it; but coming one day with some of my brethren to pay you homage, you ordered me to take the direction of the monastery; I at once obeyed without taking time to dispose of my property. This leads me now to beg that you will empower me to take the necessary steps that my obedience may not wrong my son, who is in want." St. Gregory granted the request. "All your reasons are good," he said; "we therefore give you full liberty to dispose of your property as though you had not entered the monastery."

17. Meanwhile the East had again become the scene of civil strife. The emperor Mauritius, yielding to a sentiment of avarice unworthy of a prince, ground down his subjects, wrung large sums from the fruit of their toil, and allowed twelve thousand Roman prisoners to be massacred by the khan of the Avars, a Scythian tribe, rather than ransom them at the paltry price of three thousand pieces of gold.* This unnatural conduct aroused a feeling of general indignation. The army chose a leader, and bestowed the purple upon a centurion named Phocas. The whole population of Constantinople came forth to greet the approaching Cæsar, who was crowned in St. Sophia's by the Patriarch Cyriacus (A. D. 602). Mauritius had fled to Chalcedon, whence he was now brought back to Constantinople by order of Phocas. Dragged to the shore, in sight of the palace where he had reigned, the unhappy prince was

* About twenty-seven thousand francs, French currency.

made to look upon the execution of his five sons. At each
blow that struck off a head so dear, he repeated the words of
the Psalmist: "Thou art just, O Lord, and Thy judgments are
right." After witnessing this heart-rending scene, he was himself given over to the hands of the executioner. The warning
of St. Gregory had received its fearful sanction. The Pope
availed himself of the accession of Phocas to enter a new protest against the encroachments of the court of Constantinople,
which claimed the right of confirming ecclesiastical nominations and of levying large taxes on them. It will be remembered that Theodoric, king of the Ostrogoths, first claimed this
right over the Papal elections; the Greek emperors, on taking
possession of Italy, carried out the system of exaction practised by their Gothic predecessors. A new Pontiff could not
be enthroned without their leave. When cupidity was afterward joined to tyranny, this permission was only granted for
a pecuniary consideration. Justinian had even fixed a tariff
for the principal bishoprics of the empire. St. Gregory thus
expressed himself to Phocas, in regard of simony: "This
abuse threatened to mar the halcyon days of the infant
Church. Though condemned at the time, the accursed error
still breeds its baneful offspring. It has aroused against the
Church of God not only the countless masses of the people, but
even the kingly power, if indeed we may style them kings
who hold in bondage the spouse of Jesus Christ, and whose
presuming rashness does not hesitate to barter the heritage of
Christ for sordid gain." This was one of the last letters written by St. Gregory the Great. The illustrious Pontiff, hailed
by the unanimous voice of his age with the title of Great,
which title an admiring posterity has confirmed, sank under
the weight of labors and infirmities, on the 12th of March, A. D.
304, in the sixty-fourth year of his age. The whole world seemed
oppressed by a sense of darkening gloom at the setting of this
splendid light of the Church. He had been preceded to the
grave by St. Augustine, the apostle of England, St. Leander,
archbishop of Seville, and Recarede the Catholic, king of the

Visigoths. England gave a touching proof of her gratitude for
the boon of conversion which she had received from the great
Pontiff. In A. D. 747 the Council of Cliff decreed that his anniversary should be regularly solemnized in all the English churches.
The decree was renewed A. D. 1222, by a council held at Ox-
ford, and observed until the period of the so-called Reformation. God grant that England once again return to the faith
and worship of her apostle !

18. The pontificate of St. Gregory the Great forms an era
in the history of the Church. "Catholicity and the Papacy
have hitherto appeared under two very opposite aspects.
Deadly principles of dissolution were undermining society; the
moral as well as the political world was crumbling at all
points; in the midst of all this decay which forebodes the fall
of tottering empires, a new society is springing into life; it is
Christianity. A youthful but mighty power binds together its
various elements, and this power is the Papacy. The part this
power now plays seems to us wonderfully fitted for the mission
it has to fulfil. Up to the sixth century, as we have said, it
offers two different aspects. From the days of St. Linus to
those of St. Melchiades the Popes discharged their apostolic
ministry only, in the words of the apostle, by resisting unto
blood. From St. Melchiades to St. Gregory the Great, they
lay the foundation of the Church's written law, and crush the
heresies that assail the great mystery of the Man-God. The
former were apostolic martyrs, the latter apostolic lawgivers.
The turn taken by the political world corresponded to these two
phases : the first witnessed the breaking up of Roman unity ;
the second saw modern society begin the work of its first foundation. Such we believe to be the true aspect of the first six
centuries, viewed in the light of history and philosophy. This
Christian monarchy once fixed, once advanced from the state of
mere being to that of positive power, receives modifications; that
is, it joins the political to the religious character. The popes
have appeared as apostles and lawgivers, they now become
sovereigns; it is in this new feature that we shall henceforth

be called upon to view their political and humanizing mission."[*]

§ II. Pontificate of Sabinian (Sept. 1, a. d. 604—Feb. 22, 605).

19. The death of St. Gregory the Great was followed by an interregnum of five months and a half. Sabinian, the apostolic nuncio at Constantinople, was elected on the 1st of September, a. d. 604, to a pontificate which lasted but six months. But this short interval witnessed the ravages of a great famine which desolated Rome and Italy. Sabinian threw open the granaries of the Church, and directed that the wheat should be sold to the poor at the rate of thirty bushels for a gold as. Oldoin attributes to Pope Sabinian the custom of ringing the bells at the canonical hours, to summon the faithful to the recitation of the divine office. Bells had been used in the West from the fifth century ; their invention is generally attributed to St. Paulinus, bishop of Nola, in Campania. For this reason the oldest ecclesiastical writers called them *nolæ* or *campanæ*. The use of bells was introduced into the Eastern Church at a much later date. About the year 864, Orso, doge of Venice, sent to the Greek emperor Michael a present of twelve bells, which he placed in an elegant belfry attached to the church of St. Sophia. Pope Sabinian died on the 22d of February, a. d. 605, and was buried in the basilica of St. Peter.

§ III. Pontificate of Boniface III. (February 25, a. d. 606–
November 12, 606).

20. The pontifical elections of this period plainly show the aim of the Roman clergy to gratify the court of Constantinople. Boniface was still in the Eastern capital as nuncio when elected to fill the Chair of St. Peter (February 25, a. d. 606). His exalted merit certainly warranted the choice, for when appoint-

---

[*] *Histoire des Papes*, by M. le Comte De Beaufort.

-ing him representative of the Holy See in the East, St. Gregory said of him : " He is a defender of the Church ; our long and close acquaintance with him enables us to bear ample witness to his purity and faithfulness." By placing on the pontifical throne men personally known to the emperors, a sure check was placed upon any questions which those monarchs might be disposed to raise, whether through ill-will or cupidity, against the election of a stranger. Boniface III. reigned but little longer than his predecessor. But to his pontificate was granted the glory of settling, most advantageously for the Church, the question raised by the proud Patriarchs of Constantinople to the title of *universal bishop.* Phocas, whose cruel ambition had secured the imperial crown, was the instrument used by God to carry out this act of justice. He declared, by an imperial edict, that the title could belong only to the Roman Pontiff. Eighty years before, Justinian had styled Pope John II. "the Head of all the holy Churches, the first of all the bishops."* Phocas therefore bestowed no new honor, as the centuriators of Magdeburg have tried to prove, but simply acknowledged an acquired right, as is clearly shown by Cardinals Baronius and Bellarmin. Another difficulty has also been started upon the decree, on the ground that it was issued by a tyrant—for Phocas owed his diadem only to violence and bloodshed. But besides the fact that the succession of emperors in the Lower Empire is but an unbroken series of like examples, Phocas did, after all, but ratify the decree of Justinian, whose legitimacy no one thinks of questioning. Pope Boniface III., wishing to anticipate the disorders sometimes attending the pontifical elections, called a council in St. Peter's, at Rome. The council excommunicates any one who moots the question of a successor for a living pope or bishop, and decrees, moreover, that the clergy and faithful shall not meet to elect a new pope until three days after the obsequies of the deceased Pontiff. This is the only act we have of the pontificate of Boniface III.,

---

* NOVELL. 131, chap. ii.

who died November 12, A. D. 606, eight months after his accession.

§ IV. PONTIFICATE OF BONIFACE IV. (September 18, A. D. 607 —May 25, 614).

21. After a vacancy of ten months, the Holy See was filled, on the 18th of September, A. D. 607, by Boniface IV. The new Pontiff had been connected with the court of Constantinople, and obtained from Phocas the grant of the Pantheon, of which he made a church dedicated to the Blessed Virgin and the martyrs. The anniversary of this dedication has since become the feast of All Saints. But the power of Phocas was now on the wane; his cruelty had not stopped at the members of the late imperial family; numbers of guiltless victims daily bled to expiate a suspected attachment to the memory of the murdered princes. Only one was bold enough to cry out against so many crimes. Heraclius, the aged governor of Africa, for eight years steadily faced the threats of the centuries who now dishonored the throne of Constantine. The governor was at the head of a body of troops on whose devoted attachment he could rely. Phocas dared not attack him openly. Unable, by reason of his weight of years, to take personal command of the expedition, Heraclius intrusted it to his son, who also bore his name. Favored by wind and sea, the squadron cast anchor in the Hellespont (October 4, 610). Emboldened by the sight of the friendly fleet, the people of Constantinople shake off the tyrant's heavy yoke, and hurl him from his throne. The troops that garrison the imperial city now join the people and heap curses upon the usurper whom but a few years before they had borne in triumph to the palace of the Caesars. Phocas crouches, trembling with terror, in the underground vaults of the palace. The soldiers discover his lurking-place, tear away the purple robe from his shoulders, cover him with a black mantle, and drag him, fettered, bareheaded and barefooted, to Heraclius the younger, who orders his exe

cution. Phocas had been raised to the throne by treachery and crime; he lost it by an ignominious death which he but too well deserved. After depriving him of his right hand, Heraclius ordered his head to be cut off. On the very day of this bloody execution, the Patriarch Sergius crowned Heraclius emperor and solemnized his nuptials with Eudoxia.

22. The course of the Church in Great Britain was always onward. After the death of St. Augustine of Canterbury, Lawrence, his successor, with Mellitus and Justus, his fellow-bishops, gave their attention not only to the Britons, but likewise to the Irish. Their most zealous efforts at first failed to bring the bishops of that country to the unity of Catholic discipline. The Paschal question especially gave rise to a long and warm discussion. Mellitus accordingly set out for Rome to consult the Pope on the subject. Boniface convoked a council, which also fixed all that concerned monks and the monastic life. On his return to Great Britain, Mellitus brought with him these decisions, with letters from the Pope to Archbishop Lawrence, to King Ethelbert, to the clergy, and the whole English nation. At about the same time (A. D. 610) he founded the abbey now so well known, and called, from its position, Westminster, or monastery of the West. During the same year St. Columban was driven from his convent of Luxeuil by the persecution of King Theoderic (Thierry), whom he had reproved for his dissolute mode of life. Theoderic ordered him to be conveyed to Nantes, and there to embark for some foreign port. But a steady succession of contrary winds made his departure impossible. The sailors, looking upon this as an effect of the Divine anger, refused to take him on board. St. Columban thus found himself left at Nantes, and free to turn his steps in any direction. He went to Clotaire II., who furnished him with an escort to the states of King Theodebert. Thence he sailed up the Rhine to the extremity of Lake Zurich, where he began to preach the Gospel to the inhabitants. He afterward repaired to the shores of Lake Constance, where, with the help of his disciple, St. Gall, he

founded the monastery of Bregenz. St. Columban was not the only victim of Theodoric's persecution. St. Didier, bishop of Vienne, had the courage to reprove his disorders, and was consequently banished by the tyrant, who acted through a council of court-paid bishops, held at Châlons-sur-Saône, in the year A. D. 603. God having glorified His servant's exile by several miracles, Didier was recalled. But the king's better feelings did not long prevail, and the holy bishop was murdered by three royal officers on the banks of the Chaloronne, near Lyons. Finding himself pursued by the murderers, St. Didier knelt down and recommended to God his flock and his persecutors. In this attitude he received the fatal blow which sent him to his reward on the 23d of May, A. D. 607. Theodoric's mother, Queen Brunehault, whose misfortunes throw a veil of sympathetic respect over her name, and to whom history attributes many good qualities, did not interpose her influence to stay the savage arm of her son. Some historians even assert that she used her authority with Theodoric against the holy bishop. Yet the esteem ever expressed for Brunehault by St. Gregory the Great throws a doubt upon the record of crimes drawn up against her by later chroniclers. However this may be, the tragic end of the unhappy queen came soon after this event. Her rival, the odious Fredegonda, died quietly in Paris, in the enjoyment of a prosperity of which her crimes made her utterly unworthy (A. D. 597). Brunehault, after seeing her son snatched away in the prime of life, fell into the hands of Clotaire II., who ordered her to be tied by the hair to the tail of an untamed horse. The maddened steed soon tore her to pieces, and the savage multitude burned her mangled remains with fiendish joy (A. D. 613).

23. The East likewise felt the fearful scourge of war. Chosroes, king of Persia, had opened a way into Palestine by the capture of Edessa, Apamea, Cæsarea of Cappadocia, and Damascus. The accession of Heraclius did not stay his ravages. Jerusalem fell into the power of the Persians, and was given up to the worst excesses of war. The Christians were

butchered without pity. Urged on by the highest refinement of cruelty, the Jews bought many of them, at a high price, to satisfy their savage cruelty by putting them to death under the most inhuman tortures. The Persians plundered and then fired the churches. Among the precious spoils they seized was the sacred wood of the true cross, which they carried off with them into Persia. These disasters called forth the active and sublime charity of St. John the Almoner, Patriarch of Alexandria. The wretched inhabitants who had escaped the invaders' swords, thronged into his episcopal city from all parts of Syria. St. John received them all and largely relieved their wants. He had the sick and wounded placed in hospitals, where they were cared for free of cost; and here he often visited them and personally attended to their needs. As if to add splendor to these wonders of charity by proportionable difficulties, God allowed the same year to bring a famine also in its train. The Nile withheld its yearly overflow, and wheat became exceedingly dear. St. John borrowed large sums of money, imported a quantity of corn from Sicily, and relieved the most crying want. The saint's charity did not stop with the limits of his own city; he sent money and provisions to Jerusalem, to the monasteries in Palestine, and to all the Syrian cities. The treasures of Providence seemed to multiply in proportion as he drew on them; and we might perhaps find it hard to believe so many wonders wrought by a single man, had not charity made them credible by renewing them in the person of St. Vincent de Paul, the *almoner* of the seventeenth century, the visible providence of Alsace, Lorraine, and Champagne.

24. Pope Boniface IV. died on the 25th of May, A. D. 614. Two important councils were held during his pontificate: the first at Toledo, in 610; the second at Paris, in 613. The latter was the fullest that had yet been held in Gaul. Its fifteen canons, relating to episcopal succession and jurisdiction, were signed by seventy-nine bishops.

§ V. Pontificate of Deusdedit (November 13, A. D. 614—
November 8, 617).

25. On the 13th of November, A. D. 614, Deusdedit was raised to the Chair of Peter. During his pontificate of but three years, the English Church, hardly yet firmly rooted by the care of its first apostles, was doomed to encounter a furious storm. The pious king Ethelbert, whose name the Church holds in sacrificial remembrance, had died in the course of the preceding year (616). His son, Eadbald, a prince of dissolute life, had refused the light of the faith. His accession brought back to heathenism the ready throng of fickle courtiers, who saw in religion but a stepping-stone for their ambition. The people were led by the example of the great. The East Saxons also, under the pagan rule of the sons of Saberct, first Christian king of Essex, denied the faith and banished St. Mellitus, bishop of London. Together with St. Justus, he went to Gaul (A. D. 616); but the storm was a passing one. The conversion of King Eadbald and the death of the three sons of Saberct, left the holy bishops free to return amidst the flocks intrusted to their care (A. D. 618). Pope Deusdedit died on the 8th of November, A. D. 617, and was succeeded by Boniface V. (December 29, A. D. 617).

CHAPTER VI.

§ I. PONTIFICATE OF BONIFACE V. (December 29, A. D. 617—October 25, 625).

1. Victory of Heraclius over the Persians. Exaltation of the Holy Cross.—2. Mahomet. The Koran.—3. Religious condition of England and Gaul.— 4. Ecclesiastical writers; St. Sophronius, John Moschus, St. Isidore of Seville.—5. Death of Boniface V.

§ II. PONTIFICATE OF HONORIUS (May 14, A. D. 626—October 12, 638).

6. State of the Christian World at the accession of Honorius.—7. Case of Fortunatus, Metropolitan of Gradi. Intervention of Honorius in favor of the Lombard king Adaloald.—8. Sergius, Patriarch of Constantinople, author of the Monothelite Heresy.—9. St. Sophronius of Alexandria, Patriarch of Jerusalem, opposes the Monothelite error.—10. Letter of Sergius to the Pope.—11. Reply of Honorius.—12. Council of Jerusalem held by St. Sophronius against the Monothelites.—13. Embassy of St. Sophronius to the Pope. Death of Honorius and of St. Sophronius. Capture of Jerusalem by Omar. The True Cross carried to Constantinople.—14. Situation of the West at the death of Honorius.

§ III. PONTIFICATE OF SEVERINUS (May 28, A. D. 640—August 2, 640).

15. Vacancy of the Holy See. *Ecthesis* of Heraclius.—16. Election and Death of Severinus.

§ IV. PONTIFICATE OF JOHN IV. (December 24, A. D. 640—October 22, 642).

17. Heraclius retracts the *Ecthesis*. His Death. Burning of the Alexandrian Library by Omar.—18. Revolution in the East. John IV. clears Honorius from the charge of Monothelitism. Death of the Pope. St. Eligius, St. Ouen, St. Amandus, and St. Arnulphus in Gaul. The Salic Law.

§ V. PONTIFICATE OF THEODORE I. (November 24, A. D. 642—May 13, 640).

19. Hereditary firmness of the Popes in upholding the faith. Theodore I. renews the condemnation of the *Ecthesis*.—20. St. Maximus. Interview of the holy abbot with Pyrrhus, Monothelite Patriarch of Constantinople. —21. Pyrrhus makes his abjuration into the hands of the Pope. Relapse

§ I Pontificate of Boniface V. (December 29, A. D. 617— October 25, 625).

1. The Persian arms filled the East with blood and carnage The emperor Heraclius seemed for a while to disregard the state of those rich provinces. The time was occupied in treating with the khan of the Avars, who was threatening Constantinople. The exchequer, drained by the extravagance of Phocas, also claimed attention. This seeming listlessness on the part of Heraclius was in truth a time of useful preparation for what was, so to speak, the only aim, and afterward the highest glory of this reign. In the year 622, the emperor marched out of Constantinople to meet the Persians, at the head of a numerous army of Turks, Romans and Greeks. Before setting out he knelt before the altar of St. Sophia to pray for the success of his arms. Then turning toward the patriarch, he said to him : "I leave the care of my capital and my son to God, to the Blessed Virgin, and to you." These words were received with loud applause from the army and blessings from the people. Heraclius took advantage of the enthusiasm of his troops : his first campaign amid the mountains of Armenia taught the Romans that they had not utterly lost the habit of victory. The enemy's camp, with its hoards of treasured wealth, repaid the valor of the victorious army. The war was but a series of like successes until the year 628. Chosroes II., forced to fly before the conquering Romans, saw his most flourishing cities doomed to the same fate he had so often inflicted upon the wealthy towns of Syria. In spite of his defeats, he obstinately refused the honorable terms of peace offered him by Heraclius, who held fifty thousand of his subjects as prisoners. The obstinacy of Chosroes II. hastened his ruin. His subjects

rose up against him. His own son Siroes shut him up in Ctesiphon, in the *Tower of Darkness*, which he had built to hold his treasures. Siroes forbade that any food should be given him. " Let him feed on gold," said the prince, " for which he laid waste the world, and made so many thousand victims starve." As the wretched old man still breathed after five days of the most cruel torment, Siroes ordered him to be shot to death with arrows (A. D. 628). This tragic event put an end to the war. Wishing to enjoy the fruits of his crime, Siroes accepted the terms of peace offered by Heraclius. The emperor returned to Constantinople after an absence of six years. The people, the army, and the senate joined in giving him the honor of a triumph. The conqueror advanced in a car drawn by four elephants, and preceded by the wood of the true cross, the sacred standard of Christian nations, the most glorious trophy of his victory over the Persians (A. D. 628). In the following year the emperor himself brought back to Jerusalem the sign of our redemption. The restoration of the reconquered cross to the spot where it had saved the world, was an event of immense import. On reaching the Garden of Olives, the emperor took it upon his shoulders, and followed by the clergy and a countless throng of the faithful weeping with joy, he made the stations of the Way of Sorrows, and at length laid down his sacred burden upon the hallowed hill of Calvary. The memory of this august ceremony, this magnificent sight, has been consecrated by the Church in the festival of the exaltation of the Holy Cross, kept on the 14th of September.

2. We have somewhat outstripped the chronological course of events, in order not to break off the account of Heraclius's victories and their glorious crowning. From the far East came another wave of invasion, more powerful and lasting than its predecessor, and bearing on with it to the Western world the hitherto unknown name of Mahomet, the Prophet of the Believers. Mecca, his birthplace, had seen him a poor orphan, his heritage reduced to five camels left him by his father. His

youth was divided between the labors of a shepherd's life, and the journeys made in company with his uncle Abu Taleb, as he led his merchant caravans to the fairs of Bassora and Damascus. Now (A. D. 622) Arabia's capital beholds Mahomet mighty and powerful, an eloquent warrior, an apostolic conqueror. Idolatry was the oldest form of worship in Arabia; its great centre was the temple called Caaba, in Mecca. Hither the Magi brought the Sabaism of Zoroaster, and in later days some colonies of Jewish merchants, settled on the shores of the Red Sea, made known the Mosaic law. At length the Gospel shone upon Arabia Felix, even before the Saracen Sassanidæ of the north had been converted by the desert solitaries. Thus four religions, side by side, held sway in Arabia, when Mahomet undertook to blend them into one. To impress the ardent natures accustomed to the wonders of Eastern song and legend, he assumed the tone of a conqueror and a prophet. He taught his fellow-citizens that God created all men and distributed them into nations, and then placed him in the best of all, the Arabian!—that the Creator divided the nations into tribes, and placed him in the best tribe, the tribe of the Koreish!—that He parcelled out the tribes into families, and brought him forth from the best of all families, the family of Abdul Motalleb! He announces himself as the best of men; as the one who should first knock at the gate of paradise, and whose grave should first open on the day of general judgment. He declares that Abraham had asked him from God, that Jesus Christ had announced him to the world, and that on the day of his birth, his mother, the noble Amina, had seen a great light shining from the remote East to the far West! He rehearses his nocturnal journey through the realms of space, on the winged steed El Borak (the Sparkling); he had tied the aerial courser in Jerusalem, at the very place where the prophets were wont to tie their beasts. In Solomon's temple he had spoken and prayed with Abraham, Moses, and Jesus Christ. He had mounted to heaven on a ladder of light; passing through the midst of the stars, those huge spheres hanging by golden

chains to the .empyrean dome, he had scaled the seven
heavens of diamond, emerald, sapphire, topaz, brass, gold and
hyacinth ; the angelic hosts and bands of patriarchs and prophets had paid him homage as to the Apostle of God! The
hand of the Almighty was laid upon him and sealed his forehead with the prophet's sign! He read the inscription written
in dazzling light on the throne of the Divinity : " *There is but
one God, and Mahomet is His Prophet!*" He announces that he
has been sent to re-establish the ancient worship in its full purity;
that Abraham and Ismael, the fathers of the Arab people, were
neither Jews nor Christians, but *true believers ;* they worshipped
but one God, and were never guilty of the impious sacrilege of
associating other divinities with Him. He declares a war of
extermination against idolatry. "The sword is the key of
heaven," cries Mahomet; "one night spent in arms is worth
more than two months of prayer! Whosoever falls in battle,
his sins are forgiven! Heaven is open to him! His wounds
are bright as vermilion, and fragrant as musk." The doctrine
of fatalism he stamps on the Arab mind in characters of fire.
" Who can stay the approach of death ? His steps are swifter
than the gazelle's. Death is but a bridge between time and
eternity; a sweet, a happy eternity !" Streams of milk, and
honey, and richest wines roll their perfumed waves in the
paradise promised to the poor and savage children of Arabia's
burning wastes. He carries away their imagination by the rich
and lively coloring he gives to the sensual enjoyments awaiting
the true believers. An abode beautiful with gushing waters,
murmuring foliage, rich fruits, golden couches bright with jewels,
and unending delights, was to reward the faith of those who
adore but one God, and recognize His only prophet, Mahomet.
The burning eloquence of this wonderful man, his commanding
presence and majestic aspect, the resistless power of his smile,
joined to a superior genius and a dauntless courage in the field,
subdued and fascinated the imagination of the sons of the
desert, where the Arab's tent has ever been the chosen abode
of poetry and the passion of arms. Within a space of ten

years, by the power of his sword and the mastery of his genius, Mahomet had spread his religion from the Euphrates to Mocha, from the Persian Gulf to the Red Sea. He died from the effects of poison (A. D. 632); his last words were: "O God, pardon my sins; yes, I come among my fellow-citizens on high." The Koran, the repository of his teaching, which promises to his fanatical followers every sensual delight as their reward, was received as an inspired book, and became the religious, political and moral code of the Mussulmans. Abubeker, first caliph, and successor of Mahomet, conquered Mesopotamia and Syria (A. D. 634). Henceforth Islamism was to be a power. Its birth had caused one of the most deeply felt revolutions known in history. The struggle now begun between the followers of the Crescent and the legions of the Christian emperors, ends but with the day on which Mahomet II. plants the crescent where Justinian's cross had stood upon the dome of St. Sophia.*

To give acceptance to his pretended mission, Mahomet assured his followers that the Koran was a divine work brought down from heaven by the archangel Gabriel. Whatever this spurious volume holds of truth was borrowed from the sacred writings of the Jews and Christians, which the rabbi Abdiah and the monk Boaira had made known to the Mussulman lawgiver. The Koran is a confused gathering of narrations, visions, sermons, precepts, and counsels, in which a truth is ever jostled by a lie; a rhapsody sometimes lost in the clouds, sometimes dragging in the dust, and where nearly every maxim is contradicted by a contrary aphorism. In a dogmatic point of view, Mahomet rejected the Christian idea of a Trinity, which he deemed incompatible with the Divine unity. He preached the existence of one God, without distinction of persons, whose ministers were the angels and prophets. On this principle there was no Incarnation, no Redemption. Jesus Christ was not the second Person of the Blessed Trinity,

---

* M. Poujoulat, *Histoire de Constantinople*, t. I. p. 210.

the Son of God made man. He was but a prophet like Abraham, Moses, and Mahomet himself. A true Mussulman must believe in the immortality of the soul, the resurrection of the body, the last judgment, the punishment of the wicked, and the happiness of the just. The high Christian view of God's remunerative justice and of man's free act which alone can entitle him to merit or demerit, and hence to reward or punishment, is met, in the Koran, without any pretence of avoiding an open contradiction, by the groundwork of the Mussulman's faith, the doctrine of *fatalism.* Mahomet knew its power to stimulate the fanaticism of his followers, and to urge on their spirit of conquest. The children of the Prophet learned to die like stoics on the battle-field, calmly repeating the words : *It was written.* The precepts laid down by the Koran as indispensable for salvation, are : *circumcision,* taken from the Jewish law ; *prayer,* which every true believer must make five times a day, besides the public prayer on Friday. The muezzin, or priest, standing upon a lofty minaret, calls the faithful to prayer, with the words : "There is but one God, and Mahomet is His Prophet." In Persia the muezzin adds : "Ali is the Prophet's vicegerent. Omer, Osman, Abubekér, accursed be your names." *Alms* are of obligation, to which the Koran fixes the minimum at a tenth of the giver's income ; *ablutions,* as a preparation for prayer ; the *fast* of Ramadan, to commemorate the retreat of Mahomet on Mount Herat ; the *sacrifice of animals* on certain solemn occasions ; in fine, *abstinence* from certain meats pronounced impure, and from all fermented liquors. Polygamy is allowed by the Koran, which thus destroys the holiness of the married state, breaks every family tie, lowers woman and dooms her to a shameful seclusion. The Arabian lawgiver aimed at filling his followers with a thirst for conquest and a proud disdain for all that is not Mahometan. In every Eastern province that still wears the yoke of Islamism, the Christian is to this day called by the name of *Giaour* (dog). Industry is branded by the Koran as the work of slaves. The freeman was born to bear arms in battle, to rest in time of peace, surrounded by every delight and sensual enjoyment, amid blooming gardens, plashing fountains, and the soft murmur of perfumed rills. These two principles, a religious contempt for every other people, and slothfulness raised to the dignity of a dogma, have extinguished commerce, industry, agriculture, and the arts in the East. A good Mussulman would be ashamed to show any sympathy with a Giaour by industrial or commercial relations; he would deem himself disgraced to ask his fertile plains for other fruit than that they bear untilled except by nature. Hence did Mussulman civilization leave all around it to perish when the warrior's spirit sank inert amid the enjoyments of peace and the pride of conquest. Asia was doomed to atone for the spirit of restlessness and fickle levity which had so long ruled her, by a lingering death, in listless silence, under a power which changed the East into one vast necropolis.

3. While the East was preparing these great events which were to work so powerfully upon the world, Boniface V. was closing a pontificate full of pastoral cares. The English Church was calling for his protection. King Ethelbald and St. Justus wrote to him to make known the condition of these Christian colonies and their efforts to keep them in the faith. The Pope answered St. Justus by a kindly letter, congratulating him on the success of his apostolic labor; he likewise sent him the pallium and empowered him to consecrate bishops. Edwin V., king of Northumbria, showed himself well disposed toward the Christians. In order to obtain the hand of the Catholic princess Edilberga, daughter of Ethelbald, he promised to leave her free to practise her religion; he moreover promised to embrace the Catholic faith himself, if a serious examination convinced him of its truth. Boniface wrote him a letter of earnest encouragement, accompanied by gifts for himself and his queen. Gaul was at the same period illustrated by many examples of the highest virtue. The court of King Clotaire furnished St. Arnulphus, St. Romanus, Didier, St. Faro, and St. Goeric. But the usual peaceful atmosphere of some monas-

teries had been ruffled by Agrestinus, a schismatical monk.
He had long been secretary to King Thierry (Theodoric), and
had subsequently entered the religious state under St. Eustasius, St. Columban's successor at Luxeuil; but his natural restlessness drew him from the solitary life on the plausible pretext
of preaching to the heathen.   After wandering through Bavaria
he went to Aquileia, where he soon found himself entangled in
the schism of the Three Chapters; this was the whole fruit of
his mission.   On his return to Luxeuil, St. Eustasius, finding
him still fast in the error, thought it his duty to expel him
from the community.   Agrestinus received this just sentence
as a personal affront, and thought to revenge himself by an
attack upon the rule of St. Columban; and through the intrigues of Abellen, bishop of Geneva, one of his relatives, he
obtained the convocation of a council at Macon (A. D. 620);
but instead of a triumph, it proved only a source of confusion to
him.   St. Eustasius showed how utterly groundless were all
his charges, which amounted to a complaint against St. Columban for having established rules of discipline which the critic
judged too detailed or too numerous; he went so far as to
accuse St. Columban of heresy.   The bishop, finding no ground
for the charges made by Agrestinus, exhorted him to ask forgiveness of St. Eustasius, who had the indulgence to receive
him to the kiss of peace.   Agrestinus had succeeded in winning
the sympathy of St. Romaric, who had just founded the abbey
of Remiremont, thus named in memory of its founder (*Roma-
ricimons*): it consisted of two monasteries, one for monks, the
other for nuns, and both under St. Columban's rule.   Thus did
Luxeuil become the nursery whence were transported to all
parts of Gaul so many monastic institutions.   Many holy men
left its peaceful shade only to found like retreats in the various
provinces.   St. Deicola, now better known as St. Dié, founded
the abbey of Lure, in the diocese of Besançon; St. Valery
and St. Valdalen established the celebrated abbey of St. Valery in Neustria; St. Donatus, bishop of Besançon, enriched his
episcopal city by the erection of the monastery of St. Paul,

under the rule of St. Benedict and of St. Columban. In
A. D. 625, a national council held at Rheims brought together
the most illustrious Gallic bishops. The Fathers gave particular attention to the means of rooting out the last traces of
paganism, which were still visible in Gaul. The council accordingly forbade the observance of pagan rites, the eating of meats
offered to the idols, and assisting at their sacrifices. The Fathers
then confirmed the decrees of the Council of Paris, which they
call general, doubtless because it was composed of bishops from
all the provinces of Gaul.

4. Holy doctors also lent their efforts, for the honor of the
age, in works which do not, perhaps, show the depth and genius
of past centuries, but which yet breathe the perfume of an
enlightened and tender piety, sometimes even rising to poetic
dignity. Sophronius, an Alexandrian monk, wrote hymns on the
chief events of the Gospel narrative, and many odes on the
Christian virtues. John Moschus, his friend and fellow-countryman, had gone to end his long career in Rome, where he wrote
his Spiritual Meadow, a collection of miracles and choice examples of virtue, which the author compares to the flowers that
bloom in the enamelled meadow. St. Anastasius, a priest and
monk of Mount Sinai, hence called the Sinaite, was nobly defending the Catholic faith against the various Eutychian sects which
then divided the East. His best-known work is called Ὁδηγός,
or the *Guide*, a method of controversy with heretics, written in
the close and precise form which has since received the name of
scholastic. He proposed two ways of arguing with heretics:
one of proofs resting on the authority of the inspired writings;
the other of reasonings natural to the subject, and borrowed
from the Holy Fathers or ecclesiastical writers. The science
and virtue of past ages likewise shone again upon the West,
in the person of St. Isidore of Seville, one of the Church's
brightest lights in the seventh century. St. Isidore governed
the Church of Seville for forty years, and left a name linked
with the blessing of many most useful reforms. What Boetius
had done in Italy, St. Isidore repeated in Spain. He summed

up all the human science acquired during his age, in a clear and concise style, that might make known to the new nations of the West all that was good and useful in antiquity. His chief work in this line are the twenty books of Etymologies or Origins, written at the request of St. Braulio, bishop of Saragossa, his friend and panegyrist. It forms a perfect encyclopædia, containing in substance all that the human mind had mastered in the seventh century : grammar, history, rhetoric, dialectics, arithmetic, geometry, music, astronomy, medicine, jurisprudence, natural history, and architecture. To this herculean task St. Isidore added the Chronicles, or Compendium of Universal History, from the beginning of the world until about the year 620 of the Christian era; a history of the Gothic, Vandal and Suevic kings, who had successively left traces of their rule in Spain; a catalogue of ecclesiastical writers, and a work on the life and death of the Saints of the Old and New Testament. These great works, which might well have taken up the labors of a lifetime, are not the only ones we owe to St. Isidore's untiring activity. He drew up and published a collection of the old canons of the Church, for the use of Spain; this valuable collection is known as the Spanish Collection, and the fourth Council of Toledo made the reading of it obligatory in all the Spanish churches; it is marked by a spirit of perfect order and method, and still stands as an authority; not one of its articles has ever been treated as of questionable authenticity. In the preface, St. Isidore says : " To the canons of the councils we add the decrees of the Roman Pontiffs, because their authority, standing upon the supremacy of the Apostolic See, is unquestionable. As for the canons attributed to the Apostles, since the Apostolic See does not acknowledge them, and the Holy Fathers have not adhered to them, they have no canonical authority, and are classed among the apocryphal books, without respect to what may be useful in them."

5. Boniface ended his pontificate amid this array of holy doctors, and the din of the great events which shook the East; the wars of Heraclius against the Persians, and the rise of

Mahometanism (October 25, A. D. 625). He had held the pontifical throne for a space of eight years.

§ II. PONTIFICATE OF HONORIUS (May 1, A. D. 626—October 12, 638).

6. When Honorius ascended the Chair of St. Peter, there was nothing in the religious atmosphere that could forebode the storm about to burst upon his pontificate. The onward march of Mahometanism, first confined to Arabia, had indeed now reached Jerusalem and some of the cities of Syria; but no concern was felt at an inroad of a few Arabian tribes, which was deemed but a passing episode, like those which had gone before. The victories won by Heraclius over the Persians were thought to herald those which the power of Constantinople would renew against the Moslem invader when it thought him worthy of its arms. The West still steadily followed the course which was bringing it all to the true fold. The once barbarous nations, the Goths in Spain, the Franks in Gaul, the Anglo-Saxons in Britain, now saw their kings and their bishops working hand in hand to establish Christian morals and laws. The election of the Roman Pontiff was this time confirmed, not by the emperor, but by the exarch of Ravenna, his lieutenant.

7. The new pope at once used his authority to settle some few questions which alone marred the harmony of the Western Church. The Church of Istria had not yet rid itself of the schism which had for seventy years kept its bishops at variance on the question of the Three Chapters. The wise counsels and prudent firmness of the Pontiff at length succeeded in extinguishing forever the last sparks of the dissension. But to accomplish this end the Pope was forced to depose Fortunatus, bishop of Gradi, one of the two metropolitan sees of Istria. This prelate had shown a special obstinacy in upholding the error. The case of Fortunatus was entangled in a political question. Venice, the city raised upon the bosom of the waters by a few poor fishermen flying before the victorious Attila, had b·

daily growing in size and power. Under the protection of the Roman emperors it had become a republic, and exercised a kind of suzerainty over the neighboring provinces. Istria was subject to it. Fortunatus took the leadership of a faction which sought to throw off the Venetian yoke and put itself under the Lombard power. The Apostolic See, standing amid the Christian powers as supreme moderator and guardian of all religious rights, could not by its silence countenance so great a wrong. True to the principles which ever guide the Roman Pontiffs, Honorius lent a favorable ear to the complaints of the republic against the guilty prelate, and at length deposed him (A. D. 628). The Pope also used his authority in behalf of the Lombard king Adaloald, who had just been dethroned by an Arian faction. " We have heard," he writes to the exarch Isaac, " that the bishops of the province beyond the Po have forgotten their plighted loyalty to their king Adaloald, to join the tyrant Arioald. This is a crime hateful to both God and men. We therefore beg that, as soon as you have restored Adaloald to the throne of his fathers, you will send those bishops to Rome, that we may treat their case in due form of law" (A. D. 627). A misunderstanding between the bishop of Cagliari and his clergy was laid before the Sovereign Pontiff, who summarily checked the disorder among the rebellious clerics. The same Pontiff also succeeded in bringing the Scotch and Irish clergy to the general observance of the Church in the celebration of Easter.

8. The piety and zeal of Pope Honorius, the happy issue of all his past transactions, gave fair promise of a glorius pontificate. But its hitherto unbroken flow of prosperity was doomed to interruption by the accursed spirit of division and heresy, which seemed to be an heirloom among the Patriarchs of Constantinople. The name of Heraclius, so dear to Christian hearts, was to be associated with errors destined to shake the Catholic world. The chief author of all these evils was Sergius, Patriarch of Constantinople. This New Rome, as she loved to style herself, seems to have been commissioned

by the powers of hell to breed heresies, as ancient Rome has
been empowered by Heaven to crush them all. It was Eusebius of Constantinople who planted there the great Arian
heresy. Macedonius, Bishop of Constantinople, gave entrance to
the heresy of the Pneumatomachists; it was Nestorius, Bishop
of Constantinople, who divided Jesus Christ into two persons;
it was to Eutyches, Archimandrite of Constantinople, that the
Monophysite heresy owed its spread. And now Sergius likewise seeks to make a surreptitious entrance for the Eutychian
error, by insinuating that Jesus Christ has not two wills as He
has two natures, whence his error received its name of Monothelitism (μονος θελος, single will). But the Catholic Church
admits two wills in Jesus Christ, the divine and human, never
opposed, but still ever distinct. The question had not yet
been dogmatically defined; still the controversy raised by the
Eutychians on the two natures, naturally called attention to the
operations of the will in Jesus Christ. Sergius openly professed the heresy. He maintained that none of the holy
Fathers had ever taught that there were two operations in
Jesus Christ, and that the person of Christ, subsisting in two
natures, the divine and the human, acted by a single will. To
back his assertion, he forged a letter to Pope Vigilius, signed
by the Patriarch Mennas, and expressing the Monothelite
teaching. This supposititious letter was sent to the bishops
of the principal Eastern sees. Heraclius, who was still absent
on his Persian expedition, declared himself the protector of
the new doctrine, and, in the eagerness of proselytism, he did
not disdain to dispute with the bishops he met on his marches.

9. St. Sophronius of Alexandria, of whom we have had
occasion to speak, and whose reputation was now at its meridian, had just been raised to the Patriarchal See of Jerusalem.
He saw at a glance the bearing of the false teaching which bore
the joint seal of imperial and patriarchal sanction from Constantinople. He placed at the Church's service an untiring
zeal and energy. The two Sees of Alexandria and Antioch
had been secured by the intrigues of Sergius respectively to

two Monothelite bishops, Cyrus and Athanasius, who owed their promotion only to their support of the new error. Sophronius threw himself at the feet of Cyrus, and entreated him most pathetically to forsake the heresy, and not to grieve the Church by the public scandal of a bishop, a judge of the faith, betraying its holy cause. His prayers were of no avail. Cyrus published a Monothelite profession of faith which he read to the clergy and people in the great Alexandrian basilica, and then sent to the emperor Heraclius, who gave it his approval. In nowise disheartened by this first failure, Sophronius went to Constantinople to see Sergius. In his letter to the Eastern bishops the heretic had said : " We know not that any of the Fathers have hitherto taught two operations in Christ. If any one more learned than ourself can show us that such was their belief, we are open to conviction." Sophronius had trusted to the seeming good faith put forth in this letter. He accordingly laid before Sergius a number of select passages from the works of the Fathers plainly agreeing with the Catholic teaching. Sergius met these clear and open proofs only by an unyielding obstinacy ; and Sophronius, on his return to Jerusalem, sent one of his suffragans to Rome to lay the whole matter before the Sovereign Pontiff.

10. Sergius had unfortunately taken the lead of the holy bishop, and had sent to Honorius a long and guileful letter, acquainting the Sovereign Pontiff that the emperor Heraclius, anxious to end the Eutychian heresy, had found the Eastern mind vainly agitated by the idle question whether there were two operations, two wills in Jesus Christ. "The emperor," he added, "asked my opinion, and inquired if I knew that any of the fathers had taught the doctrine of a single will. I answered affirmatively, and sent him a letter written by Mennas, Patriarch of Constantinople, to your predecessor Vigilius. It contains several passages from the fathers which speak only of one will in Jesus Christ. Yet the monk Sophronius, lately raised to the See of Jerusalem, continually imbitters the dangerous dispute. He maintains that we must admit two opera-

tions in Christ. In vain is he reminded that, to win a greater number of souls to God, our fathers used consideration and concession, without, however, yielding any thing of strict precept; and that here, in like manner, it was not fitting to dispute about a question which in nowise hurts the true faith. In spite of our efforts the two parties are warm in the strife. We have written to the emperor to urge upon him the importance of crushing a dispute which may again plunge the East into the depths of heresy, and we deemed it fit to acquaint you with the state of the question by sending the documents that bear upon it."

11. The letter of Sergius brought to Rome the first tidings of a question which had disturbed Constantinople during the past eleven years. The West, more deeply attached to the true faith, could not arouse itself to an impassioned dispute on dangerous or barren questions. Honorius, utterly unsuspicious of the heretic's crafty designs, approved the desire, so insidiously set forth in the letter, of stifling in its birth this seed of divisions and trouble. He wrote to the Patriarch as follows : "We have received your letter acquainting us with the discussions lately raised in the East. We commend your zeal in rejecting all novelties of expression, according to the advice of the apostle. Let us leave grammarians to discuss idle questions, and disdain a war of words which would bring trouble upon the Church." Such was the Pontiff's view. He hoped to see the new heresy die out before taking deep root, and he had the misfortune to treat as an idle quarrel a controversy to which time would add bitterness, which was to sow universal dissensions, and rank among the most dangerous heresies ever brought forth in the East.

12. St. Sophronius, living on the very spot, and therefore better able to judge of the true state of public feeling, did not share the pope's pious delusion. He called a council at Jerusalem. The catholic belief on the two operations or wills in Jesus Christ was clearly set forth ; a synodal letter, signed by all, was addressed to the bishops of the principal sees in the Christian

world. "Christ," said the Fathers, "remains inseparably one and
the same in both natures. But He acts in each according to its
natural quality and properties." Honorius looked upon this letter as an attempt to revive a debate which he deemed it better
to give over to lasting silence. He wrote to this effect to all the
Catholic bishops. "Let us beware," he says, "not to darken the
teaching of the Church by the clouds of our discussions. We
acknowledge that the two natures in Jesus Christ act and operate
each with the other's participation ; the divine nature operates
what is of God, the human what is of man, without division,
without confusion, without a change of the divine nature into
man, or of the human nature into God, but the differences of nature remaining wholly distinct. Let it suffice to admit this truth
without discussing the question whether we should express this
mode of action by the terms of one or of two operations in Jesus
Christ." This passage of the Pontiff's letter shows that, save
the mention of two operations, which he thought it better to
suppress for the sake of the "weak brethren," Honorius believed
and taught the same truth as did St. Sophronius in Jerusalem.
He believed Sergius of Constantinople to be of the same mind ;
and in his eyes there was question only of checking an aimless
war of words, while he thought that all agreed upon the matter.

13. St. Sophronius at last decided on sending to Rome
Stephen, bishop of Dora, his chief suffragan, to warn the Sovereign Pontiff of the state of the question, and of the dangers
which threatened the faith in the East. But Stephen reached
Rome only to learn that Honorius was no more. Sophronius
himself had gone to the grave some months before the Pope
(A. D. 638). The holy Patriarch had lived to weep over the
capture of the holy city by the Mahometans, and to see the
standard of their false prophet planted on the spot where Jesus
Christ had died for the world's redemption. Abubekér's successor, the caliph Omar, after successively taking all the cities
of Syria and the Phœnician coast, had laid siege to Jerusalem.
The emperor Heraclius, less successful against the Mussulmans than against the Persians, gave up the holy city to its

wretched fate. He had but time to convey the wood of the true cross to Constantinople. Omar entered Jerusalem less like an angered conqueror than as a pious pilgrim. He showed the deepest veneration to the places hallowed by the Saviour's passion, and visited them in a haircloth made of camels' hair. He would also visit the grot of Bethlehem, where he prostrated himself upon the ground in prayer. He inflicted no persecution upon the Christians. He gave them a general safe-conduct in these words: "In the name of Omar, son of Hittab, safeguard is granted to the Christians of the city of Ælia (so Jerusalem was called since the reign of Adrian), as well for themselves as for their wives, children and property. The churches shall neither be closed nor destroyed." This mild and measured bearing settled the fate of the conquest, and was doubtless the working of skilful policy rather than the outpouring of genuine tender-heartedness. However this may be, the Mussulman power was now, to the shame of Christian nations, implanted in the very cradle of Christianity; and all the centuries that have since rolled by have not sufficed to free the holy city from the hated yoke (A. D. 635).

14. These sad events happily awaked no echo in the West. Spain stood true to the Church. The fourth and fifth councils of Toledo (A. D. 633–636) had fixed the crown upon the head of Suenand, son of Chintilla, both zealous champions of the true faith. The councils at the same time published excellent rules of ecclesiastical discipline. The Gauls found themselves happy under the rule of an illustrious bishop, St. Eligius, who governed the kingdom as minister to King Dagobert. St. Ouen resigned his office of high chancellor at the palace to enter the religious state, and shortly after founded the monastery of Rebais, in Brie, while his two brothers, St. Ado and St. Rado, built the monastery of Jouarre on the Marne, and that of Reuil (*Radolium*, named after St. Rado). In Great Britain, King Oswald edified his subjects by his genuine piety; while Birinus came with the commission of Pope Honorius to announce the tidings of salvation to the fierce and warlike inhabitants of Wessex.

The apostle fixed his see at Dorchester. Amid these glorious surroundings did Pope Honorius close his pontificate, too happy had it not been marred by the unfortunate Monothelite question in the East (October 12, A. D. 638).

§ III. PONTIFICATE OF SEVERINUS (May 28, A. D. 640—August 2, 640).

15. An interregnum of eighteen months followed the death of Honorius. In this interval, Sergius prevailed upon the emperor Heraclius to sign a pretended edict of pacification between the Monothelites and the Catholics. This famous edict, called the *Ecthesis* or *Exposition of the Faith*, pretended to define the Catholic doctrine. The parts were changed, the emperor became Pontiff, and wished to make his bulls binding upon the consciences of his subjects. "We ascribe," he said, "all operations, divine and human, to the Incarnate Word; and by no means countenance the teaching of one or two operations. In accordance with the definition of the ecumenical councils, we maintain that it is one and the same Jesus Christ who acts both in the human and in the divine operations, and that both acts proceed from the same Word Incarnate, without division or confusion." The Ecthesis was, in fact, a law of silence in favor of the Monothelites, who could spread their false teachings with impunity under its shelter. Sergius advised the emperor to ratify the election of the new Roman Pontiff only on condition of his agreeing to sign the Ecthesis. A council of the leading Asiatic bishops, assembled at Constantinople, approved the decree as a rule of faith, and the Patriarch's intrigues were crowned with success. He died in the course of the same year (639), and left the See of Constantinople to Pyrrhus, who at once professed his adherence to the Ecthesis.

16. An interregnum of prospectively indefinite length left Rome in the hands of contending factions. The imperial officers plundered the Lateran palace. This devastation was the

work of Mauritius, the cartulary or librarian, who incited the Roman troops to seize upon the pontifical treasury. The Catholics opposed their entrance into the palace; Mauritius alone entered, sealed the wardrobe and treasury, and sent for the patrician Isaac, exarch of Ravenna. The exarch took possession of the wealth contained in the palace, and sent a portion of it to Constantinople. He had just received the Ecthesis, with an order to have it signed by the newly elected Pope. Severinus, a Roman citizen, son of Avienus, had just been raised to the pontifical throne; but the court of Constantinople refused to confirm his election until he should have signed the Ecthesis. The deputies sent to solicit the imperial confirmation met the emperor's propositions with admirable firmness. "The Church of Rome," said they, "has received the prerogative of settling questions of faith; she cannot, then, receive her belief from any other." It was during this negotiation that Mauritius and Isaac had plundered the Lateran palace to force the Pontiff elect to sign the Ecthesis. Their endeavors failed before the firmness of Severinus, and the emperor at length gave his consent to the nomination without urging an inadmissible condition, and Severinus was consecrated on the 28th of May, A. D. 640. His first care was to convoke a council at Rome, which condemned the Monothelites and the partisans of the Ecthesis. Time did not allow the Pontiff to carry out this system of fearless resistance; he died on the 2d of August in the same year (640). His short pontificate had sufficed to win a universal love and esteem for his virtue, his prudence, gentle disposition, and charity for the poor.

§ IV. PONTIFICATE OF JOHN IV. (December 24, A. D. 640—October 22, 642).

17. John IV. was elected to succeed Severinus in the Chair of St. Peter (December 24, A. D. 640). Monothelitism was still uppermost in all minds. The new Pontiff, following the example of his predecessor, called a council, in which the

Ecthesis was again solemnly rejected. John IV. made known this condemnation to Pyrrhus, Bishop of Constantinople, by a letter in which he energetically inveighed against the obstinacy of the imperial court in upholding the cause of heresy. When the pontifical rescript reached Byzantium, age and infirmities were slowly but steadily dragging down Heraclius to the grave. Alarmed at the proportions reached by a controversy in which he had rashly taken part, and freed from the wiles of Sergius, who had drawn him into the strife, he resolved to withdraw the Ecthesis. He accordingly wrote to the Pope as follows : " The Ecthesis is not mine. I neither dictated nor commanded it; but the Patriarch Sergius, having drawn it up five years ago, during my absence in the East, begged me, on my return to Constantinople, to have it published throughout the empire with my signature, and I yielded to his wish ; but seeing now to what troubles the edict has given rise in the world, I publicly declare that I am not its author." This was the emperor's last public act. The repentance, though late, could deaden the stings of conscience, but it could not repair the evil done by the Ecthesis. While the emperor, one of the last who upheld with honor the glory of the Roman arms, was sinking into the tomb, the Mussulmans under Amru, Omar's lieutenant, took possession of the rich Egyptian provinces. The followers of the false prophet sacrificed to their fanaticism the Alexandrian libraries, those vast treasuries of human learning. The caliph Omar ordered that all the books should be burned. They were used for six months to warm the public baths of the city.* " If they contain only the doctrine of the Koran," said the fierce caliph, " the Koran is enough for us ; if they are opposed to it, they must burn." Science still weeps the irretrievable loss. The original copy of the Septuagint, thus far religiously preserved in the library of the Ptolemies, shared this undiscriminating, unsparing doom.

18. The death of Heraclius (A. D. 639) left the empire a

---

* According to some historians, these baths were four thousand in number

prey to all the miseries of civil war. His will divided the
power between his two sons, Constantine III. and Heracleonas.
Neither of the two ever reigned. Constantine III. was poisoned; Heracleonas was deposed and banished. These crimes
and proscriptions ended in the rule of a child; Constans II.,
son of Constantine III., was hailed emperor in the twelfth year
of his age. During the ephemeral reign of Constantine III.,
John IV. had been able to write to him concerning the Ecthesis.
The letter shows how his predecessor Honorius, misled by the
crafty words of Sergius, could urge both parties to silence,
without a shade of heretical sympathy, and ends by entreating
the emperor to suppress an edict which Heraclius had himself
retracted. Constantine III. died before being able to comply
with the Pontiff's wish. The troubles arising out of these revolutions obliged Pyrrhus to quit the episcopal see of Constantinople. He laid his pallium upon the altar of St. Sophia, and
turned away with the words : " I abandon a froward flock, but
not the priestly character." The priest Paul, who was elected
to succeed him, followed him in his attachment to the Monothelites. Constantinople seemed to be marked as the see for heretical bishops. John IV. was stricken down by death, October
12, A. D. 642. During his reign, St. Eligius, first a goldsmith,
and afterward minister of King Dagobert, forsook the honors
of the court to embrace the monastic life, and was soon after
raised to the bishopric of Noyon. Gaul was at the same period
glorified by the virtues of St. Amandus, St. Ouen, St. Dado, and
St. Arnulphus, an ancestor of Charlemagne, and the stem from
which sprang the second race of Frankish kings. Under the
influence of these saintly personages, French legislation received
a character of humanity and gentleness until then foreign to it.
The Salic law, drawn up by the pious ministers of King Dagobert, was a marvel of wisdom, and a sign of wonderful progress for so barbarous an age. The Franks had, however, retained from their old manner of life the habit of constant
appeal to the sword. Continual murders and robberies called
for a severe check. Punishments were fixed for every fault

and the Salic law was, in some sort, the criminal code of the first period of the monarchy. By regulating the right of succession of fiefs, and by fixing the great principle of the inability of women to inherit them, it secured to authority a power and a vitality which has carried it through successive ages with ever-growing splendor, until the time at which all power seemed crushed at once under the blows of triumphant philosophy and incredulity.

§ V. PONTIFICATE OF THEODORE I. (November 24, A. D. 642—May 13, 649).

19. The Popes, on ascending the pontifical throne, seemed successively to inherit the same zeal for the extinction of heresy. The independent firmness of the Apostolic See in matters of faith was never more clearly shown than in the question of Monothelitism. Their election was always subject to the confirmation of the Eastern emperors; and yet, with all this power to rule the pontifical decisions, the emperors could not bring a Pope to subscribe an heretical doctrine which they had taken under their patronage. Severinus, though regularly elected, was able to take his seat only after a delay of several months. The imperial court even used violence to make him sign a false profession of faith. Severinus overcame all these endeavors. He patiently awaited the time when Divine Providence would remove all obstacles; and when the appointed hour came, he inaugurated his pontificate by the solemn condemnation of the Ecthesis. John IV. renewed the anathema. Theodore I., immediately upon his accession to the pontifical throne, on which his two predecessors had made so short an appearance, wrote to Constantinople to urge the revocation of the Ecthesis, and to brand the Monothelite teaching.

20. A new champion had appeared on behalf of the faith, within the very walls of Constantinople: it was the holy abbot Maximus. The lofty conceptions and masterly logic of the theologian he made attractive by the resistless eloquence of

the finished orator. Seeing the ravages of heresy in his native
land, he opposed it with untiring courage and energy. No one
had as yet taken up the spiritual weapons which had fallen
from the dying grasp of St. Sophronius: Maximus now undertook, in his turn, to wield them. He wrote forcible and
solid treatises against Monothelitism. He makes an historical
review of the heresy, and defends Pope Honorius, who enjoined silence concerning this dangerous question, without ever
becoming a party to the heresy. Pyrrhus, the exiled Patriarch
of Constantinople, met Maximus in Africa, and opened a public
conference with him (A. D. 645), where the Monothelite question
was solemnly discussed. "In what," asked Pyrrhus, "have
we hurt the integrity of the Catholic faith?" "By making
open profession," answered Maximus, "in the Ecthesis, of belief in one will acting in Jesus Christ. Now can there be
any thing more impious than to say: It is by one and the same
will that the Word created the world out of nothing, and performed, since His Incarnation, the various functions of human
life, such as eating, drinking, sleeping—all purely natural, and
proving the reality of His flesh?" "Is Christ one, or not?"
asked Pyrrhus." "He is certainly one." "If, then, He be
one, He willed as a single person, and hence could have but
one single will." St. Maximus replied: "In putting forward
a proposition, we should first clearly define its meaning. If
Christ be one, is He only God or only man? Is He not both God
and man at once?" "Certainly," said Pyrrhus, "He is God
and man." "Then," continued Maximus, "He willed, at once,
as God and as man. Therefore He willed in two ways, or in
other words, He had the two wills, divine and human, for
neither of the two natures joined in His person could be without its own proper will; and if Christ willed and acted conformably to His two natures, it is plain that He must have two
wills; this implies no division contrary to the principle of
unity of person, since the two wills subsisted each and respectively distinct in the same person, Jesus Christ." "But it is
impossible," retorted Pyrrhus, "that there should not be as

many persons willing, as there are wills." "That is an error of which you made Heraclius guilty, in his Ecthesis," said Maximus. "There are three Persons in the Holy Trinity, and yet but one will. Upon your principle we must say with Sabellius: there is in God but one will, therefore there is in God but one Person." "Since the will," persisted Pyrrhus, "belongs to the nature, and since the holy Fathers declare that the saints have no will but that of God, it follows that they are also of the same nature as God." "I have already observed," replied Maximus, "that in seeking the truth we must distinguish the meanings of words in order to avoid mistakes. When the fathers say that the saints have the same will as God, do they mean the substantial and all-powerful will of God, or only the object of His will? Had they meant the substantial will, they would have attributed to the saints the same nature as to God, which is inadmissible; but they spoke only of the object of the will, which they improperly style *the will*, as the name of the effect is often given to the cause." "Let us lay aside these subtle questions," insinuated Pyrrhus, "which the simple do not understand, and confine ourselves to the profession that Christ is true God and true man, without going into further details." "If we do," returned Maximus, "we must then condemn the councils and the Fathers who require us to acknowledge not only the natures, but their respective properties, such as being visible and invisible, mortal and immortal, created and increated. They also teach us that there are two wills, and that they are different—the one being divine, the other human." "Then," persisted Pyrrhus, "let us hold exactly to what the councils have said, without speaking of one or of two wills." "The councils," answered St. Maximus, "condemned Apollinaris for holding that there was but one will in Christ, whence it followed, in his theory, that the flesh was in Christ, consubstantial with the divinity. They condemned Arius, who also taught the doctrine of one will. How, then, can we call ourselves Catholics, unless we hold to a belief contrary to the teachings of heretics?" "Why then did Vigilius approve the letter of Mennas, Patriarch of Constantinople?" "You well know," replied Maximus, "that the heretical paper presented to the emperor during a session of the council of state, was never approved by any Pope; that is a fable due to Sergius." "I grant the case of Vigilius," said Pyrrhus; "but you cannot deny that Honorius, in a letter to my predecessor, openly taught the doctrine of a single will in Jesus Christ." "To whom should we rather refer the explanation of the letter?" continued Maximus: "to the Pontiffs who succeeded Honorius, and whose holy teaching enlightens all the West, or to those who say what they please in Constantinople?" "It would be more reasonable to rely upon the Roman Pontiffs." "Well, they all assert that it was the well-known and received design of Honorius to bury in silence a heresy of which he feared the results; and that he had never intended to give judgment in favor of the Monothelites. Pope John IV. wrote as follows to the emperor Constantine of happy memory: When Honorius spoke of a single will in Jesus Christ, he meant that in the person of the Incarnate Word, the humanity had not the two contrary wills of the flesh and the spirit, as we have them since the fall. But he did not mean that the divinity had not, in Jesus Christ, its own proper will, as well as the humanity." "My predecessor," concluded Pyrrhus, "misunderstood the Pontiff's words. But I ask pardon for him and for myself. *Ignorance was the cause of our error.* I am ready to recall my errors, and I shall prove my sincerity at the tomb of the Holy Apostles, at the feet of the Sovereign Pontiff."

21. While the close logical reasoning of Maximus was opening a way of light to the mind of Pyrrhus, Divine grace had been slowly and surely working upon his heart. The exiled Patriarch acknowledged the truth, and begged St. Maximus to accompany him to Rome. The saint consented. After paying his homage at the tomb of the Apostles, Pyrrhus, in presence of the clergy and faithful, laid before Pope Theodore an orthodox profession of faith. Great was the rejoicing

in Rome at this change of heart in the Patriarch of Constantinople. He had not been juridically deposed; and the Pontiff cherished the hope of being able to restore him to a see of which he was lawful pastor, and in which he could be of so much service to the Church. The change was unhappily not sincere. A journey to Ravenna, where he met the exarch who governed Pentapolis* for the emperor, changed the current of his thoughts, and he again professed Monothelitism. Theodore I., on learning his relapse, called a council at Rome and took measures for his solemn deposition. The sentence is said to have been written by the Sovereign Pontiff himself, with a pen dipped in a chalice containing the precious blood of Jesus Christ. Some writers say that the same rite was used by the eighth general Council of Constantinople, when Leo pronounced sentence against Photius, and again in the treaty of peace between Charles the Bald, king of France, and Bernard, count of Toulouse. In the same council, Theodore I. also condemned Paul, the intruded successor of Pyrrhus, who, besides his irregular election, had also deserved the Church's ban by his obstinate attachment to the Monothelite heresy (A. D. 648).

22. Sericus and Martin, the Pope's legates at Constantinople, had vainly urged him to sign a Catholic profession; but his obstinacy was unconquerable, and he had openly professed the error in a letter to the Sovereign Pontiff. In his eagerness to spread his false doctrine, he led the youthful emperor Constans to publish a new edict on behalf of Monothelitism. The Ecthesis had not yet been taken down from the doors of St. Sophia, where it remained posted as a law of the empire. The disasters it had caused, and the repentance of Heraclius, its author, did not hinder the young prince from the evil-fraught measure. He, too, had inherited the passion for meddling with Church matters and shaping them after his own fancy. Paul accordingly penned the new edict, to which the

---

* This name designated the territory bordering on the Adriatic from Rimini to Ancona, and extending inland to the ridges of the Apennines.

emperor affixed his name. It appeared under the name of
Type or *formulary* of faith. After a brief review of the question and the arguments brought forward by both parties, the
emperor added : " We forbid all our subjects henceforth to discuss the question of the two wills in Jesus Christ. We wish
that all abide by the teaching of Holy Writ, of the five ecumenical councils and the writings of the Fathers, whose belief
is the standard of the Church. In fine, to insure peace and
harmony between the factions, we have ordered the Ecthesis
to be torn down from the doors of St. Sophia. Whosoever
dares to oppose the order incurs our imperial indignation. If
he be bishop or cleric, he shall be deposed ; if a monk, excommunicated and driven from his abode ; if he hold any dignity,
he shall be stripped of his honors and functions ; the wealthy
shall forfeit their possessions, and others be visited with bodily
punishment or exile."

23. The execution of these threats was not long delayed.
The altar in the palace of Placidia, on which the legates were
in the habit of offering up the Holy Sacrifice, was overthrown.
Those who remained true to the Catholic faith were persecuted,
imprisoned, or banished. Meanwhile a number of bishops in
the provinces of Syria and Palestine, of Egypt and Africa,
raised their voices in several councils, against the violent measures of the imperial court. Thinking minds had been moved
by the example of St. Sophronius, lately renewed in St. Maximus. These African bishops wrote an earnest letter to Paul,
to turn him away from the heresy ; and at the same time sent
to Pope Theodore a faithful account of their conduct. " If
Paul," they wrote to the Pope, " continues to dissemble, it belongs to your Apostolic See to cut him off, by its authority,
from the body of the Church." Theodore did not falter in his
difficult mission, and Paul was deposed. But the emperors of
Constantinople deemed it a mark of skilful policy to oppose
the decisions of the Holy See. In spite of the anathema
hurled against him, Paul was kept in possession of the Byzantine Church.

24. The Monothelite difficulty had taken up the whole of Theodore's pontificate. The rest of the Catholic world was not disturbed by the madness of the new sectaries. Gaul was blest, under the influence of its bishops, with a steady enjoyment of a legislation more in accordance with Gospel principles. Ecclesiastical law began to branch off from the civil. The councils, backed by the sovereigns, established the rights and privileges of clerics. The Council of Châlons (A. D. 644) frees them from the obligation of lodging royal officers, and allows bishops alone to exercise jurisdiction over ecclesiastical property and persons, which right had hitherto been claimed by temporal lords within their fiefs. Spain followed the example of Gaul. The seventh Council of Toledo (A. D. 646) made every effort to counteract the disorders caused by monks unworthy of their holy vocation, who wandered about the towns and country places, in contempt of all rule. Bishops are enjoined to see that these vagabonds be returned to their monasteries and placed under the common rule. This council also published a liturgical canon in these words: "Should the officiating priest be seized by illness during the Holy Sacrifice, another bishop or priest shall take his place, but the sacrifice shall not, in any case, remain uncompleted." While the bishops thus watched over the deposit of faith in the already Christian countries, missionaries carried its light into the midst of heathen nations. Saints Bertin, Mummolin and Ebertran were converting the inhabitants of the Low Countries, and founded St. Bertin's abbey, which afterward became celebrated. Great Britain still gave examples of holiness and virtue to the admiration of the world. Thus the West, ever true to the faith, remained in ignorance of the troubles which were shattering the East. In spite of the Pope's opposition, Constans stubbornly upheld, as a law of the empire, the dangerous decree which silenced the faithful, confounded truth with error, and condemned the faith to mute captivity.

25. Theodore I. was preparing to take more vigorous measures, when he was surprised by death (May 13, A. D. 649).

He was the first Pope officially styled *Sovereign Pontiff*, and the last whom the bishops called *brother*. The pre-eminence of the first See and the extension of the pontifical authority were becoming more necessary in proportion as the Church spread farther her conquests. Moreover, Europe was beginning to form itself into various states: these circumstances called for a centre of unity imposing enough to counterbalance national divisions. Besides, the title added nothing to the real authority which Theodore's predecessors had wielded as widely and as energetically as himself.

CHAPTER VII.

§ I. Pontificate of St. Martin I. (July 5, A. D. 649—September 16, 655).

1. On the 5th of July, A. D. 649, St. Martin I. was raised to the pontifical throne. His name is surrounded by the halo of martyrdom. In all ages, at every period, when brute force is made to serve the purposes of the political or religious passions of a power, the victim is ever surrounded by an aureola of greatness and majesty, which raises his lowliness and sets him far above the oppressor. St. Martin had been legate of the Holy See at Constantinople. The emperor's consent was not awaited at the time of his consecration, and the tyrant afterward charged him with having taken the pontifical authority *irregularly and without his approval*—as though the usurpation of the civil power over religious authority could ever, in any length of time, constitute a prescriptive right. The tendency of the Church, ever since the first claims of this nature, had always been to protest against the abuse of power, and like endeavors, made by the monarchs of the Middle Ages, met with the same resistance.

2 The Pontiff's first official act was to convoke a council at the Lateran palace, in the church of the Saviour: one hundred and five bishops answered the call. Among them was Stephen of Dora, chief suffragan of Jerusalem and apostolic vicar of the Pope in that part of the East. The remaining bishops were from Italy, Sicily, Sardinia and Corsica. St. Martin I. opened the sessions with an account of the motives which had led him to call the council. As the statement sums up the whole question of Monothelitism from the outset, we give it in substance: "You know," said the Pope, "the errors brought forward by Cyrus, Bishop of Alexandria, Sergius of Constantinople, and his successors, Pyrrhus and Paul. Eighteen years ago, Pyrrhus published from the ambo* the nine articles, in which he asserts

---

* The ambo, as we have explained before, was a kind of pulpit placed between the sanctuary and the body of the church occupied by the faithful. Here the deacons read the passages from the Gospels or the Old Testament, on which the bishop then made his homily.

that in Jesus Christ there is but one operation of both divinity and humanity together, as taught by the heretical Acephali, with an anathema against any one who held a different belief. Sergius, Patriarch of Constantinople, in a letter to Cyrus, approved the doctrine of a single operation in Christ; and moreover, he drew up, a few years later, an heretical profession of faith, which he engaged Heraclius to adopt and to publish as an imperial decree. He maintained, with the impious Apollinaris, that there is but one will in Jesus Christ, as a result of the union of the two natures, divine and human. This edict was styled the Ecthesis. Sergius caused it to be posted up on the doors of his church, and deceived the good faith of some of his bishops into signing it. His successor, Pyrrhus, deceived many more, and drew them into the snare of heresy. Moved by repentance, he afterward laid before the Holy See a paper signed by his own hand, in which he condemns what he and his predecessors have written or spoken against the faith; but, to use the words of the sacred text, he *has again gone back to his vomit*, and has paid the penalty of his sin by a canonical deposition. Paul, ambitious to outrun his predecessors, was not satisfied with writing to our Holy See, approving the Ecthesis, but has even undertaken to defend its errors. Hence he was most justly deposed by the Apostolic authority. He likewise followed Sergius in deceiving the good faith of the prince, and persuaded him to publish the Type, which destroys the Catholic belief, by forbidding the admission of *one single will*, or of *two wills*, in Jesus Christ, as though Jesus Christ were without will or act."

The Pope here mentions the violence of Paul, the altar overthrown in the palace of Placidia, the persecuted legates, and then adds: "The world is witness of what he and his predecessors have done against the Catholics, whose complaints have reached the Holy See from all quarters, both by letter and by word of mouth. Our predecessors have continued, without intermission, to write to these bishops of Constantinople, striving to move them by prayers, and reproaches, and warnings through the legates; but all in vain. Therefore have I called you together, that we may jointly, in the presence of God, Who sees and judges us, examine into the conduct and errors of these men, having before our eyes the precept of the Apostle, to have a care of ourselves and of the flock over which the Holy Ghost has made us bishops, and to guard against the impious teachings which seek to creep in among us, since we must answer before God for our stewardship."

3. At the close of the Pontiff's discourse, the original documents were read, which might throw some light upon the question, especially the Ecthesis of Heraclius. The discussion was then opened; the Pope presided with remarkable dignity. He most clearly proved that the term *theandric act*, used by St. Dionysius the Areopagite, and quoted as a triumphant argument by the heretics, had been turned by Cyrus from its true meaning. "The term *theandric*," said the Pope, "necessarily supposes two wills, and St. Dionysius used it only to mark the union of the two operations, like that of the two natures, in a single person." The council held five sessions. The closing one was mostly devoted to reading the passages from the Fathers which bear upon the question; St. Martin then compared the errors of the first heretics with those of the Monothelites, showing the analogy between them. When the dogma had been made sufficiently clear, the council set forth its judgment in twenty canons. It proclaimed the distinction of the two natures and their hypostatic union; either nature keeps its properties, so that the Incarnate Word had two wills and two operations: one divine, the other human. It accordingly condemns all who acknowledge but one will and one operation in Jesus Christ, and it then anathematizes those who seek to forbid the assertion of one or of two wills in Christ. This was an indirect blow at the Type of Constans. Then summing up in a general condemnation the names of all preceding heresiarchs, Sabellius, Arius, and others, it adds those of the Monothelites, Theodore of Pharan, Cyrus of Alexandria, Sergius of Constantinople, and his successors, Paul and Pyr-

rhus. An express prohibition was also published against obedience to the *impious* prescriptions of the Ecthesis and Type, and in general against receiving the new expositions of faith composed by the heretics. The Sovereign Pontiff signed as follows : " I, Martin, by the grace of God Bishop of the Holy Catholic and Apostolic Church of the city of Rome, have signed, as judge, this definition which confirms the orthodox faith, and likewise the condemnation of Theodore, formerly bishop of Pharan, of Cyrus of Alexandria, of Sergius of Constantinople, and of Pyrrhus and Paul, his successors, all anathematized together with their heretical writings : the impious Ecthesis and Type published by them." The hundred and five bishops of the council gave a like approbation. John, bishop of Milan, and some others who had been unable to attend the council, sent in their signatures (A. D. 649).

4. The acts of the council were at once translated into Greek, and sent at the same time to the Eastern and Western Churches. The Pontiff's chief care was to find an entrance at the court of Constantinople for so direct a condemnation of the heresy professed and publicly upheld by the imperial edict. The legates to be intrusted with such a mission could not be chosen at random. St. Martin I. asked Clovis II., king of the Franks of Neustria and of Burgundy, for some bishops of his states to go to Constantinople. The Franks, not being subject to the Greeks, would be less liable than Italians to yield to the violence or the wiles of the Byzantine court. The Pope had been nuncio in the East; he knew better than any other the state of men and of things there, and he knew, therefore, how much his deputies would need a character of perfect independence. St. Eligius and St. Ouen both sought the honor of serving the Church in a mission fraught with peril; but motives of policy forbade their departure. The moral weakness of the monarchs of the first race, disgraced in history by the epithet of *idle kings*, called more imperatively for the presence of bishops who displayed at the same time, as did St. Eligius and St. Ouen, the qualities of great statesmen. The necessity of giving

up a design so glorious for the French Church, determined the
Sovereign Pontiff simply and openly to send the acts of the
council to the emperor, with a respectful letter, but free from
all Byzantine adulation.

5. With a view to maintaining the Churches of Syria, Palestine and Egypt in the true faith, the Pope thought it necessary
to bestow the dignity and authority of apostolic vicar for the
East upon John, bishop of Philadelphia (the ancient Rabbah-
Ammon, capital of the Ammonites). The vicar was charged
to keep the Catholic Churches supplied with orthodox bishops,
priests and deacons; to receive all heretics who might wish to
embrace the truth, first requiring of them a written profession of faith; the penitents might be reinstated in their former
orders provided there were no canonical hindrance: "For we
are," said he, "the defenders, the guardians, and not the adul-
terators of the canons." Several other letters, both from the
Pope in person and from the council in general, were sent to
the principal Eastern Churches. Those to Jerusalem and Antioch were full of exhortation and advice; they show to what a
wretched state Mahometan conquest had brought Palestine
and Syria. Besides the natural evils of invasion, the Mussulmans abetted heresy and schism; the churches, bereft of their
pastors, were given over to the Monothelites. The Nestorians
began to reappear in Syria, the Eutychians in Egypt. The Mussulmans feared the Catholics true to the Roman communion,
because of their fidelity to the imperial authority. It was the
hope of curing these evils, and of repairing so many disorders,
that led St. Martin to clothe the bishop of Philadelphia with
the dignity of apostolic legate in the East.

6. At the same time Paul, bishop of Thessalonica, sent to
the Pope synodal letters containing his profession of faith. St.
Martin found them tainted with Monothelitism. The deputies
asserted that whatever was reprehensible in the profession
should be ascribed to want of thought; that Paul was at heart
a true Catholic, and that he would prove himself ready to correct whatever his letters might contain in opposition to the

orthodox teaching. As there was no reason to suspect treachery, the Pope was satisfied with these representations, and he
feared, besides, the effects of a useless scandal; he accordingly
contented himself with directing his legates to require from
Paul the necessary recantation. But the false bishop deceived
the legates and gave them another imperfect profession of
faith. St. Martin now felt the necessity of acting vigorously.
The legates who had been guilty of receiving a questionable
profession of faith were subjected to canonical penance, and
Paul was deposed from the episcopal dignity.

7. The attachment displayed by the holy Pontiff for the
Catholic faith was paralleled by the obstinacy with which the
emperor of Constantinople pursued his perverse course. The
struggle now dropped its character of dogmatical discussion to
put on the fearful shape of persecution. Constans was powerless
to hinder the mighty and fearless voice that went forth from
the Roman See to defend the true faith, from reaching the
remotest parts of the earth. He thought that in murdering the
Pontiff, he should by the same blow crush the teaching, and to
this end he directed all the workings of his policy. His chamberlain, Olympius, was sent as exarch to Italy, with precise
orders to assassinate the Roman Pontiff. Worthy minister of
the imperial rage, Olympius prepared every thing that could
promise success to the plot. The day and hour were set.
An officer was to seize the occasion of the Pope's stooping to
give communion to the people, to strike the fatal blow. But
when the appointed hour came, whether the appearance of the
Sovereign Pontiff, or the horror of the crime he was about to
commit in the midst of so tremendous a solemnity, made too
deep an impression on the officer's mind, or whether, according
to some historians, *Divine Providence threw the ægis of its protection over the Sovereign Pontiff*, the murderer dared not attempt
the life of the august victim. He came back to the exarch,
declaring that he could never find courage to attack a holy
Pontiff whom God protected. Olympius, acknowledging the
interposition of Providence, proceeded no farther in his crim-

inal design; he threw himself at the Pope's feet, confessed
the whole transaction, begged forgiveness, which was readily
granted, then passed into Sicily with his army, to attack the
Saracens, who had already gained a footing there.

8. The emperor Constans was not disarmed by the failure
of his first attempt. He wished this time to make his revenge
sure. To this end he determined to have the Sovereign Pontiff forcibly carried off. This duty he intrusted to Theodore
Calliopas, whom he made exarch of Italy after the destitution
of Olympius. The pretexts by which Constans sought to give
color to his violence were grounded on various grievances
which he ascribed to St. Martin. He charged the holy Pope
with heresy, and reproached him with not honoring the Blessed
Virgin as Mother of God. This charge of Nestorianism was
constantly thrown up to the Catholics by the Monothelites and
Eutychians. In fine, he accused St. Martin of treachery, and
pretended that he had furnished means to the Saracens. This
last charge was founded on an act of generous liberality of the
Pope, who, on hearing of the ravages committed by the Saracens in Sicily, had sent sums of money to ransom the prisoners held by them. The malice of the Pope's enemies had so
distorted this simple act of Christian charity, that it was
currently reported in Constantinople that the Pope had sent
subsidies to the Saracens to enable them to carry on their disastrous war against the empire. On learning the designs of
his enemies against him, St. Martin withdrew, with his clergy,
into the basilica of St. John Lateran. He had already enclosed
himself there, when the exarch, Theodore Calliopas, and his
chamberlain, Theodore Peliurus, reached Rome. The Pope
was ill and could not go out to meet them, as was customary;
but he sent several of the most distinguished among his
clergy. The exarch at first made use of cunning, fearing lest
the Pope should meditate a defence; but on finding his mistake by a search both of the Lateran church and palace, he
made his appearance at the head of a body of troops. The
Pope lay ill at the door of the basilica. The soldiers entered.

under arms, without the least respect for the majesty of the
holy place. Calliopas showed the priests and deacons his
written order from the emperor to depose St. Martin and
remove him to Constantinople. The clergy with one voice
declared that *the belief of Martin was the only true one.* Calliopas feigned great reluctance in the fulfilment of his mission;
declared that *he himself held no other creed; but that the emperor's strict order obliged him to act thus.* The Pope made no
resistance, in spite of the prayers and counsels of most of his
clergy. "I would rather," he said, "die ten times than cause
the death of a single person." The only favor he asked was
that he might be allowed to choose some members of his clergy
to accompany him. The request was ostensibly granted, but
Calliopas contrived to avoid its fulfilment. On the following
night the Pope was secretly embarked on the Tiber, and the
gates of the city were shut after him, lest some of his clergy
should endeavor to follow him.

9. The guards who were in charge of the holy Pontiff
stopped at the island of Naxos, where the Pope remained
for the space of a year. He suffered severely during the
whole journey, and never left the ship which was his prison.
Until his arrival at Naxos no relief had been afforded him;
but here the bishops and faithful of the island received him
with the greatest reverence, loaded him with gifts, and did all
in their power to soothe his sufferings. But their care was
rendered fruitless by the cruelty of his guards. The soldiers
robbed him of all that had been furnished him by the charity
of the faithful, and overwhelmed him with insults and outrages;
they often even ill-treated those who dared to visit the august
prisoner. "Whoever loves this man," they said, "is an enemy
of the state." The Pope at length left Naxos and reached
Constantinople. From four o'clock in the morning until the
same hour in the evening he was left on the quay, stretched
upon a coarse pallet, and exposed to the insults of a rude and
furious rabble. He was thence transferred to a prison where
he passed three months. From his solitary dungeon he wrote

two letters to the exarch, to clear himself of the charges brought against him. One of his letters describes the sufferings and the cruelty he had undergone, and closes with these words of mildness toward his executioners: "But my hope is in God, who sees all things. When He has taken me from this life, He will vouchsafe to remember those who have persecuted me, and bring them to repentance." After three months of the strictest confinement, the Pope was carried to the treasurer's apartment, for illness left him no strength to walk. Constans had ordered the senate to meet, in order to examine the holy Pontiff; the persecutors wished to keep up some outward appearance of regularity in a case where the most sacred rights had been outrageously trampled under foot The treasurer ordered the Pope to stand; this was the refinement of cruelty. St. Martin could not obey by reason of his weakness; he was accordingly supported by two soldiers, and in this state underwent a most brutal examination.

10. And now appeared the holy Pontiff's gentle patience. The treasurer first questioned the heroic martyr: "Answer me, wretch!" said he, "what harm has the emperor done you? Did he confiscate your property? Did he inflict violence upon you?" St. Martin was silent. Deeds spoke too plainly of themselves. The angry treasurer then continued: "Do you not answer? Your accusers will soon appear." The accusers were twenty in number, mostly soldiers, or the dregs of the people. On seeing this characteristic array the Pope asked with a smile: "Are these the witnesses? Is this your trial?" Then seeing that they were required to swear upon the Gospels, the Pope, turning to the magistrates, exclaimed: "I beseech you, for the love of God, do not put them to the oath. Let them say what they will. And you, do what is enjoined you. Why thus perjure their souls?" The first false witness, pointing to the Pope, cried out: "Had he fifty heads he would deserve to lose them for conspiring in the West, with the late exarch Olympius, against the emperor." To this direct charge the Pontiff replied that he had never betrayed

the emperor's interest in political matters, but that he could not obey him when the faith was jeoparded. "Talk not of faith," said the calumniator, "we are treating of a civil offence. We are all Christians and orthodox; the Romans and ourselves." "Would to God it were so," exclaimed the Pope. "Yet on the last dread day, I shall bear witness against you concerning this faith." "Why then," he was asked, "did you not oppose Olympius when you saw him betray the emperor, his master?" "How," replied the Pope, "could I resist Olympius, who commanded all the forces in Italy? Did I make him exarch? But I entreat you, in God's name, to accomplish as soon as possible the work enjoined you. God knows what a rich reward you are preparing for me."

11. As soon as the report of this examination had been laid before the emperor, the treasurer came back and dared to lay his sacrilegious hands upon the Lord's anointed. He but obeyed the order of Constans, who looked on from a spot in which he could see without being seen. A soldier, by order of the treasurer, tore away the Pontiff's mantle, and then stripped him of his other insignia of authority. The holy Pope, reduced almost to a state of nudity, was loaded with chains and dragged through the streets of the city. Under all these outrages, the martyr's great soul was as calm as if he had stood in the midst of his pious faithful. He ever showed his executioners a mild and unruffled countenance, and never ceased to pray for them. On reaching the prætorium, he was thrown into the prison reserved for thieves and murderers: here he passed nearly a whole day without food. The Patriarch Paul had fallen ill during these unnatural events; the emperor visited and thought to please him by telling him how the Pope had been treated. Paul, heaving a deep sigh, turned toward the wall, with the exclamation: "Alas! this will set the seal upon my condemnation!" He died eight days after. Pyrrhus, whose relapse had won him back the emperor's favor, came to sit upon the episcopal throne of a city in which the Pope was pining in a dungeon. Death bereft him of the en-

joyment of his apostasy, after the short interval of five months. The emperor dared not consummate his crime by laying murderous hands upon a victim so august; the Pontiff was accordingly banished to the Tauric Chersonese. Before his departure, the faithful of Constantinople obtained permission to take their leave of him. When they looked upon the Pontiff loaded with chains, wasted by a long and severe illness, they could not restrain their tears. St. Martin, who alone *possessed his soul in peace*, said to the weeping throng: "These sufferings are my greatest happiness. Why do you pity me, instead of sharing my joy?" The Pope reached his place of exile in the month of May, A. D. 655. His sufferings, which seemed to have reached their climax, were even yet increased. "Hunger and want," he wrote to his clergy, "have reached such a pitch in this country, that bread is but spoken of, never seen." He might reasonably have expected that the Roman Church, whose alms he had always so generously dispensed, would not overlook the exiled Pontiff's distress. But the cruel precautions taken by Constans debarred the holy martyr from all relief. The Pope complains of his abandonment and misery in a tone of such true charity that we deem his words worthy of being quoted. "We are," he says, "not only cut off from the rest of the world, but in some sort buried alive in the midst of an almost wholly heathen people, destitute of the least trace of humanity, bereft of even the natural pity that dwells in a barbarian's heart. We receive but a scanty pittance from without, and I have been enabled to obtain only a measure of wheat at the cost of four golden ases. That I receive no relief is as strange as it is true; but I bless the Lord, who sends us sufferings according to His good pleasure. I beseech Him, through the intercession of St. Peter, to keep you firm in the true faith, *especially the pastor who now governs you.* As for this wretched body, the Lord will have a care of it. He is nigh. Why am I troubled? For I trust in His mercy, which will soon bring my course to an end."

12. The pastor of whom St. Martin spoke was Eugenius,

who afterward succeeded him under the title of Eugenius I. Fearful of falling into the hands of a Monothelite Pope, the faithful at Rome had chosen him to govern during St. Martin's captivity. The words we quoted above from a letter of the august exile would seem to imply that Eugenius I. was already Sovereign Pontiff, which could not be without the consent and voluntary resignation of the lawful Pontiff. Some historians, however, and Baronius among others, think that while St. Martin lived, Eugenius was but vicar of the Holy See, and that he became Sovereign Pontiff only on the death of St. Martin. Whatever may be the result of this historical discussion so long agitated, and in which the Church's enemies have claimed to find an argument against the ever-present authority which must preside over her destinies, it is certain, as we have just seen, that St. Martin did not protest against the authority exercised by Eugenius, whether it was delegated or titulary. It is evident that St. Martin, instead of calling Eugenius *the pastor of the Roman Church*, would have styled him a usurper, had he not been lawfully clothed with the spiritual power. It is, therefore, unquestionable that the authority of the Roman Pontiff had not ceased to be visible in the Church; that the light *set upon a mountain* continued, amid the most trying circumstances, to enlighten the whole world. It is of little consequence, then, to determine whether or not the pontificate of Eugenius began during the life of St. Martin. This is only an historical point, on which we have no conclusive documents. The imprisonment and exile of St. Martin account but too well for the disappearance of the written evidence which might throw light upon the matter.

13. The prayer of the august exile, that God would speedily call him to the glory of heaven, was soon granted. He died on the 16th of September, A. D. 655, a martyr of the faith he had so nobly defended. In writing his history, we have been often and forcibly reminded of great analogous misfortunes which we shall have to treat in speaking of a period much nearer to our own. In either case, material force has

been engaged with spiritual authority ; in either case, also, the Vicar of Jesus Christ, rudely torn from the pontifical city, violently dragged into exile, has shown himself worthy to suffer for the name of his Master; in either case the truth has been victorious, powerful oppression overcome, downtrodden weakness risen up triumphant.

§ II. PONTIFICATE OF EUGENIUS I. (September 16, A. D. 655— June 1, 658).

14. The death of St. Martin I. did not leave the pontifical throne vacant. Eugenius I. continued to govern the Church. His wisdom, prudence, and moderation were equal to the events which called for their exercise. Peter, who had just succeeded Pyrrhus in the See of Constantinople, and who was as much an abettor of Monothelitism as his predecessor, hoped to insnare the new Pontiff's watchfulness, and sent him the usual synodal letter, or letter of communion. It was a tissue of doubtful protestations concerning the two wills and operations in Jesus Christ. It might easily have misled any one who read it without great care. The Roman clergy had learned to mis· trust Greek faith, and they were, moreover, justly indignant against the Patriarchs of Constantinople, the authors of St. Martin's sufferings. Peter's letter was rejected. Pope Eugenius pronounced it suspicious and of heretical tendency. He sent an orthodox profession of faith to Constantinople, and recalled the legates of the Holy See in that city, who had allowed themselves to be entrapped by the intrigues of the Patriarchs.

15. The emperor still continued his system of persecution against the defenders of the Catholic faith. St. Maximus, as we have already seen, was well known as a zealous champion of the truth. In the very year of St. Martin's death, he was likewise seized and taken to Constantinople, with his faithful disciple, Anastasius, and another Anastasius, who had been *apocrisiarius*, or legate of the Roman Church. At their

arrival they were separated, and thrown, almost naked, into isolated dungeons. But nothing could shake their attachment to the faith. The fall of Eugenius's legates, held up to them as an unanswerable argument, filled the holy confessors with grief, but could not change their dispositions. "In spite of the allegations of our persecutors," wrote the disciple Anastasius to the monks of Cagliari, "we do not yield our firm belief that, according to the promise made to St. Peter, the seed of faith will remain at least in the Roman Church." St. Maximus, on the other hand, strongly urged the canonical condemnation of Monothelitism by the Council of Rome held by St. Martin I. His persecutors replied that the council was not lawful, because convoked without the emperor's order. "But," argued Maximus, "if the council's authority depends upon the emperor's orders, we must then receive the canons of Tyre, of Antioch, of Sirmium, and so many more which the emperors, misguided by Arian intrigues, convoked against the Catholic faith. We must also respect the *Latrocinale of Ephesus*, which displayed all the madness of the impious Dioscorus! Where are the canons which establish the necessity of the emperor's authority for the convocation of councils?" For this glorious confession the saint and his two companions were rewarded by banishment. This injustice was suggested to the emperor by the clergy of Constantinople, who held the new errors, and feared the resistless ascendant of a venerable doctor, to whom all the Catholics looked as to their father and guide. The three confessors were separately conveyed to the two extremities of Thrace, to the uttermost possessions held by the Romans on the frontiers. Here they were left without provisions to sustain life, and almost without clothing. But isolation and misery were not the most cruel trials they were doomed to undergo: Theodosius, heretical bishop of Cæsarea, in Bithynia, was directed by the emperor to use all the wiles of his eloquence to insnare the three exiles; but the wretched bishop's endeavors failed before the firmness of Maximus. The holy abbot explained the Catholic belief with such clearness and logical force, that

Theodosius, overcome by divine grace, and moved to tears, forgot the emperor's cruel orders, and offered to the generous
confessor all the relief at his command; but he had not the
generosity of soul that could sacrifice the honors of this world
for the sake of faith. He preferred to go on in the way of
error, and to rest upon the favor of an earthly monarch.

Maximus was then, by the emperor's order, rudely forced
away, without regard for his age and weakness, to the savage
country of the Lazi, near the dangerous cantonments of the
Alani. The aged confessor had to be carried upon a wicker
barrow; but he reached the end of his journey, overcome by ill-
usage and fatigue, only to give up to God his glorious soul, at
the age of eighty-two years (August 13, A. D. 662). His
disciple, Anastasius, had died a month before. Anastasius, the
apocrisiarius, held out through four years of cruel torture, devoting every moment of his exile to upholding the truth for
which he deemed himself happy to be offered as a victim. He
wrote works in its defence; and as the persecutors had cut off
his hand, he still contrived to write by attaching to the extremity of his mutilated arm two little sticks which held the
pen. His tongue had also been cut out at the roots; but God
enabled him to speak as plainly as before. The hatred and fury
of Constans outlived his victims; but divine justice awaited
him in Rome, whose pastors he had persecuted.

16. Pope Eugenius I. had died (June 2, 657), after a pontificate of two years. He had, during this interval, shown a
courage and firmness worthy of the successor of the Apostles.
The death of his predecessor, banished for the faith, did not
deter him from offering a steady resistance to the emperor's
solicitations. He might not perhaps have escaped persecution,
had not God otherwise ordained by calling him to Himself. The
struggle of the Sovereign Pontiffs against the court of Constantinople, and the account of the Monothelite heresy, have necessarily called away our attention, for a time, from the sight
which the West presented at the same period. Christian civilization was making vast and rapid conquests under the influence

of the bishops and the numerous councils, which had become, so
to speak, the great assizes of nations. The religious element
which they represented exercised its controlling power over
nations still bearing the stamp of their original barbarism. The
laws, manners and government were modified by degrees. This
slow but rich growth, which was to mature in the organization
of our modern society, was fostered and encouraged by the care
of the bishops and the influence of monastic orders, whose joint
action led to a common end. The benefits conferred by religious orders, whether in agriculture, science, or government,
though denied by the historical school of the last century, have
been better appreciated by those who, in our own day, have
studied out our early history with an honesty enlightened by
a more conscientious and deeper learning. The period we have
now reached saw the faith flourishing in most of the countries
wrested from the emperors, amid the people styled barbarians
by those who, in the West, bore the empty name of Romans.
Among the Goths in Spain, the Church of Toledo, their capital
city, was made the metropolitan see of the province of Carthagena, in the year 610, and during the whole of the seventh century was engaged in regulating its discipline in such a manner
as to serve as a model for the many churches of its dependency.
In this city were held eighteen councils, of which several were
national. The one held A. D. 633 presents a feature not else-
where recorded in the ceremonial of councils, but which must
have sprung from some ancient tradition. At early dawn, before the sun had risen, all the faithful were requested to leave
the church, and the doors were closed. The Fathers of the
council, that is, the bishops and their attendant priests, together
with some deacons whom it was thought proper to admit, took
the places pointed out for them. The bishops sat in a circle,
with the priests behind them; the deacons stood before the
bishops. The secretaries or notaries of the council were next
introduced. The archdeacon then gave the signal for prayer;
all at once prostrated themselves except the oldest bishop, who
stood and recited the prayer aloud. After the prayer, a deacon

vested in an alb brought the book of the canons into the midst of the assembly, and the metropolitan called up the questions for discussion, one being always settled before another was taken up. If any one from without, whether cleric or layman, wished to communicate with the council, it was always the archdeacon of the metropolitan church who received the message. No bishop was to quit the assembly before the close of the session, nor might they leave the place of meeting until they had signed the acts. The chief aim of King Sisenand, who had brought about the convocation of the council, A. D. 633, was to give firmness to his power, in which he had been substituted to King Swinthila, who had been solemnly deposed and was still living. It is worth noting that this council affords the first instance of bishops taking part in temporal government; but we must likewise bear in mind that the Gothic monarchy was elective, and that the bishops, as chief lords, had a voice in the election. In the seventh Council of Toledo, held shortly afterward, severe punishments were decreed against those who plotted the overthrow of the royal power. It was likewise ordained, at the request of the prince and nobles themselves, that no king should thenceforth ascend the throne unless he promised to uphold the Catholic faith. In respect to public penance, it was ordained that whosoever gave it up after once entering upon it, should be arrested by the bishop and be made to finish his course in a monastery. This is the first instance we have of these forced penances. The seventh Council of Toledo also shows us the already established custom of episcopal visitations. The ninth and tenth councils were held under King Receswinde, at an interval of two years. They published canons intended to repress incontinence among the Gothic clergy, so long corrupted by Arianism. The power of making wills was limited, for bishops, to the patrimonial estate they might possess before consecration. The eleventh, held under the same king, A. D. 656, shows that there was still in the Church an order of widows consecrated to God. They are forbidden to forsake their state under pain of excommunication

and of being shut up in convents for the rest of their days. As
a mark of their consecration, they wore a kind of mantle, or
rather a long veil, either black or violet, like the virgins of St.
Chrysostom's day. Spain was happy in the possession of some
bishops whose lives were shining examples of every virtue.
The most illustrious of them were St. Eugenius of Toledo, his
successor, St. Ildefonsus, and St. Fructuosus of Braganza, all
three drawn alike from monastic retreats, much against their
will, to sit upon an episcopal throne. St. Eugenius swayed an
influence equalled only by his zeal. He is well known as the
author of several learned works, both in prose and in verse, but
especially by a treatise on the Trinity, which he thought it
necessary to write against the last lingering remnants of Arianism in Spain. The works of St. Ildefonsus are equally celebrated. Besides the Continuation of the Catalogue of Illustrious
Men, begun by St. Isidore, he has left several valuable works
of his own, among others a Treatise on the Virginity of the
Mother of God. St. Fructuosus, sprung from a royal line,
showed, even in early youth, a decided taste for the holy sweets
of solitude. As soon as he had inherited the great estate left
him by his ancestors, he outran even the most zealous pro-
moters of the monastic life, by the number of his foundations.
His institute counted seven monasteries, some of them so well
filled that the governor of the province complained of it to the
king, *lest no one should be left to hold civil offices.* Whole families, fathers with their sons, daughters following their mothers,
thronged the various retreats of their respective sexes. Fructuosus sought to withdraw to the East in order to avoid the
distractions and honors of the world; but the king kept him
back by force, and, with the clergy and people, laid upon him
the burden of the episcopate, so much dreaded by his humility.
He was raised to the see of Braganza, where he did not put
aside the practices of the monastic life.

17. The same prosperous advance characterized the march
of ecclesiastical and monastic discipline in Gaul and Germany,
still subject to the Frankish rule. St. Eligius of Noyon, and

so many other holy bishops, his contemporaries, still kept their onward course, and the Lord had prepared workmen able to carry out their mission. Seconded by St. Ouen, St. Eligius had struck a death-blow at simony, in the Council of Châlons (A. D. 644). He expressed all his horror for this vice to the queen St. Bathildis, who was all-powerful in the kingdom (A. D. 656), since the death of her husband Clovis II., who left none but infant children. Queen Bathildis was of royal Anglo-Saxon blood, and had been captured by some Norman adventurers. She had been bought as a slave by Erchinoald, mayor of the palace, whose heart was won by her virtue; he offered her his hand, but she escaped the offer by flight. Her natural disposition invited her to a life of solitude, but Providence pointed to a throne : Clovis II. made her his queen. Even in the royal dignity she was rather a modest religious than a queen. She respected bishops as her fathers, cherished the poor as her own children, and only consoled herself in her dignity by making it the instrument of her inexhaustible charity. During her term of regency, she earnestly strove to root out every trace of simony, and to put an end to the cruel exactions which often obliged fathers to sell their children. Bathildis also founded the two equally renowned monasteries of Chelles and Corbie, and when her son, Clotaire III., had reached his majority, she withdrew to Chelles, where she ended her days in the austerities and virtues of the cloister. Bathildis was still in power when St. Eligius died (A. D. 659). St. Ouen has handed down to us, in the life of his illustrious friend, an inestimable epitome of the truly evangelical doctrine preached by St. Eligius with so great success and perseverance. The homilies bearing the name of St. Eligius, but not so well authenticated, are still precious for the study of contemporaneous discipline, and even show flights of oratory which sound eloquence will never disclaim. Great praise is also bestowed upon several models of the goldsmith's art practised in the beginning of his career by St. Eligius;* among other works

* A costly monument of goldsmith's work in the seventh century is still shown in the

are the shrines of St. Germanus of Paris, of St. Severinus and of St. Quentin in Vermandois; but especial praise is due to those of St. Denis, apostle of the nation, and of St. Martin of Tours. Religious retreats went on increasing under the protection of St. Bathildis. Vaning, one of the most illustrious lords of the court, founded, on his estate of Caux, the monastery of Fécamp, which was at first designed for nuns. On the death of Erchinoald, Ebroin, the very type of the savage nature blended with the craft and deceit of a more advanced civilization, succeeded by means of intrigues in obtaining the dignity of mayor of the palace. His name has come down to us as that of the most odious villain of his day. Yet he even gave something to the devotion of the period. He established and greatly advanced, by the care of St. Drausin, bishop of Soissons, the abbey of Our Lady, in that city. The same period witnessed the foundation of the famous abbey of Lobbes, on the Sambre; one at Haumont, by a nobleman named Maldegar, who entered it himself as a monk; another at Mons, which gave rise to the city of the same name, founded by Valdetrude, wife of Maldegar; another at Maubeuge, by her sister St. Aldegonda, and finally that of Hautvillers in Champagne. The great favor in which the religious life was now held won it many privileges. Lerins, Agaunum, Luxeuil, St. Denis, St. Germanus of Paris, St. Martin of Tours, St. Medard of Soissons, Corbie, and a number of others shared in the immunities readily granted by the Sovereign Pontiffs, kings, bishops, and lords. The mere record of these exemptions forms the chief part of the work known as the Formulas of Marculphus. The privilege of St. Denis, given in full by this learned and contemporaneous monk, perfectly agrees with the original, long kept in the archives of the abbey, written upon Egyptian papyrus.* The letters, the orthography, the style, every-thing proves at once the authenticity of the document

___

royal throne said to have been made by St. Eligius for Dagobert I. This witness of ancient royalty among the Franks is kept in the *Museum of Sovereigns* at the Louvre.

* MABIL., *Dipl.*, l. l., tit. 5, n. 7.

and the rudeness of the age.   Clotaire II. here announces that
Landry, bishop of Paris, deems it well to grant this privilege
to the abbey, that the monks may more quietly give themselves up to prayer.   He accordingly forbids all bishops or
other persons of authority to take possession of any lands or
serfs belonging to the monastery, even under the name of an
exchange, without the community's consent and the royal
leave.   It is also forbidden to remove chalices, crosses, altar
ornaments, books, or other furniture, with proviso that the Divine Office shall be sung day and night in the monastery, as it
was established in the time of King Dagobert, and as it is
practised in the monastery of St. Mauritius at Agaunum.   This
grant is signed by the king, by his referendary or chancellor,
and by twenty-four bishops assembled in council for the purpose.

18. As early as the second and third centuries the Gospel
had been preached in Switzerland, on the banks of the Danube
and along the Rhine.   Flourishing Churches had arisen in
Germany, and in the northern provinces of Gaul.   But the
continued inroads of the barbarians had jeoparded the existence of these rising communities, and it became necessary to
send fresh missionaries to these people, to carry the light of
faith to *nations sitting in darkness*.   This noble mission was
fulfilled by the Franks and Anglo-Saxons, the only two barbarous nations not yet blighted by heresy.   Switzerland, as
we have already stated, was evangelized toward the end of
the sixth century by St. Columban, founder of Luxeuil.   His
disciple, St. Gall, carried out the work, and laid the foundation
of the convent of St. Gall, afterward so fruitful of good to the
Church.   Frankish missionaries were at the same time visiting
all parts of Noricum, Vindelicia, and the whole of Southern
Germany.   The relations existing between the Bavarians and
the Frankish kings lightened the task of the apostolical workmen in that country.   Toward the end of the sixth century,
one of their dukes, Gumbald, father of the Lombard queen
Theodelinda, was a Catholic.   Duke Theodo, his relative, who

ruled another Bàvarian province, called to his side St. Rupert, bishop of Worms, and charged him to preach the Gospel to his subjects. St. Rupert followed the Danube to the borders of Pannonia, founded the bishopric of Saltzburg, and left the perfection of the work to the Gallic bishop Emmeran, who is accordingly deemed the apostle of Bavaria (A. D. 652). The countries lying north of Gaul stood in great need of the care of these new apostles. The once illustrious Churches of Cologne, Mayence, Strasburg, Triers, Metz, Toul, and Verdun had suffered severely from barbarian inroads. St. Amandus undertook, in 630, to convert the pagans in Belgium. He was supported by the power of Dagobert I., king of the Franks. The inhabitants of Tournai and Ghent yielded to his earnest appeals, and he founded the bishopric of Maestricht (A. D. 649). St. Omer, who was contemporary with him, labored among the heathens settled along the coast from Boulogne to the mouth of the Scheldt. He destroyed their idols and sacred groves, baptized great numbers of them, and provided for the conversion of the remainder by the establishment of monasteries.

19. England furnished hosts of saints, even upon the throne. The last two kings, Edwin and Oswald, had been found worthy of public veneration. Penda, king of Mercia, became its apostle; he brought from Northumbria and Hibernia experienced teachers, who succeeded, under his protection, in converting the greater part of the people. Oswiu, king of Northumbria, founded the monastery of Streaneshalch, which soon displayed, under the prudent government of its first abbess, St. Hilda, all the order and discipline of the most celebrated institutions. Such was the triumphant advance of the Church in the West, while the subtleties and controversies in the East threatened to turn it away from its primitive purity.

§ III. PONTIFICATE OF ST. VITALIAN (July 30, A. D. 658—Jan. 27, 672.)

20. After a vacancy of two months the Roman See was filled by St. Vitalian, a native of Campania. The hour of retribu-

tion had come for the impious monarch whose power had so
long been abused to persecute the faithful.   Constans II. had
a brother named Theodosius, a youth of the brightest promise.
The emperor forced him to receive holy orders, and to enter a
monastery.   The base and suspicious Constans still feared
Theodosius, though the young prince, in his cloistered retreat,
had laid aside all earthly ambition.   Constans had him assassinated in 659, one month after having received communion
from the hand of his unfortunate victim.   The gnawing worm
of remorse that never sleeps in the guilty heart, turned the
nights into seasons of sleepless agony for Constans.   The
bloody spectre of Theodosius haunted his dreams.   In one
hand it bore a flaming brand, the other held a chalice filled
with blood ; the spectre held it to the murderer's lips, exclaiming : *"Drink, Cain !"*   The atrocity of the crime had roused
the public indignation of Constantinople against the fratricide
emperor, who was forced to fly in haste to escape impending
death.   He gave out that he intended to transfer the seat of
government from Constantinople to Rome, as he "preferred
the mother to the daughter."   He then embarked on board a
vessel which had been secretly prepared.   He sent one of his
officers to bring his wife and three sons, Constantine, Tiberius,
and Heraclius.   But the people had been warned in time ; they
would not allow them to leave the palace, and the emperor
went alone.   As he stood upon the deck of the ship that bore
him to the shores of the Tiber, he turned to Constantinople
and spat toward it in contempt.   This act of stupid folly became the executioner of St. Martin, St. Maximus, and the two
Anastasiuses.   Landing at Tarentum, which was still subject
to the empire, he took, plundered, and utterly destroyed the
little towns of Luceria and Eclanum.   Beneventum, held by
the Lombard duke Romuald, and electrified by the preaching
of the holy priest Barbatus, afterward its bishop, held out
against all his endeavors.   The baffled emperor raised the siege
and withdrew to Naples, whence he marched straight for Rome.
He sought the extinction of the Lombard power in Italy, and

the restoration of the Roman empire. But his check at Naples had already begun to clear away the vapors of a powerless ambition. He made his solemn entrance into Rome on the 5th day of July, A. D. 663. Pope Vitalian, at the head of his clergy, met the emperor at a distance of two leagues from the city, and escorted him to the church of St. Peter, where the deceitful emperor left a costly gift, by way of hiding his real designs. On the following Sunday, after the Holy Sacrifice, at which he had been present, the emperor publicly embraced the Pope, as a token of perfect reconciliation. This was but a fresh proof of his bad faith. On the next day, before setting out for Sicily, he ordered his soldiers to plunder all the churches in Rome; he seized upon all the gifts he had made them, and carried off whatever was most costly in the city. The roof of the Pantheon, which was protected by a metal covering, did not escape the rapacity of the crowned robber. The sanctuary ornaments, the sacred vessels, respected even by the Goths and Vandals, became the booty of the grandson of Heraclius. Constans II. then withdrew to Syracuse, where he drowned all his romantic dreams of greatness in debauchery. Giving himself up to the most infamous disorders, he seemed at times to remember his dignity of emperor only to persecute the Roman Church. He urged Maurus, archbishop of Ravenna, to declare himself independent of the Pope, on pretext that his city, being the residence of the exarch, should depend, even in spiritual concerns, only on the emperor. Maurus, blinded by ambition, allowed himself to fall into the snare. St. Vitalian summoned him to appear at Rome, and on his refusing to obey, excommunicated him. Maurus appealed to the emperor. Constans II., by a decree dated Syracuse, March 1, 666, ordained "by virtue of his divinity," such are his words, "that the archbishops of Ravenna should be thenceforth always free from dependence on any ecclesiastical superior, even the Patriarch of ancient Rome." Maurus held out in his schism and died without being reconciled with the Sovereign Pontiff. His successor, Reparatus, hastened to return to the bosom of the Church. The licentious conduct of Constans was meanwhile revolting both courtiers and people against him. One of his officers murdered him in a bath (July 15, A. D. 668). He went to his grave at the age of thirty-eight years, followed by the execrations of his subjects. He was succeeded by his eldest son, Constantine IV., surnamed Pogonatus, or *the Bearded*,* who professed the Catholic faith. He returned to Constantinople, and made every endeavor to give peace to the Church. Vitalian had powerfully seconded him in an expedition against the Armenian Mizizes, a usurper, proclaimed emperor by the legions in Sicily. He showed his gratitude for the service by making every effort to uproot the Monothelite heresy, that fruitful source of so much trouble in the East.

21. While the new emperor gave to the Church such cheering hope of peace and quiet, Great Britain also brought its offering of consolation to the Sovereign Pontiff's heart. St. Wilfrid, born in Northumbria about the year 634, had begun his course of studies in the monastery of Lindisfarne. Bound by ties of closest friendship to St. Benedict Biscop, a native of Kent, they visited together France and Italy, and spent some time under the guidance of St. Delphin, archbishop of Lyons. On his return to England, Wilfrid endeavored to reform the abuse prevalent in Ireland of celebrating the festival of Easter on the fourteenth day of the moon, on whatever day of the week it happened to fall. King Oswiu, who then ruled Northumbria, opened a conference on the subject, in the monastery of Streaneshalch, of which St. Hilda was then abbess. Three bishops were present: Colman, Cedde and Agilbert. Colman had brought with him his Irish clerics. Cedde, who had been ordained in Ireland, upheld their cause, as did also St. Hilda and her community. Agilbert, bishop of the West-Saxons, was a native of Gaul, and followed the Roman custom. He had with him St. Wilfrid, two priests, Agatho and Romanus, and the deacon James. Oswiu, who was accompanied by his son

---

* He had quitted Constantinople with beardless chin, but on his return his beard had grown out, and the people called him *the Bearded.*

Alcfrid, opened the conference. "As servants of the same God," said the king, "heirs to the same heavenly kingdom, we should all follow the same rule of discipline. The only question, then, among us, should be to seek out the true tradition, in order to follow it." "The custom we follow," said Colman, "was handed down to us by our fathers. We read that it was left by St. John the Evangelist, the disciple whom Jesus loved, to the various Churches under his care." St. Wilfrid being then urged by Agilbert and by the king himself to give his view, spoke thus: "We celebrate the Paschal solemnity as we have learned at Rome, where the Apostles St. Peter and St. Paul dwelt, taught, underwent martyrdom and were buried. The same usage we observed in Gaul. We know that it is common to Africa, Asia, Egypt, Greece, and all the Catholic nations in the world. The Picts and Britons alone, who people two of the farthest isles of the ocean, oppose the general custom. St. John the Evangelist thought fit to solemnize the Pasch in his day according to the Mosaic law, because the Church still followed the Jewish rite in some points. But now that the Gospel has enlightened the whole world, there is no longer any need to bind it with Mosaic precepts. Our Lord Jesus Christ having risen from the dead on a Sunday, St. Peter ordered that the Paschal solemnity should be held on the Sunday following the fourteenth day of the moon, in March. The Council of Nice renewed St. Peter's decree and made it binding on the whole Church. The successors of St. John the Evangelist have submitted to it. You quote the authority of Columban, who observed your custom. I do not deny that he was a true servant of God, but I believe that he would have followed the rules and decrees of the Apostolic See in this matter, had he been acquainted with them. However holy your fathers may have been, is their authority of more weight than that of the Universal Church? Whatever the reputation of St. Columban, is his word to be put in opposition to that of the Prince of the Apostles, to whom our Lord said: 'Thou art Peter, and upon this rock I will build My Church, and the gates of hell shall not prevail against it; and I give unto thee the keys of the Kingdom of Heaven?'" At these words the king, turning to Bishop Colman, asked him: "Is it true that Jesus Christ thus spoke to St. Peter?" Colman answered in the affirmative. "Can you prove," continued the monarch, "that St. Columban ever received like power?" "No, my lord," replied Colman. "Then you both agree," said Oswiu, "that Christ gave principally to St. Peter and his successors the keys of the Kingdom of Heaven?" "Yes," they replied, "we admit it." "Then I declare to you," resumed the king, "that I will not oppose this keeper of the gate of heaven, lest, when I stand at the heavenly portal, I find no one to open it, if he who holds the keys is unfavorable to me." Such was the wise decision which his simple good faith prompted the half-barbarian king of Northumbria to pronounce. The Roman custom in solemnizing the Pasch prevailed from that time forward in Great Britain. Had the more civilized sovereigns of modern England, of Germany and of Russia imitated the prudence of Oswiu, what countless evils would they have spared the Church! (A. D. 664).

22. In order to bind Great Britain yet more closely to the Holy See, Oswiu, during the following year, sent Vigard, archbishop elect of Canterbury, to Vitalian, that he might receive episcopal consecration from the Sovereign Pontiff's own hands. But Vigard died of the plague on reaching Rome. The Pope wrote a remarkable letter on the subject to King Oswiu: "To our lord and most excellent son Oswiu, king of the Saxons, Vitalian, bishop, servant of the servants of God. Your highness's letters have made known to us how the grace of God led you to embrace the true faith of the Apostles, and to strive so earnestly to win the kingdom of heaven, after a long and glorious reign over your people. Happy people! who have deserved so wise a king, whose glory it is to bring his subjects to the knowledge of the true God. The priest you sent us having died, we are occupied in seeking a learned and pious man, a bishop adorned with every virtue, whom we may send you as a fellow-laborer, to pluck out from the husbandman's

field the *tares of the enemy*. As a member of the Catholic Church, your majesty should always and in all things follow the rule of the Prince of the Apostles, not only for the Paschal celebration, but for every point of ecclesiastical discipline. We have received as a pledge of everlasting remembrance, the gifts sent by your majesty for the Prince of the Apostles. In return we send to the queen, your partner, our spiritual daughter, a cross containing a key made from the chains of Sts. Peter and Paul. May your majesty soon see the whole island dedicated to the service of Christ, our Lord." The man marked out by Providence to fill the see of Canterbury, was St. Theodore, a native of Tarsus in Cilicia, once a philosopher in Athens, and afterward a religious. Thoroughly acquainted with sacred and profane literature, of pure morals and venerable age (being then sixty-eight years old), Theodore was the object of general admiration in Rome, which he had made the home of his declining years. St. Vitalian consecrated him archbishop of Canterbury, and sent him to take possession of his see, accompanied by two fellow-laborers, St. Adrian, bishop of the monastery of Niridan, and St. Benedict Biscop (A. D. 668). They met with a slight delay in France, owing to an abuse of power on the part of Ebroin, mayor of the palace, and only reached England in the following year. Theodore's first care was to place St. Wilfrid in the see of York. St. Adrian was made abbot of the monastery of St. Peter at Canterbury (670). St. Benedict Biscop founded the two celebrated abbeys of Weremouth (674) and Yarrow (675). He brought workmen from Gaul to build a stone church vaulted in the Roman fashion; for in England buildings had hitherto been made of wood and covered with boards. Glass-making was likewise unknown, and he had brought over some glaziers, who furnished the windows of the church and other buildings of the monastery with panes. Thus did these three saints, apostles at once of Divine faith and human civilization, spread both among the English people. In the year 673, St. Theodore convoked a general council of the whole of England, at Hereford; ten canons were drawn up, to this effect: "We will all celebrate the Paschal solemnity on the Sunday after the fourteenth day of the moon in March." "Bishops shall not encroach upon each other's dioceses." "A council shall be held every year on the 1st of August." "Vagabond clerics are not to be tolerated, and they shall nowhere be received without letters of recommendation from their bishop." "Foreign bishops and clerics are not allowed to exercise any of their ecclesiastical functions without leave of the diocesan." "Monks must not pass from one diocese to another without their abbot's permission." "Divorce may be granted only in case of adultery, and even then a Christian is not allowed to marry again during the lifetime of the first wife." The usual penalties of deposition and excommunication were pronounced against all delinquents. St. Theodore and St. Adrian then jointly founded the renowned school of Canterbury, and gave their personal care to the youth drawn thither in great numbers by their reputation for learning; they taught them the sacred writings, astronomy, Latin and Greek poetry, philosophy, religious chant, and ecclesiastical computation. Vitalian's wish was realized, and England had received the "learned and pious man, the bishop adorned with every virtue," whom the Pope had promised to send her; that man was St. Theodore.

23. The holy Pope had passed away on the 27th of January, 672. In a council held at Rome (A. D. 667), the Pontiff had reinstated John, bishop of Lappa, in the island of Crete or Candia, who had been wrongfully deposed by his metropolitan, Paul. The acts and the judgment of the council held on the subject in Crete, were annulled at Rome. Vitalian's erudition raises him to a level with the most learned Pontiffs, and he was certainly second to none in the zealous propagation and fearless defence of the true faith. It was during his pontificate that the Lombards inaugurated the new legislation promulgated by their king, Rotharis. They had hitherto been without written laws. The Lombard laws, like those of nearly all other barbarous nations, are little more than a tariff of compensations or

penalties or various kinds of wounds, blows and offences. They evidently belong to a people whose swords are seldom sheathed. The 176th article is somewhat remarkable. It decrees that a leper who has been cast out to live at a distance from his home and city, can no longer alienate his property nor make it over to another as a gift; for, from the day of his isolation, he is deemed civilly dead. He may be supported only by the property he has left. Lepers must certainly have been very common among the Lombards, since it was thought fit to take such severe measures against them. No like injustice is found in the code, either of the Goths, the Franks or the English; nor would it exist among the Lombards, had the bishops held the same control over their legislation as over that of the three other nations.

Pope Vitalian's charity was called into action by the ravages of the Saracens * in Sicily, where they partly destroyed the city of Syracuse (A. D. 669). In the preceding year they had made an inroad into Africa, carrying away with them more than eighty thousand prisoners, who were sold or reduced to slavery. These desolated Christian communities sent their sighs and tears to the foot of the pontifical throne. Here they were always sure to find help and protection. .We saw how Pope St. Martin was charged with treason, simply for having disposed of the Church's wealth to redeem the wretched captives. Vitalian proved himself the worthy successor of that heroic Pontiff, martyr at once to charity and to the cause of the Catholic faith.

---

* The etymology of the word Saracen, applied through the Middle Ages to all Mussulmans, is not positively fixed. Some derive it from a particular tribe of Arabia Deserta, the Saracens, who formed the chief strength of the Arab forces; others maintain that it is from the Arab word Sharkeyn, "the Eastern people," in opposition to the name of Moors, derived from Maghreb (the West).

CHAPTER VIII.

§ I. Pontificate of Adeodatus (April 11, A. D. 672—June 17, 676).

1. Revolution in Gaul.—2. St. Léger, bishop of Autun. Ebroin, mayor of the palace.—3. St. Prix or Priest.—4. St. Lambert, bishop of Maestricht.—5. Growth of Monastic institutions in Gaul.—6. Wamba, king of the Visigoths in Spain.—7. Eleventh Council of Toledo. Fourth Council of Braga. St. Julian of Toledo.—8. Death of Adeodatus. This Pope confirms the right of the Venetians to elect their doges.

§ II. Pontificate of St. Domnus I. (November 2, A. D. 676—April 11, 679).

9. Accession of St. Domnus I.—10. Constantine IV. Pogonatus repels the attacks of the Saracens. The Maronites.—11. Letter of Constantine Pogonatus to the Pope, concerning the reconciliation of the Greek and Roman Churches. Death of St. Domnus I.

§ III. Pontificate of St. Agatho (June 26, A. D. 679—August 17, 682).

12. Council of Rome to restore St. Wilfrid to the see of York.—13. Letter of St. Agatho to Constantine Pogonatus.—14. Sixth General Council, held at Constantinople.—15. Death of St. Agatho.

§ IV. Pontificate of St. Leo II. (August, 17, A. D. 682—June 28, 683).

16. St. Leo II. confirms the decrees of the sixth General Council. Death of St. Leo II.

§ V. Pontificate of St. Benedict II. (June 26, A. D. 684—May 8, 685).

17. Election of St. Benedict II. Constantine Pogonatus gives up the claim of the emperors to confirm pontifical elections.—18. The Spanish Churches receive the sixth General Council.—19. The Holy See adopts the son of Constantine Pogonatus. Death of St. Benedict and of the Eastern emperor.

§ VI. Pontificate of John V. (July 25, A. D. 685—August 2, 686).
20. Election, pontificate and death of John V.

§ VII. Pontificate of Conon (October 21, A. D. 686—September 21, 687).

21. Peter and Theodore, antipopes. Justinian II. revokes the decree giving freedom to the pontifical elections. Election of Conon.—22. Progress of the faith in the North.—23. Death of Conon.

§ I. PONTIFICATE OF ADEODATUS (April 11, A. D. 672—June 17, 676).

1. ADEODATUS, a Benedictine friar of the monastery of St. Erasmus, at Rome, was elected to succeed St. Vitalian (April 11, A. D. 672). During his pontificate, the Franks entered upon one of those crises which modern speech calls political revolutions. The descendants of Clovis, a race branded in history with the name of *fainéants*, were becoming daily more inert and powerless. All the authority was usurped by the mayors of the palace, whose power, equally hateful to nobles and people, leaned upon intrigues and violence alone. Ebroin was mayor of the palace under the nominal king of Neustria, Clotaire III.; in Austrasia, under Childeric II., a prince of the same stamp, the office of power was held by Wulfoald. Clotaire III. died A. D. 670, being then under nineteen years of age, when Ebroin at once gave the throne to the third son of Clovis, Theodoric or Thierry III., while Childeric, the second, still reigned in Austrasia. But the nobles of Neustria and Austrasia, who had not been consulted by Ebroin, offered their services to Childeric and put an army in the field. Theodoric III. and Ebroin were forced to seek shelter in the churches, and to receive the monastic tonsure (*clericalem coronam*), to be enclosed respectively in the monasteries of St. Denis and Luxeuil.

2. In A. D. 673 a new revolution restored Theodoric III. to the throne and Ebroin to power. Childeric II. was put to death, together with his wife and an infant son. This was the beginning of a series of royal murders which ended only when Ebroin himself fell, under the hand of a Frankish noble whose life he sought (A. D. 681). These deeds, it is true, belong to profane history, but they are also linked with the history of three illustrious bishops ranked by the Church among her saints; they are St. Léger of Autun, St. Prix or Priest of Auvergne, and St. Lambert of Maestricht. Léger or Leode-

garius belonged to the highest rank of Gallic nobility. Though brought up in the court of Clotaire II., he felt called at an early age to a more perfect state, and embraced the monastic life in the abbey of St. Maxentius. On the death of St. Ferreol, bishop of Autun, Queen Bathildis raised the youthful Leodegarius to the vacant see (A. D. 659). The new bishop at once devoted himself to cultivate piety, sacred learning and ecclesiastical discipline throughout his diocese. The wisdom and prudence displayed in his advice won him the unreserved confidence of Childeric II., who kept him in his court, and, under the saint's direction, the first years of his reign were marked by blessings. But the majority of the nobles, with Wulfoald, mayor of the palace, at their head, resented the influence wielded by St. Leodegarius, since it tended to repress their thirst for violence and rapine; they accordingly worked together to ruin him in the king's favor. Childeric, misled by their false charges, and not perhaps unwilling to rid himself of a troublesome censor, that he might plunge without stint into all the excesses which afterward rendered him hateful to his subjects, confined St. Léger, without even the form of a trial, in the monastery of Luxeuil. Here the venerable bishop met Ebroin, who had been a prisoner since the revolution in Neustria. Ebroin swore deathless fidelity to the holy bishop. The pledge was not destined to remain long unbroken. As soon as Theodoric III. found himself again upon the throne, the prison doors were opened to the two captives. St. Léger at once set out for Autun, where his return filled his faithful flock with joy. Ebroin followed close upon the holy bishop, but as an enemy. He came at the head of an army to lay siege to Autun, threatening the city with utter destruction unless St. Léger were immediately given up. Ebroin had just betrayed the cause of Theodoric III., and wished to force St. Léger's recognition of the shadow of a king whom he had crowned under the name of Clovis, a pretended son of Clotaire III. St. Léger declared that he would rather die than violate the pledge he had given to Theodoric. Unwilling, however, to bring a general massacre upon the city of Autun, he bade his faithful flock a lieu, and, after receiving the holy sacrament, went boldly forth and gave himself up to his enemies. They plucked out his eyes, which torture he calmly bore without allowing them to bind his hands or uttering a single groan. Ebroin ordered Duke Vaimer to take St. Léger into a solitary wood and leave him there to starve, after which his body was to be thrown into a pond, and the report spread that he had drowned himself. Vaimer led the august victim into a forest near the city of Troyes, where he was left for several days without food. But moved at length by the patient suffering of the holy bishop, Vaimer threw himself at his feet, begged forgiveness for his savage treatment, and obtained Ebroin's consent that the bishop should retire into a monastery. An interview took place a few years later between the barbarian and his victim. St. Léger and Count Guérin, his brother, were brought before Ebroin, whose wiles had again secured the mayoralty of the palace under the same Theodoric whom he had sought to dethrone. Ebroin loaded them with reproaches. St. Léger only answered: "You seek to stand above all laws and men in France, but you shall soon lose the dignity you so ill deserve." The tyrant ordered the two brothers to be separated. Guérin was tied to a post and stoned. St. Léger was dragged through a pond spread with sharp stones, which cruelly tore his feet. His face was gashed with a sword, his lips and tongue cut off, and, after being led half clothed through the streets of the city, he was taken to the monastery of Fécamp, which was to be his prison. From this retreat the holy bishop wrote to his mother, St. Sigrades, in terms of the greatest charity and mildness. "The Lord," he writes, "has freed your children from the miseries of the world, whereas you should have wept for them as dead, had you left them behind you upon earth. Can there be a higher virtue than by loving one's enemies to become a child of God, and by forgiving obtain full pardon for our own indebtedness?" St. Léger still spent two years in the monastery of Fécamp: during this short interval he learned the punishment of all his persecutors except Ebroin. Dodo, one of his bitterest enemies, after holding the see of Châlons, was deposed and put to death. Vaimer, duke of Champagne, and afterward bishop of Troyes, falling into disgrace with Ebroin, was deposed, scourged and hanged. Ebroin alone was left; but he had not yet sated his vengeful malice against his innocent victim; he seemed to thirst for the blood of St. Léger. Having degraded him, in opposition to all canonical rules, he ordered four executioners to take him into a forest and drown him. He feared that the faithful might gather up his remains as those of a martyr. His guards lost their way in the depths of the wood, upon which St. Léger said to them : "My children, why weary yourselves further? Fulfil your orders here." Three of the executioners threw themselves at his feet, asking his blessing and forgiveness for their intended crime. The fourth struck off the saint's head with his axe. The wretch perished miserably a short time afterward (A. D. 678).*

3. St. Prix, better known as St. Priest, bishop of Clermont, was a native of Auvergne. He was a friend of St. Léger and shared with him the favors of Childeric's first years of power. His virtue likewise drew upon him the hatred of the ambitious courtiers who dreaded his influence. One of them, named Agricius, at the head of an armed force, surprised him at Valvic, where the holy bishop was praying with the abbot Amarinus. Twenty of the soldiers went in and murdered the holy abbot, whom they mistook for the bishop. They were about to withdraw when St. Prix said to them : "Here is the one you seek." One of the ruffians pierced him with his dagger while he prayed for his persecutors. One of his attendants, named Elidius, shared the martyr's fate. The three saints are honored as martyrs on the 25th of January.

4. St. Lambert was a native of the city of Maestricht, which

---

* M. Sismonde de Sismondi, a Protestant writer, does not hesitate, in his *Histoire des Français*, to accuse St. Léger of plotting against the life of Childeric II. He pretends that the holy bishop of Autun was convicted of regicide and met a just doom. Every contemporaneous monument cries out against this historical calumny. (Vide *Vie de St. Léger, évêque d'Autun*, by Dom Pitra, who treats the historical question with an erudition which leaves no room for reply ·

he was to glorify by his episcopate. His youth was devoted to the study of sacred letters and the practice of every virtue; and on the death of the bishop, St. Theodard, the unanimous voice of clergy and faithful called St. Lambert to the episcopal throne. The tie of a common virtue bound him to St. Léger of Autun and St. Priest, and with them he shared the confidence of King Childeric II. as well as the persecution of the savage Ebroin by whom he was banished, on the death of the king, to the monastery of Stavelo, where he lived as a simple religious, in perfect obedience to the abbot. After passing seven years in this retreat he was restored to his see by the duke of Austrasia, Pepin of Herstal. He won many souls to God, less, however, by the winning power of eloquence than by the resistless force of example. The crown of martyrdom, bestowed upon his two friends, Sts. Léger and Priest, was not withheld from him. He was assassinated by Dodo, brother-in-law of Pepin of Herstal, whose disorders he fearlessly condemned.

5. The storm which struck down so many illustrious forms did not stay the spread of the religious life in Gaul. The age was drawn along by a resistless current, to thoughts of faith and pious institutes. St. Gumbert, archbishop of Sens, founded a monastery at Senones in Vosges; St. Deodatus, bishop of Nevers, one at Jointures; St. Hidulphus, bishop of Triers, that of Moyenmoutier; and St. Bercarius established that of Montier-en-Der, in the diocese of Châlons (A. D. 672-673.) Still the barbarian element against which religion so energetically struggled, through all these institutions, was aroused at times to fearful reactions. One of the victims of this savage spirit was St. Aigulphus, abbot of Lerins, who had incurred the hatred of some of his monks by the reforms he brought into the abbey. The discontented monks induced a neighboring lord to plunder the monastery, and under favor of the tumult the abbot was forcibly carried off, together with those of his religious who were most faithful to him. They were hurried on board a ship, their tongues and eyes torn out,

and were at length murdered on a little island near Sardinia (A. D. 675.) St. Aigulphus is commonly known by the name of St. Ayoul.

6. Spain was equally fruitful in great saints, but more blest by exemption from political strifes. Amid the mourning throng that followed King Receswinde to the grave (September 1, A. D. 672), an aged Gothic chief drew special attention by the sincerity of his grief. The venerable mourner was Wamba. A sudden impulse seems to seize upon the multitude, they press around the venerable chief, with one voice they hail him king, protesting that none other shall reign over them, and, prostrate at his feet, beg his consent to wear the crown. Wamba resists and urges his weight of years. One of the dukes rose up and said: "Either promise to be our king, or you fall at once beneath our swords. You go hence a king or a corpse!" Wamba reigned. Nineteen days after he was anointed with the holy oil by Quiricius, archbishop of Toledo. This is the first express mention we find of the anointing of Christian kings; but the tone in which Wamba's historian speaks of it, shows that it is a custom of much older date. The new monarch proved at once his courage by overcoming the rebellious Biscayans and Cantabrians, and his magnanimity in the forgiveness with which he crowned his victory. Septimania* had shared the revolt and met the same merciful fate. The archbishop of Narbonne, after offering up the Holy Sacrifice, appeared in pontifical attire before Wamba, and, throwing himself at the monarch's feet, begged forgiveness for the guilty. The king was moved to tears, raised up the suppliant bishop, and granted pardon to the rebels.

7. On his return to Toledo, he promoted the meeting of a council for the province of Carthagena; this is called the eleventh Council of Toledo (A. D. 675.) The bishops first complained of the want of councils which had been interrupted for eighteen years. They then regulated several points of disci-

* Septimania is supposed to derive its name from its seven chief cities: Narbonne, Agde, Beziers, Maguelonne, Carcassona, Elna, and Lodeva.

pline, in sixteen distinct canons. One ordains that "in every province the Divine Office shall be conformable to that of the metropolis." The fifth forbids "that any restitution or settlement be required of bishops, unless they hold personal property, or have before given it to the Church." The application of this canon is found in the barbarian legislation, in which crimes were atoned for by pecuniary compensations, often required from bishops at the expense of their Churches. This abuse the council wished to correct. We also learn from these canons that the Spanish bishops then had power to condemn to corporal punishments such as exile or imprisonment, and that the custom already prevailed of giving communion to the dying only under the species of bread. During the same year (A. D. 675) eight bishops met in the Council of Braga. This council forbids the offering of milk or grapes instead of wine in the Holy Sacrifice, and giving the Sacred Host dipped in wine; "which is," said the Fathers, "contrary to the institution of the sacrament, where our Lord distributed the bread and wine separately." Priests are forbidden to celebrate the Sacred Mysteries without having the stole on both shoulders and crossed over the breast, that they may carry before them the sign of the cross. Both councils closed their sessions by a vote of thanks to King Wamba, who had assembled them, and by prayers for the happiness of his reign. The history of this prince, who showed himself so worthy of a dignity which his humility had at first led him to refuse, was written by St. Julian of Toledo, who succeeded St. Quiricius in that metropolitan see (A. D. 680). St. Julian wrote several other works, of which only two are extant. The first is entitled *The Future*, and is dedicated to his friend Idalius, bishop of Barcelona. "You remember," he says to his friend, "that finding ourselves together in Toledo, on the anniversary of our Saviour's Passion, we withdrew into a solitary place to seek the silence becoming the august commemoration. We read the history of the Passion, comparing the four Gospels; but our reading was broken off by our tears. What heavenly sweet-

ness reigned in our souls! With what unspeakable comfort
did Divine love overflow our hearts! . Who could describe it?
We spoke then of the life to come." The sublime converse
between two hearts detached from earthly ties, forms the
theme of St. Julian's work. It contains three parts: the first,
on the origin of the death of men; the second, *on the state of
souls before the resurrection;* the third, *on the resurrection of the
dead, and the happiness of the blessed.* The author closes it
with this beautiful expression: "What else can our death be,
than reaching the kingdom without end?" Julian's second
work is a Treatise on the Sixth Age of the World. The Jews,
who were still quite numerous in Spain, notwithstanding the
expulsions to which they had been condemned, endeavored to
prove by prophecies from the Old Testament, that the Messiah
was to come in the Sixth Age. But by their calculation, the
world was only then in the fifth millennium. Therefore Jesus
Christ was not the Messiah. St. Julian meets the argument
by abundant proofs drawn from the same prophets, establishes
the divinity of Christ, and proves that according to the calculation of the seventy Interpreters, His coming really occurred in the sixth millennium. He adopts their chronology,
which has been since then generally dropped. The holy bishop
thus divides the six ages of the world: the first, from Adam
to the deluge; the second, from the deluge to Abraham; the
third, from Abraham to David; the fourth, from David to the
Babylonish captivity; the fifth, from the captivity to the coming of Christ; the sixth, from the coming of Christ to the end
of the world, "which last period," says the author, "is known
to God alone."

8. Pope Adeodatus had died on the 17th of June, A. D.
676, after confirming the right of the Venetians to elect their
doges. This fact shows the good feeling which then existed
between Rome and Venice. The Venetians, eager to free
themselves from the troubles of a democratical anarchy, had
wisely determined to choose a more firm and centralized government. They now sought to strengthen their new constitu-

tion by a sacred sanction, which would give them a new and clearer title to throw off the bondage of the Eastern emperors. The Pope, on the other hand, must have experienced great satisfaction on seeing a free people asking the investiture which it deemed necessary to its government. This was an implied admission that the temporal power at that time became an emanation from the Church's authority; and the Church, by granting to others the use of civil dominion, showed her right, and opened the way, to her own claim in some points on that dominion. Adeodatus likewise ratified the privilege granted by Crotpert, bishop of Tours, to the monastery of St. Martin, which privilege freed the monastery from the jurisdiction of the ordinary. Some historians ascribe to this Pope the first use of the formula now common to the letters of the Sovereign Pontiffs: *Salutem et apostolicam benedictionem.*

§ II. PONTIFICATE OF ST. DOMNUS I. (November 2, A. D. 676—April 11, 679).

9. St. Donus, or Domnus, a citizen of Rome, was elected to succeed Pope Adeodatus, on the 2d of November, A. D. 676. His pontificate of two years sufficed to give the world a high opinion of his piety and active zeal in the service of the Church. He repaired the basilica of St. Paul, and placed a marble pavement in the *atrium* before St. Peter's church. He received into Catholic communion the archbishop Reparatus, successor of Maurus in the see of Ravenna. This reconciliation was the death of a schism sprung from the hatred of Constans II. and the ambition of an unworthy prelate.

10. The new emperor, Constantine Pogonatus, had been engaged, since his accession, in defending his capital against the Saracen invader. The Mussulman fleet under Yesid, son of the caliph Moaviah, hemmed in Constantinople from the castle of the Seven Towers, on the Propontis, to the mouth of the Bosphorus. The Greek fire,* lately invented by a

---

* Much has been said about the Greek fire, which held so prominent a place in military operations before the invention of gunpowder. This fire burned under water, and was more

Syrian named Callinicus, destroyed most of the Turkish ships, together with their military engines. The besiegers withdrew to the harbor of Cyzicus, on the left bank of the Hellespont. For seven successive summers they renewed the attempt, and always in vain. At length the caliph Moaviah sued for peace (A. D. 678), which was granted for a term of thirty years, on condition of his paying to the imperial treasury a yearly tribute of three thousand pounds in gold, fifty prisoners, and fifty steeds of the best Arabic blood. The inhabitants of Constantinople ascribed to the most Holy Virgin the happy issue of their courageous resistance. In this war we have the first appearance of the Maronite Catholics, who had sheltered their faith in the caves of Mount Libanus, from the storm of persecution raised against it by the Persians and Mussulmans. This little nation still exists, and glories in having always held to the true faith and union with the Roman See. The Maronites take their name from St. Maro, a Syrian abbot, who lived in the time of St. John Chrysostom, and whose energetic zeal had raised, on the banks of the Orontes, between Apamea and Emesa, a renowned monastery, numbering eight hundred religious. After the retreat of the emperor Heraclius, which left the way open to the Persians and Mussulmans, some Christians took refuge in the mountains of Libanus, and in the cities of Byblas and Cæsarea Philippi. Other Christians flying before the Turkish scymitar, swelled their ranks and their strength. By gradual accessions from Antioch, Apamea and Emesa, their number soon amounted to forty thousand. John, bishop of Philadelphia, appointed by St. Martin I., vicar of the Holy See in the East, gave them as bishop, John Maro, a religious of the monastery of the same name. He was a man of great learning and piety, and had already proved his zeal by

destructive than Congreve rockets. Flame naturally rises, but the Greek fire ran downward, and took any course given to it. The inflammable materials were enclosed in tubes and thrown on board the enemy's ships. The secret of the Greek fire had been lost, but was discovered in France, under Louis XVI. That good but unfortunate king bought the secret from the inventors, forbade them to use it, and sought to bury the dangerous discovery in endless oblivion.

his writings against the followers of Nestorius and Eutyches. He was consecrated bishop of Botrys, with the title of Patriarch, to which his successors added that of Patriarch of *Antioch for the Maronites*, and they are thus styled in the pontifical bulls. The new bishop showed as much skill in the management of secular business as in ecclesiastical government, and enkindled in the hearts of his people a fearless zeal and dauntless spirit which made them the scourge of the Saracens in Syria. The Maronites made repeated inroads on the Turkish territory, and pushed their enemies as far as Jerusalem, on one side, and on the other, beyond Damascus, to the bounds of Arabia the Barren. It was in large part these ceaseless attacks that forced the caliph Moaviah to sue for peace from the emperor of Constantinople.

11. Constantine Pogonatus, thus freed from external trouble, was enabled to give his undivided attention to the Monothelite question, still agitated in the East. Peter, Patriarch of Constantinople, had died a heretic. His immediate successors, Thomas II., John V., and Constantine (A. D. 666–676), had shown themselves true to the Catholic faith, and were declared orthodox by the sixth general Council of Constantinople. But the Patriarch Theodore inherited only their throne without their Catholic spirit; he was an avowed Monothelite. Weary of this domestic strife, the emperor begged the Pope to send legates to the East, and to convene a general council for the thorough investigation and final settlement of the disputed points. "The two Patriarchs, Theodore of Constantinople and, Macarius of Antioch," writes the emperor to the Sovereign Pontiff, "make every endeavor to have the name of Vitalian removed from the diptychs. They are very willing to keep the name of Honorius, but cannot agree to insert those of his successors until more light be thrown upon the matter in dispute between the two sees." The exception made in favor of Honorius shows the belief of the Monothelites that that Pontiff had favored their error. When Constantine's letter reached

Rome, St. Domnus had passed from earth (April 11, A. D 679). The letter was handed to his successor.

§ III. PONTIFICATE OF ST. AGATHO (June 26, A. D. 679— August 17, 682)

12. St. Agatho, a monk of the Benedictine abbey of St. Eumes, in Palermo, was elected Pope on the 26th of June, A. D. 679. The ambassadors of Constantine Pogonatus, on reaching Rome, found a council of fifty bishops in session, to inquire into the unjust deposition of St. Wilfrid, archbishop of York, who had come in person to lay his case before the Apostolic See. Ermentrudis, queen of Egfrid, king of the Saxons, much offended at the high repute of St. Wilfrid at court, persuaded the king to divide the see of York into three new bishoprics, seeking thus to lessen the power of the holy bishop (A. D. 678). Wilfrid at once set out for Rome, to beg the intervention of the Sovereign Pontiff, but he was thrown by head winds upon the coast of Friesland, among an idolatrous people. Wilfrid preached the truths of the faith to these people, whom he had the happiness to bring, in great part, into the fold of Christ. But Ebroin, who seemed to look upon every virtuous man of whatever nationality as his personal enemy, wrote to Adalgise, king of Friesland, promising him a bushel of gold pieces for the head of the bishop of York. The king caused the letter to be publicly read to him at dinner, before Wilfrid, the envoys of Ebroin and several lords; he then tore it to pieces, threw it into the fire, and turning to the bearers, said to them: "Say to your master, from me: Thus may the Lord our God break the power of traitors!" In the following year (A. D. 679) Wilfrid reached Italy, after passing through Gaul, where he was everywhere received with the greatest honor. The Council of Rome annulled all that had been done against him, and he returned to England to present the pontifical judgment to king Egfrid, who refused to submit to it. Wilfrid was at first imprisoned, then banished, and it

was only the king's death that enabled him at length to return to his see (A. D. 680).

13. The Pope's attention was next called to the request of Constantine Pogonatus; he convoked a council of a hundred and twenty-five bishops, and read to them the emperor's letter (A. D. 679). The council renewed the sentence against Monothelitism, and chose the legates who were to preside for the Pope in the general council convoked at Constantinople. The legates bore a letter from the Pope to Constantine: "Do not expect," wrote the humble Pontiff, "to find our envoys gifted with brilliant eloquence, nor even with a thorough knowledge of the Scripture : how could these acquirements have been preserved amid the din of arms, by bishops forced to earn their bread by daily toil? The only thing they have been able to save from the general wreck in which the patrimony of the Church has become the prey of barbarians, is the treasure of the faith such as our fathers left it, without addition or lessening." The modesty displayed by the Sovereign Pontiff was doubtless necessary to disarm false science, the sophistry and vain subtleties of the Greeks, especially as they were about to see five or six of their Patriarchs condemned. For it must not be forgotten that at the very same time, the Sovereign Pontiffs were sending to England truly learned men, who awakened in those yet savage tribes a taste for letters, art and science. If the holy Popes did not tell it themselves, lest the good deed should lose its merit, it belongs to history to speak of it : it is the duty of grateful Europe to treasure its memory. In the same letter, St. Agatho refuted the Monothelite heresy by the constant tradition of the Roman Church. "The Catholic world," says the Pope, "looks up to this Church as the mother and mistress of all the others. By the grace of Almighty God, it will never be convicted of having wandered from the path of apostolic tradition or of yielding to the waywardness of heretical teachings. The faith which she received from her founders, the princes of the Apostles, she has kept unstained, according to the promise made by our Lord to St. Peter : 'I

have prayed for thee that thy faith fail not; thou being converted, confirm thy brethren.' In virtue of this Divine promise
the Apostolic Pontiffs, whose unworthy successor we are, have
always upheld the cause of the faith. So that when the bishops
of Constantinople strove to bring heretical novelty into the
spotless Church of Christ, my predecessors of apostolic memory
never ceased to exhort, to warn and to entreat them to forsake
their false belief, or at least to hush questions so dangerous.'
These closing expressions evidently relate to the letters of
Pope Honorius I., who, misjudging the import of Monothelitism
at the outset, had too lightly deemed that it might be easily
extinguished by forbidding any controversy on the subject.

14. On the arrival of the priests Theodore and George, and
the deacon John, legates of the Pope and bearers of his letter,
as well as of minute personal instructions, the sixth general
council was opened at Constantinople on the 7th of November,
A. D. 680, in a hall of the palace, called in Latin *Trullus*, or the
Dome. Constantine Pogonatus was present in person; on his
right were the legates; on his left, George, Patriarch of Constantinople, the successor of Theodore, who had been lately
banished, and Macarius, Patriarch of Antioch. The book of
Gospels was, as usual, placed in the middle of the hall. One of
the legates then rose and thus addressed the emperor : " It is
now about forty-six years since the prelates of your capital,
Sergius, Pyrrhus, Paul and Peter, as well as Cyrus of Alexandria, Theodore of Pharan, and several other bishops, spread
through the Eastern Church doctrines opposed to the truth,
teaching that in Jesus Christ there is but one will and one
operation. The Apostolic See condemned the error and repeatedly urged them to forsake it; but it vain. Hence we beg
your imperial majesty to order that these abettors of new
teachings point out their source and tell us where they learned
them." The emperor ordered George of Constantinople and
Macarius of Antioch, the two leaders of the Monothelite party,
to explain their belief. Macarius answered: "We hold no
new belief, but one that is taught by the ecumenical councils,

the holy Fathers, the Sovereign Pontiff Honorius, by the
Patriarchs of Constantinople just mentioned, and by Cyrus of
Alexandria. Like them and with them, we believe, we teach
that in Jesus Christ there is but one single will, one only operation, and we are ready to bring forward our proofs."   The
discussion was opened on this ground, and took up eighteen -
sessions of the council, which entered upon a thorough examination of all the texts of the Fathers, and other writings brought
forward by the Monothelites in defence of their heresy.   The
imperial library furnished all the necessary original documents.
The notorious letter of Mennas to Pope Vigilius, so much talked
of in this controversy, was carefully examined ; it was proved
a forgery, penned by an heretical hand, and surreptitiously
added to the acts of the fifth general council.   The three rolls
on which it was written were in a different hand, and wanted
the cipher and signature which marked the remaining pages of
the book. St. Agatho's letter was then read : no sooner had the
assembled fathers heard the clear and strong definition of the
Catholic belief of the two wills of Jesus Christ, than they
cried out with one voice : " Peter has spoken by the mouth of
Agatho !   We believe with him that there are two wills in
Jesus Christ.   Anathema to whosoever upholds the contrary
opinion !"   George of Alexandria, overcome by this general
profession, came back himself to the true belief, and was the
first to propose that the names of Pope Vitalian and his successors should be restored to the sacred diptychs.   Macarius
of Antioch alone stood out for the heresy.   " I would rather
die a thousand deaths," he exclaimed, " than acknowledge two
wills in Jesus Christ !"   In spite of the entreaties of his fellow-
bishops, and of his friends who had gone over to the Catholic
side, he persisted in his error ; the council deposed him in the
same session. His disciple, the monk Stephen, sought to
defend him, but he only aroused the indignation of the bishops,
who cried out: " The question is cleared up, drive out the
heretic !" Every text quoted by the legates had been compared
with the originals and found perfectly correct. It remained

to examine the letter of Honorius, addressed to Sergius of Constantinople, in which the Pope treats the rising question of Monothelitism as an idle dispute, which would be destroyed by mere contemptuous silence. We spoke of this in treating of the pontificate of Honorius. The Pontiff, deceived as to the real state of minds in the East, soon saw that the heresy threatened to grow until strong measures should be needed to cope with it. He had recalled his decision; but the first letter still existed, and furnished the Monothelites with several imprudent expressions which they held up as decisive in their favor. It was accordingly put to a severe test and condemned by the council. We must not omit to state here that Cardinal Baronius and other learned writers look upon the acts of the sixth general council, condemning Honorius, as apocryphal. But the majority of conscientious critics are of a contrary opinion. They agree in acknowledging, 1st. That, according to the expression of Pope John IV., a contemporary of Honorius, the latter Pontiff, in his letter to Sergius, did not teach Monothelitism, but forbids its discussion as an empty war of words. 2d. They think that he was condemned in the sixth general council for the indifference he showed in so serious a matter, for the carelessness with which he jeoparded the authority of the Apostolic See, by rashly despising a heresy so fraught with baneful results. It is allowed on all hands that in the letter to Sergius, condemned in the sixth general council, Honorius did not intend to define a dogma of faith; he defined neither the Monothelite teaching nor the Catholic belief which is its opposite. He simply recommended what he then deemed the most prudent course, not to disturb the peace of the Church by sowing in its bosom the seeds of dissension through the introduction of a new controversy.* His condemnation then

---

* "If the natural and grammatical sense of Honorius's letter is blamable, its general bearing at least has been clearly justified; hence it does not affect the infallibility of the Church in matters of faith. Besides, Honorius continued till the hour of his death to profess and defend the truth, to entreat and threaten the very Monothelites whose opinions he was afterward charged with supporting."—(Hist. de la Papauté, par M. le Baron Henrion, 2e edit., Paris, in-12, p. 128).

proves nothing against the infallibility of the Sovereign Pontiff's speaking, *ex cathedra*, in matters of faith. When the council had ceased its labors, the definition of faith was read. The fathers spoke thus : " By the inspiration of the Holy Ghost, in agreement with the dogmatic letter of our Holy Father and Sovereign Pontiff Agatho, we acknowledge in Jesus Christ two natures with two respective wills and acts. We anathematize Theodore of Pharan, Sergius, Paul, Pyrrhus, and Peter of Constantinople, Cyrus of Alexandria, and the letter of Pope Honorius in so far as it is favorable to them. We likewise condemn Macarius of Antioch, and Stephen his disciple. We have followed the teaching of the Pope, as he has followed the traditions of the Apostles and the Fathers. If we have worsted the enemy, the great chief of the Apostles fought with us, for we were led by his imitator and heir, the successor to his throne, the holy Pontiff whose learning is the glory of Catholic truth. O Prince, new Constantine arisen to meet a new Arius, ancient Rome holds out to you a profession of faith coming from God himself. A letter from the West has brought back the light of truth. Peter has spoken by the voice of Agatho." This discourse was subscribed by one hundred and sixty-five bishops; the acts of the council were sent to St. Agatho, "in order," wrote the fathers, " that his Holiness might vouchsafe to confirm and stamp them by his venerable rescripts." Before leaving Constantinople, the legates obtained from Constantine Pogonatus the remission of the three thousand gold ases required by the emperors at every pontifical election, and it was agreed that the tax should no longer be paid by the Holy See. The abuse inaugurated by Athalaric had been kept up by all the Eastern emperors. Constantine however held to the condition that the Pontiff elect should only be consecrated when approved by the emperor.

15. St. Agatho died (January 10th, A. D. 682) before the return of his legates to Rome, and was succeeded (August 17th, A. D. 682) by St. Leo II., a Neapolitan by birth.

§ IV. PONTIFICATE OF ST. LEO II. (August 17, A. D. 682—June
28, 683).

16. The new Pope reigned less than a year, during which
space, however, he had time to examine and confirm the acts
of the sixth general council. Constantine sent them to him
with a letter bearing the superscription: "To the holy and
blessed Leo, Pontiff of *Old Rome,** and ecumenical Pope."
"The letter of Pope Agatho," writes the emperor, "was unanimously acknowledged to agree with the Scriptures, the councils
and the teaching of the holy Fathers. We saw with the soul's
vision, the Prince of the Apostles himself, in the person of his
successor, divinely opening out the mystery of the Incarnation
and saying to our Lord: 'Thou art Christ the Son of the living God!' Macarius and a few of his disciples alone obstinately
held out against the teaching of the Apostolic See. They asked
to be sent to your Holiness, which request we have granted,
and now leave them to your fatherly judgment." Constantine
ends by a request that the Pontiff would send a legate to represent the Holy See at Constantinople in all ecclesiastical, matters. Leo II. hastened to send the acts of the sixth general
council to the Spanish bishops, none of whom had been present
at the Council of Rome held by St. Agatho in 680, where the
instructions had been drawn up by which the legates were
to preside in the general council. Peter, a notary of the
Roman Church, was charged to present them to St. Julian,
archbishop of Toledo, with a pontifical rescript by which the
Pope directed the prelate to acquaint all the bishops and faithful of Spain with the definition of the Council of Constantinople; to have it subscribed by the bishops, and to send the signatures to Rome to be placed near the confession of St. Peter.
The Sovereign Pontiff himself examined them most diligently,
and in the following year sent as legate to Constantinople a

---

* It will be remembered that, in the style of the imperial chancery, Constantinople was
called *New Roma.*

regionary sub-deacon of the Apostolic See, named Constantine. He bore to the emperor a letter dated May 16, A. D. 683, in which the Pope thus speaks of the acts: "On examination we find them to agree with what the legates had reported: we have ascertained that the sixth council exactly followed the instructions of the Apostolic See, and that it agrees with the definitions of the five former ecumenical councils. For this reason we have consented to the publication of the decrees; we ratify them by the authority of St. Peter, and wish them to have the binding power of laws, like those of the five preceding general councils. We anathematize all those whom it has anathematized, especially Macarius, formerly Patriarch of Antioch, with all his accomplices. We have made every endeavor, as you urged in your letters, to enlighten them and bring them back to the true faith; but they have remained fixed in their obstinacy." This was St. Leo's last pontifical act; he died on the 28th of June, A. D. 683. This Pope was much attached to solemn church music; he perfected the style of Gregorian chant and made several new arrangements in the manner of singing sacred hymns. He also regulated the ceremony of the *kiss of peace* at mass, and the *sprinkling of the people with holy water.*

§ V. PONTIFICATE OF ST. BENEDICT II. (June 26, A. D. 684—May 8, 685).

17. St. Benedict II., a native of Rome, was raised to the Sovereign Pontificate on the 6th of June, A. D. 684. "He was brought up in poverty," says Fleury, "and showed great mildness, patience, liberality, application to the study of sacred literature, and a great knowledge of the rules of ecclesiastical chant." Constantine IV., who was personally acquainted with him, and could appreciate his lofty qualities, decreed that the Papal elections should no longer need the confirmation either of the emperor or of the exarch of Ravenna. Rome had long sought this favor in vain; and now it was doomed to be but

short-lived, for Justinian II., son and successor of Constantine Pogonatüs, regardless of his father's decision, renewed the abuse by charging the exarch of Ravenna to confirm the election of Pope Conon.

18. King Ervig, who had succeeded Wamba in the government of Spain, received a letter (A. D. 684) from the new Pope, urging him to require the subscription of the Spanish bishops to the decrees of the sixth general council. Provincial councils were accordingly held throughout the whole of Spain. The belief of the Roman Church was universally received. The fourteenth of Toledo, besides the subscription of its eighteen bishops, sent to Pope Benedict a special work, treating the Monothelite question *ex professo*. The Sovereign Pontiff found in this memorial several doubtful expressions which might give rise to errors or disputes, but refrained, through delicacy, from mentioning the fact in the letter of acknowledgment addressed by him to the archbishop of Toledo. He merely spoke of it to the deputies of the Spanish bishops, who replied in the course of the same year by a full explanation and vindication of their memorial. Meanwhile the Pope was doing his utmost to bring back Macarius of Antioch, still an exile in Rome. He gave him a final delay of six weeks, and daily sent a Catholic doctor to confer with him; but the heretic would not bend, and the Pope was forced to confirm the condemnations pronounced against him.

19. The last days of Benedict II. were marked by a political event showing the importance of the position now held by the Papacy. The declining years of Constantine Pogonatus were not free from care concerning the future welfare of his two sons, especially of Justinian, the elder, whom he designed to make his successor. Conspiracies were rife even in the bosom of the court, headed by the emperor's two brothers, uncles to the young princes; moreover, he had met with several repulses from the Bulgarians, to whom he had been forced to pay tribute. In these intricate circumstances, Constantine IV. deemed it prudent to secure for his sons the protection of the Sovereign

Pontiff, and with this view he sent to Rome tresses of their hair, which were received by the Pope, the clergy and the army. This was the ceremony of adoption then in use, and he who received a youth's hair was looked upon as his father. The Holy See was indeed the only institution which then showed signs of lasting firmness. Whoever wished to live, must lean upon that support. Pope Benedict II. died soon after this adoption, which placed the Cæsars of Constantinople under the care of the Roman Pontiff (May 8, A. D. 685). Constantine IV. outlived him but a few months (September, A. D. 685), and left behind a high reputation as a pious, skilful, wise and valiant prince. His son and successor, Justinian II., proved himself unworthy of the apostolic adoption, and seemed bent by his misrule and disorders upon increasing the general regret for his father.

§ VI. Pontificate of John V. (July 25, A. D. 685—August 2, 686).

20. John V. was elected on the 25th of July, A. D. 685, to succeed St. Benedict II. He was one of the legates sent by Pope Agatho to the sixth general council, where he had shown a depth of learning equalled by his ability and moderation. His election was carried out according to the lawful system so long departed from, that is, without interference of the civil power by the Eastern emperor. He was proclaimed Pope in the Lateran palace by the unanimous voice of clergy and people, and was at once escorted to the pontifical palace, where he was consecrated on the next day by the three bishops of Ostia, Porto and Velletri. He reigned but a year, during which time, however, he brought back the Churches of Sardinia to the jurisdiction of the Roman See, from which they had been transferred to that of the archbishops of Cagliari; but as these prelates began to abuse the right, a decree of Pope Martin I. had already withdrawn it. In spite of this prohibition, Citonatus, archbishop of Cagliari, had consecrated Novellus for the Church

of Torres, without asking leave from John V.; the Pope called a
council, which restored Novellus to the immediate jurisdiction
of the Holy See by a formal act kept in the archives of the Roman Church. John V. died on the 2d of August, A. D. 686, worn
out by a long life of toil devoted to the service of the Church.
The shattered state of his health hardly allowed him to perform
form the episcopal ordinations which the ancient authors always
reckoned among the Pope's most regular duties.

§ VII. PONTIFICATE OF CONON (October 21, A. D. 686—September 21, 687).

21. Justinian II. had revoked his father's decree in favor
of pontifical elections, and made them again subject to the
approval of the exarch of Ravenna. The odious measure soon
bore its natural fruit. Two antipopes, Peter and Theodore,
upheld respectively by the clergy, and the civil and military
power, contended for the pontifical throne during two months
after the death of John V. At length the clergy determined
to do away with all irregularity by giving their votes to Conon,
a native of Temeswar, in Lower Mysia. The newly elected
Pontiff was a venerable old man, upright, plain, peaceable, a
stranger to the spirit of faction, but little skilled in business.
He was obliged to ask the consent of the exarch of Ravenna
for his consecration.. Justinian II. sent two letters to the exarch ordering the recognition, and as if to smooth over the
unjust imposition by a largess, the ward of the Holy See, so
soon freed from tutelage, remitted the tax paid to the court of
Constantinople by the ecclesiastical property in Brutium and
Lucania; he likewise ordered the restitution of the serfs attached to the property, as also those of Sicily, who were held
by the troops as hostages.

22. During the quick succession of pontificates in Rome,
from Domnus to Conon, the faith was making great progress
under the zealous workmen who enlightened the pagans of Germany St. Willibrord, a native of Northumberland, disciple

of St. Wilfrid, and St. Vulfran, born at Maurillac (now Milly, near Etampes), devoted themselves to the conversion of Friesland, and were struggling by a life of wonders against the cruelty and superstition of Radbod, duke of that country. The two saints Ewald, apostles of the Saxons, died for the faith on the banks of the Rhine. St. Kilian, who belonged to an illustrious house in Great Britain, sought and obtained leave from Conon to preach the Gospel in Franconia. His mission was very fruitful at Wurtzburg, where he however incurred the unjust hatred of Geilana, wife of Duke Gosbert, who ruled the territory. Whilst the holy bishop and his companions were singing the praises of God, they were seized by order of Geilana, and shortly afterward suffered martyrdom with a courage worthy of the palmiest days of the early Church.

23. Conon died at Rome (September 21, A. D. 687), after a pontificate of little less than a year. He is accused of too weakly yielding to the wiles of the Syracusan deacon Constantine, upon whom he bestowed the dignity of elector for the patrimony in Sicily. The governor of the province was obliged to take legal measures against him on account of the repeated complaints of the Sicilians, whom he worried by unjust lawsuits.

CHAPTER IX.

§ I. Pontificate of St. Sergius I. (December 15, A. D. 687—September 8, 701).

1. Antipopes Pascal and Theodore. Election of St. Sergius I.—2. Fifteenth and sixteenth Councils of Toledo.—3. Seventeenth Council of Toledo.—4. Council in *Trullo*. Attempt upon the life of Sergius I.—5. Taking of Carthage by the Saracens, and extinction of the Roman rule in Africa.—Justinian II., Rhinotmetus, banished to the Tauric Chersonesus.—6. Antipope John in Rome. Death of Sergius I.

§ II. Pontificate of John VI. (October 30, A. D. 701—January 12, 705).

7. John VI. defended by the Romans from the attacks of Theophylactus, exarch of Ravenna. Attachment of the Italians to the Sovereign Pontiffs.—8. Council at Nesterfield in England. St. Wilfrid arraigned as a criminal. He appeals to John VI. in a council held at Rome, and is declared innocent.—9. Pilgrimage to the Holy Land. Advance of the religious movement in England.—10. Death of John VI. Mosque of Damascus.

§ III. Pontificate of John VII. (March 1, A. D. 705—October 18, 707).

11. Arribert II., king of the Lombards, makes over the Cottian Alps to the Holy See.—12. Restoration of Justinian II., Rhinotmetus.—13. John VII. refuses to confirm the acts of the council in *Trullo*. His death.

§ IV. Pontificate of Sisinnius (January 19, A. D. 708—February 7, 708).

14. Election and death of Sisinnius.

§ V. Pontificate of Constantine (March 25, A. D. 708—April 9, 715).

15. Ravenna plundered by the troops of Justinian II.—16. The Pope goes to Constantinople.—17. Bardanes Philippicus dethrones Justinian II. and declares himself the protector of the Monothelites. His successor Anastasius restores the true faith in the East.—18. The Moors in Spain.—19 Death of Constantine.

§ I. PONTIFICATE OF ST. SERGIUS I. (December 15, A. D. 687— September 8, 701.)

1. CONON'S pontificate had been too short to crush the existing party spirit. After his death a new division arose among the Roman people. One party elected the archdeacon Pascal, the other the archpriest Theodore. The partisans of the archpriest obtained possession of the interior of the Lateran palace; the whole of the exterior was held by their opponents. The tumult waxed fierce and threatened to end in bloodshed. The clergy, magistracy, and people at length cast their votes in favor of the priest Sergius, whom they led in triumph to the Lateran palace. The doors opened before them, and Theodore was one of the first to salute the new Pontiff and bow to his authority. Pascal would not yield; he was accordingly degraded and shut up in a monastery, where he died impenitent. Thus did Sergius inaugurate, in the midst of a tempest, a pontificate which was yet to weather many more fierce storms, though its first years were peaceable enough.

2. The fifteenth Council of Toledo, held in the reign of Egica, son-in-law and successor of Ervig, confirmed the acknowledgment of the sixth general council, and gave an orthodox explanation of the propositions to which Benedict II. had objected in the memorial of the archbishop of Toledo (May 11, A. D. 688). Four years later (693), the sixteenth Council of Toledo published a number of disciplinary canons. The most noteworthy among them relate to the condition of the Jews in Spain, to the material state of the churches, and to the administration of the Blessed Eucharist. Converted Jews are freed from the tax paid by them to the treasury, but those who hold out in their unbelief are to remain subject to the same stern legislation as before. There were many abandoned churches in Spain too poor to support a pastor. The Holy Sacrifice was seldom offered in them, and they were crumbling

into ruins. The council came to their help by ordering the bishops to devote one-third of the income of country churches granted them by the canons, in repairing the deserted temples. Some priests in celebrating the Holy Mysteries used a common loaf, from which they cut a round slice. The council orders that for this sacred service, a form of bread should be used, white, made especially for the purpose, and in small quantities, *since it is not bodily food, but spiritual nourishment*, and should be easily kept in a small receptacle. The hosts for the service of the altar from that time began to be made very much as we have them now.

3. The seventeenth Council of Toledo was held the following year (A. D. 694) in the church of St. Leocadia. The Spanish Jews, who had just been proved guilty of plotting against the state, were condemned to bondage and their property declared confiscate. The elective royalty of the Goths suffered greatly from the daily renewed undertakings of that people, ever conquered but never crushed, and this circumstance explains the severity of the council in their regard. An old law was also revived, forbidding the widows of kings from contracting a second marriage, doubtless on the political principle of giving more lasting security to the actual reign. The remaining canons treat of liturgical matters. Bishops and priests are recommended to strip the altars of all their ornaments on Holy Thursday, which ceremony is observed to this day. It is also particularly enjoined to observe the washing of feet on the same day, in memory of what our Lord Jesus Christ did at the Last Supper.

4. While Spain, thus united in submission to the Roman Pontiff, secured herself under the laws of strict discipline, the Church of Constantinople, yielding to its innate passion for change and novelty, was again sowing the seeds of trouble and discord. From the time when he ascended the imperial throne, Justinian had always shown feelings of hatred and wickedness. The stern and presumptuous emperor cherished the dream of a universal monarchy under his single sway. He even thought

of adding the spiritual authority to the sceptre of the Cæsars. His order that the pontifical elections should be submitted to the exarch of Ravenna, his lieutenant in Italy, was suggested by these ambitious projects. Under the pretext that the sixth general council had published no canons of discipline, he assembled a false council in Carthage, generally known as the *council in Trullo*, or council of the dome, as it was held in the hall of the dome at the imperial palace. It is sometimes also called quini-sext, being meant to supply what was wanting in the fifth and sixth general councils (A. D. 692). The bishops gathered together by the emperor's order, showed a most disgraceful slavishness, leaving the spiritual authority utterly at the discretion of the temporal power. Priests were allowed to marry, in contempt of every canonical law, whether of the Eastern or Western Church. Pope St. Gelasius and the Roman Church had classed as apocryphal the canons *of the Apostles*. The council *in Trullo* pronounced them authentic and binding, though one of them openly teaches the doctrine of the rebaptizers. The one hundred and two canons drawn up by this assembly, which pompously styled itself an *ecumenical council*, but was more properly called by Venerable Bede the *erratic council*, were sent to the Sovereign Pontiff for his approval, which was refused. Justinian II., irritated by this opposition, publicly ordered Zachary, his armor-bearer, to seize and bring the Pope to Constantinople. The imperial minion found all Rome in arms to defend its pastor. The military force of the exarchate hastened to the scene for the same purpose; the city resounded with cries and threats (A. D. 693). Zachary was forced to fly for his life and sought shelter in the very apartment of the Sovereign Pontiff, humbly craving his protection. The Lombard ambassadors residing in Rome had meanwhile sent couriers to Ravenna asking for troops to deliver Sergius. The report is suddenly spread that by a combination of cunning and inexplicable boldness, the Pope has been carried off and embarked on the Tiber. The troops from Ravenna at once surround the palace, with tumultuous demands for the Pope's appearance, threatening to break in the doors, if they are not at once opened. Zachary, crouching beneath the Pontiff's bed, trembling with the dread of a surprise, begs Sergius not to forsake him. Sergius promises his protection, orders the doors to be opened, and appears among the people and the soldiery, who press forward to kiss his hands and his garments. The time had passed when an emperor could forcibly carry off a St. Martin. The shameful cruelty inflicted upon that holy martyr was still remembered, and it was not believed that Justinian II. would prove less barbarous than his grandfather Constans II. The Pontiff's presence soothed the popular feeling. Sergius blessed the faithful multitude and asked forgiveness for Zachary, which was granted by acclamation; but he was required to quit Rome at once, with full liberty to go back and tell his master that the imperial power must henceforth bow to the strong defence enjoyed by the Pontiffs in the undying affection of their people.

5. From that hour the emperor began to feel the weight of Divine justice. No impious hand may be laid with impunity upon the Lord's anointed. A disastrous war, rashly undertaken by Justinian II., ended in the loss of Africa. The emperor had first sent against the Mussulman force before Carthage, the patrician John, a great captain whose first fields had been continual scenes of triumph. But in the following year (A. D. 696) the Saracens, returning in greater numbers, at length took Carthage with all the neighboring country, and thus extinguished the Roman power in Africa, where it had ruled for eight hundred and fifty years, from the year 608 of Rome, the period at which Carthage was captured by Scipio Africanus. Meanwhile Justinian himself was carrying on the war against the Bulgarians. A bloody defeat sent him back a fugitive to Constantinople. A body of Sclavonic auxiliaries had betrayed him; in a cowardly and barbarous spirit of revenge the emperor ordered that all the women, children and old men of that hated race, in Constantinople, should be thrown into the sea. General indignation was aroused by this deed

of senseless cruelty. The baffled tyrant's helpless rage suggested the thought of a general massacre of the imperial city during the night. The patrician Leontius, informed of the horrible design, seizes upon the emperor, orders his nose to be cut off,* banishes the mutilated tyrant to the Tauric Chersonesus and assumes the purple, which was torn from his shoulders two years later by a new usurper Tiberius Apsimar (A. D. 698).

6. Rome had meanwhile fallen into the hands of new factions. An antipope named John, backed by the credit of the exarch of Ravenna, had banished St. Sergius I. The noble Pontiff remained seven years far from his beloved flock, who bore all the usurper's violence with ever-unshaken fidelity to their lawful pastor. On his return, Sergius pronounced the excommunication and anathema against John and his abettors. The Pope's winning gentleness brought back to Catholic unity the archbishop of Aquileia and his suffragans, who had hitherto refused to subscribe the acts of the Council of Chalcedon against the *Three Chapters.* The remainder of his pontificate was devoted to seconding the efforts of the apostolic laborers in Germany. He consecrated St. Willibrord bishop of the Frisians, with the rank and rights of metropolitan, and appointed solemn processions for the three chief festivals of the Blessed Virgin Mary: the Annunciation, the Nativity, and the Assumption, which was then called *Dormitio Beatæ Virginis.* St. Sergius died on the 8th of September, A. D. 701, after a pontificate of nearly fourteen years.

§ II. Pontificate of John VI. (October 30, A. D. 701—January 12, 705).

7. John VI. was a Greek by birth, and was elected Pope on the 30th of October, A. D. 701. The emperor Tiberius Apsimar, on hearing of this new exaltation, sent to Rome the patrician Theophylactus, exarch of Ravenna, to compel the rati-

---

* It was owing to this circumstance that Justinian was thenceforth called Rhinotmetus.

fication of some unjust measures. But the Italian forces, which had already so intrepidly defended St. Sergius I., declared that they would avenge any attempt made upon the person of the Sovereign Pontiff. These were no longer the days of Calliopas and Zachary. The indignant soldiers and people would have laid violent hands upon the exarch had not John interposed. Baronius here takes occasion to point out the hold which the pontifical rule must have taken upon the affection of Italy, since every fresh attack of the emperors awaked a new rising of the people for their pastor's defence. From this period the power of the exarch began to wane, while the pontifical authority was daily strengthened by calling about it every principle of order, wisdom and stability in government. Thus when Charlemagne, at the close of the eighth century, established the temporal power of the Papacy and made it independent of political revolutions or imperial whims, he did but answer the general call of public opinion, and satisfy the most earnest wish of nations. And yet this change in the situation of the Church, which brought the Roman Pontiffs from out the darkness of the catacombs to the splendor of the Vatican, is brought about without intrigues, without slaughter or bloodshed, without costing humanity a single tear. It was natural enough, since the Popes use their influence only for the good of the people. Amid the jarring din of political revolutions so disastrous to those ages of transition and trouble, their voice arose but to still the storm with gentle words, their deeds were ever stamped with the seal of charity. In A. D. 702, Gisulphus, the Lombard duke of Beneventum, suddenly broke into Campania, at the head of a formidable army, burning towns, plundering dwellings, monasteries and churches, and dragging a host of captives in his train. John VI. at once sent bishops supplied with large sums of money from the treasury of the Roman Church, and charged to buy a peace as well as to pay the ransom of all the prisoners. In this noble and generous policy John VI. was but carrying out what the example of his predecessors for the past three centuries had taught him. What wonder then that such a power could gather around it influence, moral force, and the full confidence of the public mind? By such circumstances, by such means, did the Popes gradually become temporal-sovereigns of Rome and part of Italy; indeed they held that power *de facto* long before it was granted them *de jure*. People, downtrodden by tyrants of every nation and of every class, saw no other sheltering power than the fatherly rule of the Sovereign Pontiffs, to which they hastened with grateful affection.

8. In A. D. 703, Alcfrid, king of Northumberland, assembled the English bishops in a council at Nesterfield, about five leagues from Ripon, over which Bretwald, archbishop of Canterbury, presided. St. Wilfrid, still an exile by the king's injustice, was summoned before the council to answer the charges brought against him. The venerable bishop appeared with a countenance full of modest but firm dignity, and showed the letters of rehabilitation received from Pope St. Agatho twenty-three years before. But Alcfrid's hate was not yet glutted. By his order a formal renunciation of the see of York was laid before St. Wilfrid, with a direction that he should be forced to sign it. The holy bishop answered with noble firmness: "Why seek to force me to the disgraceful extreme of condemning myself? Would it not be a subject of scandal for all Great Britain, where it is well known that for forty years, though unworthy, I have borne the episcopal character? I appeal to the Holy See concerning the violence which is done me, and I call upon those who wish my deposition to come with me to Rome, on this very day, to ask a solemn judgment of the case there." Wilfrid indeed set out himself and again sought redress from the Holy See. Bretwald's emissaries followed him. John VI. called a council to examine the case more thoroughly, and St. Wilfrid's innocence was again solemnly declared. The Pope sent him back with letters for Alcfrid, and Ethelred, king of Mercia, whom he begged to restore St. Wilfrid to his metropolitan see of York. The saint reached England only to learn that Ethelred had withdrawn into a monastery to prepare, by a

holy life, for a heavenly crown; Alcfrid showed no more respect for the advice of John VI. than for that of St. Agatho.
But his death soon restored St. Wilfrid to freedom (A. D. 705),
and he took possession of his Church, where he died full of
days and merits (A. D. 709).

9. This period inaugurated among the Western Christians
the pilgrimages to the Holy Land.   A Gallic bishop named
Arculphus, and Peter, a Burgundian hermit, visited the holy
places, went through Palestine, Syria, and Egypt, and returned
by sea to Constantinople.   The account of their journey was
taken down from their own lips by St. Adamman, abbot of a
monastery in the island of Hi, on the western coast of Great
Britain, where the two pilgrims were cast ashore, by a storm, on
their return (A. D. 705).   England was still rich in models of
ecclesiastical virtue and learning.   St. Ceolfrid, the disciple and
successor of St. Benedict Biscop, governed the two joint abbeys of Weremouth and Yarrow, and succeeded in doing away
with the abuse concerning the Paschal celebration.   He also
introduced among the English clergy and monks, the Roman
custom of wearing the whole round tonsure.   Hitherto the
English priests had only worn it over the forehead.   Ceolfrid
died at Langres, as he was passing through France on his way
to Rome (September 25, A. D. 716).   Another light of the English Church was St. Althelm or Aldhelm, first bishop of Sher-
burn, which see was afterward removed to Salisbury.   He was
versed in every branch of learning.   Besides poetry and English versification, to which he first gave attention, he studied the
Roman laws, philosophy, canon law, the exact sciences and
astronomy.   So wide-spread was his reputation that strangers
came from the most distant countries to consult him.   We have
a letter of his, addressed to the king and clergy of the West
Saxons, on the Paschal question, and a Treatise on Virginity,
written in the style of mingled prose and poetry of Sedulius.
The verses often halt with Greek words; the prose is too full
of synonyms and of unnecessary epithets; in a word, its learning betrays a want of method.   Yet if we remember that St.

Aldhelm is the first Anglo-Saxon who undertook to write in Latin, we must give him credit for much true talent. His death occurred in 709.

10. Pope John VI. had ended his pontificate in A. D. 705, the very year in which the caliph Walid was raising the celebrated mosque of Damascus. The caliph is said to have offered the Christians a large sum of money for their cathedral, which they refused. The haughty Mussulman seized the church by force, tore it down, and on its ruins raised his mosque to Mahomet. Islamism and Christianity were soon to measure weapons on vaster fields.

§ III. PONTIFICATE OF JOHN VII. (March 1, A. D. 705—October 18, 707).

11. John VII. was raised to the Chair of St. Peter on the 1st of March, A. D. 705. "In his reign," says Paul the Deacon, the Lombard historian, "King Aribert II. gave back to the Holy See the territory of the Cottian Alps, which had once belonged to the Roman Pontiffs, but had since been seized by the Lombards. Aribert sent to Rome the deed of gift, written in letters of gold."* The Cottian Alps, named after King Cottius, a contemporary of Augustus and ally of the Romans, reached, according to Paul the Deacon, from the Tuscan Sea, on the east, to Gaul on the west. They took in the cities of Aix, Dertona, Bobbio, Genoa, and Savona. These events are worthy of note. We called attention to the fact that under the pontificate of St. Gregory the Great, the Roman Church already held possession of the cities of Gallipoli, Otranto, and Naples Providence was plainly opening the way for the temporal sovereignty and independence of the Popes, and Charlemagne but gave the finishing strokes to the work.

12. Justinian II. had in the mean time found means to escape from his prison, and suddenly appeared in Constantino-

* The gift was afterward ratified by the Lombard king Luitprand, under Pope Gregory II.

ple at the head of a Bulgarian army (A. D. 705). Tiberius Apsimar and his predecessor Leontius were arrested, loaded with
irons and thrown into a dungeon. Before their execution they
were cast prostrate in chains beneath the throne of the emper-
or; and Justinian, planting a foot on each of their necks, con-
templated above an hour the chariot race, while the people,
whose base inconstancy was worthy of such masters, shouted,
in the words of the Psalmist: "*Super aspidem et basiliscum am-
bulabis: et conculcabis leonem et draconem.*"* Justinian closed
the games by ordering their heads to be struck off. During
the remainder of his reign the city was a constant scene of proscription and murders. Whilst Justinian was in exile, he one
day found himself in a violent tempest on the Black Sea, when
one of his pious companions said to him: "My lord, we shall
be lost! Deserve the mercy of God by a vow of general forgiveness, should He restore you to the throne." "Of forgiveness?" replied the monster; "may the Almighty whelm me in
the waves if I consent to spare a single head of my enemies!"
And never was vow more scrupulously performed than the
oath of revenge which he had sworn amidst the storms of the
Euxine.

13. In his misfortune Justinian had neither learned nor
forgotten. He returned with the avowed intention of forcing
from John VII. a confirmation of his council *in Trullo*, which
St. Sergius I. had refused to approve. His first care, accordingly, was to send to Rome two metropolitans bearing the acts
of the so-called council, and a letter in which the emperor
begged John VII. to confirm what he deemed good in the decrees, and to reject what might be evil. He doubtless reserved
to himself the right of taking exception to the distinctions
that might be made by the Pope, and to distort the partial approval of a few indifferent canons into a general approval of all
the acts of his false council. But John VII. saw the snare and
was careful to avoid it. He sent back the acts without reading

* "Thou shalt trample on the asp and basilisk, and on the lion and dragon shalt thou
set thy foot!"

them, "for the reason," he wrote to the emperor, "that the council *in Trullo* was not lawfully assembled with the presence of legates from the Holy See." The Pontiff's prudence has not been fairly appreciated by some modern writers. The dishonesty of Justinian II. and his Greek subjects claimed indeed to interpret the Pope's silence as a tacit approval, and the argument is still used by Greek priests who seek to uphold the lawfulness of their custom regarding the marriage of clerics.* But history should never subserve the interests of human passions. The council *in Trullo* was never confirmed by the Apostolic See; its decrees are powerless; it is a cabal, not a council. By rejecting these acts John VII. ran a considerable risk, as it is impossible to tell to what extreme Justinian's rage might have carried him, had not death come to the rescue of the Sovereign Pontiff, on the 17th of October, A. D. 707.

§ IV. PONTIFICATE OF SISINNIUS (January 19, A. D. 708—February 7, 708).

14. Sisinnius was elected Pope on the 19th of January, A. D. 708, and scarce had time to wear the pontifical tiara. He died suddenly twenty days after his promotion (February 7, A. D. 708). Within that short space of time he consecrated some bishops for the island of Corsica, and designed to raise the walls of Rome to shelter the city against any hostile blow from without. When death surprised him he had already gathered many of the materials necessary for the undertaking, which the ceaseless wars of that period made so necessary.

§ V. PONTIFICATE OF CONSTANTINE (March 25, A. D. 708—April 9, 715).

15. The next occupant of the Pontifical Chair was Constantine, a Syrian by birth (March 25, A. D. 708). The first pon-

* The false council in *Trullo* solemnly recognized the right of priests to marry.

tifical act of the new Pope was the consecration of Felix, as archbishop of Ravenna. This ceremony was attended by a somewhat remarkable event. Felix, backed by the secular power of the exarch, sought to revive the claims of his predecessor Maurus, and refused to make the usual promises of submission and dependence to the Roman Church. This conduct should have won him the favor of Justinian II. But that monarch had made it his mission to devote the second part of his reign to avenging the wrongs he thought he had received during the first, and he had not forgotten the protection granted by the inhabitants of Ravenna to St. Sergius, against the attempt of the imperial officer Zachary. In the year 709, the patrician Theodore, commander of the Sicilian forces, received orders to moor his fleet under the walls of Ravenna. By feigned professions of friendship he drew the principal inhabitants of the city into his tent upon the sea-shore. As they entered the tent they were seized, gagged and led by a hidden way to the fleet, where they were thrown into the hold of a ship, as prisoners; among the victims of this treachery was Felix, the archbishop. The city thus dispeopled was given up to plunder; the prisoners were taken to Constantinople and subjected to various kinds of punishment. Felix, after having his eyes torn out, was banished to Pontus.

16. Justinian still showed his irritation at the refusal of Rome to receive his council *in Trullo*, but, hopeless of doing any thing by force, he thought to win the desired approval by professions of friendship. He accordingly sent an embassy to the Sovereign Pontiff, urging him to visit Constantinople (A. D. 710), as he had many things to settle in conjunction with his Holiness. He also gave signs of a desire to change his line of conduct and to atone for his faults, thus inviting the Pope to come and encourage him in his designs of mercy and repentance.

The expedition of the preceding year against the wretched inhabitants of Ravenna was hardly a good omen; but the fearless zeal of Constantine could not hesitate to undertake the journey: offering up the sacrifice of his life, should the emperor have the boldness to attempt it, he set sail on the 5th of October, A. D. 710, accompanied by a numerous train of deacons, priests, and bishops. He was everywhere received with marks of the deepest respect. An imperial order directed all officers to show the same honor to the Pope as to the emperor himself. Tiberius, Justinian's son, accompanied by the patricians and chief nobles, came forward seven miles from Constantinople, to meet the Sovereign Pontiff, who made his triumphal entry into the city, robed as was his wont on solemn days in Rome. He was escorted by all the nobles and his own suite, mounted upon the noblest steeds of the imperial stables, richly caparisoned with jewelled bridles, saddles, and trappings of cloth of gold. The emperor was absent; Constantine was taken to the palace prepared for him. As soon as Justinian, who was then at Nice, heard of the Pontiff's arrival, he sent him a congratulatory letter, and begged him to meet him at Nicomedia, whither he at once repaired in person. At their first meeting, the emperor, crowned as he was, threw himself at the Pontiff's feet, which he reverently kissed.* They then embraced amid the acclamations of the people. Their conversation on the council *in Trullo* was private. The Pope found no difficulty in removing the prejudices which the theological ignorance of the emperor had so long fostered in respect to this false council. He gave the charge of the discussion to his deacon, afterward his successor, Gregory, who was thoroughly conversant with canon law, the Scriptures, and the Fathers. His clear, close and logical replies deeply impressed the emperor, who declared himself satisfied with the conference, and as a public proof of his joy, he assisted on the following Sun-

---

* Since that time the greatest monarchs have always shown the same mark of respect to the Popes: Luitprand, king of the Lombards, to Gregory II.; Rachis, king of the same nation, to Zachary; the emperor Charlemagne to Adrian I.; Louis the Pious to Stephen IV.; Sigismund to Eugenius IV.; Frederick Barbarossa to Alexander III.; Stephen, king of Hungary, to Benedict VII.; Charles VIII., king of France, to Alexander VI.; Charles V., emperor of Germany, to Clement VII. and Paul VIII.; Charles III., king of Naples, and since Catholic king, to Benedict XIV.

day at the mass celebrated by the Pope, from whose hand
he received the Holy Sacrament. Not satisfied with these
passing tokens of regard, the emperor renewed the privileges
bestowed by his predecessors upon the Roman Church. At
last he allowed the Pontiff to return to Italy. Constantine
re-entered his pontifical city in A. D. 711, after an absence of a
year, stronger, more powerful, more really a sovereign than ever.

17. It were hard to say how long this state of good feeling
between the Pope and the emperor might have lasted, had
not a fresh revolution snatched from Justinian both his sceptre
and his life (A. D. 711). Bardanes Philippicus, the moving spirit
of the revolution, took the imperial purple. While still a youth
his ambition had been aroused by the prediction of a Syrian
hermit, who coupled with his promise of a throne this injunction : " Remember, when you come to power, to annul all that
was done in the sixth council against the Monothelites. Such
is the will of God." The first part of the prophecy now fulfilled, Bardanes sought to make good the second. The Monothelites, who had kept aloof since the reign of Constantine
Pogonatus, raised their heads once more. All that was Greek
in the East, became Monothelite ; the vacant sees were filled
by the abettors of the heresy. Even orthodox bishops
yielded to fear or interest. Germanus, bishop of Cyzicus, and
Andrew of Crete, both renowned for virtue and learning,
and some of whose pious works are still extant, weakly
yielded to the general impulse and anathematized the sixth
general council; this shameful defection, however, they afterward repaired by their tears and by their noble defence of
Catholic truth against Leo the Isaurian. Bardanes showed
mercy only to Felix, archbishop of Ravenna, whom he had
known as an exile in Chersonesus, and restored the bishop to
his see, with all honor. But Felix had been learning in the
stern school of misfortune, where experience had taught him
the shifting nature of the things of earth; he therefore cast
off all the ambitious aims that had blighted his episcopate,
and, bowing submissive to the Holy See, sought the bond of

Catholic unity, the only foundation that cannot fail. The Monothelite reaction which had begun with Bardanes, fell with him too. He had hastened to write to Pope Constantine in defence of his heresy. The Pontiff refused to answer. The faithful at Rome would not allow the emperor's image to be carried to the church as was customary, nor would they have his name uttered during the Holy Sacrifice. The following year (A. D. 713) brought the tidings that the emperor Bardanes Philippicus had been dethroned, and succeeded by Anastasius II. The new emperor was a Catholic. At the ceremony of his coronation, the bishops, clergy, and people, gathered together in the church of St. Sophia, cried out with one voice: " We embrace the faith of the sixth general council : it is holy, it is ecumenical !" Anastasius joined his voice to that of the multitude. He then wrote to the Pope, professing his attachment to the Catholic faith, and his example was followed by the Patriarch of Constantinople. Such was the Greek empire, the home of fallen morals and slavish minds, ready by turns to take up and to throw aside the most opposite tenets, according to the impulse of the times or the ruling powers.

18. While the East was being thus rent asunder by ceaseless change, Spain was the theatre of a most important movement. Islamism was advancing with conquering strides into the heart of this rich province. Roderic had just mounted the Gothic throne to sully it by his vices. A slave to the most shameful passions, he spared neither age nor rank. He carried off the daughter of Count Julian, governor of Ceuta, the only city then held by the Goths on the African coast. Julian's despairing grief whelmed the thought of his country's claims in the burning thirst to revenge the cruel outrage on a father's honor. He accordingly proposed to Musa, Walid's lieutenant in Africa, to help him in the conquest of Spain. The skilful commander saw at a glance the advantages of Julian's alliance; the agreement was made. Twenty-five thousand Turks, under Taric, landed on the coast of Algezire (April 28, A. D. 711), seized upon Mount Calpe, now Gibraltar (*Gibel Tarick*, Tarick's

Mountain). The Goths, enervated by a long season of peace, had unlearned the art of war; besides, one party was already devoted to the enemy's cause. The engagement was fought near Xeres (July 17, A. D. 711), and the Goths were defeated. King Roderic had disappeared amid the confusion of the battle. At this news Musa himself crossed the Strait, took Toledo, Seville and Merida, and within fifteen months the whole of Spain was under the Prophet's standard. The Visigoth power fell, after a duration of nearly three centuries since its first establishment at Toulouse (A. D. 419). Cordova became the capital of the new Mussulman caliphate. The Christians who remained faithful sought shelter in the mountains of Asturias, under the leadership of Pelagius, whom they made their king. Pelagius chose Oviedo as the capital of his new empire, which was to battle for seven centuries in behalf of the national faith and independence. When the Moors saw the fugitives building up a government, they sent to Pelagius one of their generals named Aliaman, with his sword in one hand and gold in the other. Pelagius received him in the celebrated grotto of Cavadonga, which was held sacred to the Mother of God. Aliaman's interpreter was the apostate bishop of Toledo. "You know," said the traitor to Pelagius, "that all Spain has submitted to the Arabs. What can you hope from a few fugitives lurking in the hollow rocks of these mountains?" "We hope," answered Pelagius, "that from these mountain dens will go forth the salvation of our land which you have betrayed, and the restoration of the Gothic empire. Traitor bishop, go back to the unbelieving race in whom you trust, and tell them that we fear not their numbers. The Almighty, after punishing His faithless servants, will show His mercy toward dutiful children." Thus was the gauntlet thrown down between Christianity and Islamism. The heroic handful of faithful warriors in the mountain fastnesses of Asturias bore the fate of the world in the folds of their banner.

19. On the 8th of April, A. D. 715, Pope Constantine closed his pontificate of seven years, at Rome. He was the eighty-

ninth successor of the Prince of the Apostles. Of this number, forty Sovereign Pontiffs had been chosen from among the
Roman people; the remaining forty-nine were of various na-
onalities: Galileans, Tuscans, Athenians, Syrians, Greeks, Africans, Dalmatians, Spaniards, Sardinians, Corsicans, Sicilians
and Neapolitans. These elections must surely have been ruled
by a pious impartiality. They could have been dictated only
by zeal for religion. What respect must the world have felt
for so unwonted a spirit of charity, fairness and justice! Rome
could not be charged with keeping her See for her own children alone. This wise management, meeting every schism,
every division, contributed largely to increase the power of the
Holy See. Weighty motives have since made modifications
necessary; for the measures which best serve to *establish* are
not always those which best *preserve*. In these changes in the
discipline of the pontifical elections, the unprejudiced historian
sees but a new proof of the watchful care of Divine Providence
over the Church's welfare.

CHAPTER X.

§ I. Pontificate of St. Gregory II. (May 19, a. d. 715—February 12, 731).

1 Situation of the world at the accession of Gregory II.—2. Monastic discipline in Italy. Progress of Christian missions in Germany. St. Boniface, archbishop of Mayence.—3. Venerable Bede.—4. Leo the Isaurian drives back Soliman from the walls of Constantinople.—5. Leo the Isaurian becomes an Iconoclast.—6. St. John Damascen.—7. The Pope opposes the impious measures of Leo the Isaurian.—8. The Pope besieged in Rome by the exarch of Ravenna and the Lombard king Luitprand.—9. Death of St. Gregory II.

§ II. Pontificate of St. Gregory III. (March 18, a. d. 731—November 28, 741)

10. Election of St. Gregory III.—11. The Iconoclast heresy most unpopular in Italy.—12. St. Gregory III. places the Holy See under the protection of Charles Martel.—13. Invasion of Gaul by Abderahman.—14. Battle of Poitiers.—15. Importance of the battle of Poitiers with respect to the Holy See.—16. Council at Rome against the Iconoclasts.—17. Charles Martel uses his influence with Luitprand on behalf of the Holy See. Death of Charles Martel, of Leo the Isaurian, and of St. Gregory III.—18. Various acts of this pontificate.

§ III. Pontificate of St. Zachary (December 3, a. d. 741—March 15, 752).

19. Election of St. Zachary.—20. Treaty of peace between the Pope and Luitprand.—21. Labors of St. Boniface, archbishop of Mayence.—22. Heresies of Samson and Virgil.—23. Heresies of Adelbert and Clement.—24. Council of Cliff. Penitentiary and pontifical codes of Egbert. Ceremony of the royal coronation.—25. Revolt of Artabazus.—26. Carloman at Monte Cassino.—27. Pepin the Short, king of the Franks.—28. Death of St. Zachary.

§ IV. Pontificate of Stephen III. (March 18, a. d. 752—March 20, 752).

29. Death of Stephen III. before his installation.

§ V. Pon. .ficate of Stephen IV. (March 26, a. d. 752—April 8, 757).

§ I. Pontificate of St. Gregory II. (May 19, a. d. 715—February 12, 731).

1. The period at which Gregory II. ascended the pontifical throne (May 19, a. d. 715) was one fraught with difficulties. Luitprand had just assumed the Lombard crown (a. d. 712). His uncommon energy and skill inspired him with the idea of subjecting the whole of Italy to his sway. The influence of the Popes, which stood in his way and balked his ambitious views, led him to take a stand hostile to the Holy See. The Saracens, now masters of Spain, pushed their advance-guard even into Gaul, and threatened the independence of Christendom. Leo the Isaurian had followed the Catholic Anastasius on the Greek throne, and was about to give up the East to a heresy more fierce than any of its predecessors. The mission of the Sovereign Pontiff in so serious a juncture was beset on all sides by dangers. St. Gregory II. proved himself worthy of his position. A fearless courage, joined to a moderation and prudence proof against every assault, carried him triumphant through all the intricacies which so beset his pontificate.

2. His first thought was to restore monastic discipline in Italy. The monastery of Monte Cassino, destroyed by the Lombards one hundred and fifty years before, had never been raised from its ruins. Gregory charged a holy religious, named Petronax, to revive the cenobitic life and high ecclesiastical studies which had made this favored abbey the most illustrious of St. Bennet's rule. Not content with spreading the fostering influence of the Papacy through the countries near to Rome,

Gregory at the same time sent the bishop Martinian, the priest George, and the sub-deacon Dorotheus, all members of the Roman clergy, to enlighten the yet heathen people of Bavaria (A. D. 716). Three years later (A. D. 719), Winfrid, better known as St. Boniface of Mayence, came from England to lay before the Sovereign Pontiff his plan of an apostolate in Germany. Winfrid had provided himself with *dimissory* letters from Daniel, bishop of Winchester, in which diocese he had received holy orders. St. Gregory empowered him to preach the Gospel among all the heathen nations in Germany, and to baptize them according to the Roman rite. Winfrid began his mission in Bavaria and Thuringia, where he reaped a most plentiful harvest. The Pope, on hearing of the wonderful work which God had wrought through his ministry, directed him to return to Rome (A. D. 723), where he consecrated him, with his own hands, metropolitan prelate of Germany, at the same time changing his name of Winfrid into that of Boniface (*doing good*), in allusion to the services already done and still promised to the Church by the apostolic laborer. On his return, the newly consecrated bishop, strong in the support of Charles Martel, to whom he had been recommended by St. Gregory, converted nearly all the inhabitants of Hesse and Thuringia. He made it his particular care to found monasteries, in order to perpetuate, by living example, the holy traditions of Christian life in the countries he evangelized. After fifteen years of untiring toil, St. Boniface repaired to Rome for the third time and received from Gregory III. the archiepiscopal pallium, as a mark of his jurisdiction over the whole of Germany. He chose Mayence as the seat of his archbishopric, and had thirteen suffragan sees; to all these churches he gave a strong and lasting organization. Satisfied that he had thus provided for the permanence of his work, he gave up his see and consecrated his successor. Entering again upon the apostolic career, he undertook the conversion of Friesland, hitherto proof against all the efforts of missionaries. Here the crown of martyrdom awaited him. After his death his body was taken to the abbey of Fuld, one of his own foundation, where God glorified his servant by many miracles.

3. St. Boniface, we have said, was an Englishman. Great Britain, full worthy at this period to be called the *Isle of Saints*, promised to furnish apostles for all the other nations of the earth. It also possessed in its bosom a bright light of the Church, in the Venerable Bede. This title was bestowed upon him even during his own lifetime, and has been kept by Christian antiquity, on account of his reputation for virtue and learning. Bede was one of the most illustrious doctors of that age of transition from the old Latin literature to that of modern nations. Trained in the monasteries of Weremouth and Yarrow, under the eye of St. Ceolfrid, he had early acquired a taste for ecclesiastical studies. By a dispensation granted to his merit he was ordained deacon at the age of nineteen years, though the canons required twenty-four. His long life was devoted to the writing of many works still extant. The most important are the History of the English Church, in five books, a precious monument of national erudition, and the Chronicles or Treatise on the Six Ages of the World, an abridgment of universal history from the creation to his own day, in which he briefly points out the designs of Providence on mankind in general, on the posterity of Abraham in particular; in fine, on the multitude of nations joined together in Christ and in His Church. His writings on grammar, orthography, and versification did much in the West, with those of Cassiodorus and St. Isidore of Seville, to give their distinctive character of regularity and clearness to modern languages, which were just springing into existence by a mingling of Latin with the Teutonic dialects. Bede died A. D. 735, at the age of sixty-three years, abbot of the monastery of Yarrow. His greatest glory is to have been the master of Alcuin, Charlemagne's preceptor.

4. Whilst the West was rejoicing the world by these offerings of saintliness, the hopes of Christendom were suddenly clouded by the apparition upon the Eastern throne of a name

that boded evil. Leo III., the son of a poor Isaurian peasant, wore the purple of the Cæsars (A. D. 716). He was the fourth emperor raised within three years to the Byzantine throne by the fickle Greeks.* The keen eyes of the Mussulmans did not miss this spectacle so disgraceful to the Lower Empire in the eighth century; they thought its knell had already sounded. A Turkish fleet of eighteen hundred sail, under the caliph Soliman, formed its crescent on the bosom of the Propontis (A. D. 717). Leo the Isaurian wished to treat with the caliph. Soliman replied that " he did not reason with the conquered, and that he had already detailed the force that was to garrison Constantinople." The insolent bravado rekindled all the old Roman pride in the bosom of the empire. They swore to drive back the invader or to die beneath their country's ruins. Leo encouraged the national spirit and took an admirable advantage of it. A month later the Turkish fleet had been destroyed and Soliman died of shame at his disgrace. By this feat of arms Leo the Isaurian had saved Constantinople and the empire. Happy constancy, had he always remained satisfied to be the champion of Christianity, and not lent his name to swell the list of its most bitter persecutors!

5. Amongst the stories of the emperor's youth, it is told of him that whilst still in his father's cabin amid the mountains of Isauria, he once heard some Jews blaspheme and curse an image of the Redeemer. One of them turned to him and jokingly remarked: "Were you emperor, would you not destroy all those impious images?" "I swear," replied the boy, "that I should not spare a single one!" The imperial crown recalled his oath. In A. D. 726 he published a decree announcing that in gratitude for the favors heaped upon him by God since his accession, he wished to destroy the *idolatry* which had crept into the Church; that the pictures of Christ, of the Blessed Virgin, and the saints, were idols, to which honor was

* Bardanes Philippicus (A. D. 713), Anastasius II. (A. D. 714), Theodosius III. (A. D. 715). Leo the Isaurian (A. D. 716).

given that was only due to a jealous God. He accordingly ordered their removal from the churches, oratories and private dwellings, and at length doomed their existence as well as their use. When the edict was presented for his signature to Germanus, Patriarch of Constantinople, he refused his name. "The Christians do not worship images," said he to the emperor, "but only honor them as memorials of the saints and of their virtues. Painting is but an epitome of history for Christians, not an idolatry. You must distinguish between direct and relative veneration." But Leo was unwilling to understand so clear and simple an explanation. He again ordered St. Germanus to receive his decree, with the alternative of banishment or even death in case of refusal. "Remember," said the Patriarch, "your coronation oath to change nothing in the tradition of the Church." The emperor struck the venerable confessor and caused his deposition by the senate. Germanus, taking off his pallium, said to the tyrant: "My person is in the prince's power, but my faith bows only to the decision of a council." The intrepid champion of Christ already numbered fourscore years. The emperor banished him and gave his see to a priest named Anastasius, who did not blush to barter his faith for the empty honor of a usurped title. From that hour an unparalleled fanaticism wreaked its fury upon every sacred symbol. The troops of the Isaurian broke into the churches and private dwellings, destroyed every pious work of art, and murdered all who dared to oppose them. Their profession named the heretics Iconoclasts (breakers of images). The emperor found it profitable to confiscate a number of gold and silver statues, costly vessels used in the service of the altar, jewels which enriched the images of Mary, so dear to the faithful hearts of the empire, and destroyed a large brass crucifix with which the piety of Constantine the Great had adorned one of the porticos of the imperial palace. It had always been held in special reverence by the inhabitants of Constantinople; some women of the lower class rushed upon the officer who had executed the impious order, and murdered him. They had but given the signal for a savage slaughter, and were put to death with a number of other Catholics. The martyrs were covered with a coat of pitch, and burned upon a pile of sacred images; their calcined bodies were then thrown to dogs. The celebrated Byzantine library was contained in a basilica situated between the imperial palace and the church of St. Sophia. This basilica, called the Octagon, from the eight splendid porticos which gave entrance to it, was the residence of the professors of belles-lettres and theology, paid by the state. The emperor directed these scholars to subscribe to his decree, which they refused to do, at the same time opposing the monarch's opinions with respectful firmness. Unable to convince, the emperor determined to destroy them, and, with a cruelty far beyond that of the caliph Omar, he doomed the books, the basilica and its learned inmates to the flames.

6. Yet even from the very bosom of the East a voice was raised to brand the excesses of this savage cruelty. It came from a monk whose eloquence won him the title of Chrysorrhoës, (Golden stream). St. John Damascen was born of an illustrious Christian family of Damascus, in the decline of the seventh century. His father, who was grand vizier at the court of the Ommiad caliphs of Damascus, was one day looking at some Christian prisoners exposed in the public square : those who were about to be led to execution, threw themselves at the feet of one of their number, recommending themselves to his prayers. He was an Italian religious, named Cosmo, taken with the others at sea. The grand vizier asks him who he is : " I am a poor monk," he replied, " whose days have been spent in the study of philosophy and the sciences, and I confess that I regret to die before being able to impart my acquirements to others." The vizier had long been seeking a teacher who might give his son a fitting education. Delighted at the thought of having found this treasure in a prisoner about to suffer death, he hastened to ask the caliph for him, and easily obtained his request. Cosmo was freed. He became the father's friend, the son's preceptor; his pupil made quick and

steady progress in the study of grammar, dialectics, algebra,
geometry, music, and astronomy,* but especially in theology,
or the science of religion. The caliph was not blind to the
qualities of John Damascen, and soon made him vizier. But
that generous soul soared high above the sphere of worldly
honors ; he obtained the caliph's permission to live in retirement, and availed himself of his freedom to enter the monastic
state. This was the doctor who took in hand the defence of
Catholic truth against the blind fury of Leo the Isaurian. He
wrote a work against the Iconoclast heresy, which soon won
popularity in the East. He thus begins his first discourse on
the subject : " Conscious of my own unworthiness, I ought perhaps to have kept an unbroken silence ; but at the sight of the
Church tossed by a violent storm, the words break of their
own accord from my lips, for I fear God more than any earthly
emperor." He then goes on to discuss the question with resistless depth, clearness and learning. He proves the lawfulness
of venerating images, by Sacred Scripture, Catholic tradition
and sound logical arguments. "A picture is to the ignorant
what a book would be to the learned. The picture does the
same office through the sight as the word through the hearing.
Holy images are a memorial of the Divine works. Besides,"
he concludes, " the decision in such matters falls not within the
province of princes, but of councils. It was not to kings that
Jesus Christ gave power to bind and to loose ; it was to the
apostles and their successors, the bishops and doctors of the
Church. Let these rash innovators recall the words of the

---

* It is a remarkable fact that the learning of Greece and Rome was first brought to the
court of the caliphs of Damascus by a poor Italian monk, a captive doomed to death.
"Who," says M. Charles Lenormand, in his Course of Modern History, " opens the list of
those master-minds that inspired the genius of Arabia ? It is a very good Catholic, a
Father of the Church, St. John Damascen, who initiates the Arab mind into the reasonings of Greek philosophy, not at the court of the Abassides, but a century later in that of
the Ommiad race; not in Bagdad, but at Damascus. The illustrious Father, John Damascen, who enjoyed the highest consideration at the court, yet had left it for the religious
cell, and was certainly the most renowned character of his day in the East, introduced the
Arabs into the sphere of Aristotle's philosophy." Cosmo was afterward raised to the
episcopal see of Majuma, and won the martyr's palm (February 21, A. D. 743).

apostle St. Paul: Should an angel come down from heaven to preach to you another gospel than that which you have received . . . We will not finish the text, but leave them time for repentance. But if—what God forbid—they obstinately cling to their error, we may then add the rest: *Let him be anathema!*" This work created a deep sensation in the Catholic world. Leo sought to revenge himself on its author by means of a most infamous fraud. He caused a skilful forger to counterfeit the handwriting of the holy doctor, and to address a supposititious letter from him to the emperor, inviting him to march upon Damascus, which he promised to place in his power. . The emperor then sent the false document to the caliph as a pledge of his friendship and a proof of his desire to preserve peace between them. The caliph, too much angered to listen to John, ordered his right hand to be cut off. The author of his life relates that after the bloody punishment, the saint threw himself upon his knees before an image of the Blessed Virgin, begging her to intercede with her Divine Son for the restoration of his mutilated hand, that he might still defend the cause of holy images. His prayer was granted; struck by the miraculous cure, the caliph loaded the saint with favors.

7. The Pope was meanwhile rallying about him all the powers of the West to meet the Iconoclast Leo. The wounded hearts were most earnest in resisting the savage doctrine of the imperial heresiarch. In the beginning of his reign, Leo had as usual sent to Rome his own pictures crowned with laurels; for though he could not abide the veneration given to images of saints, he did not the less require honor for his own as well as for his imperial person. But on learning the lengths to which he had gone in respect to holy pictures, the Roman people trampled the imperial statues under foot. Gregory II. at the same time wrote to Leo, clearly laying down the Catholic teaching on the subject. The maddened emperor sought to rid himself of this powerful opponent by a crime, and charged Marinus, his lieutenant in Rome, to organize a conspiracy against the Pontiff's life. The chief conspirators were dis-

covered and suffered capital punishment. On learning this event, Paul, exarch of Ravenna, assembled his troops and prepared to take Rome in order to force the election of another Pope. The Romans likewise took up arms, and soon saw their numbers swelled by the Florentines, the Lombards of Spoleto, and the people of all the neighboring country, who hastened to defend the city and person of the Sovereign Pontiff. Paul was forced to beat a disgraceful retreat before the imposing array of faithful arms. Though the Saracens still pressed Constantinople, yet the emperor would arm only against the Catholics, and showed more concern at the Pope's resistance than at the progress of Islamism.

8. The senseless rage of Leo wasted itself upon the Holy See only to hasten two results of vast importance, never dreamed of in the furious tyrant's thoughts of vengeance. These vain attacks were preparing the speedy realization of the temporal independence of the Popes, and the establishment of the Frankish instead of the Greek power. Since the imperial commander's check before the walls of Rome, Marinus had been vainly endeavoring to murder the Pope. The inhabitants had driven him from the city, and, longing for a more quiet and milder form of government, they loudly called upon Gregory to take in hand the reins of government. Thus may the temporal power of the Popes in some manner date from this period. Still Leo the Isaurian would not acknowledge himself worsted. He opened negotiations with the ambitious Lombard king, Luitprand, and persuaded him that it was their common interest to join their forces and crush the pontifical power The gates of Rome are again beset by the combined armies of the exarch and Luitprand, lost in astonishment at finding themselves side by side in a common cause. Their camp-fires crown Monte Mario, and at length they stand by Adrian's mausoleum (the castle of St. Angelo.) The Pontiff, preceded by his clergy, goes forth from the gates of the city, like another St. Leo, again to save the capital of the world. He convinces Luitprand that the misfortunes of the Eternal City will prove those

of the whole of Christendom; that the Saracens will have more cause than the emperor to rejoice in the disasters of this Church, mother and mistress of all the others. Gregory's pathetic eloquence moved the Lombard king to tears; he prostrated himself at the Pontiff's feet. The church of St. Peter was close at hand. Gregory points out to the monarch the sacred spot where stands the tomb of the Apostles. Luitprand, overcome, advances toward the basilica, kneels before the confession of St. Peter, strips off his royal ornaments, and leaves them, together with his military scarf, his sword and golden crown, before the tomb; he then begs the Pope to forgive his enemies; Gregory utters the solemn pardon, and Luitprand, having sworn eternal friendship, goes back to Pavia. Minds enlightened by prudence foresaw all the moral power bestowed upon the Church by these events. They could daily convince themselves of the necessity of obedience to the Sovereign Pontiff, since they had just beheld the most powerful monarch of Italy prostrate at his feet.

9. St. Gregory II. neglected no political means to secure the help of the Western princes. He had written to ask the protection of Charles Martel for the Holy See. The royal Frank promised his aid. Strong in all these allies, Gregory once more wrote to Leo the Isaurian, upbraiding him with his unworthy conduct. "The eyes of the West are turned upon our lowliness," he said, "and it looks to us as the arbiter and moderator of public peace. Should you dare to tempt the issue, you would find it ready even to go to Constantinople, there to avenge the wrongs of your Eastern subjects." The tone of this letter is the best proof of the sway then held by the Papacy over the world. The Iconoclast emperor replied only by the most insulting threats. He promised to Gregory II. the fate of Martin I., but the time was past when an emperor of Constantinople could renew such scenes of violence. Besides, the toils of a long and stormy pontificate had wrecked the already shattered health of St. Gregory II., who sunk at last on the

10th of February, A. D. 731. His pontificate was a reign of wisdom, glory and courage.

§ II. PONTIFICATE OF ST. GREGORY III. (March 18, A. D. 731— November 28, 741).

10. Gregory III. was unanimously elected to succeed Gregory II., five days after that Pontiff's death. But as it was still necessary to await the confirmation of the exarch of Ravenna, his coronation was delayed till the 18th of March, A. D. 731. The Papacy might now deem itself strong enough in Italy to do away with an abuse against which it had ever protested since the days of Athalaric, king of the Visigoths, who first enforced it by open violence. Moreover, Leo the Isaurian had made himself odious enough to the Church to have forfeited all claim to patronize it in any way. But the very existence of these unfriendly relations between the courts of Rome and Constantinople was a new and powerful motive for shunning all occasion of rupture. The bearing of the Popes is a sufficient reply to the assertions of some historians that the Sovereign Pontiffs of this period all acted from motives of personal ambition, and were ready to seize the most trifling pretexts to throw off the Eastern yoke. But this endeavor must naturally have ceased with the successor of Gregory III., since the power of Constantinople had finally fallen in Italy. The election of Gregory III. was a triumph. During the funeral ceremonies of his predecessor, the people bore him to the Lateran palace with enthusiastic acclamations.

11. The emperor still carried on his persecution against those who would not join him in destroying holy images. The Iconoclast heresy was by far the most unpopular of all in Italy. Pagan Rome, after the Grecian conquest, had hailed the arts with enthusiasm: Christian Rome now earnestly defended the same arts which were likewise to prove her glory. Gregory III. adorned the interior of St. Peter's, on one side with images of the Saviour and the apostles, on the other with

those of the Blessed Virgin and the most illustrious martyrs. At the same time he wrote a most dignified and energetic letter to the emperor Leo, in reply to the invectives of the Iconoclasts, addressed to the preceding Pontiff. "You think to terrify us with the threat: I shall destroy the statue of St. Peter at Rome, and seize Pope Gregory as did the emperor Constans II. Pope Martin. We do not fear your empty threats. The Sovereign Pontiff has an inviolable abode in Campania." A second letter followed close upon this one, clearly tracing the line of separation between the temporal and the spiritual power, between the empire and the priesthood. Both these letters were intrusted to a priest named George, who did not deliver them to the emperor, but returned to Rome to confess that his courage had failed him on the way. The Pope subjected him to a course of penance for his weakness, and sent him back as bearer of the same dispatches. But Leo, hearing of his departure and the end of his mission, had him arrested and held for nearly a year in Sicily.

12. Luitprand again began to show unfriendly feelings toward the Holy See. Charles Martel, to whom Gregory had appealed in like circumstances before, had hitherto been hindered from any active display of good-will by the unsettled condition of his own authority in France. Gregory sent him a solemn embassy charged to commit to his guard the keys of St. Peter's tomb. The grandfather of Charlemagne, laying his powerful hand upon the sacred symbols, declared himself the protector of the Holy See, and swore that neither the emperor of Constantinople nor the Lombard king should, without his leave, open the tomb of the Prince of the Apostles. It was on this occasion that Gregory III. bestowed upon the duke of Austrasia the title of Most Christian Prince, which Pope Pius II. afterward (A. D. 1460) declared hereditary in the person of the French kings. The institution of pontifical nuncios in France dates from this embassy sent by Gregory III. to Austrasia. It bore some resemblance to that of the *Apocrisiarii*, or legates of the Holy See accredited by the Popes to

the court of Constantinople. The nuncios were subsequently recognized as ministers of a directly sovereign power. Charles was not slow to prove himself worthy of the title bestowed upon him by the Pope.

13. A most fearful tempest was now bearing down upon the whole of Christendom. In A. D. 732 a countless host of Saracens, under Abderahman, swarmed through the defiles of the Pyrenees. They seemed to follow the footsteps of Hannibal in his Italian invasion. But here they displayed a knowledge of strategy for which they had never yet received credit, for they would not enter the enemy's country without guarding their flanks against the Gauls. Abderahman marched his army in two divisions. The first followed the banks of the Rhone and the Saône, to the river Yonne. Captors of Avignon, Viviers, Valence, Vienne, Lyons, Mâcon, Châlons, Besançon, Beaune, Dijon and Auxerre, the Saracens at length besieged Sens. But the bishop St. Ebbo, after a fervent prayer to God for help in their necessity, made a bold sally at the head of the besieged, and drove back the horde of unbelievers in hasty flight. Meanwhile, Abderahman in person led the second division of his army into Aquitaine. The cities of Béarn, Oléron, Auch, Aix, Dax, Lapurdum (now Bayonne), Bordeaux, Agen, Perigueux, Saintes, and Poitiers were plundered or burned. The Saracens marked their course by tracks of blood. Their scymitars gave to many a martyr his blood-dyed palm. The diocese of Puy-en-Velay honors St. Theofred, more commonly known as St. Chaffre, abbot of the monastery of Carmery. At Marseilles, in the convent of St. Saviour, the abbess St. Eusebia and forty of her religious gashed and otherwise disfigured their countenances, to escape the outrages of the Mussulmans. The infidels murdered the heroic virgins, who were buried together in a chapel since known as the *Chapel of the Confession.* The monastery of Lerins, under St. Porcarius, the second of the name, numbered more than five hundred monks, who were massacred by the Saracens. Only four religious, by a kind of miracle, escaped this fearful slaughter.

and came back to restore the monastic life upon the graves of their glorious brethren. St. Pardoux (Pardulphus), abbot of the monastery of Varecte (Guéret), likewise received the martyr's crown.*

14. "Charles Martel did not wait† to declare war until the enemy knocked at the gates of Orleans and Sens. He had not quitted Gaul that year, but held himself in readiness to balance the scales of war by the weight of his sword. The appearance of Eudes, king of Aquitaine, conquered, flying, a general without an army, a king without a realm, showed him that the danger was more threatening than he had deemed it. During the summer of 732 the Roman clarions and German horns kept alive the echoes of Neustria and Austrasia. The most impenetrable marshes of the Northern Ocean, the pathless shades of the Black Forest, gave forth a swarm of half-naked warriors, who poured on toward the Loire, in the rear of the heavy squadrons of iron-clad Austrasians. This huge mass of Francs, Teutons, and Gallo-Romans crossed the Loire at Orleans, rallied the broken fragments of the Aquitanian army, which had sought shelter in Berry and Tourraine, and at length stood face to face with the Arab host under the walls of Poitiers, in the month of October, A. D. 732. Here Abderahman had gathered together the countless battalions of his two armies. The history of the human race scarce records a more solemn moment. Islamism stood before the last bulwark of Christianity The North and the South had met. The contemporary chronicler, Isidore de Beja, did not misname the Frankish host when he styled it the European army. If this army falls, the world is Mahomet's. What would have been the future of mankind, had the European civilization of the Middle Ages, our mother, been thus stifled in the cradle? At the moment of the great crisis, Arab civilization, at some

---

* The monastery of Varecte became renowned in Gaul, and gave its rise and name to the city of Guéret.

† We borrow the account of the battle of Poitiers from M. Henry Martin's History of France, which won the first prize in the Academy of Inscriptions and Belles-Lettres.

points presented an appearance of chivalry; but we should not deceive ourselves as to the real value of these outward, shining qualities, nor allow our eyes to be dazzled by the elegant monuments of literature and art which were given to the light in Cordova, Granada, Bagdad, or Shiraz. Relatively to European convictions, Islamism was no new development of humanity, but a fatal leap backward. The Koran revived the fatalism of the ancients, and doomed woman to the disgraceful yoke of polygamy, which had been broken by Christian civilization, both Greek and Roman. The boundless submission of the Mussulmans to the decrees of fate and to the Prophet's representative, destroyed in them all human personality as well as all political existence, and must cast them without transition from a blind and rash fanaticism into a stupid inactivity.* The Frank and the Saracen are about to throw for the fate of the world. The Austrasian warriors little knew what destinies were to be shaped by their swords that day; yet they seemed to feel an indistinct apprehension of the vast importance of the struggle now before them. The Mussulmans faltered for the first time. For seven days the East and West watched each other with fear and hate; the difference of physiognomy, costume, and tactics inspired the two armies, or rather the two worlds, with mutual wonder. The astonished eyes of the Franks reviewed those myriads of swarthy hue, with many-colored turbans, white cloaks, round bucklers, crooked sabres, and light lances, curveting about on their uncurried steeds. The Mussulman sheiks galloped back and forth before the

* In his conference of December 21st, 1845, Fr. de Lacordaire eloquently remarked: "See the Mussulman! He is six centuries behind us. Mahomet had the Gospel within his reach; he could copy it, and so he did. And now! What is the Mussulman? What are Greece and Syria under his rule? What has become of their cultivated fields? Where is the landscape which, with so many other illustrious recollections, had recalled the poetic memories of its mountains and valleys? The very earth refuses to live under the degrading power whose twelve hundred years have not yet taught it to protect a single grain of wheat. I say nothing of the rest. God gave them the fairest portions of the earth, after even giving them subsequence to His Gospel, to teach us by their example, as near as it is striking, what will be the fate of nations that reject the Gospel already taught and known."

Gallo-Teutonic lines to gain a better view of the northern giants with their long light locks, their burnished helms, buff mantles or heavy coats of mail, their long swords and huge battle-axes. At length, on the seventh day, a Saturday near the end of October, the muezzin's cry at early dawn drew forth the Arabs and Moors from their tents, to prayer. They formed iu line upon the plain, and after the morning devotion Abderahman gave the signal. The Christian army never flinched before the hail of darts poured by the Berber archers on their ranks. The serried masses of the Mussulman cavalry then, fiercely pealing their well-known war-cry, *Allah ak-bar!* (God is great!), bore down like a hurricane upon the Christian front. The long French line stood firm and quailed not before the fearful shock; *hard as a wall of iron, firm as the front of an iceberg, the pale hordes of the north stood shoulder to shoulder like marble statues.* Twenty times the maddened Turks turned rein to take a wider field and try the charge again with the speed of a thunderbolt; twenty times their fiery charge was dashed like the breaker's foam from off the unbroken lines. The Austrasian giants rose in the stirrups on their great Belgian war-horses, received the Arabs on the point of their swords, and smiting the diminutive sons of the desert with downward stroke, clove them in two with their frightful long sabres. The struggle lasted throughout the whole day, and Abderahman still hoped to weary the Christians' stout resistance, when toward the tenth hour (four o'clock after noon), king Eudes, who with the remainder of his Vascons and Aquitanians had turned the Saracen flank, fell upon the Moslem camp and dispersed the guards. *The icy bulwark* breaks at last; Charles and his Austrasians charge in turn, and bear down all before them. Abderahman and the flower of his host disappear, crushed beneath the heavy mass of iron." Charles had fairly won his name *Martel,* for like a hammer he had crushed the might of the Saracens.

15. The results of the battle of Poitiers were incalculable. The duke of Austrasia dispatched a messenger from the battle-

field to bear to Pope Gregory III. the glad tidings of the Christian victory. The courier's progress through the country, stricken with terror by the Moslems' march, was a continued triumph. Every church in France and Italy resounded with solemn anthems of praise to God. The envoys reached Rome, loaded with the conqueror's gifts for the church of the Apostles. They were directed to inform all the enemies of Gregory III. that his son, Charles Martel, protector of Christendom, after having received such signal protection from Jesus Christ, would never allow the least insult to be offered to His vicar upon earth. The emperors of the East could now see the protectorate of the Holy See, which they had so often changed into persecution and violence, pass to a nation more worthy of the charge. The Lombards acknowledged the necessity of bowing to the new power now rising up before them. Charles Martel showed himself worthy of the noble stand he now took before the Catholic world, and his glory would have been stainless had he not allowed himself to be led into an unjust persecution of St. Eucherius, bishop of Orleans, and St. Rigobert, archbishop of Rheims, who had held him over the baptismal font. St. Eucherius, a monk in the abbey of Jumiéges, and afterward raised to the bishopric of Orleans, was accused of plotting against the state. The duke of Austrasia, without taking time to examine the charges, banished the holy bishop to Cologne, and afterward to the monastery of St. Trudo or St. Tron, where he died, April 20, A. D. 738. St. Rigobert succeeded St. Reol in the see of Rheims, about the beginning of the eighth century. His saintly virtue won the esteem and friendship of Pepin of Herstal, and he showed a particular zeal for the maintenance of clerical and monastic discipline in his diocese. The bishop's great prudence kept him aloof from the unceasing strifes which divided the ambitious courtiers, and refusing to take part with Charles Martel in a movement against the Neustrians (A. D. 717), the duke deposed him from his see, and gave it to an intruder named Milo. St. Rigobert died in the monastery of Gernicourt, on the

4th of January, A. D. 740, on which day the Church honors his memory.

16. Iconoclasm, backed by the power of Leo the Isaurian, daily grew into threatening proportions. Pope Gregory III., unable to transmit his letters to the emperor, assembled a council of ninety-three bishops in St. Peter's church at Rome. The Roman nobility, clergy, consuls and people were present (A. D. 732). An anathema was hurled against the Iconoclast heresy. Every profaner and even every contemner of images was declared unworthy to partake of the body and blood of Jesus Christ, and was cut off from the communion of the Church. The Pope once more endeavored to send the decisions of the council to the emperor, but in vain. The priest Constans, to whom they were intrusted, was thrown into close confinement, stripped of the papers he bore about him, and was only released a year later, overwhelmed with threats and ill treatment. An embassy from the whole of Italy, sent to beg of the emperor the restoration of holy pictures, met with a like reception. The Pope wrote on the subject to Leo and to his creature Anastasius; his complaints and steady opposition only served to rouse the emperor's fury to its highest pitch. He armed a fleet for the subjugation of Italy; but it perished in the Adriatic Sea. The troops landed on the shore of Ravenna, were attacked and utterly routed by the inhabitants (A. D. 733). The Iconoclast's madness knew no bounds; he redoubled his cruelty toward the Catholics, and, powerless in every other respect against the Church of Rome, confiscated all its domains in his states. He moreover issued an imperial edict withdrawing from its immediate jurisdiction all the provinces between Sicily and Thrace, comprising Greece, Illyria and Macedonia, and declared them henceforth subject to the Patriarchate of Constantinople. The tax of Sicily and Calabria was increased by a third; and, not to exempt even children, it was ordered that they should be entered upon the rolls of contribution on the day of their birth.

17. Each new deed of violence from Constantinople only

tended to estrange Rome and Italy farther from its sway.
Luitprand deemed this juncture favorable for the execution of
the plans of aggrandizement which still filled his mind. He
attacked Thrasimund, duke of Spoleto, who immediately fled
to the shelter of the Sovereign Pontiff and the Romans. A
successful engagement between them and the Lombard forces
restored Thrasimund to Spoleto. Yet Luitprand threatened to
besiege Rome with all his forces, and Gregory feared that the
city would yield to his attacks unless speedily succored. In
this extremity he thus wrote to Charles Martel, who had declared himself the champion of the Holy See: "Such is the
grief into which we are plunged that we cease not, day and
night, to shed bitter tears over the sad state to which we see
the holy Church of Christ reduced. All that we had laid up
during the past year, for the support of the Roman poor, in the
territory of Ravenna, has been destroyed by fire and sword.
The Lombard kings, Luitprand and Hildebrand, respect nothing.
They mock us with the bitter taunt, 'Bring on that Charles
Martel whose help you entreat! Let the French arms save
you from our hands, if they can!' Most Christian son! help
the Church of St. Peter and its wretched children. Turn not
a deaf ear to our prayers, that the Prince of the Apostles may
be equally favorable to you at the gates of heaven" (A. D. 737).
Charles Martel, detained at home by a fresh inroad of the
Saracens, could not come in person to defend the Holy See.
Since Abderahman's bloody defeat at Poitiers, the infidels
every year poured a flood of Mussulmans upon the southern
provinces of France, and every year the *Hammer* of Christianity
crushed the fresh host of enemies. Yet the duke of Austrasia
used his influence to advantage in the Pope's favor. He wrote
to his ally Luitprand, asking him to abstain from hostilities
toward Rome, and the powerful recommendation produced its
effect on the Lombard king (A. D. 739). This was one of the
closing acts of Charles Martel's great and long administration.
He was only fifty-four years of age. With the new career now
opened to him as titulary champion of the Roman, and conse-

quently of the Universal, Church, he might yet have looked forward to many years of power and glory. But death came upon him at the castle of Quercy-sur-Oise. He left two sons, Carloman and Pepin: the former received Austrasia, Suabia, and Thuringia; the latter inherited the provinces of Neustria, Burgundy, and Provence. But to the younger it was given to gather under his single sway the vast possessions of his father, and to found the Carlovingian dynasty. Death at the same time seized upon the Iconoclast emperor, Leo the Isaurian, at Constantinople (A. D. 741). The persecutor and the defender of the Holy See, together stood before the tribunal of its Divine Founder; and, as if to close completely this eventful act, the 28th of November of the same year (741) ended the glorious pontificate of Gregory III.

18. This Pontiff had continued to encourage the missionaries in Germany, and established the four bishoprics of Saltzburg, Freisingen, Ratisbon, and Passaw, under the metropolitan jurisdiction of St. Boniface of Mayence. Out of his own purse he raised the walls of Rome and Centum-cellæ, a work designed by Sisinnius (A. D. 708) during his short pontificate. He bought from the duke of Spoleto, for a great sum of money, a stronghold which often troubled the peace of the Roman territory; in a word, he availed himself of the very troubles of the times to shelter the freedom of the Catholic Church from the despotism of the Eastern emperors. He saved Europe, and indeed the whole world, from the wretched alternative of degrading itself under the degenerate rule of the Greeks, or of being lowered by the brutal domination of the Saracens. Gregory III. is one of the Pontiffs to whom the whole world owes a debt of lasting gratitude. Even Photius, the most unfriendly of the Greek historians, could not but praise Pope Gregory III., and his successor, St. Zachary. "How," he writes, "can I pass in silence the Roman Pontiffs Gregory and Zachary, men of lofty virtue, who have enlightened the world with the teachings of divine wisdom, and made their day illustrious by their gift of miracles?"

§ III. Pontificate of St. Zachary (December 3, a. d. 741—March 15, 752).

19. The whole world was undergoing a change of rulers at tho same time. While Carloman and Pepin inaugurated their rule over the Franks, St. Zachary mounted the steps of the papal throne (December 3, a. d. 741). Neither the emperor nor the exarch of Ravenna was consulted in his election, and the consecration took place without that formality, which was thenceforth entirely abolished. At Constantinople the sceptre of Leo the Isaurian passed into the hands of his son, Constantine V., surnamed Copronymus,* who succeeded his father on the throne, but far surpassed him in impiety.

20. Luitprand's ambition still disturbed Italy. The Lombard had just despoiled the duke of Spoleto, Thrasimund, the late ally of the Holy See, whose bad faith and ingratitude had forced St. Zachary to withdraw the protection with which Gregory III. had formerly favored him. Luitprand profited by the chance to seize upon Spoleto and Beneventum. Thrasimund was imprisoned in a monastery. The Pope determined to turn the unfriendly dispositions of the Lombard king by a personal meeting at Terni. Luitprand received the Sovereign Pontiff with the highest honors. Peace was concluded between the two powers, and Luitprand gave back to the Holy See the four cities of Ameria, Horta, Polisartium, and Blera, which he had hitherto unjustly held. He added to this personal restitution that of the estates of Narni, Sabinium, Osimo, and Ancona, which the Lombards had successively seized during the past half century. The treaty between Zachary and Luitprand presents a feature worthy of note—it is to the Pope that the restitution of all the estates is made. There must, therefore, even then have existed a recognized, immediate, sovereign pon-·ifical power, with which the Lombard king treated on terms

* His surname was derived from his having defiled his baptismal font.—Copronymus being a compound of the Greek words κόπρος, filth, and ὄνομα, a name.

of equality (A. D. 742). In the following year the prayers of the inhabitants of the exarchate, still harassed by the restless ambition of Luitprand, once more called St. Zachary to meet the king at Pavia, where he held his court. As Pontiff of the God of peace, he came to implore the clemency of a prince whose ambition ever kept his sword unsheathed. Luitprand could not resist the Pope's earnest eloquence; he withdrew his troops from the territory of Ravenna, and voluntarily gave up all the usurped provinces. Thus did the Papacy ever prove the refuge and stay of the downtrodden, against their oppressors, and grateful nations hailed it as a guardian power.

21. The benefactor of Italy, whose various states he so faithfully guarded, won the same title of gratitude from Germany, where his missionaries steadily spread the light of faith. He likewise labored to restore to Gaul the discipline which Mussulman inroads and civil wars had so sadly shaken. St. Boniface of Mayence received the title of vicar of the Holy See for all the Churches of Germany. Three new bishoprics were founded at Wurtzburg, Buraburg, and Erfurth, the capital of Thuringia. The tireless apostle of Germany, St. Boniface, gathered all the bishops of his jurisdiction in a national council (A. D. 742), which published disciplinary canons relating to matters peculiar to the times. The council dwells particularly upon the prohibition to all ecclesiastics to bear arms or to take part in the numerous wars then desolating the world. A great number of clerics, bishops and priests had not scrupled, in the war against Abderahman, to place themselves at the head of the troops and fight in the foremost rank. The council reminds them that the hands of a priest should not be stained with blood, and that their only mission on the battle-field is to bear the last consolations of religion to the dying. Princes are allowed to take almoners or chaplains with them on their military expeditions; but all clerics are forbidden on pain of excommunication to bear arms. As a more effectual separation from the rest of the world, and a safeguard to the honor of their ministry, they are enjoined to wear a long black garment,

different from the common mantle. Such is the origin of the present ecclesiastical costume. Hunting was at that period the favorite pastime of kings, nobles and lords. In that age this mimicry of nobler war could not but please, and even ecclesiastics had allowed themselves to be drawn into the current of the prevailing passion. "We forbid all bishops, priests, clerics or monks," decreed the Fathers of the council, "to hunt in the forests with packs of hounds, sparrow-hawks or falcons." The newly converted Germans found it hard to strip themselves of their old heathen superstitions in the idolatrous worship of Odin, Thor and the Scandinavian gods. The council dwells particularly on this point. "We ordain that every bishop, within the limits of his own diocese, forbid all heathen superstition, such as sacrifices to the *shades** of the dead, spells, charms, the immolation of victims, and the sacrilegious fires called *nodfirs*."† Another German council convoked during the following year (A. D. 743) at Leptines (now Lestines), royal residence of the diocese of Cambray, renewed all the above ordinances and added the following remarkable canon, published with the consent of the Fathers under the name of Carloman: "To meet the expenses of the wars now forced upon us, we have determined, by the advice and consent of all the bishops, to withdraw for a time the income of ecclesiastical property, to appropriate it to the support of our army." This willing sacrifice of their means to the defence of the land, showed in the bishops of Germany a noble example of disinterested attachment to their sovereign. St. Boniface sent the acts of the two councils to St. Zachary. The Pope was gratified by these happy beginnings of reform, and answered by a circular letter to the German clergy, congratulating them on their return to the rules of canonical discipline. "If the clergy in your land," writes the Pontiff, "strictly follow out the rules of discipline and chastity as the canons decree, and brother Boniface teaches in our name, no other peo-

---

* The chief of the Scandinavian gods, Odin, dwelt in the palace of Valhalla, in the region of the clouds, where he received the shades of the heroes who fell in battle.

† The Northmen honored fire as a divinity, and paid it a superstitious worship.

ple can stand before you." St. Boniface had worn the pallium
and borne the archiepiscopal rank and responsibilities since the
beginning of Gregory the Third's pontificate, but had hitherto
been without any fixed see or metropolitan church. He was
now raised to the archbishopric of Mayence, with jurisdiction
over the twelve churches of Strasburg, Spires, Worms, Cologne,
Liege, Augsburg, Wurtzburg, Buraburg (since transferred to
Paderborn), Erfurth, Eichstadt, Constance and Coire.   The
archbishop was the soul of Christianity in the northern part of
Europe. All business was brought before him, every difficulty,
every doubt was dispelled by his lights, every misfortune found
a support and defence in his charity. His voluminous correspondence with St. Zachary, who had appointed him legate,
shows his respectful submission to the Holy See, and the importance he attached to the close union of Germany with the
centre of Catholic unity. Boniface had to meet obstacles of
every kind; and one of the most formidable was the decline
of ecclesiastical studies, which had fallen into neglect in those
times of confusion and war. The consequent ignorance of the
clergy had reached a degree which in our days would awake
the deepest contempt. Many of them hardly understood the
formulas used in administering the sacraments. This gave rise
to a curious question put by St. Boniface to the Pope. The
archbishop asked if a baptism should be deemed valid in which
the priest used these words devoid of all meaning: *Ego te bap-
tizo in nomine Patria, et Filia, et Spiritua Sancta.* St. Zachary
answered that a baptism thus administered in the name of the
Trinity and with the intention of doing what the Church does,
has the qualities essential to the sacrament, and that mere
ignorance of the language, without any mixture of doctrinal
error, could not invalidate it.

22. Innovators took advantage of the dearth of theological
studies to broach the most absurd doctrines. Thus a Scotch
priest named Sampson came to Germany and taught that baptism was a useless formality, and that the imposition of the
bishop's hands was enough to remit original sin. Another

priest, of German blood, named Virgil, taught that there were
men living *under the earth,* not redeemed by Jesus Christ. St.
Zachary wrote to Boniface to excommunicate the reckless innovators. Some modern writers, instigated by hatred for the
Catholic Church, have made the condemnation of Virgil an
argument against the Papacy, alleging that St. Zachary condemned the teaching of those who held the existence of the
antipodes. Their system would exalt Virgil's ignorance into
lofty astronomical acquirements, and hold him up to the world as
a scholar whose genius has outrun his age, whose splendid dis-
coveries were rewarded by the anathemas of the Church. This
is but another historical sophism added to the many which the
misbelieving world has already received. Zachary's condemnation touched but one point of dogma, utterly foreign to questions of astronomy or cosmography. It was aimed solely at
certain heretics teaching the existence of a race of men not
descended from Adam and not redeemed by our Lord.

23. Pepin was not behind his brother Carloman in zeal for
the establishment of religious discipline in his states. In the
year 744 he assembled twenty-three bishops in council at
Soissons. The canons bore the sanction of the Frankish prince.
They renewed the ordinances of Leptines and the German
council, and issued some new regulations contained in ten articles. The council directed that the old canons of the councils
should be published throughout the kingdom, in order to restore
the primitive purity of discipline. The transgressors of canonical laws were made subject to fines. The same council condemned the two heretics, Adalbert and Clement. These two
fanatical impostors called themselves bishops, and led many
astray by a hypocritical show of piety. At a more enlightened period an open publication of their teaching would have
been its speediest death. Adalbert pretended to have been
sent by God to put an end to the idolatry of churches and
temples. "The only temple fit for the Divine Majesty," said
he, "is the temple of the universe." It appears by this proposition, that the teaching of the German illuminate was some-

what similar to that of the Eastern Iconoclasts. He based his mission upon an epistle which he mysteriously showed to his followers, as having been written by the very hand of the Son of God, and dropped from heaven at Jerusalem. The crowds, ever eager for novelties, followed the impostor's steps in great numbers. He gathered them together in the country, in the open air, around little crosses which he set up at every stopping-place. The characteristic feature of Clement's heresy was a contempt for tradition. Clement rejected, in a body, all the canons, councils, and writings of the holy Fathers. Such a doctrine was of course easily received in an age ruled by ignorance. The Council of Soissons condemned the two heresiarchs, and in the following year (A. D. 745) St. Zachary confirmed the sentence in a council of eight bishops held at Rome. Both sects were very short-lived, and left not a single trace either in Germany or in France.

24. Great Britain also had its council, at Clove-shoe (Cliff), in the beginning of September (A. D. 747): *Our Lord Jesus Christ reigning forever*, in the words of the Acts. St. Cuthbert, archbishop of Canterbury, presided, and King Ethelbald was present in person. The thirty canons drawn up by the council contain a few interesting particulars. "Every priest should be able to explain, in the language of the country, the Creed, the Lord's Prayer, the words used in celebrating the Holy Mysteries, in administering baptism, and in the other offices of the Church. The rule of the Roman Church, which we have in writing, shall be followed in all the liturgy." The council blames the growing abuse of substituting alms at will for the canonical penances imposed by the priest in satisfaction for sins committed. The subject of canonical penances had lately been settled in England by the Penitential Code of Egbert, archbishop of York. The holy prelate, who was a brother of Edbert, king of Northumberland, composed, at the same time, a celebrated pontifical, in which appeared for the first time the ceremonial for the royal unction. The Church has a twofold object in pouring holy oil upon crowned heads: she wishes to awake in the people a feel-

ing of reverence for authority by placing it under the immediate
sanction of God, while warning rulers that their mission is an
apostolic one, and that the greater and more sublime the power
they wield, the more directly it depends upon God, "Who judges
justice and holds in His hand the hearts of kings." According
to St. Egbert's pontifical, the ceremony began by the following
oath on the king's part: "I swear to keep the Church of God
and the Christian people under my rule in peace; 2d, to repress injustice, from whatever source it may come; 3d, to
blend, in all my judgments, justice with mercy. So may the
good and most clement God forgive us all in His eternal mercy!"
The king was next anointed with holy oil. The chief nobles
then drew near, and, together with the bishops, gave the sceptre
into his hand. The archbishop then began the acclamations:
" Be he ever magnanimous and victorious! Be all his judgments wise and just! Be his reign blest with peace and his
triumphs bloodless! Be his life but an unbroken chain of prosperous days! And after his earthly reign, may he enjoy one
of endless bliss in heaven!" The people then thrice called out,
Vivat rex in œternum! Very low must be the moral standard
of the heart which does not feel that such a ceremony laid a
far more lasting foundation for a reign than the shouts of the
streets or popular clamors.

25. While the saintly archbishop of York was drawing up
these touching ceremonies of coronation for the Anglo-Saxon
kings, to remind princes that wise counsels and lofty conceptions are born in heaven, the brutal impiety of Constantine
Copronymus was deeply disgracing the Eastern throne. This
monarch, the too worthy heir of Leo the Isaurian, did not hesitate openly to deny the Catholic faith. His sacrilegious blasphemies revolted even the Patriarch Anastasius, that creature
of an Iconoclast emperor. From the very pulpit of St. Sophia,
Anastasius swore by the Holy Cross that he had heard Copronymus, in his own presence, deny the divinity of Jesus Christ, and
outrage the name that saved the world. Constantine V. plunged
the empire into mourning and ruins. He sought to immortal-

ize his reign by persecuting the faithful who refused to join the Iconoclast heresy. To this period of desolation and blood the Christians could apply the words of the Gospel : "The hour cometh, that whosoever killeth you will think that he doth a service to God. And these things will they do to you because they have not known the Father nor Me." But Copronymus soon became so intolerable to his downtrodden subjects that they rose up and deposed him in favor of his brother-in-law Artavasdes. With all his vices, Constantine V. was unquestionably brave. He gathered six thousand soldiers under his command, besieged Constantinople, in which his rival had taken shelter, reduced it by famine, and gave it up to be plundered by his pretorians. Artavasdes and two of his sons had their eyes plucked out by the emperor's order. The Patriarch Anastasius was publicly scourged in the hippodrome, and afterward led through the streets of Constantinople upon an ass, with his face toward the animal's tail, as a punishment for favoring the attempt of Artavasdes. Yet the prelate kept his patriarchal throne. "The emperor," says Theophanes, "could not have found a worse one to put in his place." Anastasius was indeed one of the warmest Iconoclasts in the empire.

26. Far different was the example given to the world by a Frankish prince at the same period. One day in the year 747, a stranger knocked at the gate of the monastery of Monte Cassino. On being admitted he threw himself at the abbot's feet and said to him : "I am a wretch loaded with crimes. I have voluntarily forsaken my country to make myself worthy of a heavenly home." He was accompanied by an attendant; both were received among the novices. After a year of trial they made their profession to the abbot Optatus, successor of St. Petronax. No one knew the names of the new brethren. One of them was sent to serve in the kitchen, which duty he accepted with joy, but, through want of experience, doubtless, discharged rather ill. The cook, seeing his dishes spoiled, was so far excited as to give the unhandy scullion a blow. The humble religious uttered but the expression : "May God and Car-

loman forgive you!" But his companion, who had witnessed
the brutal punishment, unable to withhold his indignation, seized
a pestle close at hand and struck the cook a violent blow, with
the exclamation : "May neither God nor Carloman forgive
you!" The abbot made this a crime in the stranger monk, and
asked him before the whole community how he had dared to
strike an officer of the monastery. "It is," replied the culprit,
"because I could not see so much nobility and virtue so basely
treated. This unknown religious is Carloman, the son of Charles
Martel, and lately sovereign of half of Gaul, who has been led
by the love of Jesus Christ to forsake the glory and power of
the world."* It was indeed Prince Carloman ; weary of human
greatness, he had left his states to his brother Pepin, and came
to seek rest and quiet in the solitude of Monte Cassino. Foremost among the religious in humility, he begged the lowest
offices of the convent as a favor. He kept the flocks belonging
to the monastery. Such examples of royal humility were not
few at that period. The same monastery of Monte Cassino
soon saw another crowned head bowed beneath the yoke of
religious discipline. After the death of the Lombard king
Luitprand (A. D. 744) and the ephemeral reign of Hildebrand,
Rachis, duke of Friuli, was elected to succeed them. The new
king at first showed friendly dispositions, and renewed the alliance made by Luitprand with the Romans. But he shortly
afterward determined upon seizing Pentapolis, and laid vigorous siege to Perugia. St. Zachary at once came forth from
Rome accompanied by the chief members of his clergy and the
citizens, and sought the king in his very camp. He not only
persuaded the monarch to raise the siege, but spoke to him so
feelingly of his eternal welfare and the hollowness of every
earthly interest, that Rachis yielded to the resistless voice
of inward grace, forsook the royal dignity, received the reli-

---

* This occurrence, which may seem somewhat extraordinary in our time, is related by
Reginon, abbot of Prum, and by contemporaneous chronicles; some modern writers object
to it on the ground of its romantic coloring, but offer no solid proofs in support of their
view.

GENERAL HISTORY OF THE CHURCH.

gious habit from the Pontiff's own hands, and sought a cell in the holy shades of Monte Cassino, where he ended his days in peace. Three hundred years later the passing stranger was still shown a vine which bore his name; he had planted and trained it with his own hands. His brother Astolphus succeeded him on the Lombard throne (A. D. 750).

27. Pepin, now left sole master of Gaul by his brother's retreat, still possessed but the modest title of mayor of the palace. A king in fact, he was by right but the minister of a royal phantom, Childeric III., a weak and powerless prince. A change of dynasty was imminent. The nation had long been prepared for it by the slothfulness of the sluggard kings, degenerate scions of the great Clovis. The crown of the Franks was originally elective, but the genius of Clovis had fixed it in his family. His descendants, however, had made this hereditary right odious by their luxurious incapacity. The blood of Charles Martel, the champion of Christendom, was now endeared to the Franks, and the duke of Austrasia had won for his race a royal crown on the field of Poitiers. Pepin was about taking a step which would secure him a throne; he wished to sanction his enterprise in the eyes of nations by the approval of the highest authority in the world, that of the Vicar of Jesus Christ. "In the year 751," says Eginhard, "Burchard, bishop of Wurtzburg, and Fulrad, chaplain of the Frankish prince, and afterward abbot of St. Denis, were sent to Rome to obtain from Pope Zachary an answer to the following question: 'Who has the better right to the name of king, he who holds nothing of royal authority but the name, or he who possesses it all without the name?' The Pope replied: 'It is just and reasonable that he who has all the royal power should also have the name of king.' In the following year (A. D. 752) Pepin the Short* was elected king of the Franks, consecrated by the holy bishop of Mayence, St. Boniface, and

* The diminutive size of his body, to which he owed his surname, was accompanied by prodigious strength. The story is well known of his display of muscular power in killing a lion and a bull in the arena, before the courtiers who rallied him on his low stature.

raised, according to the national custom, upon the great shield of the city of Soissons."

The decision of Pope Zachary, in this matter, has been made the subject of the most various criticisms. It has been taxed with injustice, as depriving a lawful king of a power belonging to him by deed and by right. It has been called a pontifical encroachment on the temporal domain of kings. Not to moot a fruitless discussion, we purpose merely to quote the opinions of three French writers, whose names alone should be authority enough: they are Bossuet, Fénelon, and M. de Châteaubriand. "The Pontiff is consulted," says Bossuet, "as in an important and doubtful question, to decide whether it be lawful to give the title of king to him who already holds the royal power. He replies that it is lawful. The decision, coming from the highest authority in the world, is deemed just and binding. By virtue of this authority, the nation itself takes the kingdom from Childeric and transfers it to Pepin. The Pope was not asked to take or to give away the kingdom, but to decide that the kingdom might be taken or given away by those whom he thought empowered to act in the case."[*] "Pope Zachary," says Fénelon, "simply answers the question of the Franks, as the chief doctor and pastor, whose duty it is to clear up particular cases of conscience in order to quiet troubled souls."[†] "Thus the Church neither deposed nor set up temporal princes; she only answered the nations that consulted her on matters of conscience relative to oaths and contracts. This is not exercising a juridical and civil power, but one merely of direction and ordination, as proved by Gerson."[‡] "To treat Pepin's accession to the crown as a usurpation," says M. de Châteaubriand, [§] "is one of those old historic lies which have become truths by dint of repetition. There can be no usurpation where the monarchy is elective: it is the hereditary succession which, in this case, constitutes the

[*] Bossuet, Defensio Cleri Gallic., lib. ii., ch. 34.

[†] Œuvres complètes de Fénelon, Versailles, tom. ii., p. 381.

[‡] Ibid., t. ii., p. 384.

[§] Études Historiques, t. ii., p. 243.

usurpation. Pepin was elected with the knowledge and consent of all the Franks; such are the words of Fredegarius's first continuator. Pope Zachary, when consulted by Pepin, could lawfully reply : It seems to me just and reasonable that he should be king who wields the power though he have not the name, rather than he who holds but the title without the power."

28. St. Zachary's decision in regard to the Carlovingian dynasty was his last pontifical act. He died on the 14th of March, A. D. 752. In the course of his fatherly administration, he rescued a number of slaves whom the Venetian dealers wished to take to Africa for sale to the infidels. The Venetians seemed to be departing from the system of moderation which had satisfied them with a wise mode of government under the protection of the Sovereign Pontiffs. Love of wealth led many merchants of the republic into a desire to stretch their commercial relations at any price. But commerce is not like industry, which tempers its egotism by a national and patriotic feeling which can excuse it to a certain extent. The commerce of the Venetians showed itself, from the outset, what trade too often proves to be everywhere, thoroughly cosmopolitan, without respect for religion or one of its noblest teachings, that which discountenances slavery.* St. Zachary gave a momentary check to this scandal. This Pontiff has left us some *Letters* and *Decrees,* and a translation from Latin into Greek of the Dialogues of St. Gregory the Great.

§ IV. Pontificate of Stephen II. (March 18, A. D. 752—March 20, 752).

29. After the death of Pope Zachary, the clergy and people elected, as his successor, a priest named Stephen, and placed him in possession of the Lateran palace, but he died suddenly on the second day after his promotion. As he was never crowned, many historians do not rank him among the Sovereign

* M. Artaud de Montor, *Histoire des Souverains Pontifes,* 1ᵉʳ vol., *Pontificat de Saint Zacharie.*

Pontiffs. But the official list of Popes, published yearly at Rome, by the *Diario*, with the approbation of the Holy See, mentions Stephen II. in his proper place. We have deemed it safe to follow an opinion consecrated by the pontifical authority itself. Moreover, this system is preferable from the fact that it establishes a more regular nomenclature for the remaining Popes of the same name.*

§ V. PONTIFICATE OF STEPHEN III. (March 26, A. D. 752—April 26, 757).

30. The clergy and people, gathered together in the church of St. Mary Major, elected by acclamation a new Pope, under the name of Stephen III. (March 26, A. D. 752). So lively was the joy awakened by his election, that the enthusiastic multitude bore him upon their shoulders to the basilica of St. John Lateran. The usage has since been renewed, at the installation of each new pontiff, and was the origin of the *sedia gestatoria*—the pontifical chair, borne by twelve of the Noble Guards. This imposing ceremony gives to the Roman pomps a splendor never equalled by any other sovereign court.

31. The Pontiff soon found himself in trouble with Astolphus, king of the Lombards, who had just seized upon Ravenna. Eutychius, the last exarch who ever ruled the city as lieutenant of the Byzantine emperors, fled to Greece. The exarchate was abolished after an existence of one hundred and eighty years. In the views of Astolphus this was but the first step toward the rule of all Italy—that unreal vision pursued through numberless vicissitudes by so many monarchs, who have repeatedly atoned for their ambitious folly by such cruel reverses. In the plan of Divine Providence Italy must remain divided, that the Rome of the Popes may ever be independent; and since its dismemberment at the fall of the Roman Empire in the West, it

---

* Novaes and the other historians who reject Stephen II., are obliged to mention the other Pontiffs of the name with this qualification: Stephen II., *styled Stephen* III.; Stephen IV., *styled Stephen* V, and so on till Stephen IX., *styled Stephen* X.

has been given to no human power to restore the disjointed
fragments. The Lombard king was far from sharing this elevated view of the subject. At the head of all his forces he
marched into the Roman territory. Stephen III. succeeded in
his first endeavor to obtain peace. Astolphus signed a treaty,
which was to last for a term of forty years; it was broken
within four months, and Astolphus again stood at the gates of
Rome. The city was in a state of the utmost consternation.
The Pope sent a courier to Constantinople to warn the emperor
that the hour had come to strike a decisive blow and save Rome,
if he wished to keep an inch of ground in Italy. This token of
faithful loyalty on the part of the Sovereign Pontiff was the
more meritorious, as the Eastern emperors, instead of protecting, had, for the last century, most relentlessly persecuted the
Holy See. Copronymus was too far below such magnanimity
to know how to reply to it. Besides, he had just made extensive military outlays to attack the Turks and profit by the
civil feud which had just broken out between the house of the
Ommiades and that of the Abbassides. Astolphus availed himself of the inertness of the Eastern emperor to show himself more
impracticable than ever. He threatened to put all the Romans
to the sword if they refused to bow to his authority. The
juncture urged the Pope to a great resolution. He ordered a
solemn procession, to beg the Divine mercy for his wretched
people. Barefooted, his head covered with ashes, and followed
by a weeping throng, the Pontiff bore upon his shoulders a
miraculous image of our Lord Jesus Christ. The treaty of
peace violated by the Lombard king was attached to the processional cross. A deputation secretly left Rome, on the following day, to bear to the Frankish king, Pepin the Short, the
cry of distress from Italy and the Holy See. Stephen III.
sent the following message to the king: "Send ambassadors
to Rome, ostensibly to invite me to come to you." The mere
course of events thus naturally brought on one of the most decisive events in history. The political precedence was now to
be finally transferred from the East to the West, France would

take her stand at the head of the nations, and open a new era
in the history of man.

32. The deputation, to whose keeping was intrusted the
welfare of the Church and of the world, escaped the watchful
jealousy of Astolphus, and safely reached the Frankish court.
Since his accession, Pepin had proved himself worthy to rule
the *most Christian* nation. He had utterly expelled the Saracens from the South of Gaul, and had marched into Spain as
far as Barcelona. In the second year of his reign (A. D. 753)
he had turned his victorious arms against the idolatrous Saxons,
who still persecuted their missionaries and burned the Christian
churches. When he had destroyed their strongholds, the king
granted them peace, on condition that the teachers of the Gospel should enjoy full liberty to preach and baptize. Pepin the
Short received the Pope's envoys as his heroic father Charles
Martel would have done. He promised to place the sword of
the Frank at the disposal of the Sovereign Pontiff, to help him
to resist the pretensions of Astolphus, and immediately sent
St. Chrodegang, bishop of Metz, and the duke Autcharius,
to bring Stephen III. to Gaul (A. D. 753). When the royal
ambassadors reached Rome, they found the Pope on the point
of setting out to implore once more the clemency of Astolphus.
On the 14th of October (A. D. 753), Stephen III. passed out of
his pontifical city, followed by a weeping throng of his faithful
people, who earnestly strove to turn him from a course so
fraught with danger. St. Chrodegang and Autcharius accompanied him to Pavia, but Astolphus was unyielding. The two
ambassadors demanded, in their sovereign's name, that the
Lombard should at least grant the Pontiff a safe-conduct to
Gaul, where their master awaited his presence. This demand
surprised Astolphus, who knew nothing of the preceding negotiations; but, after a stubborn resistance, he was at last forced
to yield. But he had no sooner given the safe-conduct than
he repented the deed, and sought to hinder the Pontiff's journey. It was too late. Stephen III., little trusting his gener-

osity, had already crossed the frontier, with George, bishop of Ostia, and Vilcarius, bishop of Nomentum.

33. On his arrival at St. Mauritius, in Valais, Stephen III. found Fulrad, archchaplain of the palace, and Duke Rotard, whom Pepin had sent to meet him. The king himself was occupied with a military expedition in Saxony, but on learning that the Pope had crossed the Alps, he hastened back to France. The meeting occurred at Pontyon, in Champagne. The king advanced to meet the Pontiff, dismounted, and humbly prostrated himself to the earth, with his wife and children, as well as all the lords of his court. The escort then moved on, the king, on foot, held the bridle of the Pontiff's horse, thus acting as groom to the Vicar of Jesus Christ. As he set his foot upon the threshold of the hospitable palace of Pontyon (on the feast of the Epiphany, January 6, A. D. 754), Stephen III. intoned a canticle of thanksgiving. The deep religious emotion of the flying Pontiff may be imagined, on finding, in a strange land, children as respectful as they were devoted. He offered pious gifts to the king and princes. On the next day Stephen, with his clergy, appeared before the whole court, barefooted, in sackcloth and ashes. Yesterday the Pontiff was entering the palace of a king; to-day the suppliant, the fugitive, begs for help and protection. Prostrate before King Pepin, he beseeches him, by the divine mercy, to rescue the Holy See and the Roman people from the tyranny of the Lombards, and keeps his humble posture until the Frank holds out his royal hand as a pledge of the promised help. The scene left a deep impression upon the lords who witnessed it, and they all swore, with the king, never to sheathe the sword until the Lombard's insolence had been punished. The Pope then took up his residence in the monastery of St. Denis. Fatigue and grief had undermined his health; he fell seriously ill. He attributed his recovery to St. Denis, and left to the monastery his pallium, which has been kept until very lately as a precious memorial of the Pontiff's visit. Frankish envoys had been sent to ask Astolphus to

cease hostilities against the Holy See, now under the protection
of Pepin.   Astolphus replied in terms of haughty contempt.

34. Pepin the Short assembled all the nobles of his kingdom in a *Champ de Mai* (field of May),* at Quercy-sur-Oise
(April 14, 754).   The Pope was present in person, and the
Italian expedition was resolved upon.   The bishops availed
themselves of the Pope's presence to settle various questions
of discipline already treated in the previous year (A. D. 753),
in the local council of Verberie.†   Nineteen points were proposed : ten on marriage, five on baptism, four relating to the
clergy.   The articles on marriage relate mostly to its indissolubility.   It is forbidden to confer baptism with wine.   It is
allowed, in case of necessity, to administer the sacrament by
pouring water upon the head from a shell or with the hands.
This decision relates to the custom then in use of baptism by
immersion.   Pope Stephen III. resolved most of the cases proposed, on the authority of the ancient decretals of St. Leo, St.
Innocent and St. Sericius, or by the canons of Chalcedon, Antioch, Neocesarea and Carthage.   Two months after the field of
Quercy (July 28, A. D. 754), the Franks were again called
together by an august solemnity.   In the church attached to
the monastery of St. Denis, the Sovereign Pontiff renewed the
ceremony of Pepin's coronation.   He poured the holy oil upon
the monarch's forehead, and at the same time anointed his
queen, Bertrade, and their two sons, Charles, afterward Charlemagne, and Carloman.   After this unction Pepin led his army
toward the boundaries of Italy.

35. To avert the storm about to break upon him, Astolphus
was at length reduced to supplications.   He apologized for his
insulting replies to the Frankish ambassadors.   Hoping to
secure a more favorable reception of his embassy by Pepin, he
intrusted it to the man who should have been most acceptable

---

* This was the name given to the usual gathering of lords called by the French kings,
in the spring of each year, to prepare military expeditions.

† A town in the department of Oise, near Senlis.   It contained a famous palace built by
the kings of Neustria.

to him : it was Carloman, the humble religious of Monte Cassino.* The king of the Franks received his brother with marks of the truest friendship; but told him, concerning the mission on which he had come, that the Franks were bound by solemn oath to the Sovereign Pontiff's cause, and could not now withdraw. The army therefore marched on, followed by Stephen. Pepin sent forward a small force to seize the Alpine passes. At the sight of this handful of troops, Astolphus suddenly fell upon them with a strong force. But the courage of the Franks made up for want of numbers. The Lombard host was cut to pieces; Astolphus himself owed his safety to a shameful flight, and took shelter within the walls of Pavia. Pepin led the remainder of his army across the Alps, entered Italy, and besieged Astolphus in his own capital. Yet Stephen III. could not forget that he was a father. His pity was moved, and he begged the royal Frank to spare the shedding of Christian blood. His peaceful intervention secured a treaty between the Romans, the Franks and the Lombards. Astolphus and his nobles solemnly promised to restore Ravenna and all the usurped cities. Pepin required hostages, and then returned to France. Stephen III., the Liberator of Italy, was at length free to return to his pontifical city. On his way to Rome, escorted by Prince Jerome, brother of Pepin the Short, by Fulrad, and other Frankish nobles, he was met in the field of Nero, near the Vatican, by the Roman clergy and people, uttering cries of joy. Tears filled every eye. "Our father has come back to us!" cried the people with deep emotion. "After God, he is our hope!"

36. But the treachery of the crafty Astolphus soon changed the joyful shouts into cries of fear. On the 1st of January, A. D. 755, the Lombard king again stood before the walls of

---

* Carloman died at Vienne, in Dauphin, on his way to Italy (A. D. 754). Pepin, who was closely attached to his brother, enclosed his body in a golden coffin and sent his sacred remains to Monte Cassino. Some martyrologies mention Carloman as a saint on the 17th of August, the day of his death; but no public veneration is paid him. His ashes repose under the high altar at Monte Cassino, in an urn of onyx stone; a splendid inscription was placed upon it in the year 1628.

Rome, to which he laid vigorous siege. For three months the
city was so closely invested that the Pope found it almost impossible to send the letter by which he once more called upon
Pepin to come to the rescue of the Holy See. "You will doubtless have learned from other sources," he writes, "that the
impious Astolphus has violated the conditions of peace to
which he had sworn. He has again laid siege to Rome. He
has sent the following message to the Romans: 'Open the
Salarian gate; give me up your Pope, or I shall tear down your
walls and put you all to the sword.' The whole neighboring
country has been wasted by fire and carnage. They have
burned dwellings and churches, violated monasteries, broken
the sacred images and outraged the Holy Mysteries. Children
are murdered at the mother's breast; the vines have been cut
down to the roots, the harvests trodden under their horses'
hoofs; and now, to the horrors of war are added the pangs of
hunger. For fifty-five days have they besieged this wretched
city, hemming it in on all sides: night and day they renew the
assault and make new breaches in the walls. They taunt us
with the cry: 'Let your Franks come on now! your brave defenders! Let them snatch you from our grasp!' Their hosts
now press so closely round us that we have hardly been able
to send you these lines bathed with our tears. Hasten, then,
beloved prince, to our rescue. What people ever appealed to
the gallant nation of the Franks and found not relief? How
much more should it be your glory to save the Apostolic See .
and the Holy Church of God!" To these plaintive prayers he
added another letter, written in the name of St. Peter, whose
successor he was, and of the whole Roman Church. By a bold
and eloquent personification, the Prince of the Apostles addressed the king of the Franks, exhorting him to hasten to the
help of his Church.* Pepin was not deaf to the appeal. Like

---

* In this letter Fleury finds matter for incredibly bitter criticism. "Stephen's letter,"
he says, "is valuable as an index of the spirit of his age, and shows how far the gravest
men could push a fiction when they found it useful. Moreover, it is like the former one,
full of ambiguities. It makes the Church consist not in the assembly of the faithful, but in
the temporal property consecrated to God; Christ's flock is made up of the bodies, not the

a thunderbolt, he once more crosses the Alps and the Lombard territory, and invests Pavia, in which Astolphus had hardly had time to throw himself with his army. The spirit of the Franks was irresistible. The city was on the point of falling under their attack, when the Lombard king sued for quarter, promised to fulfil the terms of the treaty made in the preceding year, and to give up all the places mentioned in it. Pepin made them all over to the Holy See, by a solemn deed, which was placed in the archives of the Roman Church. While the articles were being drawn up which made the Popes successors to the former power of the Eastern emperors, Gregory, chief secretary of Constantine Copronymus, and John the Silentiary, entered Pavia as ambassadors of the Byzantine court. They had come to put forward their master's claims to the provinces which Pepin was about to bestow upon the Sovereign Pontiffs. Copronymus had stood aloof in the hour of danger, and now came forward to share the spoils. These representatives of a fallen power, found the whole of Italy opposed to their claims. It seemed to them supremely absurd that the sword of the Franks, the *most Christian nation*, should have conquered only in the interest of an Iconoclast emperor. Pepin understood this. The two envoys were dismissed; the gift to the Holy See, in the person of Pope Stephen III., was solemnly ratified. Pepin took such steps as should insure the execution of the Lombard's oath. Ravenna, Rimini, Resaro, Fano, Cesena, Sinigaglia, Jesi, Forlimpopoli, Forli, Castrocaro, Montefeltro,

souls; the temporal promises of the Old Law are mixed up with the spiritual ones of the Gospel, and the most sacred motives are urged in an affair of state." It seems in no wise doubtful to us that Fleury's desire to criticise a pope has made him forget the first principles of Christian faith. Rome is to the people under the New Law, to all Christianity, what Jerusalem was to the people under the Old Law. There is no one nation whose interest is not bound up in the independence of Pontifical Rome, the centre of Catholic unity, the seat of supreme authority. This fact did not escape Bossuet, whose words we here quote in opposition to Fleury: "That the Apostolic See," says the illustrious prelate, "has received the sovereignty of the city of Rome and of other territory, in order more freely and securely to wield its apostolic power throughout the universe, is a fact on which we congratulate not only the Holy See, but the whole Church; and we pray Heaven with all the fervor of our hearts, that this sacred sovereignty may be preserved in every particular, safe and unimpaired."

Acerragio, Montelucari, supposed to be the present Nocera, Serravalle, San Marigni, Bobio, Urbino, Caglio, Luccoli, Eugubio, Comacchio and Narni, were evacuated by the Lombard troops; and the keys of the twenty-two cities were laid, with King Pepin's deed of gift, upon the Confession of St. Peter. The independence of the Holy See was established. Of all their former Italian possessions, the Eastern emperors now held but a few towns in the duchy of Beneventum.

37. Constantine Copronymus, entirely given up to his iconoclastic rage, suffered all these disgraces with indifference. He thought that he had done enough for his own glory and the safety of the empire, by devoting some Catholic monks to the contempt of the rabble in the arena of the hippodrome. In the year 754 he had convoked his famous Iconoclast council in the church of St. Sophia; one hundred and thirty-eight Eastern bishops, fawning slaves, condemned the veneration of images and anathematized those who honored them. Special canons were directed against painters and sculptors, forbidding them to represent on canvas, wood, stone, marble, gold, or brass, any religious subject whatever, under pain of excommunication, by which punishment, however, they were not exempted from those decreed by the imperial laws.* The work of devastation, the plundering of churches and monasteries, and the shedding of Catholic blood, were resumed with the same savage fury as in the days of Leo the Isaurian; and the Iconoclast heresy did as much to swell the martyr ranks of the Church, as the paganism of Nero and Diocletian. Holy priests, virgins consecrated to the service of the altar, persons of every rank and condition,

---

* "Cold, rigid Protestantism," says M. Poujoulat, "devoid of greatness and life (Spennheim-Gibbon), is enthusiastic in its admiration of the Iconoclast council of A. D. 754. With Leo the Isaurian and Copronymus, it raises the cry of idolatry! superstition! on seeing our churches decorated with the masterpieces of great artists. Asserters of free thought, leave us our artists! cease to fetter the intellect! Allow Raphael to give us the *Transfiguration*, the *Holy Family*, the pure and heavenly lineaments of the Mother of God. Permit Buonarotti to bequeath his *Last Judgment* to the admiration of posterity! Let Rembrandt's pencil take us to witness the *Descent from the Cross*, let Rubens show us *Christ healing the Sick*, and withhold not Canova's chisel, as it bows over the crucifix the weeping figure of the *Repentant Magdalen!*"—(*Histoire de Constantinople*, t. I., p. 235.)

covered with blood and loaded with chains, were savagely dragged through the streets of Constantinople, and then plunged into dark dungeons, to die of hunger and misery. The most celebrated martyrs who owe their crowns to the persecution of Copronymus, were St. Stephen, abbot of the monastery of St. Auxentius, St. Andrew the Calybite (or *recluse*), from the isle of Crete, and St. Peter the Stylite. When Stephen was brought before Constantine, he drew from his bosom a coin bearing the emperor's effigy, and presented it to the tyrant, with the words, "Whose image and inscription is this, my lord?" "It is ours," replied the astonished emperor. The holy abbot thereupon threw down the piece of money and trampled upon it. The attendants were on the point of hewing him in pieces, to avenge the outraged imperial dignity. "Alas!" cried the holy confessor, "if we are punished for dishonoring the image of a mortal monarch, what shall be the punishment of those who dishonor and burn the image of Jesus Christ and His holy Mother?" A few days later St. Stephen was given up to the rage of the Byzantine rabble, who tied his feet with a rope and dragged him through the streets, until his body had been literally torn into shreds. Peter the Stylite suffered the same punishment. Constantinople had become but one vast scene of bloody executions. The sight was everywhere met by scenes of mutilation: here a Catholic had his eyes torn out, there another lost his nose; more were torn with whips, and many cast into the sea. An invocation of the Blessed Virgin, the act of entering a church, or assisting at any religious office, was deemed a treasonable offence, and won for the culprit torture and death. These inhuman orders were executed at Constantinople by the patrician Antony, the master of offices Peter, and the soldiers of the imperial guard. The provincial governors vied with each other in seeking the emperor's good graces by their cruelty toward the Catholics. St. Andrew the Calybite came from the island of Crete to Constantinople, to sustain the courage of the faithful in the midst of the persecution. As the emperor was one day present at one of these bloody executions, St. Andrew pierced the crowd, made his way through the imperial retinue, seized the emperor's bridle, and addressed him: "Prince, if you believe in Jesus Christ, how dare you thus treat the Christians, his living images?" The guards seized him and would have put him to death, but Constantine checked them. He spoke to Andrew with more than his usual mildness, and tried to win him to his cause by the promise of the highest honors. "Why is it," asked the fearless athlete of the faith, "that while you punish those who insult the emperor's image, you still order insults to be offered to images of Jesus Christ, who is far greater than the emperor?" "Well," replied Copronymus, "since your own acknowledgment condemns those who show a want of respect to the emperor's image, what do you deserve, who have insulted the emperor in person?" And the holy hermit was given up to the fury of the rabble. They stripped him, tore him with whips, broke his jaw, and fastened a rope about him with the intention of dragging him through the streets of the city; but one of the monsters struck at him with such fury as to cut off one of his legs, upon which the holy martyr immediately expired.

38. The peculiar hatred entertained by Constantine Copronymus against religious was chiefly due to the fearless eloquence of the holy monk John Damascen, whose reputation was as wide as the boundaries of the East. His genius seemed to grow with the indignation everywhere aroused through the Catholic world by the cruelty of the Iconoclasts. His works followed each other with wonderful rapidity. In the immense work called the Source of Science, addressed to his early preceptor, Cosmo, bishop of Majuma, he treats the whole collection of human acquirements, and crowns them all with the divine science of theology. He met the various heretical systems with the truths of faith, and proved, by powerful reasoning and a captivating eloquence, the absurdity of Iconoclasm. To popularize devotion toward the Blessed Virgin and the saints, whose images Constantine destroyed, he wrote hymns

full of sublime poetical beauties. It is especially in singing the praises of the Mother of God that his soul kindles with inspiration, and finds expression in words of fire : " Mother of life," he writes, "kill in me the passions of the body, which are the death of the spirit. Protect my soul when it leaves this earthly tabernacle to soar above, to a better world. The storm of passion plays wildly round me now, the billows of iniquity hurry me on to the gulf of despair. Star of the sea, still the foaming surge. The roaring lion seeks to devour me. Leave me not to his fury, O Immaculate Virgin; thou who didst give to the world the divine Child Whose hand hath broken the lion's teeth." Ever in the breach, John was always found where the foes were thickest. The Manicheans, under the name of Paulicians, were again beginning to multiply in Syria, under cover of the Mussulmans' hatred of Catholicity. About the eleventh year of his reign, Constantine Copronymus conveyed a number of these heretics into Thrace, whence they infested Bulgaria, under the name of Bogomili, and afterward spread into the West as Albigenses and Patarini. To protect the faithful of his day from their snares, St. John Damascen wrote a dialogue refuting all their impious systems with a masterly logic. His energetic zeal was equally tireless against the Eutychians, the Nestorians and the Monothelites. Catholicity found in him a champion of the stamp of Augustine and Athanasius. As he was a subject of the Ommiades and enjoyed their protection, he had nothing to fear from the savage cruelty of Copronymus, who vented his powerless rage upon the saint in the disgraceful surname of Mansour. St. John Damascen died about the year 756. He has been called the *Thomas Aquinas of the East*, because, first among the Greeks, he applied Aristotle's logic to the study of theology. He is looked upon as the father and founder of scholastic divinity.

39. A fresh revolution had meanwhile broken out in Italy. Astolphus, who had so often perjured himself for the sake of subjecting the Roman Church, was killed by a fall from his horse, while hunting (A D. 576). Didier, whom he had made

duke of Tuscany, assembled the troops to seize the crown. But Rachis, the former king of the Lombards, tired of his cloistered obscurity, quitted Monte Cassino, headed another army, and claimed his throne. Wretched example of human weakness and inconstancy, sighing for repose when surrounded by greatness, and poisoning the delights of solitude by a longing wish for the cares of a throne! Didier placed his claims under the patronage of Pope Stephen III., whom the Frankish sword had made supreme arbiter of Italy. His protection at length secured the Lombard throne to Didier, and Rachis went back to tend his vine at Monte Cassino. Happy if Christian faith gave him the true resignation which can make up every loss, and is better far than a royal crown! This was the last act of Stephen's glorious pontificate. He died on the 6th of April (A. D. 756), leaving to his successors a power increased by his fearless constancy in the midst of the most critical junctures and the most varied fortunes.

CHAPTER XI.

§ I. Pontificate of St. Paul I. (May 28, A. D. 757—767).

1. As long as the Roman empire ruled the world, the Sovereign Pontiffs took their share with all the faithful, in the persecutions and triumphs of Christianity; at one time protected by a Constantine or a Theodosius, at another oppressed by a Constans or a Julian. But when the Roman power fell to make way for so many others that rose upon its ruins, as widely different in views as in interests, then was displayed the design of Providence that the Popes should be independent and wield a power which, without being formidable, might at least secure them in the free exercise of their spirit

nal authority, unhampered by any outward influence. This
change had been effected by the arms of Pepin the Short,
under Pope Stephen III., whose brother and successor, St.
Paul I., accordingly inaugurated the temporal sway of the
Vicars of Jesus Christ upon earth. Paul's election was for a
moment contested, and a part of the Roman clergy and people
supported the pretensions of an antipope named Theophylactus. But all party spirit soon disappeared before the winning
virtue of Paul I., who was crowned on the 29th of May, A. D.
757. His first care was to acquaint Pepin with his promotion
to the pontifical throne: "Be assured that both we and *our
people* will ever be true to the friendship established between
the holy Pontiff, our brother, and yourself." Pepin answered
the Pope's letter as became a most Christian prince, exhorting
the Romans to show a lasting fidelity to the Holy See. Pepin
understood the importance of the trust he had received from
Heaven, and the glory of having established the temporal independence of the Church, and he fulfilled the sacred charge
with affectionate devotion. A few months afterward, at the
birth of his daughter Gisela, he wished the Pope, though absent, to be her godfather, and accordingly sent Ulfard, abbot
of St. Martin of Tours, to bear to the Pontiff the white veil in
which the princess had been enveloped on coming from the
baptismal font. To this gift he added a portable altar made
of a single precious stone. During the following year (758),
the Pope, in return, sent King Pepin several works for his
royal library; they consisted of an antiphonal, a responsory,
the works of St. Dionysius the Areopagite, Aristotle's logic, a
geometry, a treatise on orthography, and a grammar. To this
literary gift he added the then rare present of a clock. The
books of the divine office were to introduce the Roman liturgy
and Gregorian chant into Gaul. The Gallican Church had
hitherto admitted into its liturgy many usages at variance
with those of Rome. Acting in concert with the bishops of
his kingdom, Pepin ordered that for the greater union of
prayers and sentiments, the customs of the Holy See should

thenceforth be observed. The Roman liturgy was then solemnly received in Gaul, except in the case of a few observances which some churches still kept from the old rite.

2. The alliance of the Frankish king was now more necessary to the Sovereign Pontiff, as King Didier seemed disposed to break off friendly relations with the Holy See. Fraudulent policy seemed to be an apanage of the Lombard crown. Didier owed his power to the Roman Church. As a token of his gratitude he secretly opened relations with the emperor of Constantinople, engaging to seize by open force the territory of the exarchate and the cities given by Pepin to Stephen III. The king of the Franks, hearing, through the Pope, of these crafty intrigues, sent to Rome a solemn embassy, consisting of his brother Remigius, archbishop of Rouen, and Duke Autcharius (A. D. 760). The Pope gave the king the following account of their mission : "Rejoice, most happy prince. By the power of your arms, your spiritual mother, the Catholic Church, has triumphed over her enemies. We make known to your most Christian Majesty that your brother Remigius, beloved of God, and the illustrious Duke Autcharius, lately came to Rome and engaged Didier, king of the Lombards, to make full satisfaction to St. Peter, and to restore all the estates, rights and territory of the various cities of the Roman republic. He has already begun to make good his promise, and protests that he is ready to carry it out to the full. Powerless as I am fitly to express my gratitude to you for so many favors, it is my consolation to think that there is a Supreme Judge in heaven Who will not forget to reward. The name of the French people stands far above the other nations, in its glorious privilege of being ruled by kings who are known as the champions of the Catholic Church."

3. The watchful care of St. Paul I. did not overlook the sad state of Catholicity in the East. He wrote to Constantine Copronymus, begging him to forsake the Iconoclast heresy, and sent legates to bring him back to the Catholic faith and the veneration of holy images. But the emperor obstinately ad-

hered to his error, scoffed at the fatherly advice of the Pontiff, and treated the legates with great cruelty. "The part taken by Italy in this war of images," says a French historian, " has been too much overlooked. Every theological discussion of the councils on abstract questions was not within the people's understanding; but the blows of an axe to destroy a picture or statue was within the universal capacity; and then the most ignorant as well as the most learned might become at once client and judge. To rob the people of those religious emotions awakened within them by the paintings and sculpture of the churches, was to wound them in their tenderest sensibilities. Subjects from nature, living in objects of art, speak to the mind and heart, raise the soul above its wonted sphere : how, then, could religion help receiving the veneration of images, since she calls for higher endeavors and sacrifices than vulgar human virtues could bear, and therefore needs to keep before her children's eyes the deeds of Christian heroes, who gave up all the world's allurements and even life to gain heaven?"* "What holy intensity of motherly love," says the learned Cardinal Maï, "has often been inspired by the sight of the Virgin holding her Divine Child in her arms! What is that nimbus which surrounds the heads of the blessed, but the supernatural brightness which every Christian should strive to reach? Why the martyr's palm that waves in the hand of that virgin saint? Though marked by the bloody stains of recent torture, does it not portray, more vividly than the most eloquent words, the glorious reward sent down beforehand from heaven to earth?"†

4. Constantine Copronymus still cherished designs unfriendly to the Roman Church, and spared no pains to break the bonds that bound it to the Frankish king. He asked of Pepin the hand of the princess Gisela, for his son Leo, the presumptive heir to the Byzantine throne. The emperor's ambassadors presented to the king, from their master, the first

---

* M. ARTAUD DE MONTOR, *Histoire des Souverains Pontifes*, t. I., p. 422.
† *Spicilegium*, t. vi., Preface, pp. xv. and xvi.

organ ever seen in France. From the descriptions of contemporary historians, there can be no doubt that it resembled our modern instruments. They represent it as consisting of a bellows and brass tubes, through which the passing air gave a sound, sometimes like rolling thunder, sometimes resembling the harmonious softness of the flute or the lyre. But with all these baits, the Byzantine envoys failed in their mission. To their requests, Pepin made answer that it was not the custom of the Frankish kings to form alliances with houses so distant, and, to save his subjects from any danger of Iconoclasm through the communication from Constantinople, he called a council at Gentilly, near Paris (A. D. 767), at which the emperor's envoys were present. The council published the Catholic definition of the procession of the Holy Ghost and of the veneration of images. The acts reached Rome just as the Pope St. Paul I. had passed from earth (June 2, A. D. 767).

5. The Gallic councils were held with a truly edifying regularity. They had become, in some sort, the great national assizes. The Council of Compiègne, held a few years earlier, had dwelt at length upon the marriage question—a question of vast importance amid a people in which the religious element had still to struggle with native barbarism, and whose passions, but ill-subdued by Christian teaching, had kept the native fire of the Frankish blood. Leprosy was allowed, by the Council of Compiègne, to constitute a lawful ground of separation, with leave to the sound party to contract another marriage. This canon is opposed to the true discipline of the Church on the indissolubility of the marriage tie. The Franks, and even the bishops, were not sufficiently instructed on so important a point, and the history of Charlemagne will give us further proofs of this ignorance. It was no unwonted occurrence, in those days of dissension and trouble, to see whole families stained with blood by deeds of private revenge. The law called Faïde, allowed the relatives of a murdered man to retaliate upon the assassin wherever they might meet him. To escape the law, most of the murderers left their country, for-

saking their wives and children. The Council of Compiègne forbids those who have thus left their homes to escape the law, to marry again in their place of refuge; the same prohibition holds for their wives. About this time (A. D. 758), St. Chrodegang, bishop of Metz, established in his church the first community of regular canons mentioned in the history of France. The name *canons* (*canonici*) was given to those clerics who lived in common under a particular rule, in imitation of the clergy of St. Augustine and St. Eusebius of Vercelli. They were so called because they were to live in a more particular observance of the ecclesiastical canons. St. Chrodegang gave his clergy a rule which has since been adopted by all like institutions. The chief regulations are the following: The canons were not bound to strict poverty, but they were to make over their property to the Church, keeping only the use of it. They had the free disposal of the alms received for masses or other ecclesiastical functions.* No woman was admitted within the cloister, and laymen might enter only with the bishop's leave. The daily chapter was to be held after the office of Prime The rule then goes into minute details on the article of food: it may be remarked that it allowed two meals a day, from Easter to Pentecost, and the use of meat during the same period, except on Fridays. It was ordained that the older canons should every year receive a new choir-dress, and the old ones were given to the younger members of the chapter. The canons were to make an extraordinary confession to the bishop twice a year. This is a modification of the old monastic rule which reserved the confessions of the religious to superiors alone. Such was the beginning of the institution of canons, which has since spread throughout all dioceses.

| * This is the first mention we find of these alms or stipend for ecclesiastical functions.

§ II. PONTIFICATE OF STEPHEN IV. (August 7, A. D. 768—February 1, 772).

6. The death of St. Paul I. was closely followed by that of Pepin the Short. Borne down rather by labors than by years, the monarch died at St. Denis (September 24, A. D. 768), just as his long struggle in Aquitaine, with Waifre, another Vercingetorix, ended in victory. The whole of Gaul was thus brought under the sole sway of the Frankish kings, and Pepin left his name enshrined in the glory of having founded, with a new dynasty, a kingdom displaying territorial unity. Two sons inherited his states : Charles, the elder, so well known as Charlemagne, twenty-four years of age, and Carloman, twenty-two. A descendant of Pepin of Herstal, and following close upon two generations of heroes, Charles was yet destined to outshine the glory of his predecessors. "Claimed by the Church as a saint, by the French as their greatest king, by the Germans as a fellow-countryman (he was born in the castle of Saltzburg, in Upper Bavaria), by the Italians as their emperor, this great monarch stands at the head of every branch of modern history."* He received the title of Great (Magnus) almost during his life, and so thoroughly embodied has this title become in his own name, that its removal would, of necessity, confuse all our historical memories. The partition of Pepin's domain between his two sons was made according to the old custom which gave to each of the co-heirs an equal share, both in the territory of the Franks and in the Roman province of Gaul. Carloman received Austrasia and Burgundy; Charlemagne's share was Neustria, together with Aquitaine, hardly yet conquered, and already in a state bordering on revolt.

7. The death of St. Paul I. had thrown Rome into the midst of countless troubles, which left the Holy See thirteen months vacant. Duke Toto, who was at Nepi with a troop of soldiers, had his brother Constantine proclaimed pope, though

* M. SISMONDI DE SISMONDI: *Histoire des Français*, t. xi, p. 217.

only a layman. After this irregular election, the antipope was taken to the Lateran palace, where George, bishop of Præneste, was forced to give him the clerical tonsure; on the next day the same bishop ordained him sub-deacon, and on the following Sunday, closing the ordination *per saltum*, he anointed the usurper as Sovereign Pontiff. At the close of the ceremony, Constantine sent a false account of the proceedings to King Pepin the Short. But the Frankish king, having doubtless learned from another source the irregularity of the election, paid no heed to the antipope's letters, and they remained unanswered. But Rome was under martial law, and no one was allowed to leave the city lest this mystery of iniquity should be noised abroad. Christopher, primiciarius of the Holy See, and his son Sergius, determined to put an end to the scandal and to overthrow the usurper. They obtained leave to quit Rome, for the ostensible purpose of entering the monastery of Monte Cassino. Protected by the habit of their new calling, bestowed upon them by the Pope's own hands, they passed all the posts. Once clear, they went to Didier, king of the Lombards, obtained the command of an armed force, and returned to attack the troops of Duke Toto. The most complete success crowned their enterprise. The Romans, freed from the yoke under which they had bent for a whole year, thronged round the antipope's palace, seized his person, and, according to the cruel practice of the time, put out his eyes. They then proceeded to hold a regular election, which raised Stephen IV. to the Apostolic dignity, with the unanimous consent of clergy and people (August 7, A. D. 768).

8. The new Pope at once wrote to the king of the Franks, acquainting him with his election, and requesting him to send some Gallic bishops to the council he was about to call at Rome to try the antipope Constantine. The legates reached Gaul to learn that Pepin had died, and the letters were given to his sons, Charlemagne and Carloman, who received them with respectful submission, and sent twelve bishops to the Council of Rome. They were Villicarius of Sens, Lullus of Mayence,

Gavienus of Tours, Ado of Lyons, Herminard of Bourges, Daniel of Narbonne, Filpin of Rheims, Herulf of Langres, Heramburt, Babulf, and Gislebert, whose sees are not known. The council was opened in the basilica of St. Saviour, at the Lateran palace (April, A. D. 769). The sightless antipope was brought in, and persisted, before the Fathers, in upholding the regularity of his election. He was degraded, in presence of the assembled bishops. The sub-deacon Maurian, taking off his orarium, or stole, trampled upon it, and then cut off his sandals, which at that time constituted part of the insignia of pontifical authority. The antipope was confined in a monastery, where he spent the remainder of his days. All the acts of his administration were annulled. The bishops and priests ordained by him were required to make their submission to Stephen IV., who was left at liberty to confirm or to suspend them in their ministry, as might seem best to him. Finally, to hinder the recurrence of like scandals, it was decreed that "no one should be eligible to the pontificate who was not already priest or deacon;" and laymen were forbidden, under pain of excommunication, to be present at the Papal election, which belongs exclusively to the Roman bishops and clergy. The closing session of the council was devoted to the examination of the Iconoclast heresy, which still raged in the East. The teaching of the Church on the subject was established by the writings of the holy Fathers and the decisions of the Apostolic See. The council thus sums up the question: "If we desire hereafter to enjoy the society of the blessed, we must honor them here by a solemn veneration, and respect the images that recall their virtues. A heathen named Antiochus once asked St. Athanasius why the Christians adored the images of saints. 'The faithful,' replied the illustrious Patriarch of Alexandria, 'do not adore the images of the saints; that would be idolatry; but they honor them, because they awake feelings of devotion and charity in the heart.' If, therefore, any one henceforth refuse to honor the images of our

Lord Jesus Christ and of His holy Mother, or the saints, let him be anathema!"

9. The year 769 found Didier yielding to the political current which seemed destined to sweep along successively all the Lombard kings; he aimed at taking from the Holy See the lands of the exarchate. Repairing to Rome, ostensibly to venerate the tomb of the Apostles, he there threw off the mask, arrested several Roman nobles, and had their eyes put out. Not satisfied with this cruel deed, he invited the Pope to come and confer with him on the interests of Italy. Stephen IV. agreed to meet him in the church of St. Peter. The Pope had no sooner entered the basilica than Didier ordered the doors to be closed upon him, intending that the Pontiff should there die of hunger. Christopher and Sergius, who had already given proof of their devotion to the Holy See, at the time of Stephen's election, succeeded in freeing the Pope. Their intrepid virtue soon received the reward too often given to noble and virtuous actions in those barbarous ages: Didier caused their eyes to be plucked out. The Lombard's hatred surrounded the Holy See with difficulties. He had lately placed an intruder upon the archiepiscopal throne of Ravenna, by armed force, and sought to compel the Pope's approval of this usurpation. But Stephen IV. was the successor of him who answered the chief-priests: *Non possumus.* He steadily rejected all the proposals of the Lombard king. So powerful was the action of his legates at Ravenna that the people drove the intruder from the city. He was brought to the Pope, who merely confined him in a monastery and had a bishop lawfully elected to fill the see.

10. The ill-will of Didier was proof against all these failures. Hoping ultimately to turn away the two kings, Charlemagne and Carloman, from their alliance with the Holy See, he proposed to them the double marriage, of his own daughter, Desiderata, to one of the two monarchs, and of Gisela, their sister, to Adalgise, his son and heir. While these negotiations were pending, Queen Bertrade, widow of Pepin the Short and

mother of the Frankish kings, reached Italy (A. D. 770). Didier
received her at Pavia with extraordinary magnificence, and
prevailed upon her to approve the double alliance proposed.
Bertrade saw in it a means of quieting Italy and France, and of
drawing closer the ties of friendship between Charlemagne and
Carloman, which seemed about to break asunder. She knew no
higher policy. The royal brothers were already married; but
this circumstance was not of a nature to deter her. We have seen
that the Franks were but ill-informed on the indissolubility of the
marriage-tie, and Bertrade trusted to her influence with her two
sons to lead one of them into a divorce that should enable him
to marry the Lombard princess. The Sovereign Pontiff could
not countenance the intrigue. He had not been slow to catch
the hidden aim of Didier's policy. The Lombard sought an
alliance with France only to be better able to assail the independence of the Holy See. The Pope opposed Didier's endeavor
with all the force of his apostolic authority. In a letter addressed to Charlemagne and Carloman, he reminds them of the
indissolubility of Catholic marriage, dwells upon the importance
of this essentially Christian law, which has hallowed society in
the family, where it begins, and confirmed the restoration of
woman to her social dignity. He then warns the two kings to
beware of the advances made by a ruler unfriendly to the Holy
See, and recalls the example of their father, Pepin, who had
refused the hand of their sister, the princess Gisela, to the son
of Constantine Copronymus, because the emperor was not in the
Roman communion. The Holy Father solemnly laid the letter
upon the altar of the Confession of St. Peter, on which he then
offered the Holy Sacrifice, as if to consecrate it more especially
by this impressive ceremony. He then sent it to the Frankish
kings by two legates, Peter and Pamphilus, whom he charged
to urge most earnestly the remonstrance, which ended with
these touching expressions: "This exhortation, these entreaties
which we address to you, have been laid upon the Confession
of St. Peter. We have offered the holy sacrifice over them,
and now send them to you bathed with our tears. And now,

if any one dares to oppose this rule, may he incur the excommunication of St. Peter and be excluded from the kingdom of God!" It may be noticed that the closing formula is about the same as that now used by the Sovereign Pontiffs, successors of Stephen IV.

11. The ephemeral interests of an immoral policy were unfortunately of more weight with Bertrade than the reasons, prayers, or threats of the Pope. She succeeded in persuading Charlemagne to put away his first wife to marry Desiderata. But her arguments failed with the princess Gisela, who would have no other spouse than Jesus Christ. She took the religious habit in the monastery of Chelles, of which she died abbess. Carloman himself was carried off in the flower of his age (A. D. 771), which unlooked-for death overturned all Bertrade's calculations. Carloman left two sons by his queen, Girberga, but the young princes did not inherit their father's realms. The bishops and nobles, using their unquestioned elective right, gave themselves with one accord to Charlemagne, happy to be ruled by a youthful hero whose name was already a synonym for glory, and who had just illustrated his arms by a series of brilliant triumphs over the revolted province of Aquitaine. This political revolution made Charlemagne master of all France. We shall now behold him, in this position, achieving the great deeds which have made his reign illustrious. His union with Desiderata, contracted under auspices so unfavorable, had been neither long nor happy. After a year of conjugal unhappiness, Charlemagne had sent her back to her father. He felt powerful enough to waive all consideration, and had just espoused Hildegard, a Suabian princess, in contempt of all ecclesiastical laws, of which he did not perhaps understand the full weight. The Lombard king was touched to the quick by the outrage thus put upon him, and with a view to avenge his wounded feelings he received Girberga, Carloman's widow, at his court, took her two sons under his protection, swore to restore them to the throne of their father, and with this aim began to conciliate Stephen IV., from whose hand he wished them to receive

the royal unction. But the Pope died on the 1st of February,
A. D. 772, after a toilsome pontificate of three years.

§ III. PONTIFICATE OF ADRIAN I. (February 9, A. D. 772—December 26, 795).

12. The promotion of Adrian I. to the Chair of St. Peter
(February 9, A. D. 772) coincides with the first year of Charlemagne's rule over the united monarchy of the Franks. The
two names of the Pontiff and the king, are bound by ties of the
closest friendship. With all the irregularity of his frequent
marriages, it is Charlemagne's glory that he was truly a Christian hero. This great historical figure, whose influence pervades a whole epoch, looms up through the lengthened perspective of bygone ages, surrounded by a double aureola of power
and religion. The part of defender of the Church, bequeathed
to his race by Charles Martel, the conqueror of the Saracens,
and taken up by Pepin the Short, grew into colossal proportions in the hands of Charlemagne. It was in defence of the
Catholic faith that he was about to carry his arms into Spain,
and that Roland, one of his paladins, fell at Roncesvalles; it
was for the propagation of that divine faith that his formidable
sword so often smote the stubborn Saxon, ever worsted, yet
ever unconquerable; that savage race so essentially opposite to
the Frankish nation, since the latter had begun to soften their
manners by the influence of Roman religion and civilization. In fine, it was to secure the liberty and independence
of this faith that his powerful hand crushed Lombard nationality, the unbending enemy of the Roman Pontiffs. Charlemagne
then made himself the sword of the Church whose Pontiff was
Adrian. And the Church knew how to proportion the glory
of the reward to the splendor of the services rendered.

13. In the year 772, the missionaries in Saxony, harassed
in their apostolic labor, in spite of the promise made by the
Saxons to Pepin the Short, threatened that fierce people with
"the arms of the great empire," for Charlemagne's kingdom

had already won this significant name. The boldness of St.
Lebwin, who uttered the threat, nearly cost him his life; his
church at Daventer was burned. When these tidings reached
Charlemagne, he assembled his Franks at Worms, and marched
straight upon Ehresburg, the chief Saxon sanctuary, which contained the celebrated idol *Irmensul*,[*] raised by the Germans to
their God Teutas. This statue, armed *cap-à-pié*, held a pair
of scales in the left hand, and in the right a banner bearing the
figure of a rose; on its buckler, a lion; at its feet, a flowery
mead. This was the heathen figure of Saxony, whose fertile
fields and flowery meadows were inhabited by a nation of lion
hearts, whose only justice, rule, or law was the sword. Irmensul fell beneath the blows of the victorious Franks, and the
Saxons, surprised in their forest fastnesses, gave up twelve hostages, one for each tribe. The triumphant Frank was met on
his return from this expedition by letters from Pope Adrian I.,
calling for his presence in Italy. The Lombard king, Didier,
had reopened with the new Pontiff the negotiations broken off
by the death of his predecessor, Stephen IV. He still cherished the design of restoring the sons of Carloman, Charlemagne's nephews. But Adrian I. had plainly and decidedly
refused to share in an enterprise which would have sown the
deadly seeds of division in a friendly kingdom. Didier broke
through all bounds, seized upon the exarchate, and was marching upon Rome accompanied by the two disinherited princes.
Charlemagne's safety and honor were as much at stake as those
of the Holy See; still, he took up arms only after a fruitless
appeal to the presumptuous Lombard to *restore the domain of St.
Peter to the Sovereign Pontiff*. The king of the Franks entered
Italy and besieged Pavia and Verona. They made a long
resistance, but at length opened their gates to the youthful
conqueror. Didier was sent to the monastery of Corbie, where
he ended his days; his son Adalgise managed to reach Constantinople. Thus fell the Lombard power, after an existence

---

[*] *Herman-Soul*, Herman's pillar.

of two hundred years. Charlemagne took the title of king of
the Lombards, and placed the iron crown upon his brow, thus
leaving to the conquered nation its political being with its national constitution. His conquest was secured by the presence
of judges and a garrison (A. D. 774).* The conqueror then
returned to Rome, where Adrian I. received him with marks
of distinguished honor. Charlemagne confirmed, with some
additions, the gift made by his father to the Apostolic See. It
comprised the island of Corsica, Parma and Mantua, the exarchate of Ravenna, the provinces of Venetia and Istria, with
the duchies of Spoleto and Beneventum. The last-named
estate still forms a part of the pontifical dominion, though included within the boundaries of the kingdom of Naples. The
deed of gift was duplicated and received the royal signature.
The king left one copy upon the altar of the Confession of St.
Peter, and kept the other in the royal archives.

14. Six expeditions against the Saxons under their unconquerable chief Witikind, and a successful inroad upon the Saracens in Spain, occupied, until the year 781, the tireless activity
of Charlemagne. The continual risings of the Saxons forced
him to a rigorous though necessary measure. He required the
rebels to give him up four thousand of their most restless
spirits, whom he put to the sword (A. D. 780). Witikind, the
new Arminius of Germany, *that torch which enkindled so many
wars*, had again succeeded in escaping the conqueror's search.
Charlemagne deemed nothing done so long as that foe was
alive. But the grace of God now showed itself more powerful
than Charlemagne, and undertook to effect alone this great

* This turn of affairs left the sons of Carloman, Pepin and Siagrius, in the hands of their
victorious uncle, Charlemagne. It was feared—and some unscrupulous historians have
worked up the doubt into the semblance of a fact—that Charlemagne might have given way
in their regard to acts of violence that would have sadly tarnished his glory. Bossuet received from the abbey of Saint Pons, at Nice, a manuscript which proves the existence of
Siagrius as a monk in that monastery. After holding the episcopal see of Nice, Siagrius was
ranked among the saints, and to Bossuet was reserved the grateful duty of clearing the
memory of Charlemagne from this foul imputation of unnatural crime. Pepin's name does
not occur in history; but it is most probable that he was, like his brother, confined to a
monastery.

victory. On Easter-Day, in the year 785, the royal guards
brought to the king a beggar arrested at the gate of the palace
of Attigny,* where the court was then held. A Frankish
nobleman, in giving him an alms, caught sight of a crooked
finger on the right hand, which he had often had occasion to
notice in battle. The pretended beggar was Witikind. "What
motive has led you to wear this disguise?" asked Charlemagne.
"I wished to make a close examination of the ceremonies of
your Church," replied the Saxon, "and I deemed this disguise
most favorable for my purpose." "Well," asked the king,
"what did you notice?" "On the day before yesterday, my
lord, which you call Good-Friday, your face was clouded with
gloomy sadness. To-day I saw you, in the beginning of the
ceremony, thoughtful and recollected; but when you and the
nobles in your court approached the table in the midst of the
temple, I saw all your countenances lighted up with a joy so
deep that I was at a loss to conjecture the cause of this sudden
change. A supernatural emotion filled my heart. It seemed
to me that the priest placed upon your lips a little infant
bathed in heavenly brightness. Prostrate in tearful awe, I
adored, without knowing Him, your God, who shall henceforth
be my God." "Happy are you," cried Charlemagne, "who
have enjoyed a favor granted neither to me nor to my priests!"
Then ordering Witikind to be clothed as became his rank and
dignity, he explained to him the teaching of faith concerning
the august mystery of our altars.† Witikind was converted
and baptized. Charlemagne, to use an expression of the times,
wished himself to *raise* him from the baptismal font. The late
chief of the Saxons now became their apostle, and obtained from
the Frankish king some missionaries to preach the faith to
his people. The city of Minden was erected into a bishopric,

---

* Attigny (Ardennes), near Vouziers. The Neustrian Merovingians had raised a royal
residence here. It was the seat of several councils; among others, that in which Louis the
Mild did public penance.

† This episode was found in the annals of the reign of Charlemagne. Its authenticity
is not unquestionable. It seemed to us to afford a very good example of the spirit of
those ages of simple and ingenuous faith, as well as of the state of Charlemagne's court.

and St. Herembert was its first incumbent. Charlemagne lost
no time in acquainting Pope Adrian I. with this happy event,
and begged him to order public prayers in all the churches, in
solemn thanksgiving to God. This great monarch's devotion
thus shone forth on all occasions. In the year 781, he had
visited Rome a second time, to celebrate the Easter festival,
and to have his two sons, the young princes Pepin and Louis,
baptized and anointed by the Sovereign Pontiff. The former
received the title of King of Italy, the latter that of King of
Aquitaine. The period of this second journey corresponds with
the death of Queen Hildegard, who was succeeded by Fastrade.
Charlemagne was a third time called to Rome by the revolt of
Arigise, duke of Beneventum, who endeavored to shake off
the yoke of the Papal authority. The presence only of the
hero who had overcome the Saracens, the Saxons, and the
Lombards, was enough to crush the uprising. The king added
to the gift already made to the Pope in 774, the cities of Sora,
Arces, Aquin, Arpi, Theano and Capua, which he had just taken
from Arigise. Thassillon, duke of Bavaria, availed himself of
Charlemagne's presence in Rome, to seek the Pope's mediation
for the termination of certain old feuds between the king of the
Franks and himself. Adrian I. accepted the office, and settled
all the difficulties with Charlemagne ; but when the time had
arrived for signing the treaty, the Bavarian ambassadors, with
a view to gain time, stated, according to their master's order,
that they had no power to sign. To punish this want of good
faith, Adrian I. excommunicated Thassillon and his party. This
is the first instance we find in history of a Sovereign Pontiff
passing judgment upon the claims and di putes of two princes.
For the world's happiness, the Papacy was to keep this character of mediator, and to wield the authority of the God of
peace only to secure the happiness and quiet of nations.

15. The West, thus controlled by the blended influence of
the king of the Franks and of the Pope, presented a magnificent spectacle of union and harmony. Yet this peace was
ruffled by the appearance of a heresy. The Adoptionist error

tore the bosom of the Spanish Church, already rent with grief by the Mussulman domination. The very rise of this heresy would be enough to establish the necessity of having but one liturgy for all Christendom, that the form of prayer might become the rule of faith. Some misinterpreted words of the Mozarabic liturgy gave rise to the new error. Elipandus, archbishop of Toledo, and Felix, bishop of Urgel, taught that Jesus Christ, according to the human nature, is only by adoption and appellation the Son of God. This supposed two persons in Jesus Christ, and renewed the heresy of Nestorius. The error spread rapidly through the Asturias and Galicia, and beyond the Pyrenees, into Septimania, now Languedoc. Adrian I., on receiving tidings of the heresy, wrote to all the Spanish bishops, exhorting them to stand fast to the principles of the true faith; yet Elipandus of Toledo was not a whit the less earnest in spreading the Adoptionist error, which was as steadily met by Beatus and Etherius, two monks of Asturias. Charlemagne, who never lost sight of the dangers which threatened the Church, had the heretics condemned in the two councils of Narbonne and Friuli (A. D. 792). Another council, at which the emperor was present, in Ratisbon, personally condemned Felix, bishop of Urgel, who then apparently forsook his error and placed his recantation in the hands of Pope Adrian, who was moved by his seeming repentance to restore him to his diocese. The heretic's abjuration proved to be but a hypocritical feint, for on reaching Urgel he still continued to teach his false opinions. The Pope, repeatedly consulted by the Spanish bishops, wrote them a lengthy and full refutation of the new heresy. Elipandus and Felix continued as obstinate as ever, and were at length solemnly condemned and deposed from the episcopate, by the Council of Aix-la-Chapelle, in 799, in the pontificate of Leo III., successor of Stephen IV.

16. During this period, Constantine Copronymus closed thirty-four years of Catholic persecution by a frightful disease, the result of his debauched life (A. D. 775). He is said to have

exclaimed, while struggling in the agonies of death: "I am given up alive to flames of inextinguishable fire." Hoping to atone for his crime and to disarm the vengeance of God, he ordered the restoration of the images of the Blessed Virgin and the saints, the destruction of which had formed the occupation of his lifetime. Alas for him that his atonement came so late! What tears could ever cleanse the stains of blood that sullied the annals of his reign? His son and successor, Leo IV., had contracted an alliance with a descendant of one of the most illustrious Athenian houses of ancient Greece, whose rare intellect and surpassing beauty had won her the distinction of being chosen by Constantine himself as the spouse of his heir. Irene was a Catholic, and abhorred the mad excesses of the Iconoclasts. While Copronymus lived, she had been forced to hide her true belief, yet hoping one day to use her power for the Church's good. The keen, and seldom faulty, instinct of the masses led the people of Constantinople, weary of Constantine's cruel 'violence, to lay their secret, deeply cherished hopes at the feet of Irene, whom they already hailed as their deliverer. At the accession of Leo IV., surnamed Porphyrogenitus, from the fact of his having first seen the light in the porphyry apartment of the imperial palace, the Catholics fondly believed that the end of their trials was at hand. But he proved only too worthy to succeed his father, whose hatred for holy images he fully inherited, and the city was once more given up to the senseless brutality of the Iconoclasts. Leo one day found under the empress's pillow an image of Christ and His most holy Mother. The sight of these *idols* threw the emperor into a fit of furious anger. The empress left no means untried—tears, blandishments, promises, repentance—to disarm the fury of the Iconoclast prince. He was unappeasable, and drove the empress from his palace as the last of ungrateful wretches. But she soon returned, more powerful than ever, after a disgrace which ranked her among the Catholics as a martyr of the faith. The death of Leo IV., prematurely stricken down in the prime of life, reopened to her the palace gates. By his marriage with Irene, the late emperor left a son ten years of age, who was crowned, with the title of Constantine VI., and the regency was confided to the empress, his mother. The rule of Irene brought back Constantinople from its disgraceful wanderings of the past three centuries. Peace was restored to the wretched Churches of the East; a Catholic Patriarch, Tarasius, filled the see of Byzantium. In A. D. 782, Irene sent ambassadors to Charlemagne, to ask his alliance and the hand of his daughter, Rotrudis, for the youthful emperor, Constantine VI. This alliance might have changed the fate of the world. It might, perhaps, have given a lasting firmness to the empire of Constantine the Great. Charlemagne was not blind to the fact, and received the proposal with unfeigned satisfaction. The all-conquering sword which ruled Europe, and had lately driven the Western Saracens to the banks of the Ebro, would as readily have borne back the Eastern caliphs to the barren retreats of their desert home. The marriage was settled, and the time fixed for the majority of the two children; but the delay gave time to court intrigue to break off its fulfilment. The great lords of Constantinople, slavish panderers to the interests of the hour, saw in this union but a foreign influence calculated to deprive them of positions of which they felt themselves unworthy. "Reflect," they said to Irene, "that in Charlemagne you give us a master, and not an ally." These paltry considerations, inspired by the most disgraceful selfishness, were powerful enough, however, to lead Irene to break off the proposed match, and Constantine VI. married an Armenian named Mary.

17. In the midst of all these political cares, Irene did not lose sight of the interests of the Church, so long weighed down by the storm of Iconoclastic persecution. The friendly relations of Rome and Constantinople, broken off during the reigns of Constantine and Leo, had just been re-established by the new Patriarch Tarasius, who had seized the first occasion after his promotion to send his synodal letters and profession of faith

to Pope Adrian I. The empress Irene likewise wrote to the
Sovereign Pontiff to express her desire of repairing the evils inflicted upon the Church by the last emperors, and urged him to
convoke a general council for the purpose of confirming the
Catholic tradition respecting the veneration of images, and thus
quiet all minds. The letters filled the pious Pontiff's heart
with joy; they blotted out nearly fifty years of schism. Still,
Adrian found in the empress's letter, an expression which he noticed with some energy, in his reply; Irene had styled Tarasius
Ecumenical or *Universal Patriarch.* "We know not," wrote the
Sovereign Pontiff, "whether this expression be the result of
ignorance or of a hidden germ of heresy. But We beg your
Majesty not to use it again, since it is contrary to the canons
and to the decrees of the holy Fathers. The precedence of all
the Churches was given by Jesus Christ to St. Peter, and, in
the person of the Apostle, to all the Roman Pontiffs, his successors, to which rank We have been raised in spite of our
unworthiness." Adrian, however, congratulated Irene and her
son on their zeal for the re-establishment of the true faith. When
all these preliminary steps had been regulated, the seventh general council was opened in the church of St. Sophia, at Nice,
under the presidency of the Pope's prelates, Peter, archpriest
of the Roman Church, and another Peter, abbot of the monastery of St. Sabas (September 27, A. D. 787). Three hundred
and seventy-seven bishops were present. The question of the
veneration of images was solemnly defined, according to the
rules of oral and written tradition. The council anathematized
the false council held by the Iconoclasts (A. D. 724) at Constantinople, under Copronymus. The following decree was then
adopted: "After mature deliberation and a deep research into
the merits of the question, we decide that the sacred images of
our Lord Jesus Christ, those of His holy Mother, and of the
angels and saints, shall be restored to their place of honor in
the churches, oratories and private dwellings; they are to be
honored with a special worship, not with that of adoration or
latria, which belongs to God alone, but with that of reverence

and honor; for in honoring the image we honor the person rep
resented by it. Such is the teaching of the holy Fathers and
the tradition of the Catholic Church, known throughout the ·
world." It would seem that plain common sense should suffice
to master truths so palpable; and it will ever remain one of the
most disgraceful stains in the annals of the Lower Empire, that
half a century of violence and bloodshed should have been
needed to teach it this elementary lesson. The acts of the seventh general council, signed by Irene, Constantine VI. and all
the bishops present, were sent to Pope Adrian I., who had them
translated from Greek into Latin. He sent the translation to
Charlemagne, with tidings of the happy event which gave back
peace to the Eastern Church.

18. Charlemagne received the Pontiff's communication at
Frankfort, where the bishops of Germany and Gaul had met
to condemn the errors of Elipandus and Felix of Urgel (A. D.
790); the king communicated to them the acts of the General
Council of Nice. An unfortunate mistake of the Latin translator,
who had rendered both Greek words προσκύνειν* and λατρεύειν†
by the same Latin verb *adorare*,‡ misled the Frankish bishops
as to the value of the Council of Nice. "We have been asked,"
they say, "what is to be thought of a new council held by the
Greeks at Nice, which anathematizes those who do not pay to
images of the saints the worship of adoration due to the Holy
Trinity. We have unanimously condemned the error, and forbidden all adoration of images." A fuller refutation of the supposed heresy of the Ecumenical Council of Nice was then composed, in four books, which were sent by Charlemagne to the
Pope, and from the name of the donor they were called the
Carolin Books. Adrian answered the French king's communication with great mildness, explaining the error which had given

---

* Προσκύνειν properly signifies to prostrate one's self, to salute with a low bow.

† Λατρεύειν means to adore, in the sense of the highest worship (*latria*) due to God.

‡ *Adorare* does not convey precisely the same idea as our verb to *adore*. In the Old
Testament it almost invariably means προσκύνειν, to salute with a low bow. In the New
Testament and in the works of the Latin Fathers, it generally conveys the meaning of
λατρεύειν, to adore by an act of the highest worship.

rise to the misunderstanding, and showed him that the Catholic
teaching which the French bishops thought it necessary to defend against the Fathers of Nice, was precisely that which the
seventh ecumenical council had just promulgated against the
Iconoclasts.

19. The news of Pope Adrian's death reached Frankfort
almost simultaneously with his letter (December 25, A. D. 795).
His pontificate of twenty-three years was one of the most glorious for the Roman Church.   Adrian possessed, in fact, all the
qualities of a great Pope : a tender and active piety, an ardent
zeal, tempered with cautious prudence and unchanging mildness.
Charlemagne mourned him as a father and a friend.   He has
left us a monument of his grief, in the epitaph which he composed himself and had engraved on Adrian's tomb, where it still
remains.   The great king's sensitive affection is here displayed
in its most touching form.   "You were my father and the object of my affection," says the king.   "You are now the cause
of my tears.   As an emblem of the union of our hearts, I here
blend our names : Adrian, Charles.   I am the king, you the
father.   O best of fathers! deign to remember your son; obtain that your disciple may yet again be with his father."   Holy
and noble friendship, that bound these two great hearts of Pontiff and king, for one common end : the happiness and glory of
their age!   The name of Adrian closes the third period of
Church History.

CHAPTER XII.

HISTORICAL REVIEW OF THE THIRD PERIOD OF THE CHURCH.

1. The Middle Ages.—2. Barbarian inroads.—3. Protective authority of the Popes.—4. St. Gregory the Great.—5. Temporal power of the Popes.—6. Benefit of this power.—7. Form of government among the Barbarians.—8. Feudal laws.—9. Legislation.—10. Letters, arts and sciences.—11. Monastic orders.—12. Ecclesiastical doctors and writers.—13. Religious monuments of the Third Period.—14. Islamism. The Iconoclasts in the East.—15. Worship.—16. *Missa Catechumenorum.*—17. *Missa Fidelium.* The use of communion under *one* kind established in the earliest ages of the Church.

1. THAT part of the world's history known as the Middle Ages begins with the third period of Church History. The Middle Ages take in the period between the settlement of the barbarians in the Western provinces of the Roman empire, in the fifth century, and the literary *renaissance* in the fifteenth, which gives it a duration of about ten centuries (A. D. 476–1494). The face of the world was changed. Historical events appear upon a new field, where the action of Christianity takes a special form. It is now Western Europe; no longer that old Europe so familiarly known, but a Europe that seems just springing into being, the abode of foreign races, raising up over the ruins of Roman power a new social order, and though ever triumphant and victorious, bowing down mind and heart to the religion of the conquered countries. In those lands, and in those days, when, to use Herder's beautiful expression, *the bark of the Church bore the destinies of the world*, the Church appears before us under an aspect hitherto unknown, wielding an influence which she could now for the first time exercise. Strong in the

lights and civilization of the Roman world, which she had appropriated, powerful by her mission and by the unity of her unbroken hierarchy, she now becomes the guardian of the new European races; this title gives her immediate cognizance of all public and private relations, carries her jurisdiction even into purely civil cases, and rests in her chief, now at the height of his power, as arbiter and judge between princes, subjects, people, and state.

2. Every new race of barbarians that sets foot upon Roman soil, successively brings a fresh harvest to be gathered into the Church's garners. Missionaries need no longer seek a distant strand to find subjects for their apostolic zeal: the nations themselves come to seek the missioner. "And in the last days the mountain of the house of the Lord shall be prepared on the top of mountains, and it shall be exalted above the hills, and all nations shall flow unto it."* The Heruli merely pass through Italy (A. D. 476–493); they are followed by the Visigoths (A. D. 493–553). The Lombards (A. D. 568–774) are equally short-lived. The fruitless endeavor of these various tribes to fix a lasting throne in Rome, is not a little remarkable. A Divine power seemed to drive them to Milan, to Pavia, and to Ravenna, as if to make room for another empire prepared by Providence. These divers races, sometimes pagan, sometimes Arian, or even at times Catholic, yet always barbarous, by their contact with the centre of religion, with the heads of the Church, found their rude manners softened by degrees, and were preparing that blending of conqueror and conquered which has at length resulted in our modern society. The inhabitants of Italy, left defenceless to the inroads of these conquering hordes, betrayed by those whom they thought their protectors, forgotten by the emperors of Constantinople, who still pretended to call themselves *Roman emperors*, harassed for two hundred years by the Huns, the Goths, the Heruli and the Lombards, at length turned their suppliant looks with one accord to the

---

* "Et erit in novissimis diebus præparatus mons domus Domini in vertice montium, et fluent ad eam omnes gentes."—ISAIAH, ch. ii, v. 2.

guardian power of the Popes, the only sure bulwark and retreat. In the midst of these indescribably frightful calamities,
the Roman Pontiffs had become the only refuge of all the
unfortunate.

3. This stand forced upon the Papacy gave it a new importance before the world, and brought on the crowning event of
the third period—the temporal sovereignty of the Holy See.
This is perhaps the only example in history, of an empire created without the help of arms, preserved without violence, acquired without even the appearance of usurpation. It was the
people's gratitude that gave the Sovereign Pontiffs their crown.
The great Pontiff St. Leo had, by the mere mastery of his virtue, twice saved Rome and the Romans from the fury of Attila
and of Genseric. For twenty-seven years St. Gregory shielded
the holy city from the sword of the Lombards. These fierce
conquerors felt their hot rage and burning threats cool on their
lips, and their swelling pride break into empty foam, at the feet
of the unarmed Roman Pontiff, as before the very apparition of
an angel of the Lord. And the nations did not await desperate
crises to appeal to the Popes; they were consulted from all
quarters and on all subjects. Nothing of importance was undertaken without their advice. In the sixth century, Pope
Agapetus, on behalf of the Italians, negotiated a peace between Theodoratus, king of the Goths, and the emperor Justinian. When Athalaric and Theodatus made some important
gifts to the Roman people, it was Pope Vigilius who, in his visit
to Constantinople, obtained from Justinian an imperial constitution, chiefly in order to the confirmation of the gift. At
about the same period, Cassiodorus, a Roman senator, made
præfect of the prætorium, thus wrote to John II.: "You
are the chief and the guardian of the Christian people; as
Father you direct every thing; the public safety depends upon
your power and name. In the civil government we have but a
small share of solicitude and authority; you bear these burdens
in their full weight. You are indeed the spiritual shepherd of
the flock; but you cannot neglect its temporal welfare: it be-

longs to a true father to watch at once over the temporal and
eternal welfare of his children." The surprise that might he
awakened on hearing such expressions from a præfect of the
prætorium, or, in other words, from one of the chief officers of the
empire, will cease when we learn that desolated Italy had long
and vainly called upon the emperors for help in its distress. The
people were dying of hunger and misery; cities were dismantled and burned, and the country laid waste; the scattered inhabitants wandered about in homeless destitution, at the mercy
of the barbarians. In this deplorable condition, Italy found its
first, nay its only hope of relief in the authority of the Holy
See and the charity of the Popes. Their protection became
necessary not only to the poor, but to the very exarchs, who
were obliged, in spite of themselves, to beg their assistance,
sometimes to meet the expenses of the administration in the
provinces, sometimes to calm the popular passions, and at times
even to treat in their favor with the Lombards. In a word, the
very force of circumstances, the crying need of their presence
and authority, had made the Sovereign Pontiffs the centre of
all administrative power and public business in Italy. It was
an involuntary, but yet a no less real and necessary sovereignty.*

4. St. Gregory the Great was the most striking personification, the noblest and most touching type of this singular sovereignty, which was felt only by its beneficent love of man, and
which was cast upon the Roman Pontiffs by the resistless power
of events, the miseries of the times, and the grateful love of
nations. That holy Pontiff is usually found discharging the
duties of a temporal lord and almost of a sovereign, for the government and protection of Italy; he administers provinces, pro-
vides for the defence of cities, and sends governors, enjoining
upon the people to obey them as they would himself. "We
have charged Leontius to take upon himself the government of
your city," he writes to the citizens of Nepi. "It is our wish

---

* Monseigneur DUPANLOUP, bishop of Orleans, *On the Temporal Sovereignty of the Pope.*
Paris, 1849, pp. 34, 35, 37, 38, 39.

that his watchful care should overlook nothing, and that he should personally decide and regulate all that he deems proper for your good and that of the commonwealth. Whoever opposes his orders, by the very fact resists our authority." He sends military officers to command the garrisons in places threatened by the enemies of the empire. Many of his letters were written to arouse the vigilance and zeal of bishops, for the protection of cities, for the defence of the walls, and the supply of fortified towns. He gives orders to the commanders of armies, treats in person with the Lombards for peace, and facilitates the success of negotiations, at one time by his liberality, at another by repeated representations to the exarchs, to the emperors, or to the Lombards themselves. In fine, his authority, compelling equal respect from prince and people, from Romans and barbarians, becomes the centre of government and of all the political interests of Italy. Such was the obligation imposed upon this great and holy Pope by the wants and miseries of his people, no less than by the charity which burned in his breast; he says of himself that his life was divided between the duties of pastor and those of temporal prince. He thus wrote to the empress Constantina, wife of the emperor Mauritius: "For twenty-seven years have we dwelt in this city, under the swords of the Lombards. But even such a life we must buy at the price of a daily ransom which I dare not name. To give you an idea of it in a few words, I may say that as the emperor takes care to keep a treasurer in Ravenna, to provide the daily supplies of the chief Italian army, so am I the emperor's treasurer at Rome, to look to the wants of this unfortunate city, incessantly assailed by the Lombards." St. Gregory's successors inherited both his power and his charity. Gregory II. thus wrote to the emperor Leo: "The entire West is looking to our lowliness. It looks upon us as the judge and regulator of peace and public tranquillity."

5. These facts make it easy to follow up the generation of the temporal power of the Papacy. From the days of Gregory II. there has existed a *real sovereignty*. The learned have

called it a *provisional sovereignty* ; but under whatever name it
be known, it was real; it existed *de facto* and *de jure ;* it
was sanctioned by time, by public custom, and by the gratitude of nations.   It was unquestioned, and even the East paid
it the tribute of involuntary but striking homage.   Rome and
Italy now awaited but the hour marked by Providence—the
hour when this great institution should be solemnly confirmed
and proclaimed to the world as part and parcel of the public
law of nations, and should take, amid the new powers of the
West, without prejudice to any, the exalted rank assigned it
by the designs of God upon His Church.   "In the decline of
the empire," says Bossuet, "when the Cæsars were hardly able
to defend the East, where they had shut themselves up, Rome,
abandoned for nearly two hundred years to the fury of the
Lombards, and forced to call upon the Franks for protection,
was constrained to withdraw from the emperors.   Nor was this
decisive step taken until the last degree of suffering and want
had been endured, and when the capital of the empire was
looked upon by its emperors as a country cast off, and left a
prey to every passing marauder."   The protectorate of the
Holy See thus passed from the empire of Constantinople to the
French monarchy, which places its sword at the command of
the Papacy ; and not content with securing its independence,
it must establish on a lasting foundation the temporal rule
of Christ's Vicars.   We have given full details of events so
glorious for France.   In the name of Pepin the Short, Fulrad,
abbot of St. Denis, visited all the cities given up or *restored* by
the Lombards to the Roman Church, received the keys of their
gates, and laid them with religious reverence upon the tomb
of St. Peter, together with the deed of perpetual cession and
transfer made by the Lombard king in favor of the Holy See.
These cities were twenty-two in number, comprising the greater
part of the exarchate of Ravenna, and chiefly situated within
a space of forty leagues along the shores of the Adriatic.   Charlemagne, of deathless memory, carried out and crowned the
work begun by his father, in a style of royal magnificence.

Besides ratifying the donation already made, he went to Rome and ordered his chaplain, Estherius, to draw up a deed of much more ample gift, which secured to the Holy See the lasting possession of the exarchate of Ravenna, the Island of Corsica, the provinces of Parma, Mantua, Venetia, and Istria, with the duchies of Spoleto and Beneventum. The deed was signed by the conquering hand which had just put an end to Lombard monarchy. The paper was then laid upon the altar of St. Peter, and Charlemagne, with all the French chieftains, swore to maintain the Holy See in its possession of the states now restored to it. The first use made by the Papacy of this officially acknowledged power was, to rebuild the Western Empire to the advantage of its illustrious benefactor. The sword of the Cæsars was placed in the hands of a French prince, the champion of St. Peter. Grateful nations sanctioned this token of gratitude on the part of the Sovereign Pontiffs, and posterity caught up and renewed the contemporary gladness which showered blessings upon the two names of Leo III. and Charlemagne.

6. No earthly power, other than that just bestowed upon the Church in its Pontiffs, could stem the torrent of barbarian invasion, and heal the hurt it caused to society. Utterly unacquainted with science, art, or civilization, the savage conquerors of the West had no other pastime than the chase and war, respected no higher law than force, sought no brighter glory than that of mere conquest; and, far from acknowledging the disorder and the irregularity of this savage state, they expressed a sovereign contempt for a more polished manner of life. It is true that the Christian religion, which these nations successively embraced, gradually tamed their native fierceness; but this precious result of their conversion was slow and imperceptible. With the greater part of them, it was the reluctant work of years to give up their old habits, their violent and irritable temper, a passionate love of hunting and fighting, a hearty contempt for science and art, but especially that spirit of restless independence which seemed to constitute the most

deeply-rooted element of their character. We may now form some idea of the obstacles which the Church had to overcome before reaching a practicable ground in these savage natures. It was necessary to humanize them before the work of Christianizing could begin. The whole political and social system of the barbarians was a perfect chaos. Their government, legislation, literature, sciences and arts, all had been swallowed up in a fearful flood. The Church undertook to restore every thing, and this was her ceaseless toil through the whole course of the Middle Ages. We shall speak in a summary way of each point separately.

7. Most of the monarchies founded in Europe, since the fourth century, on the ruins of the Roman Empire, were elective, at least to the extent that the sovereign could be indifferently singled out *from among all the princes of the reigning family.* The crown was thus, strictly speaking, neither *purely elective* nor *purely hereditary*, but both elective and hereditary at once: hereditary, inasmuch as the choice was confined to the reigning family; elective, by the fact that the selection was not limited to any single prince of the blood royal, but might fall upon any one of them indifferently. All the children of the deceased monarch enjoyed an equal right to the throne, which they sometimes shared among themselves as a particular succession, with the expressed or tacit consent of the nobles, to whose approval this right was subject, as they were free to oppose the division of power, and to choose the new king from among all the relations of the deceased, even to the exclusion of his children. The latter, indeed, might claim a hope, nay, an incipient though not a full and unquestionable right, of succession. They could be deemed the *natural and probable* successors of the late king, though not his necessary successors, since they were liable to be passed over by the nobles, in whose hands were the results of the elections. Such was the order of succession to the throne among the Visigoths in Spain, the Anglo-Saxons in England, the Franks under the second race of their kings, according to most historians, and even under the first,

as is asserted by many reliable authors.   This was especially
the character of the new Empire of the West, where this form
of government lasted much longer than in the other European ·
states.   That great historical event, the accession of Pepin the
Short, and the decision of Pope Zachary, which has furnished
so much material for the spleen of writers unfriendly to the
power of the Holy See, rested upon the principle of public
right generally acknowledged in the Middle Ages : the *blending of the elective and the hereditary succession* in the royal races.[*]
It must be readily seen how greatly the elective element
brought into the monarchical succession, increased the influence
of the clergy in the political affairs of that period.   The bishops
and the abbots of the leading monasteries, independently of
the religious character which compelled public respect, represented the most enlightened portion of society.   Their sentiment was always controlling in the general assemblies which
discussed the great interests of the nation.   The first duty, the
chief obligation imposed upon the newly-elected sovereign, was
to show and to enforce respect for the laws of religion and the
Church.   " The title of king (*rex*)," said a canon, " is intended
to express the *rectitude of conduct* which should distinguish the
monarch ; for if he rule with piety, justice, and goodness, he
may lawfully hold his title of *rex ;* if he want these qualities,
he is no longer a king, but a tyrant.   The highest duty of the
king is to rule and guide the people of God with justice, and
to endeavor to keep them in peace and harmony.   His greatest
glory must be to defend and protect the Church and the servants of God—widows, orphans, the poor, and all the needy."
The Church conferred blessings upon the royal races in return
for the favors they bestowed upon her.   Her influence gradu-

---

[*] It is the opinion of able critics that Pepin was of the royal blood of the Merovingians.
They thus establish the succession of French princes from Meroveus to Pepin and Hugh
Capet : Sigebert, king of the Ripuaril, brother of Childeric I. ; Cloderic, killed by Clovis;
Munderic, king in Auvergne ; Bodegesilus, king in Austrasia ; St. Arnoul; Asigise, Sigo-
bert's mayor of the palace ; Pepin of Herstal, who had two sons—Charles Martel, founder
of the Carlovingians, and Childebrand, founder of the Capetians.   On this hypothesis, and
with the existing constitution, the accession of Pepin the Short cannot be called a usurpation.

ally moulded hereditary succession into the regular form in
which we see it now. It was no unwonted sight in the Middle
Ages to see Sovereign Pontiffs adopt royal orphans, and shield
their rights from usurping encroachments.

8. After the conquest the barbarians took possession of
the soil of Europe. The conquered were bound to the glebe as
serfs. The conquerors kept for themselves the profession of
arms, and had the right of life and death over their serfs.
Within their own estates they severally enjoyed an independent authority, for which they were answerable only to the king
to whom they were vassals. To him they swore fealty, and
furnished men-at-arms for his military expeditions, as standing
armies were still unknown. In case of war, an assemblage of
lords and vassals was called, and the subject paid military duty
to his suzerain by bringing his vassals to swell the royal ranks.
Such was the principle of the feudal system. The Churches,
having received vast estates from the liberality of kings and
lords, were thus bound to military duty as fiefs. This often
gave rise to serious abuses. Some bishops, forgetting their
peaceful character as ministers of Jesus Christ, took personal
command of their forces, and fought amid the armed ranks.
But the passing contempt of discipline was soon checked by the
influence of councils, and then the feudal system appeared only
in its beneficial and protective character. The bishops found
their natural position between the lords and their vassals, as
the representatives of mercy. Their intervention softened whatever of inhuman rudeness the still savage nature of masters
might have lent to serfdom. They began by giving the example of a gentle and tutelary authority, and, until the extinction
of the feudal system, the truth had passed into a by-word, that
no man could be happier than a serf of a church or monastery.

* The writers of the eighteenth century have spread the most absurd calumnies about
the feudal system; but history cannot be made the organ of malicious accusations. Feudalism was a political system, a form of government, and, like all other constitutions, possessed
both good and evil traits. Many attempts have been made, but to this day we have not
succeeded in setting up a blameless form of government; this fact should be borne in mind.

As temporal lords the bishops had the right and even the obligation of taking part in the deliberations of the great national assemblies or *diets*, which met every year. Their influence was always evident in the useful regulations made on behalf of the people, and it moreover gave to these meetings the tone of mixed councils, looking at once to the welfare of Church and state.

9. The changes brought into the West by barbarian inroads, necessitated deep modifications in legislation. A glance at the Frankish laws may serve to give an idea of the various legislative systems of the barbarians. The Salic law mostly related to harm inflicted upon person or property; for, in a period of ceaseless revolutions, these must have been the most common crimes. Every offence was to be cancelled by a pecuniary satisfaction proportioned to the nature of the offence, the rank and condition of the offending party. The sentence of capital punishment was reserved to the prince, who could send the criminal to death and decide the manner of the execution. We saw how Clovis used this power in the case of the soldier of Soissons; and, according to the then acknowledged principles, he did no more than he had a right to do. A freeman was never imprisoned for debt. His punishment consisted in the plundering of his property, and his consequent ruin; no one might shelter him, and he was thus forced to an involuntary self-exile. The master was responsible for thefts committed by his slaves or damages done by his cattle. Justice was administered as nearly as possible in a uniform manner. The present magistracy was then unknown. Each class and profession had its own tribunal, laws, and customs. In villages, the executive officer was a centurion; in cities, a count; in the provincial metropolis, a duke. Men-at-arms were judged by military tri-

Feudalism would seem to be the fittest form of government for the infancy and youth of nations. Russia still lives under its influence, without exciting any complaint. It was long the law in France, whose history certainly lacks not splendor or greatness. The system doubtless had its abuses, and what system was ever entirely free from them? Nations, like individuals, share the failings of the age in which they live. Years may modify, but cannot utterly eradicate them.

bunals, and clerics answered before an ecclesiastical court appointed by the bishop; this system was called *being judged by one's peers.* Widows and orphans were under the especial protection of the bishop, and were never prosecuted without his knowledge. The weak were thus intrusted to the guardian care of the Church, the only power that gave any promise of weathering the social storms which convulsed that period. In lawsuits, the parties were put on oath. The defendant was allowed to clear himself by oath only on procuring the same testimony from witnesses, whose number varied according to the importance of the case and the merit or rank of the individuals. The oath was administered in the church, on the cross, the Gospels, the tombs of the saints, or the shrines enclosing their relics. In all this we can readily trace the germs of true legislation. The Roman law, into which Justinian's labors had infused something of the morality of the gospel, was at once the most complete and best fitted to the wants of nations. In this respect, humanity had been falling back; but the Church gradually improved the laws by wiser thoughts and sounder principles. The councils were the true legislative assemblies of the Middle Ages; and we may more than once be struck by their useful and wholesome influence.

10. The fifth century was fatal to letters. The torrent of barbarian invasion sweeping down from the North overwhelms the literary treasures, bears down all the monuments of the South. The light of intellect is extinguished, or finds shelter within the seclusion of the cloister. A thick and lasting gloom settles down upon Western Europe. Rome, the home of the arts, four times taken and sacked by the Goths, the Vandals, the Lombards, and the troops of Belisarius, saw its countless masterpieces crumble beneath the ruthless hands of the savage sons of the North. Then did the bowels of the earth receive the treasures so eagerly sought by the modern delvers of the Roman soil. It was doubtless in the designs of Providence that ancient Rome should thus bury herself with all her idolatrous, heathen superstitions, that the glorious monuments of the

new and Christian Rome might rise up over the ruins of lost polytheism. While Rome and the fine arts sunk under these cruel disasters, literature met with severe misfortunes in other quarters. A conflagration, which visited Constantinople in the fifth century, destroyed one hundred and twenty thousand volumes, among which are said to have perished the complete works of Homer, written in letters of gold. In the seventh century, the blind bigotry of the caliph Omar applied the torch to the celebrated Alexandrian library, and snatched from the world the most precious monuments of human genius. The East thus found in the Mahometan invasion the counterpart of the barbarian inroads in the West. Still, the Byzantine empire yet stood, and might have given shelter to science and literature now banished from the West. But the degenerate Greeks, sunk in indolence and corruption, wasted their time in fruitless discussions; their fickle nature seized with delight upon every heresy or new opinion that offered itself. The remains of civilization which they still possessed were rather a monument of their degeneracy than the germs of a new life; and, threatened as they were on all sides by the Saracens, the Ruriskchs, and the Bulgarians, they gave but scant promise of a brighter future.

11. To repair the wide-spread ruin, the Church now brought forth those generations of religious who made it their mission to keep alive the sacred fire of literature, science, and art, for the benefit of a more worthy age. The rule of the Egyptian monks was brought into Provence, in the beginning of the fifth century, by Sts. Honoratus and Cassian, who founded two monasteries respectively at Lerins and Marseilles. These nurseries produced learned and zealous apostles of the Christian faith and cenobitic life, among whom was St. Patrick, first founder of the monastic colonies of Ireland. The religious orders in the West followed various rules, until the Benedictine held all the Latin monasteries under its discipline. This celebrated order owes its beginning and rise to St. Benedict of Nursia, who, in the year 529, built the monastery of Monte Cassino,

which was to become the mother house of a numerous congregation. The rule to which St. Benedict subjected his monks prescribed manual labor and study, and bound them by the three vows of poverty, chastity, and obedience. Sanctioned by the approval of St. Gregory the Great, in 595, it spread rapidly through all the provinces of the Latin Church. The important services rendered by the Benedictines to religion, humanity, and literature, endeared them to all the faithful. Their monasteries became seminaries which sent forth preachers to carry the light of faith to barbarous nations, and with it, and by it, to widen the bounds of civilization. Their hands cleared the dense forest; of the most barren wastes their patient toil made rich and smiling fields. In fine, it is to their devoted care we owe the preservation of the great masterpieces of Greek and Latin antiquity. So many and so great blessings would naturally draw from their favored contemporaries a corresponding return of grateful liberality. The endowments showered upon monasteries soon exceeded the estates of the Churches. These means would of course result in wholesome effects. When the burden of public teaching afterward fell upon the religious orders, their wealth enabled them to attract the greatest minds within the sanctuary of science, and the constant communication kept up between the various monasteries gave action and union to the intellectual world. 　　•

12. The great vital power which had given such marvels of learning and eloquence to the fourth and fifth centuries, though weakened during the vicissitudes of the third period, was not utterly destroyed. St. John Damascen appeared in the East, the worthy successor of an Athanasius and a Chrysostom. In the West, St. Fulgentius, St. Cesarius of Arles, and St. Gregory the Great, were bright links in the glorious chain of the Church's doctors. Poetry, hitherto the chief vehicle of polytheistic teaching, changed its object and nature under the pen of Claudian. It became Christian, and was represented by St. Sidonius Apollinaris St. Fortunatus, and Boetius. The general corruption of taste appeared less strikingly in poetry than in

prose, and the inspirations of the Christian muse found interpreters well worthy to render their lofty flight. Profane history saw its last heathen representative in the person of Ammianus Marcellinus, a writer of the fourth century. The writers of the third period are of an exclusively Christian stamp; they are true religious chroniclers. We mentioned, in due course, St. Gregory of Tours, St. Isidore of Seville, and the Venerable Bede. The path marked out by the learned bishop of Tours was carefully followed by the Goth Jornandes, bishop of Ravenna (A. D. 552), in his works *De Gothorum origine et rebus gestis; De origine mundi*, and by the Burgundian Fredegarius (A. D. 650), in his *Chronicles*. The most valuable and reliable historical monuments of the fifth and sixth centuries are the letters of those who played a prominent part in Church or state. The epistolary collections of St. Sidonius Apollinaris, of Cassiodorus, and St. Gregory the Great, are full of the highest interest. Christian philosophy was worthily represented by the illustrious Boetius, who established the first alliance between theology and the Aristotelian method, to which the Church afterward owed all the advantages of the *scholastic* system.

13. The arts of design were already in full decline when the Northern invasion gave them their death-blow. This epoch witnessed the ruin of more temples than could be numerically replaced by the churches raised in the same length of time. But still, while the masterpieces of classical architecture* fell under the unsparing mallet of the barbarians, the Christian religion clothed itself with the splendors of the fallen worship, and thus saved the most precious remains of antiquity. It had already raised a great number of basilicas under Constantine; the work was nobly carried on under the Theodosian emperors. But the only sacred monuments of the period de-

---

* This is the term applied to Grecian architecture, of which the principles and later developments had been adopted in the Roman monuments, in opposition to the style called the Gothic, to which Christianity owes so many masterpieces, and of whose first appearance we shall have occasion to speak in the twelfth century.

serving of special mention, from their boldness of design or colossal dimensions, are the Rotunda at Ravenna and St. Sophia at Constantinople. These last two works of art are associated with the names of a royal barbarian and of an emperor—Theodoric and Justinian. After their period, the disordered state of the West and the unsteadiness of the imperial power in the East forbade princes to undertake great architectural works. Mussulman inroads and Iconoclastic fury struck a fatal blow at the fine arts, especially painting and sculpture, which had begun to decay long before architecture showed signs of weakness. The valuable service rendered to the arts by the energetic struggle of the Papacy against Iconoclasm, is too generally overlooked. It took to its protection those gifted sons of genius whose inspirations it has ever guided and fostered with a mother's care, and by this noble protection consecrated the temporal authority just bestowed upon it by the gratitude of the West.

14. While the pontifical power was thus upheld by the love and veneration of nations, the East felt the want of a firm and vigorous authority. The inertness of the Greek emperors gave way to the Mussulman encroachments, which might have been stifled in their birth. To this sad truth Constantine's degenerate descendants awoke too late; the Prophet's standard was already reflected in the waters of the Bosphorus, and all the East was bent before him. All was over. The religious and political system under which the East still languishes was thenceforth a power. This indelible stain was fixed upon civilization. The fairest countries on the face of the earth were doomed to a lasting barrenness. Not more utterly does the burning simoom of the desert wither every trace of vegetation, than does Islamism every germ of prosperity, greatness, and life. What has been the fate of the flourishing cities of Asia Minor, Syria, Palestine, and Egypt, under a government which dispeoples by polygamy, which breaks up the sanctuary of the family circle by the sensual ties of the seraglio, which

lowers woman, which degrades conscience by the teachings of fatalism, clogs every energy, raises sloth to the dignity of a dogma, looks down upon industry and agriculture as fit only for slaves, and palsies commerce by an official contempt for whatever is not of the Prophet?* It seemed to be the mission of Islamism to weigh down the East in the deep sleep of death, as a monumental stone presses upon a grave. But this material and sensual religion will crumble into dust at the first shock it receives from a powerful hand. The fanaticism that now bears it up is but the passing reaction of a degraded race fighting for its sensual institutions, armed to keep the right of dying unnerved and spent by the voluptuousness of the harem. Moreover, the empire of Constantinople was fated to atone, by its ruin, for the shameful crime of leaving humanity enslaved to this infamous yoke. Viewed in this light, the much-abused crusades were the highest political undertakings, fraught with the greatest benefits to mankind, had God willed to crown them with success.

Instead of turning their weapons against the Mahometans, those enemies of all civilization, the Greek emperors were entirely given up to fomenting religious quarrels. All the great heresies of this period were born in the East. The Church of Constantinople, far removed from the guardian care of Rome, and given up to the ambitious aims of its Patriarchs, was ever the home of innovation and error. The discussion on the Three Chapters was followed by the heretical stubbornness of the Eutychians and the rage of the Iconoclasts. Three general councils successively anathematized the error, but could not entirely uproot it. The Photian schism was coming on, to gather up all the scattered fragments of division and ruin, and to herald the final cutting off of the Greek Church.

15. When Christianity came forth in triumph from the catacombs, the Catholic worship displayed its splendors with

* It is notorious that in the East the Christians are known only by the name of *Giaour* dog).

all magnificence. The outward pomp of the sacred ceremonies deeply impressed the minds of the barbarians, and drew numbers to the faith. Clovis, dazzled by the unearthly splendor of the church of Rheims, on that glorious Christmas midnight that gave the French nation to the Christian fold, asked St. Remigius : " Father, is this the Heavenly Kingdom of which you told me ?" The clergy now wore particular ornaments on solemn days and in the discharge of certain ministerial functions. The dress which marked the bishop, consisted, in the East : 1. Of the stole (ὠράριον), first called *orarium*, and afterward *stola*. 2. An ornament made of white woollen stuff, worn on the shoulders (ὠμοφόριον, *pallium*), as a symbol of the lost sheep mentioned in the Gospel, sought and carried to the fold by the Good Shepherd. The pallium, also used in the West, was, from the sixth century, sent by the Popes to the metropolitans as a sign of communion and of dependence. 3. The *tiara* or *mitre*, made of costly stuff, often adorned with gold and precious stones, was, both in the East and in the West, the badge of episcopal authority. 4. In the West, the ring and crozier were also assigned as part of the bishop's insignia. The clergy, in humble imitation of monks and slaves, wore their hair cut close, or at least had it shaved on the crown, in a tonsure (*tonsura Petri, signum passionis*), which was afterward worn by all the clergy. Toward the close of the sixth century, it was found necessary to complete and improve the liturgical work of previous ages ; for the liturgy, like the creed of the Church, like its code of discipline, must receive new wealth from the tide of time, though it can never undergo any essential change. St. Gregory the Great undertook the work of reform ; we have mentioned his labors in this field. The grave and solemn religious chant that bears his name, was taught in a special school founded by the great Pontiff, and thence spread throughout the whole Church. In the lapse of time, church music became more artistic. At length the swelling strains of the majestic organ—echo of heaven's harmonies—accompanied the solemn Gregorian chant.

16. In the beginning of the fourth century a hammer and a plate of metal, and from the seventh the sound of bells, called the Christians to the churches for morning and evening prayer, or the celebration of the Holy Mysteries. This celebration consisted of two principal parts. The first (*Missa Catechumenorum*) was free to the catechumens, and even to pagans; none but baptized Christians could witness the second. The mass of the catechumens opened, according to the various liturgies, either by the singing of psalms or by reading a portion of the Sacred Scriptures. All those present chanted the Psalms in unison, though the custom prevailed in the East, from the fifth century, and in the West, since the time of St. Ambrose, of singing the Psalms in alternate choirs composed of all the faithful present. The first Psalm was sung in the style of our Introit (*Introitus*); then, according to the oldest liturgies, followed the same invocation we now make to the Divine mercy (κύριε, ἐλέησον), and the more or less fully developed doxology (*Gloria*). The bishop next saluted the people with the words *Pax vobis*, and offered up a prayer on behalf of the whole congregation (*collecta, quia fidelium vota ab eo quasi colligebantur*). Then he seated himself upon his throne, and the lector ascended the ambo to read a passage from the Epistles or from the Old Testament—generally from a book in which the *lessons* were disposed according to the season. This reading was followed by the singing of a psalm (*gradualis*),* after which the lector again read the Gospel (though after the sixth century this duty was always discharged by the deacon), which the bishop, standing either at his throne or the altar, explained with practical and familiar reflections (ὁμιλία, *tractatus*), or he made a discourse upon a text chosen at will (*sermo*). After the homily, the deacon removed the unbelievers, catechumens, and penitents, and, closing the doors, called upon the faithful, privileged to remain in the temple, to pray for the afflicted, for travellers,

---

* So named because generally chosen from among the fifteen Psalms called gradual (*graduales*).

for the sick and the agonizing, the clergy, the Church, for all classes of people, friends and enemies. This prayer corresponds to the one still preserved in the churches of France, under the name of *prône* (πριονaος).

17. Then began the second part of the sacrifice, with ceremonies exactly corresponding to those in use at the present day. From the offerings of bread and wine made by the faithful, the deacon and sub-deacon took what was necessary for the communion. This offering is styled, in the offertory (*offertorium*), a *sacrifice of propitiation* for our sins, the *sacrifice of the spotless Victim* born of the Virgin Mary. The use of incense at the Holy Sacrifice is mentioned in the fifth century. After the offertory, the deacon brought water to the bishop to wash his hands. The people were exhorted to raise their minds and hearts to heavenly sentiments (*præfatio*, πρόλογος). "Let us lift up our eyes to the Lord, with fear and trembling; let us raise up our hearts, *sursum corda.*" "We raise them up to the Lord," answered the people. "Let us give thanks to the Lord our God," again chanted the bishop, and the people again answered, "It is right and just." The preface ended with the angelic chant: "Holy, holy, holy is the Lord God of hosts." And now began the principal part of the tremendous Mysteries (ἀναφορα, *actio*, *secretum*), called the *canon* since the time of St. Gregory the Great. Then, as now every, word was carefully regulated. The addition of a single line to the canon of the Mass was an event that interested the whole Church, and must be known to all succeeding ages.* There was a commemoration of all the faithful, of the bishop or patriarch, the ruling monarch, the benefactors of the Church, and both in the East and West

---

* Joannes Diaconus thus speaks of it: "To the canon of the Mass Pope Gregory added the words: *Diesque nostros in tua pace disponas, atque ab æterna damnatione nos eripi et in electorum tuorum jubeas grege numerari.* This addition, which expresses a petition for peace, would seem to refer to the year 594, when Agilulph, king of the Lombards, laid siege to Rome; the city, being then ungarrisoned, was thrown into a state of the utmost consternation. St. Gregory, interrupting his labors on the prophet Ezekiel, by his ceaseless prayers and energetic zeal seconded the courage of the Romans, and rescued the city after a year's siege.

especial mention was made of the Pope, whose name was written for the purpose in the sacred diptychs. When the bishop was about to consecrate in the Oriental rite, the curtain which hid the sanctuary was drawn aside, and the bishop raised the consecrated Host, changed by the words of divine institution into the body of Jesus Christ, and the faithful bowed down in prostrate adoration. The custom of elevating the Host was not introduced into the West until some time later; but according to Sts. Ambrose and Augustine, the Blessed Sacrament was adored before the Communion. Next followed the *Pater*, the *Agnus Dei*, and the *kiss of peace* given by the bishop, and communicated in hierarchical order till it reached the simple faithful. The same order was observed in the communion: the bishops, priests, the inferior clergy, ascetics, monks, religious, and laymen successively received the sacred species of bread and wine with the words: "May the body, or may the blood of our Lord Jesus Christ keep thy soul unto life everlasting." After a closing prayer, the congregation was dismissed (*Missa. Demissio*). The general communion was usually given under both forms, as we have just stated, though it was evidently always believed that the substance of the Sacrament is wholly contained under either form, as is plainly expressed by the apostle: "He who eateth or drinketh unworthily," &c. Besides, the Christians, in the first age of persecution, or before setting out on a long journey, especially by sea, were allowed to keep the Blessed Eucharist in their houses; this privilege was especially enjoyed by monks who had no priest in their solitude. Now in such cases, as also in administering it to the sick, the Eucharist was always given under the *one* form of bread, and this communion was deemed as holy, as full, as that under both kinds. It is equally certain that communion was given to little children only under the form of wine, as was the early custom. As to the kind of bread used for the Eucharist, both the East and the West used *leavened bread*. It was not till the time of Photius that the use of unleavened bread pre-

vailed.   In both Churches was observed the primitive usage
of mingling a little water with the wine.

Such was the state of the Church when the re-establishment
of the Western Empire, in the person of Charlemagne, gave a
new impulse to the world, and constituted all Europe into a
powerful unity.*

---

* We have borrowed the materials for this chapter from the various works of MM.
Alzog, Dupanloup, Las-Casas, Des Michiels, Doellinger, Rohrbacher, Guéranger, &c.

FOURTH PERIOD

OF

THE HISTORY OF THE CHURCH.

From the Re-establishment of the Western Empire (A. D. 800) to the Pontificate of Sylvester II. (A. D. 999).

CHAPTER I.

§ I. PONTIFICATE OF ST. LEO III. (December 26, A. D. 795-. June 12, 816).

1. THE third period of Church history opened at the downfall of the Roman empire in the West; the re-establishment of the Western empire under Charlemagne inaugurated the fourth. Begun under the auspices of a hero, the impersonation of a whole century, this period, despite the bright promise of its

opening years, proved a season of sore trial to the Church. The whole East broke from the fold, and plunged into a lamen⁴· able schism, which still lasts. The West, ravaged by the Normans and Saracens, fell into all the disorders that ever follow in the train of anarchy. The monks and secular clergy became relaxed; the taste for ecclesiastical studies died away, the bonds of discipline were weakened; even the Papacy was subjected by the Tuscan kings and German emperors. Yet the Divine protection, ever watchful of the Church's interest, did not fail her at this critical juncture. The Holy See, armed with the temporal power bestowed upon it by the liberality of Pepin and Charlemagne, ever stood forth the centre of truth, the unshaken bulwark of the faith against its various enemies. The purity of Catholic teaching was jealously guarded, and the Gospel continued to make new conquests among the barbarians.

2. On the 26th of December, A. D. 795, St. Leo III. was raised to the Chair of St. Peter, and after his consecration was crowned on the lower steps of the Vatican basilica. Now that the Pope was a king, it was fitting that he should be crowned as other monarchs; and the tiara, the triple diadem that encircled his brow, represented the threefold royalty of the episcopate, the pontifical primacy, and the temporal sovereignty.* This was the origin of the ceremony called the *possessio* or *taking possession*, renewed with such majestic pomp at the enthronement of each new Pope. St. Leo III. hastened to acquaint Charlemagne with his election. The king had just won a complete triumph over the Huns, whose capital he gave up to be plundered by his troops. Here were hoarded up the captured treasures of Italy from the days of Attila. With his letter of congratulation to the new Pope, Charlemagne sent the most costly articles found among the spoils. The royal hand of a Frankish hero thus gave back to the Rome of the Sovereign Pontiffs, the monuments of art wrested by the *Scourge of God* from the nerveless grasp of the degenerate heirs of Cæsar and

---

* The tiara only took its present form in the pontificate of John XXIII. (A. D. 1413).

Augustus. " We had fully prepared," wrote Charlemagne, "to
send to your predecessor of holy memory, one of our dearest
servants, Engilbert, with the spoils which the God of armies
has given us out of the hands of the barbarians, the enemies of
His holy name; when we received tidings of the loss which I
still weep. The fond affection I had sworn to Adrian fills my
eyes with tears at only the mention or very thought of him.
Be it yours, worthy successor of that holy Pontiff, to assuage
my bitter grief by concerting measures with Engilbert, in conformity with Adrian's views, for the exaltation of the Church,
for the honor of your august dignity, and the glory of my patrician rank.* Ours it shall be, by God's help, ever to wield the
sword in defence of His holy Church; without, against the inroads and ravages of infidels; within, against the attacks of heretics." To these proofs of royal interest and generosity Leo
replied by a solemn embassy bearing to Charlemagne the keys
of the Confession of St. Peter and the municipal standard of
Rome; and, to perpetuate the memory of the Frankish hero's
patrician dignity, the Pope ordered a mosaic for the great hall
of the Lateran palace, representing the Apostle St. Peter giving a standard to the prince, and at the same time a stole to
the Pope.†

3. The promotion of St. Leo was hailed with unmingled
joy throughout the Christian world. Offa, king of the Mer-
cians, on the occasion of a visit to Rome, at the time of Leo's
election, increased the tax formerly levied by Ina for the support of an English college at Rome. This tax afterward
received the name it now bears, of Peter pence, from its being
paid at Rome on the feast of St. Peter Ad-Vincula. Kenulf,
Offa's successor, soon after wrote to congratulate Pope Leo on
his accession, and begged that the bishopric of Litchfield
might be joined to the archiepiscopal see of Canterbury,
which request the Pontiff saw fit to grant. Catholic Spain

---

* Charlemagne, and before him Pepin the Short, took the title of Roman Patrician, bestowed upon them by the Popes, in consideration of their protectorate over the Holy See.
† This monument is still in a state of preservation.

was ruled by Alphonso the Chaste. This great king, worthy
to be, the friend of Charlemagne, begged the new Pope's
prayers for the success of his arms against the Moors. Alphonso's faith was rewarded by the capture of Lisbon, which
awakened new hope in the hearts of this Christian people,
so few, but yet so great in courage. The East, Catholic for
the time, under the rule of Irene, lent its voice to swell the
general acclamation, and promised faithful obedience to the
new Pontiff. The death of Constantine VI., ordered by his
own mother (A. D. 797), left the imperial power wholly in the .
hands of that able but ambitious woman, who stopped at
nothing on the road to power. She sought, too, to cover the
remembrance of her crime by the prosperity heaped upon her
subjects, and the new impulse given to the empire. Had she
not sacrificed every natural claim to love of power, her name
had remained enshrined in glory in the Church's annals.

Under favor of all these promising circumstances, so full
of bright and cheering hope for Leo's pontificate, a plot was
formed, in the very heart of Rome, against the Pontiff's life.
Two priests, Pascal and Campulus, whose ambitious views
had been thwarted by the Pontiff's election, planned his assassination. On the 25th of April, A. D. 799, Leo was on horse-
back, in the solemn procession of the feast. of St. Mark. The
unarmed attendants are scattered by the two assassins with
their band of cut-throats; the Pontiff is assailed with blows
and wounds, and his eyes and tongue cut out. The ruffians
then drag him in a dying condition to the church of Sts. Stephen
and Sylvester, where they heap new outrages upon his sacred
person, and throw him at length into a gloomy dungeon. Rome
heard with horror the details of the execrable crime. His
chamberlain Albinus, backed by all the faithful, demands that
the prison doors be opened, breaks the august captive's fetters,
and restores him to liberty. On the very next day, Viginisus,
duke of Spoleto, appeared at the head of his army hastening
to the Pope's rescue, offered him an asylum in his states, and
escorted him to his capital with the highest honors. Here the

Pope miraculously recovered the use of his eyes and tongue, which wonderful cure is attested by all contemporary authors, and hardly admits of a question. Banished from Rome, still in a state of insurrection, the Sovereign Pontiff determined to seek in France the help never yet withheld from the Holy See. Charlemagne prepared to receive the holy Pope as a martyr of the faith, and went forward to meet him at some distance from Paderborn, where the interview was held. The countless throngs of soldiery and people, who had come to witness the solemn sight, stood around in an immense circle; Charlemagne, as he stood in their midst, towered above all around him. As soon as the Pope appeared among them, the immense multitude, soldiers, civilians, and clergy, three times prostrated themselves at the feet of the Vicar of Jesus Christ; three times the Pontiff gave them his blessing, and prayed for them. Charlemagne himself, the hero of the West, reverently bowed before Leo, the pastor of the world. They then embraced, with tears of joy and affection. Leo III., with tremulous voice, intoned the angelic hymn, *Gloria in excelsis*, which was continued by his clergy. Charlemagne led him thus in triumph to the church of Paderborn, where a service of solemn thanksgiving was performed. The moral effect of scenes so imposing upon the minds of new nations has, perhaps, been too much overlooked. This impressive figure of the union existing between the Papacy and the empire, tended to give a kind of divine sanction to power in the eyes of subjects, at a time when force was the great law of the material world. The interview of Paderborn was not without effect in Rome. The Pope's enemies trembled before the sword of Charlemagne; and a few months later (A. D. 799) Leo III. re-entered his pontifical city amid the acclamations of a whole people wild with joy at the return of a beloved father.

5. The humble and pious Pontiff thought himself called upon to answer, before a council of bishops, the slanderous charges uttered against him; but the prelates, with one voice, exclaimed: "It belongs not to us to judge the Apostolic See,

the head of all the Churches. That See and its Pastor are our judges rather." The Pope took up the book of Gospels, and, ascending the ambo, before the assembled multitude, uttered this solemn oath: "I, Leo, Pontiff of the Holy Roman Church, of my own free-will and inclination, swear before God, Who reads the innermost thoughts of the heart, in the presence of His angels, of the blessed Apostle St. Peter, and of you all who hear me, that I have neither done nor ordered any of the deeds imputed to me. So help me God, before Whose tribunal we must all appear, and in Whose sight we now stand. This I do without compulsion from any law, and by no means wishing to establish a precedent for my successors."

6. This scene was witnessed by Charlemagne, who had followed close in the footsteps of the Sovereign Pontiff, in order, by his presence, to restore perfect calm in the capital of the Christian world (A. D. 800). Since his accession to the Pontificate, Leo III. had been maturing a design of immense import. The hour of its execution was now at hand. The sceptre of the Frankish hero stretched over all the provinces formerly included in the Roman Empire of the West, from the Ebro to the Baltic, from the Theiss to the Atlantic, from the Northern Ocean to the Vulturnus. The remotest nations, most widely different in language and manners, longed to own the sway of a monarch who gloried in reigning for Jesus Christ.* The empire was virtually restored; nothing was wanting but the name. On Christmas Day (A. D. 800), Charlemagne, wearing his insignia as Roman patrician, came to the basilica of St. Peter to assist at the office of the solemnity. As he entered the church, which seemed but one blaze of light, the enthusiastic throng, forgetting for a moment the holiness of the place, broke forth into long and joyous acclamations. Charlemagne silenced the

* All Charlemagne's decrees were issued under this memorable formula: "Our Lord Jesus Christ reigning forever. I, Charles, by the grace and mercy of God, king of the Franks, avowed defender and humble ally of the Holy Church of God." "Regnante Domino nostro Jesu Christo in perpetuum. Ego, Carolus, gratia Dei, ejusque misericordia donante, rex et rector regni Francorum, et devotus sanctæ Dei Ecclesiæ defensor humillusque adjutor."—BALUZ, Capit., t. i., p. 210

multitude, and prostrated himself before the altar. A solemn stillness reigned in the vast assembly; every heart seemed instinctively to await some great event. Charlemagne alone was at a loss to account for this unwonted manifestation. But now the Pontiff Leo, already vested for the celebration of the divine mysteries, approached the kneeling monarch and placed upon his brow a diadem sparkling with jewels. The lofty arches of the basilica rang with the heartfelt acclamations of the people : "Long life and victory to Charles, the most pious Augustus, crowned by God the great and pacific emperor of the Romans!" The crowd, unable to satisfy their enthusiasm, filled the lofty dome with their repeated salutations. How often, in the course of ages, have like acclamations hailed an ephemeral reign! But here the splendor of the scene was hardly above the hero. His brow received the royal unction at the hands of the Pope, who then paid the first homage to the new emperor. The Roman Empire of the West, overthrown three centuries before, was now restored, and this great event opened the ninth century (December 25, A. D. 800). It added nothing, indeed, to the power of the Frankish king, but it clothed his authority with a splendid prestige. This event shaped the future rather than the actual condition of the Western nations, and completed the German invasion and the legal reconciliation of conqueror and conquered.

7. The empress Irene understood the immense significance of this glorious event, and hastened to send an embassy to the new emperor, for the ostensible purpose of renewing the treaties of alliance formerly made between the Byzantine court and the king of the Franks. But a union which should join the two worlds must be the result of a more private negotiation. The empress of the East was seeking a means of offering her hand to the emperor of the West, and the gigantic project was perhaps not altogether impracticable. Charlemagne sent an embassy to Constantinople. This movement was apparently satisfactory to the passion or the policy of Irene, who was, however, dethroned by an unexpected revolution (A. D. 801),

which resulted in the coronation of her former chancellor, Nicephorus. Irene had taken refuge in the palace of Eleutherius, where the imperial treasure was secured. Unattended and unarmed, Nicephorus presented himself before her, and respectfully assured her, with the confirmation of an oath, that not a hair of her head should be hurt if she would but give up to him the fortune of the Cæsars. "Nicephorus," replied the fallen empress, "you know me as the world has known me. I aimed at a crown; nothing should stand in the way of my ambition, not my own son, nor the sons of Copronymus. You, Nicephorus, I spared. You alone I left to snatch my sceptre from me. I did not mistrust you. May your clemency toward her whom you have torn from the throne, at least win you the mercy of the usurper who shall supplant you in turn! The imperial treasury is in your hands. Since my husband's death it has served me to corrupt those who gave you the crown and betrayed me." What a lesson is contained in every word of this reproachful speech! Irene exacted an oath from Nicephorus that he would restore her to freedom, and always treat her as an empress; but Nicephorus made light of oaths, and his victim, reduced to the last depth of misery, earned a scanty subsistence by the labors of her distaff in her solitary banishment in the isle of Lesbos. Thus died the first woman who ever held the sceptre of the Cæsars in her own name (A. D. 803). Nicephorus hastened to recognize Charlemagne as emperor of the West, and the boundaries of the two empires were fixed without dispute. Istria, Croatia, and Dalmatia passed into the hands of Charlemagne; and, while Constantinople thus ratified its decline in the West, each successive day witnessed the dismemberment of some one of its provinces in the East. Asia Minor, Pontus, Thrace, Macedonia, Greece, and a part of Illyria, alone remained to own the sway of the Byzantine sceptre; and this remnant would hardly have been withheld from the power of the Saracens or the Bulgarians by Nicephorus, for he was a bloodthirsty, vile, cowardly, and covetous prince. The Bulgarians burned him alive, together with his army, in a

Thracian valley, in the year 811, which event gave rise to the first joyful emotion felt by the people during the eight years of the tyrant's reign.

8. The failure of the attempted alliance between the two imperial courts was compensated by the number of foreign princes whose presence adorned the court of Charlemagne. Egbert, the youthful king of Sussex, and Eardulf, king of Northumberland, sought to profit by closer intercourse with the more polished civilization of the Franks. Lope, duke of Biscay, was also a pupil of the same polite court. Catholic kings and Spanish emirs followed him even into the Bavarian forests. Alphonso the Chaste displayed for his acceptance the rich tapestries taken at the siege of Lisbon. He received an embassy from the Edrisites of Fez. But all these demonstrations yielded to that of Haroun Al Rashid, caliph of Bagdad, who professed the most unbounded admiration for Charlemagne. Chief among the rich presents sent by the caliph were the keys of the Holy Sepulchre, emblem of the sovereignty which he granted to the emperor over the city of Jerusalem; a monstrous elephant,* which threw the Franks into a state of astonishment equal to the terror of the Romans at the sight of Pyrrhus's enormous chargers; and a hydraulic clock, with hands which told the hour by means of little balls falling upon a metallic plate, and by the simultaneous appearance of miniature horsemen. There were also Bengal apes, and such a profusion of perfumery, says the chronicler, that "it seemed as if they had drained the East to supply the West." But the monarch was doubtless more highly gratified at the homage paid to his glory by Eastern adulation. "Your power is great, O emperor!" said one of the Eastern envoys, "but it is surpassed by your renown. We Arabs and Persians fear you more than we do our master Haroun. What shall we say of the Mace-

---

* He was called Abul-Abbas. In the treasury of the basilica of Aix-la-Chapelle is still shown Charlemagne's great hunting-horn, which is said to have been made of one of this monster's teeth.

donians and Greeks, who dread your greatness more than the
billows of the Ionian sea!"

9. To appreciate the wondrous influence wielded by Charlemagne over the spirit of his age, we must not look upon him only
as a conqueror; this gives but one view of his great genius.
"Charlemagne," says Hallam, "stands alone like a beacon upon
a waste, or a rock in the broad ocean. His sceptre was as the
bow of Ulysses, which could not be drawn by any weaker
hand. In the dark ages of European history, the reign of
Charlemagne affords a solitary resting-place between two long
periods of turbulence and ignominy, deriving the advantages
of contrast both from that of the preceding dynasty and of a
posterity for whom he had formed an empire which they were
unworthy and unequal to maintain." The patron of literature
and science, a skilful ruler, essentially endowed with a talent
for organizing, lawgiver to an immense empire, equally wise
and Christian in policy, Charlemagne, in the varied effulgence
of every kind of glory, compels the admiration of all posterity.
His hand held aloft the torch of literature and science which
dispelled the gloom of barbarous ignorance, and his court became the rendezvous of the most distinguished men of the
age. Whenever he met a scholar, a writer, a poet, whether
Frank, Lombard, Goth, Saxon, or English, he at once made him
his friend. The Lombard historian, Paul Warnefrid, so well
known under the name of Paulus Diaconus, was King Didier's
chancellor. Charlemagne, after the capture of Pavia, sent him
word that he made war upon rebels, but not upon scholars, and
assigned him to his former rank in his own court; and when,
some time afterward, disgusted with the honors of the world,
of which he had so good reason to know the emptiness, Paul
retired to the monastery of Monte Cassino, Charlemagne still
kept up an epistolary intercourse with him. The emperor
sometimes wrote in verse to beg the prayers of the pious monk,
who was eminently worthy of this honorable intimacy. His
merit is proved by the various works we have from his pen:
1. *Historical Miscellanies*, or *Compendium of Roman History*,

of which the materials were furnished by various authors, and chiefly by Eutropius. 2. *History of the Lombards*, from the time of their migration from the Scandinavian forests to Luitprand (A. D. 744). Erchampert carried out this work to the year 888. 3. *Chronicles of the Bishops of Metz*, composed at the request of Engelram, bishop of that city. 4. *Life of St. Gregory the Great.* 5. *A Collection of Homilies*, made by order of Charlemagne, and recommended by the monarch to his subjects throughout the empire. 6. A vocabulary dedicated to Charlemagne, but never printed. He is also supposed to have written some poetical works, and to him is attributed the hymn of the feast of St. John Baptist : *Ut queant laxis.* Charlemagne won another trophy of the same kind in Lombardy, in the person of St. Paulinus, patriarch of Aquileia, whom he always kept near him, and consulted in the most important matters of state, with unbounded confidence in his piety, zeal, and enlightened judgment. Theodulf, another Lombard, who has also left us some writings, was taken from the imperial court to fill the see of Orleans, in which he revived the taste for sacred literature and ecclesiastical discipline. The poet Sedulius Scotus, whose elegant compositions have but lately found an editor in the learned Cardinal Mai, dedicated his *Book of the Christian Kings* to Charlemagne, whom he thus addresses in the preface : "In my wanderings through the enamelled meadow of holy writings, I have gathered for your majesty the freshest and most fragrant flowers, to adorn a sceptre which glories in reigning for Jesus Christ." But by no one was Charlemagne so ably seconded in the restoration of letters as by the Englishman, Alcuin, the learned disciple of Ven. Bede. The year 782 already found him established in the French court, and intrusted with three important abbeys : Ferrières in Gâtinais, St. Lupus of Troyes, and St. Josse in Ponthieu. Alcuin was now the confidant, the adviser, the doctor, and, so to speak, the intellectual minister of Charlemagne. His time was chiefly given to the three great duties of teach-

ing, correcting and restoring the manuscripts of ancient literature, and the foundation of schools.

10. The continual wars and political revolutions which filled
the period included between the sixth and eighth centuries, had
left both sacred and profane manuscripts to possessors or copyists, whose ignorance had almost irremediably disfigured the
texts thus committed to their keeping. To the correction of
this evil and the restoration of the rules of orthography and
grammar in these manuscripts, Alcuin gave the labors of a
lifetime; he also constantly recommended it to his scholars,
and was always supported by the authority of Charlemagne.
The Capitularies contain an ordinance worded thus : " Desirous
to revive in our empire, by assiduous labor, the cultivation of letters, which the inertness of our ancestors had
almost consigned to oblivion, we have directed that the text of
the ancient manuscripts be submitted to a board of revisers.
which we have established in our palace." Alcuin thus furnished a purified edition of the books of the Old Testament,
after carefully collating the texts of the best manuscripts, and
dedicated it to Charlemagne, " unable," as he said, " to offer to
the emperor of the earth a more magnificent gift than the books
containing the Word of the God of heaven." The emulation of
Charlemagne, aroused by such a work, moved him to undertake
the direction of a corrected edition of the four Gospels, with
the help of several learned Greeks and Syrians.   Such examples, confirming such orders, could not fail to prove effectual,
and a general mania at once arose for the reproduction of old
manuscripts.   As soon as a correct revision of some work had
been produced by Alcuin, or by some one of his disciples, new
copies were at once made and distributed to the principal
churches and abbeys.   A skilful copyist was on the high road
to glory and fortune.   The production of neat and exact manuscripts made the reputation of a monastery.   The abbey of
Fontenelles and two of its monks, Ovo and Hardwin, won a real
renown in this line.   Rheims and Corbie strove to equal them.
The uncertain and confused characters which had been used for

the past two centuries, gave way to the Roman. Monestic libraries rapidly enlarged their store of volumes. A vast number of manuscripts bear the date of this period; and though religious zeal devoted itself chiefly to sacred literature, still the profane was not neglected. Alcuin himself revised and copied the comedies of Terence.

11. While deeply engaged in restoring the texts of manuscripts, and thus rendering to studies the eminent services of which the scholars of succeeding ages have profited, without, however, sufficiently acknowledging their indebtedness, Alcuin also labored to re-establish the schools, which had fallen from their original splendor. An ordinance, inserted by Charlemagne into the Capitularies, made it obligatory upon every bishopric and monastery to open a scholastic course, in which the youth of the day might be trained to the knowledge of divine and human science. This period marks the rise of most of the schools, which soon gained a wide renown, and sent forth the most distinguished men of the following century : Fuld, in the diocese of Mentz, St. Martin of Tours, Richenau, in the diocese of Constance, and Fontenelle or St. Vaudrille (Vaudregisile), in Normandy. Most of the teachers who illustrated their chairs had been disciples of Alcuin; for besides his constant devotion to the task of founding schools, he also taught in person with distinguished success.

12. The first lessons of the illustrious master were not given within the cloister nor in more public institutions of learning. From A. D. 782 to 796, the period of his residence at the French court, Alcuin presided over a domestic school, called the *Palace School*, which had its seat wherever Charlemagne happened to find himself, being composed of the princes, great lords, and noble strangers who followed in the emperor's suite.* From this domestic chair Alcuin imparted his first teachings to three sons of Charlemagne: Charles, named king of France and Burgundy; Pepin, king of Italy; and Louis,

* The *Palace School* was the germ of the Palatine Academy, founded by Charlemagne at about this period, and the first institution of the kind known in modern history.

king of Aquitaine, and afterward emperor ; to Adalard, grandson
of Charles Martel, and his sister Gundrada; Engilbert and
Eginhard, sons-in-law and counsellors of Charlemagne, who
used to call the former his Homer, because of his high poetical
attainments; the latter has left us two important works : the
Annals of the French Kings, and a *Life of Charlemagne*, written
in a style which recalls the classic elegance of antiquity;
Riculf, archbishop of Mentz; Rabanus Maurus, his successor in this see, whose principal works, *On the Institution of
Clerics and the Ceremonies of the Church*, and *On the Ecclesiastical Calendar*, are both equally able and useful; Benedict, son
of the count of Maguelonne, who, at the age of twenty years,
retired into solitude, and is so well known as St. Benedict of
Aniano, the restorer of monastic discipline and the second patriarch of the religious orders in the West; William, duke of
Aquitaine, an accomplished prince, to whom Charlemagne, with
great difficulty and many tears, granted leave to withdraw into
the solitude where he won his title to a place in the Church's
calendar; Rigbod, archbishop of Trêves; both the princesses
Gisela, sister and daughter of Charlemagne ; and, above all,
Charlemagne himself.   The monarch had studied grammar under the deacon Peter of Pisa; under Alcuin he pursued the
higher studies of rhetoric, dialectics, astronomy, and theology
Latin was as familiar to him as his own mother-tongue; he was
well versed in Greek, and possessed some knowledge of the
Hebrew and Syriac.   The writings of the Fathers gave him the
greatest pleasure.   The imperial library at Vienna still contains
a manuscript *Commentary on the Epistle to the Romans*, under
the name of Origen, corrected by Charlemagne himself.   So
thoroughly had this great prince and the companions of his
studies become imbued with the spirit of their labors, that in
their familiar correspondence they assumed literary names borrowed from both sacred and profane antiquity.   Charlemagne
signed himself David; Alcuin took the name of Flaccus (the
surname of Horace—Quintus Horatius Flaccus); Adalard called
himself Augustine; Engilbert assumed the name of Homer ;

Riculf that of Damœtas; Gundrada was Eulalia,* &c. Filled with an ardent zeal to equal the science of the ancient Fathers, Charlemagne one day uttered the exclamation: "O that I had twelve clerks as learned and eloquent as Jerome and Augustine!" "What!" replied Alcuin; "the Creator of heaven and earth has but two men of such merit, and you wish for twelve!" To supply the want of Jerome and Augustine, Alcuin was obliged to minister to the intellectual greed of his imperial disciple. Of two hundred and thirty-two of his letters, now extant, thirty are addressed to Charlemagne, and treat various questions of astronomy, cosmography, chronology, ecclesiastical computation, the exact sciences, history, grammar, liturgy, and law. Charlemagne had brought together, in his palace school, a great number of youths, some from the highest ranks of the nobility, others of a middle state in life. He very reasonably judged that community of studies would arouse a useful spirit of emulation in the young princes, his sons; and watched, with great interest, the progress of the students. Returning from one of his military expeditions, he examined the results of the labors executed during his absence; they were all in favor of the poorer class. "Continue," said Charlemagne, "the studies you have so well begun; strive to make new progress; hereafter I shall bestow upon you offices and rank. As for you, whose effeminate nobility pales at the thought of labor, and languishes in sloth and ignorance, by Him who rules the heavens! I make little account of your rank; unless you very soon atone for your negligence, never look for the favor of your king." He then called out the most successful of the poor scholars, and, upon the spot, appointed him clerk of his imperial chapel. On receiving the tidings of the death of one of his bishops, Charlemagne asked how much he had bequeathed to the poor. "But two silver livres," was the reply. "A scanty viaticum for so long a journey," observed the youthful chaplain, who was present. "If this bish-

---

* Eulalia (eloquent), from the Greek εὐλαλία (to speak well).

opric were bestowed upon you, would you make a better provision for the journey?" asked the emperor. "My lord," replied the youth, throwing himself at the monarch's feet, "that is in the will of God and your power." "Then be bishop," said Charlemagne; "but, for the sake of your own soul and mine, forget not the viaticum."

13. Alcuin's constitution at last yielded under the weight of his labors, and he begged the emperor's leave to end his days in solitude. After a long resistance, Charlemagne at length granted his petition, and gave him as a home the abbey of St. Martin of Tours, one of the wealthiest in the kingdom. Alcuin hastened to his desired retreat, whence he kept up a correspondence with the emperor, which cheered without wearing out his declining years. His life of retirement was by no means one of idleness; he restored discipline in the monastery, enriched its library with manuscripts copied at York, and, by his teaching, gave to its school a celebrity to which it had never before aspired. "I am engaged," he wrote to Charlemagne, "in gathering for some the sweets of the Sacred Writings; I try to inebriate others with the old wine of the study of antiquity; some I nourish with the fruits of grammatical studies, while striving to enlighten the eyes of others with the order of the heavenly bodies and the wonderful economy of the world. But I feel the want of some of the best works of scholastic learning, which I had obtained, at home, either through the devoted care of my master, the Venerable Bede, or through my own efforts. I therefore beg your majesty's leave to send some of my servants to bring those British flowers into France. In the morning of my days I sowed the seeds of learning in that beloved Britain; now, though the sunset of life has chilled my blood, I still continue to sow them in France, and I trust that, by the grace of God, they may prosper in both countries."[*]

* Alcuin died at Tours (A. D. 804). Besides several commentaries on the Sacred Scriptures, some works on theological and pious subjects, and some lives of saints, he has left various treatises on the liberal arts; on grammar, logic, and rhetoric; and, finally, two hundred and eighty pieces in verse, mostly on occasional subjects. Perfect purity of morals

Such were the language and habits of these great men. The death of Alcuin did not check the zeal of Charlemagne for the cultivation and encouragement of letters; and in the year 804 he signed the diploma of foundation for the celebrated school of Osnabruck, which he at the same time endowed with imperial munificence. He begged the Pope to send him Roman chanters, to restore the Gregorian chant in the churches of Germany and Gaul. "Whence do we draw the purest water?" asked the emperor of his clerks, "from the stream or from the fountain-head?" "From the fountain-head, of course," replied they. "Then return to the source," said the monarch, "for you have evidently corrupted the ecclesiastical chant." Two schools of Gregorian chant were accordingly established, one at Soissons, the other at Metz. The Roman clerics taught the Franks the use of organs, whose recent introduction into Gaul we lately had occasion to mention. Walafrid Strabo, a contemporary writer, states that a woman, on hearing for the first time the sound of the wonderful instrument, died in an ecstasy of delight.

14. All these occupations did not withdraw Charlemagne's attention from the more serious cares of government. Under the Carlovingian dynasty the monarchical principle was restored to its necessary relations with that of representation; the two elements were thus seen combined without detriment of either to the other, both combining as truly for the maintenance of order as for the development of national power. Charlemagne himself convoked more than thirty general assemblies, or diets. "If the season was favorable," says Archbishop Hincmar, a contemporary writer, "they met in the open air, otherwise in two large halls, one for the bishops, the other for the counts; the two chambers were at liberty to hold their deliberations separately or together. Several other apartments (*diversa loca*)

---

and a burning zeal for the defence of the Catholic faith won for Alcuin the title of saint, as we learn from the author of his life, from Flodoard, from the chronicles of St. Martin of Tours, and of Rabanus Maurus, archbishop of Mentz, his disciple, who gives him a place in his Martyrology. But the Church, as yet, allows him no public honors.

were assigned to the other members of the assembly (*cætera multitudo*), who were called *minores;* they consisted of the notables and the *scabini* (*échevins*, or selectmen of towns and districts), who accompanied the governors and counts to the general assembly." In these large assemblies Charlemagne perfected his great legislative work called the *Capitularies*, from the division of the decrees into chapters (*capita*). He sealed these ordinances with the hilt of his sword, saying: " These are my orders, and this is the steel that shall win them respect." The constant aim of Charlemagne's legislation was to modify and to fuse, so to speak, the laws of the Ripuarii, Saxons, Lombards, Bavarians, and various other nations which made up his vast empire, to bring them to the unity of the Roman law. The prominent feature of this immense labor is a religious attachment to the Church, and a profound respect for canon law, which is made binding in all its prescriptions. Charlemagne sincerely discharged the duties of *exterior bishop*, which title he used to assume, in imitation of the great Constantine. From this source the legislation and jurisprudence of European nations derive something of the mild and humane spirit which essentially characterizes the legislation and jurisprudence of the Church. To insure the execution of his laws, and to acquaint himself with the real condition of the masses subject to his rule, the emperor every year sent commissioners into the various provinces, whose duty it was to see and hear every thing, and to make a faithful report of all to the head of the state. Two of these envoys, a bishop and a duke or count, were appointed for each province, with the title of *missi dominici,* the same officers are used by different modern administrations by the name of *inspectors.* We may close our account of the laws and government of Charlemagne with the words of Montesquieu: " This great monarch made admirable laws; but what is more, he put them into execution. The influence of his genius was felt throughout the whole empire. His legislation shows the spirit of prudence which takes in every thing, and a certain power which sweeps away all obstacles; pretexts

to evade duties are removed, negligence corrected, abuses reformed or prevented; if he knew how to punish, he knew still
better how to pardon. The simple execution of vast designs
proves him a master in the art of doing the greatest deeds with
ease, and the most difficult with readiness. He traversed all
parts of his vast empire with unfailing energy, ever present
where the support of his strong hand was needed, settling every
question as soon as it arose. Never was prince better calculated to brave dangers, or to prevent them; he made light of all
perils, and chiefly of those which always threaten great conquerors: I mean conspiracies. Yet this great prince was ex-
tremely moderate, mild, and simple in his manners, and loved
to mingle with those who were attached to his court. His
expenses were admirably regulated; his estate assessed with
wisdom, care, and economy; a father could learn, from his laws,
to govern his private household; and his *Capitularies* tell us the
pure and sacred source whence he drew his rich treasures of
legislative wisdom. I may conclude with the single remark,
that he ordered the eggs of his farm-yards and the useless weeds
of his gardens to be sold, and he had distributed among his people
all the riches of the Lombards and the immense treasures of
the Huns, who had pillaged the whole world."*

15. To the Church he owed his imperial title; the Church
Charlemagne strove to glorify throughout his empire. In A. D.
803 he received Pope St. Leo, who once more sought the counsel and assistance of the great king in the troubles raised in
Italy by the ambition of the Venetians. The doge had lately
driven from his see Fortunatus, patriarch of Gradi, one of the
islands subject to the republic. It was to be feared that the
Greeks would avail themselves of these dissensions to seize the
city, which had been the barrier to their desire for the fertile
plains of Italy. The Pope and the emperor spent the time of
the Christmas festival at Quercy-sur-Oise, where they decided
upon the measures necessary to pacify the peninsula, after

* MONTESQUIEU, *De l'Esprit des Lois*, l., xxxiii., ch. 38.

which the Pope returned to Rome. Charlemagne gave the greatest care to the restoration of canonical order in the hierarchy. The election of bishops by the joint suffrages of clergy and people had been almost entirely done away with by his predecessors, in their ambitious desire to monopolize the nominations. The emperor had himself made use of this right, such as he had found it, in the beginning, and we saw an instance of it in the nomination of the young clerk before mentioned; but he soon gave it up, and enforced the strict observance of the ancient discipline on this point. He reformed another and more hurtful abuse, which had long since been introduced into the churches of Germany and Gaul, by the ignorance and sloth of certain prelates, who intrusted the greater part of their duties to the *chorepiscopi*, who had, in the majority of cases, received no higher order than the priesthood. On this subject Charlemagne consulted St. Leo III., "in order," he said, "to conform to the wish expressed in the holy canons, that all important cases should be referred to the Apostolic See." The Pope replied that the chorepiscopi should be forbidden to exercise episcopal powers, and their ordinations held as null. The pontifical decree was put into execution, though, indeed, the chorepiscopal office fell of itself in the following century. We have already had occasion to record the prohibitions of councils against bishops and clerics bearing arms. In spite of the wise regulation, some bishops still continued personally to lead their vassals in military expeditions. Their obligation to contribute to the defence of the state, by reason of the great domains or fiefs they held; the necessity, even, of protecting ecclesiastical property against the inroads of rival lords; but, above all, the prejudices of a nation wholly martial in all its instincts, holding the profession of arms in the highest honor, had hitherto overruled all principle. But awaking at last to higher views and feelings, all orders of the state, in general assembly, presented a petition to the emperor, begging him to put an end to such disorders. The following engagement was entered into by the nobles: "In order that the bishops and other ecclesiastics may have no ground to suspect that we disarm them with a sacrilegious design to invade more freely the Church's estates, we all, while holding straws in our right hands, and casting them upon the ground,* protest before God and His angels, before you, our bishops, and in presence of the assembled people, that we will neither commit this crime ourselves, nor suffer others to perpetrate it." Charlemagne, delighted at finding in his subjects dispositions so conformable to his own, received the petition most favorably, and embodied it in a capitulary forbidding any bishop or cleric to appear in the army, unless in the capacity of chaplain or almoner. He was always the first to show the filial respect and obedience due to the laws of the Church. The Council of Frankfort had forbidden bishops to absent themselves from their dioceses for a longer space than three weeks at a time ; Charlemagne laid before the council Pope Adrian's permission that Engelram, bishop of Metz, should always reside at the court, and begged that Hildebold of Cologne might also be left with him, as he had obtained for him a like permission from the Holy See.

16. In the third Council of Toledo, the Spanish bishops had inserted into the symbol of Constantinople the famous expression *Filioque*, which holds, against the Greeks, that in the Blessed Trinity the Holy Ghost proceeds from the Son as well as from the Father. The usage was gradually introduced into Gaul of singing the Creed, with this addition, in the churches, or at least in the royal chapel. The same custom prevailed in a community of Frankish monks, established in the Holy Land, by the Mount of Olives, and who held to the Latin rite. Stigmatized by the Greeks as heretics, they laid their complaints before Charlemagne, who at once called a council at Aix-la-

---

* This ceremony of the straw is here a fact worthy of note. The Franks took possession of a domain or other piece of property by receiving a straw ; while, on the other hand, to throw down a straw was to renounce all claim to the property. A like form was in use among the ancient Romans in their contracts ; hence the words to *stipulate* and *stipulation*, from *stipula*, a straw.

Chapelle (November, A. D. 809), with the determination to give their calumniated faith a splendid vindication. As an additional sanction to the decision pronounced in favor of the *Filioque*, the pious monarch resolved to have it approved by the Sovereign Pontiff. The council sent as envoys to St. Leo III., Vernarius, bishop of Worms; Adalard, abbot of Corbie; and Smaragdus, abbot of St. Michael's (now in the diocese of Verdun). To the last-named deputy, who was present at the conference held on the subject in Rome, we owe the details of its acts. The Pope received the envoys in a hall of the basilica of St. Peter, and heard their statement of the procession of the Holy Ghost from the Father and the Son, established on the testimony of the holy Doctors. The Roman Church had never entertained a doubt on this subject more than any other Western Church; but for reasons but too clearly justified by after-contentions between the Greeks and Latins, it had not been deemed expedient to insert the formal expression of this belief into the Creed. The prudent Pontiff, to whose care was intrusted the general welfare of Catholicity, assured the deputies that he believed as sincerely as themselves the truth expressed in their addition, but that he could not approve the addition itself. "If it be a truth of faith," said the envoys, "should it not be taught?" "I should be slow," replied St. Leo, "to sit in judgment upon the fathers of an ecumenical council, who have written their profession of faith under the inspiration of the Holy Ghost. I do not feel at liberty to suppose that they could not foresee as well as ourselves the consequences of their reserve, and of their absolute prohibition to make any addition, whether this or any other, to their formula." "If the Creed is still sung in the churches,"* urged the deputies, "with the omission of this term, all the faithful will be led to think that it is against faith. What do you advise us to do, in order to avoid this

---

* The custom of singing the Creed had not yet been introduced at Rome, but was confined to the churches of Gaul and Germany.

difficulty ?" " Had I been consulted earlier," replied the Pope, " I should have advised the omission of the *Filioque*. What occurs to me now—but I do not impose it as an obligation— is the gradual discontinuance of the practice of singing the Creed in the imperial chapel. Thus what was introduced without the sanction of authority would disappear by degrees. This would perhaps be the best means to guard against the danger of your innovation, without any detriment to the faith." Such is the sum of the celebrated conference of St. Leo III. with the deputies of the Council of Aix-la-Chapelle (A. D. 810). What the Pope discountenanced in the practice of the Franks was not the addition itself, in so far forth as it concerned the dogmatic question, but the unseasonableness of the addition, made without the necessity which only arose at a later period, and without the authority necessary for an object of so great moment. Besides, this conference seems to have had no re- sults, since every thing remained as before. In Gaul the Creed was still sung with the inserted *Filioque*. Rome did not think it proper to make the addition, nor even to begin to sing the Creed. St. Leo even had it engraved, without this addition, upon two large silver escutcheons, each weighing about a hun- dred pounds, in Latin upon one and in Greek upon the other. They were then hung up on the right and on the left of the Confession of St. Peter, as public and religious monuments, as marks of the care taken by the Roman Church to preserve the symbol just as she had received it. The subsequent Greek schism sufficiently proves the wisdom of this foresight, and the better results which would have followed a faithful conformity to the policy of the mother and mistress of all the Churches.

17. Hitherto Charlemagne has appeared before us as the happiest monarch of his time, as he was certainly the most illustrious. But for his old age there were sorrows in store, which all the greatness of the world is powerless to assuage. The visitation began in what was nearest and dearest : his son Pepin, king of Italy, was snatched from him in the flower of his age. The pale reaper, Death, once at work in this august

family, mowed down, in the same year (810), the princesses
Gisela, the emperor's sister, the prudent and pious abbess
of Chelles, whom he so tenderly loved, and Rothrudis, his
eldest daughter; and struck a fatal blow at once at his policy
and his tenderness, in his eldest son, Prince Charles. Thus, of
his three sons, all capable of governing, and already sharing
the provinces of his vast domination, was spared but Louis,
king of Aquitaine. Pepin left a son named Bernard, upon
whom the diet of Aix-la-Chapelle bestowed the kingdom of
Italy (A. D. 813). The rest of the empire fell to the lot of
Louis, the only surviving son of Charlemagne. The emperor,
on calling him to share his power, thus addressed him: "My
son, beloved by God, by your father, and by this people, whom
God has left the only solace of my declining years, you see
me fast sinking; even my old age flies from me; the gloom of
the grave is gathering about me. God vouchsafed me the
honor of being born of the Frankish race. He has granted
me to sway the sceptre of my fathers; I leave it no less
glorious than when I received it. First among the Franks,
I have borne the title of Cæsar, and brought over to the
Frankish rule the dominion of the race of Romulus. Receive, my son, with Christ's consent, the crown and the em-
blems of the royal power." Then raising his voice, he exhorted
the prince to love and honor God, to keep His commandments,
to protect the Church, to treat the princes of his family with
kindness, to love his people as his own offspring, to have a care
of the poor, to confer offices only upon faithful and religious
officers, never to confiscate a fief without sufficient reason and
regular form of law; in fine, to lead a life blameless in the
sight of God and man. "Are you disposed, my son, to fulfil
all these duties?" asked the venerable monarch. Louis gave
his promise with many tears. "Then take the crown" (it had
been placed upon the altar), "place it upon your brow, and be
mindful of your promise." The young prince obeyed, amid
the acclamations of the nobles present at the ceremony. The
weeping father then sent back the youthful monarch, loaded

with costly gifts, to his kingdom of Aquitaine; he was never again to behold his youthful heir on earth. Though stricken so deeply in the tenderest affections of his heart, the mind of the great emperor was still keenly alive to the frightful portents which now loomed up in the political horizon of Europe. As he was one day sitting down to table in a city of Narbonese Gaul, some Scandinavian pirates made a descent upon the coast, and carried on their plundering depredations even in the harbor, under the very eyes of the aged emperor. Chase was given to the light vessels, which, however, escaped untouched. Charlemagne, says the chronicler, stood at a window looking toward the East, and wept bitterly. No one dared question him as to the cause of his grief; turning, at last, to his barons, he asked them: "Do you know, my faithful friends, why I weep so bitterly? Certainly, I do not fear the harm which those barbarians can do me by their wretched plundering; but I am deeply grieved to think that while I am still alive, they should dare to touch my shores; and I foresee, with heart-felt pain, the evils they will bring upon my descendants and their subjects." And yet he could not foresee the devastation of the whole of Gaul, the burning of the palace at Aix-la-Chapelle, the asylum of his old age, which he took pleasure in adorning, only to be at a future day the prey of the Normans (*Northmen*).

18. His last thoughts were still of the Church, whose armed defender he had ever been through the whole course of his long and glorious reign. In 813, as many as five councils were held in different parts of the empire: at Arles, Châlons-sur-Sâone, Tours, Rheims, and Mayence. Their disciplinary canons were sent to Aix-la-Chapelle, where the emperor laid them before a large assembly of bishops and lords (September, A. D. 813?), and made them binding upon all his subjects by a special capitulary. This was the last act of his reign. He felt the approach of the fatal stroke on the 20th of January, A. D. 814, and was the only one to face the danger with all the heroism which had ever characterized him in so many perilous encounters. On the seventh day of his illness he received the holy

viaticum at the hands of his archchaplain, Hildebold, archbishop of Cologne, without betraying a single human emotion during the whole ceremony, seemingly absorbed in religious sentiments; and when the last moment had come, summoning up all his remaining strength, he signed himself with the sign of salvation, and, murmuring the words of the Psalmist, "Into thy hands, O Lord, I commend my spirit," he gently breathed his last, at about nine o'clock in the morning of the twenty-eighth day of January, A. D. 814, in the seventy-second year of his age, the forty-seventh of his reign, and the fourteenth of his empire. He was buried in the church of Aix-la-Chapelle, which he had built, and where his splendid monument is still preserved. With him would most probably have died out the torch of civilization in the West, had not the Papacy been alive to feed the flame.

19. The fate of the East, far removed from the wholesome influence of the Sovereign Pontiffs, and wholly given up to the weak despotism of princes equally devoid of nobleness and of faith, shows but too plainly what must become of nations which forsake the centre of Catholic unity. The emperor Nicephorus, whose shameful accession and yet more inglorious end we have already recorded, had devoted the greater part of his reign to the persecution of two Catholic priests, St. Plato and St. Theodore the Studite,* who maintained, according to the teachings of faith, that princes are as much subject to the rules of the Church, concerning marriage, as the simple faithful. The interest of Nicephorus in this question was due to the fact that he had, by an adulterous alliance, united his son to the Athenian Theophano, who was already married. A council, consisting of fifteen court-paid prelates, had the baseness to depose the two courageous priests, and Nicephorus banished them to an island near Constantinople, where they were confined in two separate prisons. From their place of exile, the holy confessors addressed

* St. Theodore owed his surname to the monastery, near Constantinople, of which he was abbot.

the following admirable letter to St. Leo, to beg his protection: "To your Holiness we repeat the words which the Prince of the Apostles addressed to our Lord, when the waves threatened to ingulf his bark: 'Save us, Supreme Pastor of the Church! Save us, we perish.' Imitate the Divine Master, stretch forth a saving hand to our Church, as the Saviour did to St. Peter. There is but one point of difference between the two situations, and it is to our disadvantage. Peter had only begun to sink into the waters, whereas our Church is already overwhelmed by the billows of heresy. Remember the great Leo, whose name and whose virtues you now revive. Like a lion, he met the rising heresy of Eutyches. Do you likewise, Holy Father, denounce this new heresy. If the enemies of the faith have dared to assume the right of holding a heretical council, though, in truth, they have not even the right to hold an orthodox council without your knowledge, according to the canons and traditional usage of the Church, how necessary should it not seem that your Holiness call a legitimate council for the triumph of sound doctrine and the truth!" This letter of the two holy sufferers recalls that which was addressed to Pope Symmachus by the whole Eastern Church. Both recognize, in the face of Heaven and earth, that the safety of all Christendom consists in its union and submission to the Roman Church. Time and experience have both combined to prove the truth of this principle. Every individual Church which has forgotten or discarded this truth, like a branch severed from the parent stock, has lost its sap and vital power, sunk into degradation and bondage, and become the sport of every passing barbarian, Arab, Turk, or Muscovite. St. Leo's reply to the two confessors is a noble specimen of courageous faith. He made every effort to obtain their release from Nicephorus, who refused to hear any mention of terms until his son's adulterous union had been approved; and with this fixed resolve, he joined the Manicheans, or Paulicians, as they were then called, hoping to find some countenance for his disorders in that degraded sect. This event marks the period of the first appearance of Manicheism in Thrace, and, later, throughout the West. The most baneful errors, if traced back to their source, will generally be found to have taken their rise in the heart of an abandoned monarch. The new Patriarch of Constantinople, also called Nicephorus, and successor to St. Taraisus, could never obtain the emperor's leave to send his synodal letter to the Pope, and to ask for the confirmation of his election. The victory of the Bulgarians (A. D. 811), which cost the heretical emperor his life, was followed by the reign of the just and virtuous Michael I., Rhangabe,* a reign too short for the happiness of the East and for the peace it gave to the Church. The Patriarch Nicephorus availed himself of the passing truce to send to St. Leo III. a long profession of Catholic faith, in which he assures him of his attachment to the teachings of the Church, and receives the seven general councils held up to his time. His influence with the new emperor also obtained the enactment of severe measures against the Manicheans, and the release of St. Plato and St. Theodore the Studite. Plato, borne down by years and infirmities, died in the act of praying for his persecutors (March 19, A. D. 813); and Theodore, returning to his holy retreat, by his wise and saintly government soon made it one of the most flourishing monasteries in Christendom. The bright anticipations excited by the beginning of Michael's reign were but short lived. The Lower Empire was too unworthy of even the unwonted boon it now enjoyed, and, as usual, did not keep it long. Leo the Armenian betrayed and supplanted the generous master who had loaded him with favors and given him the chief command of his forces. The nobles, the senate, and the people of Constantinople, urged Michael to resist the usurpation. "No," replied the emperor, "no, I would not have a drop of Christian blood shed in my quarrel. I leave a throne which I never coveted, and on which I was placed in my own despite." This noble sentiment would certainly have shown heroic self-denial in a private individual, but it must be deemed

---

* Michael was called Curopalates (grand master of the palace), from his having filled that office under Nicephorus, his predecessor.

a mark of fatal weakness in a sovereign, who would spare a few drops of blood shed in the struggle against a usurper, at the risk of torrents which were sure to flow under the rule of a tyrannical power. Michael put off his imperial insignia and sent them to Leo, with the acknowledgment of his sovereignty. Thus was the throne usurped by Leo V., the Armenian, to whom his contemporaries gave the surname of *Chameleon*, from the facility with which he adopted the most different and opposite doctrines. He became a furious Iconoclast, and his reign revived the persecutions of Leo the Isaurian, Copronymus, and Leo IV. (A. D. 813).

20. Pope Leo III. did not long survive his friend, the emperor Charlemagne. He died after a pontificate of more than twenty years. In 813 he restored the feast of the Assumption, already celebrated by Pope Sergius I., but now fallen into desuetude. In the fervor of his piety he used to celebrate the Holy Sacrifice as often as eight or nine times a day, as nothing had yet been fixed on this point. The number of daily masses was left to the devotion of the priests and faithful. The present practice was only established by Alexander II., in the eleventh century. During the last year of his reign, the life of St. Leo was threatened by a conspiracy ; but the indignant Romans seized upon the conspirators and put them to death. The Papacy, thus leaning upon the affection of its subjects, was ever invincible.

§ II. Pontificate of Stephen V. (June 22, A. D. 816—January 22, 817).

21. The election of Stephen V. to the Sovereign Pontificate (June 12, A. D. 816) was contemporaneous with two late accessions, which placed Louis the Mild, the son of Charlemagne, on the throne of the West, and gave to Leo V., the Armenian, the sceptre of the East. The government of the world had thus passed into new hands. The reputation for justice, moderation, and courage, acquired by Louis, during his father's life-

time, in the government of Aquitaine, encouraged the hope that
he would prove himself the worthy descendant of four heroic
ancestors, and that he would add a fifth illustrious name to the
French annals, already emblazoned with those of Pepin of Herstal, Charles Martel, Pepin the Short, and Charlemagne. His
goodness to his fellow-men, or his piety toward God, had won
him the title of the Pious.* The fatherly prejudice or the tenderness of Charlemagne saw a son worthy of himself in the
prince who had subdued the Gascons, driven back the Saracens
to the Ebro, and covered himself with glory in Italy. Could
the virtues which adorn a private individual equally serve to
make a great king, Louis had undoubtedly been such; but he
lacked energy, loftiness in his views, and firmness. It was
said of him that there was in him more of the monk than of
the king, and to his easy compliance he owed his surname, *the
Mild*.

22. Yet the first years of his reign were peaceful. The
momentum acquired under Charlemagne still kept the empire
in its onward course, and it would require time to disorder the
well-adjusted machinery. Pope Stephen V. repaired to Rheims
to crown the new monarch. Louis sent the archchaplain of
the palace; Hildebold, archbishop of Cologne; Theodulf, bishop
of Orleans; and John, archbishop of Arles—all in full pontificals,
and accompanied by all the clergy—to meet the approaching
Pontiff. The emperor himself came forward within a mile of
the monastery of St. Remigius. On approaching the Pontiff
he dismounted, helped the Holy Father to alight, and prostrated
himself at his feet, with the words: " Blessed is he that cometh
in the name of the Lord." " Blessed be God," replied the Pope,
" who has granted us to look upon a second King David." They
then embraced, and passed on through the glad throngs of the
faithful, who now fondly believed that they had not yet lost
Charlemagne. On the following Sunday, in presence of the
whole clergy and people, Stephen V. anointed Louis the Mild,
and crowned him with a costly golden diadem, bright with pre-

* The Latin word *pius* is applicable in either of these relations.

cious gems, which he had brought from Rome. He likewise
crowned the empress Irmengard, and bestowed upon her the
title of *Augusta*. Stephen and Louis profited by this interview
to concert various measures for the reform of the clergy and
monastic orders. The fruit of these conferences appeared in
the ordinances published by Louis at this period. The same
year (816) was marked by the assembling of another council
at Aix-la-Chapelle, chiefly to take into consideration the reform of the canons and clergy. Amalarius, a deacon of the
Church of Metz, was charged to draw up a complete treatise
on the subject. The one hundred and forty-five chapters of
which this work consists are but the development of the admirable rule of St. Chrodegand, save in one peculiar ordinance,
which afterward became the origin of an important institution.
Every cloistered canonry was required to have a common hall,
where children and the young clerks were to be lodged, under
the care of a prudent man, advanced in years, whose duty it
was to advance their intellectual and moral culture. Here we
have the cradle of the ecclesiastical schools, which afforded, together with the monasteries, the only shelter and salvation to
letters and public instruction, during the whole period of the
Middle Ages. To these cloister-schools the world was indebted
for its greatest men, in every department of life, and to them
the Council of Trent owes the fruitful idea of ecclesiastical seminaries. Louis sent the regulations of the council to all the
metropolitans throughout the empire, with directions to communicate them to their suffragans, and he fixed the term of one
year within which they must be put into practice. The principle of reform was applied to the court and to the civil administration with the same energy as to the ecclesiastical bodies;
but, too weak to support his own good intentions, Louis only
succeeded in arousing the flames of hatred, of which he was
soon to become the victim. His first step was to rid the court
of his own sisters, whose loose conduct was equally offensive to
religion and propriety. The officers who supported the offensive levity were either punished or exiled. The seeds of dis-

content which these perhaps too hasty measures had cast into
the public mind were fostered by the exile of two ministers
who had commanded all the confidence of Charlemagne; -St.
Adelard buried in the retreat of the monastery of Noirmoutiers,
and Count Wala, in that of Corbie, the talents which might
still have long been usefully devoted to the service of their
country. The storm of angry feelings aroused by this unsea-
sonable severity soon bore down in full fury upon the defence
less head of the unfortunate Louis.

23. The year of the Council of Aix-la-Chapelle (A. D. 816)
also witnessed one at Celchyt, in England. Here we find precious traces of the perpetuity and conformity of the faith in
the various Churches, as also the tradition of pious observances
by which they are necessarily accompanied. It was decreed
that sacred edifices should be dedicated by the diocesan with
the sprinkling of holy water and the other ceremonies prescribed in the Roman ritual. It was also ordained that the Blessed Sacrament should be kept in the churches, enclosed in
boxes prepared for the purpose. The acts of the council also
inform us that baptism by infusion was beginning to be practised in cold countries.

24. Meanwhile, Leo the Armenian had entered upon his intended plan of persecution against the Catholics. He first sought
to gain the Patriarch Nicephorus, and to prevail upon him to
reject the veneration of sacred images, "which filled the East,"
as he says, "with trouble and discord." "We yield to none,"
replied Nicephorus, "in our love of peace. It is you, prince—I
say it with heartfelt grief—it is you who disturb it. Do not
all the Churches agree in the veneration of images? Will
Rome, Alexandria, Antioch, and Jerusalem consent to forsake
it? If your faith is weak, we are not only willing, but in duty
bound, to strengthen it; but we neither can nor may encourage
the hopes of convicted and condemned heretics." The emperor,
who was at best but a tolerable theologian, was at a loss for
further arguments, but brought in Iconoclast doctors, the nobles
of the empire, the whole senatorial body, and a great number

of military officers, sword in hand, to carry out the discussion with the Catholics. Fearless of this imposing and threatening array, the Patriarch addressed the nobles : "Answer me : can that fall which does not exist?" As the astonished lords looked at one another, perfectly ignorant of the meaning of this enigma, Nicephorus added : "Did not the images fall under Leo the Isaurian and Constantine Copronymus?" The heretics answered in the affirmative. "It is evident, then," concluded the Patriarch, "that they must have been subsisting before. Hence the Iconoclastic doctrine is opposed to Catholic tradition and teaching." Hopeless of shaking the faith of the intrepid prelate, the emperor assembled a cabal of venal bishops, who took measures for his deposition. Without giving them time to act, Nicephorus sent in to the emperor his resignation, in these terms : "Heretofore I have used my best endeavors to defend the truth, at the cost of the most shameful treatment. To such a pitch has the opposition been carried, that persons calling themselves bishops have come to insult me, backed by mobs armed with swords and staves. Nor did their madness find its limit in these measures ; these enemies of the truth have sought to deprive me of my see, or even of my life ; and for this reason alone, to prevent the excesses which must render your majesty odious, I reluctantly yield to the necessity which tears me from my Church, and receive with joy whatever it may please Heaven to ordain in my regard." The emperor could not control the satisfaction afforded him by this letter ; he ordered a troop of soldiers to carry off the Patriarch in the dead of night, and to imprison him in a monastery. On the morrow he spread the report, in Constantinople, that the Patriarch had abandoned his see, which was then given to an imperial minion named Theodotus, a man of worse than doubtful morality, utterly ignorant of the first principles of theology, and bred amid the license of camps (A. D. 816). Like Copronymus, Leo must also have his Iconoclastic council, and he assembled in the basilica of St. Sophia the bishops who had basely yielded to his seductive offers. The seventh general council was condemned, and the veneration of images again proscribed. The persecution was renewed with all the fury that had characterized it under Leo the Isaurian and Copronymus. The sectaries had dragged to their meeting some orthodox bishops whom they hoped to pervert; but, finding their efforts fruitless, they tore their pontifical robes in pieces, rudely threw the bishops upon the ground, and each one of the actors placed a foot upon the prostrate victim's throat; they were then made to retire backward, spit upon, and struck in the face with such brutal violence that many of the sufferers were covered with their own blood. They were at last given in charge to imperial satellites, who thrust them into prison. The most illustrious martyrs in this persecution were Michael, bishop of Synnas, Theophylactus of Nicomedia, Emilianus of Cyzicus, George of Mitylene, and Euthymius of Sardis. Among the abbots who gave their lives in the same cause were St. Nicetas, St. Theophanes of Singriana, and St. Macarius of Pelicita, whose numerous and wonderful miracles obtained for him the name of Thaumaturgus (A. D. 817).

25. While his children thus nobly fell for their faith in the East, Pope Stephen V. died at Rome, on the 22d of January, A. D. 817, after a pontificate of five months, which short reign still raised bright hopes for the glory of his pontificate, had God been pleased to grant him length of days.

CHAPTER II.

§ I. Pontificate of St. Pascal I. (January 25, A. D. 817—May 11, 824).

1. Election of St. Pascal I.—2. St. Benedict of Aniano. Clerical and monastic reforms.—3. Revolt of Bernard, king of Italy.—4. Public penance of Louis the Mild, at Attigny.—5. Various forms of *Judgments of God.*—6. St. Adelard. New Corbie. Progress of the faith.—7. Persecution of Leo the Armenian in the East.—8. Revolution in Constantinople. Michael the Stammerer.—9. Death of St. Pascal I.

§ II. Pontificate of Eugenius II. (June 5, A. D. 824—August 27, 827).

10. Eugenius II. causes the Romans to swear fealty to the emperor.—11. Disguised Judaism of Michael the Stammerer.—12. Council of Paris.—13. Heresy of Claudius, bishop of Turin.—14. The Capitularies.—15. Council of Rome.—16. Death of Eugenius II.

§ III. Pontificate of Valentine (September 1, A. D. 827—October 10, 827).

17. Election and death of Valentine.

§ IV. Pontificate of Gregory IV. (January 1, A. D. 828—January 11, 844).

18. The Saracens in Sicily.—19. Gregory IV. rebuilds the city and walls of Ostia.—20. Revolution in France. Revolt of the sons of Louis the Mild.—21. The field of *the Lie.*—22. Diet of Compiègne.—23. Council of Aix-la-Chapelle. Death of Louis the Mild.—24. War of succession at the death of Louis.—25. Theophilus the Unfortunate. Michael III., Porphyrogenitus, emperor of the East. End of the Iconoclast heresy.—27. Norman invasion. Death of Gregory IV.—28. False decretals. Paschasius Radbertus. *Treatise on the Body and Blood of our Lord.*

§ I. Pontificate of St. Pascal I. (January 25, A. D. 817— May 11, 824).

1. On the 25th of January, A. D. 817, by the joint vote of the Roman clergy and people, Pascal, a priest of the Roman Church, first of his name, ascended the pontifical throne. Deeply versed in the knowledge of Sacred Scripture and of the

interior life, the new Pontiff was distinguished by the most tender piety, by the austerity of his life, and by a lively and feeling
charity for the poor and strangers. He at once sent a special
legation to make known his accession to Louis the Mild, who
replied by an imperial patent confirming the grants already
made to the Holy See by Charlemagne and Pepin the Short.
The islands of Corsica, Sardinia, and Sicily are included in the
enumeration of the pontifical estate. This particular item has
awakened doubts in the minds of some modern writers, concerning the authenticity of Louis's patent, since the island of Sicily
still belonged, in 817, to the emperors of Constantinople. But
we know, by a letter of Leo III., that the island of Corsica
had been given to the Church by Charlemagne. Even in the
pontificate of St. Gregory the Great, the Holy See already held
considerable estates in Sardinia and Sicily. Louis only meant
to confirm the Sovereign Pontiff's claim on these various domains. Hence the validity of the deed cannot suffer from this
clause. Others have found a cause of suspicion in another
clause, which decrees that it shall henceforth suffice that the
newly-elected Pontiffs send legates to the king of France.
Now several of St. Pascal's successors have still asked and
awaited the emperor's confirmation before proceeding to their
coronation. But we can readily see, in this act of writing to
monarchs to secure their approval and protection, that these
Popes already were, and sought still to remain, on good terms
with sovereigns whose patronage had always proved so useful
to the Church. The intention of Louis on this point does not
admit of a doubt; for, in a capitulary issued at about this time
from Aix-la-Chapelle, he speaks thus: "Conformably to the
decrees of the sacred canons, we wish the Church to enjoy its
rights without any let or hindrance; and it is our desire that
the bishops be elected by the suffrage of clergy and people,
without any other consideration than that of personal worth."
At about the same time, Florus, a learned deacon of Lyons.
on the authority of this capitulary, published his *Treatise on
Episcopal Elections.* "The usage," says the author, "lately in

troduced into several kingdoms, of consecrating no bishop until the prince has been consulted, was established only to preserve harmony between the two powers, and not to give to the consecration the validity or the authority which no royal power can give, but only the will of God and the consent of the faithful; for the episcopacy is not a human institution, but a gift of the Holy Ghost."

2. The emperor also put forth some admirable regulations for the honor of the episcopacy and the priesthood. "It was at this time," says a contemporary writer, "that the clerics and bishops began to lay aside their gold-embroidered sashes, their diamond-hilted swords, the costly spurs and other accoutrements which they had hitherto worn." It now remained to reform the monastic orders, to which the faithful chiefly looked for edification, but which the misfortune of the times had sadly turned from their primitive purity. Louis intrusted this important duty to St. Benedict of Aniano, and gave him, as assistants, the most exemplary abbots of France and Italy—such men as Arnul of Noirmoutiers, Apollinaris of Monte Cassino, Alveus of St. Hubert in the Ardennes, Apollinaris of Flavigny, Joshua of St. Vincent's on the Vulturnus, and Agilul of Solignac. The laxity of monastic discipline arose chiefly from the diversity of binding observances. Though most of the monasteries professed to follow the rule of St. Benedict, there was yet a great variation in many practices, due to the successive changes in the manners of the age, which the patriarch of the cenobitic life could not have foreseen. It was accordingly decided to establish a uniformity of discipline, by means of constitutions explanatory of the primitive rule. These regulations enter into the most minute details. The use of flesh meat is forbidden to the religious, except for the sick, and during four days in the Christmas and Easter seasons. Still the daily use of lard is allowed, as the poorer classes made use of it where oil was scarce and dear. From this permission, however, are excluded the twenty days preceding Christmas, and every Friday throughout the year.

In cases of unusual fatigue, a slight refection is allowed in the evening, even during Lent; this is the origin of the collation on fasting-days. Each religious was to receive a pound and a half of bread, in the dough; and a hemina of wine;* in countries where grapes are not plentiful, double this allowance of beer might be substituted. The claims of the government upon the monasteries were also regulated, as they were very different. Some abbeys were bound to military service, some owed presents like our gratuitous gifts, and others, in fine, the tribute of their prayers. Of the first class we can count fourteen, among others St. Benedict-on-the-Loire, Ferrières, Corbie, Stavelo, St. Eugend, now known as St. Claude and Notre Dame de Soissons. The monastery of Fuld, afterward so powerful, only held a second rank with the thirteen whose indebtedness amounted only to gifts. The third and most numerous class comprised two hundred monasteries, which were bound only to the tribute of prayer. All these ordinances were published in the Assembly of Aix-la-Chapelle (A. D. 817), and were subsequently esteemed of authority hardly less than that of the Benedictine rule, though the greatest difficulty was felt, in the beginning, to secure their enforcement. The reform of a whole kingdom could hardly have presented greater difficulties than was met in that of some single monasteries. But the persevering and prudent tact and mildness of St. Benedict of Aniano triumphed over all obstacles, and the dying moments of the great man were soothed by the consoling assurance that his reform had been adopted in nearly all the monasteries (A. D. 821).

3. The Assembly of Aix-la-Chapelle also apportioned the States of the empire among the sons of Louis the Mild: Lothaire, the eldest, shared the government of the empire; Pepin received the kingdom of Aquitaine, and Louis that of Bavaria. The Italian sceptre remained in the hands of Bernard, the grandson of Charlemagne. To use the words of Mably:

---

* About the quantity contained in an ordinary drinking-glass; a hemina being equal to a half-setier, and a setier to half a pint.

"When Charlemagne crowned his sons, he only gave himself so many lieutenants; the weak Louis, in bestowing crowns upon his, set up as many rivals for himself," who soon became his masters. The patent setting forth these important dispositions had indeed been solemnly received by the lords and the people at large, who bound themselves by oath to respect it; it had, it is true, received the approbation and apostolic sanction of St. Pascal I., who also crowned Lothaire emperor, at St. Peter's in Rome, on Easter Day (April 5, A. D. 823); but all this was vain while no stronger arm than that of Louis the Mild was at hand to make good its provisions. Yet the first attempts at revolt were vigorously met. Misled by imprudent counsellors, Bernard, the youthful king of Italy, valiant, magnificent, and adored by his subjects, expressed himself dissatisfied with the allotment of the imperial domain. He raised a body of troops to support his claims, and marched to the Alps; but on the approach of Louis, at the head of a formidable army, the rebel prince, forsaken by the greater part of his followers, was forced to throw himself upon the promises of the empress Irmengard, who offered her mediation. All the conspirators were tried and sentenced to death; Bernard was condemned to lose his eyes, and died of the frightful torture thus inflicted (A. D. 818). The three young princes, Drogo, Hugh and Theodoric, sons of Charlemagne, were confined in monasteries, and forced to take the religious habit, though perfectly innocent of any participation in Bernard's rebellion. Louis alienated all minds by this untimely severity; he had put off his natural disposition in sentencing the rebels, and he now resumed it to give way to all the horrors of remorse. He taxed himself with crime in the death of Bernard, which the wisest statesmen agreed in pronouncing a lawful punishment; and he bitterly reproached himself with the oppression of his three brothers, by which he had violated the solemn pledge given at the death-bed of Charlemagne.

4 He determined, in his despair, to give a signal proof of repentance. A general diet of the empire was called at the

palace of Attigny-sur-Aisne (A. D. 822). His sons, Lothaire, Louis and Pepin were present, together with the bishops and chief lords of their respective realms. Drogo, Hugh and Theodoric were brought from their monastery, to assist at the solemn reparation. Louis appeared before this assembly, and, in presence of all his people, stripped of the imperial insignia, clothed with sackcloth, prostrate at the feet of bishops, he confessed what he called his crime, and asked to expiate it by a public penance. The moving sight of an all-powerful monarch thus voluntarily humbling himself before a whole people, had not been witnessed since the days of Theodosius the Great. But the act which won for the Roman emperor the admiration of his civilized subjects, drew upon the imperial Frank the contempt of a race but half redeemed from barbarism, whose brutal pride blushed at the sight of repentant royalty. The scene of that day taught the sons of Louis their father's weakness. Adelard of Corbie, at the same time a great statesman and a fervent religious, remarked, in speaking of this event and of the fine regulations which were then promulgated : " It were hard to treat better of the public good, in theory; Heaven grant that the execution and obedience correspond."

5. The bishops present at Attigny met in council, and, on motion of Agobardus, archbishop of Lyons, one of the most enlightened prelates of his day, forbade the use of the various kinds of judicial tests, known by the name of Judgments of God, and hitherto perpetuated by the national customs and superstitions. The trial of the *cross* was conducted thus : both parties, accuser and accused, stood motionless before a cross ; he who first fell lost his case. In the ordeal of the *hot irons*, the accused party took up or trod upon a red-hot iron ; his escape unhurt was the proof of his innocence. A similar test was applied with boiling water. The ordeal of *cold water* consisted in throwing the accused person into the water ; if he floated, he was pronounced guilty—if he sunk, innocent. But the practice in which the most shocking cruelty was joined to

superstition, was the ordeal of the *duel*. The culprit was first
made to swear to his innocence, and if the accuser was not
satisfied with this testimony of his guiltlessness, the judge
ordered the combat; and such is the origin of the false point
of honor which still disgraces civilized humanity, and thinks
to wash out in blood the insult of a word. Should the parties feel unwilling to defend their respective causes personally,
there were always a number of professional *bravos* at hand,
ready to take their destiny upon them, and to fight in their
stead. What makes this blindness appear more stupid is the
fact that these strange ordeals were used, not only in cases of
criminal charges, but in questions of law and order. When
the question arose in Germany whether the representation
should proceed in a direct line, it was decided by a single combat. When the Spanish Church was hesitating between the
Roman and Mozarabic liturgies, both books were cast into the
flames, which were expected to decide the case by sparing the
ritual approved of Heaven. The Council of Attigny denounced
these superstitious practices with great vigor, and the watchful zeal of the Popes, seconded by the imperial authority, soon
blotted out these disgraceful stains from European legislation
and manners.

6. The abbot Adelard of Corbie, one of the brightest lights
of the Council of Attigny, had occasion during the same year
(822) to display his zeal beyond the boundaries of Gaul, even
in the remotest parts of the Western empire. The Saxons,
newly converted and still weak in faith, stood in great need of
guides and models in the way of salvation. With a view to
keep before them these needed lessons and examples of evangelical perfection, Adelard founded among them a monastery, to
which he gave the name of the New Corbie: situated in a beautiful valley, on the bank of the Weser, it was long used as a
school and seminary for the northern missions now springing
again into active existence. The conversion of Saxony opened
a way for the missionaries into the kingdom of Denmark, which
had long been kept before their minds by the renowned

audacity of its people, their maritime enterprises, and their repeated inroads into Southern Europe. Harold, their king, driven from his throne by a civil war, had taken refuge in the court of Louis the Mild, where he sought instructions in the truths of the Catholic faith, asked and received baptism at Mentz, with all the officers in his retinue. Ebbo, archbishop of Rheims, with a monk named Halitgar, afterward bishop of Cambray, had first been sent on a fruitless mission to Denmark In the Old Corbie, Harold found a pious and learned man, with all the necessary enterprise and energy, who had been pointed out to him by St. Adelard. This monk was destined to become the apostle of Denmark and Sweden, as St. Boniface had been of Germany. It was St. Anscharius. After seeking, in holy retreat, a fullness of apostolic spirit, he received from his superiors the mission of enlightening the barbarous and idolatrous Danes. Accompanied by his colleague Autbert, he presented himself at the court of King Harold, and labored with cheering success in the conversion of these infidels. He found an efficacious means of fostering the seed cast by his preaching, in the purchase of young slaves whom he trained up in the fear of God, and formed into a numerous school. But a fresh revolution once more deprived Harold of his crown, and stayed the onward course of Christianity in the full tide of success. Autbert died, and Anscharius returned to the French court, whence he was at once sent to Sweden, whose king had begged Louis to send missionaries into his states. The saint was again accompanied by a religious of Corbie, who had solicited the mission. The two apostles set out together, loaded with gifts from Louis to the king of Sweden; but they were robbed on the way by pirates, and appeared among the barbarians bearing only the good tidings of salvation. They were favorably received by the king, and made many conversions: among the first trophies of Divine grace was the governor of the city, who immediately gave proofs of his sincere piety by the erection of a church, and by his steady adherence to the principles he had embraced. When the increase of the faithful

warranted the measure, Hamburg was made an archiepiscopal
see, with St. Anscharius as its first incumbent. He devoted
himself with unwearied energy to the cultivation of the field
intrusted to his zeal. His manner of life was most austere,
his diet consisting only of bread and water. He often withdrew to a little retreat he had himself constructed there in
the intervals of his pastoral duties, to take some moments of
rest and to pour forth his heart without restraint before God.
He was favored with the gift of miracles, and healed many
diseases by the power of his prayers. On finding himself
attacked by his last illness, the holy prelate was much grieved
that the hopes of his lifetime were not to be fulfilled, and that
he was not to shed his blood for the faith. "Alas!" he exclaimed, "my sins have deprived me of the grace of martyrdom." Feeling the approach of his last moment, he gathered
his remaining strength to exhort his disciples to the love of
God and the support of his dear mission. The rising Church,
spread by the labors of St. Anscharius even to the shores of
Greenland, was for a time swept by a fierce storm, in an invasion of the barbarians; but the precious seeds sown there by
the apostle survived the fury of the blast, and flourished by
the care of his zealous successors.

1. While the West thus bowed to the gentle violence
of the faith, the East presented a vastly different sight. Leo
the Armenian had banished all the Catholic bishops and
abbots. He ordered all the paintings in the churches to be
destroyed, and the workmen who executed his orders were
worthy to be classed with the Vandals, by the destruction
of so many masterpieces of art. The sacred vessels, on which
were represented pious subjects, were broken; the paintings
executed on wood disappeared under the blows of the axe,
and the remains were burned in the public square. The
emperor, not satisfied with silencing the defenders of the truth
by banishment, wished to win them over to his cause, and
thus seduce the faithful by their example. With this view
he recalled several of the exiles to Constantinople, assuring

them that no violation of their consciences was meant; that
they need only communicate once with the Patriarch Theodotus, after which they were at liberty to retire quietly to their
monasteries. Deceived by this stratagem, they had the weakness to comply, and received communion from the hand of
Theodotus. Among the prelates was St. Nicetas of Medicion,
whose venerable age, virtuous and austere life, won him the
filial love and veneration of all the monks. He had no sooner
yielded this weak compliance than his soul was torn by the
most stinging remorse. Resolved to repair his fault by a
public retractation, he would not return to his monastery, but
remained in Constantinople, loudly protesting that he had
been guilty of shameful weakness, and that he had nothing in
common with the Iconoclasts. Leo sent for him and inquired
why he had not returned to his monastery, like the other
abbots. "Know, my lord," replied Nicetas, "that I disclaim
what I did through a cowardly compliance, and that I have
never been less disposed to communicate with your sect. Do
with me what you will, I shall never change my sentiments!"
The holy abbot was banished to a distant island, where he lin-
gered in painful captivity until the death of the emperor. St.
Theodore the Studite, who had also been proscribed in the
beginning of the persecution, made use of his hours of exile
to defend the Catholic faith by his eloquent writings. The
persecutors thought to hush this importunate voice, by bury-
ing it in the remote province of Anatolia. "Take me where
you will," said the saint, "I am content; the whole earth is
the Lord's. But you can never fetter my voice, for I have
consecrated it to the cause of the God of truth." The emperor, maddened by this courageous resistance, ordered the
confessor to be scourged to blood. Theodore removed his
own tunic, saying: "I have long desired to suffer outrages
for the name of Jesus Christ." The sight of that body, worn
by macerations, filled the executioner with a holy dread of
sacrilege. Under pretext of decency, he caused all the by-
standers to withdraw; then bringing in a sheepskin, he dis-

charged upon it a number of lusty blows, distinctly heard
without. He even drew blood from his own arm to stain the
scourges, which he took care to expose to public view. The
holy abbot continued to devote both voice and pen to the
interests of the true faith. In order to collect proofs of the
unanimity of all the Churches in the veneration of holy images,
he wrote to all the bishops and Patriarchs throughout the Christian world. His letter to the Patriarch of Alexandria gives
a lengthy description of the Iconoclast persecution, with which
he supposed the prelate to be but partially acquainted, because of the difficulty of communicating by sea, owing to the
continued depredations of the Saracen corsairs. "In the very
centre of Christendom," says St. Theodore, " the altars of Jesus
Christ are overturned, His churches devastated. The Arabs who
oppress you would blush at such acts of violence. Bishops,
priests and monks are held in universal contempt; some have
entirely lost the faith, while others think to keep it still, though
associating and communicating with heretics. Yet some there
are who have not yet bowed the knee to Baal, and they have a
worthy guide and patron in our glorious Patriarch, Nicephorus;
but many of these confessors have been cruelly outraged and
scourged, many thrown into dungeons and reduced to a few
ounces of mouldy bread, a few drops of impure water to sustain their daily life; some, in fine, have been sent into exile.
The unfortunate monks have been driven to seek a voluntary exile, with no roof save the leafy forest boughs, their
only dwelling the mountain dens. Some have ended the
martyr's course under the executioner's lash; others have
been thrown into the sea in bags. The possession of a sacred
image, shelter afforded to a hunted victim, or the slightest
relief administered to a prisoner, is sufficient to incur immediate arrest, scourging and exile." The holy abbot had previously written to Pope St. Pascal I., urging him to interpose
his apostolic influence and authority in favor of the confessors
of the faith. "You," he wrote, "who are clothed with the
Divine power, intrusted with the keys of the kingdom of

Heaven, appointed by God pastor over the whole flock of Christ, rock upon which is founded the Catholic Church, for you are Peter, since you fill his chair; come to the assistance of your children, never more cruelly exposed to the rage of the ravenous wolves of heresy. Let the whole earth know that you have anathematized those who persecute Jesus Christ in his worshippers. Thus shall you support the weak, confirm the courage of the strong, raise up the fallen, and gladden the whole Church. Obedient, like your predecessors, to the voice of the Holy Ghost, you will acquire undying glory for the Roman Church, the refuge and harbor of all the oppressed." This letter, signed by the abbots of nearly all the monasteries in and about Constantinople, was well received by the Sovereign Pontiff, who replied in terms of the most affectionate tenderness, promising to use all his influence in behalf of his persecuted children, exhorted them to persevere, and hastened to send legates to Constantinople. But the emperor's heretical prejudices had reached their highest pitch, and the only effect of the legation was to inspire the Catholics with renewed courage, on seeing the Holy See openly arrayed in their defense (A. D. 818). In order at least to afford a home to the most violently persecuted sufferers, the Pontiff established a monastery of Greek monks at Rome, near the church of St. Praxedes, which he had lately rebuilt. The knowledge that St. Theodore had addressed his complaints to the Pope, redoubled the emperor's rage against him. The holy confessor received a hundred lashes, so cruelly delivered that he was left breathless and motionless upon the ground. It was only by a kind of prodigy that one of his disciples, confined in the same prison, succeeded in bringing him back to life. But even the consolation of companionship in distress was denied him, and he was removed to a solitary dungeon, where his keepers threw him a piece of bread every second day. The archbishop of Smyrna, one of the leaders of the Iconoclasts, seeing that nothing could shake the constancy of Theodore, said to him, on leaving for Constantinople: "I shall beg the emperor to

order you to lose your tongue or your head." But Divine
justice struck the tyrant too soon to allow the fulfilment of
this threat.

8. A veteran from the imperial army, a native of Upper
Phrygia, whose occupation had been that of a horse-trader,
hardly able to read, and altogether ignorant of the art of
writing, a man almost bereft of the faculty of articulate speech—
in a word, Michael the Stammerer, had succeeded, by means of
dishonesty and intrigues, in reaching the highest military dignities. These secured, he now covets the imperial purple, con-
spires, is arrested, judged, and condemned by the emperor to
be burnt alive in the furnace of the imperial baths. The sentence, pronounced on the 24th of December, A. D. 820, was to
be carried out on the morrow, Christmas Day. The empress
Theophrano urged that the sacred anniversary would be profaned
by an execution. "I grant your request," said Leo; "God
forbid that, in seeking to save my soul, you expose my body
to the weapons of the assassins." During the night the clergy
of St. Sophia came as usual to sing matins in the imperial
chapel. In the ecclesiastical habit, but with swords under
their robes, four of Michael's accomplices crept unnoticed into
the chapel, under favor of the imperfect light and similarity of
dress. Leo was present at the Christmas office. At the fatal
signal, the conspirators, brandishing their swords, encompassed
on all sides the royal victim. Unarmed, unfriended, the emperor grasped a massive silver cross and stood at bay against
the hunters of his life. He struggled long and well, but was
at last hurled to the ground, and cried aloud: "Mercy! mercy!
in the name of the sanctuary!" "This is the hour not of
mercy, but of vengeance," replied a conspirator; and seizing
the prostrate emperor by the hair, he severed his head from
the trunk. A moment more, and Michael the Stammerer is
borne, ironed hand and foot, from the felon's dungeon to the
throne of the Cæsars. The keys of his fetters had been
secured by Leo; they were broken with hammers. Michael
was proclaimed emperor. The officers of the palace, thunder

struck, come in trembling crowds to pay their homage, while
the conspirators chant the Psalmist's words, in the Christmas
office : "*Ad vesperum demorabitur fletus, et usque ad matutinum
lætitia.*"[*] The bloody tragedy had been enacted under the
shades of night, while Constantinople was buried in slumber.
The morning's light brought the conviction that God will
sooner or later chastise the persecutors of his Church, as at the
dawn of this 25th of December it revealed the head of Leo the
Armenian, the Iconoclast persecutor, exposed upon the point of
a lance in the midst of the hippodrome. The fickle populace
now heaped curses and outrages upon the idol they had but
yesterday so zealously incensed with adulations and false homage, and now their cry arose with equal fervor : "Michael II.,
Augustus! Long life to Michael II. !" The new emperor, on
the strength of his happy accession, recalled the exiled Catholics ; but only to resume the persecution under a new form.

9. While the East was cowering in terror under these
ceaseless revolutions, a violent sedition at Rome threatened
the life of St. Pascal I. Two factions had arisen against the
Pontiff. The imperial party, ignorant of Lothaire's good intentions, used the weight of his name in their demands for absolute
authority in his behalf ; while the Roman faction sought a
very doubtful independence, and strove to throw off the authority of the Holy See. The contest had already cost the lives of
Theodore, primiciarius, and Leo, nomenclator or secretary of
the Roman Church, when the presence of Lothaire restored
peace and order. The Pontiff did not long survive this sad
event, and died on the 11th of February, A. D. 824, after a
pontificate of seven years. It is universally allowed that the
title of cardinal[†] was first officially granted in his reign to the
principal ministers in the Roman clergy. They were, however, few in number. Under Nicholas III., A. D. 1277, their
whole number amounted to seven ; under John XXII., A. D.

---

[*] "In the evening weeping shall have place, and in the morning gladness."—Ps. xxix. 6.

[†] Cardinal, from the Latin word *cardo*, a hinge—the cardinals being, so to speak, the hinges upon which rest the *gates* of the Church.

1330, it had increased to twenty ; and at the time of the Council of Constance the number was thirty-four. This number was increased by Leo X. to sixty-five ; by Paul IV., in 1556, to seventy ; and Sixtus V., in 1586, decreed that, as seventy was the number of the *Seniores* in Israel, as also of our Lord's first disciples, it should remain at that standard. Of the seventy cardinals, six are cardinal-bishops, fifty cardinal-priests, and fourteen cardinal-deacons. The election of the Pope is now confined to the college of cardinals, and it will be seen hereafter how this wise regulation was first established.

§ II. Pontificate of Eugenius II. (June 5, A. D. 824—August 27, 827).

10. Eugenius II. was elected Pope on the 5th of June, A. D. 824, and won by his tender charity the title of *Father of the People.* Yet his election was disturbed by that of an anti-pope named Zizimus ; but the schism was crushed at the very outset by the care of the youthful emperor Lothaire, whom Louis had sent to Rome to take possession of the throne of Italy, left vacant by the death of Bernard. In order to put a stop to these disgraceful cabals and disorders, and to keep the Roman nobles and people within the limits of obedience, Eugenius and Lothaire concerted together the following measures : the Pope. issued a decree enjoining upon the Roman clergy to swear fidelity to the emperors, according to this formula : " I promise, in the name of Almighty God, by the holy Gospels, by the Holy-Rood, and by the body of blessed Peter, prince of the Apostles, that I will ever be true to our lords, the emperors Louis and Lothaire, *saving the faith I have pledged to the Sovereign Pontiff.* I will never consent that the election of the Pope proceed otherwise than according to the canons and justice, nor that the Pontiff elect be consecrated before taking, in the presence of the people and the emperor's envoy, an oath similar to that

pronounced by Pope Eugenius himself, for the preservation of all."* The emperor Lothaire, on his part, published, under the portico of St. Peter's, a constitution in nine articles. The chief clauses are as follows : " Agents appointed by the Pope and the emperor shall give to the latter a yearly account of the administration of justice by the dukes and magistrates. The senate and people of Rome shall be consulted on the legislation to be adopted among them ; that is, they may choose between the Roman law and the law of the Goths or of the Lombards, both equally authorized in Italy, that they may henceforth be subject to a uniform law by the authority of the Pope as well as of the emperor. Officers to that end appointed shall at once put the Sovereign Pontiff and the Church in possession of the ecclesiastical property unjustly withheld. Finally, whoever seeks the emperor's favor must in all things show obedience and respect to the Sovereign Pontiff."

11. In Constantinople, Michael the Stammerer had not granted a long truce to the faithful. He belonged to the sect of Paulicians or Melchisedechians, a sect of mixed Jewish and Christian observance, who practised the ceremonies of the Mosaic law together with the pagan superstitions of the Samaritans. Michael II. made vigorous efforts to restore the old Hebrew law. In the palace he changed the time of the Easter celebration, and substituted the observance of the Jewish Sabbath for that of the Christian Sunday. Refusing to recognize Christ as the Messiah, he placed Judas in the calendar of the saints. Over the bloody disorders with which he filled the empire, he would have thrown the darkness of ignorance, in

---

* " Promitto ego, per Deum omnipotentem, et per ista sacra quatuor Evangelia, et per hanc crucem Domini nostri Jesu Christi, et per corpus beatissimi Petri, principis apostolorum, quod, ab hac die in futurum, fidelis ero dominis nostris imperatoribus Illudovico, et Illotario, diebus vitæ meæ, juxta vires et intellectum meum, sine fraude atque malo ingenio, salva fide quam repromisi domino Apostolico ; et quod non consentiam ut aliter in hac Sede Romana fiat electio Pontificis nisi canonice et justa, secundum vires et intellectum meur : et ille qui electus fuerit, me consentiente, consecratus Pontifex non fiat, priusquam tale sacramentum faciat, in presentia missi domini imperatoris et populi cum jurarnaoto, quale dominus Eugenius papa sponte pro conservatione omnium factum habet præscriptum."
(Cont. Paul. Diac., t. I., p. 617.)

which he was himself so deeply buried, and accordingly proscribed the study of belles-lettres and religion. The recall of
the exiles was but a passing lull, soon followed by a bloody
persecution. Michael thought that in favoring the heresy of
the Iconoclasts he should sooner reach his end of destroying
the true faith by the divisions thus raised in the Church. To
veil his violent measures, he sent an embassy to Louis the
Mild, with a letter bearing this superscription: "Michael,
faithful to God, emperor of the Romans, to our dear and honored brother Louis, king of the Franks and Lombards, named
their emperor." After a false statement of the manner of his
accession to the throne, he protests his desire to preserve peace.
Then passing to the question of images, he asserts that the
Catholics give them a worship of adoration, and that he must
necessarily interfere to prevent this idolatry. After urging
Louis to convoke a council in his states to discuss the question
of images, he adds that, as an earnest of his union with the
Holy See, he sends to St. Peter's Church a copy of the Gospels, bound in gold, enriched with costly gems, and a richly-
jewelled gold paten.

12. In the question of sacred images, the Gallic bishops had
left it in the unsettled ambiguity of the word *adorare*, of which
the twofold sense of mere *veneration* and of *latria* had not been
distinguished in the Council of Frankfort (A. D. 790). The
council assembled at Paris, in 825, by Louis the Mild, threw
no new light upon the subject. The bishops present mainly
endeavored to show that the worship of *latria* is not to be
paid to holy images, and they collected all the texts from the
Fathers that bear upon the point. Still, they would seem to
have been but slightly acquainted with the state of things in
the East; and their ignorance is easily explained by the difficulty of communication, not yet established by navigation or
commerce, and by the want of serious historical studies.

13. The heresy of Claudius, bishop of Turin, drew the attention of the Western bishops to the question of image-wor-
ship, and taught them what they must think of the Iconoclasts.

Claudius, a Spaniard by birth, had acquired in the school of Felix of Urgel a passion for novelty, to which he soon joined its wiles and violence. Skilled in the art of dissimulation, he won the esteem of Louis the Mild, who called him to his court, where he devoted himself, with great success, to preaching and the publication of sacred works, and even acquired reputation as a learned writer by some commentaries on the Sacred Scriptures. About the year 822, he was raised to the episcopal see of Turin. Now that he had reached the object of his ambitious aims, he no longer hid his real sentiments, but made open profession of the Iconoclastic heresy. In his first episcopal visitation he broke all the crosses, statues, and images in the various churches, which sacrilegious proceeding revolted all his pious and faithful subjects. The crying scandal, on the part of a bishop, aroused the whole of Gaul and Italy. All the doctors of the period, Theodomir, Eginhard, Jonas, bishop of Orleans, Agobardus, archbishop of Rheims, and Walafrid Strabo, abbot of Reichenau, entered the lists, and levelled their eloquent writings at the heresy brought into the West by Claudius of Turin. The heretic, on the other hand, issued in defence of his error a swarm of libels, in which indecency and impiety seem to contend for the mastery. "If those idolators," he writes, "will have us adore crosses because Jesus Christ was fastened to a cross, we must, then, also adore all mangers, because He was laid in a manger ; we must adore every fishing-boat, because He preached from one ; we must even adore *asses*, because Jesus Christ chose to ride upon an ass. No ; God does not command us to adore the cross; He commands us to bear it."

The blasphemies uttered by Claudius of Turin, against holy relics and pious images, produced a directly opposite tendency in Gaul. Never was more honor given to these sacred objects ; and the translations of relics were multiplied to an extent almost incredible. The monastery of Andein, in the forest of Ardennes, was enriched by the translation of the body of St. Hubert, by Valcan, bishop of Liège (A. D. 825).

Hilduın, abbot of St. Denis and of St. Medard of Soissons, by his credit with Pope Eugenius, obtained a considerable portion of the relics of St. Sebastian. Eginhard brought to his monastery of Seligenstadt the bodies of St. Marcellinus, a priest, and of St. Peter the Exorcist (A. D. 826).

14. At about the same period, Ansegise, abbot of Fontenelles, published his collection of the Capitularies of Charlemagne and of Louis the Mild (A. D. 827). These ordinances had hitherto been scattered about on loose sheets; and Ansegise, fearing that they might, in course of time, be forgotten or lost, gathered them into one work, which he divided into four books. The first contains the capitularies of Charlemagne on ecclesiastical matters, in one hundred and sixty-two articles; the second includes the ecclesiastical capitularies of Louis the Mild, in forty-eight articles; the third embraces the capitularies of Charlemagne on profane matters, in ninety-one articles; the fourth, those of Louis, on the same subjects, in seventy-seven articles. This collection of the abbot Ansegise has always been held in high esteem, and is quoted in imperial decrees, subsequent to its publication, as a public authority.

15. The state of the times demanded of Eugenius II. the greatest moderation and prudence. At Constantinople, the Iconoclasts, supported by the emperors, burned all books unfavorable to their error, mutilated or falsified others, and used all manner of deceit and violence toward the Catholics. From the depths of their solitary dungeons or remote exile, the supplicating voice of the Catholic bishops and abbots reached the successor of St. Peter, now their only hope. In the West, the unfaithful translation of the seventh ecumenical council had opened the way for the insidious error. The wily Greek thought, by insnaring the French bishops and emperors, to insure the triumph of the heresy. It was particularly important to dissipate the prejudices of the French bishops, by the gradual introduction into the West of a more complete system of education; for ignorance was the paramount evil of the age, and gave a striking proof of its sway in the very council

assembled at Rome (A. D. 826), by Pope Eugenius II., to combat it. So fallen was the cultivation of belles-lettres, that it was found necessary to copy the opening discourse from a council held under Gregory II., as it would have been too difficult to find any one able to write an original one. The canons of the council are all directed to the restoration of studies. Ignorant priests were to be suspended by their bishops from the exercise of their functions, until they should have acquired the necessary instruction. The same line of conduct was prescribed to metropolitans in regard to their suffragans. Schools were to be founded in each bishopric and monastery, under the care of masters of acknowledged ability and dependent upon the bishops. Finally, priests were forbidden to devote their time to agricultural pursuits, which turned them away from the true spirit of their vocation.

16. Eugenius II. died on the 27th of August, A. D. 827, shortly after the closing of the council, and was buried in the Vatican.

§ III. Pontificate of Valentine (September 1, A. D. 827—October 10, 827).

17. Elected on the 1st of September, A. D. 827, Valentine had hardly been seated upon the pontifical throne, when he was called away from the high but dangerous position. He closed a pontificate of forty days, on the 10th of October, A. D. 827, to the grief of the Roman people, who had already learned to love the piety, liberality, and gentleness of their new Pontiff

§ IV. Pontificate of Gregory IV.(January 5, A. D. 828—January 11, 844).

18. After a vacancy of over two months, the Apostolic Chair was filled by Gregory IV., who was raised to the lofty dignity, like his illustrious namesake, St. Gregory the Great, only with great violence to his own humility. He had fled to

a monastery, whence he was borne by the whole people, in spite of himself, to the pontifical throne (January 5, A. D. 828). His pontificate was a fresh proof that a sincere aversion for worldly greatness by no means unfits for great deeds. The Spanish Saracens, obliged to yield before the ever-advancing energy of the Christians of the Asturias, had transplanted their colonies to the Grecian isles, where they did not meet the same resistance : they had possessed themselves of this new domain without meeting a single vessel to oppose their movements. The Eastern emperor, Michael the Stammerer, was too busily engaged in persecuting the Catholics to feel much interest in the gradual dismemberment of the empire. The Saracens fixed the seat of their power in the Archipelago, and in Crete they raised the walls of Candia, which has since given its name to the whole island. Sicily was, at the same time, invaded by the African Mussulmans, who found admittance through the shameful faithlessness of an imperial officer; just as the invasion of Spain had been brought on by the most disgraceful passion. Euphemius, general of the imperial troops in Sicily, had dared, with sacrilegious audacity, to carry off a religious from her convent with the intention of marrying her. Michael the Stammerer had to reproach himself with the same scandal, for he had also espoused, against her will, a virgin consecrated to God, Euphrosine, grand-daughter of the empress Irene. By a strange inconsistency, of which history affords many other examples, the emperor would have punished in his lieutenant a crime of which he had himself been guilty. But Euphemius anticipated his imperial master, and called upon the emir of Africa, who took possession of the whole of Sicily (A. D. 827). When the tidings of the loss of this island reached Constantinople, Michael II. said to Ireneus, one of his ministers : " I congratulate you on being freed from the administration of an island so remote; you are now eased of a weighty burden." "My lord," answered Ireneus, "two or three similar reliefs will free you from the care of your empire." But provided he found the executioners to carry out his bloody orders, Michael thought himself powerful enough. The holy monk Methodius, afterward Patriarch of Constantinople, received seven hundred lashes, by order of the emperor, and was then thrown into a dungeon where he languished fifteen years. Euthymius, bishop of Sardis, expired under the torture. St. Theodore the Studite died in exile for the faith he had so eloquently and so valiantly defended, and was soon followed by the holy Patriarch St. Nicephorus. The intruder, Theodotus, died in possession of his usurped see, and was succeed by a furious Iconoclast, Anthony of Sylea, who spent the eleven years of his intrusion in persecuting Catholics.

19. The shameless inertness of the Iconoclast emperors of Constantinople had allowed the Saracen power to grow into formidable proportions. Masters of the richest provinces of the East, of Egypt and of Africa, commanding the Mediterranean by their strongholds in the Archipelago, they made Spain and Sicily, those two gates of the West, their advanced posts against all Christendom. The only power that could have stayed their invading march was the Empire of the Franks; but Louis the Mild was satisfied with having driven them back from his frontier to the Pyrenees, and did not concern himself about enemies who were not immediately in his way. Besides, Charlemagne, in leaving him the sceptre, could not bequeath his genius with it, and the unfortunate emperor would soon have enough to do to resist the attacks of his own sons. The Papacy was thus left the sole bulwark of Christendom, and then appeared the wisdom of the providential plan which had given it an independent temporal domain. Gregory IV. understood his mission. He opposed all the means in his power to the incursions of the Mussulman fleets on the coasts of Italy, in Calabria, Tuscany, and even in Lombardy. As a protection to the mouth of the Tiber, where the hostile fleets found an easier landing, he undertook an immense labor. The ancient city of Ostia, now but a mass of ruins, was raised anew, surrounded with lofty walls and deep ditches, defended by a strong garrison and naval force, and thus be-

came an impregnable post. A nation's gratitude bestowed
upon it the name of its founder, and called it Gregoriopolis
(A. D. 828).

20. But meanwhile a lamentable revolution was preparing
in the Frankish empire. The Council of Paris (A. D. 829) had
offered Louis a wise counsel, of which he did not, however,
avail himself. "The greatest obstacle to order," said the council, "is the gradual interference of princes with ecclesiastical
matters; while bishops, whether through ignorance or cupidity,
give more attention than is proper to temporal affairs." The
empress Judith, his second wife, had borne to Louis a son,
Charles, afterward known as the *Bald*. Now the emperor
perceived the mistake he had made by the premature division
of his estates among the sons of his first union. He was
unwilling to leave Charles without a realm, and yet he could
furnish him with one only at the expense of the other princes.
An imperial decree bestowed upon Charles the territory of
Rhetia, Suabia, and Burgundy Transjurana. This was the
work of Bernard, count of Barcelona, prime minister of Louis.
The empress Judith, by means of caresses and skill, drew from
Lothaire a promise to respect the new allotment, and even to
act as guardian and protector to the young prince. But ambition overcame brotherly affection. A powerful league was
formed between Lothaire and his brothers Pepin and Louis,
with the ostensible end of withdrawing their father from the
power of Count Bernard, whose pride and pomp had incensed
all minds, and whom report accused, though perhaps unjustly,
of an intrigue with the empress Judith. The league counted
among its confederates some of the most influential characters
of the age: Hilduin, abbot of St. Denis and archchaplain;
Ebbo, archbishop of Rheims; Jesse, bishop of Amiens; Elias,
bishop of Troyes; St. Agobardus, archbishop of Lyons; St.
Bernard, archbishop of Vienna; Paschasius Radbertus, the
most celebrated doctor of the period; the illustrious and pious
Vala, abbot of Corbie, a former minister of Charlemagne, who
stifled the voice of flesh and blood to array himself against

the count of Barcelona, his own brother-in-law. Their example led the whole body of great lords, who all appeared at
Compiègne, under the leaders of the confederation (A. D. 828).
Louis had promptly removed Count Bernard at the very
moment when he most needed his services. But this act was
not enough for the factious nobles. They obliged him to send
the empress to the monastery of the Holy Cross, at Poitiers,
there, in the religious habit and discipline, to atone for the
crimes laid to her charge. They even sought to make him
abdicate and retire also to the confinement of a cloister. Lothaire had engaged some religious, whose influence with the
emperor he knew to be very weighty, to lead him to this
determination. The pious cenobites, more loyal than Lothaire
would have wished them at that moment, offered their services
to him whom they looked upon as their lawful sovereign.
The great point was to disunite the three rebel princes. Gundebald, a monk of easy and persuasive manners, betook himself
to the kings of Bavaria and Aquitaine, appealed to their conscience, their filial affection, and even their very interests, and
succeeded in bringing them back to their duty. The diet
which was to declare the fall of Louis the Mild was on the
eve of assembling. It was important that it should not be
held in Gaul, where the party of Lothaire ruled paramount.
The influence of Gundebald obtained its convocation at Nimeguen, where the Saxons and Frisians, who had vowed eternal
gratitude to Louis for the clemency he had shown them, might
have a decided majority. "All Germany," says a contemporary historian, "hastened to the rescue of its emperor." This
concourse alarmed the rebels, who insisted that Lothaire should
either resort to arms or withdraw his claim. A whole night
was spent in ceaseless parleying in the tent of that prince.
When informed of his irresolution, Louis sent for his son, who
dared not disobey.

A great tumult immediately arose in the camp, which would
soon have been a scene of bloody sedition, but the father and
son appearing before all in a mutual embrace, by this appear-

ance of reconciliation at once calmed the popular commotion (A. D. 830). The principal leaders of the conspiracy were arrested, judged, and sentenced to death; but the mild monarch wished them no worse evil than the imprisonment of a cloister, seemingly forgetful that egress was not impossible. The empress was recalled from her convent; but Louis hesitated to receive her in their former relations, as she had meanwhile pronounced her vows. A council held in the following year (A. D. 831) at Aix-la-Chapelle, removed the canonical difficulty, and with it the scruples of the pious monarch. Judith protested, under oath, that she was wholly guiltless of the charges made against her, and was re-instated in her rights as spouse and empress. The rebel princes were pardoned and sent back to their respective kingdoms. The count of Barcelona alone remained in disgrace, and his charge was bestowed upon Gundebald, who had done such signal service to his sovereign.

21. The peace was short. The first revolution had sprung from the ambition of the princes; the second was due to that of the fallen minister, Bernard. He imbittered the minds of the three princes against their father, and a manifesto soon appeared throughout the whole extent of the empire, complaining of the tyranny of Judith, who was accused of secretly plotting the overthrow of the three first sons of the emperor, to extend the domain of the young Charles. The proclamation concluded with an appeal to arms, to serve *God, the king, and the empire.* Every means that could awake the national honor was put into play; and the three unnatural sons, Lothaire, Pepin, and Louis, soon found themselves at the head of a formidable army (A. D. 833). To give to their undertaking a sort of sacred sanction in the eyes of the world, the three brothers begged Pope Gregory IV. to visit their camp, alleging a wish to use his mediation between their father, the emperor, and themselves. The Sovereign Pontiff, deceived by the crafty message, and hopeful of restoring peace to France, accepted the duty. He appeared in the camp at Rothfeld (Redfield), a vast plain in Alsatia, between Basle and Strasburg. The princes, meanwhile, putting

quite a different interpretation upon the Pontiff's visit, spread
the report among the troops and the people that the Pope had
given to their criminal designs the sanction of his apostolical
authority. Louis the Mild, also misinformed on the subject,
allowed himself to be deceived by public report; yet he did
not give up. Rousing himself to an energy and activity of
which no one supposed him capable, he gathered about him a
strong force and pitched his camp at a short distance from that
of the confederate princes. Had the emperor seized the moment to give battle while the ardor and good disposition of the
troops were at their height, victory had assuredly crowned his
standard. His wisest counsellors advised it, the troops themselves asked to be led on to the fight. But Louis was more
ready to hear the inspirations of a father's heart than the counsels of policy, however prudent. Before resorting to arms, he
wished to make terms. Negotiations were prolonged, during
which Lothaire and his royal brothers secured certain influences
in the imperial camp. Meanwhile, Gregory asked to be allowed
the exercise of his ministry as mediator. Robed in full pontifical attire, and surrounded by a numerous train of bishops, he
advanced into the space between the two armies. Louis, still
laboring under the false impression received at the outset, did
not come forward to meet him. Pope Gregory passed through
the imperial lines, approached the emperor, and gave him his
blessing, with the assurance that all his own proceedings had
been inspired by the truest desire for peace. "You are not received among us," said Louis, "with the honors which our fathers loved to pay to the Sovereign Pontiffs, your predecessors;
for your conduct has been far different from theirs!" "Like
our predecessors," replied Gregory, "we have but one aim,
that of maintaining peace in the kingdom of Jesus Christ." He
then acquainted the emperor with the real motive of his presence, and a conference ensued between the Pope and the emperor, which might have produced the most happy results; but
Lothaire and the two kings sought no such object; their intrigues had undermined the fidelity of their father's troops, who

deserted to the enemy's standard in the course of a single night.
The morning found Louis surrounded only by a handful of
faithful followers. "Go!" said the emperor, as his eyes filled
with tears, "go, too, and join my sons; I would not have your
devotion cost you your lives." The wretched father himself
appeared in the camp of his sons, asking only that the lives
of the empress and of Charles, his son, might be spared. Thus
did he humble himself for the sake of these objects of his lawful tenderness. Lothaire, Pepin, and Louis saw themselves
victors, without striking a blow; but can there be a deeper disgrace than a victory which humbles the most indulgent of fathers? The princes were incapable of this view. Louis was
confined in the monastery of St. Medard, at Soissons; Charles
the Bald, a poor child of ten years, whose youth would have
touched and drawn any heart other than those of his cruel
brothers, was separated from his mother, and placed in the
monastery of Prum, in the Ardennes; Judith was sent to Tor-
tona, in Lombardy. The people expressed their sentiment at
this sad sight by naming the plain of Rothfeld the *Field of the
Lie* (Lügenfeld) (A. D. 833). The constitution of 817 was
restored. The abbot Vala, withdrawn from his retreat at Corbie, to approve the deed, exclaimed with a sigh: "Alas!
every thing has been provided for, save the interests of justice."
Pope Gregory IV., whose good faith had been so shamefully
deceived, returned to Italy, filled with hopeless grief.

22. Louis had not yet drunk his bitter cup to the dregs. In
October, A. D. 833, a general assembly of bishops and nobles
met at Compiègne. Ebbo, archbishop of Rheims, presided, and
Louis the Mild was arraigned before it. Prostrate upon a sackcloth spread upon the ground, he read aloud a confession, acknowledging himself guilty of homicide, in the case of his
nephew Bernard, king of Italy; of sacrilege, in violating the
act of partition solemnly ratified in 817; of tyranny, by
the exile and death of faithful subjects; and of the ruin of the
State, by his capricious and inconstant policy. His only crime
was his incorrigible facility of disposition. The wretched prince

confessed his pretended crimes with many tears. Then handing to the bishops the confession, signed by his own hands, he
placed his helmet, cuirass, and military belt upon the altar, and
clothed himself with a sackcloth garment. While he lay prostrate upon the ground, the bishops went through the ceremonies usual on such occasions, of the imposition of hands and
penitential prayers. The three kings pretended that the act of
public penance, according to the canon law, carried with it inability to bear arms again, or take any part in business of
State; this was false, even in respect to private individuals,
who were forbidden to take part in public affairs only during
the course of their penance, and was altogether inadmissible in
regard to sovereigns. They therefore appeared with heartfelt
satisfaction at this odious ceremony, as at the degradation of
a father whose sovereignty was to them intolerable. Far different was the bearing and sentiment of the multitude. The
humiliation of a sovereign whose goodness was so popular revolted all hearts, and the reaction was not long delayed: Lothaire himself hastened it by his proud and haughty bearing
toward his brothers. The bond of unnatural treachery was
soon severed; Pepin and Louis conspired together against
Lothaire. At the tidings of their armed preparation, Lothaire
hastily quitted Aix-la-Chapelle, dragging along, in his flight,
the unfortunate emperor, whose penitential dress and cruel misfortunes everywhere won the most feeling expressions of compassionate pity. At Paris, the public sympathy took the form
of directly hostile demonstrations. Lothaire, leaving his august captive at St. Denis, fled in terror to his kingdom of Italy.
The lords, the bishops, and the military officers, now freed
from the tyrant's yoke, hastened in a body to St. Denis, and,
throwing themselves at the emperor's feet, begged him to resume the marks of his dignity. Even Louis and Pepin came,
as humble suppliants, to beg forgiveness for the past. Lothaire
alone continued to wage a civil strife; but forsaken, at length,
as his father once had been, he was forced to crave the forgiveness of a sovereign he had so basely and so cruelly outraged.

Louis the Mild forgot the past, restored his sons to their respective thrones, but would put off his own penitential humiliation only by the decree of a council. Forty-seven prelates, assembled at Thionville (A. D. 835), annulled all that had been done at Compiègne the year before. Ebbo laid before the council a resignation, in these terms: "I, Ebbo, an unworthy bishop, deeply impressed with the enormity of my crimes, and wishing to save my soul by a salutary penance, hereby renounce the sacred functions of the episcopate, which I have profaned, that a pastor may be consecrated in my stead, more worthy to govern the Church. I have signed this deed with my own hand." The resignation was submitted to the Pope, and accepted. Louis was solemnly freed from the penance imposed upon him, and resumed the imperial insignia only to extend his clemency to all who had betrayed him. Agobardus of Lyons, Jonas of Orleans, and the other bishops returned to their dioceses. Had they needed a defense, they might easily have alleged the critical state of affairs at the time; but the emperor was satisfied with a simple promise of fidelity to his authority, without reverting to actions which he wished to bury in endless oblivion. Ebbo himself was allowed to withdraw into a monastery of his own choice; though he was subsequently brought forward again, with the imperial consent, to fill the see of Hildesheim. Desirous to consecrate the anniversary of his restoration by a solemn festivity, and in compliance with the expressed wishes of Gregory IV. and all the bishops, Louis decreed that the feast of All Saints should be solemnized in the Churches of Gaul and Germany, on the 1st of November, as it had been kept in Rome for the past two hundred years, according to the decree of Boniface IV. One of the hymns of the feast, in which occurs the following petition: "Deliver thou the Christian soil from the foul pollution of the heathen's tread,"

> Auferte gentem perfidam
> Credentium de finibus,

refers to the Norman inroads, then wasting the Gallic territory.

During the year 835, they had entered the Island of Noirmontiers, and plundered its monastery.

23. The reparative measures which now gave back peace to France were confirmed in a council held at Aix-la-Chapelle (A. D. 836). The question of the distinction between the ecclesiastical and civil powers was treated here. The bishops acknowledged that they had allowed the current of public opinion to carry them too far in the difficulty between the emperor and his sons. "Wherefore," said they, in their address to Louis, "we think it necessary in order to preserve peace, that, leaving to the bishops the spiritual power they hold from Jesus Christ, you freely use all that which belongs to you as father and emperor." An ordinance was then passed for the restoration of all church property usurped by Pepin, king of Aquitaine, and the nobles of his kingdom. The emperor's order, following close upon the petition of the bishops, secured the restoration of the estates. The pious monarch seemed fated to find even this well-earned rest denied him. The clemency which springs from weakness rather emboldens than represses disorder. Louis, king of Bavaria, the emperor's son, a third time took up arms against his aged father, on the occasion of a new addition made to the estate of Charles the Bald. The emperor left Poitiers to meet the rebel; but, ere he reached Mentz, death cut short the term of his reign and of his misfortunes. He was assisted in his last moments by his brother Drogo, bishop of Metz and archchaplain of the palace. His last words were of forgiveness to the ungrateful son whose revolt had perhaps hurried him to a premature grave (June 20, A. D. 840). Thus ended the sad career of a prince whose only fault was his goodness, who owed all his misfortunes to his royal title!

24. A succession so bitterly contested during the lifetime of the incumbent could be but a heritage of strife and discord. Pepin of Aquitaine had followed his father to the grave. Louis of Bavaria and Charles the Bald were unwilling to acknowledge any real suzerainty in the person of Lothaire. The dispute was referred to the test of arms, in spite of all the con-

ciliatory efforts of Pope Gregory IV. Three legates had vainly
offered them the mediation of the Holy See. The contest took
place in the field of Fontenay (A. D. 842). All the contemporary chroniclers agree in the statement that " never did Frank
meet Frank in so disastrous a combat." They estimate at
forty thousand men the loss of Lothaire, who fled defeated to
Aix-la-Chapelle. Then might he recall his shameful triumphs
over his injured father. The empire of Charlemagne disappeared in the blood of Fontenay ; the hero did not live whose
arm could give back its lost unity. He of modern times, who
would fain have revived the greatness of Charlemagne, without
his religion and justice, had indulged that dream ; but, raised to
power by a tempest, he was sent to die upon a lone rock, beat-
en by the billows and storms of the ocean. Pepin, Louis, and
Charles divided the states given them by this victory, and
pledged to one another, each in the language of his brother's
subjects, an inviolable fidelity. The oath pronounced by Louis
of Bavaria, in favor of Charles the Bald, designated to the
throne of France, is the first monument of the French language ;
it is thus worded : " Pro Deo amur, et pro Christian poblo, et
nostro commun salvamento, dist di in avant, in quant Deus savir
et podir me dunat, si salvare io cist meon fradre Carlo, et in
adjudha, et in caduna cosa, si cum om per dreit son fradre sal-
var dist, in o quid in mi altre si fazet. Et ad Ludher nul plain
nunquam prindrai, qui, meon vol, cist meon fradre Carlo in
damno sit."* Lothaire had naturally been forgotten in this
partition. In the course of the following year he was reconciled with his brothers, and the final division was then made
(A. D. 843). All that part of Gaul lying to the west of the
Meuse, Saône, and Rhône, with that portion of Spain comprised
between the Pyrenees and the Ebro, was bestowed upon
Charles the Bald ; and this was the new kingdom of France.

---

* For the love of God and the Christian people, and our common salvation, from this day
forth, in so far as God grants me light and ability, I promise to support my brother Charles,
here present, by assistance, and in every particular, as it is right to support a brother, as
long as he does the same for me. And I will never enter into any agreement with Lothaire
that may prove detrimental to my brother.

The whole of Germany to the Rhine, was given to Louis. Lothaire, with the title of emperor, joined to Italy all the eastern portion of France, from the sea of Provence to the mouths of the Rhine and Scheldt. This long and narrow belt, cutting off all communication between Louis and Charles, was called the kingdom of Lothaire, *Lotharii Regnum, Lotharingia*, the present province of Lorraine.

25. We may now turn from this stormy picture of civil discord in the West, to the Eastern empire, which had meanwhile changed masters by the death of Michael the Stammerer (A. D. 829), who was succeeded by his son Theophilus, surnamed the Unfortunate, from his constant defeats in the war against the Saracens. He was the last and most violent persecutor of the faithful. In concert with his creature, John Lecanomantis,* whom he had placed in the see of Constantinople at the death of Anthony of Sylea, the new emperor undertook to secure the triumph of Iconoclasm by dint of persevering cruelty. He not only forbade the veneration, but even the making of sacred images. The prisons were crowded with painters, sculptors, Catholic priests and bishops, and especially with pious solitaries, toward whom the emperor had a particular aversion. Racks, scorpions, all the old instruments of torture, were again brought to light; Christian blood once more deluged the empire. A painter of Constantinople, for simply sketching a religious scene upon canvas, had his hands burned by order of Theophilus. Two Catholic monks, Theodore and Theophanes, were branded on the forehead, as *guilty of the crime of idolatry*. Theophilus wished to witness the infliction of the punishment, to enjoy their torture. "My lord," said Theophanes, "the words with which you brand my forehead are ineffaceable; you will read them hereafter at the bar of the Sovereign Judge." Both religious expired under the torture. The holy monk Methodius, imprisoned, or rather en-

---

* Lecanomantis, so called from the Greek words λεκάνη (a basin) and μάντις (prophet), as the impostor pretended to utter oracles by means of a metal basin which gave forth mysterious sounds.

tombed alive, during the reign of Michael the Stammerer, had lately come forth from his confinement, more a living skeleton than a human being; yet he still used his learning and elo- ' quence to warn the faithful against error. Theophilus, on learning his existence and zeal, sent for him, and said to him: "After the punishments you have suffered for your vain disputes, will you never cease to excite dissension and trouble for a subject as trifling as that of images?" "If these sacred images are contemptible," replied Methodius, "why do you wish that yours should be honored and daily multiplied, while those of Jesus Christ are everywhere destroyed?" * The emperor ordered him to be stripped to the waist, and torn, before his eyes, by a thousand lashes. Half dead with loss of blood, the confessor was let down through an opening in the floor, into an underground vault, whence some compassionate persons drew him up during the night to dress his wounds. Yet, in the midst of this bloody persecution, on the very steps of the imperial throne, rose up a name dear to the faithful—the only hope of the Church for a brighter future. The empress Theodora, whose surpassing beauty had deserved the honor of a throne, venerated sacred images, and was maintained in her good dispositions by her mother, Theoctista, who was often visited by her imperial grandchildren. Theophilus once asked them how they were received by their grandmother, and what took place during their visits, which seemed to afford them so much pleasure. Pulcheria, the youngest of the princesses, with the unsuspecting sincerity of childish innocence, showed the emperor some little statues and sacred images given them by Theoctista, adding, at the same time, that she had some larger and much finer, which she made them kiss with respect. The

---

* By a flagrant contradiction of his avowed system, Theophilus the Iconoclast squandered upon profane sculptors and statuaries the treasures so much needed for the defence of the empire. His reign was a period of unbridled luxury in Constantinople. Contemporary historians mention a tree with golden branches, in the great hall of the palace, on which a number of golden birds, hidden in the foliage, gave forth a concert of harmonious sounds. On either side of the imperial palace was a lion of massive gold, whose roar was a perfect imitation of that of its living model.

imperial Iconoclast dissembled his anger. He dared not openly break out against his mother-in-law, a woman of superior genius and intrepid piety, who had won all hearts by her own eminent qualities and through the winning graces of her daughter, the empress. Theophilus was at last stricken down (A. D. 842); but even the agonies of his deathbed could not tame the fiendish thirst for blood, and in his last moments he demanded, on the instant, the head of Theophobus, his sister's husband. This accomplished prince had refused the crown offered him by the army, and the emperor rewarded his fidelity with a dungeon. Some assassins brought him the victim's head upon a silver dish. Seizing it by the hair, he held it up, all dripping with gore, and exclaimed, with fiendish exultation: "I shall soon no longer be Theophilus; but you are now no longer Theophobus!" With these words he expired. The empress was declared regent for her son, Michael III., Porphyrogenitus, still an infant. Her first care was to restore the veneration of holy images. Lecanomantis was driven from the patriarchal throne, which he profaned by his heresy and his notorious disorders. A council, held in the church of St. Sophia, anathematized the enemies of sacred images. Lecanomantis was solemnly deposed and the see given to the holy confessor Methodius, who had so cruelly suffered for the faith under the last two reigns (A. D. 842). The Iconoclast heresy was extinct after a reign of about one hundred and twenty years. On the first Sunday in Lent, the new Patriarch, Methodius, together with the empress and all the faithful, spent the night in prayer, in the church of Our Lady of Blachernes, whence they proceeded in the morning, in solemn procession, to St. Sophia, where the holy sacrifice was offered up, and the sacred images restored. An anniversary feast was instituted in the East, to mark this event, called the *Feast of Orthodoxy*.

26. These glad tidings filled with joy the heart of Gregory IV., and alleviated the grief he felt at the sad state of the West. Christianity stood in terror of two enemies, one in the North, the other in the South of Europe. The Normans still

carried on their depredations; and such was the terror inspired
by their very name, that the help of God was publicly invoked against their fury.* They traversed the seas with wonderful rapidity, in little boats, with sails or oars, ascended
inland rivers, visited different places in such swift succession
as to appear everywhere at once, everywhere spreading terror
by carnage, conflagration, ruined cities, temples profaned,
crimes and atrocities hitherto unknown and unheard of. The
sea-board territory of Neustria, too soon known to them for its
fertility and wealth, was the first scene of their wasting depredations. They entered it by the Seine, plundered the city of
Rouen and burned the monastery of St. Ouen, sailed on to
that of Jumiéges, which they also gave to the flames, spoiled
and burned all the villages lying along the shores of the Seine
(A. D. 841). In another inroad they came down upon Nantes,
which they took by assault. The bishop, St. Guihard, withdrew into the church with all his clergy a multitude of people, and the religious of the Isle of Aindre, who had brought
their property here, as to a safe retreat. The barbarians broke
in the doors and windows and butchered the whole multitude;
they then sacked and burned the church, and carried off the
inhabitants who had escaped the massacre, to be sold as slaves.
While the barbarians of the north came into France from the
ocean, the Saracens made their appearance in the south by
way of the Rhone, landed at Arles, and loaded their vessels
with an immense booty. In the absence of Lothaire, who was
warring against his brothers, they made several descents upon
the coast of Italy, and were very near taking Rome itself.
They plundered the church of St. Peter, not yet enclosed by
the city walls (A. D. 842). The rich treasures of Monte Cassino also became their spoil.† To prevent the occurrence of

---

* In the manuscript rituals of the Middle Ages is found this invocation, sung in the
Litanies: *A furore Normanorum, libera nos, Domine.* (From the fury of the Normans, O
Lord, deliver us.)

† This monastery was not really pillaged by the Saracens. They received its wealth
through Siconulphus, duke of Beneventum, who sought to buy their help against his rival
Radalgisc The booty thus received by the Saracens amounted to one hundred and thirty

like disasters, Gregory IV. began to fortify Rome, and to surround it with a strong rampart; but death interrupted the useful labor (January 11, A. D. 844). He had reigned sixteen years, and won universal admiration for his rare prudence in the intricate circumstances of his administration.

27. Two celebrated works appeared in this pontificate: the *False Decretals* and the *Treatise on the Body and Blood of the Lord.* The False Decretals, bearing the name of Isidore Mercator, in the first part, simply reproduce the Spanish collection perfected by St. Isidore of Seville two centuries before. The second part comprises some fifty supposititious letters, attributed to the Popes of the first three centuries, whereas they are in truth made up from shreds of decretals issued by Pontiffs of the four following centuries. The pseudonymous author has moreover interpolated several authentic letters, by the insertion of passages which do not belong to them. This collection, of which the author has not yet been discovered, was never approved by the Church. In 831, Paschasius Radbertus, the learned abbot of New Corbie, published his famous Treatise on the Body and Blood of the Lord. He lays down the teaching of the Church concerning the sacrament of the Eucharist, as the monks of his monastery, charged with the instruction of youth, were to explain it. He quotes the testimony of the Fathers: Sts. Cyprian, Ambrose, Hilary, Augustine, Chrysostom, Jerome, Gregory, Basil, Isidore, and Venerable Bede. Nothing can be more formal, more precise, than his words concerning the real presence of the Saviour in the sacrament of our altars, and of the miracle of Transubstantiation. Unable to elude the irresistible clearness of this monument of Catholic belief, Protestant writers have asserted that Paschasius Radbertus, *an ignorant monk of the ninth century, invented* the dogma of Transubstantiation. Besides the palpa-

pounds of gold and eight hundred and sixty-five of silver, in crowns, crosses, challices, and other sacred vessels; thirty-two thousand sous in gold coin, a gold crown enriched with emeralds, estimated at five thousand gold sous—all precious testimonials of the pious liberality of Christian princes.

ble fact, that if this Treatise had offered to the world a new doctrine, a thousand voices would at once have been raised to condemn it, Paschasius was not the only writer of his age who uttered the same sentiments on the same subject. Haymo, bishop of Alberstadt, wrote a work, under the same title, embodying the same teaching. Amalarius, in his Treatise on the office of the Mass; Florus, in his work on the Sacrifice of the Mass, and Rabanus Maurus, writing on the same subject, all teach one and the same Catholic dogma. The Protestant assertion, therefore, springs either from gross ignorance or shameless insincerity.

CHAPTER III.

§ I. Pontificate of Sergius II. (January 27, a. d. 844—(January 27, 847).

1. Sergius II. was raised to the Chair of St. Peter (January 27, a. d. 844) without awaiting the arrival of the emperor Lothaire's deputies. This haste was warranted by the peculiar exigency of the times. A deacon, named John, had gathered a factious crowd to oppose Sergius, and gain his own promotion to the Papacy by open violence. He had already broken into the Lateran palace with an armed force, and gave reason to fear the most alarming excesses as a consequence of his schism. The nobility of Rome at once arose in defence of the lawful Pontiff. The mob was dispersed; the schismatical deacon was subjected to close confinement, and only owed his life to the clemency and urgent solicitations of Sergius II. The

emperor, whom the news of these events had not yet reached, at first showed some displeasure that his ambassadors had not been awaited for the consecration of the new Pope. He sent to Rome his eldest son, Louis, with the title of king of Italy, and attended by a numerous escort of nobles and bishops, headed by his uncle Drogo, bishop of Metz, and archchaplain of the empire. Sergius received the noble embassy with the highest honors. Surrounded by all the Roman clergy, the Pope received the young king at the head of the steps before St. Peter's basilica, but yet the doors were closed. On the arrival of the prince, the Pontiff thus addressed him: "If you come here for the good of the Church and of the State, I shall order the doors to be opened to you; otherwise they remain closed." The king protested that his thoughts were only of peace and good-will; the doors were opened, they entered together and prostrated themselves before the Confession of St. Peter. A council was held in Rome under the presidency of Drogo, and recognized the election of Sergius II. as lawful. Louis then received the royal unction at the hands of the Pope, as king of Italy, or of the Lombards. The iron crown was placed upon his brow, and the Pontiff's hands girded him with the royal sword. The young prince was desirous that the Romans should swear fealty to his person, according to the formula drawn up by Eugenius II.; but Sergius II. showed him that the oath could be exacted only in the name of the emperor, in whom alone a sovereign protectorate was recognized by the Holy See; and such, in fact, was the form in which the Romans renewed it to Lothaire, through the new king of Italy, in St. Peter's church (A. D. 844). The Pope then conferred upon Drogo the title and dignity of vicar apostolic in Germany and Gaul; and the ambassadors went back to their imperial master, who expressed his satisfaction at the result of their mission.

2. Peace and harmony existed between the three royal brothers, Lothaire, Louis and Charles the Bald. The Gallic churches availed themselves of this season of quiet to restore

the true spirit of discipline by numerous councils, successively held at Verneuil, Beauvais, Meaux, Paris, Soissons, Quercy-sur-Oise, Thionville, and Mentz. It is a true saying, that laws are more abundantly multiplied in proportion as their execution is less strictly enforced. Reasoning from this principle, the churches of France and Germany must, at this period, have been in a sad state of relaxation; for the statutes and regulations on the same subjects were every year reproduced by the successive councils. Particular stress was laid upon the necessity of subjecting monasteries to episcopal visitations, for the maintenance of canonical discipline. The councils decree the severest censure, and most rigorous chastisement in respect of the blind piety of certain religious women, who cut their hair and assumed the dress of the other sex, to gain admittance into the communities of monks most celebrated for their austerity. The ever-recurring prohibition is again found necessary against the armed presence of clerics in military expeditions. Princes are instructed that they should not exact personal military service from bishops, but that it should be sufficient to enlist under their standards the vassals of ecclesiastical estates. In the present state of civilization, these provisions may appear pointless. But the tendency of human minds, abuses, and manners change with the passing ages. If the public mind is, in some respects, improved, it is due to the constant efforts of the Church in that direction. If there still remain abuses to repress, prejudices to overcome, dangerous tendencies to curb, the mission of improvement is still for the Church. She is ever armed, ever in the breach, to do battle for the faith in every age. The modern historical school of the eighteenth century has endeavored to convict the Frankish bishops, under the Carlovingian dynasty, of assuming temporal power to which they were not entitled. The very position of the bishops, in Church and State, made it impossible for them not to take part in political events; and the general result of their intervention has been to check the natural tendency of minds and movements, and to render wars and revolutions far less bloody. The bishops of the first centuries were responsible only for the people of a single city, or at most of a diocese limited in extent. The Frankish bishops, on the other hand, besides their own diocese, were obliged to guide, to form, to educate a whole nation, kings and subjects, warriors and magistrates. The task was the same in nature, but on a vastly larger scale. It was also embarrassed by all the difficulties arising from a spirit still imbued with barbarism. These points we must keep in view, to form a just estimate of their position.

3. The diocese of Langres drew the public attention at about this period, by a new kind of abuse, astonishing even to that ignorant and superstitious age (A. D. 844). Some wandering monks came to Dijon, bringing relics of a saint, whose name they had forgotten, and deposited them, without episcopal sanction, in the church of St. Benignus. The city of Dijon was at that time within the jurisdiction of the diocese of Langres. The bishop, Theobald, would not receive the pretended relics on information so vague and unsatisfactory. Notwithstanding his prohibition, they were exposed to the veneration of the people, and popular credulity soon had attracted a prodigious concourse. The most singular feature of the case is, that St. Benignus became the scene of convulsions exactly similar to those which the Jansenists exhibited seven centuries later, at the tomb of the deacon Paris. The report of these wonderful scenes soon brought together a great number both of spectators and of actors; as many as four hundred at a time were seen indulging in their sacrilegious extravagances. Theobald consulted his metropolitan, Amolo, archbishop of Lyons. The prelate's reply was such as became a prudent and enlightened pastor. "Arm yourself," he said, "with episcopal zeal and severity, to banish these scandalous innovations from the sanctuary. Order that each one bring his vows and his offerings to the Church in which he was baptized, where he receives the other sacraments, participates in the sacred mysteries, and is to receive the last rites of religion.

When public credulity ceases to lavish upon impostors the
alms due to the suffering members of Jesus Christ, profit-
less imposture will fall of itself. Should some fanatic, more
obstinate than common, persist in these ridiculous practices,
he should be made publicly to confess his deceit." Theobald
followed the advice, and with immediate success. Such seems
to have been the duration and end of this sect.

. 4. The measures adopted by the empress Theodora for the
conversion of the Manicheans or Paulicians who desolated the
churches of the Eastern empire, were not crowned with the
same happy result. Mildness and conciliation failed to move
these sectaries. Supported by the Saracen power, they came
forth from their retreat in the city of Argaous, in Armenia,
and made frequent inroads upon the territory of the empire.
Theodora sent a considerable force against them, and many of
them paid for their plunder with their lives. Their doctrine
of community of property and equality of condition had many
points of resemblance with the various systems reproduced in
more modern times under the name of socialism. The leaders
of the sect soon found themselves surrounded by a host of
worthless outcasts and malcontents, naturally drawn to a sys
tem of extreme radicalism, destructive of all principle, government, or form of society. They became the terror of the East,
and were powerful enough to build two cities, Amara and
Tibricus. From this time their fury knew no bounds. The
remnants of the Iconoclast party were more easily reconciled
to the Church. St. Methodius, Patriarch of Constantinople,
treated them with the most merciful indulgence; retaining in
their sees the bishops who abjured their error; and in all
things following the true spirit of the gospel. Yet his conduct gave offence to some bishops whose zeal was not "according to knowledge." "He relies," said the dissatisfied, "upon
the testimony of the subjects he ordains, and seems to be
under obligations to those who receive his ordination!" The
feeling of discontent finally reached such a pitch, that fears
were entertained of schism, and not without reason; the exer-

SERGIUS II. (A. D. 844-847).

cise of the imperial authority and the banishment of several
of the most turbulent prelates only added to the misunderstanding. It is hard to say where the evil would have ended
but for the vigorous efforts of the holy solitary Joannices, in
the labor of reconciliation. His well-known sanctity eminently
fitted him for the difficult office of mediator. After twenty
years of solitude on Mount Olympus, in Bithynia, he had
come to Constantinople, as St. Anthony of old to Alexandria,
on learning the imminent danger which threatened the Church.
All hearts yielded to the influence of his mild and winning
eloquence, and to the heavenly piety which shone in his countenance : availing himself of this ascendency, he convinced the
most clouded understandings of the prudence of the Patriarch's
measures, and leaving all minds at rest, he returned to his
beloved retreat, where he soon afterward died, at the age of
eighty-one years. St. Methodius followed him the 14th of
June, A. D. 846. The holy confessor's jaw had been broken
during the persecution, which obliged him to wear a bandage
under his chin to support it. Respectful remembrance is still
preserved of this mark of the saint's confession of the faith,
in the similar bandage worn by the Patriarchs of Constantinople when in full pontificals. The saint was followed by a
worthy and no less illustrious successor, in the person of St.
Ignatius, who showed his attachment to the centre of Catholic
unity, with all the constancy of a saint raised up by God to
hinder, or at least to delay, the consummation of the Eastern
schism. His happy pontificate is contemporaneous with two
other equally cheering episodes in the history of religion : the
conversion of the Khazars and the Moravians. The Khazars
inhabited Tauris (the present Crimea), with Chersonesus as their
capital. Their worship was a mixture of Judaism and Mohammedanism. Their petition to the empress Theodora for Catholic
missionaries was answered by St. Ignatius, who at once sent
them the priest Constantine, called the Philosopher ; the
envoy of the Church invoked upon his mission a powerful
patronage by assuming the name of Cyril. The conversion of

a whole nation was the reward of his earnest zeal. The Moravians, a people of the Sclavonic race, occupied the present Moravia, Bohemia, Silesia, Pomerania, and Mœsia. Their king, Ratislas, addressed to the empress Theodora a petition similar to that of the Khazars. Cyril, on his return from the first mission, at once set out for Moravia, accompanied by his brother, St. Methodius, and with the two holy brothers these favored people received the twofold light of faith and civilization. They gave to the Moravians their alphabet and translations of the Sacred Writings; thus do the Sclaves recognize in them at once their apostles and the fathers of their literature (A. D. 846).

5. Providence now sent two illustrious prelates to fill the two principal Frankish sees. Hincmar was consecrated, at the Council of Beauvais, archbishop of Rheims, in the month of April, A. D. 845, and Rabanus was raised to the see of Mentz, in June, A. D. 847. Hincmar belonged to an illustrious Gallic house, and early won the admiration of his age by the loftiness of his views and his untiring energy. He was one of the most learned men of his day, and has scarcely been surpassed, at any period, in knowledge of canon law. It has been said that he was far less conversant with the writings of the Fathers than with the canons; yet he has proved himself much better versed than his critics in the deepest passages of St. Augustine, since he drew from them the very doctrines constantly recognized, and again confirmed, by the Church in later ages. During his episcopate he was one of the most zealous defenders of the faith and of discipline, and one of the greatest lights of the Gallic Church. Yet he is sometimes, perhaps justly, charged with too great a love of power, and the occasional display of a naturally harsh and violent temper. Rabanus was a native of Mentz, and a pupil of Alcuin; according to the prevailing custom among the learned men of his time, he added the surname of Maurus to his own. Called to the chair of theology in the monastery of Fuld, he acquired for its school an unequalled renown: the annals of Christian

literature owe to his training some of the brightest names in
the list of doctors—it may suffice to mention Walafrid Strabo
and Lupus of Ferrières. At the death of Eigil, abbot of Fuld,
Rabanus was called to succeed him; but his was a genius destined to shine in a wider sphere, and notwithstanding his years
—for he had reached the term of threescore and ten—he was
raised to the archiepiscopal throne of Mentz (A. D. 847). In
this responsible post he seemed to regain all the activity and
energy of youth; his name became the terror of heresy
and the bulwark of the faith, in the theological discussions
excited by the errors of Gotescalc.

6. Meanwhile, Pope Sergius II. had died at Rome, on the
27th of January, A. D. 847. His last days, like those of his
predecessor, Gregory IV., were imbittered by the ruinous inroads of the Normans and Mussulmans. The Normans, under
Regnar Lodbrog, appeared before the very walls of Paris,
whose weak monarch, Charles the Bald, purchased with gold
the safety of his capital. These spoilers were the terror of
the Franks, who neither dared to fight them nor to till the
soil. The region between the Seine and Loire became over-
spread with dense forests. In the month of August, A. D. 846,
the African Saracens, who began to be known as *Moors*, ascended the Tiber in light vessels, forced the passage of Ostia,
and covered the Roman territory with their swarming legions.
Defended by the walls begun by Gregory IV. and finished by
Sergius II., Rome resisted the attacks of the infidels; they
pillaged the churches of St. Peter and St. Paul, not yet enclosed within the city bounds; all the ornaments and wealth
of these splendid temples, even the silver altar over St. Peter's
tomb, became the Moslem's spoil. At this critical period
death deprived the Romans of a wise and able leader in the
person of Sergius II.

§ II. PONTIFICATE OF ST. LEO IV. (April 12, A. D. 847—July
17, 855.)

7. The funeral obsequies of Sergius II. were not yet over
(January 30, A. D. 847), when the unanimous voice of the
Roman clergy and people bestowed the tiara upon a priest
whose merit and virtue had won all hearts. St. Leo IV., the
new Pontiff, was raised by Providence to be the savior of
Rome, and the bulwark of all Christendom against the Saracens. The existing circumstances required dispatch; the
emperor's consent was not forthcoming. Yet Rome was in
critical need of a head. After two months of useless delay,
it was determined to proceed at all hazards; the new Pope
was consecrated, but with the protest that no detriment was
intended to the honor and fealty due to the emperor Lothaire
as protector of the Holy See. The Saracens had meanwhile
been freighting their ships with an immense booty, and put out
to sea. A fearful tempest destroyed their fleet; the waves
washed up along the Italian strand, with the bodies of these
enemies to the Christian name, some portions of the treasure
taken from St. Peter's church, which were gathered up and
brought to Rome with pious reverence (A. D. 847). St. Leo
IV. removed the last traces of the passing infidels by the truly
royal magnificence with which he repaired that august temple.
He had also conceived a gigantic project which would, alone,
have been a splendid glory for a sovereign and a Pontiff. With
a view to shield the basilica of St. Peter from any fresh outrage, he resolved to join it to ancient Rome by means of a new
city, surrounded by walls. The emperor Lothaire, to whom
the Pope communicated his design, received it with real enthusiasm, and at once contributed considerable largesses toward
the immense outlay that must necessarily attend its execution.
This immortal work was begun in 848. A whole army of
laborers from Italy, Gaul and Germany answered the call of
the Holy Pontiff, who watched the progress of the work with
active interest, and devoted to it all the leisure left him by the

many cares of his pontificate. As if in scorn of these defensive preparations, the Saracens, in the following year (849), landed at Ostia a force superior to that of any former expedition. But now they were doomed to meet a second Poictiers on the shores of Italy, a second Charles Martel in the person of St. Leo IV. Here, however, we prefer to quote the testimony of an author who is not wont to lavish praise upon the Christian Pontiffs.* "When attacked by the Saracens," says Voltaire, "Pope Leo IV., by his defence, proved himself worthy to be Rome's sovereign. He had used the Church's wealth to raise the walls, to build towers, to stretch chains across the Tiber. He armed a force of militia at his own expense, engaged the citizens of Naples and of Gaëta to help in the defence of Ostia's coast and harbor, without neglecting the wise precaution of securing hostages from them, mindful that those who are powerful to do us good may equally use their power for our harm. He visited all the posts in person, and met the Saracens at their approach, not in the iron harness of a warrior, but as a Pontiff come to exhort a Christian people, as a king watchful of his subjects' weal (A. D. 849). Leo was born a Roman; the courage of the first ages of the republic glowed in his breast; and amid the decline and corruption of a-ruined age, he stood erect, like one of the firm and lofty columns that rear their heads above the fragments of the Roman forum. His courage and prudence were ably seconded, and the invading Saracens met a bold resistance : the advantage leaning to the side of the Christian arms was quickly. though less gloriously, decided by a storm which shattered half the Moorish fleet; those who escaped the hostile sword or a watery grave met but a merited prison and chains, and were usefully employed by the Pontiff to restore and embellish the walls and sacred edifices they had attempted to subvert."†

8. Leo IV. had forever freed the Eternal City from Mus-

---

* VOLTAIRE, *Essai sur les Mœurs*, t. 1, chap. xxviii.

† The pencil of Raphael has traced for succeeding ages, in the halls of the Vatican, a monument of this undying service of the Papacy to Christendom in the West.

sulman profanation. The Prophet's crescent never again appeared before the walls of Rome. The security thus gained enabled the Pope to prosecute with redoubled ardor the building of the *Leonine* city. Four years completed the work, and the inauguration was celebrated with the most solemn pomp (A. D. 852). The Pontiff knelt successively at the three gates of the new city, and offered up a fervent prayer. "May the scourge of Thy anger, O Lord, never touch the city founded by Thy help. May it ever triumph over its enemies, nor ever become a by-word among misbelieving nations." By the unwearied activity of the Holy Pontiff, the falling city of Porto was raised (A. D. 852), and peopled by a colony of Corsicans driven from Bastia by the fear of the Saracens. Brave, hardy, devotedly true, and inured to a life of arms, the Corsicans were fitly placed by St. Leo to guard the Italian coast against the Mohammedan power. Centumcellæ (Civita Vecchia) also owned its restoration to the care of the pious and vigilant Pontiff.

9. Gaul and Germany were troubled by the restless presumption of a Saxon monk who aspired to treat the most intricate questions of theology. Gotescalc, a son of Count Bern, had been trained in the monastery of Fuld. His restless and roving disposition made the religious habit too burdensome, and on the pretext that his engagement had been forced, he put it off. But the world could not satisfy his ardent mind, and shortly afterward, Gotescalc, once more a monk, in the monastery of Orbais, in the diocese of Soissons, was eagerly perusing the works of the Fathers, especially of St. Augustine. What would have been a sanctifying influence to any other man proved his ruin. His bold imagination and superficial mind ventured to sound vast and uncertain depths ; and besides, his learning wanted the two indispensable pillars of piety and humility. He would plunge into the mysterious abysses of predestination, and give his fancies to the world as the teaching of St. Augustine. The charitable care of some true friends, who saw the danger of his position, afforded him a wholesome

warning. "I cannot too warmly urge you, my dear brother," wrote Lupus of Ferrières, "to release your mind from the fatiguing study of questions which it would perhaps be better not to sound too deeply. Is there nothing to which we may more usefully devote ourselves? Let us apply ourselves to the study of the Sacred Text, seasoning our application with humility and prayer. God will teach us what it is fitting we should know, provided we follow not too curiously what He would withdraw from our search." Gotescalc was not a man to relish this brotherly advice. In a council held at Mentz, under the presidency of Rabanus Maurus (A. D. 848), he maintained that *predestination so binds man that, even though he wish to be saved, and strive, by the help of grace, to work out his salvation by faith and good works, yet he can do nothing, unless predestined.* This is but one of the forms of the fanaticism reproduced in the seventeenth century by Jansenius. The council anathematized the error and its author, who was sent, under guard, to his metropolitan, Hincmar, archbishop of Rheims. Rabanus Maurus, on behalf of the assembled prelates, wrote to Hincmar, defining the new heresy with theological precision. "The dangerous error of the wandering monk, Gotescalc," he writes, "consists in teaching that God predestinates to evil as well as to good; that there are men who cannot overcome their sinful nature or their errors, because dragged on by predestination to unavoidable destruction, as though God had created but to damn them." The question raised by Gotescalc was an intricate one, and touched upon the stoniest tracts of theology: free-will, Divine foreknowledge, predestination—subjects so deeply discussed by St. Augustine in his works against Pelagianism and semi-Pelagianism. Gotescalc maintained that predestination irresistibly draws man to good or evil. This was the point of his error; for God, who foresees by his eternal knowledge the good or bad use we shall make of our will, yet does not deprive us of its freedom. Ratramnus, abbot of Corbie, Amolo, archbishop of Lyons, and Florus, one of his deacons, defended the Catholic belief with a degree of clearness and learning which show none of the effects of a period of literary darkness. But the doctrine of the Saxon heretic contained a secondary point still more ambiguous. He asserted that predestination was of two kinds—one to everlasting life, the other to eternal loss. To make the proposition absolutely and rigorously true, the condition is necessary that neither kind of predestination takes away man's free-will; so that predestination to life everlasting can take effect only by the free co-operation of man and his voluntary correspondence with Divine grace; just as predestination to eternal loss is nothing but the Divine foreknowledge that a certain man will be lost, because he will voluntarily make a bad use of his free-will; since it is indeed impious, remarks Rabanus Maurus, in his letter to Hincmar, *to hold that God created men to be necessarily damned.* This second point of Gotescalc's error gave rise to several ambiguous expressions in the writings of otherwise unimpeachable doctors—such men as St. Prudentius, bishop of Troyes,[*] and even Hincmar of Rheims, who maintained that predestination is not twofold; "for God, he says, "does not create man to destroy him." By predestination to eternal loss, these writers understood the fatality which should lead man to eternal death in spite of himself, by destroying his free-will. The work most at variance with the Catholic teaching on this point was the treatise on predestination by Scotus Erigena.[†] Scotus Erigena, a man of more erudition than judgment, a superficial sophist, but little versed in theology, a subtle, bold, and biting spirit, had been called to the French court by the favor of Charles the Bald.[‡] Scotus then maintained, against all the Fathers of the Church, that there is but one kind of predestination—

[*] We know, from a letter of Hincmar of Rheims, that St. Prudentius is the author of the *Annals* known under the title of St. Bertin, from the name of the monastery in which they were discovered.

[†] *Erigena*, a native of Erin, the early name of Ireland.

[‡] The following repartee is attributed to Scotus Erigena: Charles the Bald, who admitted him familiarly to his table, asked him one day, in the course of a repast, "What difference is there between a Scot and a sot?" "My lord," answered the sophist, "there is precisely the width of this table." A man of this character was hardly fitted to treat with propriety one of the most delicate points of theological discussion.

that to eternal life ; that as to eternal loss, God can neither predestinate nor even, in strictness, foresee it. A new controversy arose on this point between Scotus and the other doctors. Charles the Bald was passionately fond of these theological disputes, and kept them alive by the interest he seemed to take in them. But Gotescalc was solemnly and definitively condemned by a council held at Quercy-sur-Oise, under Hincmar, archbishop of Rheims (A. D. 849). He pleaded in vain for the privilege of testing the truth of his doctrine by the ordeal of fire or of boiling water, instead of which he was even subjected to the penalty decreed by the Council of Agde, and by the article of St. Benedict's rule, which condemns an insubordinate monk to flagellation and confinement. The sentence was put into rigorous execution. He was publicly whipped in the presence of the king, obliged to burn his writings, and finally enclosed in the monastery of Hautvilliers, in the diocese of Rheims. The controversy on predestination fell of itself, to rise with renewed force a few centuries later ; and the prudence of the Frankish bishops sufficed to stifle the error at its birth, or at least materially to check its poisonous contagion. It does not appear that it necessitated an appeal to the Apostolic authority. The two Councils of Soissons (A. D. 853) and Valence (855) closed the discussion with these remarkable words : " We are desirous carefully to shun all novelty in word, all rash disputes, which can but breed scandals ; to cling firmly to the Sacred Text, and to its true interpreters—to Cyprian, Hilary, Ambrose, Jerome, Augustine, and other Catholic doctors. We openly confess the predestination of the elect to everlasting life, and the predestination of the wicked to eternal death ; but, in the choice of those who shall be saved, the mercy of God precedes their merit; and in the condemnation of those who are doomed to be lost, their demerit precedes the judgment of God."

10. The erection of Brittany into an independent kingdom, by Nomenoe, is referred to this period (A. D. 850). This prince established three new bishoprics : Dol, St. Brieux, and Tré-

guier, and bestowed the metropolitan dignity upon the see of Dol, which he selected as the place of his coronation, thus cutting off the whole of Brittany from the metropolitan jurisdiction of Tours. Dol enjoyed the metropolitan dignity and privileges for three hundred years, in spite of the canonical objections of the Frankish bishops.

11. The Christians now began to suffer a cruel persecution in Spain. The kings of Asturias and Leon no longer dwelt in the dens and hollows of the mountains. From the time of Alphonso the Chaste, whose victorious reign of fifty years had raised the courage of his subjects to the highest pitch, the Christians, once so shamefully oppressed, began to make their persecutors tremble. They had taken several cities from their oppressors: Leon, Tuy, and Astorga, among others (A. D. 816).[*] The Franks still held Eastern Iberia, or Catalonia, beyond the Pyrenees; the cities of Barcelona, Girona, Urge and Elna (now Perpignan) were within the metropolitical jurisdiction of Narbonne. In the midst of these mountains arose a third power, whose example led many Christian heroes to erect independent sovereignties at the expense of the Spanish Moors, whom they daily straitened more and more, and at length entirely crushed. Inigo, count of Bigorra, finding the weak government of Charlemagne's degenerate heir unable to protect him from the barbarians, conceived the manly design of defending himself, and was acknowledged by his countrymen as their king, about the year 830. He gained sufficient power, in a few years of successive victories, to leave a well-established kingdom to his successor Ximenes, who transmitted it, in turn, to his son Inigo II., one of the worthiest scions of his noble race. The youthful hero rested not within the narrow realm acquired by his predecessors, but, widening out its limits by his own endeavor, took the important city of Pampeluna, and gave all its wealth, with enduring firmness, to the kingdom of Na-

---

[*] It is said that the body of St. James the Greater was, at this period, found at Compostella. This agrees with the common belief of the ninth century, confirmed by the oldest traditions, that St. James was the first apostle of Spain.

varre. Such was the beginning of this crown, one of the oldest
and most illustrious in Spain. The brilliant and continued
success of the Christian arms aroused the bitter hatred of the
Moors, and the whole of Spain was whelmed in blood by a persecution equal in violence to the fiercest struggles of paganism
with the Church. The heroism of the early martyrs was revived in all its splendor. At Cordova, a holy priest, named
Perfectus, was brought before the cadi. "What is your belief
of Jesus Christ and of Mohammed?" asked the magistrate.
"Jesus Christ," replied the confessor, "is God, most holy.
Mohammed, your false prophet, is one of those corrupters,
mentioned in the Gospel, who are to lead their followers to
eternal ruin." He had hardly time to utter his closing words,
when the judge ordered him to be taken to a plain near Cordova, on the banks of the Bœtis, to be beheaded. The same punishment was inflicted upon Isaac, abbot of the monastery of
Tuban, and thirty of his religious. The virgins Flora, Maria,
Liliosa, Colomba, Aura and Nathalia, by the same constancy,
won the same glorious crown. St. Eulogius, a priest of Cordova, to whom we owe the account of their martyrdom, was at
length seized, and shared the triumph of those whom he had
defended and encouraged during life (A. D. 850). For sixty
years these bloody scenes were incessantly renewed. Abderahman II., caliph of Cordova, the author of the persecution,
was suddenly stricken down, in the very act of feasting his
eyes upon these cruel executions, from a terrace of his palace.
Far from heeding this fearful warning of Divine vengeance, his
son and successor, Mohammed, carried his impious rage to still
greater lengths. But to sate his mad and sacrilegious hate
would have been to dispeople his realm, and remain the crowned
master of a desert waste. He was forced to turn to the bishops, that they might keep the faithful from presenting themselves to claim the palm of martyrdom. A council was held at
Cordova, in 852, for this singular object; but the ardor and
constancy of the Christians suffered no diminution in consequence. Policy now drove Mohammed to adopt a different

course, and to change his bloody violence into a more secret persecution. He strove to crush the Christian religion under the weight of public contempt; he removed the Christians from all their offices, drove them from the palace, tore down all the churches raised within the period of Moorish domination in Spain, and laid heavy taxes upon the worshippers of Jesus Christ. The rack and sword were reserved for bishops and priests, whom he still continued to put to death, hoping to kill religion in his States by destroying the perpetuity of the priesthood.

12. The provinces of Germany and Gaul still suffered from Norman inroads. A fleet of six hundred sail, under Roric, moved up the Elbe to Hamburg, which was given up, for the space of a day and two nights to the licentious fury of the barbarians (A. D. 855). Friesland was laid waste, its monasteries and churches sacked and burned, the inhabitants massacred or led away into bondage. Holland, the valley of the Rhine and of the Wahl were not spared. Godefriel, another of their leaders, had meanwhile penetrated Gaul, even to Beauvais, which was sacked. Passing thence into Aquitaine, the Normans besieged Bordeaux, which was betrayed into their hands by the treachery of the Jews; they left it stripped of its immense wealth, a heap of smoking ruins. Rouen once more became their prey; and, in the following year (857), the same lot befell Tours and Le Mans. The monastery of Marmoutier was given to the flames, and its religious inmates, to the number of one hundred and sixteen, were put to the sword. The relics of St. Martin, the holy patron of Gaul, had been conveyed to Orleans, to save them from the barbarian sacrilege; it was again found necessary to transfer them to Auxerre, for the Normans, following the course of the Loire, took Orleans and Blois, and attacked even the city of Chartres, which the courageous resistance of its heroic bishop, Erobald, was powerless to save from devastation and ruin. During the same invasion, the Normans again insulted Paris, burned St. Geneviève and all the churches of the city and neighboring country, with the excep-

tion of three : the Cathedral, St. Germain-des-Prés, and St. Denis, which Charles the Bald rescued at an immense price. Such were the scenes of blood and horror by which these men *of the North*, as impervious to all sentiment of pity or gentleness as the rude rocks and bergs of their own chilly home, changed the smiling face of our rich and fertile land into a black and desert waste. We may now form some idea of the labor and pain it must have cost the Church to bring forth anew these Norman infidels to Jesus Christ, and to present them at last to her Divine Spouse, one of the most faithful people of the most Christian kingdom.

13. The pontificate of St. Leo IV. was drawing to a close in the midst of these bloody scenes. He had succeeded in preserving union and harmony between the Holy See and the emperor, in spite of the efforts of a party formed in the very heart of Rome, for the purpose of bringing back the pontifical domain to the condition of vassalage to the Eastern emperor. The holy Pope died on the 17th of July, A. D. 855. The Chair of St. Peter lost a great Pontiff, all Christendom a great hero. In Leo IV. the rarest virtues had met together : prudence, liberality, piety, humility, courage, love of justice, and an exhaustless charity. His name will ever command respect and admiration.

§ III. Pontificate of Benedict III. (September 1, A. D. 855— March 10, 858).

14. The unanimous voice of the Roman clergy and people called Benedict III. to fill the Chair of St. Peter, left vacant by the death of Leo IV. When the multitude came to escort him from his church of St. Callixtus, to place him upon the pontifical throne, the humble priest, throwing himself upon his knees and clinging to the altar, exclaimed, with tearful eyes : " Do not, I beseech you, take me from my church ; I am utterly unable to bear so great a dignity !" In spite of his resistance, he

was borne to the Lateran palace, amid the hymns and pious canticles of the enthusiastic people. They placed him upon the throne of Leo IV., the decree of election was drawn up and signed by the clergy and nobles, and sent, as usual, to the emperor Lothaire. Under the rule of the Gothic kings and their successors, the Greek emperors, civil intervention in the pontifical elections had been a source of ceaseless evils. In restoring the Western empire, the Popes had thought it safe to intrust the protectorate of the Roman Church to the descendants of Charlemagne. But this measure also became a fruitful source of fresh troubles. The spiritual authority must have a free and independent sphere of action; all outward control tends to become, in time, an odious tyranny. The history of the ninth and tenth centuries is but too replete with sad proofs of this fact. The deputies sent by the emperor to confirm the election and receive the oath of the new Pope, found, on their arrival in Rome, a faction supporting the nomination of a schismatical priest, named Anastasius, formally excommunicated by St. Leo IV. The antipope succeeded in gaining the imperial deputies. At the head of an armed troop, he entered the Leonine city, ordered the doors of St. Peter's church to be opened, and took possession of the basilica, tearing down, with Iconoclastic fury, the image of our Lord and His Blessed Mother. The clergy met on the next day in the church of St. Emiliana. The imperial envoys proposed to acknowledge Anastasius as Pope; but the assembly, with one voice, replied: "We will not have for Pope a priest solemnly deposed in council by Leo IV. Let him be anathema!" All efforts failed to shake this constancy. The cry arose on all sides: "Benedict is the lawful Pope! We will obey no other!" The ambassadors were at length obliged to yield to the public wish. Benedict III. was borne in triumph to the church of St. Mary Major, and solemnly consecrated on the 1st of September, A. D. 855.

15. A calumnious fable, accredited by the ignorance and bad faith of the age, seeks to thrust upon the pontifical throne, between the reigns of Leo IV. and Benedict III., the famous

Pope Joan.* The defenders of the calumny pretend, though without quoting a single contemporary authority in their favor, that a woman of superior genius, named Joan, a native of Mentz, had succeeded in hiding her sex, and entered into orders under the name of John of England. Raised by her talents to the highest ecclesiastical dignities, she had been elected Pope, in 856, under the title of John VIII. The story here runs into a strain of gross obscenity. During a solemn procession, the female Pope, seized with the pangs of childbirth, is delivered at the very portals of St. John Lateran. We pass over the disgraceful ceremony of the *Sedia*, which a modest pen must refuse to transcribe. The fable was at first eagerly examined by the disciples of Luther and Calvin, but has since been triumphantly refuted by the most enlightened Protestants, by David Blondell, Samuel Mares, Wagenseil, and Marquard Freer; it now remains but as a historical proof of the disgraceful extreme to which party spirit is capable of leading its victims.†

16. The same year that saw Benedict ascend the pontifical throne, saw the emperor Lothaire descend into the grave (A. D. 855). He had proved himself an ungrateful and unnatural son, a ruler without ability and without character. His declining years were imbittered by remorse for his shameful treatment of the best and most indulgent of fathers. He abdicated the throne and sought relief in the cloistered solitude of Prum, where he ended his days in the holy practices of a penitential life. Of his three sons, Louis, the eldest, kept the kingdom of Italy and assumed the title of emperor; Lothaire ruled the states watered by the Rhine and Meuse, thus confirming the name, already given to this territory, of Lorraine (*Lotharii regnum*); Charles inherited Provence and the adjacent country

---

* The anonymous authors of this absurd and sacrilegious fable do not even agree on the name of their female Pope. She is variously called by them Agnes, Angelica, Margaret, Jutta, Dorothea, Gilberta, and Isabella. The name of Joan at last prevailed.

† The most remarkable work produced by this question is the *Dona son exere stata Pontifiex*, by Fr. George Scherer, S. J. (Vienna, 1586, in 4to; Venice, 1636)

as far as Lyons. Thus was Charlemagne's inheritance cut up into disjointed fragments.

17. The accession of Michael III. to the throne of Constantinople was contemporaneous with the promotion of Benedict III. The unworthy son of the saintly empress Theodora was one of the most shameless defilers of the imperial dignity. Like another Nero, his highest study was to excel in the ignoble arts of the hippodrome. Surrounded by worthless debauchees, the partners of his midnight orgies, he delighted in travesties of the august ceremonies of religion. Theodora was condemned to a shameful banishment from the court, after suffering foul outrages from the jesters of her son, if such he may be styled. He confined her in a monastery, and ordered her to receive the religious habit at the hands of the Patriarch St. Ignatius. "Prince," said the intrepid Pontiff, "when I assumed the government of the Church of Constantinople, I swore to do nothing against your glory. If you seek to disgrace yourself by violence toward the one who gave you life, I cannot lend my ministry to further such an outrage." The empress died in prison, and her name is ranked with those of the saintly princesses whose memory is honored by the Church (A. D. 857). Michael III. had placed all his confidence in the patrician Bardas, his uncle, upon whom he conferred the title of Cæsar. Bardas was one of those ambitious characters who deem any road the right one, provided only it lead to power. A skilful politician, a friend of science, a patron of the learned, he everywhere made himself creatures, and he easily won the pardon of Michael for his superiority, by affecting to share all the imperial orgies. Making it his whole study to profit by his nephew's vices, his own life was a public scandal. He repudiated his wife to marry his daughter-in-law. Finding warnings of no avail, the Patriarch Ignatius was at length forced to excommunicate him. The furious minister would have dyed his sword in the prelate's blood; but the tranquil majesty of the holy archbishop was too powerful even for his sacrilegious hate. Yet he ever after made it his constant study to ruin St.

Ignatius. He banished him to the island of Terebintha : he had long since chosen the tool whom he intended to thrust into the vacant see.

18. Bardas commanded the fellowship of the eunuch Photius. Poet, mathematician, orator, grammarian, jurist, theologian, and statesman, Photius possessed at once the most refined intellect and the most perverse heart of his age; the most vast and cultivated, the boldest and most artful mind. His nobility of birth was heightened by alliance with the imperial family,* and illustrated by his two distinguished offices of master of the horse and of chief secretary, and by a celebrated mission to Syria. His was the power of wealth, of credit, of facility in making partisans, of giving plausibility to his guilty projects, and of even deceiving men of true worth. Religion, which he always regarded as a jest, had every thing to fear from an enemy of such a character. The Eastern Church, long since fallen from its first splendor by the neglect of holy teachings, by the overshadowing of every correct principle, now only needed the impulse of an unfriendly hand to plunge into the abyss of ruin. Photius became the instrument of this fearful catastrophe. In contempt of all canonical rule, and without even the form of an election, he was consecrated by the bishop of Syracuse, and on Christmas Day, A. D. 857, the future author of the great Eastern schism ascended the Patriarchal throne of Constantinople.

19. Benedict III. hardly outlived this fatal accession, so fraught with unknown evil for the future. He died on the 10th of March, A. D. 858, after a reign of two years. Endowed with a tender piety, full of meekness and charity, visiting the sick, ever accessible to the poor, his was the glory to see his very enemies pay an admiring and reverential tribute to his many virtues.

* He was son of the patrician Sergius and of Irene, daughter of the empress Theodora.

CHAPTER IV.

§ I. Pontificate of Nicholas I. the Great (April 25, a. d. 858—November 13, 866).

1. The approaching struggle between the Papacy and the Patriarch of Constantinople called for a Pontiff of consummate prudence, firmness and ability. God is watchful of His Church's destinies; He holds in reserve, in the treasures of His mercy, those noble souls destined to control the evil passions of an age; and when the hour has come, sends them forth into the world. Nicholas I., upon whom an admiring world bestowed the title of Great, was raised to the pontifical throne, on the 25th of April, a. d. 858. His humility suffered

violence in this elevation, and it was necessary to tear him from the church of St. Peter, in which he had sought to shelter himself from the dreaded dignity. He was taken in triumphal procession to St. John Lateran, for the ceremony of the *possessio*, and the emperor Louis II., who was then in Rome, would hold the bridle of the Pontiff's horse. Nicholas soon showed that his lively conviction of the obligations and perils of the pontifical charge would but nerve him to greater efforts in the faithful discharge of its duties.

2. Six days had sufficed to carry Photius through the inferior orders of the church to the Patriarchal dignity. Michael III. and his worthy minister, Bardas, were satisfied. Their former boon companion now ranked among the princes of the Church; he could hardly prove as unmanageable a censor as Ignatius, whose see he had usurped. Such an intrusion could not but result in the most disastrous consequences. It is worth observing that the Eastern schism, like most of the great heresies which have desolated the Church, had its root in the corrupt heart of an adulterous Cæsar striving to stifle the rebuking voice of a worthy ambassador of Christ, and found a minister in the unprincipled infidelity of an ambitious courtier. The seeds of schism had been sown in Constantinople, in the second general council, in 381. But it was reserved to Photius to give the final expression to the separation, and to bring it forth with all its political and religious perils. He tore the branch from the trunk, and the branch withered away, because it had not the life-stream which could come but from the great heart in Rome. He established a *Greek Church*, whereas Jesus Christ founded but the *one Catholic Church*, whose see St. Peter fixed at Rome. In division is death; in union is life and power. When the prophet's crescent threatens the Byzantine empire, and the suppliant cry of alarm is borne from Constantinople to the Roman Pontiffs, masters of Europe in the Middle Ages, the Popes, who could have guided the warlike spirit of the West to rescue the trembling East from the devouring surge of invading Islamism, and snatched

Constantinople from the grasp of Mohammed II., are overcome
in the effort by the treachery of the Greeks.

3. To hush the universal cry of indignation excited by his
sacrilegious intrusion, Photius strove to deceive Nicholas I. into
an approval, by an artful letter, a very tissue of lies and flat-
tery. "When I reflect," he wrote, "upon the weight of the
episcopal dignity, upon human weakness, and my own in particular, I cannot express the deep grief which fills my soul
when I find myself under this fearful yoke. But the emperor,
considerate to all others, reserves all his cruelty for me; as
soon as my predecessor had resigned his dignity, the assembled
metropolitans, clergy and people, moved I know not by what
impulse, with one voice uttered my name. Regardless of my
excuses and urgent prayers, they imposed upon me the episcopal dignity; they have done violence to my feelings, they have
done their will in spite of my tears and my despair." These
false protestations were presented to the Pope by an embassy
from Michael III., accompanied by four Greek bishops. In
order more completely to veil this imposture, the deputies were
instructed to ask the Pontiff for two legates to the East, for
the thorough extinction of the Iconoclastic heresy, which in
truth had now no existence whatever. The consummate prudence of Nicholas, and his fidelity to canonical observance,
saved him from the well-laid snare. "We cannot," he said, in
reply to the emperor, "by any means approve the irregular
promotion of Photius, until Ignatius declare before our legates
why he has resigned his see, and we ourselves canonically approve his demission, if there be valid reason for it. As soon
as we have received an exact and satisfactory report of these
facts, we shall take the steps best calculated to promote peace
and quiet in the Church of Constantinople." The legates of
the Holy See, Rodoald, bishop of Porto, and Zachary, bishop
of Anagni, set out for the East, with instructions to make
juridical inquiries (A. D. 859). Michael III. was but little concerned in the matter; his days were spent at table, in the company of his jesters. "Theophilus," he used to say, with a

laugh, "is my Patriarch" (Theophilus was the chief of his boon-companions); "Photius is the Patriarch of Bardas; and Ignatius is the Patriarch of the Christians." He hardly knew how truly he had spoken.

Photius and Bardas acted with greater energy. During the absence of their Roman embassy they had called a council at Constantinople, in which three hundred and eighteen bishops appeared. St. Ignatius was deposed on the ground that his election had not received the emperor's approval. The Papal legates had in the meantime reached Constantinople. Blinded to the true state of the case, ensnared by the intrigues of Photius, a perfect master in the art of deception, they had the weakness to betray their trust and to share in the deposition of the holy Patriarch. Ignatius was brought into the assembly and stripped of his pontifical vestments. As each part of his dress was successively removed, the guilty legates joined their voices to those of all the Greek bishops, to utter the Greek formula of degradation: Αναξιος (he is unworthy)! But even Photius, conscious of the glaring irregularity of this proceeding, sought to obtain a formal resignation from Ignatius. The Patriarch resolutely refused to give it, and was imprisoned in the empty tomb of Copronymus, whose ashes Michael III. had scattered to the winds. Here he was subjected to the most frightful torture. Overcome by suffering and hunger, stretched almost lifeless upon the imperial sarcophagus, the Patriarch was visited by a man whose features were hidden behind a mask, and who overwhelmed him with blows; then guiding the victim's nerveless hand, into which a pen had been forcibly thrust, he traced with it a cross upon a blank parchment, and took it to Photius, who wrote these words above the martyr's sign: "I, Ignatius, unworthy Patriarch of Constantinople, confess that I assumed the episcopal dignity without regular election, and that I have *tyranically* governed the Church intrusted to my care." Photius read the false instrument to the people, and then gave a copy of it to the legates, who were to present it to Pope Nicholas. They returned to Rome, accompanied by an ambassador from Michael III., bearing letters from the false Patriarch and the emperor to the Sovereign Pontiff.

4. The letter of Photius was worded thus: "Charity, which straightens the bonds of love, and breaks the toils of discord, should, by a stronger reason, remove all that could separate the father from his children. I write to justify my own position, not to contradict you. The reproaches addressed to me by your Holiness have been keenly felt; but I ascribe them wholly to your personal affection for me, and zeal for the discipline of the Church. Yet it is true that I am much more deserving of sympathy than of censure. I was elected in spite of my tears, my protestations and my despair. I have been guarded, confined like a criminal. I have been torn from the peace and quiet which I enjoyed amid a circle of virtuous friends devoted to the study of wisdom and truth. Your Holiness well knows the difficulties of the position in which I have been placed; the froward people, their seditious bent, their aversion for all authority. But, it may be said: You should have resisted violence. Are reproaches due to him who suffers, or to those who persecute? I have perhaps resisted more than was proper. Alas! had I not feared even worse consequences, I should have resisted unto death. Why, it may again be asked, violate the canons, which forbid the promotion of a layman to the episcopate? The Church of Constantinople, Most Holy Father, had not yet received the canons said to have been violated. And even in the West, would the Latins dare to condemn St. Ambrose, the glory of their Church?* I speak not in a spirit of opposition and resistance, for I have since advocated, in full council, the canonical precept, and I have caused the adoption of the rule that henceforth, throughout the East, no one shall be raised to the episcopate without having previously passed through all the antecedent orders of the clergy.†

---

* It will be remembered that St. Ambrose, then Governor of Milan, was a layman when the unanimous voice of clergy and people called him to the episcopal throne of that city.

† We may now clearly see how wise it would have been always to observe (save in the

But, for the present, it would be an insult to our fathers to give a retroactive effect to a recent law." Photius must have enjoyed a triumph, among his fellow-debauchees in the palace, for the craft and cunning of this lying letter. The legates, bound to fellowship with the impostor, gave a report correspondingly faithful. They dwelt upon the wisdom displayed in the last Council of Constantinople, upon the merit of Photius, "the most wonderful man who had illustrated the East for centuries, and whose talent had alone compelled his election, in spite of his natural modesty." Nicholas was not to be surprised by these deceptive reports, but wrote at once to the Patriarchs of Alexandria and Antioch, and to all the Eastern metropolitans, forbidding them to hold communion with the intruder. Wishing to inflict a signal punishment upon the scandalous connivance of his legates, he called a council at Rome (A. D. 863). Rodoald and Zachary, convicted of having basely betrayed their trust, were deposed from the episcopate and excommunicated. The false Council of Constantinople was solemnly annulled, and placed on a level with the Latrocinale of Ephesus. Sentence was thus pronounced : "Photius has dared, during the lifetime of our venerable brother Ignatius, Patriarch of Constantinople, to usurp his see, and *has entered the sheepfold like a robber;* he has, in contempt of all law and justice, caused the condemnation and deposition of Ignatius by a cabal; he has violated the law of nations to corrupt the legates of the Holy See, obliging them not only to infringe, but even to oppose, our orders; he ceases not to persecute the Church, and to inflict barbarous outrages upon our brother Ignatius. Wherefore, by the authority of Almighty God, of the Apostles St. Peter and St. Paul, Photius is hereby deprived of all priestly honor. As to our brother Ignatius, driven from his see by the violence of the emperor and the prevarication of our legates, we declare, in the name of Jesus Christ, that

few rare exceptions sanctioned by an extraordinary merit and approved by the Holy See) the rule laid down by St. Paul: Non neophytum; ne in superbiam elatus, in judicium incidat diaboli. (Tim. I iii. 6.)

he has never incurred either deposition or anathema, and we
maintain him in his episcopal dignity and functions." Photius
did not quail before this act of apostolic vigor and authority,
but forged a letter by which the Pope was made to approve
most fully of his ordination and of the false council of A. D. 859.
Secret as had been his manœuvres, they were speedily discovered by the public indignation, which soon rose to such a height
that Bardas, who had shared in the plot, was forced to satisfy
the public clamor by instituting inquiries. An unknown monk,
chosen by Photius as an accomplice in the disgraceful affair,
was publicly scourged; the tool was punished by the hand
that used it. But the emptiness of all these forms appeared
soon after, when the same monk, through the credit of Photius,
received an office in the magistracy of Constantinople itself.

5. The intruder's insolence did not stop here. In 866 he
summoned a fresh council in the church of St. Sophia, and
there pronounced sentence of deposition and excommunication
against Nicholas I. and his adherents. This unheard-of outrage against the authority of the Holy See was based upon a
thousand imaginary crimes heaped by Photius upon the Holy
Pontiff. The emperor, Michael III., all the senators of Constantinople, three legates in the East, magistrates, generals, and
more than a thousand bishops and priests signed the act of
deposition, which was then sent to the Pope himself, to all the
Churches of Asia, and to the Bulgarians, whom Nicholas had
lately received into the fold. Photius followed up this sacrilegious act by a circular declaring that the *Greek Church* is the
first and only true Church; that it must thenceforth remain
separated from the Church of Rome, "which has corrupted the
primitive purity of the faith." He then spoke thus of the
Latins : "Men have come forth from the darkness of the West
to alter the sacred traditional heritage of our fathers. Wandering wide from the way of truth, and plunging into the impious
errors of Manes, they take upon themselves to condemn the
Divine institution of marriage, and make it a crime in their
priests. Secret disorders and hidden immorality naturally fol-

low such a measure. They have crowned their impiety by the
addition of new words to the sacred symbol of our faith, declaring that the Holy Ghost does not proceed from the Father
only, but likewise from the Son. They also admit two principles in the Trinity, and confound the properties of the Divine
Persons." Thus the event justified the far-seeing prudence of
Pope Leo III., who had opposed the French bishops in their
untimely addition of the *Filioque*. Photius closed his circular
by applying to the Catholic priests the name of ministers of
Antichrist, and public corruptors. The indignation awakened
by his first acts of violence only served to call forth fresh out-
breaks from the bold schismatic. The sentence of excommunication issued by Pope Nicholas I. against the intruder had
caused a great sensation in Constantinople, and many of the
faithful refused to communicate with the schismatical Patriarch.
Photius visited all such demonstrations with the punishment
due to rebellion and sedition. The Catholic bishops who dared
to oppose him were deposed and banished to distant cities.
The holy Patriarch Ignatius, still on the list of proscription,
saw a price set upon his head. He had fled his mother's
palace, disguised as a porter, just in time to escape the assassins sent by Bardas to murder him. Wandering and a fugitive,
he escaped the searches and pursuits of his enemies only by a
continued miracle. Photius, ever impelled onward as he gave
freer reign to the hatred and vengeance that burned within his
breast, aimed at nothing less than the utter ruin of the Roman
Church. He undertook to tear from the communion of the
Pope all the countries under Frankish domination, which formed
so considerable a portion of the Western world that they were
commonly called the Empire or the Kingdom or the Christians.
To gain the emperor Louis I., he had bestowed upon him, in
his false council, the titles of Imperator, Cæsar, and Augustus,
regardless of the claims so loudly put forth by the Byzantine
chancery, since the time of Charlemagne, against the usurpation—such was their term—of the Frankish kings. The
empress Ingelberga, who wielded a great influence over the

mind of her husband, had been also honored with the titles of Augusta and Second Pulcheria. The acts of the council were sent with gifts and adulatory letters, begging Ingelberga to use her influence with the emperor to drive Nicholas I. from Rome, as deposed by an ecumenical council.

6. In the midst of all these negotiations, a revolution, fraught with mighty results, was preparing in the East. Its accomplishment was intrusted to a man of strange and varied fortunes. In the year 851 a wretched captive, a native of Adrianople, dragged into bondage by his Bulgarian captors, had succeeded in breaking his chains, and came to Constantinople to seek a livelihood. Destitute and hopeless of obtaining a lodging in the imperial city, he laid his weary limbs upon the steps of the church of St. Diomede, without the city walls. The keeper of the church found the homeless wanderer there, and, moved by pity, took him in. Basil, the unknown mendicant, had learned among the barbarians the art of taming the most unruly horse. Michael III., in his youthful days, was passionately devoted to horsemanship, and had in his stables a splendid Arabian steed, which no man had yet ventured to mount. In a fit of impatient anger, he orders the noble animal to be hamstrung, when some courtiers mention Basil as a man who can tame the new Bucephalus. The fractious beast is brought into the hippodrome, where an immense crowd had assembled to witness the trial. After a few moments of flattering caresses, Basil masters the fiery steed, and rides him round the circus, amid thunders of applause. The enthusiastic emperor names him, on the spot, chief groom of the palace. "What a master-horseman they have given me!" said Michael to his mother, Theodora. "My son," replied the empress, "this horseman will be the ruin of our house." The prediction was received by Michael III. with an incredulous smile. In 854 the groom was made great chamberlain. Bardas was a stumbling-block in his way to honors, and Basil persuaded the emperor that his minister was plotting his murder. The credulous emperor resolved to anticipate the deed by the death of its

NICHOLAS I. (A. D. 858-867).   499

intended author; but this act of imperial rigor would have blasted
all the hopes of Photius, who accordingly used every means to
reconcile the emperor and his minister. On the feast of the
Annunciation (A. D. 866), the emperor, Basil and Bardas were
all present at the Holy Sacrifice in the church of St. Sophia.
After the consecration, Photius, holding in his hand the sacred
host, turned to the emperor and his chamberlain, and made
them swear not to attempt the life of Bardas. Then, dipping
a pen into the blood of Jesus Christ, he made them sign the
solemn promise. Three days had not passed away when the
chamberlain stabbed Bardas, in the emperor's apartment (April
7, 866), and before another year the same dagger had drunk
the blood of Michael III. himself, in the hour of intoxication
(September 24, 867). Thus Basil* possessed himself of the
throne, to which he restored its long-lost dignity. The administration of the Empire was reorganized. The venal judiciary
was removed; the active pursuits of commerce, agriculture,
science, art and industry illustrated his reign. Constantinople
and the great cities of the Empire were adorned by the erection
of churches, hospitals and educational institutions. The Latin
of Justinian's code was not the tongue of Byzantium; and this
co-operated with legislative madness—unmistakable token of a
declining nation—to throw confusion into the legislation of the
Empire. Basil wished to dispel the darkness, and to let in the
light of simple, clear and settled principles, for the restoration
of justice. He gave his attention to the revision of the statutes,
and the Justinian code disappeared, to make way for the *Basilics*, which held their deserved authority until the fall of the
Greek Empire and the rule of the Koran.† Two days after
his accession, Basil removed Photius from the Patriarchal See,

---

* Basil was called the Macedonian, from his long captivity in that province. The keeper
of the church of St. Diomede was not forgotten by the crowned beggar. He was made
treasurer of St. Sophia, and *Syncellus* of the Patriarch.

† In 1830 the celebrated but unfortunate Capo of Istria named a commission to revise
the *Basilics*, which he, in great part, applied to the government of the new kingdom of
Greece.

as a disturber of the public peace; St. Ignatius was recalled, and the schism seemed extinct; but this was only a momentary pause in the career of Photius.

7. The tidings of this temporary restoration had not yet reached Nicholas I. He wrote to the bishops of Gaul, then in council at Troyes, to warn them against the schismatical attempts of Photius (A. D. 867). "Of all the troubles which weigh upon our pontificate," wrote the great Pope, "the condition of the East is that which most grieves our heart. The emperor Michael III. has plunged his Empire into a schism, because of our refusal to sanction the irregular election of the intruded Patriarch, Photius. A false council, held in Constantinople, has even dared to outrage the rights and honor of the Apostolic See. They make it a crime in us to teach the Catholic doctrine of the procession of the Holy Ghost from the Father and Son. They accuse us of condemning marriage, because we enjoin celibacy to our clergy. They dare to assert that, by removing the seat of the Empire to Constantinople, the emperors also transferred with it the primacy of the Roman Church and the prerogatives of honor and apostolical supremacy. Photius has even assumed the title of Universal Patriarch. As it is impossible to convene you all in Rome, to take measures against these bold attempts, we earnestly exhort you to meet in provincial councils, to examine the complaints and claims of the Eastern Church, that the unanimous voice of the West may crush this rising calumny." (A. D. 866.)

8. The Churches of Gaul and Germany, thus addressed by the Holy Pontiff, had for the past ten years been the theatre of scandalous disputes. While imperial dissipation, the corruption of an adulterous minister, and the ambition of an intruded prelate had plunged the East into a sea of misery, the guilty passion of a Frankish prince had destroyed the peace of the West. In 856, Lothaire II., king of Lorraine, a year after his union with Teutberga, became madly enamored of Waldrada, sister of Gunthier, archbishop of Cologne. The time had passed when a Frankish king could tie or break the conjugal bond at

will. The Church, by insisting upon the indissolubility of the
marriage tie, besides maintaining the respect due to the sanctity
of a sacrament of Divine institution, secured the quiet of individuals, the peace of the domestic circle, the regular transmission of inheritance, the dignity of woman, union among brothers,
all the bonds and duties of the family—without which nations
soon become degraded, the light of civilization pales and gradually becomes extinct: witness Mohammedanism sunk in the
shameful luxury and barren idleness of the seraglio. The
immense services thus rendered to modern nations by the
Papacy are not sufficiently understood. But for the unyielding
perseverance of the Sovereign Pontiffs, the barbarian elements
reigning in the midst of European society, during the ninth
and tenth centuries, would have triumphed over the most
sacred moral principles; and the world, buried in the mire of
vice, would never have reached the high degree of civilization
of which we are so proud, but yet so far from grateful.

9. Blinded by his adulterous passion, and determined to
have it legalized by the Holy See at any cost, Lothaire had
recourse to a shameless deceit: he brought against the empress
an infamous charge, capable of securing the dissolution of their
marriage, according to the laws of the Church. Teutberga
availed herself of the justification then accredited by popular
superstition—the *judgment of God* by the sword. The champion
chosen to defend her honor came forth unhurt from the combat,
and, in conformity with the ruling custom, Lothaire was forced
to give back to Teutberga her rank of queen and spouse. But
he could not give back a heart whose affection was all centred
in another object. The apparent reconciliation was but short-
lived; Lothaire banished Teutberga from the royal palace (A.
D. 859), and openly lived with Waldrada. Sinful example is
contagious; the court of the royal adulterer soon became a
mere brothel. Boson, count of Burgundy, deemed it a safe
asylum for his incestuous partner, Engeltrudis. Baldwin,
afterward count of Flanders, also sought impunity here for a
crime of the same nature. He had outraged the royal family

by the elopement of Judith, daughter of Charles the Bald, and
cousin-german to Lothaire, who was too utterly steeped in licen-
tiousness himself to oppose corruption in another. He still
strove to win the sanction of the Church for his scandalous
connection with Waldrada. An assembly of eight bishops, at
Aix-la-Chapelle, pronounced the dissolution of his former marriage with Teutberga; the injured queen was sent to a monastery, and Lothaire solemnly espoused Waldrada (A. D. 862).
But from the depths of her solitary prison the prayers of
the wronged and innocent queen had reached the foot of St.
Peter's throne. The Sovereign Pontiff learned the fearful
alternative to which she was exposed, either to dishonor herself
or to be exposed to the direst extremes of suffering. "Should
your Holiness learn," said she, "that I have at length made the
lying confession required of me, be persuaded that violence
alone can have wrung it from a wretched queen, more shamelessly ill-treated than the lowest slave." With this secret
communication the tidings also reached Rome of Lothaire's
solemn union with Waldrada. Nicholas I. did not hesitate an
instant between the wronged and powerless victim and the
crowned oppressor. He belonged to the race of iron Pontiffs,
who "stand," in the words of the Sacred Text, "like a firm
wall against the criminal attempts of the wicked." The bishops
of Gaul and Germany received a pontifical decree, enjoining
them to meet in council at Metz, to cite Lothaire, and to pronounce a canonical sentence against him. Rodoald, the faithless bishop of Porto, was returning from his legation in Constantinople, where he had betrayed his trust. The Pope, still
ignorant of his defection, sent him, together with John, bishop
of Ficolo,* to preside, in his name, at the council, which was
opened in the month of June, 863. All the prelates of Lothaire's kingdom were present, save the bishop of Utrecht.
By unlimited largesses and honors Lothaire had disposed the

---

* The present Cervia, in the States of the Church, about eleven miles southeast of
Ravenna.

leading prelates far more favorably than he could have done
by any process of law or canonical jurisprudence. Even the
legates yielded to these disgraceful arguments. Rodoald of
Porto proved as unworthy of his high mission at Metz as he
had been at Constantinople, and his shameful example was
followed by his colleague. The last Council of Aix-la-Chapelle
was confirmed, the marriage with Teutberga declared null, and
the union with Waldrada acknowledged as lawful. Adultery
was triumphant. Gunthier, Waldrada's brother and archbishop
of Cologne, and Teutgald, bishop of Triers, the two leading
spirits in the work of iniquity, were deputed by the Council
of Metz to accompany the legates to Rome and present the
scandalous decision to the Sovereign Pontiff.

10. Nicholas I. was, perhaps, of all the Popes the most
impervious to the miserable calculations of human respect, and
his sagacity in unravelling the most skilfully concerted plots
was equalled by his courage in the defence of injured innocence. "Senseless indeed," exclaims a contemporary annalist,
speaking of the two prelates, "if they flattered themselves
that their vain subtleties could cast a shadow impenetrable to
the torch of the Apostolic See." On their arrival they found
all the Italian bishops convoked by the Pope to annul the acts
of the Council of Metz. Gunthier and Teutgald were brought
before the assembled prelates. Nicholas received them with
imposing dignity. When the renegade bishops timidly presented the decrees of Metz, signed by their own hands, with a
request that he would give them his apostolic sanction, the
Pontiff only replied: "Withdraw; the council will call you
when your presence is needed." And in a few days they
were summoned to hear the condemnation of their Council of
Metz; and as they persisted in maintaining its lawful authority, they were both deposed from the episcopate. The same
punishment was inflicted upon the faithless legates. Rodoald
was already under the weight of the excommunication uttered
against him while on his way to France, for his disgraceful
conduct at Constantinople. The Council of Rome pronounced

sentence in these terms: " By the judgment of the Holy Ghost
and the authority of the Prince of the Apostles, we annul the
acts of the Council of Metz, composed of bishops who have
anticipated our decision and dared to violate the regulations of
the Holy See. We remove from episcopal dignity and functions Teutgald, archbishop of Triers and primate of Belgium,
with Gunthier of Cologne, both convicted, by their writings
and open confession, of having led that irregular assembly.
Upon the other bishops, their accomplices, we pass the same
sentence, if they persist in their error; but, should proofs of
their sincere repentance reach the Apostolic See, they shall lose
neither their rank nor dignity." Lothaire II. was also threatened
with excommunication unless he would put away Waldrada.
Throughout the whole kingdom of the Franks, the liveliest
indignation had been excited by this scandal. Charles the Bald
and Louis of Bavaria befriended the unfortunate queen Teutberga, and were preparing to support her rights by force of
arms. Lothaire, terrified by the dangerous consequences of his
passion, yielded to the pressure against him, and put away the
cause of all these evils (A. D. 865). But his resolution was
too weak for his love, and in the following year he resumed his
scandalous life. This time St. Nicholas launched the thunders
of the Church against Waldrada, and called a council at Soissons to end the deplorable affair (A. D. 866). In a letter to
Adventius, bishop of Metz, the Pontiff warned the French
bishops against the allurements held out by the temporal
power, and settled the limits within which they might freely
exercise their episcopal independence. " You pretend," he
writes, " that you are subject to your prince, because the
Apostle says : ' Be ye subject ...... to the king as excelling.'
In this you are right; but first see whether princes command
only what is just : otherwise they are rather to be looked upon
as tyrants than as kings, and their orders should be opposed
rather than obeyed; for by compliance we become accessory to
their disorders. Be subject, then, to the king, as excelling by
his virtues, and not by his vices. Be subject to him for God's

sake, according to the Apostle, and not against God."[*]   The
Council of Soissons restored the tarnished honor of the French
episcopate. The shameless Lothaire was unanimously condemned; the acts of base connivance and venal weakness of
Aix-la-Chapelle and Metz were rescinded.

11. The noble Pontiff was called to engage in a struggle
of another sort with Hincmar, archbishop of Rheims. This
prelate, yielding too readily to a personal prejudice, had deposed and imprisoned Rothade, bishop of Soissons, one of his
suffragans, on the ground of too great rigor used by the bishop
in interdicting a priest of his diocese, who appealed from his
sentence to the judgment of the metropolitan. The bishop, in
turn, appealed to the Holy See. Mature deliberation convinced
the Pope of Rothade's innocence, and Hincmar was directed to
restore the bishop to his see within a month after the reading
of the pontifical letters. In his irritation against Rothade.
Hincmar resorted to a subterfuge, unworthy of himself, to
elude the pontifical decree. Learning its contents before
opening it, he would not read the letter, thus sheltering himself by the clause which granted a delay of a month after the
reading of the bull for restoring the deposed prelate. It is painful to meet such a display of bad faith in the life of a prelate
like Hincmar; but the highest and greatest are also subject to the
petty passions of fallen humanity, and it is the continued miracle
of the Church that she remains ever pure, ever intact, despite
the miseries and weakness of her ministers. On learning the in-
delicate course pursued by the archbishop, Nicholas might have
used harsh measures; but justice and mercy were enthroned
with twin power in his great and noble soul, and he was satis-

---

[*] These words of Nicholas I. have furnished matter for long discussions on the obedience due to the secular power. It is pretended that they tend to set subjects in judgment
upon their rulers. This interpretation seems to us utterly without foundation; it would,
moreover, be in direct opposition, if we may so speak, to the constant policy of the Holy
See. To us it seems evident that when the Pope speaks of resistance he refers only to
spiritual matters. The tyrants of whom he speaks are the princes who abuse their power,
as did Lothaire II., in the order of religion. Hence there can be in this no incitement to
revolt, nor to the seditious instincts of the masses.

fied to write him a second letter, using the precaution necessary
to insure its reception. "You once asked us," wrote the Pontiff, " to confirm, by our Apostolic authority, the privileges
granted by our predecessors to the Church of Rheims. What
can be the value of these privileges, if you ignore the power
which instituted them?" Then, laying open the greatness of
his fault, the disorders to which it could give rise in the hierarchy, he urges him to free Rothade from his confinement.
Still Hincmar but half obeyed the Holy Pontiff's orders. The
bishop was released from prison, but only to be sent to Rome,
that his case might be examined there. Hincmar's letter to
the Pope on the subject breathes too much the subtle reasoning
of the law, and is far from the spirit of true submission which
should ever bow the heart of every bishop to the common
Father of all the faithful. "Most Holy Father and reverend
lord," writes the prelate, " we send you Rothade, accompanied
by our deputies; nor do we appear as the accuser of the bishop
of Soissons, but as ourself arraigned, wishing to justify ourself
by representing to your Holiness our proceedings and intentions. Our respect for the first See, the Sovereign See of the
Church of Rome, is too great to allow that we should weary
its Pontiff with minor causes, which the canons of councils and
the decrees of the Popes authorize metropolitans to decide in
provincial councils. *We know, too, that we can expect obedience
and respect from our inferiors only in proportion as we show ourselves submissive toward our own superiors.* Should the merciful
compassion of your Holiness deem it proper to reinstate the
bishop of Soissons, the prelates who acted with us in the
council by which he was deposed would not look upon the act
of authority as an injustice. They recognize their dependence
on the Roman Pontiff, in virtue of the supremacy of St.
Peter." After a serious and deliberate examination, which
lasted ten months, the Pope relieved Rothade from the censures
laid upon him by his metropolitan, fully reinstated him in his
episcopal office, and wished him to officiate pontifically in one
of the churches of Rome. For Rothade, whose conduct during

the whole proceeding seems to have been irreproachable, had faithfully observed the interdict, though deeming it unjust, and had not, accordingly, offered up the Holy Sacrifice. Nicholas then sent him back to his Church of Soissons, and wrote, at the same time, to Charles the Bald to interpose his authority in favor of Rothade, while threatening Hincmar with excommunication, if he offered further opposition to the execution of the Apostolic sentence. The archbishop submitted. His bearing had been in direct contradiction to the principles he always maintained in his writings; but this is not the first example in history of the ruinous power of passion over even the greatest minds. In a treatise on the indissolubility of the marriage tie, Hincmar thus speaks of the supremacy of the Holy See: " In all doubts on matters of faith we must consult the Roman Church, the mother and mistress of all others, and follow her salutary counsels. And this filial submission may more readily be expected from those who inhabit Italy, Gaul, Spain, Africa, Sicily and the neighboring islands, where the faith was certainly planted by evangelical laborers who had received their mission from St. Peter or his successors."

12. This faith, intrusted as a sacred deposit to the Church of Rome, was hourly making new conquests. The Western emperors helped to the conversion of the Danes, the Suevi, and generally of all the German nations; the emperors of the East sent missionaries to evangelize the Sclavonic race, whose conversion opened a way, for the faith of Christ, into the empire of their Russian neighbors. They readily admitted the light of faith, and the emperor Basil profited by the circumstance to conclude a treaty of peace with them; and having softened their natural fierceness by timely presents, he sent them a bishop consecrated by Ignatius, Patriarch of Constantinople. The miracles wrought by the holy bishop overcame the people's incredulity; they eagerly sought and devoutly received the sacrament of regeneration. The Bulgarians were likewise indebted to the East for the blessing of faith. In their war against the Greek emperor Theophilus, the barbarians had lost

an important battle, and the sister of their king was among the
captives who had fallen into the victor's hands. The princess
was taken with the captive train to Constantinople, where she
was detained for a space of thirty-eight years. This long
interval she improved by studying the teaching of the true
faith, and was at length baptized. On her return to her
brother's court, the princess earnestly and perseveringly pressed
him to embrace Christianity. Her unwearied endeavors moved
the king, and Heaven seemed to league with her to subdue the
royal infidel. An appeal to the God of his sister suddenly
stayed the ravages of a destructive plague. The prodigy was
convincing: the king was baptized. The Bulgarians rose up
against their Christian king, and laid siege to his palace; but,
strong in the confidence of Heaven's assistance, he came forth
with a handful of faithful followers, and scattered the seditious
throng. The rebels were forgiven. This act of mercy opened
their eyes to a clearer view of the Christian faith, and they too
were folded with the flock of Christ. The king now sent
deputies to the Holy See to beg for evangelic workmen, and to
obtain light on several points of faith and morals. The Pope
was touched by the sight of the new Christians coming from
afar to receive the teaching of St. Peter's successor; he received
them with paternal affection, answered all their questions, and
sent them back rejoicing, accompanied by two bishops of known
wisdom and virtue. The establishment of each new Church
affords another example of the ready homage paid by all the
missionaries to the primacy of the Roman See. All the apostles
sent from among the Anglo-Saxons and Franks seek their war-
rant directly from the Holy See, and place the people converted
through their means under its immediate jurisdiction; the missionaries sent from the East look at once to Rome for the
decision of every important question, and bow submissive to
her decree. Providence would seem to have doomed the Greek
Church to pronounce its own condemnation in the face of the
whole world, some years before its schism.

13. These consoling events threw a ray of happiness over

the last days of Nicholas I., who ended a pontificate of nine years on the 13th of November, 867. His lofty conceptions and unbending resolution appeared in the immense labors of his pontificate. At home, he had to meet the evils of the age, to provide for the necessities of the poor and the safety of Rome; abroad, to check the efforts of schism, refute calumnies, and protest against the wanderings of rulers, without moving subjects to revolt. Yet Nicholas trod the dangerous ground with firm and steady step. With all his multiplied occupations, he still found time to answer the questions put from all parts of the world. A collection of more than a hundred letters of the energetic Pontiff shows the vast but sure sweep of his great mind.[*] His death threw a veil of mourning over the face of the world. Crime alone exulted in its dark retreats; but its guilty hopes were doomed to bitter disappointment.

§ II. Pontificate of Adrian II. (November 13, a. d. 867—November 25, 872).

14. The death of Nicholas I. revived in the depraved heart of Lothaire II. the criminal hope of seeing his adultery at length legalized. The fearless Pontiff had thus expressed himself in a letter written a few days before his death: "We are told that Lothaire intends to come to Rome, notwithstanding our prohibitions. Dissuade him from the step; represent to him that while he is under the Church's ban he could not be received in this city with the honors due to his rank, which he can claim only after the fulfilment of promises so often violated." The state of many minds presented serious difficulties. It had been with Nicholas I. as with all men who wield their power with energy: he had made enemies of all those whose excesses or sinful endeavors he had checked; while those who had been the ministers of his justice, or had held office in his pontificate, were his avowed partisans. One

---

[*] These alone have reached us. Anastasius Bibliothecarius had collected more than double the number, and yet, as he himself testifies, his collection was far from complete.

class hoped for every thing from a new Pontiff; the other feared lest the acts and the memory of Nicholas should be compromised. The event justified neither their hopes nor their fears. A venerable priest, of seventy-six years, Adrian II., the mildest of men, was borne in triumph by the clergy, the senate, and the people to the Lateran palace, where he was consecrated on the 13th of November, 867, with the consent of the emperor, Louis II. The lion was followed by the lamb; and by a wonderful dispensation of Providence, the gentleness of Adrian was destined to keep unharmed the heritage of his stern predecessor. The new Pope's accession was marked by deeds of mercy. Teutgald, archbishop of Triers, and the faithless legate, Zachary of Anagni, were freed from the censures imposed upon them, and restored to ecclesiastical communion. Serious fears were entertained by the friends of the preceding Pontiff. Anastasius Bibliothecarius* thus wrote to his friend, the archbishop of Vienne: "I write you sad tidings. Alas! our great Pontiff, Nicholas, passed to a better life on the 13th of November, leaving us overwhelmed with the deepest grief. The wicked men whom he so vigorously rebuked for their crimes now openly strive to overturn all the great works of his pontificate. Communicate this sad intelligence to all the Gallic bishops, and do whatever your zeal may suggest for the Church of God. The new Pope, Adrian, is likewise a man of exemplary life, but we cannot yet know whether he possesses the active energy of his predecessor." The archbishop of Vienne, to whom this confidential letter was addressed, was the illustrious Ado, who had just published his Roman Martyrology, a most estimable work, from the wholesome spirit of criticism which distinguishes it. In common with the other Gallic prelates, he wrote to the new Pontiff, exhorting him to honor the memory and respect the acts of his predecessor.

---

* Anastasius received his surname from his office of librarian of the pontifical archives. In 869 he was present at the eighth general council held in Constantinople, and translated its acts into Latin. He is the author of the Liber Pontificalis, which contains the biographies of the Popes from St. Peter down to his own time, and also of an Ecclesiastical History.

16. Adrian determined to remove all doubts, and to give a positive character to his pontificate. It was customary for the Popes to gather into the Lateran palace, on Friday in Septuagesima week, all the religious present in Rome. This assembly always counted some deputies sent by various princes to assist at the solemnity. Adrian II. added to the august character of the meeting (A. D. 868); he waited upon all the religious, washed their feet, as our Lord had done for His Apostles, and finally sat at the same table with them. At the end of the meal the Pope knelt with all the assembly, saying: " Let us pray, my brethren, for the Catholic Church, for our most Christian son, the emperor Louis; that God may humble the pride of the Saracens by his arms. Pray, too, for me, that God may grant me strength to govern His Church in holiness. As prayers for the good should be but real thanksgiving, I beg you to thank God for having given to His Church our lord and lamented Father, the very holy and orthodox Pope Nicholas, to defend it like another Joshua." The Pontiff was here interrupted by loud applause, and the unanimous cry arose: " Long live Adrian, our Father and our lord! No evil report shall hurt him! Let envy hide its poisoned dart! Long life to Adrian, chosen of God, Sovereign Pontiff and universal Pope!" The Pontiff motioned for silence, and then proceeded in a grave and steady voice: " To the holy and orthodox lord Nicholas, established by God, Sovereign Pontiff and universal Pope, be undying memory! May deathless life and glory crown the new Elias! Eternal salvation to the new Phineas, worthy of the everlasting priesthood!" Not content with this public expression of sentiment, Adrian wrote to the bishops of Gaul: " We exhort you to inscribe the name of Pope Nicholas in your sacred diptychs. We likewise enjoin you rigorously to resist all princes or clerics who may attempt any thing contrary to his teachings or decrees, for we shall never consent to any such proceeding. Yet we would not act harshly toward those who implore the mercy of the Holy See, after a reasonable satisfaction, provided they do not strive to

free themselves by accusing that great Pope, who is now before God, and whom no one dared to accuse while on earth." He also wrote thus, in reply to the archbishop of Vienne: "I purpose to uphold my predecessor's decrees as I would defend my own. Still, I have no desire to lay aside the quality of mercy. If the juncture obliged him to be severe, nothing can hinder us from acting otherwise, under different circumstances." These few words contain the whole of Adrian's policy. He knew that, to gather the fruit of Nicholas' vigor, the timely application of gentleness was necessary, and that the inviting paths of mildness would call back the souls which unyielding sternness might estrange forever.

16. Lothaire sought to avail himself of Adrian's indulgent disposition to obtain readmission into his communion. He sent to Rome the bishop of Metz, Adventius, accompanied by his chancellor, and bearing letters to the Sovereign Pontiff, in which he said: "I have bowed to the authority of Pope Nicholas, or rather to the authority of the Prince of the Apostles, with a docility unknown to my predecessors. I have followed the paternal advice and exhortations of his legates, even to the prejudice of my dignity. I have never ceased to beg that I might be heard at Rome, in my own defence, in the calumnies uttered against me. This he ever refused me, and forbade my visiting the Holy See, of which my ancestors have ever been the willing defenders." Lothaire now gave his whole attention to the means of furthering the interests of his passions in this journey. He sent before him to the Sovereign Pontiff the wretched queen Teutberga, so wearied and broken by the ill-treatment suffered during the last ten years from the royal adulterer that she even begged to be freed from the bond of a union which could bring to her but tears and misery. She asked to spend the remainder of her days in a monastery, there to find consolation, at the foot of the altar, for the bitterness of royalty and the sorrows of her life. Adrian II. replied that he could not grant her request; but promised to convoke a council for the mature consideration of so vexed a question

recommending her, at the same time, to return to Lothaire, to whom he wrote to treat Teutberga as his lawful spouse, and to give her the abbeys which he had promised her, that she might not be left in utter destitution. So unrelenting had been the persecution against Teutberga, that a holy Pope, who could not but censure the abuse of giving up benefices to laymen, was forced to sanction such a proceeding as an alms to a wronged and needy queen.

17. Lothaire received Teutberga, hoping thus to win the Pontiff's favor, and Waldrada asked for absolution from the anathema pronounced against her by Pope Nicholas. She engaged the intervention of Louis II., who assured the Pontiff of her sincere repentance. Relying upon the emperor's word, Adrian wrote to absolve Waldrada from the censures she had incurred, to enable her to enter the churches, there to assist at public prayers and ceremonies, and to communicate with the faithful; but yet he forbade her any communication whatever with Lothaire. Deeming the opportunity favorable to his views, Lothaire set out for Italy, accompanied by the empress Engelberga, as witness to the sincerity of his penance and promises. The interview between the Pope and the king took place at Monte Cassino (A. D. 869). The artful prince showed all the submission which he thought capable of gaining the Pope. Already he exulted in the success of his false protestations. The day was fixed for his solemn rehabilitation and the ceremony of communion, which he wished to receive from Adrian in person, to give more splendor to his reconciliation with the Church. He saw not the arm of Divine justice as it descended upon him now, to show to the world, in the person of an adulterous prince, one of the most fearful punishments of sacrilegious communion. At the end of the pontifical mass, celebrated in the presence of all the nobles of the court, of a numerous body of the clergy, and of an immense multitude of the faithful, attracted by the grandeur of the solemnity, Adrian II., holding in his hands the sacred body of the Lord, turned toward the king, and addressed him in a clear and distinct

voice: "Prince, if you are guiltless of the crime of adultery,
since the warning given you by our holy predecessor Nicholas;
if you have firmly resolved to hold no further communication
with Waldrada, come with confidence to receive the sacrament
of everlasting life; but if your repentance be not sincere, dare
not profane the sacred body and blood of the Lord, and thus
consummate your own damnation." Lothaire must have shud-
dered inwardly, at least, at the words which awakened in
the depths of his heart the horrible sense of his past life, and
of the fresh crime he was about to commit. But his resolution was taken; he would not withdraw; he added perjury to
sacrilege, and rather than stay the fatal step, he plunged into
the abyss so plainly yawning at his feet. The Pope addressed
these words to each of the nobles who communicated with
Lothaire: "If you have neither contributed nor consented to
the adulterous connection of your master with Waldrada, and
have held no communication with any of the other persons
condemned by the Holy See, may the body of the Lord be to
you a pledge of eternal life." Terrified at the prospect of
open sacrilege, some, and they were the few, abstained from
receiving the sacred Eucharist, but the greater number shared
the crime of their king. Lothaire strove to drive away the
remorse which tore his heart at the thought of this terrible
scene. He hastened his departure, wholly intent upon the
object of his blind and sinful passion, whom he longed to
rejoin. But his course was stayed at Lucca by an unknown
disease, the effects of which were at that time without example.
The hair, the nails and even the skin fell from his body, as by
an anticipated death incessantly renewed. All those who had
shared his sacrilege also shared the punishment, and perished
before his eyes; among them was Gunthier, the unworthy
archbishop of Cologne. They alone who had withdrawn from
the holy table were spared. Lothaire expired in fearful torments, without the least sign of repentance (A. D. 869). Teutberga wept her faithless spouse as though he had never given
her cause of grief. Waldrada took the veil in the monastery

of Remiremont; happy if tears of sincere repentance could blot out the disorders of her past life, and the remorse of having perhaps caused the eternal loss of a soul by her artifices and unchaste allurements.

18. The states of Lothaire II., who had died without issue, should of right have reverted to his brother, Louis II. But Charles the Bald, though unable to defend his present territory against the Norman inroads, still showed himself none the less eager to acquire more. He marched into Lorraine, had himself proclaimed king, to his nephew's detriment, and was crowned by Hincmar, archbishop of Rheims. Adrian II. could not allow so glaring a usurpation. He sent legates to Charles to insist upon the rights of the emperor Louis, and to show him the shameless injustice of despoiling a Christian prince, his own nephew, who was then engaged in fighting the Saracens in Italy, thus devoting his life to the cause of the whole of Christendom. Some historians, slaves to party considerations, have sought to convict Adrian II. of interfering, without any right whatever, in a question of temporal domain entirely foreign to his jurisdiction. The Pope could not overstep the bounds of duty by taking in hand the cause of right and justice. The emperor himself had intrusted his interests to the Pontiff's keeping. Had the voice of the Holy See not been disregarded, France would have been spared a great convulsion and torrents of her children's blood. However this may be, a fresh dispute arose on this point between the Holy See and Hincmar, who showed again how little he could keep within the limits of submission and respect due to the Apostolic Supremacy. Charles vainly endeavored to obtain the Pope's approval of his usurpation, which force alone could now make good. But Adrian's attention was called to the East by matters more essential to the peace of the Church.

19. The ambassadors of the emperor Basil, who had set out immediately upon the expulsion of Photius, reached Rome after the death of Nicholas I. and Adrian's accession (A. D 868). They brought tidings of immense import, which were

received by the new Pontiff with transports of joy. He at
once dispatched three legates to Constantinople: Donatus,
bishop of Ostria; Stephen, bishop of Nepi; and Marinus, one
of the seven deacons of the Roman Church; bearing letters to
the emperor and to the holy Patriarch Ignatius. The Pontiff
thus addressed Basil: "Heartfelt and sincere is the joy of the
West at the expulsion of Photius by an act of your impartial
justice. For the measures to be taken concerning the other
schismatics, our legates will confer with our venerable brother
Ignatius. We are disposed to use the greatest possible indulgence toward them all save Photius, whose consecration must
be wholly rejected. We approve the convocation of a general
council, over which our legates will preside, for the final judgment of the guilty, the annulment of the false council of
866, which outraged the dignity of the Holy See, and to sign
the decrees of the Council of Rome against Photius." The
legates were awaited with signal impatience by the emperor,
the clergy and the people of Constantinople; their arrival
amid the acclamations of the people and every testimony of the
public joy was a real triumph (September 24, A. D. 868). The
emperor Basil, surrounded by all the officers of the crown,
received them in the Golden Hall of the palace. Rising at
their approach, he took from their hands the pontifical letters,
which he kissed respectfully, and thus addressed the legates:
"The Church of Constantinople, rent by the ambition of Photius, has already experienced the unerring guidance and fatherly
affection of Pope Nicholas. Since his death we have been
awaiting, with all the Patriarchs of the East, the judgment of
the Roman Church, our mother. We beg you to restore immediate order and harmony among us." The legates expressed
their earnestness to second a zeal so praiseworthy, and steps
were at once taken for the convocation of the eighth general
council, which was opened at Constantinople on the 5th of
October, A. D. 869.

20. The temple consecrated by the great Constantine to
the Eternal Wisdom, and restored by Justinian, on a scale of

splendor which has provoked comparison with that of Solomon, was the august sanctuary in which the Roman primacy found, in the very heart of Greece, its strong defence and most glorious triumph. On the appointed day, one hundred and nine Fathers took their places upon seats placed in a semicircle. The book of Gospels, as usual, and the portion of the true cross preserved at Constantinople, were placed in the midst of the assembly. The three legates held the places of honor. Beside them sat Ignatius, the intrepid Patriarch of Constantinople, whose persecutions and sufferings were more than compensated for by the joy of this great day ; next in order were the Patriarchs of Antioch and Jerusalem. A place was reserved for the legate of Alexandria, who had not yet arrived. The bishops were brought in who had suffered exile and torture, during the reign of Michael III., for the cause of Catholic unity. At the sight of these venerable old men, covered with the scars of a glorious combat, the august assemblage rose in a body, to do homage to the band of aged martyrs. The Roman legates exclaimed : " Come forward, incomparable bishops, whose lot we envy ! Come and take your fitting rank ! You are worthy to hold your place among us !" This glorious testimonial to the holy confessors was received by the council with enthusiastic acclamations. After reading the formula of faith sent by the Pope through his legates, the council proceeded to reinstate the bishops and clerics who had communicated with Photius in spite of the prohibition of the Holy See. Each, in turn, presented himself with the protestation : " We have had the weakness to yield to the violence and threats of the schismatics. With contrite and humble hearts we have recourse to your clemency, ready to perform whatever penance may be imposed upon us by the holy Patriarch." " We receive you," said the legates, " to the communion of the Church, by the authority of Pope Adrian, whose representatives we are : and we admit you to a share in the labors of the council." Several of the schismatical bishops stubbornly adhered to their error, and remained deaf to all

remonstrance. The emperor Basil united his entreaties to
those of the council. " If you so much dread this wholesome
confusion," said the emperor, " I will give you the example of
self-humiliation. Forgetful of my purple and my diadem, I
prostrate myself before you. Trample under foot the body of
your emperor; I am ready to do and to suffer any thing to
restore peace and harmony to the church, and to procure the
salvation of your souls!" These noble and touching words
moved not their hardened hearts! The council was forced to
utter the sentence of excommunication against the rebellious
prelates. Photius himself stood before his judges. " Is this
the man," asked the legates, " who for seven years has unceasingly outraged the Roman Church; who has rent the Church
of Constantinople, and filled the East with the fruits of his
madness and revenge?" Photius seemed indeed another man.
He was no longer the artful and eloquent sophist whose words
were clothed with such alluring charms; he had assumed another character, and now played the part of injured innocence.
To all the questions of the Roman legates he made but two
replies : " The God who guards the innocent hears me without
the help of words." When told that his silence would not
save him from condemnation, he only answered : " The very
silence of Jesus Christ was also condemned." A delay was
granted him to prepare whatever defence he might wish to
present. He was again brought before the council at its next
session. Again he had changed his character and action.
Feigning weakness, he leaned upon a long and curved staff,
somewhat like the crozier used by Eastern bishops. He was
made to lay aside the significant emblem, an insult to the
august assemblage. He then began a crafty speech full of recriminations against the Holy See. " In what is contrary to
reason and the canons," said he, " though the messenger come
from Rome or Jerusalem, or were he even an angel from
heaven, I obey not!" " When schism or heresy," said the
Fathers, " have rent the bosom of the Church, is not safety
always sought in adherence to the Roman See and to the other

Patriarchates? To-day the united voices of Rome, Antioch, Jerusalem, and Alexandria condemn you; what authority can you bring in your defence?" "That of the canons," replied the schismatic; "they are my rule and my judges!" In presence of such obstinacy, there was nothing left but to pronounce the sentence. The legates spoke : "We utter no new judgment; we but promulgate that which was long ago pronounced by the holy Pontiff Nicholas, since confirmed by Pope Adrian. We cannot deviate from their paternal decision. Tell us whether you approve this sentiment; for it is that of the holy Apostolic See which we represent. Should you not confirm it, we shall rise, as upon a lofty mountain, above the council, and publish with all our power the sentence already pronounced, with the grace of the Holy Ghost, by the voice of our holy Fathers Nicholas and Adrian." All the Fathers assented. Twenty-seven canons containing the judgment of the council were read, approved, and signed by the legates, the Patriarchs, the emperor Basil, and the bishops. It was declared that Photius was never really a bishop; that the ordinations conferred by him were null, as well as all the acts performed by him during his intrusion. He and his partisans were excommunicated. The primacy of the Roman See, the independence of the spiritual power, and the freedom of councils, were recognized and proclaimed. The prohibition to raise neophytes to the episcopate was renewed; the evils resulting from its neglect were too numerous to allow the omission of this step. The acts of the false council of 866 were then brought into the assembly. The book in which they were contained was presented by John, metropolitan of Sylea (Perge) in Pamphylia, and committed to the flames, together with all the false and schismatical writings of Photius. The Eastern and Western Churches were one again; the schism was at an end. The emperor Basil, wishing to give solemnity and the sanction of imperial authority to the labors of the council, thus addressed the assembled Fathers : " Peace is at last restored to the Church. We have at length reached the object of all our endeavors, of our painful labors, amid obstacles which seemed insurmountable to our predecessors. Ministers of God, bishops intrusted with the salvation of His people, guard with jealous care the saving doctrine, bring back the wanderer to the fold, preserve the union you have just restored. And you, magistrates, officers, governors, laymen placed in authority, remember that it becomes us not to discuss the affairs of religion. Have not the rashness to touch the rights of bishops. However little be the prelate's merit, he is always a pastor while teaching the truth. Beware, then, of judging your judges, and of trying to lead those whom God has appointed your guides." With these wise counsels, so long misknown and so soon forgotten, ended the eighth general council (A. D. 870).

21. Yet the sad truth was too soon disclosed that the spirit of independence generated by the schism of Photius had struck root too deeply in the Eastern soil to be so speedily uptorn. The Bulgarian king Bogoris sent deputies to the council to ask whether the Bulgarian bishops were to derive their authority immediately from the Patriarchate of Constantinople or from the Roman See. The last session of the council had been closed eight days before. The Fathers, however, reassembled to discuss this question. The legates gave their opinion thus : " We have ended the mission upon which we were sent by the Holy See. We have no special authority to judge in this matter. But since the Bulgarian king has submitted, together with all his subjects, to the Roman Church, and as his kingdom is still evangelized by our priests, we decide, as far as in us lies, that Bulgaria should depend upon the See of Rome." But the Eastern prelates claimed that Bulgaria had once formed part of the Greek empire, under the name of Dardania, and as, at the time of the conquest, the Bulgarians had found Greek, not Latin, priests in the country, it should be deemed under the jurisdiction of Constantinople. " This is not a question of political divisions," replied the legates, " but of hierarchical order. It cannot be a matter of

doubt that Dardania, as well as all Illyria, was first under the government of the Roman Church; so that Rome has deprived Constantinople of nothing. She has but resumed, at the request of the Bulgarians themselves, the exercise of those rights which their irruption and heathenism had interrupted." As the discussion waxed violent by mutual contradiction, the legates at length said : " The See of Peter, the See whose primacy you must acknowledge, does not appoint you judges or arbiters in the case. It will condemn your decision with an ease equal to your haste in pronouncing it." " It is rather strange," returned the Orientals, " that you, who have thrown off the yoke of the lawful emperors, to bend to that of the Franks, should now claim any jurisdiction in our master's states! Bulgaria shall remain under the See of Constantinople." And so it did, in spite of Adrian's protestations. The legates only reached Rome two years afterward: Basil, in his irritation at this discussion, had allowed them to go without an escort, and they were captured by a band of Sclavonic pirates, from whose destructive grasp they hardly saved the acts of the glorious council over which they had just presided. The Pope hastened to write to the Greek emperor. " Our legates," he says, " have just returned to us after two years' captivity among a barbarous people. It is a subject of great surprise that you have utterly neglected to provide for their safety. Having so eagerly requested their presence, you might at least have followed the example of your predecessor, Michael, who, tyrant as he was, still furnished an escort to those who were sent to him. There is yet another act by which you have cancelled all the marks of good-will shown by you toward the Holy See: it is that our brother Ignatius has dared, with your consent, to consecrate a bishop for the Bulgarians. Rectify this abuse of power, and cease to usurp the rights of the Roman Church, if you would avoid canonical judgment and the condemnation of the Holy See." This protest was also without fruit; and Bulgaria has always recognized its dependence upon the see of Constantinople.

22. This was Adrian's last pontifical act, as he died on the 25th of November, A. D. 872. The Normans had made a descent upon the English coast in the preceding year, destroyed the monasteries of Lindisfarne, Tynemouth, Yarrow, Viremouth, Streaneshalc and Ely, and put all their inmates to the sword. At the approach of these formidable marauders, St. Ebba, abbess of Coldingham, assembled her religious and exhorted them to save their honor even at the cost of their lives. She gave the example by mutilating her nose and upper lip, in which she was followed by her companions. The Normans came on the next day; yet the sight of these self-mutilated virgins failed to touch their ferocious hearts. Setting fire to the monastery, they cast into the flames these heroic victims, worthy of speeding their way to the nuptials of the Lamb. At Croyland, the abbot, Theodore, was murdered at the altar. St. Edmund, king of East Anglia, had the misfortune to fall into the hands of these barbarians, who bound him to a tree and shot him to death with arrows. Thus, in each age, was the Church forced to witness the flow of her children's blood ; but this blood fell back upon their persecutors in a dew of graces and salvation, and the martyrs went to heaven to pray for the conversion of their murderers. The Normans profited by the weakness of Charles the Bald, and treated Gaul no better than England. The Franks were outraged that the grandson of Charlemagne should meet these formidable foes with gold instead of steel, and offered the crown of Neustria to Louis of Bavaria (A. D. 856–858), who advanced as far as Pontyon, where he was joined by most of the nobles. Charles the Bald appeared in battle array at Brienne; but through mistrust, whether of himself or of his troops, he retreated, leaving the whole kingdom to his rival. Once in possession of the crown, Louis thought as little as his vanquished rival of defending it against the Normans. The haughty bearing of the Germans irritated the Neustrians, and Charles recovered, as bloodlessly as he had lost, the throne of which he was so unworthy. Meanwhile the Normans grew in numbers and in

daring. A body of these pirates held the island of Oissel, near Paris, which they had occupied since A. D. 856. Another detachment had ascended the Somme, sacked Amiens, and spread terror throughout all Picardy. Charles conceived the hope of destroying the Normans by means of the Normans themselves, and offered three thousand pounds of silver to those on the Somme on condition of their ejecting those on the Seine. The bargain was concluded. They marched, under their leader, Wieland, upon the island of Oissel, which they took by assault; but the two bands soon united, and, far from quitting France, they settled on the banks of the Seine, from its mouth to Melun (A. D. 861). Robert-le-Fort (Robert-the-Strong), count of Anjou, founder of the third dynasty of our kings, did more than Charles the Bald for the defence of the land, and Charles rewarded his services with the duchy of France (comprising the country between the Seine and Loire). Notwithstanding Robert's valor, Hastings, formerly a peasant of the neighborhood of Troyes, but now one of the most redoubtable Norman chiefs, by his depredations compelled the king of France to sign one of the most humiliating treaties, by which he obtained four thousand pounds of silver, the return or ransom of all the Franks who had escaped from his captivity, and a restitution in money for every Norman killed by the Franks in the late inroads. Such were the disgraceful terms which Charles could accept without a blush. As soon as the stated sum had been all paid the Normans on the Seine withdrew. Those of the Loire still carried on their ravages. Robert-the-Strong attacked them with his wonted daring, but fell at Brissarthe (A. D. 866), by the hand of the fierce Hastings.

CHAPTER V.

§ VIII. Pontificate of Romanus (September 17, a. d. 897—February 8, 898).
28. Election and death of Romanus.

§ IX. Pontificate of Theodore II. (February 12, a. d. 898—March 3, 898).
29. Election and death of Theodore II.

§ X. Pontificate of John IX. (March 12, a. d. 898—March 26, 900).
30. Council of Rome.—31. Council of Ravenna.—32. Death of John IX. End
of the ninth century.

§ I. Pontificate of John VIII. (December 14, a. d. 872— December 15, 882).

1. John VIII. ascended the Pontifical throne to look upon a world already beginning to show symptoms of fearful convulsions. The East, where the General Council of Constantinople should have established a lasting peace, was soon to find a new source of dissension in its unceasing restlessness. The West, peopled by nations still unformed and full of unfermented blood, was but one vast battle-field, where the Saracens in the South, the Normans in Gaul, the kings of France, Germany and Italy, contended for some fragments of territory, which they deluged with blood. Upper Italy enjoyed comparative rest under the emperor Louis II. But he had no heir, and the prospective succession was jealously watched, on one side by the Franks, on the other by the Germans. Lower Italy, divided, torn by the contentions of the Greeks, who still held some towns, a remnant of their former rule by the Saracens, who made continual inroads upon the land, and by the Lombard dukes and counts, each a petty sovereign in his own stronghold, was alternately wasted and plundered by each in turn. Gaul, unceasingly harassed by the Normans no longer kept at bay by the powerful sword of Charlemagne, which the weak grasp of his grandson, Charles the Bald, was powerless to wield—divided in interests and policy by Charles's sons—Charles, Louis and Carloman, rebels to the paternal authority—now lacked the

undivided and powerful control under which its people could
have achieved great deeds. Amid the din and confusion of
this universal conflict was inaugurated the reign of John VIII.,
"an indefatigable Pontiff, eminently skilled in political transactions, equally vigorous and moderate, who only needed a less
stormy reign to have been ranked among the greatest Popes."[*]

2. The emperor Louis II. died in 786. Charles the Bald,
whose cupidity of acquiring new territory was only equalled
by his inability to defend it, hastened to Rome, to secure the
succession, which Louis of Bavaria might have rightfully disputed, but which he was too slow in claiming. John VIII.
crowned Charles as emperor of the Romans, and required an
oath that he would defend Italy against the Saracens, its
eternal enemies. The clergy, the senate and people swore
fealty to the new emperor in these terms : " To the most illustrious prince, crowned by God, great and pacific emperor, our
lord Charles Augustus, we, bishops, abbots, counts, and other
lords of the kingdom of Italy, wish endless peace and prosperity. Since the Divine goodness, through the merits of the
holy Apostles and their vicar, our most Holy Father John,
Sovereign Pontiff, universal Pope, has already raised you to
the empire, by the election of the Holy Ghost, we unanimously choose you as our protector, lord, and defender. We
gladly submit to your rule, and faithfully promise to observe
all that you may decree for the good of the Church and for our
safety." The same high-sounding language that might have
befitted a Charlemagne! While Charles the Bald was setting
a second crown upon the one he already wore and so ill
defended, Louis led an army into his Gallic possessions. The
emperor hurried from Italy, but the death of Louis freed him
from a formidable rival (A. D. 876).

3. John VIII. hoped that the official defender of the Holy
See would now turn his attention to Italy, which the Saracens
were again devastating. " Christian blood is shed," he wrote

to Charles. "Those who escape the sword of the infidel are dragged away into bondage on a foreign shore. The cities and fields are left a lonely wilderness. Bishops separated from their wretched flocks, come to seek shelter and food in Rome. In the last invasion, the enemy reaped the harvest which we had sown; this year we have been unable to sow, and we have not even the hope of a harvest. But why complain of the unbelievers, while the Christians themselves act no better? The neighboring lords, whom you call marchiones,* plunder the patrimony of St. Peter. They put us to death, not by the sword, but by hunger; they do not lead us away captives, but reduce us to a state of servitude. Under God, you are our refuge, our consolation, our only hope. Stretch forth your hand to raise up this desolate people, this noble and faithful city, to help the Church your mother, who crowned you with the twofold diadem of royalty and faith, and lately raised you to the imperial dignity before your brother." The evils mentioned by John VIII. were assuming yet more fearful proportions, as some of the Italian nations, far from checking, only helped to increase them. The Neapolitans and the neighboring people had formed an alliance with the Saracens, and came by sea to the very gates of Rome. The Pope used every means to break the league; he sent two bishops, Valbert of Porto and Peter of Ostia, to urge this measure upon Pulcherius, præfect of Amalfi, and especially upon Sergius, duke of Naples, the chief author of the treaty. John, deceived by their promises, several times repaired to Gaëta to conclude the affair.

4. The legates charged to deliver the Pope's letter to Charles the Bald found the emperor at Compiègne (A. D. 877). Their earnest petitions moved Charles to hurry at once to Rome. John VIII. came forward to receive him; they met at Verona, and journeyed together as far as Pavia, where the Pope solemnly crowned the empress Richilda. The ceremony

---

* This title was bestowed upon the governors of the marches or borders. This is the origin of the present title of marquis.

was hardly concluded when Carloman, eldest son of Louis of
Bavaria, who had crossed the Alps at the head of a large
army, attacked Charles the Bald, and called him to an account
for usurping the imperial title belonging, by right, to his father.
A terrible panic seized upon the troops of Charles ; their chief
was not more courageous ; he preferred to fight with gold
rather than with the sword. He hastily fled, almost alone, a
prey to a burning fever ; and at the foot of Mt. Cenis he lay
down to die, poisoned, perhaps, by his Jewish physician, Se-
decias. Louis, possessed of more power than he was worthy
to wield, more awake to the call of ambition than of glory,
more crafty than prudent, more covetous of conquests than
able to hold them, bequeathed his crown and his weakness to
Louis III., the Stammerer, who allowed Carloman, king of
Bavaria, to snatch his imperial title from him. The blood
which had produced Pepin of Herstal, Charles Martel, Pepin
the Short, and Charlemagne, had now ceased to course in the
veins of heroes (A. D. 877).

5. By the death of Charles the Bald, Italy was left open
to all its enemies, Moor and Christian. John VIII. searched
in vain among the Carlovingian princes for a noble heart or
stalwart arm to stem the destructive torrent. Carloman, ·
grasping at an imperial crown through streams of blood, ordered his lieutenant in Italy, Lambert, duke of Spoleto, to
march upon Rome and make himself master of the city.
Lambert but too well obeyed these tyrannical orders ; the Roman territory was given up to fire and sword. Yet the Pope,
hoping to turn the duke's hostile weapons against the Saracens, his real enemies, met him as a friend ; Lambert could
not share the Pontiff's Christian views. He passed, as an
angry conqueror, the gates which had been voluntarily opened
to him, took military possession of Rome, and imprisoned the
Pope in St. Peter's church. For the space of a month the
altar remained stripped of every ornament ; the desolate basilica was no longer hallowed by the wonted sacrifice or sacred
office. The Pontiff succeeded in eluding the watchful eyes

of his keepers, and, sailing from the port of Ostia, landed on
the hospitable shores of Provence, where the Papacy had
always found an unfailing home and brave defence. John sent
to ask Louis III. where he might hold an interview with him.
Troyes was named, and thither the Pope proceeded. He convoked a council; but the bishops beyond the Rhine refused
their presence. The Pontiff's call was unheeded; Rome
seemed forsaken. All were ready to receive at her hands their
crowns and titles; but no one was found to draw the sword
in her defence. The council was solemnly opened on the 11th
of August, A. D. 878, and expressed its regret at the disgraceful outrage put upon the Sovereign Pontiff by Carloman and
his lieutenant. Wise regulations were made to maintain the
independence of the bishops against the encroachments of the
civil power. There were noble words; but other arguments
were needed to beat back the Saracens and check the growing
insolence of rebel lords. John VIII. was keenly alive to this
truth. "I conjure you, my brethren," said the Pontiff, "to
arm your vassals for the defence of the Holy See and of all
Italy. Give me a final answer on this point." His prayers
were vain. The grief-stricken Pastor recrossed the Alps and
sought Rome once more.

6. Convinced that he had nothing more to hope for from
the Western rulers, he turned toward Constantinople, where
Basil the Macedonian reigned with glory. His victorious
arms had driven back the Saracens from Asia Minor, from
Pontus, Armenia, Cappadocia, and Mesopotamia, and only
stayed their conquering career beyond the Euphrates, whither
the Roman eagles had never ventured to wing their flight
since the days of Heraclius. The Pope believed that this was
the hero destined by Providence to save Italy, and tom becoe
the bulwark of Christianity in the West. He sent two legates
charged to propose to him this noble mission. But Constantinople had undergone a great change since the eighth general
council. Photius was no longer the schismatic deposed by the
Fathers, proscribed by the emperor, forced to fly from public

contempt and indignation. He had now gained access to the
monarch's intimacy, dwelt in the imperial palace, appeared in
pontifical attire, and enjoyed an unbounded influence at court;
and this great metamorphosis was due to a skilful imposition
of his perverse mind. Basil, though born of a lowly family
of Adrianople, was, like nearly all upstarts, covetous of a
pedigree. Photius had the address to profit by this petty
vanity. He improved his hours of exile in engrossing in .
Alexandrian characters, upon an old parchment, in a moth-
eaten cover, a genealogical table which carried back the family
of Basil to King Tiridates, so famous in Armenia. Theophanes,
a cleric at the court, and an intimate friend of the intruder,
undertook to place the dusty manuscript upon the shelves of
the imperial library. He then presented it to the emperor as
a most precious literary monument. " Unfortunately," added
he, " the characters are unknown to us. There is but one man
in the East who might decipher it." " Who is the man?" demanded Basil. " Photius." Photius was summoned, examined the book which he understood better than any one else,
and said that he could make known its contents to no one but
the emperor, as it revealed important secrets. Basil fell into
the snare. Photius's exile, which had lasted seven years, was
at an end. The crafty politician, once in the master's favor,
soon had him under full control (A. D. 878). The death of St.
Ignatius now left the way open for him to resume his Patriarchal dignity in Constantinople. The legates, Paul and
Eugenius, were so utterly overcome by the crafty machinations
of the Greeks, as publicly to announce that they were charged
to restore Photius to his former rank. The Eastern bishops,
terrified into submission by the proofs of wonderful power so
lately shown by Photius, dared not oppose his restoration, and
the wily schemer had the satisfaction of seeing all his plans
crowned with the most brilliant success.

7. The ambassadors bearing the letters of the Greek emperor
to John VIII. had reached Rome. Basil wrote to urge the
Pope's approval of Photius's nomination. This was the price

of his protectorate. The Pope was thrown into a state of cruel perplexity. The condition of Italy, growing daily worse, called for prompt relief; Basil alone could afford it; on the other hand, the reinstatement of Photius, deposed by a general council and still suspected of attachment to the schism, presented considerable difficulties. In so delicate an alternative, John VIII. took counsel of necessity. The course which he adopted was dictated by unquestionably serious reasons of policy. "You ask," he at length wrote to the emperor, "that, opening our heart to the call of mercy, we should, by our Apostolical authority, consent to the restoration of Photius to the honors and dignity of the Patriarchate. In order to conform to your petition, to heal the division and scandal existing in the Church, now so long harassed, and yielding to stern necessity, we consent to grant the pardon of Photius and his restoration to the Patriarchal throne. This we do, without detriment to the Apostolic Constitutions, without annulling the regulations of the holy Fathers, and upon this principle alone, that there are occasions in which we must yield to the force of circumstances and act contrary to the ordinary traditions of the Church. We therefore absolve Photius from the ecclesiastical censures laid upon him; we allow him to resume the Patriarchal See, in virtue of the supreme authority granted us in the person of the Prince of the Apostles, by Jesus our Lord, Who said to St. Peter: 'I will give unto thee the keys of the kingdom of heaven. And whatsoever thou shalt bind upon earth, it shall be bound also in heaven; and whatsoever thou shalt loose upon earth, it shall be loosed also in heaven.' Yet we give our consent under four conditions: 1st, That, on the death of Photius, his place shall not be filled by a layman. 2d, That the Patriarch claim no jurisdiction whatever over the province of Bulgaria. 3d, That the bishops and clerics ordained by Ignatius shall all hold their present rank and positions, and suffer no persecution. 4th, That Photius convoke a council to receive the disavowal of his past conduct."

8. The last clause was particularly offensive to Photius.

Its fulfilment would have cost his pride too dear, and he did not hesitate to elude it in his usual way. He took upon himself to translate the Pope's letters into Greek; and in the translation purposely omitted the pontifical reservations concerning the acknowledgment of his faults, the relinquishment of all claims upon Bulgaria, and the plea of pressing necessity which alone could have relaxed the strictness of ecclesiastical discipline in his regard. He even inserted the expression, which the Pope had never used, that the general council of 869 had been guilty of injustice in deposing Photius, and that all its acts were annulled. These blasphemous lies were publicly read, as coming from the pen of John VIII., in a false council over which the intruder presided in person, regardless of the honor due to the papal legates, still in Constantinople. The guilty envoys neither complained of this dishonor nor protested against the shameful expressions ascribed to the Vicar of Jesus Christ, whom they were sent to represent. They carried their base compliance to the extent of presenting the pontifical vestments to Photius with their own hands, in the ceremony of rehabilitation. And, when this scene of intrigue and disgraceful weakness was over, they came to tell the Pope that peace was at length restored and consolidated for ever in the Church of Constantinople.

9. But the Pontiff had in the mean time received full and precise details of their faithlessness and the intrigues of Photius. Ascending the ambo of St. Peter's church, in the presence of the assembled clergy and faithful of Rome, and holding in his hands the book of Gospels, John VIII. renewed the anathemas uttered against Photius by Nicholas I., Adrian II., and the eighth general council; and afterward fulminated a sentence of excommunication against the cowardly legates who had so basely betrayed their trust. The deacon Marinus, one of the legates who had presided over the eighth general council, was again sent to Constantinople to acquaint the emperor Basil and the intruded Patriarch with the sentence just pronounced. Marinus proved himself worthy of the confidence

reposed in him. In spite of the emperor and of Photius, he publicly appeared in the ambo of St. Sophia, and, in the name of the Pope, announced the annulment of all that had been done in favor of the intruded Patriarch. The fearless ambassador was, by order of Basil, thrown into a dungeon, from which he succeeded in making his escape, and reached Rome in safety to give an account of the dangerous duty he had discharged at the risk of his life.

10. The Pope thus saw the hopes he had cherished for the defence of Italy successively blighted. The East was barred against him, the West was deaf to his entreaties; yet was he not disheartened, for his energy seemed to gain strength as obstacles grew before him; and it was a noble sight to behold a devoted Pontiff struggling with unflagging spirit against the indifference or opposition of his age. In 880, he thus wrote to Charles the Fat, king of Germany and brother of Carloman : " We are equally exposed to the outrages of the Saracens and the rebellion of the Christians themselves. The husbandmen leave their furrows unsown; the ministers of God are endangered by the very discharge of their sacred office. If you hasten not to the help of Rome and the Apostolic See, you will answer before God for the loss of Italy." Charles III. would have made as light of this appeal as he had done of so many others before ; but the death of Carloman (A. D. 881) left the empire vacant. Charles hastened to Rome to receive the imperial crown at the hands of the Pope. He fully intended to take upon him the implied obligation, but was equally determined to disregard every claim of gratitude, as his predecessors had done before him. The Pontiff did, indeed, require the usual coronation oath, that he would use the sword given him by the Church in her defence ; he forgot his oath as soon as its fruits were within his grasp. John VIII. vainly renewed his petitions, prayers, and threats ; and the unfortunate Pontiff died (December 15, A. D. 882) without having accomplished the great object of all his hopes and endeavors during the ten years of his reign—the rescue of Italy. History, which must

judge the endeavor and not the result, is forced to pay an admiring tribute to such loftiness and firmness of character. Resolved to secure the safety at least of Rome against the barbarians, he bought a peace from the infidels, at the cost of an annual tribute of twenty-five thousand silver marks.

§ II. Pontificate of Marinus I. (December 23, a. d. 882— February 23, 884).

11. The intrepid legate, Marinus, who, in the words of an annalist, "had just covered his name with immortal glory in the prisons of Constantinople and the fetters of Basil the Macedonian," was already marked, by universal esteem, as the successor of John VIII. He was raised to the Pontifical Chair on the 23d of December, a. d. 882. The Greek emperor and his false Patriarch in vain protested against his consecration. Marinus answered their interested protestations by renewing the excommunication of Photius and issuing a decree that henceforth the orders of the Eastern emperors should not be awaited for the Pope's consecration. The authority of the Carlovingian princes, weakened by their personal incapacity, and by their domestic strifes in Germany and Gaul, was utterly lost in Italy. The energy and apostolic firmness of Marinus justified the brightest and most sanguine hopes for the Church's future; but they were unhappily doomed to a speedy disappointment by the Pontiff's death, after a short reign of fourteen months (February 23, a. d. 884).

12. A few months before his death, he had received ambassadors sent by Alfred the Great, king of England, bearing rich offerings from their sovereign for the tomb of the Apostles, in gratitude for his wonderful success against the Normans. Alfred was justly convinced that no power short of the Almighty's arm could have wrought the unlooked and unhoped-for prosperity with which his kingdom was now blessed. It had once, like its neighbors, felt the blighting tread of the Normans

and Danes, who had possessed themselves of his states, re-
ducing him to the necessity of seeking shelter, with his family,
in a forest fastness, surrounded by almost impassable marshes.
For six months the august fugitives enjoyed no nobler shelter
than the hovel of a poor shepherd, no daintier fare than the
fish they drew from the neighboring ponds. But in winter
an icy barrier cut off even this scanty supply of subsistence. One day a houseless beggar knocks and asks for
food. "What have you to give?" asked Alfred of the queen.
"We have but a single loaf," answered the royal fugitive.
"Thank God!" exclaimed the king; "He who with five loaves
could feed five thousand men can well supply our need with
half a loaf. Give the other half to this poor wanderer." The
noble deed of charity could not go unrewarded, and God
bestowed a throne for the piece of bread given in His name.
A short time after this occurrence, Alfred learned that, notwithstanding the desperate state of his affairs, some Englishmen
had dared a last desperate encounter. Hubba, the Danish
chief, and the author of St. Edmund's martyrdom, had been
slain in a bloody engagement. The king came forth from his
retreat, rallied his scattered subjects, fell like a thunderbolt
upon the Danes, and gained a complete victory (A. D. 878).
Those who escaped the carnage sheltered themselves in one of
their strongholds, which Alfred speedily compelled them to
surrender at discretion. Those who refused to forsake idolatry
were banished from the island, while estates were bestowed
upon the others. The new Christians, headed by their king,
Gunthrum, who received at the font the name of Ethelstane,
settled in the provinces assigned them by Alfred. Thus he
peopled with a bold and trusty race the two kingdoms of East
Anglia and Northumberland, which the invasion had almost
made a tenantless desert. To perfect the work of their civilization, he gave them laws which have since become the universal code of England. The closing years of Alfred's reign were
as glorious as its beginning had been gloomy and unpromising.
His higher glory is to rank among the Church's sainted sons.

The splendid figure of Alfred the Great sheds a ray of glory upon a gloomy page of history, and he stands out in noble contrast to his weak and faithless contemporaries on the Frankish throne. We have several works from the pen of Alfred the Great; among others, a *Treatise on the Different Fortunes of Kings*. In this work, at least, he might speak with the authority of experience.

13. During the reign of Louis the Stammerer (A. D. 881), the Normans burned the monastery of Corbie and the city of Amiens. Entering Lorraine by the Wahl, they destroyed Nimeguen, Liège, Maëstricht, Tongres, Cambray, Cologne, Bonn, Zulpich, Juliers, and at length Aix-la-Chapelle, where they used Charlemagne's imperial chapel to stable their horses. Champagne was laid waste, Rheims sacked and given to the flames. Hincmar had fled with the treasure of his church and the precious relics of St. Remigius, and sank under exhaustion and grief at Epernay, on the 21st of December, A. D. 882. Lupus of Ferrières, his administrator, speaks of him as "a generous prelate, full of good works, of lofty views and surpassing wisdom." We have had occasion to observe that his character was at times too much controlled by the spirit of the age. As a writer he displays more learning than taste; his style is diffuse, obscure, clogged by parentheses and overloaded with quotations. He is far inferior to his contemporary, Ratramnus, a monk of Corbie, whose works, especially the *Treatise on the Eucharist*, are models of elegant and pure Latinity.

While Germany and Gaul groaned beneath the Norman yoke, Italy was not more gently treated by the Saracens. The infidels plundered the lands of Beneventum and Spoleto, and pushed on to the very walls of Rome, regardless of the compact made with Pope John VIII. The religious of St. Vincent's-on-the-Vulturnus were put to the sword, and their monastery destroyed; Monte Cassino met the same fate, though its former abbot, St. Bassacius, had given it a crown of walls and towers which made it as strong as a fortress. But the unquenchable avarice of the Arabs was resistless; the convent was sacked and burned, and the abbot, Bertarius, with most of his monks, fell beneath the pitiless scimetars of the fierce Moslem (A. D. 884). The few survivors succeeded in reaching the priory of Theano, bearing with them the annals of the monastery, and the hope of one day raising it again from its then ruined state.

§ III. PONTIFICATE OF ADRIAN III. (March 1, A. D. 884—July 8, 885).

14. Adrian III. had hardly taken possession of the See left vacant by Marinus I. when he received urgent letters from Basil the Macedonian. Still under the influence of Photius' infernal power, he begged the Pope to recall the censures pronounced against the false Patriarch by Marinus I. and John VIII. Adrian's only reply was a plain and formal refusal and the confirmation of his predecessors' sentence. Having inaugurated his reign by this act of Apostolical authority, he turned his attention to the means of rescuing Italy from the galling yoke of the Saracens. The emperor, Charles the Fat, invited him to France, to anoint his natural son, Bernard, as heir presumptive to the imperial throne. The Pope, hoping to find in the French monarch the liberator of Italy, set out upon the journey; but death overtook him at St. Cesarius, a little village near Modena, where he died on the 8th of July, A. D. 885. Adrian's charity, prudence, and fearless intrepidity, had awakened the brightest hopes for his pontificate; their realization was left to his worthy successor.

§ IV. PONTIFICATE OF STEPHEN VI. (July 25, A. D. 885—August 7, 891).

15. On his accession (July 25, A. D. 885) Stephen VI. found Rome in a most lamentable condition. The countless woes inflicted by the Saracens were still increased by a cruel

famine and a withering drought which threatened the failure of the coming crops. It was found necessary forcibly to remove Stephen from the house in which his humility had concealed him, to avoid the burdensome dignity imposed upon him by the unanimous voice of clergy and people. "My shoulders are too weak for the immense weight!" exclaimed Stephen. Heedless of his prayers and tears, the people bore him in triumph to the Lateran palace. As if to pledge approval of the happy choice, even while the enthusiastic throng was still on its way, Heaven sent a plentiful and refreshing rain to save the parched and drooping harvest. On the next day the Pope went to visit the Roman churches and the pontifical palace. The altars had been profaned, all their ornaments had become a prey to the sacrilegious Saracen; the treasury was empty, the furniture, granaries and storehouses plundered. Yet he must provide for the wants of the clergy and military, ransom the captives, and feed a whole people wasting away with the pangs of hunger. The exhaustless charity and energy of Adrian met every demand. His illustrious lineage placed an immense fortune at his disposal. His entire patrimony was sold, and liberally bestowed to relieve the crying want. His own household was put upon a most severe footing. Tried and spotless virtue was the only passport to the offices of his court. The Pontiff's table was daily shared by a certain number of orphans, whom he made the favorite children of his great adoptive family, the Roman poor. The sinking hearts of the Romans were cheered with new and hopeful courage, and the fearful unbelievers dared not approach the Eternal City, so strongly defended by the virtues of her Pastor.

16. Photius thought to revenge himself upon the Roman Church by calumniating the faith of the Latins in respect to the *Filioque* and the procession of the Holy Ghost. He accordingly published a pamphlet, claiming to prove, by texts of Holy Writ and quotations from the Fathers, that the Holy Ghost does not proceed from the Son. The work was ad-

dressed to Adrian III., and accompanied the insulting letter of the emperor Basil in reply to the Pope's renewed excommunication of the intruded Patriarch. Stephen VI. received the dispatches addressed to his predecessor, and answered them with the same firmness that Adrian himself would have shown. "If God," he wrote to the emperor, "has bestowed upon you the government of the political and civil world, He has intrusted to Peter and his successors the government of the religious and moral world. You accuse the Apostolic See of breaking off all relations with the Church of Constantinople. Where is the head of that Church, that the Sovereign Pontiffs may communicate with him? You have no Patriarch. We cannot hold official communication with Photius, a mere layman."

17. This letter reached Constantinople in the midst of a fresh revolution (A. D. 886). Photius had placed one of his tools in charge of Basil, to keep the imperial mind in the channel marked out by the false Patriarch. Theodore Santabaren proved himself well worthy of the shameful charge. The emperor was already in the decline of life; Leo, his son and heir, whose love of study and science had already dignified him with the surname of the Philosopher, made no secret of his aversion for Photius, whose insincerity was well known to him. Santabaren made known these unfriendly dispositions to Photius, and together they planned the prince's ruin. The intruder's ambition made light of deceit. In obedience to his directions, Theodore went to the young prince. "Why," said the hypocrite, "do you not carry some weapon about you when you go with your father to the chase? Aged and weak as he is, you leave him without defence against the fury of the hunted beasts." It was customary at the court of Constantinople to hunt with no other weapon than the boar-spear, with which the animal was struck when run down. In the morrow's imperial hunt, Leo secreted a sword under his garments, in order not to alarm his father. Santabaren whispered to the emperor: "Your son is plotting against you, and intends to

murder you in the forest. As a proof, order him to be
searched." Anxious to avoid excitement, Basil feigned to
need a knife; the unsuspecting prince offered his own. The
misguided father asked no further proof, but ordered his son
to be thrown into a dungeon and tried at once. The members
of the imperial family, fully convinced of Leo's innocence,
filled the palace with their cries and tears. A general mourning reigned in the court. Every effort was made to open the
emperor's eyes to the infamous plot of the two impostors.
Basil was inflexible; Photius and Theodore triumphed. Basil
had one day entered more than usual into the spirit of the
banquet, when suddenly a favorite parrot broke in upon the
general hilarity of the feast with the piteous cry: "Alas! alas!
my lord Leo!" The poor bird had heard this sad expression
incessantly uttered in the court during the past three months,
and now repeated it for the first time. The cry paralyzed
the flowing mirth. A gloomy silence, broken only by a few
stifled sobs, reigned around the festive board. At length a voice
arose: "Sire, that bird condemns us. We are here in festive
gladness, while your son Leo, the heir to your crown, is pining
in a dungeon, the victim of an infamous calumny. If he is
guilty, we are all armed to punish him; if innocent, then are
we all guilty." The emperor, deeply moved, summoned the
prince, and learned from his own lips the infernal plot of which
he had himself been the dupe. Theodore purchased safety by
a hasty flight, not waiting to betray his partner, Photius, who
continued to enjoy the imperial favor. But his triumph was
short-lived. Basil died of a fall received in escaping from a
stag which had rushed upon him in the chase (A. D. 886). He
was now, but too late, enlightened upon the conduct of Photius,
and his last words to his heir were words of warning against
his own evil genius: "My son, beware of Photius; he has
opened a fearful abyss beneath my throne." He was right.
Posterity would have ranked Basil the Macedonian among the
greatest monarchs, for the rare prudence, the too-long-unknown
virtues with which he graced the Eastern throne, had he not

met in Photius a rock against which was wrecked all the glory of his reign.

18. Leo VI., the Philosopher, was not regardless of his father's dying injunction; had filial love been wanting, motives of personal vengeance were strong enough to insure its fulfilment. The new emperor immediately sent two of his chief officers to the church of St. Sophia, where they published from the ambo a detailed account of the schismatical usurper's intrigues, and the sentences of excommunication pronounced against him by the predecessors of Stephen VI. The false Patriarch was then banished from Constantinople, this time not to return. His career of intrigue and deceit was at an end; the hour of vengeance had come. His expulsion crushed the Eastern schism to which he gave his name. Photius was born to achieve great deeds, had not his daring mind plunged too rashly into crooked paths and endless deceits. He was, unquestionably, one of the best writers of his day. The chief works we have from him are: 1st, his *Bibliotheca*, an analysis of the various works read by him in the course of his Syrian embassy. This collection is one of the most valuable monuments of ancient literature and a model for literary journals, perhaps hitherto unsurpassed. It contains extracts from two hundred and eighty works, some of which have not reached us in the original. 2d, The *Nomocanon*, or Harmony of the laws and canons, a collection of the acts of all the councils, from the apostolic days to the seventh general council, compared in their relation to the imperial decrees. 3d, *Syntagma Canonum*, or classification of the canons under fourteen titles. The original of this work was first brought to light and published by H. E. Cardinal Mai, in the seventh volume of his Spicilegium Romanum. It is a remarkable feature of the two last works, that they contain not a single word in favor of the schism. Photius quotes, entire and without gloss, the canons establishing the supremacy of the Roman Pontiff and the right of appeal to the Pope. In this respect the writer and the private individual seem to have nothing in com-

mon. Impartiality and love of truth, banished from his heart, had made their seat in his intellect; his pen proclaims the uprightness and honesty which were wanting in his character and his deeds.

19. Immediately after the banishment of the intruder, Leo VI. raised to the vacant See his own virtuous brother Stephen, who was consecrated toward the end of the year 886. A solemn embassy was then sent to Rome, to acquaint the Sovereign Pontiff with the happy downfall of the schism which had lasted thirty years. Stephen VI. answered the Greek emperor by letters conveying all his joy and that of the Western churches at the glad tidings. He requested Leo to send him some Eastern bishops, that they might agree together upon some necessary measures touching the irregular ordinations conferred by the schismatical Patriarch. These negotiations necessarily entailed a long delay, and when the deputies sent by Leo VI. to treat these matters reached Rome, Stephen VI. had ceased to reign on earth (August 7, A. D. 891). His Pontificate witnessed the most formidable Norman invasion recorded in history. The light skiffs of these savage *sea-kings* covered the Seine for a distance of more than two leagues, and so close together that the surface of the water was not visible at any point within their lines. Their king, Sigefrid, presented himself before Goslin, bishop of Paris, saying that he required but the right of transit, to which the bishop proudly replied : " The emperor, Charles the Fat, has intrusted us with the safety of the city. We shall defend it to the death." He was true to his word. With the help of Eudes, count of Paris, worthy son of Robert the Strong, whose heroic valor on this occasion won him a well-deserved throne, Goslin, with a display of great personal prowess, in spite of the canonical prohibition, withstood for a whole year the desperate efforts of the Normans. Cowed by this unwonted opposition, the barbarians, who were fonder of plunder than of battle, found means to carry their boats overland to a point above the city (A. D. 886-887), where they again embarked. Following the course of

the Seine and Yone, they sacked and burned the city of Sens, wasted Burgundy, and carried terror to the very heart of Gaul.

§ V. Pontificate of Formosus (September 19, a. d. 891— April 4, 896).

20. Formosus, bishop of Porto, affords the first example of a bishop transferred from another See to that of Rome, to which he was raised on the 19th of September, a. d. 891. These translations were, as yet, very unusual in the West, truer to this point of discipline than the East. We shall soon see how keenly sensitive was the public mind on this subject, by the excesses springing from the use of a dispensation granted to Formosus only for the greater good of the Church. The bishop of Porto was raised to the Sovereign Pontificate solely in consideration of his unfeigned attachment to religion, his zeal and exemplary virtues, his energy and experience, his thorough knowledge of the Scriptures and holy Fathers—a rare combination of high endowments in any age, but especially in his time, and deemed much more necessary to the head of the Church than to a simple bishop. He had labored with fruit among the Bulgarians, and won general esteem for his learning and the edifying regularity of his life.

21. Formosus gave his first thoughts to the question of the ordinations conferred in the East by the schismatical Patriarch Photius. The Pope's legates set out for Constantinople with minute instructions on the subject. "First of all," said the Sovereign Pontiff, "the condemnation of Photius shall remain asting and irrevoc   We are willing to pardon those whom he has ordained. They must present to the metropolitan an acknowledgment of their fault, signed by themselves, after which they may be received into lay-communion, but deprived of all rank in the hierarchy of the Church." This letter is the last act of the Holy See concerning the Photian schism, which thenceforth officially disappeared; but the final separation of

the Greeks, long under the fostering influence of jealous
rivalry, hastened by heresies which degenerated into a kind of
irreligion, and at length consummated by the daring artifices
of the most seductive of party-leaders, was but for a moment
checked. The seed was sown deep in the bosom of the Eastern Church, and only awaited the favorable moment for breaking forth with new power to beget a ruin hitherto irretrievable (A. D. 891).

22. Fulk, Hincmar's successor in the See of Rheims, and
one of the most illustrious by birth and personal qualities of all
the Frankish 'prelates, hastened to write to Pope Formosus, to
pay his homage to the worthy successor of St. Peter, and congratulate the Roman Church upon an election which he pronounced "a token of the divine protection over the whole
Church." In the following year (A. D. 893), Fulk proclaimed
and established in France the royalty of Charles, son of Louis
the Stammerer, and asked the Pope's guidance and protection
for the youthful monarch. The prince, then but fourteen years
of age, was the only legitimate descendant of Charlemagne.
After the rescue of Paris, public gratitude had bestowed the
crown of France upon Eudes, and Charles, an uncrowned
child, owed his safe retreat into England to the care of a few
followers still true to the Carlovingian dynasty. Here he remained until a fitting opportunity offered of regaining his lost
rights; some rising troubles in Aquitaine called Eudes far
from the centre of his states; the loyal nobles seized the moment and brought Charles to Rheims, where he was crowned
by Fulk, at whose request the Sovereign Pontiff wrote in the
young king's behalf to his two powerful rivals, Eudes and
Arnold, king of Germany. Whatever may have been the influence of a mediation, so respectable in itself, but yet so seldom honored in like cases, the continual dissensions between
France and Germany proved much more useful to Charles,
who kept at least the title of royalty, though branded with the
deserved epithet of *the Simple*. Eudes held the provinces
stretching from the Seine to the Pyrenees, while Charles

was confined within the narrow limits of the Seine and Meuse. At the death of Eudes, Charles the Simple was generally acknowledged in Neustria, Burgundy, and Aquitaine; this submission was readily made, as it amounted to nothing more, on the part of the nobles, at least, than a barren recognition. Feudalism, grown powerful by the weakness of the Carlovingian kings, and secure within its strongholds, now braved the monarch's authority and too often wasted the nation's blood in petty wars and personal disputes. The struggle now begins between the royal power and its often more powerful vassals. Happy if, in the midst of unceasing strifes, the common father of the faithful had ever been the arbiter, or had his peaceful mediation been always respected!

23. It would seem that the necessity of clinging closer to the centre of Catholic unity must now have seized more forcibly upon all minds. In 895, Arnold, king of Germany, called a general council of all the states under his sway, at Tribur, near Mentz. "Pastors of Christ's flock," said the king, addressing the assembled bishops, "faithfully fulfil your trust, and be sure that I shall religiously discharge my duty of battling against the enemies of the Church and yours." The Fathers published canons of discipline and took measures to restore public penance, so little regarded in the midst of continual wars and dissensions, to its first conformity with the spirit and laws of the primitive Church. They concluded with these remarkable words: "We must honor the holy and apostolic Church of Rome in memory of the Apostle St. Peter, and as being for us the mother of the priestly dignity and mistress of the ecclesiastical power. It therefore becomes our duty to yield a pious submission to her orders."

24. Though this solemn tribute of homage came to the Holy See from the midst of the German nations, it was oppressed at home by its own children contending for the imperial power. The emperor Guy died in 894. His son Lambert, recognized as his heir and successor, had been crowned by Formosus, and now reigned with his mother, Agiltrude, an

ambitious princess, whose power soon degenerated into tyranny. A portion of Upper Italy was at the same time in the hands of king Berengarius, who thought to seize the imperial sceptre while the public mind was still imbittered by the despotism of Lambert and Agiltrude. War was declared; the whole country, not excepting Rome, was divided into two parties, for or against either competitor. To quell the disturbance, Formosus appealed to Arnold, the German king, whose noble and generous tone at the Council of Tribur we had occasion to quote. Arnold answered the Pontiff's call (A. D. 896). At the head of a powerful German army he wrested Rome from the hands of Lambert. Formosus received him with joy, crowned him emperor, and made the people swear fealty to him as such. But this act only complicated instead of clearing up the difficulties. There were now three emperors, three parties, and three armies face to face. The division had become a real anarchy. Arnold, after a series of alternate victories and defeats, was forced back into Germany. Lambert and Berengarius agreed to share Italy as their booty. Formosus was spared any further scenes of blood and misery by death, which came to his release April 4th, A. D. 896.

25. While the West was shaken by the universal clash of resounding arms, many chosen souls, mysteriously drawn after the sweet perfume of a life of holy solitude, sought, in the forests of Germany and Gaul, retreats far removed from the tumultuous passions and strifes of men. Holy contemplatives built themselves cells in the very midst of noisy cities, against the wall of some church, with which they communicated by means of a window. There, alone, between the sanctuary and the world, they stood as suppliants unceasingly imploring the divine mercy for the people. One of these solitaries, named Grimlaic, composed a rule for their use—an angelic legislation of that peaceful kingdom whose judge was conscience, the love of God its sanction, and everlasting joys the reward. At the same period a lonely but delightful vale, at the foot of the mountains of Auvergne, received St. Gerald, more proud of his

coarse monk's cowl and habit than of the knightly mail and earldom he had just forsaken. Here he founded a monastery, which afterward gave rise to the city of Aurillac. Thus did " piety," which is " profitable to all things," continue, during the ninth century, its work of saving souls and civilizing the world.

§ VI. Pontificate of Boniface VI. (April 11, A. D. 896—April 26, 896).

26. The death of Formosus left Rome in a state of dissension and torn by the rival factions of the three emperors. In the midst of this confusion, a regular election was out of the question. The faction of Berengarius, in a tumultuous assembly, bore to the throne Boniface VI. (April 11, A. D. 896). The lawfulness of this election, carried by force of arms, is doubtful enough. But the incumbent only left his name in the pontifical annals, as he died fifteen days after his promotion (April 26, A. D. 896).

§ VII. Pontificate of Stephen VII. (May 2, A. D. 896—August, 897).

27. The party which had elected Boniface VI. was still powerful enough to manage the choice of his successor, though somewhat more in accordance with canonical propriety, and Stephen VII. ascended the pontifical throne (May 2, A. D. 896). Fulk of Rheims wrote to him, as he had done to his predecessors, to testify his veneration for the Apostolic See, and his desire of visiting Rome to pay his homage to the tomb of the Apostles. The new Pontiff's reign lasted but a year, and is marked by a singular occurrence, which helped to its untimely end. Formosus had been transferred from the See of Porto to that of Rome, contrary, as we stated above, to the received notions of discipline in the West. Stephen VII. thought it due to the honor of strict canonical discipline to return to the past. A council assembled, by his order, in Rome, ex-

amined the question and instituted the trial of Formosus, as if the sentence could now affect him. His election was declared irregular, and the ordinations conferred by him, as Sovereign Pontiff, were annulled. An unwarrantable extreme of rigor, too clearly showing the spirit of the times, violated the grave of the man whose memory it would doom to ignominy. The corpse of Formosus, unearthed and robed in full pontifical attire, was placed upon the apostolic throne, in the midst of the assembly. "Bishop of Porto," said Stephen VII. to the lifeless form, "why did your ambition lead you to usurp the Roman See?" The sentence of deposition was then pronounced, the body, stripped of the sacred vestments, deprived of the three fingers with which the pontifical benediction was usually given, was finally cast into the Tiber. The memory of Formosus still lived in Rome; they who had received ordination from him were many. These friends to the cause of the outraged Pontiff seized Stephen VII., threw him, loaded with chains, into a dungeon, where he was strangled (August, A. D. 897). Were we ignorant of the degree of fury to which party spirit too often raises the minds of men, such a scene might be pronounced incredible. But it is doubtless to deeds of like atrocity that this unfortunate period owes its name of *the iron age*. We must bear in mind, too, that the odious scene we have just described bore no relation to any question of dogma, and that the unheard-of conduct of Stephen in nowise touches the infallibility of the Holy See. "The deed," says Baronius, "shows a despotic violence in the fact, but no error of faith. Let us not forget that we are dealing with the ninth century."

§ VIII. PONTIFICATE OF ROMANUS (September 17, A. D. 897— February 8, 898).

28. History presents us with the mere record of the election and death of Romanus, which were hardly more than simultaneous. Flodoard extols his virtues and piety, which the age was unworthy to enjoy.

§ IX. PONTIFICATE OF THEODORE II. (February 12, A. D. 898—
March 3, 898).

29. The chair of Peter seemed, at this sad period, to have
become a mere thoroughfare. Theodore II., its next incumbent,
reigned but twenty days, which short period he improved by
faithful labors for the restoration of quiet to the public mind
and edification in the Church. He recalled the banished
bishops, reinstated the clerics ordained by Formosus, and
solemnly deposited in the Papal vaults that Pontiff's body,
which had been found by some fishermen. These acts of
justice and moderation enshrined in benedictions the too rapid
pontificate of Theodore II.

§ X. PONTIFICATE OF JOHN IX. (March 12, A. D. 898—March
26, 900).

30. The death of Theodore left two parties contending for
the choice of his successor. A priest named Sergius, who
eventually occupied the chair of St. Peter, was violently
upheld by one faction; their opponents, however, triumphed,
and John IX. was elected Pope (March 12, A. D. 898). His
promotion was approved by the wisdom and piety which illustrated his short pontificate. His first care was to confirm the
action of his predecessor, in the reinstatement of Formosus.
In order to sap the very foundation of the evil, he called a
council at Rome, to make fresh inquiries into the matter, and
the following decree was unanimously adopted: "We disown
the outrages done to the memory of Pope Formosus when his
disentombed remains were violated and cast into the Tiber. No
one of our predecessors was ever known to be guilty of a like
excess. We now, by the authority of the Holy Ghost, forbid
the recurrence of similar scenes. A corpse cannot be called
to trial. Yet, as the bishops who took part in that disgraceful
deed now confess that they were carried away by the heat of
party spirit, and acknowledge their fault, we, of our own

authority, hereby pardon them, and will not have them troubled on that account." The council next turned its attention to the factions now rending the whole of Italy. Arnold was in his agony in far-off Germany. Lambert had secured the recognition of his power. John IX. and the Fathers of Rome thought it just, in order to remove the germs of dissension, to proclaim in right a power which already existed in fact. They accordingly confirmed the election and imperial title of Lambert. Measures were also taken to end a disgraceful abuse introduced into Rome by the civil wars and frequent vacancies in the Holy See. The council issued the following decree on the subject: "The death of each successive Pontiff throws the Roman Church into the most shameful scenes of violence. The excited mob plunders the Lateran palace, and even carries its licentious madness into private dwellings. To guard against the return of similar disorders, we decree that henceforth the election and consecration of the Pope shall not be carried on without the presence of the emperor's deputies, whose duty it shall be to secure freedom of election." The Papacy must indeed have sadly felt the effects of the unquiet period, since it was forced to appeal to temporal princes to protect the elections of its Pontiffs. The Church risked the disadvantage of the imperial patronage, rather than remain subject to the violence of popular sedition; it was the less of two evils.

31. In the following year, John IX. presided over another council, at Ravenna, where all these decrees were confirmed. The emperor Lambert wished to attend the sittings in person. He declared his intentions to be upright, and announced his readiness to accept the high and noble mission of *Defender of the Holy See,* which Charlemagne had ever esteemed the most glorious of his lofty titles. "Should any Roman," said he, "cleric or layman, of whatsoever rank, claim our protection, no one can oppose it without incurring our imperial indignation." This solemn league between the Empire and the Papacy justified the most sanguine hopes. But Providence had other-

wise ordained. Lambert died of a fall from his horse, while hunting in the forest of Marengo, a name which a coming day would render brilliant with imperishable glory (A. D. 898). Arnold, his rival, died at Mentz in 899, and, as though death had scorned any other harvest than crowned heads, in that year, Eudes, the terror of the Normans, also died in France. His last words were spoken to his barons : " Go, swear fealty to Charles the Simple, and unite the whole kingdom under one empire." His disinterestedness was the more remarkable as he had a nephew, Robert, duke of France, and grandfather of Hugh Capet. But the royal dignity, disgraced by Carlovingian princes, afterward attached itself to the heroic race of Eudes and Robert the Strong. The sceptre now passed into the hands of Louis III., styled the Blind, and late king of Arles. Arnold was succeeded on the German throne by his son Louis. The archbishop of Mentz thus acquainted the Pope with the circumstances of this accession : " We were for some time in doubt as to the choice of our sovereign ; but the prospective dissolution of the German States overcame our hesitation, and we have elected the eldest son of Arnold, notwithstanding the prince's youth. We sought in this to follow the ancient usage of choosing the Frankish kings from the same race. If we have acted without your permission, we are convinced that you know the reason, which was the difficulty of communicating with Italy, on account of the barbarian occupation of the frontier lines.* Now that we enjoy the opportunity of writing to you, we beg that you will confirm our election by your episcopal authority."

32. John IX. closed the rapid series of illustrious deaths, and ended his earthly career on the 12th of March, in the year 900. His pontificate closes with the ninth century. This eventful age, opened by Charlemagne with a splendor which

---

* These barbarians, who infested the boundaries of Germany and Italy, were the Hungarians, a Scythian race, who had for the past ten years harassed the French empire. Moravia, Bavaria, and Northern Italy were successively made the theatre of their inroads and barbarous devastation.

has pierced the gloom of even that dark period and sheds a bright radiance over all the after pages of history, now wanes in the midst of inglorious revolutions, of dismembered kingdoms and falling empires, to the din of the tempests raised by the Saracens and the Normans at either extremity of the West, deluged in a sea of blood shed by obscure rivals contending for shreds of territory. The Papacy, now but the sport of factions, gave to the world a series of ephemeral Pontiffs, unheeded by the battling world around. All taste for useful studies was lost; ignorance, immorality, violence reigned supreme. Humanity was entering upon one of those crises which go before and prepare great events. The ninth, tenth, and eleventh centuries were to mature in the hearts of European nations that renewal by faith which bloomed with so much splendor in the bright phase of the middle ages, in deeds of holiness, greatness, and glory. The Sovereign Pontiffs were the first to come forth from the oppressive gloom, and to sound the signal for the advance. Protestant criticism has inveighed with unsparing bitterness against two or three Popes more especially pointed out to its shafts by 'contemporary testimony, generally the fruit of party spirit. The unbiased historian never abstracts from the period and surroundings of his characters, to judge them, thus isolated, by ideas and habits not their own. Through all its successive phases of development, society still lives upon a fund of ideas common to all. Master minds may radiate the scintillations with greater brightness over the world, but they are as much the mirrors as the foci of their times. By what uncalled-for prodigy could the Holy See, surrounded by general decline, at a time when the standard of both prince and people was so irretrievably lowered, claim the unheard-of privilege of transmitting the tiara through a succession of exceptional men, standing alone upon the summit of genius or holiness? To St. Peter and his successors was promised infallibility, not essential impeccability. Of two hundred and fifty-nine Popes, history can point to but two or three of more or less questionable virtue. No empire can show a list of emperors, a line of kings, lasting through nineteen centuries, so free from blame or blemish. "The heretics," said Mabillon, "seize upon a few examples of irregularity in the Popes to attack the incorruptible truth and unity of the Roman Church. Whatever may have been the private character of most of the Popes upon whom they discharge the venom of their calumny, it can in no degree prejudice the Catholic Church, spread through the whole world. We must say, with St. Augustine : 'We shall receive no crown on account of their innocence; we shall suffer no punishment for their perver sity.'"

CHAPTER VI.

§ I. Pontificate of Benedict IV. (April 6, A. D. 900—October 20, 903).

1. The tenth century opens with the pontificate of Benedict IV. "With his reign," says Baronius, "begins a new century, to which the depth of moral depravity, the rule of crime and utter absence of all good, have given the name of *the iron age*, and which might as justly be styled *the age of lead*, so gloomy and chaotic is the appearance it presents."

"The barbarism of the age," says Pagi, "was beyond measure fearful. Ecclesiastical estates, bishoprics, and benefices were shamelessly usurped by laymen, and even by married men." The frequent changes in the Apostolic See aggravated the evil. "The generation of doctors and ecclesiastical writers," says Novaes, "seemed forever extinct. Ignorance would have held unbounded sway had not a few religious, in their lonely cells, kept alive a spark of the sacred fire, and devoted their hidden life to transcribing, for a happier age, the monuments of ancient literature."

"The bishops," says Tiraboschi, "were reduced to the shameful necessity of inquiring into the ability of their priests to read. The universal decline had dragged down the public morals in its fall, and corruption gained ground in proportion as intellect failed. Peter Damian thus wrote to a Pontiff concerning a candidate for the episcopate : 'He is entirely ruled by avarice and vanity ; he shamelessly canvasses for the episcopal dignity ; but, if all this be no obstacle, I must make known to your Holiness that he is yet the best of all.'"

2. Before entering upon the relation of events, it will be useful to settle the true character and the historical value of the charges brought against several Pontiffs of this dark period. The Pope, being at once the first prince of Italy and the Head of the Universal Church, had necessarily a paramount influence in the choice of the emperors. The different factions were also deeply interested in securing the election of a Pontiff favorable to their own views, and the worsted parties would infallibly traduce the Pope elected by their opponents. Our own age has better reason than any other to know how carefully we have to guard against the passionate and hostile invectives of contemporaries. The ecclesiastical history of the tenth century was long without any other annalist than Luitprand. Born in the beginning of the tenth century, Luitprand was at first sub-deacon of the church of Toledo, in Spain, then deacon of the bishop of Pavia, and finally bishop of Cremona. He was always a member of the party opposed to the Italian faction, headed by Adalbert, marquis or margrave of Tuscany, and the chief nobles of Rome. The six books of his *History of the Western Empire*, written under such influences, betray the political passions and irascible disposition of the author. "His style," says Fleury, "shows more wit than judgment. The display he makes of his acquaintance with Greek is really boyish. (This was a reminiscence of his two journeys to Constantinople.) His pen is always guided by passion ; heaping gross insults upon some, lavishing extravagant praises upon others," according to the whim of the

moment. The followers of Luther and Calvin have zealously
studied Luitprand's charges or injurious insinuations against
two or three Popes of the tenth century, and received them as
unquestionable proofs. Coming down to us with so many
varied echoes, the solitary voice of Luitprand has reached the
ears even of Catholics as the testimony of a *host of witnesses*.
Muratori (A. D. 1672–1750) was the first to proclaim that the
deafening chorus was but the noisy repetition of a single voice,
but yet refuted by a more weighty and disinterested contemporary witness. This opposing voice is that of Flodoard, who
was born at Epernay, in 894, and died, a canon of Rheims, in
966. Flodoard commanded universal esteem by his exemplary
life and *more than human wisdom*, to use the words of a contemporary annalist. He won no less distinction for his style as
an author than for his virtue as a priest. His *Lives of the
Popes*, from St. Peter to Leo VII. (A. D. 939), unknown to
Baronius, give a true coloring to many facts misrepresented
by Luitprand, and serve as a counterpoise to the calumnies
of the bishop of Cremona. With these premises, we have
only to say, with Bellarmine: "As we have not exaggerated the qualities of former Pontiffs, we shall not, in
speaking of their successors, hide what may be blamable,
for we are satisfied that Divine Providence will draw greater
triumphs from all things, since in the midst of so great disorders He has kept untarnished the spotless splendor of His
Church. The Roman pontificate owes its preservation neither
to the guidance nor to the prudence of men; it has been preserved because the *rock* is so truly of divine establishment, is
so deeply set, so constantly protected, that these *gates of hell*,
persecutions, heresies, the scorn of strong minds, the spread
of baneful writings, the craft and wickedness of men, have
never prevailed against it."

3. The reign of Benedict IV. was happily inaugurated by
the tidings of a brilliant victory won by Alphonso the Great
over the Moors, in Spain. The Spanish monarch, whose successful arms gave new realms to the crown of Asturias, shared

the warlike valor of his contemporary, Alfred the Great, of England, but lacked the milder virtues which endeared the Saxon hero to his subjects. Alphonso illustrated his reign by more than thirty campaigns against the Moors. To his original States he had added Galicia, a part of Portugal, Old Castile and the kingdom of Leon. In gratitude to God for the success granted to his arms, he rebuilt the church of St. James of Compostella, on a magnificent scale (A. D. 899), endowed the church of Oviedo, for which he obtained the metropolitical dignity and jurisdiction (A. D. 900), and founded bishoprics in the cities of Porto, Braga, Viseu and Tuy. While the Ommiad caliphs of Granada were doomed to see their limits daily narrowed before the triumphant march of Alphonso the Great, the Abassides of Bagdad, more favored in the East by the voluptuous inertness of Leo the Philosopher, coasted the shores of Macedonia and Greece, attacked Thessalonica, the second city of the empire, gave it up to fearful carnage, and led away twenty-two thousand of its citizens into bondage. The African Saracens had, at the same time, made a descent upon Sicily, which was doomed to all the horrors of pillage and devastation. The advance of the Saracens in the East and in Italy, with the unchecked career of the Normans in Gaul, seemed to foreshadow that the two barbarian powers would yet meet and shake hands in mutual congratulation over the ruins of a conquered world. In 903 the fierce followers of Rollo fired the basilica of Tours and the celebrated monastery of Marmoutier, the very heart of the French Church.

4. Louis IV., King of Arles, had received the imperial diadem, in Rome, at the hands of Pope Benedict IV. (A. D. 900). But the honor cost him 'dear, for he had enjoyed it but two years when he fell into the power of Berengarius, king of Upper Italy, who burned out his eyes by a cruel process practised in the East at this barbarous epoch.* To this brutal

---

* This punishment consisted in passing a red-hot iron before the victim's eyes, which were thus destroyed without causing death.

punishment the unfortunate Louis owes his epithet, the Blind.
Benedict IV. made his pontificate a season of blessings by the
spirit of moderation, mildness, and wisdom which marked it
throughout. He reinstated Argrim, bishop of Langres, who
had been unjustly deposed from his see. Rome looked forward
to brighter times under the auspices of a Pontiff worthy
of the Church's palmiest days; but the unsparing hand of
death snatched him from his children's love and bright anticipations (October 20, A. D. 903).

5. Holiness, that crown of Christ's spouse, did not fail,
even in these disastrous times, to give to the world its usual
display of pious and wholesome examples. The monastery of
St. Gall was a nursery of saints; its school was at this time
illustrated by the learning and virtue of Radbertus, Notker,
and Tutilo, whose mutual friendship was purified by the divine
love which gave it birth in their hearts. Salomon, bishop of
Constance, also acquired within the cloisters of St. Gall that
love of study which he still cherished in the midst of ecclesiastical dignities. St. Radbod, bishop of Utrecht, a descendant
of Friesland's royal line, revived the memory of the great
bishops of the early Church. When asked by Arnold, king of
Germany, to do him some service of a temporal nature, the
holy prelate replied : " It is just to obey superior powers ; but
who can be ignorant that bishops may not interfere in secular
matters, since they are the leaders of the spiritual arm ?
Clothed with the armor of faith, they must pray for the welfare of kings and subjects, strive to win souls, and not earthly
possessions. As to business of state, it is the duty of the
officers loaded with the king's favors to transact it. St. Fulk,
archbishop of Rheims, showed the same episcopal vigor in
France, and died a martyr to his zealous defence of the
Church's interests. He had excommunicated Baldwin II.,
count of Flanders, for an unjust usurpation of Church property
attached to the arch diocese of Rheims ; a land a assassins,
in the pay of the count, murdered the intrepid bishop (A. D.
900). Harvey, Fulk's successor, fulminated an excommunica-

tion against Baldwin and the assassins of the saintly prelate.
"Let them be accurst in city and country!" says the sentence.
"Evil betide their offspring, the fruits of their lands and of
their flocks! May they die the ignominious death of Arius!
And as we extingush and trample upon these torches, so may
their light be forever extinguished!" Here we have a proof
of the antiquity of the ceremony, practised in the publication of
an excommunication, of extinguishing tapers or lamps. Thus
did the Church wield her spiritual weapons to resist the violence of a still half-savage period.

§ II. PONTIFICATE OF LEO V. (October 28, A. D. 903—December
6, 903).

6. Hardly had Leo V. ascended the Pontifical throne, than
he was thrown into a dungeon by Christopher, one of the priests
to whom he had intrusted all his confidence for the government
of the Church. Leo died of privations and grief; and the Roman people made not the slightest effort to avert the fate of
their legitimate pastor. The minds of men, at this sad stage
of the world's history, had become so habituated to acts of
injustice and violence, that they looked upon them with
indifference and basely bowed to every kind of oppression!
The anti-Pope, Christopher, did not long enjoy the triumph of
his ingratitude. He was seized by the faction of Adalbert,
duke of Tuscany, and imprisoned in a monastery, where he
perished miserably; and Sergius III. was called by the ruling
party to the Sovereign Pontificate.

§ III. PONTIFICATE OF SERGIUS III. (June 9, A. D. 905—December 6, 911).

7. The name of Sergius III., who was recalled from exile
to fill the chair of St. Peter, is one of those upon which the
enemies of the Holy See have most delighted in heaping oppro-
brium. On the strength of Luitprand's testimony, his morals

have been deeply calumniated. The name of Marozia, wife of Adalbert of Tuscany, a notorious character intimately connected with all the scandals of the day, is mentioned in connection with these foul reports, perpetuated by shameless pens. We may quote contemporary writers on the character of Sergius III. "This Pope," says Flodoard, "already proposed for the Sovereign Pontificate at the time of the election of John IX., was recalled amid the unanimous acclamations of the people, and received the consecration long since destined for him. The seven years of this Pontiff's reign were a season of grateful joy to his subjects throughout the world." Another contemporary author, John the Deacon, thus speaks of the same Pontiff: "After his consecration, Pope Sergius III. was much grieved at the dilapidated condition of the basilica of St. John Lateran, which had fallen into ruins in the time of Stephen VI., and he had recourse to the divine goodness *in which he ever placed his trust.* He undertook to restore the noble pile; he happily succeeded in his holy work, and adorned the new basilica with the most costly ornaments." The epitaph inscribed upon the Pontiff's tomb by a grateful people fully bears out the testimony of Flodoard and John the Deacon: "Returning from his exile at the earnest prayer of the people," says this precious monument, "the good pastor showed equal love to all classes of his flock, and met all usurpers with apostolic energy." These three witnesses, who speak of Sergius as a Pontiff not only of unexceptionable moral virtues, but full of faith, piety, and zeal, are contradicted by Luitprand's partial voice alone. And so ill-informed is that hostile author on this period of history, that he places the pontificate of Sergius immediately after that of Formosus, and ascribes to him the shocking scene so disgraceful to the annals of Stephen VI. We believe that the dawn of truth is now breaking upon the life of Sergius, and that history has too long been the unsuspecting accomplice of a partial and ill-informed annalist.

8. During the seven years of his pontificate, Sergius was esteemed by the Christian world as a Pontiff worthy of the

highest veneration. The new archbishops of Cologne and
Hamburg respectfully solicited and obtained the pallium from
him. With a view to facilitate the spread of the faith among
the heathens of the North, he definitely placed the bishopric
of Bremen under the archiepiscopal jurisdiction of Hamburg.

9. His pastoral care reached every want of the Church.
Learning that the Greeks were reviving the errors of Photius
concerning the procession of the Holy Ghost, Sergius III. made
known the attempt to the Western bishops, that they might confirm the point of faith in provincial councils. The acts of one
of these councils, held at Trosly* by Harvey, archbishop of
Rheims, are still extant. The opening discourse and the canons are valuable monuments of contemporaneous history. "The
religion of Christ," says Harvey, "seems to be upon the brink
of destruction. The whole world is given up to the prince of
darkness, and the bolts of divine wrath give us no respite. In
contempt of all law, divine and human, heedless of the wholesome warnings of their pastors, men follow no guide but their
passions. Oppression reigns everywhere; men have become
like the fishes of the sea, the great devour the small. Even
we who are honored with the episcopal dignity, how are we
found wanting? Alas! we bear the glorious title of bishop
without fulfilling the bishop's sacred duties. We here receive
the name and rank of pastors, but when we shall stand before the
dread tribunal of the Sovereign Judge, where will be our flock
to present to the divine Shepherd?" This vehement protest
of an indignant heart does honor to Harvey's character and to
the episcopate of which he was a member. The same complaints are repeated in the canons of the councils, which, indeed, might rather be styled exhortations than decrees. There
was, in truth, far less need of new regulations than of vigorously enforcing the observance of the old ones. After condemning the blasphemies of Photius, the Fathers of Trosly
continue: "To so low an ebb has the observance of monastic

---

* Near Soissons.

discipline now fallen, that we despair of finding words to express or means to restore it. In punishment for our sins, desolation has fallen upon the house of the Lord. Of the numerous monasteries founded by our fathers, some have been burned by the heathens, others spoiled of their property and nearly ruined. And even where some material remains still stand of what was once a cloister, the utter wreck of religious discipline has left no trace behind. The rule is unknown. And all this ruin and disorder may be traced to the indigence and relaxation of the monks, but chiefly to the abuse of giving them lay superiors and abbots. Poverty obliges the religious to leave their cloisters and take part in worldly business; and the Prophet's wail might but too aptly be uttered in our own day and country: *Dispersi sunt lapides sanctuarii, in capite omnium platearum** (A. D. 909). The evil was indeed fearful, though not irretrievable. The zeal of these bishops was in itself a beginning and cause of reform. In the following year (910), St. Bernon, a man raised up by God to be the restorer of monastic discipline, laid the foundation of the monastery of Cluny, which became the well-spring whence the true spirit of religious vocation gradually flowed to all parts of the Church. Bernon, accompanied by St. Hugh, then a monk of St. Martin of Autun, begged of William-le-Débonnaire, duke of Aquitaine, the quiet and unfrequented vale of Cluny as a site for his monastery. The duke replied that he had appropriated it to his hounds, and asked them to choose any other suitable spot in his domains. "My lord," answered St. Bernon, "drive out the hounds and receive the monks." The fervor of the new community soon bore fruits, for good example has also its attractions and allurements; and now the dawn of a true monastic reform began to break through the heavy gloom that weighed upon the age.

10. The Church of Constantinople, so lately freed from the tyranny of Photius, was again given up to new struggles

---

* The stones of the sanctuary are scattered in the top of every street.—LAM. JER. iv. 1.

and deeds of violence. Leo the Philosopher, whose wisdom seems to have resided in his title alone, had been thrice married. In 905 he wished to legitimate his union with Zoe, his concubine. The Eastern Church looked upon the fourth nuptials as a state of polygamy. Nicholas the Mystic,* then Patriarch of Constantinople, deposed the priest who, won by the emperor's largesses, had blessed the union without the prelate's order. The unbending firmness of the Patriarch cost him his see and a sentence of banishment. The Pope, however, sent legates to the East to examine the question. Acting upon the true spirit of ecclesiastical discipline in the matter, they authorized the emperor's marriage, and thus restored peace to Constantinople (A. D. 907). In the West, where the Roman Church had taught the necessity of looking more to the essence of religion than to shifting customs, such a case would not even have excited a question.

Sergius III. died on the 6th of December, A. D. 911, after a pontificate of nearly seven years—guiltless, as we firmly believe, of the faults laid to his charge by Luitprand and other equally partial or misinformed historians.

§ IV. PONTIFICATE OF ANASTASIUS III. (December 6, A. D. 911 —June 6, 913).

11. While Anastasius ascended the Pontifical chair at Rome, Alphonso the Great died in Spain, dethroned by his own son, Garcias. The illustrious monarch, but unhappy father, found, in the bosom of his own family, foes more fatal than the formidable Paynim he had so often routed on the battle-field. The same year also closed the reign of Leo the Philosopher, at Constantinople, leaving the crown to the infant Constantine VII., *Porphyrogenitus*.

12. France was now the theatre of events full of the

---

* *Mystic* (*syncellus* or *secretary*), from the Greek word *secretary*. Nicholas had previously held that office in the imperial court.

brightest promise for the glory of the Church and the peace of
the world.   Rollo, the most daring and skilful of the Norman
leaders, had just met with a disastrous repulse, while besieg-
ing the city of Chartres.   This was the first time, for thirty
years, that the *Raven*, the sacred standard of the Normans, had
suffered such disgrace.   The inhabitants attributed their deliverance to the protection of the Blessed Virgin, whose tunic
they kept as a most precious treasure.   This sacred relic is
said to have been sent by the emperor Nicephorus to Charlemagne.   Charles the Simple thought the occasion favorable for
a conference with the Norman chief, and accordingly deputed
Franco, archbishop of Rouen, to treat with Rollo.   The intrepid
prelate stood before the formidable barbarian and addressed
him with unwonted firmness: " Great captain, will you fight
unto death, or do you deem yourself immortal ? Are you a god,
or a man formed from the earth, doomed to return to the dust
whence you sprung ?   Should you die as you have hitherto
lived, in deeds of blood and plunder, you can look forward only
to endless torments in the world to come.   But if you forsake
the superstition and fury of Paganism, you will enjoy the
sweets of peace both in this life and in the next.   King Charles
invites you to this course by the gift of this province of Neustria, wasted by yourself and Hastings ; and as a pledge of his
friendship he also offers you the hand of his daughter Gisela."
Such terms as these, offered by a king of France to a bandit
chief, are indeed somewhat revolting to national honor.   But it
was esteemed a favor, at that period, that Rollo accepted them
at all.   The dreaded Norman appeared at the court of Charles
the Simple, where his very presence was an event.   He ratified the treaty, placed his hands within those of the monarch,
and swore fealty to him, as was customary at the time.   But
when it became necessary, according to the ceremonial form in
use, to bend and kiss the royal foot, Rollo remembered that he
had a hundred times made this shadow of a king tremble upon
his throne ; and he would not bend.   Yet he allowed one of his
officers to discharge the duty in his stead.   The subject was

as proud as his master : in seizing the king's foot to embrace
it, his action was so ungentle as to throw the prince completely
off his feet.   This incident, however, did not break off the negotiation ; Neustria was thenceforth known as Normandy.
Rollo was instructed and baptized by Franco, the same prelate
who had been the ambassador of peace.   "Before sharing these
lands among my people," said the wolf now changed into a
lamb, " I wish to present a portion to God, to the Virgin Mary,
and to the other saints of whom you have spoken to me, and
whom I wish to make my patrons and protectors."   The converted barbarian showed himself as skilful to organize as he
had been fierce in battle.   The five remaining years of his life
repeopled deserted cities, placed religion in a state of prosperity, restored fallen churches, and established laws among his
people.   To Rollo's Normans, theft became a name unknown.
Religion had bowed this people to its gentle sway, and the
Normans edified the world in which they had so long spread
terror and dismay (A. D. 912).

13. Anastasius III. did not long survive the conversion of
the Normans.   He died on the 6th of June, A. D. 913, leaving
behind him an unassailable reputation for gentleness, wisdom,
and prudence.

§ V. Pontificate of Lando (December 4, A. D. 913—April 25,
914).

14. Lando survived his election just long enough to leave
his name to the pontifical annals as successor of Anastasius
III.   "At the date of his accession," says Platina, " a fierce
war had just broken out between the Italians and the Germans, for the possession of the empire.   The Italians wished
to have an emperor from their own nation.   This was a noble
and praiseworthy sentiment, but there was wanted the powerful
mind and strong arm to give it effect.   The great lights of
Italy had set; the strong and lofty tree which spread its great
boughs far and wide, was now dead to the core !"   Pope Lando

lent his pacific mediation, which resulted in a suspension of hostilities between Berengarius, king of Italy, and Rudolph of Germany. Lando died five months after his election (April 25, A. D. 914).

§ VI. Pontificate of John X. (April 30, A. D. 914—July 2, 928).

15. Lamentable in the extreme was the condition of Rome and Italy at this period. In the South, the Saracens, intrenched on the banks of the Garigliano, wasted the estate of the Church. In the North, the princes and municipal powers, far from leaguing against the common enemy, did but help his ravages by domestic feuds. The state of Italy called for a Pope who could lead the imbittered spirits into the ways of conciliation and peace. John X. was elected to the Sovereign Pontificate (April 30, A. D. 914). He had been nine years archbishop of Ravenna, and yet Luitprand does not hesitate to state that he was transferred to the Sovereign See of Rome within a year after his appointment to that of Ravenna by Pope Lando. It is important to correct this error, for upon it depends an entire system of accusations brought against the morals of John X. Luitprand himself confesses that he gathered the facts alleged against the Pontiff from a *Popular Life of Theodora*, mother of Marozia. The infamous character of these intriguing and abandoned females plainly shows that his authority could have been but a mere pamphlet. Such is the basis upon which hostile historians have built up all their charges against John X. Flodoard, on the other hand, thus speaks of the same Pontiff: "His prudent and virtuous life have won for him a throne in heaven." The reader is free to chose between these two contemporaneous but contradictory statements. Whatever may be imputed to the private individual whose name has been made a mark for the lying calumnies of writers unfriendly to the Papacy, the Pontiff was unimpeachable, and the Church blesses the reign of John X. To

an impartial mind this must be a strong presumption in favor of his innocence. Moral depravity is an unwonted appanage of great characters.

16. John X. was endowed with a great soul and rare political acumen. His first aim, was to settle the imperial power in Italy upon a solid foundation, and he accordingly crowned Berengarius emperor (A. D. 915). He secured to the new Cæsar friendly relations with the court of Constantinople, and with the princes of Capua, Salerno, Beneventum, and Spoleto, petty sovereigns who held nearly the whole of Italy. The combined forces of these various powers met in Rome. John X. took personal command, and by his presence gave unity, vigor and promptness to all the movements of the troops. It was a noble sight to see a Pope, in the tenth century, trampling upon difficulties, until then insurmountable, and in-augurating the holy crusade for the life of Europe and of civilization. While a Greek fleet skirted the coasts to cut off all re-enforcements to the Saracens from Sicily, John X. attacked them on the Garigliano, defeated them after a long and bloody battle, utterly annihilated their army, and forever freed Rome and its territory from the insults of the Crescent. The news of the victory was received with enthusiastic joy, and John X. made his triumphal entry into Rome amid universal transports of gratitude (A. D. 915).

17. The fourteen remaining years of John's pontificate were eminently useful to the Church. In 916, Harvey, archbishop of Rheims, sought his advice concerning the treatment of the newly converted Normans, some of whom afterward fell back into idolatry or into those savage and sacrilegious excesses with which they had been so long familiar. The Pope's reply is far more in keeping with the holiness proper to the Apostolic See, than with the moral depravity ascribed to the organ which now gave forth its teaching. "Were they among the older children of the Church," wrote the Pontiff, "they should be judged with all the rigor of the sacred canons; but as they have been so lately subjected to the yoke of the faith, it would be unjust to

insist upon the strictest observance of the law, lest the burden, to which they are not yet accustomed, appear too weighty at the very outset. As to the infliction of canonical penance, you are in a better position than we to judge of its reasonable application. Use your own judgment and prudence, and, aiming only at the salvation of souls, your apostolic zeal for the conversion of the Normans will entitle you to share the everlasting crown of the great St. Remigius, the apostle of the Franks." The Church seemed destined to enjoy no respite from hostile arms. One host disappeared only to give place to another equally formidable. The Magyars, a nation of Finnish stock, took the place of the converted Normans, and became in turn the terror of the West. After a long sojourn between the Don and Dnieper, they entered Hungary, toward the end of the ninth century. The people, terrified by the appearance of these savages, with shaven heads, dark features and fierce taciturnity, who seemed to live by blood and slaughter, and without any apparent home on earth, believed that the hosts of Gog and Magog, foretold by Ezechiel and the Apocalypse, had actually invaded the Christian world. From A. D. 912 until 920, the Magyars plundered and wasted Thuringia, Franconia, the valley of the Upper Rhine, and Bavaria. Bremen was laid in ruins (A. D. 917). The barbarians soon crossed the Rhine, overran Lorraine and Burgundy, and appeared even in the southernmost provinces of France.

18. Austrasia and Germany were ruled by princes more worthy of the empire than the degenerate heirs of Charlemagne. Louis IV., the young king of the Germans, having died in the beginning of the year 912, the Austrasians elected Conrad, duke of Franconia, to succeed him. In the regular order of succession, Charles the Simple should have been acknowledged as king by the Eastern as well as by the Western Franks; but the powerless monarch had fallen into universal contempt in Europe. The nobles at first offered the crown to Otho, duke of Saxony. With a disinterestedness seldom paralleled in history, Otho refused the crown, on the plea of his

advanced age, and, with generous magnanimity, urged them to choose Conrad of Franconia, his personal enemy, whom he declared worthy of the throne. Conrad, thus raised to power by the influence of his noble enemy and by the choice of the people, had his claim confirmed by the national council of Aldheim, in which were present the legates of John X. (A. D. 917). He proved himself worthy of his high position, and the seven years of his reign were fruitful in blessings of peace and prosperity both for Church and state. In his last moments, Conrad remembered his former enemy, Otho of Saxony, whose son, Henry the Fowler, was already known for his distinguished courage and prudence. He summoned his brother, Eberhard, who should, in the natural order, have been his successor, since he died without issue, and gave him his dying injunction: "Take the badges of royalty, the crown and sceptre, and when I am gone give them to Henry of Saxony; he is worthy of them." Eberhard pledged himself to obey the will of his dying brother; and thus was Henry the Fowler[*] raised to the throne of Germany, in which position he realized the bright promise of his youth. We can find few pages in history adorned with traits of equal generosity.

19. Ambition, ever on the alert in a season of ceaseless troubles and revolutions, multiplied the intrigues and difficulties attending the episcopal elections. John X. was called upon to regulate a number of cases of this nature at Narbonne, Cologne, and Rheims. His decisions were everywhere received with respectful submission, and, in this regard, no pontificate ever witnessed more of these applications to the Holy See—the best proof of confidence, esteem, and filial veneration.

A fresh revolution had, in the mean time, changed the religious aspect of the East. Romanus Lecapenus expelled the empress Zoe, regent during the minority of Constantine Porphyrogenitus, and seized the imperial sceptre. He was crowned

---

[*] Henry was called the *Fowler* from the circumstance that he was found engaged in that amusement when the royal insignia were brought to him by Eberhard.

in 920, and immediately set about putting an end to the schism which had divided the Church of Constantinople since the question of the fourth nuptials of Leo the Philosopher. The Patriarch Nicholas was recalled, and an account of the proceedings sent to Pope John X., that he might confirm them by virtue of his Apostolic authority. "You know," wrote the Patriarch to John, "the afflictions we have suffered for nearly fifteen years. But when we least expected it, Jesus Christ has stilled the storm, and we are all happily united."

20. These letters reached Rome just as a political revolution plunged the Church into deep mourning. John X. had been assassinated in a dungeon to which he had been consigned by the orders of Marozia and her husband Guy, marquis of Tuscany (July 2, A. D. 928). "From the gloomy dungeon," says Flodoard, "to which he had been doomed by the treacherous marchioness, the soul of John X. winged its flight heavenward to possess the throne prepared for him." John X. had reigned fourteen years. He proved himself above his age; and it was his misfortune to have lived at a time of such utter confusion that innocence and crime are placed side by side, unrecognized and undistinguished!

§ VII. Pontificate of Leo VI. (July 6, A. D. 928—January 20, 929).

21. Leo VI., whose ephemeral pontificate only appeared amid these violent tempests (July 6, A. D. 928), reigned but seven months. "To bring back the citizens to thoughts of peace, to settle the Italian troubles, to crush intrigues—such seems to have been the aim of Leo VI., who died on the 20th of January, A. D. 929." The rapid succession of the Popes and the violence of party spirit at this period have given rise to the suspicion that hostile factions more than once did away with an obnoxious Pontiff by means of poison. We may believe any thing of political passion; and the general disorder

which characterized it forbids the tenth century to protest against any charge, however serious.

§ VIII. PONTIFICATE OF STEPHEN VIII. (February 1, A. D. 929 —March 12, 931).

22. Stephen VIII. was proclaimed Pope on the 1st of February, A. D. 929, and lived in the midst of the factions contending for power in Rome. His pontificate of two years has left no trace in history. We do, indeed, find the praises of Stephen's piety and gentleness; but the record of his public life remains unknown—buried, no doubt, beneath the numerous party intrigues which made light of the election and death of the Sovereign Pontiffs.

23. It is cheering, in the midst of scenes so lamentable, to be able to turn our looks to some historical character bearing the almost forgotten stamp of sanctity. Sigismund, bishop of Alberstadt, was distinguished by his talents and eminent piety. King Henry had, before his accession, espoused Ratburga—a wealthy widow, already bound by vow to the religious state. Sigismund never ceased to multiply counsel, reproof, exhortation, and threats, until the scandal was removed. Henry saw in his promotion only a stricter obligation to give an example of regularity and observance of the laws. Breaking the ties which bound him to Ratburga, he contracted an alliance, at once more sacred and more honorable, with Matilda, a member of the illustrious race of Witikind.

24. The Church of Spain, ever persecuted by the unbelieving Moors, also found consolation in the virtues and enlightened zeal of many of its bishops. Special mention is made of Sisenand of Compostella, and Gennadius of Astorga, both honored as saints. They lived during the reign of Ordogno II., who succeeded his brother Garcias on the throne of Asturias (A. D. 914). The name of Sisenand was not unknown in Rome, and when John X. sent a legate on a pilgrimage to the tomb of St. James, at Compostella, he wrote to ask the saintly

bishop's frequent prayers in his behalf, at the shrine of the holy apostle. Sisenand sent his answer to the Pope's letter by a priest of Compostella, to whom king Ordogno likewise intrusted letters and costly gifts for the Sovereign Pontiff. The envoy of a holy bishop and of a king true to the religion of his fathers was received at Rome with the highest honors. During his sojourn of a year in the Eternal City, he held several conferences with the Romans touching the ritual then followed in Spain, and called the Mozarabic Liturgy. On his return to Galicia, he acquainted his bishop with what he had seen and learned in Rome. The points of difference in the two liturgies were carefully and impartially examined and discussed, and were found equally conformable to Catholic faith. It was not therefore deemed necessary to make any changes in usages worthy of reverence from their very antiquity. It was, however, decided to follow the most literal interpretation of the Roman rite in the formulas of consecration.

25. St. Gennadius had been transferred to the see of Astorga from the monastery of Viezo, or St. Peter's of the Hills, which he had founded after clearing away, by the sweat of his brow, the surrounding country, bristling with thorns and savage undergrowth. When raised to the episcopate, he strove to rebuild the ruined monasteries of his province, destroyed by the Saracens. With the rise of the material walls, he also revived the stronger defence of regular discipline and the study of ecclesiastical science. As books were very scarce at this period, Gennadius, with a view to the spread of knowledge by their greater diffusion, engaged the various religious communities to a mutual interchange of the few volumes they severally possessed. To this circumstance we owe our acquaintance with the catalogue of a monastic library in the tenth century. The list is very limited : 1st, a Psalter or Vade-Mecum ; 2d, an Antiphonal ; 3d, a Manual of Prayers ; 4th, a Manual of the Passions, or, in other words, a Martyrology. These four works constituted the common and indispensable stock of every church. Those which were mutually lent con-

sisted of: 1st, the Bibliotheca, that is, the whole Bible; 2d,
Commentaries on the books of Job, the Pentateuch, and Ruth,
in one volume; 3d, the Lives of the Fathers; 4th, a book of
commentaries upon Ezechiel; 5th, the books on the Trinity,
apparently by St. Augustine; 6th, St. Jerome's Letters; 7th,
the Book of Rules, which seems to have been the collection of
St. Benedict of Aniano. Thus the Western Churches, so sadly
desolated by the barbarian inundation strove, at least, to stem
the destructive tide of ignorance and disorder which followed
in its train.

§ IX. PONTIFICATE OF JOHN XI. (March 20, A. D. 931—February
5, 936).

26. John XI., the second son of the notorious Marozia and
Guy, duke of Spoleto,* owed his promotion to the intrigues of
his mother (March 20, A. D. 931). He was but twenty-five
years old at the time of his accession, a very unsuitable age
for the common father of all the faithful. His own brother,
Alberic, had seized upon all the power in Rome, and held the
youthful and unfortunate Pope in subjection. Lest his victim
should escape, he even doomed him to three years of close
confinement in the castle of St. Angelo.

During his captivity, Alberic forced from him the confirmation of the patriarchal authority of Constantinople, conferred
by order of the emperor Romanus Lecapenus, upon his son
Theophylactus, a youth of sixteen (A. D. 933). Ambassadors
were sent to Rome to obtain the necessary ratification of so
irregular a promotion. John XI., closely guarded by his
brother Alberic, yielded to coercion, and signed all that was
demanded of him.

27. Such scenes, in the very heart of Rome, shocking as
they may and must appear to us, will cease to seem so strange

---

* Here again Luitprand is guilty of a gross error, in attributing to John XI. a scandalous
extraction. A number of historians, either misled or hostile, have endorsed the calumny
utterly refuted by later critics.

if we turn our eyes to the other quarters of the world at the same period. Anarchy and confusion reigned throughout; feudalism was rising up from the ruins of monarchical power; the nobles, established in their own independence, made war upon each other and upon the common sovereign; they had seized upon, or rather they had abolished, the municipal and ecclesiastical elections; for how else could Hugh, styled the French Prince, king of Provence and Italy, have given to Manasses, already archbishop of Arles, the bishoprics of Verona, Mantua, and Trent, or the count of Vermandois introduced into the see of Rheims his son Hugh, a child of five years? How could an Eastern emperor have bestowed the see of Constantinople upon his son, a boy of sixteen, to shock the world by the unprecedented spectacle of a patriarch leaving the altar to visit one of his horses, and then returning to finish the office? In such a state of society, is it cause of wonder that petty tyrants, holding alternate and ephemeral sway in Rome, should dispose at will of the Holy See in favor of their children or their creatures? Unquestionably, these were immense evils; but they show more admirably the wonderful workings of Divine Providence, which has always preserved the teaching of the Church untainted in the midst of the foul atmosphere of scandal and crime through which it has had to pass. Heresy and impiety have eagerly but vainly searched the archives of this dark period; their efforts have but served to prove the unfailing truth of His word, who commissioned Peter and his fellow-apostles to "teach all nations," promising to "be with them all days, even to the consummation of the world." Not a single decree, even though issued in those days of disorder and ignorance, has afforded a clause containing aught at variance with faith and morals, or with the general discipline of the Church.

John XI. died in captivity (February 5, A. D. 936), a victim of the ambition of his own kindred.

28. While lawless license ruled supreme in the highest orders of the ecclesiastical hierarchy, a work of holy regenera-

tion was maturing in the retired shades of monastic life. The grain of wheat cast into the ground must needs pass through the cold and frost of winter before it may hope to ripen; the rich harvest of true greatness, virtue, and holiness which the Church was to reap in the thirteenth century was slowly and silently, but yet surely, developing its germs through the gloomy winter of the tenth. St. Benno, archbishop of Metz, gave up the honors of the episcopate for a poor and lowly cell, hallowed, forty years before, by the presence of the holy hermit Meginrad. He entered upon this eremitical heritage of the desert, and thus became the founder of the celebrated monastery of Einsiedeln, so well known as Our Lady of the Hermits. St. Benno was succeeded in the see of Metz by St. Adalbero, of the royal blood of Lorraine. He emulated his predecessor's zeal for monastic reform, and received into his diocese the holy abbots Einold and John of Vandières, who restored discipline and piety in the convent of Gorza. He charged St. Cadro, an Irish monk, with the reformation of the monastery of St. Clement, in Metz. St. Gauzelin, bishop of Toul, introduced the rule of St. Benedict, in its primitive purity, into the monastery of St. Evro. William Long-sword, duke of Normandy, restored the ruined abbey of Jumièges, and cherished the hope of coming to close his eyes in its peaceful shade. He kept prudently concealed in his palace the tunic and cowl which he hoped to wear at a future day. The hopes of the pious prince were prematurely thwarted by assassination (A. D. 943). But the restorer of monastic discipline, whose name is linked with this wholesome reform, is St. Odo, abbot of Cluny. Never was more tender piety, more feeling and amiable charity, joined to the austere rigor of strict discipline. It could literally be said of Odo that all the unfortunate were his children. He used to say to his religious: "The blind, the lame, and the needy will be the porters of the heavenly kingdom. We should take good care, then, not to shut our doors against them while on earth." Odo succeeded St. Benno, and was made abbot of Cluny at the death of its blessed founder (A. D. 927). Under his government the community was soon distinguished above all others, by strict observance, a holy rivalry of virtue among the brethren, the study of religion and the sacred writings, but especially by an inexhaustible charity toward the poor. St. Odo dwelt particularly upon the obligation of silence, and this was the starting-point of all his reforms. " Silence," he was wont to say, " is the parent of holy thoughts and of great deeds. Peace and charity make their abode in a community where silence reigns." The good odor of Christ shed abroad by this community drew to its cloisters many men of distinguished rank and virtue. Odo composed special rules for their direction, and thus gave rise to the congregation known as the order of Cluny. Princes and nobles hastened to place the monasteries of their dependence under that of Cluny, that St. Odo might bring them to the same standard of discipline; thus the reform soon spread throughout France, and even into Italy. The principal monasteries which then embraced it are: Fleury-sur-Loire, in the diocese of Orleans; St. Pierre-le-Vif, in Sens; St. Julien, at Tours; Carlieu, in the diocese of Macon; St. Paul of Rome, and St. Augustine of Pavia. The only hope of civilization and faith was thus cherished in the monasteries, far from the scenes of violence and corruption which disgraced humanity.

§ X. Pontificate of Leo VII. (February 14, A. D. 936— August 23, 939).

29. Leo VII.* proved himself worthy to fill the Papal throne, to which he was raised, against his will, on the 14th of February, A. D. 936. Far from seeking a dignity coveted by so many rash intruders, who saw but its splendor, he had done all in his power to avoid it, according to the old and now forgotten maxims. He did not, in his new dignity, abandon

---

* Some modern writers call this Pontiff Leo VI, looking upon the successor of John X as an intruder. This opinion is now rejected by sound criticism.

his usual application to prayer, his wonted rule of life, and constant meditation. Lofty in his views, prudent in resolve and execution, he possessed the faculty of winning the heart by the grace and mildness of his words. Such is he represented by Flodoard, who lived on terms of intimacy with the Pontiff.

During his pontificate, Gerard, archbishop of Lorck (which see has since been transferred to Saltzburg), came to Rome, to consult the Sovereign Pontiff both on his own behalf and on that of the bishops of France and Germany. The answer, addressed to all the bishops of Gaul and Germany, shows what were the questions proposed to the Pope. He declares that there is no guilt in visiting the full rigor of human laws upon sorcerers, augurs, and enchanters; though they should first be exhorted to do penance. He requests bishops to follow the custom of the Roman Church in saying the *Pax Vobis* on all feast-days and Sundays when the *Gloria in Excelsis* is said. "Another question," he says, "has been proposed to us, and one worthy of tears. Some apostate priests, renouncing the honor of priesthood, have publicly contracted matrimonial engagements. May the children sprung from these sacrilegious unions be promoted to orders?" The reply is in the affirmative. "For children," said the Pope, "cannot be made answerable for the faults of their parents." From this fact it appears that the ecclesiastical discipline on the conditions of admission to orders was not yet canonically fixed (A. D. 938).

30. Some time previous to these events, Leo VI. had proved the sincerity of his fatherly solicitude. Alberic, still master of Rome, was at enmity with his father-in-law, Hugh, king of Provence and Italy. Leo VII., aware of the merit and reputation of Odo, abbot of Cluny, summoned him to Rome, to effect a reconciliation. The saint wrought the two-fold wonder of reviving the natural feelings long since stifled in the hearts of both princes, and of moving Alberic to forgive an insult received from Hugh, who had, in public, struck him in the face. Alberic conceived for the venerable abbot of

Cluny an esteem bordering upon enthusiasm. Odo was one day met in the country by a peasant, to whom he was unknown, and who raised his hand to strike him. Alberic would have had the offending limb at once cut off; the wretched peasant owed his pardon only to the intercession of the saint himself. Thus we see that the manners and morals of the age still retained all their primitive rudeness and violence. All the barbarian elements brought together for the formation of the present state of society were then in process of fusion. Even while a prince of the tenth century seemed to bow to the sway of religion, the half-savage nature would show itself in some direction. Leo VII. ended his reign by a premature death on the 23d of August, A. D. 939.

§ XI. PONTIFICATE OF STEPHEN IX.* (September 1, A. D. 939—
January 15, 943).

31. The pontificate of Stephen IX., who was raised to the Papal chair on the 1st of September, A. D. 939, was almost wholly devoted to the settlement of a dispute relative to the archbishopric of Rheims, arising from a purely political cause. At the death of Charles the Simple, a captive in the tower of the castle of Peronne (A. D. 930), the throne of France had been given to the usurper Raoul. The queen, Ogina, fled before the rebels, taking with her to England the last scion of the Carlovingian stock, the youthful son of Charles the Simple, afterward Louis d'Outre-Mer. When Raoul died (A. D. 930), the nobles remembered the royal exile. Herbert, duke of Vermandois, whose revolt had caused the father's death, could not rejoice at the succession of the son; he accordingly used all his power to thwart the partisans of Louis d'Outre-Mer. With this view, he laid siege to Rheims (A. D. 940), whose archbishop,

* Baronius and Fleury say that Stephen IX. was a German, and elected by the German faction, in spite of the Roman clergy; that the Romans, in hatred of his unpopular nationality, seized upon his person, and, after loading him with outrages, fearfully mutilated his countenance. Other documents, however, show Stephen to have been of Roman origin. At such contradictory accounts are not unfrequent in the annals of this sad period.

Artold, was one of the most stanch defenders of the legitimate
sovereign. Six vigorous assaults compelled the city to open
its gates. Artold was made to sign his abdication, and confined in a monastery. In the following year (941), the Duke
of Vermandois assembled the bishops of the province, and,
regardless of Artold's appeal to the Pope, the see of Rheims
was bestowed upon Herbert's son Hugh, a young man of
twenty. It is painful to record these shocking abuses, but
such was the depravity of the age, that no authority was competent to quell the disorders. The Pope was obliged to yield
to the force of circumstances rather than expose the Church of
Rheims to the last extremities, and he accordingly sent the
pallium to the youthful prelate. He also availed himself of
the right to which this favor entitled him, and charged the
duke of Vermandois to recognize Louis d'Outre-Mer as lawful
sovereign. Hugh seems to have done nothing unworthy of the
dignity to which he had just been raised; and history lays to
his charge none of the excesses so common at that time, even
among members of the episcopate.

Stephen IX. died on the 15th of January (A. D. 943), after
a pontificate of three years.

§ XII. Pontificate of Marinus II. (January 22, A. D. 943—
August 4, 946).

32. Marinus II. was elected, on the 23d of January, A.D. 943,
to succeed Stephen IX. From the hopeless sterility which
marks the annals of the Church at this period, we turn with
satisfaction to the spectacle offered by Germany, happy under
the religious and wise administration of kings truly worthy of
the throne. Henry had reigned with glory, and was succeeded
by Otho the Great, who received the royal unction from Hilde-
bert, archbishop of Mentz (A. D. 937). "Receive this blade,"
said the prelate, as he girded him with the royal sword, "to
smite the foes of the Lord, whether barbarians or bad Christians; since, with the Frankish crown, God gives you the mission

to protect the whole of Christendom." Otho remembered the solemn words, and applied them faithfully to every act of his reign. Boleslas, the heathen king of the Bohemian Sclaves, had lately thrown off the German yoke and disclaimed all allegiance to Otho. Cruel persecutor of the Christian name, he had murdered the king, his brother St. Wenceslas, to seize the crown. A war of fourteen years resulted in the submission of the Sclaves, who promised to embrace the Christian religion and to remain faithful to the sovereigns of Germany. Churches and monasteries arose in Bohemia, and the converted nation at length entered the pale of true civilization. Otho now turned his victorious arms against the Danes, and compelled their king, Harold, to sue for peace, which was granted on the condition of his embracing the true faith. Harold hesitated. A priest called Poppo was striving to prove to him the divinity of Christ. " Are you ready," asked the king, " to test in your own person the truth of your assertions?" These proofs, by judgments of God, were, as we have stated, conformable to the spirit of the times. An iron was heated, which Poppo held in his hand, unhurt, until the king, convinced by the test, ordered that the idols should be destroyed and Christ adored. Jutland or Denmark was divided into three bishoprics, which the Holy See made suffragan to the metropolitan see of Hamburg. In virtue of his newly conferred powers, St. Adaldagus, archbishop of Hamburg, erected the three episcopal sees of Sleswig, Rippen, and Arhus, to which he gave the charge of the Christian communities already established beyond the Baltic, in Finland, Zealand, and Sweden. From this period Christianity rapidly gained ground throughout the North.

33. Since the death of Leo the Philosopher, the Eastern empire had again fallen into the succession of revolutions and intrigues so familiar to its annals, and necessarily following from the system of elections which placed the power in the hands of every fortunate ambition. Constantine VII. was too young at the time of his father's death to take the power into his own hands. The regency was at first intrusted to his uncle

Alexander, whose excesses surpassed those of the worst princes that ever disgraced the throne of Constantine, and who ended his shameful career in 912. The empress Zoe, a woman equally devoid of modesty and genius, succeeded in obtaining the guardianship of her son. The imperial admiral, Romanus, surnamed Lecapenus, worked himself into the good graces of the empress, used her ignominious favors as stepping-stones to the imperial power, and, once sure of the throne, imprisoned the empress in a monastery, where she died in despair. An unknown hand traced upon her tomb this epitaph : " Here lies a daughter of Babylon !" To give to his usurpation some show of justice among the people, Romanus reigned in the name of Constantine VII. In Constantinople he appeared as mayor of the palace. He caused the young emperor to marry his daughter. Meanwhile the Bulgarians were under the walls of the imperial city ; they formed a league with the Saracens, and now Constantinople seemed threatened with unavoidable ruin. Lecapenus bought a peace by giving his second daughter to the king of the Bulgarians and the imperial treasures to the caliph. It was then that he placed upon the patriarchal throne of Constantinople his son Theophylactus, a youth of fifteen years, who disgraced the pallium by his embezzlements and licentious excesses. He sold the bishoprics to the highest bidders, and every religious heart was saddened by the orgies which profaned his palace. The Greek Church was spared no scandal. The Patriarch, finding the ecclesiastical ceremonies too monotonous, enlivened them by the introduction of fantastic games, songs, and dances. These songs, mingling with the solemn ritual chant, allied, says an author, " the worship of the devil to that of the Divine Majesty." This sacrilegious abuse continued to profane the churches of Constantinople until the twelfth century. It even crossed the ocean and appeared in some churches of the West. Such is doubtless the origin of the burlesque ceremonial of the *feast of fools*, or that of the *asses*, of which we still find traces in the ritual of some cathedrals in the middle ages. But the other sons of Lecapenus, for whom he had severally obtained the title of Augustus, impatient to enjoy the power alone, clothed their father in the habit of a monk, and conveyed him by night to a monastery situated on an island in the Hellespont (A. D. 944). The weeping exile repeated these words of the Scripture : " ' I have brought up children, and exalted them; but they have despised me.' Like the High-Priest Heli, I am punished for my culpable fondness." Constantine VII. emerged from his long torpor, and seemed for a while to reign. The sons of Lecapenus perished by the sword or by poison; Theophylactus was replaced by the Patriarch Nicephorus (A. D. 945). But Constantine, who had reached the age of forty years without a thought of governing, found the weight of the imperial power beyond his strength. Basil, his chamberlain, and his daughter-in-law, Theophano, ruled him, as Lecapenus had done before. Leaving the reins of government in their hands, he was content to be the emperor of scholars and scientific men, and literature flourished through his care in Constantinople. He forgot that literary pursuits should be the recreation of a monarch, who, indeed, illustrates his reign by their diffusion, but speedily falls into public contempt if they are made paramount to the more serious and important duties of royalty.

34. Marinus ended his pontificate of three years on the 4th of August, A. D. 946. He had nobly struggled against the overwhelming tide of ignorance which desolated the Church. There is still extant a letter of the Pontiff's, in which he severely reproaches the bishop of Capua for his neglect to familiarize himself with the canonical regulations and the first elements of letters. Unfortunately, these efforts proved unavailing against the thick gloom of an age of darkness. Marinus stands out in bright relief against the universal darkness and disorder, showing some of that pious energy which animated the Sovereign Pontiffs in the primitive days of the Church.

§ XIII. PONTIFICATE OF AGAPETUS II. (August 9, A. D. 946—
March 18, 956).

35. The Chair of Peter found in Agapetus II. (August 9,
A. D. 946) a worthy successor to Marinus, and the government
of the Church received a new impulse during a reign of ten
years, one of the most glorious in the annals of the tenth
century.

The three councils of St. Pierre-de-Mousson, Ingelheim, and
Triers (A. D. 948) ended the difficulty in the archbishopric of
Rheims which had been raised under Stephen IX. The policy
which had deposed Artold in favor of the infant Hugh was in
a state of reaction, and would now have removed Hugh to
restore Artold. Louis d'Outre-Mer had overcome the hostile
artifices of the count of Vermandois. His first thought was
to bring about the deposition of Hugh, son of the rebel lord,
and to restore the see to Artold, who had never been canonically removed. The three councils mentioned above met for
this end. The deposition of Hugh and the reinstatement of
Artold were unanimously decreed, and submitted for ratification to the Sovereign Pontiff. In a council assembled at Rome
(A. D. 949), Agapetus II. confirmed both acts, and gave them
the sanction of the Apostolic See. But their execution was
attended with more than one difficulty. Notwithstanding his
earnest endeavor to restore the royal authority in France,
Louis was not master in his own realm. The feudal system
had raised the vassal's power at the monarch's expense. The
death of Herbert, which occurred at this date, might have
simplified the situation of affairs by depriving the false archbishop of Rheims of his natural support; but Hugh the Great,
count of Paris, had assumed the duty of protecting his nephew,
the archbishop, who was also preparing to make good his pretended rights by force of arms. The struggle lasted a whole
year. Pope Agapetus intervened, with a view to a general
pacification, which was at length effected under the

auspices of the Pontiff and of Otho the Great. Artold was restored to the see of Rheims, which he succeeded in holding against the subsequent attempts of his rival, Hugh.

36. The power of Otho the Great was on the increase in Germany. The Western Empire, restored by Charlemagne, had ceased to exist in 911, with the infant king Louis IV. The rival ambitions of the kings of Italy, France, and Germany had fallen together by mutual annulment, and no prince had since received, with the imperial title, the mission of protecting the Church. This was likewise one of the causes which led to the fearful decline witnessed in the tenth century. The dukes of Tuscany had made themselves masters of Rome, and the Papacy, thrown upon its own resources alone, was too often made a mere plaything in their hands. Otho daily added to his realm. He had lately made the acquisition of Lombardy, where they had invoked the aid of his sword to defend the people against the tyranny of their kings. On Christmas Day, A. D. 951, he took possession of his new territory, and married St. Adelaide, widow of Lothaire, late king of the Lombards, thus seating virtue and glory side by side upon the throne of Germany. It was not hard to foresee the day on which the empire was to be restored in his person; he foresaw it himself; but the time was not yet. Wishing to sound Pope Agapetus on the subject, he asked leave to come to Rome, to receive the imperial crown at the Pontiff's hands. Agapetus very prudently refused; he wished that facts should first prove the advantages to be derived from the power which it was proposed to re-establish. The Church had already suffered too much from princes crowned by her own hands, to risk any rash experiments. Otho accordingly returned to Germany with his bride, whose piety, sweetness, and boundless charity drew upon her power and name a people's blessing. He was also accompanied by the learned Ratherius, formerly bishop of Verona, now banished from his see by the revolutions in Italy. Ratherius revived the literary tastes of Germany, and was intrusted by Otho with the education of his youthful brother Bruno, who

was at a later period to illustrate by his holiness the archiepiscopal throne of Cologne.   The learned preceptor was afterward rewarded by promotion to the see of Liege (A. D. 953).[*]
On his return from Italy, Otho, who deemed it the first
duty of a Christian king to guard the existence of strict discipline in the Church, assembled a council of the German and
Lombard bishops, at Augsburg.   The canons published by this
council are a sad evidence of the depravity which ruled the
age.   They are nearly all directed against the immorality
and disorders of priests and clerics ; an appeal to the secular
arm was even found necessary to restrain their irregularity
(A. D. 952).   The king and nobles pledged themselves to
secure the observance of these decrees in all the provinces subject to their authority.

37. Even in abandoned Italy a powerful voice was raised
to protest against the general contempt of canon law and the
abuses which had crept into the Church.   Atto, bishop of Vercelli, had just published his *Treatise on the Sufferings of the
Church*, a noble burst of anguish wrung from a conscience outraged at the prevailing darkness and corruption of the age.   No
abuse, of the swarm that disgraced the Church, escaped the
brand of the eloquent bishop.   The superstitious recourse to
the judgments of God, the bestowal of bishoprics upon children,
simony, the usurpation of church property, the incontinence of
clerics, are lashed with a vehemence worthy of the apostolic
times.   To shield his own diocese from the general blight, the
bishop of Vercelli addressed his clergy in a circular, called the
Capitulary, divided into a hundred chapters, in which he quotes
the decrees of the councils, the decretals of the Popes, and
especially the capitularies of Theodulf, bishop of Orleans.   The
serious and solemn warning, coming like an echo of bygone

---

* Ratherius is the oldest author of the Middle Ages who has left us a grammar for the
use of children.   He called it the *Serva Dorsum* (Save-tho-back), to signify that it would
shield studious scholars from the whips and rods then in wholesome use.   Ratherius did
not long remain in the see of Liege.   His pure morality and real talents were not calculated
to win the affections of such a period.   The people of Liege rose up and obliged him to
resign the government of that Church (A. D. 956).

ages, was not unheeded.   St. Bruno, brother of the great Otho,
lately raised to the archbishopric of Cologne (A. D. 955),
emulated the zeal of the prelate of Vercelli.   The clergy and
the monasteries subject to his rule soon became very models
of regularity, piety, and strict canonical observance.   St.
Udalric, bishop of Augsburg, whose name it shall be our pleasing task to record again with such glorious surroundings, was
also nobly laboring in the work of clerical reform.   They were
followed by St. Adaldagus, bishop of Hamburg.   St. Aimard
and St. Mayeul, abbot of Cluny, inherited the zeal and virtue
of their predecessor, St. Odo.   St. Guibert of Gemblours, St.
Gerard of Brogne, and St. Gerard of Toul, were carrying on the
same holy work amid the silence and solitude of the cloister.
Providence thus placed the remedy side by side with the evil;
and the examples of holiness, sent from on high, were gradually working upon the masses and opening the way for the
regeneration of the West.

   38. The East was not blest with a like spiritual fruitfulness.   Its annals present, at this period, but two names worthy
of another age, and working against the general downward current.   Two hermits, St. Luke the Younger and St. Paul of
Latra, gave back to the desert the long unknown wonders of
an Anthony and a Hilarion.   As if hoping to counterbalance
the barrenness of his own age by the examples of an earlier
day, Simon Metaphrastes,* chief treasurer at the court of Constantinople, undertook to gather into one general collection the
Lives of the Saints, scattered through a thousand different
works.   In this immense labor he employed copyists, stenog-
raphers, and correctors, who wrote under his orders.   The
Lives of the Saints, thus collected, are divided into three cate-
gories.   Some are simply the full and complete reproduction
of the original documents and acts of the martyrs; others but

---

* Metaphrastes is derived from the two Greek words μετα and φρασις (translation). Metaphrastes means at once translator, commentator, and interpolater.   The name was bestowed upon Simon because he selected the most important passages from the *Lives of the
Saints*, already published, which he translated and paraphrased.

partially reproduce the originals, and have been retouched by
Metaphrastes; while many are altogether his own. The
criticism of the seventeenth century, represented by Adrian
Baillet, has not always dealt justly by Simon Metaphrastes.*
The collection for which we are indebted to the learned
treasurer, is certainly one of the most valuable works
of the kind left us by Christian antiquity. The fidelity with
which he performed his herculean task has been shown by Fr.
Montfaucon. The illustrious Benedictine quotes a Greek manuscript of the ninth century, containing lives of saints for the
months of May, June, July, and August, as they were before
passing through the hands of Metaphrastes. The compiler
contented himself with some improvements in the style, but
with a most scrupulous regard to the statement of facts.

39. Germany once more resounded with the clash of arms.
In the year 955, the Hungarian Magyars poured into Germany
in countless hordes, ravaging all the provinces between the
Danube and the Black Forest, and finally laid siege to Augsburg. The walls of the city were but ill calculated to resist
the assaults of the barbarians. But Augsburg was defended
by an insurmountable bulwark in the virtue of its holy bishop,
St. Udalric. With no stouter armor than his pastoral stole, the
dauntless prelate placed himself at the head of the warriors,
distributed the posts, and remained all day exposed to the enemy's darts. On the following morning he celebrated the Holy
Mysteries, blessed the troops, and exhorted them to put all
their trust in God. At the moment when the barbarians were
scaling the walls, Otho appeared at the head of a formidable
army, attacked the Infidels, and inflicted upon them a most disastrous defeat. In thanksgiving for this unexpected success,

---

* The seventeenth century, imbued, almost unconsciously, with the spirit of Jansenism,
showed an open disposition to banish from ecclesiastical history every fact that departed in
the least from the natural order. Under cover of sound criticism, the doctrine of miracles
was really rejected. But faith in miracles is the essence of the Church, whose very existence is a standing miracle. In Baillet's system, the Lives of the Saints consisted of a general panegyric on all the virtues, squared by the two dates of birth and death.

he founded and richly endowed the bishopric of Merseburg
(August 10, A. D. 955).

40. The glory of Otho the Great was now at its height.
Abderahman, emir al Moumenin* of Cordova, sent ambassadors
to congratulate him. Otho sent him back a deputation headed
by the holy abbot, John of Vaudières. The saint was obliged
to wait long after his arrival in Cordova for an audience. At
length, on the appointed day, he was notified to appear in court
attire before the emir. "The poor of Christ," he replied "have
no change of apparel." On learning this reply, Abderahman
ordered a considerable sum of money to be given him. The
faithful religious received it, but at once distributed it among
the poor of Cordova. "I like that monk's firmness," said the
emir, when he heard of the generous deed. "Let him come in
a sack, if he choose, I shall be no less pleased to see him."
The Christian ambassador was then ushered into the presence
of Abderahman, and fulfilled his mission with a freedom which
completely won the emir. He dwelt with particular earnestness upon the persecutions which the Christians suffered from
the Saracens, and begged the prince to put a stop to them.
While taking leave, he announced his intention of returning at
once to Germany. But Abderahman graciously replied: "After
so long a delay, the sojourn should not be so short." In a second
audience the emir held a long conversation with the abbot,
on the exploits of King Otho, on his lofty character, on the
advantages and disadvantages of the feudal system in Germany,
and finally dismissed him loaded with presents. The account
of this embassy, written by John of Vaudières himself, is one
of the most curious monuments of the tenth century.

Meanwhile, Pope Agapetus II. had ended in Rome a pontificate glorious for the Church (March 18, A. D. 956).

---

* This title signifies *Prince of the Faithful.* The Franks of the Middle Ages changed the
name into Miramolin, which epithet they applied without distinction to all the Saracen
chiefs.

CHAPTER VII.

§ I. PONTIFICATE OF JOHN XII. (March 23, A. D. 956—May 14, 964).

1. Condition of Italy at the accession of John XII.—2. Election of John
XII.—3. Otho the Great, Emperor.—4. John XII. forsakes the party of
Otho the Great.—5. Hostility of Otho toward the lawful Pope.—6. A
council at Rome deposes John XII. and elects an antipope, under the name
of Leo VIII.—7. Reinstatement and death of John XII.

§ II. PONTIFICATE OF BENEDICT V. (May 19, A. D. 964—July 5, 965).

8. Benedict V. banished to Hamburg. Usurpation and death of the antipope
Leo VIII.

§ III. PONTIFICATE OF JOHN XIII. (October 1, A. D. 965—September 6, 972).

9. State of the Catholic world at the accession of John XIII.—10. The political life of Germany centres in the person of Otho.—11. Otho's efforts to
extend the triumphs of Christianity.—12. Embassy of Luitprand, bishop
of Cremona, to Constantinople.—13. Otho II. espouses Theophano, a Greek
princess.

§ IV. PONTIFICATE OF BENEDICT VI. (September 22, A. D. 972—March, 974).

14. Benedict VI. dies by poison.

§ V. PONTIFICATE OF DONUS II. (April 5, A. D. 974—October, 975).

15. Election and death of Donus II. St. Mayeul refuses the tiara.

VI. PONTIFICATE OF BENEDICT VII. (December 19, A. D. 975—July 10, 984).

16. Boniface VI., antipope.—17. The Russians before Constantinople.—
18. Social crisis in the tenth century.—19. St. Dunstan, archbishop of
Canterbury.—20. St. Bernard of Menthon.—21. Roswitha.—22. Death of
Benedict VII.

§ VII. PONTIFICATE OF JOHN XIV. (October 19, A. D. 984—August 20, 985).

23. Election and death of John XIV.

§ I. Pontificate of John XII. (March 23, a. d. 956—May 4, 964).

1. The death of Agapetus II. left Italy broken up into rival factions. Otho the Great held the Suzerainty of Lombardy; but, at the request of the empress St. Adelaide, he had left to Adalbert, son of Berengarius II., the administration of a portion of his former domain. Alberic, duke of Tuscany, and husband of Marozia, had just died, leaving his power in the hands of his son Octavian, a youth of eighteen years, who, regardless of his previous engagement in holy orders, hastened to seize the reins of government. Pandulf, duke of Capua, sought to build up an independent power in the territory called the *Laborini Campi*. The absence of a firmly constituted sovereignty, like that created by Leo.III. in favor of Charlemagne, resulted, for Italy, in domestic strifes, disorder, and bloodshed. The union of the Papacy and the empire seemed necessary for the safety of the world. Unhappily, the homogeneous elements essential to its lasting consolidation were now wanting. The restoration of the empire, to the advantage of the German princes, was not destined to afford the protection and stability looked for by the Holy See.

2. Octavian, already a cleric of the Roman Church, and at the age of eighteen master of the temporal power, was ambitious to join the spiritual supremacy to his actual sovereignty. He was elected Pope on the 23d of March, a. d. 956. His

promotion was a disgraceful calamity. He brought to the
Chair of St. Peter only the vices and dissolute morals of a
young debauchee; and though Luitprand must have exaggerated the disorders of this Pope, yet there remains enough
of truth in the account to have brought down the scandal of
the pontificate through succeeding ages, like a loud blasphemy,
which makes angels weep and hell exult. Octavian assumed
the name of John XII. This first example of a change of
name on ascending the pontifical chair has since passed into a
custom with all the Sovereign Pontiffs.

3. John XII. looked upon his new dignity only as a means
of more fully indulging his licentious passions. Immediately
after his accession he assembled his troops and marched against
Pandulf, prince of Capua; but his arms were unsuccessful.
He came back to Rome completely defeated, and this reverse
left him defenceless against the seditious attempts of Adalbert,
king of Upper Italy. Powerless to free himself from this
tyranny, the Pope appealed for help to Otho the Great. That
prince came to Rome in 962, and was hailed as saviour by
clergy and people. The youthful Pontiff immediately crowned
him emperor. Thus was the Western empire restored, after
an interregnum of fifty years. The Romans swore fidelity to
Otho the Great. John XII. solemnly promised never to contract an alliance with his enemies. Otho, on his part, confirmed the gifts made to the Holy See by Pepin and Charlemagne. The original copy of this precious deed, written in
letters of gold, was kept in the castle of St. Angelo. The
emperor engaged to claim for himself or his successors no
right of government or of jurisdiction in the Pontifical States
"*unless it be officially required by him who, at the time, holds the
government of the Holy Church.*" The decrees of Eugenius II.
relating to the papal elections were also renewed: "The Roman
clergy and nobles, by the necessity of existing circumstances,
and to punish injustice toward the people and the reasonable
demands of the prelates, shall make oath to follow exactly the
canons relating to the election of the Pope, and not to allow

the Pontiff-elect to be consecrated without the presence of the
emperor's deputies."

4. John XII. soon violated the oath he had pledged. Otho
the Great was still at Pavia when he learned that the Pope had
concluded a treaty offensive and defensive with Adalbert, to
expel the Germans from Italy. Unable to credit the report,
the emperor sent deputies to Rome to ascertain its truth. The
leading citizens loaded the Pontiff with accusations but too
well founded. His manner of life was most infamous. He
said that *if he preferred Adalbert to the emperor, it was because
he found an accomplice in the former, and a judge in the latter.*
Otho heard these accusations with a certain amount of reserve,
charging upon his youth the odious deeds imputed to the Pope.
"He will improve," said the emperor, "with age, and by the
examples and advice of good men." Otho contented himself
with visiting his indignation upon Adalbert, and he accordingly
laid siege to Montefeltro, where that prince had taken shelter.
At this juncture, a deputation from the Pope, consisting of Leo,
chief secretary of the Roman Church, and Demetrius, a person
of distinction in Rome, arrived in the imperial camp. They
bore a promise from John XII., to reform in his conduct what
had been the effect of the fire and passion of youth. He then
complained that the emperor exacted an oath of fealty to himself, and not to the Apostolic See, from the cities in which he
established his power. Otho replied by exonerating himself
from the charges contained in the pontifical letter. He sent to
Rome Landobard, bishop of Munster, and Luitprand of Cremona, the historian of this gloomy period, with vassals, who
were to prove their master's innocence by the ordeal of the duel,
according to the barbarous usage of the times, should the Pope
refuse to receive their testimony. John XII. would hear of no
excuse, and called the troops of Adalbert to Rome.

5. On receiving the account of the Pope's bearing, Otho
pressed the siege of Montefeltro, and, toward the end of the
summer, came to Rome in person. John and Adalbert, not
daring to await his approach, fled with the treasure of St.

Peter's Church (A. D. 963). Hitherto, so far as we may judge by the testimony of contemporary writers, Otho's conduct had been unimpeachable. Led away by the counsels of German bishops ill versed in the knowledge of canon law, and justly angered by the inconstant and scandalous conduct of John XII., he hazarded a step of fatal consequence, and thought himself justified in causing the deposition of the Sovereign Pontiff. Whatever he might be as an individual, John XII. was lawful Pope; any attempt against his spiritual authority was, of right, null. The eighth general council had just decreed, in its twenty-first canon : " If any one, strong in secular power, seek to expel the Sovereign Pontiff from his See, let him be anathema !" St. Avitus of Vienne, summing up the Catholic teaching of his day upon this point, had said : " How can the Head of the Universal Church be judged by his inferiors ? If any one of the other pontiffs stray from the right way, he can be reformed ; but when the Pope is arraigned for judgment, it is no longer a single bishop, it is the whole episcopate, which is impugned." In a similar case, when the bishops of France had met at Rome to examine the charges brought against Leo III. (A. D. 860), they had all joined in the solemn protestation : " We dare not sit in judgment upon the Apostolic See, the chief of all the churches of God. It belongs to that See and to its Pontiff to judge us all, being himself subject to no other judgment, according to the traditions of ancient discipline." This should have occurred to the bishops assembled, by order of Otho, to judge Pope John XII. Their meeting was but a pseudo-council, their decrees contrary to all canon law, and the Pontiff of their election could be but an antipope.*

6. The false council accordingly assembled (A. D. 963) in St. Peter's church, Luitprand acting as interpreter for the emperor, who knew no other tongue but the Saxon. The most serious charges of immorality, simony, and enormous crimes,

---

* Such is the view taken of this assemblage of German bishops by Baronius, Maraton, Mansi, Becchetti, de Marca, Natalis Alexander, and Kertz.

were alleged against John XII. When the accusations had all been read, Otho addressed the assembly, Luitprand translating each sentence of the discourse into Latin. "We know by experience," said the emperor, "that the spirit of slander and envy often attacks those who are constituted in authority. Hence am I slow to give too ready ear to the charges just read. I entreat you, then, in the name of God, Who cannot be deceived; in the name of the Virgin Mary, His mother; in the presence of the Apostle St. Peter, whose body rests here in our midst, to utter nothing against the Pope but real facts, well known, and witnessed by men worthy of belief." It is evident, from his words, that Otho felt the serious nature of the proceeding, and sought to shield the unprecedented act by every possible guard. The clergy, nobility, and people of Rome testified to the truth of the charges. "If John," they exclaimed, "is not guilty of all these crimes, and of many more too disgraceful to be spoken in words, may the Prince of the Apostles, on the day of our death, refuse us entrance into heaven! If you believe not our witnessing, at least believe the evidence of your whole army, which has, for the last five days, seen him upon the opposite bank of the Tiber, girt with a sword, bearing a buckler, corslet, and helmet, in contempt of the holy canons!" With this overwhelming evidence before him, Otho still deemed himself bound, before taking further steps, to write to John XII. " On reaching this city, we inquired of the bishops the cause of your absence. They replied by charging you with deeds which would have been unworthy of common stage-players. All, both clergy and laity, accuse you of homicide, perjury, sacrilege, and incest. We therefore beg of you to come at once and justify yourself upon all these heads. If you fear the violence of the people, we promise you, with an oath, that nothing shall be done at variance with the canons" (November 6, A. D. 963). John answered by a threatening letter to the council. "We learn," he said to the bishops, "that you intend to elect another Pope. Should you dare to proceed, then, in the name of Almighty God, in virtue of our apostolic authority, we pro-

nounce you excommunicated, and forbid you to confer any
ordination or to celebrate the Holy Mysteries." The bishops
were not daunted by this vehement language. In another session the emperor urged them to pronounce judgment. The
following sentence was adopted : "An unexampled evil requires
an unprecedented remedy. Did the moral depravity of John
XII. injure no one but himself, he should be borne with ; but
his example is contagious, and perverts souls. We therefore
beg that he be expelled from the holy Roman Church, and that
his place be given to an edifying and virtuous Pontiff." Otho
consented. The secretary of the Roman Church, who had been
deputed by John to the camp at Montefeltro, was elected, under the title of Leo VIII. Otho, though undoubtedly with pure
intention, yet too readily yielding to a zeal which was not according to knowledge, had just created an antipope (A. D. 963).
Believing that he had thus restored peace to Italy, he set out
on his return to Germany.

7. Still, John XII. was not without partisans. After the
emperor's departure he entered Rome in triumph ; Leo VIII.
had hardly time to fly. John, a deacon, and the chief secretary, Azo, who had shown a marked attachment to the antipope, were treated with the last degree of cruelty. John lost
his right hand ; Azo was deprived of his tongue, his nose, and
two fingers. After this deed of revenge, John XII. held a
council to annul the last. "You are aware, well beloved brethren," said the Pope, "that I was kept from my See for the space
of two months by the violence of the emperor. I ask you, then,
if, in accordance with the canons, the name of council can be
given to an assembly irregularly convoked in my church during
my absence ?" "It is an outrage in favor of the antipope Leo !"
exclaimed the council. "He should, then, be condemned !"
said John. "He should !" replied the bishops. This trait of
cowardly compliance shows the spirit of that abandoned age, for
most of the bishops who now spoke had, three months before,
used the same words against John XII. Leo VIII. was excommunicated. No other punishment could be inflicted upon

him : he was safe at the court of the emperor. As soon as
John had secured this triumph over his enemies, he plunged
more deeply than ever into his former dissolute excesses. The
avenging blow was not long delayed ; his end was suited to his
criminal life. Stricken down by a sudden disease, in the very
midst of his infamous pleasures, he died at the end of eight
days, unable to receive the holy Viaticum (May 14, A. D. 964).
O Holy Roman Church! Mother and Mistress of all others!
how often, while recording the annals of this gloomy period,
have we sighed at the degradation to which the disorders of an
unworthy Pope have doomed thee! Two hundred and fifty-
nine Pontiffs have succeeded each other from St. Peter to Pius
IX. Two or three, in a period of nineteen centuries, have profaned the august character of representative of Jesus Christ.
Scandals *must* come into the world : St. Paul has said it. Fatal
must! which has been verified even upon the apostolic throne.
But at least the sacred deposit of faith, even when intrusted to
unworthy keepers, has never been altered. It has ever remained
pure and unmixed ; and this is the ever-enduring miracle of
the Church.

§ II. Pontificate of Benedict V. (May 19, A. D. 964—July
5, 965).

8. The Romans cherished a heartfelt hatred against the
German rule. At the death of John XII., regardless of the
antipope Leo VIII., they raised to the vacant See (A. D. 964)
Pope Benedict V., whose virtue and learning are recorded by
even the German historians. But Otho the Great, who had
conferred his dignity upon Leo, wished to uphold his work ; he
accordingly hastened at the head of an army to besiege Rome.
The feeling of hatred was equal on both sides. The Germans
treated the besieged with unfeeling severity. The Romans defended themselves with the energy of despair. Pope Benedict
V. spared nothing that could raise their courage ; he appeared
upon the walls to threaten the emperor and his army with ex-

communication. Still, Otho did not abate the rigor with which
he had prosecuted the siege, and Rome, yielding to famine
rather than to arms, opened its gates (June 23, A. D. 964).
Leo VIII. entered with the emperor.

The antipope assembled a council in the church of St. John
Lateran. The emperor was present with the bishops of Rome,
Italy, Lorraine, and Saxony. Benedict V. was introduced, in
pontifical attire. The antipope tore off his pallium, broke the
pastoral staff he held in his hand, deprived him of his chasuble
and stole, and at length pronounced sentence in these terms:
"We deprive Benedict, the usurper of the Holy See, of all pontifical and sacerdotal dignity. Yet, at the emperor's request,
we allow him to keep the order of deaconship which he held at
the time of his intrusion, but on the express condition that he
may not stay in Rome, but be sent into exile" (June, A. D. 964).
Leo could refuse nothing to the emperor who had just restored
him to a usurped throne. He published a decree granting to
Otho and to his successors "the right of choosing themselves a
successor in the kingdom of Italy, of *establishing the Pope*, and
of investing bishops; so that neither Pope, bishop, nor patrician
can be elected without his consent; and all this under penalty
of excommunication, perpetual banishment, or death." Nothing is wanting to fill the measure of cowardly and sacrilegious
impiety which marks this decree. Usurpers have always lowered the standard of the authority taken from the lawful pastor.
Benedict V. was banished to Hamburg. The emperor soon
after quitted Rome, and spent the rest of the winter in Upper
Italy, where a violent plague decimated his army. Leo VIII.
did not long enjoy his usurped authority in the bosom of the
Roman Church. He died in the beginning of April, A. D. 965.
Otho had been able to learn something of the virtues of Benedict, whose name was held in benediction at Hamburg, and indeed
throughout Germany, and he was taking measures to restore
the Pontiff to the Roman See, when death anticipated his plans
by removing the holy exile (July 5, A. D. 965). The legiti

mate Pastor and the usurper appeared almost together before
the tribunal of God.

§ III. Pontificate of John XIII. (October 1, a. d. 965—September 6, 972).

9. The train of local events has withdrawn our attention
from the general state of Europe and the Catholic world at
the moment when John XIII. ascended the pontifical throne
(October 1, a. d. 965). A rapid glance at the various sovereigns of Christendom will suffice to restore the broken thread
of succession. England, always under Saxon rule since Alfred
the Great, has seen its throne successively filled by Edward,
Athelstan, Edmund, Edred, Edwy, until the reign of Edgar
"the Peaceful" (a. d. 957-975). Guided by the wise counsels of St. Dunstan, archbishop of Canterbury, of St. Ethelwold of Winchester, St. Oswald of Worcester, and of the pious
chancellor Turquetul, Edgar perfected the legislation of Great
Britain, giving it a true character of uniformity and of Christian wisdom and mildness. France, under the government of
Lothaire, eldest son of Louis d'Outre-Mer (a. d. 954-986),
was really ruled by Hugh the Great, count of Paris, and was
preparing to give the crown of the Carlovingian dynasty to the
Capetian race. Spain, true to the blood of Alphonso the Great,
had witnessed the successful struggles of Ramires II. (a. d.
950-955) and Ordogno III. (a. d. 956-967) against the renowned Caliph of Cordova, Abderahman. Ramires III. (a. d.
967-982) carried on the work begun by his fathers, and, under
his guidance, the Catholic kingdom widened the bounds of its
conquests. The East was ever a field of bloody revolutions.
Constantine VII., Porphyrogenitus, a distinguished scholar, but
below mediocrity as an emperor, died in 959, from the effects
of poison administered by his own son, Romanus II. The
parricide soon fell, in turn, before the intrigues of Theophano,
the daughter of an inn-keeper, whom he had married, seconding
the ambitious efforts of a skilful general, Nicephorus Phocas,

who, with the purple, assumed the name of Nicephorus II.
(A. D. 963–969).

10. The heart of the civil life of the West was Germany,
now raised by Otho the Great to the highest pitch of power.
This monarch, who might, under more favorable circumstances,
have recalled the glorious days of Charlemagne, now began to
bestow extensive fiefs upon prelates, with privileges similar to
those of noble laymen, in order to offer a species of counter-
check to the excessive power of the latter. Otho the Great
was thus the author of the temporal greatness of the German
clergy, so often ascribed by ignorance or bad faith to the usur-
pations and encroachments of the Church. Otho understood,
as well as his detractors, the danger of multiplying independent
vassals, who would eventually use their power against royalty
itself. But the point had now been reached at which it would
have been as difficult to check this growing force as it was
dangerous to show any fear of it. Yet, to guard against any
abuse of the new power thus placed in the hands of bishops
and abbots, he decreed that it might be used only with the
concurrence and under the direction of the imperial officers.
If the German clergy afterward freed themselves from this restraint, the reason must be sought for, as in the case of all other
holders of fiefs, in the great weakness of the royal authority.

11. Otho spared no pains to exalt the Church and to
advance the Catholic faith, of which he had, at his coronation,
proclaimed himself the champion. The archbishopric of Magdeburg, erected for St. Adalbert, had lately been placed, by a
decree of John XIII., upon an equality with the three great
metropolitical sees of Germany—Cologne, Mentz and Triers.
In the course of a mission among the Rugi (Pomerania), St.
Adalbert had the happiness to convert Olga, queen of these
barbarians. A flourishing church was founded in their midst,
which the emperor was careful to provide with apostolical laborers. The bishopric of Prague was founded at about the same
time and with the same object as that of Magdeburg. Ditmar,
a Saxon monk, was its first incumbent. Boleslas the Cruel, the

murderer of his brother, St. Wenceslas, had left the crown to his son, of the same name as his father, but, unlike him, surnamed the Good (A. D. 967). The young king, sincerely attached to the Christian faith, erected into an episcopal see the church in which were venerated the relics of his uncle, St. Wenceslas. John XIII., in ratifying the election of Ditmar as bishop of Prague, forbade the use of the Sclavonic language in the offices of the Church, and required that the Bohemians should, in all points, conform to the Latin rite. The kingdom of Denmark, of which we had occasion to mention the conversion, under the pontificate of Agapetus II., was marching steadily onward in the newly opened path of faith and true civilization. The Poles, at about this time, also appealed to the Sovereign Pontiff for bishops to instruct them; the Pope sent Egiel, bishop of Tusculum, to this new province of the Christian realm. Thus did the Church extend its conquests among the nations of the North.

Otho's attention was now called to Italy. The seditious factions in Rome had dared to lay irreverent hands upon the Vicar of Christ (A. D. 965). John XIII. had been seized and banished to Campania. The emperor, at this news, hurried to Rome, where his presence alone sufficed to restore order (A. D. 966). But the mere submission of the factions could not, in the emperor's estimation, repair the outrage upon the majesty of the Sovereign Pontiff. Twelve of the chief conspirators were put to death. Peter, præfect of Rome, who had played the leading part in the revolt, was suspended by the hair to the equestrian statue of Marcus Aurelius, upon the public square of the Capitol, then led through the streets of the city upon an ass, and finally sent into exile. Such examples of severity were indispensable in a period of continual disorders.

12. Otho was now maturing the plans of an enterprise which would alone have sufficed to immortalize his reign—the expulsion of the Saracens and Greeks from southern Italy. The Eastern Empire still held Otranto and a few other towns, the last remnants true to the memory of Constantine. Tho

whole of Sicily was occupied by the Saracens, who thus continually commanded the entrance of Italy, properly so called,
through the disputes of the dukes of Beneventum and Capua,
who could unblushingly call in, to second the views of personal
ambition, the most cruel enemies of the Christian name. The
power which he now wielded, and the imperial crown firmly fixed
upon his brow, gave him sanguine hopes of succeeding in the
twofold undertaking. He sought first to deal with the Greeks
by diplomacy. His son, Otho II., had lately been associated
to the government of the empire, and crowned by the hands of
John XIII., on Christmas-Day, a. d. 967. The emperor meditated an alliance between his son and a young Greek princess,
daughter of Romanus the Younger and Theophano. Luitprand,
bishop of Cremona, and historian of the tenth century, was sent
to make the proposals to the emperor Nicephorus II. It was
a delicate mission. The empire of Germany had not yet been
recognized by the court of Constantinople, whose etiquette,
always more obstinate in proportion as its power declined,
looked upon these German barbarians as usurpers. Otho
thought the bishop of Cremona equal to such a mission, since
he had already acted in the East as ambassador of Berengarius
II. His familiar acquaintance with the Greek language and
manners seemed to fit him more particularly for the management of this important affair. The emperor's expectations were
doomed to disappointment. The haughty bearing of the ambassador only imbittered the proud susceptibilities of the Eastern emperor. Luitprand was received without any of the
honors usually paid to the envoys of sovereigns. "I could
have wished," said Nicephorus, "to give you a more honorable
reception; but the conduct of your master forbids. He has
seized upon Rome as if it were an enemy's city. He has tried
to subject by violence several other cities of my empire, and
now has doubtless sent you here as a spy." Luitprand replied:
"The emperor my master did not seize Rome by violence; but
only rescued it from the tyranny of the dukes of Tuscany, under which it groaned. While the popes pined away in dun-

geons at home or in exile abroad, subject to the most shameful
treatment, what was the bearing of your predecessors, who
kept the title of Roman emperors without the burden of its
responsibilities? Otho the Great came from the farther end of
Europe to secure the freedom and dignity of the vicars of Jesus
Christ. He punished rebels according to the laws of Justinian,
Valentinian, and Theodosius." "But you are not Romans!"
cried Nicephorus, "you are only Lombards!" "All," answered
the Bishop of Cremona, "whether Lombards, Saxons, Germans,
or Franks, we know no worse insult to offer a man than to call
him a Roman. To us that name bears with it all that is worst
in baseness, cowardice, avarice, impurity, and dishonesty!"
History has recorded this spirited reply. It could certainly
contribute little to the success of the embassy, but it is valuable as a witness to existing facts. The Roman people—that
kingly race—had then carried its victorious arms to every quarter of the known world, had heaped up conquests and glory,
only to feel its haughty front bowed to the yoke of nations yet
uncivilized by the cultivation of art and science—of rude and
ignorant men who ruled the world, in turn, by the sword, the
axe, and fire! The negotiation failed, and Luitprand found
consolation for his ill success, in writing the curious relation of
his embassy.

13. Since the Greeks would not be his friends, Otho no
longer hesitated to treat them as enemies. He led an army
into Apulia and Calabria, which still acknowledged the sway of
the Eastern emperors. Hostilities had already begun, when an
unforeseen occurrence caused their suspension. Theophano, who
had already caused the death of her first husband, Romanus the
Younger, now indulged a new caprice by doing away with the
second. She then offered the throne and her hand to the murderer, John Zimisces. John accepted the throne, but rejected
her hand. Theophano received the chastisement due to her
crimes, and died in the confinement of a monastery in Armenia (A. D. 969). The policy of the East, under the guidance
of John I., took a new direction. The negotiation which had

failed with Luitprand, concerning the union of the young emperor Otho II. with a Greek princess, was now resumed. Zimisces himself made the first overtures, which were accepted; Gero, archbishop of Cologne, was charged to repair to Constantinople, at the head of a solemn embassy, to conclude the treaty of alliance. The youthful princess, who inherited the name and the beauty without the vices of her mother, Theophano, reached Rome on the 14th of April, A. D. 972, accompanied by a splendid escort. John XIII. celebrated her union with Otho II., then bestowed upon her the diadem and the title of Augusta. Theophano shed honor on the German throne to which she had thus been allied. And now was realized the constant dream of Charlemagne, the union of the two empires of the East and West. John XIII. did not long outlive the event which seemed the prelude of happier days for the Church. He died on the 6th of September, A. D. 972, after a pontificate of seven years.

§ IV. PONTIFICATE OF BENEDICT VI. (September 22, A. D. 972—March, 974).

14. The death of John XIII. was the signal for a new series of calamities and disorders in the Church. The election of the Sovereign Pontiff again became a subject of dispute among factions. Benedict VI. was raised to the chair of St. Peter, on the 22d of September, A. D. 972. The emperor Otho died soon after, on the 7th of May, A. D. 973. The wisdom of his administration; his vigor, which was maintained as steadily as the jealous pride of the great vassals of the empire would allow; his glorious feats of valor; all his imperial and Christian virtues, have deservedly won him the title of Great. He was succeeded by his son, who had already been crowned emperor. The seditious spirits in Rome received the tidings of the emperor's death as a signal of deliverance. Crescentius placed himself at their head, seized upon Benedict VI. and imprisoned him in the castle of St. Angelo, where he was stran-

gled (March, A. D. 974). This calamitous age, in which the
Papacy was at the mercy of popular passion, seemed to have
put on the character of the heathen persecutions which made
the pontifical chair a throne of martyrdom.

§ V. PONTIFICATE OF DONUS II. (April 5, A. D. 974—October, 975).

15. The name of Donus II. figures for a moment on the list
of pontiffs in the midst of these dissensions and bloody strifes.
The piety and virtues of Donus would have graced the Papal
chair in better days. His reign lasted but a few months, if we
may trust the somewhat doubtful chronology of contemporary
historians. When the Pontiff died, Otho II. and his mother, the
empress Adelaide, wished to secure the vacant see to St.
Mayeul, abbot of Cluny, whose exalted merit seemed to them
suited to heal the lamentable troubles of the Roman Church.
The holy abbot unhesitatingly replied: "I wish to die as I
have lived, in poverty and obscurity." They used the mediation of bishops who entreated him to undertake the noble task.
After a long time spent in prayer, to discover the will of God,
St. Mayeul answered, in a tone which left no room for hope:
"I am far from possessing the qualities necessary for the gov-
ornment of the universal Church; but I think myself, if possible, less fit to rule the Romans. There is a far greater distance
between their manners and mine, than between the countries
which have given us birth." This refusal, which could not be
overcome in St. Mayeul, must be viewed as perhaps the most
wonderful trait in all his history. A touching proof of his ascendency over the mind of the youthful emperor was afforded
soon after. The ambition of favorites and flatterers, jealous of
the influence of the empress-mother, had labored so successfully
to sow dissensions between her and her son, that the holy
princess was soon afterward compelled to withdraw to the
court of her brother, Conrad, king of Burgundy. This was a
source of affliction to all good men; and St. Mayeul, resolving to
put an end to the fatal separation, sought out the emperor at

Pavia. The holy abbot, with touching energy, represented to the emperor the duty of honoring his mother, and especially such a mother. Otho was moved to tears, and, falling on his knees at the feet of St. Adelaide, promised to be henceforth a most tender and devoted son. The reconciliation was sincere and lasting. St. Adelaide, the wife, mother, and grandmother of the three first Othos, became the living oracle of her illustrious family. She guided and supported the pious resolutions of her daughter-in-law, Theophano. Wholly detached from all earthly goods, she seemed to be the nurse of the poor; and public gratitude bestowed upon her the title of *Mother of the Kingdoms*. The pious empress died in 999.

§ VI. Pontificate of Benedict VII. (December 19, a. d. 975—July 10, 984).

16. Benedict VII. had hardly ascended the Papal chair, when Franco, one of the murderers of Benedict VI., had himself proclaimed antipope, under the title of Boniface VII. His partisans were numerous among the seditious Romans, who ranked him as one of their leaders. Backed by their arms, he plundered the treasury and costly furniture of the Vatican, and indulged in the worst excesses. The speedy outbreak of public indignation drove him to seek safety in flight by sea to Constantinople.

17. At the time of his arrival there, the Eastern empire was threatened by a formidable barbarian invasion. A hundred thousand Rurikschs, pouring down from their icy Scythian wastes, covered the Golden Horn with their countless vessels. Zimisces, whose courage, talent, integrity, and public-spirited devotion would have made him worthy of the crown, had he not purchased it at the cost of crime, led his legions in person against this swarm of barbarians. He inflicted upon them a loss of forty thousand men, and drove them back to the banks of the Borysthenes. The Rurikschs buried themselves in the solitude of their immense steppes, where the light of Christian

faith was soon to reach them, and·lead them on to new and splendid destinies. This still savage people was called, by its arms, its commerce, and political genius, to become one of the most formidable powers in the world; and in our own day we have seen the Ottoman empire of Constantinople tremble before its threatening advance. Zimisces returned to his imperial city in triumph; but his glory could not shield him from the ingratitude of a traitor. One of the eunuchs whom he had loaded with favors, poisoned him on the 10th of January, A. D. 976. Basil II. and Constantine VIII., sons of Romanus the Younger and Theophano, ascended the throne together, and reigned simultaneously.

18. Thus did the East hurry on in the career of crimes and revolutions which ever hastens the downfall of empires. The West, as we have already seen, presented a lamentable scene of disorder and anarchy; yet between the two situations there was a wide difference. In Constantinople, a succession of emperors, each the murderer of his predecessor, eunuchs assassinating their imperial masters, a base and dégraded standard of character ready to bow before every successful crime, every crowned ambition, are but the symptoms of a civilized decline—an irreparable evil. In the West, new nations, in the effervescence of yet untamed passions, are carried away by the energy of a half-savage nature : this is the crisis which precedes the maturity of our modern society; the long and painful labor which is to bring forth the great deeds of succeeding ages. This view is justified by the religious barrenness of the East; while the West, with its fulness of vital power, gave to the world wonderful fruits of holiness and virtue, in the midst of the general confusion and corruption of the age.

19. Prominent in the ranks of this generation of saints, struggling against the destructive tide of vice and bad example, was St. Dunstan, archbishop of Canterbury. In ascending the episcopal throne left vacant by St. Odo, he brought all the virtues of the apostolic ages to adorn the first see in England. Ho

induced King Edgar to inflict severe punishments upon the ministers of the Church who dishonored their profession by incontinence, or lowered its dignity by a passion for hunting, by
secular traffic, or meddling in secular affairs, by seeking lucra-
tive offices or earthly gain. By this noble and prudeut discipline, he so enhanced the dignity of the ecclesiastical vocation
in England, that the most illustrious houses rejoiced to see
their children embrace it. The kingdom was cleared of robbers, perjurers, parricides, sacrilegious and seditious characters,
and infamous females. The hand of the saint gave the first
impulse and the finishing stroke to all these good works; and
his firmness fully equalled his activity and benevolence. King
Edgar, forgetful of the religious principles he professed, had
been guilty of the scandal of seizing a virgin consecrated
to God. St. Dunstan, filled with bitter grief, presented himself to the guilty monarch, who rose at his approach and extended his hand, as usual. The archbishop drew back. "What!"
he exclaimed, "would you dare, with your hand stained by
impurity, to touch the hand consecrated by the immolation of
Mary's Son? Think not to conciliate the *friend of the bride-
groom* by the flattering marks of your affection; I reject the
friendship of the enemies of Jesus Christ!" Edgar believed
his crime unknown. Struck as by a thunderbolt, he fell at the
saint's feet, acknowledged his fault, and did canonical penance.
To compensate for the scandal he had given, the king, in a
council held at Winchester, gave his sanction to the measures
most proper for the repression of disorders among the clergy.
"To me God has given the sword of Constantine," said the
king, in his address to the bishops, "but to you He has confided that of Peter : let us join them together to purge the house
of God of the crimes which dishonor it." Then turning to St.
Dunstan, in particular, he said to him : "Here are Ethelwold
of Winchester, and Oswald of Worcester, who will courageously
second your efforts. To all three I leave my royal authority,
that by its union with the episcopal power, you may free the
Church from scandalous priests, and give their places to edify-

ing ecclesiastics." St. Dunstan and his fellow-workmen, the two bishops designated by the king, proved themselves worthy of the royal confidence. The illustrious prelate of Canterbury died at an advanced age, on the 29th of February, A. D. 992.

20. At the same period, a holy priest, sprung from one of the noblest houses of Savoy, devoted himself to the most painful labors of evangelical zeal, founding establishments which still bear his name, and whose public usefulness has been acknowledged by the voice of impiety itself. St. Bernard of Menthon, archdeacon of Aosta, moved to pity at the ignorance which prevailed among the inhabitants of the Alps, the majority of whom were still heathens, devoted himself with dauntless and unwearied zeal to their conversion. He enlightened them, and destroyed the idols which still remained upon the peaks of the steepest rocks. The man of God did not stay his charitable zeal within these limits. He had often witnessed the dangers run by the German and French pilgrims on their way to Rome. Amid the snows and glaciers of the Alps, he founded, for their convenience, two convents, which are now celebrated throughout the world for the generous hospitality extended to all travellers over the Great or Little St. Bernard. The zealous founder also carried the light of faith into several cantons of Lombardy where it had not yet shone. After making many conversions here he went to Rome, to obtain the pontifical approval for the religious institute charged with the care of the two Alpine convents. St. Bernard of Menthon died at a ripe old age, with a rich store of good works attached to his name.

21. Another glory of the tenth century was unfolding itself, unseen, save by the eye of God, in the cloistered shades of Gandersheim (in the present kingdom of Hanover). Roswitha, a simple and modest religious, whose name and literary works, so long buried beneath the dust of the monastic libraries, have lately been brought to light and hailed by the admiring criticism of the nineteenth century, was born about the year 940.

---

* The works of Roswitha, or, more, properly, Hroswitha, were published at Nuremberg in 1501, and at Wittemberg in 1717. The translation of the *Theatre* of this humble religious,

Without quitting her pious retreat, she learned Latin, Greek, the philosophy of Aristotle, music, poetry, and the liberal arts. Her only instructors were two nuns of the same monastery. Would not even the golden age of Louis XIV. have gloried in this literary prodigy, when it could so extol the learning of Madame de Sévigné, because she read St. Augustine in the original, and gave a reputation to Mother Angélique Arnaud, of Port Royal, because she understood the Latin of her breviary? The gifted nun of Gaudersheim never saw her undiscovered learning crowned with the light of glory; the poetry of her heart was breathed out like the wasted sweetness of the desert flower. Her poems relate to subjects of two very different classes—history and drama. The first category comprises: 1. *The Panegyric of the Othos*, of which the materials were gathered from oral, and, in some sort, confidential accounts; it forms a kind of private memoir of the ducal and imperial family of Saxony. 2. A *History of the Blessed Virgin Mary*. 3. On the *Ascension of our Lord*. 4. *The Passion of St. Gendulf*, commonly known as St. Gengoul. 5. *History of St. Pelagius of Cordova*. 6. *The Fall and Conversion of St. Theophilus*. 7. *History of the Passion of St. Denis the Areopagite*. 8. *History of the Passion of St. Agnes, Virgin and Martyr*. In the preface to this volume of poems, Roswitha thus expresses herself: "The style of this little work will doubtless be found wanting in elegance, but it has at least received the zealous care of the author. I have been obliged to work in my solitary retreat, deprived of literary resources, and still far from the age of maturity. My only aim, in fact, has been to save from the rust of inaction the poor talent intrusted to my care. I have endeavored, with the hammer of devotion, to draw from it some few harmonious sounds to the praise of God." Roswitha's dramatic pieces, composed for religious, and intended to be represented by them, are devoted to the triumphs of virginity. "I have tried," she says, "according to the powers of my feeble mind,

presented to the literary world by M. Magnin (1845), has called attention to this too long neglected monument of literature and true poetry.

to replace the pagan passions, which dishonor the profane drama, by the triumphs of the Christian heroines, the chaste spouses who are admitted to the *nuptials of the Lamb*." These pious dramas, seven in number, are written in running verse, in the style of Terence. The lonely nun of Gandersheim thus used her talent for the edification of her sisters, never dreaming that her poetic inspirations were at a future day to stamp her name with literary immortality. She was far more ambitious of the endless glory of heaven.

22. The pontificate of Benedict VII. ended on the 10th of July, A. D. 984. Contemporary historians are silent as to the details of his reign. May we not hope from this, that, unlike its stormy predecessors, it passed away in peaceful quiet? The Pope had been preceded to the grave by Otho II., in 983. Though but twenty-eight years of age, this prince had already given proofs of a precocious cruelty, which would, perhaps, have eventually outweighed the pious solicitude of his mother, St. Adelaide.

§ VII. Pontificate of John XIV. (October 18, A. D. 984—August 20, 985).

23. John XIV.* ascended the Papal throne just as the sceptre of Otho II. had passed into the hands of Otho III., a child of three years. The Papacy had now but a feeble champion, and the factious Romans seized the occasion to renew their disorders. John XIV. had been chancellor to Otho II.; had that prince still lived, he would have speedily crushed all seditious movements. The antipope, Boniface VII., hurried from Constantinople to Italy, to turn the current of events in favor of his ambitious views. He headed the rebels, seized upon the person of John, confined him, as he had done Benedict VI., in the castle of St. Angelo, and left him there to die

---

* John XIV., before his promotion, bore the name of Peter Cassavnova. Through respect for the Prince of the Apostles, he changed his name of Peter, which none of the Popes have ever borne

of hunger and neglect (August 20, A. D. 985). He then inaugurated his usurped power by arms and violence; but the hour of vengeance was not far off. He became the victim of a popular storm. His dead body was pierced with lances, dragged by the feet through the streets of the city, and left in a state of nudity on the Capitol Square, before the equestrian statue of Marcus Aurelius (December, A. D. 985).

§ VIII. PONTIFICATE OF JOHN XV. (December, A. D. 985—December, 985).

24. John XV. did not even sit upon the blood-stained throne of his predecessor. He died within the month of his election, even before his consecration.

§ IX. PONTIFICATE OF JOHN XVI. (April 25, A. D. 986—April 30, 996).

25. The accession of John XVI. to the pontifical chair corresponds to a change of dynasty in the kingdom of France. The Carlovingian race had long been under tutelage. The more vigorous blood of Robert the Strong had already produced three generations of heroes: Eudes, Hugh the Great, and Hugh Capet. The latter, under Lothaire (954–986), and Louis *the Sluggard** (986–987), really exercised the royal power. The death of Louis the Sluggard, a death shrouded in the gloom of mystery, left Charles, the brother of Lothaire and son of Louis d'Outre-Mer, the last representative of the Carlovingian family. As uncle of the last king, Charles should, in regular order of inheritance, have succeeded to the throne of France. But he had sworn fealty, as duke of Lower Lorraine, to Otho III., emperor of Germany. When he put forward his claims to the crown, he received this answer from the French

---

* History has preserved to Louis V. the epithet of *Sluggard*, (Fainéant—*nihil fecit*); but the shortness of his reign allowed no proofs of the fitness or injustice of its application.

nobles, then in solemn assembly at Noyon: "In renouncing your nationality to become the vassal of a foreign prince, you have, by a stronger reason, forfeited all your natural rights to the throne." This was no doubt a mere pretext. The real motive was the influence of Hugh Capet, upon whom all were accustomed to look as sovereign. He was unanimously proclaimed king, and crowned on the 8d of July, in the church of Rheims, by the archbishop, Adalberon. A short struggle between the French hero and his rival, Charles of Lorraine, decided the question in favor of the former. The house of Charlemagne had ceased to reign.* The Capetian dynasty was established. "Hugh Capet," says Guizot, "was raised to the throne by no general league or cabal. He took the name of king; few of the nobles were disturbed by the act, since their influence suffered no detriment from it; they had long since ceased to trouble themselves about the royal power. Hugh Capet was at first recognized by his own vassals, who could but gain by the elevation of their Suzerain; the various feudatory lords, gradually won by his concessions and promises, successively acknowledged the superior title he had assumed; and this was the whole Capetian revolution. Since the death of Charlemagne, feudalism had subjected society; by his assumption of the royal title, one of its chief members proclaimed himself its leader, thus acquiring, for the time, a new dignity rather than actual power. The feudal republic was but prospectively threatened, and certainly entertained, as yet, no fear of coming danger. Never was revolution more insignificant in its action; never, when accomplished, more fruitful in great results."† Religion suffered no harm from this revolution. It began, on the contrary, to recover, in France, its ancient lustre and youthful vigor. The kings of the third race gave back to the government the nerve and energy which keeps

---

* The descendants of Charles of Lorraine held the landgraviate of Thuringia until 1248, and the county of Hohenstein, in Hartz, until 1593, at which period the race of Charlemagne finally died out.

† M. GUIZOT. *Essai sur l'Histoire de France*, p. 85: 1823.

peace and order in the Church, while securing the safety of the
State. This line of princes, so worthy to rule, who for eight
centuries kept the empire within their own family, and by its
very duration—the longest by far of all the dynasties—endeared
it to the hearts of their subjects; these fathers of the people
and dutiful children of the Church were worthy models for the
other sovereigns of the West.

26. A political revolution had just ended in the north of
Europe, with results far less favorable to the Church. Swein,[*]
son of St. Harold, king of Denmark, had taken up arms against
his father. The aged monarch, defeated and wounded in a
bloody battle, was forced to fly for shelter to Sclavonia, where
he died soon after (A. D. 980). Swein promised the heathens
who would help him in his parricidal enterprise, to restore the
worship of idols; and he kept his word. The most violent
persecution was opened against the Danish Christians. But
reverses softened the heart of Swein. Twice defeated by the
Sclaves, and driven from his states by Eric, king of Norway,
when he again ascended the throne (A. D. 990), he restored
the Christian religion, and under its auspices once more found
happiness and victory. The Russians now saw their savage
wastes illumined by the light of faith. Wladimir was their
first Christian chief. This duke—for such was still the title of
those sovereigns, who were, at a later day, to raise so high
the name and power of the czars—having seized, in 988,
the city of Chersonesus, in Tauris, announced to the Greek
emperors, Basil II. and Constantine VIII., that he would march
upon Constantinople, unless they granted him the hand of their
sister, the Princess Anna. The Court of Constantinople, terrified by the threat, acceded to the demand, on condition of
Wladimir's conversion to Christianity. Anna was thus the
angel of peace sent to soften the savage nature of the Russian
prince. Wladimir received baptism, and, on his return to Kiew,
his capital, destroyed all the idols in the empire. Unwilling

---

[*] Sueno, or Swein, in the Swedish tongue, means *warrior*.

to use too much violence toward his subjects, or to force their acceptance of a new worship, which many rejected, Wladimir adopted measures for their enlightenment. The pious works which had been translated into the Sclavonic dialect by Sts. Cyril and Methodius, in the ninth century, were certainly known to the faithful in Kiew. But the number of the believers was small, and the pagan population remained in their original state of ignorance. Wladimir founded public schools for the young men, in which the liturgical language was taught. This good work was then deemed a tyrannical innovation. Mothers might be seen weeping the lot of their children forced to learn *"that dangerous art of writing, invented by sacrilegious magicians."* Thus literature entered Russia, hand in hand with the religion of Jesus Christ. Since the days of Wladimir, the Russians have two languages—the vernacular, and the learned, ecclesiastical, or liturgical language. The Code which bears his name, the Poem of Igor, and the Russian romances of chivalry which appeared in the reign of Wladimir, were written in the common Russian dialect. The learned tongue, of which a dictionary was published at Moscow, in 1704, by order of Peter the Great, is the dialect of Thessalonica, with a mingling of Illyrian and Sclavo-Servian. This is the idiom of the liturgical works and of the Chronicles of the monk Nestor, the father of Russian history. But, having received the Christian faith under the auspices of Constantinople, Russia was doomed to share the schism of Michael Cerularius. The daughter would not prove truer than the mother to Catholic unity.

27. A belief was gaining ground in Constantinople, favored, doubtless, by the troubles and discord of this unhappy epoch. Popular superstition thought them the forerunners of the world's dissolution, announced by the Gospel, and it was everywhere believed that Antichrist was to appear in the year '1000.* The approach of the much dreaded millenary cycle contributed to alarm the already fearful minds. St. Abbo,

---

* St. Abbo testified that he had, in his youth, heard the doctrine preached in Paris.

abbot of Fleury (St. Benedict-upon-Loire), undertook to comfort his contemporaries. His learning and piety, which had
induced St. Oswald, bishop of Worcester, to call him to England
for purposes of monastic reform, gave him additional authority
and credit. St. Abbo is the author of a Collection of the
Canons and Decrees of the Councils (A. D. 992), a work held in
the highest esteem.

John XVI. assembled a council at Rome (A. D. 993), to
proceed to the canonization of St. Udalric, bishop of Augsburg, whose death had occurred in 973, twenty years before.
After the reading and discussion of the life and miracles of
Udalric, the Pope pronounced judgment, in these words: "The
memory of the holy bishop shall henceforth be honored with
piety and devotion in the Church, since the honor we show to
the relics of martyrs and confessors, the servants of God, is
given, in their persons, to Jesus Christ our Lord. And if any
one dare to oppose this privilege, or transgress what we order
for the glory of God and the honor of St. Udalric, we anathematize him by the authority of the Prince of the Apostles, whose
seat we occupy." This is the first historical mention we find
of a solemn canonization. Hitherto, each bishop used the
faculty in his own diocese; but from this period the court of
Rome has restricted this right to itself, to prevent the abuses
that might creep into a proceeding of so much importance
(A. D. 993).

28. The following year is made memorable by the death of
St. Wolfgang, bishop of Ratisbonne, who was remarkable for
his zeal in reforming the monasteries of his diocese, infected
by the prevailing contagion of the tenth century—relaxation
and corruption. The holy bishop used to say: "Had we but
monks, the rest would not fail us." When he was answered
that their number was already too great, "Of what avail," he
said, "is a holy habit without a saintly life? Fervent monks
are angels; relaxed religious are but very devils!" His last
days were consoled by the restoration of strict canonical discipline among his clergy and religious (A. D. 994).

Pope John XVI. did not long survive St. Wolfgang. He died in the same year with Hugh Capet, king of France (A. D. 996).

§ X. Pontificate of Gregory V. (May 19, A. D. 996—February 18, 999).

29. As Pope John XVI. ended his earthly career in Rome, the emperor Otho III., who had just reached his majority, was on his way to Italy, where he wished to receive the imperial diadem. He was met at Ravenna by the deputies of the Roman clergy, who acquainted him with the death of the Pope. The thought occurred to Otho, that by choosing a successor to the Papal throne from the imperial family of Germany, the bond of union between the two powers would be materially strengthened. He accordingly cast his eyes upon his nephew Bruno, a young cleric of extensive literary acquirements,* and proposed him to the suffrages of the Romans. The youthful candidate was unanimously elected, though but twenty-four years of age, and promoted to the Apostolic See under the title of Gregory V. He was the first German Pope. The new Pontiff crowned his uncle emperor, in the church of St. Peter, on the Feast of the Ascension, A. D. 996.

30. The presence of Otho had restrained the factions which never failed to disturb Rome at the election of a new Pontiff. As soon as the emperor had returned to Germany, Crescentius, whose name we have already had occasion to record in connection with the most bloody revolutions, headed a band of revolters, expelled Gregory V., and caused the election of the Greek, Philagathos, as antipope, with the title of John XVII. (A. D. 997). On learning the news of the sedition, Otho III. recrossed the Alps, met Gregory V. at Pavia, and marched with him toward Rome. The antipope sought to

---

* Bruno was familiar with the German, Latin, and Italian tongues—three languages most useful to a Sovereign Pontiff at that period.

escape punishment by a hasty flight; but he was overtaken by
the imperial officers sent in pursuit of him; they cut off his
nose and tongue, burned out his eyes, and threw him into a
dungeon, where he atoned for his ambition by a wretched death.
The holy solitary, St. Nilus, who dwelt upon a desert rock in
the mountains of Calabria, obtained leave to bring the consolations of religion to the imprisoned antipope. The holy hermit
opened the eyes of the captive's soul, and showed him, in
another world, a throne far above all earthly greatness. In
the very midst of these sad strifes, these deadly struggles,
Christian piety still treasured up for the victims of human passions a store of resignation and hope. Crescentius, the author
of the revolt, was seized, after a stout resistance, in the castle
of St. Angelo, and beheaded by the emperor's order (A. D. 998).

31. Gregory, once more settled in the quiet possession of
the Holy See, could give his active attention to the general
administration of the Church. Robert the Pious, who succeeded Hugh Capet on the throne of France, had lately married the princess Bertha, daughter of Conrad, king of Provence
and Burgundy-Transjurana, whom he loved most passionately.
The close relationship existing between the king and Bertha,
constituted an invalidating impediment to the union. But
passion is blind; and, in spite of his sincere attachment to the
Church,—which won for him his surname,—Robert the Pious
did not stop at this obstacle, but accomplished his design. In
the very bosom of a people trained to the deepest veneration
for the laws of the Church, the scandal was immense. Gregory
V. acted in the case with unyielding firmness, and resolved to
break off this incestuous connection. Robert sent St. Abbo of
Fleury, with orders to solicit from the Sovereign Pontiff a delay
"necessary," pleaded the king, "to make suitable provision for
a princess allied to the most powerful families of the French
kingdom." This was, in fact, but the temporizing policy of a
passion powerless to overcome itself. The Pope granted a
short respite; but as the king continued to put off the final
separation, Gregory called a council in Rome to examine the

question and pronounce judgment (A. D. 998). The sentence was withering to Robert. "King Robert," said the decree, "shall put away his relative, Bertha, whom he has married in contempt of the canon laws. He shall perform a penance of seven years, according to the discipline of the Church concerning incestuous marriages. If he refuse to submit, let him be anathema! Archibald, archbishop of Tours, who pronounced the nuptial blessing, and all the bishops present, are suspended from Catholic communion until they have come to make reparation to the Holy See." The pontifical censure was immediate in its effects; the French at once broke off all commerce with their excommunicated prince.* But two attendants remained with him, and even they were careful to purify by fire every thing that was used by the king. Robert yielded at last; his piety triumphed over his love. He put away Bertha and married Constantia, daughter of William, Count of Arles and Provence. The reign of the prince, after this generous sacrifice, was marked by a long succession of good works. He built as many as fourteen monasteries, among others, those of St. Aignan and St. Vincent, in his native city, Orleans; that of St. Germain-en-Laye, and one at Poissy. His piety was unusually fervent. He spent the nights before Christmas, Easter, and Pentecost, in watching and prayer. From Septuagesima to Easter he slept upon the bare ground, and spent the whole of Lent in devotional pilgrimages. He was assiduous in his attendance at the offices of the Church, and with a devotion foreign to our modern ideas, but in perfect harmony with the

---

* Gregory V. is charged with having thus placed the kingdom under interdict. This is a misunderstanding. The Pope, bound to guard the observance of the canons, did but his duty. He warned, he begged, he waited; at length, following the decision of a council of twenty-eight bishops, he pronounced the nullity of the marriage and the canonical penance then attached to such unlawful unions. The sentence did not deprive Robert of his crown; and the French people, whose faith was then so fervent, did not cease to regard him as their king. But by refusing to hold relations with a prince under the censures of the Church, they compelled him to bow to a law as binding upon him as upon the meanest subject in his realm; by his submission he gave a bright example to the whole nation, and, on this point, the disorder was at an end. Far from throwing blame upon any one, in this circumstance, it must be allowed that each one did his duty—the Pope, the people, and the king.

notions of his day, he sang in the choir, wearing a cope, and sceptre in hand. He is said to be the author of the response found in some Gallican breviaries : *O Constantia Martyrum.* Queen Constantia, who had no knowledge of Latin, had asked him to write some verses in her praise. She felt quite flattered at hearing her name, never suspecting the innocent irony of the former husband of Bertha.

32. Less consoling was the issue of the disorders of Bermudo II., king of Leon. After forsaking his lawful wife to marry another, the king still continued an incestuous concubinage with the two sisters. The Moors were made the instruments of the divine vengeance. Mohammed-Almanzor, grand vizier of Issem and caliph of Cordova, led a formidable army against the city of Leon, which he took, after a year's siege, and levelled to the ground (A. D. 990). Then, entering Portugal, he devastated the land with fire and sword, pushed on into Gallicia, took the city of St. James of Compostella, which he gave up to pillage (A. D. 997). The disastrous days of the first Saracen invasion seemed to have returned to Spain. The stern teaching of misfortune was not lost upon Bermudo ; he found in reverses the hereditary energy of his race. He rallied the few warriors who had remained true to his cause, joined them to those of Garcia, king of Navarre, and of Fernandez, Count of Castile, and defeated the grand vizier in the celebrated battle of Calatanazor (in Old Castile), by which the Saracens lost all their late conquests. Almanzor was hurried by despair to an untimely grave (A. D. 998).

33. Gregory V. died in the flower of his age (February 18, A.D. 999).* With his pontificate ends the sad epoch of the tenth century. It has often been said that nations are like individuals : they pass through all the phases of human life; their rise is slow and laborious; and at their meridian they shed abroad

---

* The profound erudition of Gregory V., his virtues, and his great qualities of mind and heart, merited for him the name of Gregorio Minore, or Gregory the Less, in allusion to St. Gregory the Great, whose virtues were truly revived in him.

a lustre proportioned to their energy and to the greatness of
the obstacles they have had to overcome; at last they wane,
until the hour of the final catastrophe. The Church of
Christ, thrown into the great human mass, like leaven into
the dough, has undergone, in the course of its history, the various political changes of Society. It has also been carried
through those states of transition of doubtful issue for nationalities, of which the solution is left to the future. Such
is the nature of all things human: darkness goes before the
light; the night precedes the dawn. The tenth century was
one of those gloomy periods which jeopard the existence and
the after-fate of society ; its record forms the saddest, darkest,
most lamentable page of modern history. The humanizing impulse given to the world by Charlemagne, seemed on the point
of dying out. The degenerate heirs to his immense empire had
allowed their heritage to be rent in their hands. They were
borne down by the torrent, which they did not even attempt to
resist; the dynasty of Charlemagne was replaced by that of
Hugh Capet. The Papacy, now the sport of rival factions, was
forced to struggle at once against the claims of sovereigns or
their onerous protectorate, against the encroachments of bishops, against ignorance and corruption, both clerical and monastic, and the native barbarity of new races. The little remaining
life of the social body could be discerned only by the force of
its convulsions. But the Papacy triumphed over the horrors
of this deep night, and was the first to break forth from its
heavy gloom, far ahead of all the other powers. A space of
nine centuries intervenes between Charlemagne and Louis
XIV. But one century separates St. Nicholas I., the Great,
from Sylvester II., the learned predecessor of the heroic St.
Gregory VII. The Capetian dynasty, taking its seat upon the
French throne, inflicted a blow upon the preponderance of the
German empire, from which it never recovered. Gerbert, in
ascending the pontifical throne, assumed, in history, the high
rank which the Papacy was to keep until our own day. ' The
Church stands erect over the cradle and the tomb of nations,

and directs their destinies. From the lofty eminence of her immortality, she sees them rise and fall at the foot of the rock upon which she has been founded by the Almighty Hand of God.

CHAPTER VIII.

HISTORICAL REVIEW OF THE FOURTH PERIOD.*

1. Moral and political state of the world during the Fourth Period of the History of the Church.—2. The clergy.—3. Rome and the Papacy.—4. Slanders of Luitprand against the Popes of this epoch.—5. Elements of good; examples of learning and holiness during the Fourth Period.—6. Conclusion.

1. The appearance of Charlemagne at the opening of the fourth period is like a flash of lightning between two storms. The dark night of ignorance, dispelled by the bright splendor of his reign, settles down again behind him with thicker gloom. Alcuin, Hincmar, Rabanus Maurus, Eginhard, Paul the Deacon, Ratramnus, Amalarius, Prudentius of Troyes, and Usuard, all pass away and leave no successor behind them. No one comes forward to raise the fallen sceptre of science and refinement, just as none of the great emperor's heirs was able to hold with steady hand the helm of the empire. Ignorance and barbarism once more swept the world; and though this twofold character does not equally apply to every part of this period, though it has often been exaggerated by passion and malignity, yet it cannot be denied that the tenth century, compared with those which preceded and followed it, presents a truly sad and afflicting sight. With the exception of a few solitary seasons of quiet and peace, under the influence of certain rulers more firm and able than the others, we behold on all sides a society without order, government without strength, laws without authority, the deepest moral depravity. The hopes excited by the reign of Charlemagne were soon blighted by the weakness of his successors, the abuses of the feudal system, and the

* A rapid glance will suffice, after the detailed narrative of events.

renewed inroads of the Normans, Saracens, and barbarians into all parts of Europe. This disastrous combination of events threw back society into the barbarism from which it had just begun to emerge; and nothing can be more lamentable than the picture of the disorders to which the world was doomed from the reign of Charlemagne to the pontificate of St. Gregory VII. For the reign of Sylvester II. was, so to speak, but a breathing-spell, in which the Papacy, under the guidance of a great Pontiff, resumed its influence and prepared the way for the resurrection of order. But the thorough restoration dates only from the pontificate of St. Gregory VII. "The world," said St. Peter Damian, "is madly rushing into the bottomless abyss of all wickedness, and the nearer it approaches to its end, the more enormous grows the mass of its iniquities. Ecclesiastical discipline is almost entirely unheeded. Priests no longer receive the respect due to their dignity, the sacred canons are trodden under foot, and the earnestness which should be devoted to the service of God, is wholly given to the pursuit of worldly gain. The lawful order of marriage is overturned, and, to the disgrace of the Christian name, men live in it like Jews! What state is now free from fraud and robbery? Who now blushes at the guilt of perjury, impurity, sacrilege, and the most fearful crimes? We have long since forsaken all virtue, and disorders of all kinds everywhere abound. Some evil genius is hurrying on the human race into a gulf of crime, everywhere sowing the seeds of hatred and jealousy, the sources of dissension. Wars, armies, hostile inroads, are multiplied to such an extent, that the sword is now more destructive than the infirmities and diseases attached to the condition of humanity. The whole world is like a sea upheaved by a storm; dissensions and discord, like angry waves, disturb all hearts. The fearful crime of homicide appears everywhere, and seems to overrun all the land, to reduce it to a state of dreadful barrenness."

2. The clergy, it must be confessed, was not always at the height of the mission intrusted to it under circumstances so

fatal. The bishops were not, until the sixth and seventh centuries, chosen from among the barbarous nations. Taken from the ranks of the conquered, trained to Roman studies and discipline, they proved themselves worthy of their charge as civilizers and apostles. But when the barbarian element was admitted into the sanctuary, it brought in with it that warlike spirit and turbulent disposition which called for the vigorous measures adopted by the various councils against it. This disorder was increased by the disturbance attendant upon the manner of elections. Temporal sovereigns assumed this right, while seemingly faithful to the canonical form which required that the bishop should be chosen by the bishops of the province, and the clergy and people of the episcopal city. This was the period which saw the episcopal throne disgraced by the unbridled passion of boys of fifteen; "prelates," says a contempory writer, "whom the master's rod had better suited than the bishop's crosier." The wealth of the clergy, and the rank of nobility which it procured them, were another fruitful source of abuses. So true it is that the very best things have their mingling of evil too! The bishops too often forgot their divine character of pastors of souls, to attend to their part as great vassals and feudal lords. The decline of studies and its natural result, the neglect of the holy canons, swelled the destructive flood, and, to crown all this fearful train of evils, the Papacy, given up like a plaything to the caprices of a few Italian tyrants, lacked the firmness and influence to stay the fatal course of events.

3. We have dwelt long enough upon the sad state of Rome and of Italy at this period. The great imperial unity established by Charlemagne had fallen to pieces when his own mighty arm no longer supported it. To all the reproaches uttered by history against the weak and unhappy Louis the Mild, we must add the blind tenderness for his unworthy children which parcelled out the territory of the empire. Every province then became a seat of war amid the ambitious views of pretenders. Political divisions, wholly arbitrary and without grounds in the

manners of the various countries, gave rise to endless struggles
The wars of succession were multiplied for each fraction of territory; and while princes were contending for shreds of provinces, the Saracens, Normans, and Magyars were pouring over
their boundaries on the North and South. The absence of a
strong and respected imperial power left the Popes defenceless
against the brutal violence of the Tuscan dukes and the Italian
nobles disputing for influence in Rome. We have but too
often been called to record its fatal consequences. The authority of the Sovereign Pontiffs, outraged by those cruel and
bloodthirsty princes, was no longer exercised with freedom,
energy, and unrestraint. Their reign, often shortened by a
violent death, was too ephemeral to allow of great results.

4. We have pointed out the source of the calumnies heaped
upon the character and private morals of some of the Popes of
this period. Some, even of the most reliable historians, have
received them upon the testimony of Luitprand—a passionate,
and therefore doubtful author. However that may be, it must
be borne in mind that the infallibility of the Sovereign Pontiffs,
in matters of faith, could not suffer from their vices or personal
failings. The firm and dignified bearing of the Holy See, in the
case of the Photian schism, was that of a power determined to
command respect for the spiritual authority intrusted to its
care. The zeal of the Popes was rewarded by the return of
unity. The restoration of the empire, under Otho the Great,
was another deed of lofty policy, brought about by the Popes
of the tenth century. Thus, if the Papacy shared the common
lot of society, in this period of decay, it was yet the first to
shake off the universal lethargy and degradation.

5. Moreover, to do justice to an age so generally decried, it
must be admitted that all the elements of good, every virtuous
principle and germ of holiness, had not entirely disappeared.
According to the judicious remark of Monsignor Palma, we
have now, for the truer appreciation of that period, monuments
unknown to Cardinal Baronius, when he painted the tenth cen-

tury in such gloomy colors.* Ratherius, bishop of Verona, tells us that in his time the ecclesiastical schools of Verona were in a flourishing condition, training up a great number of young men in the knowledge of canon law and sacred literature. Atto of Vercelli was establishing institutions of the same nature in his own diocese. The congregation of Cluny, under its holy abbots, Benno, Odo, and Mayeul, spread the taste for pious studies and the example of religious discipline throughout all the monasteries of the West. Muratori has published a catalogue of the books in the monastery of Bobio, in the tenth century, which shows the zealous care of the religious to preserve both sacred and profane authors from oblivion. The Vatican library employed twenty-three librarians at the same period, and all equal to their scientific mission. We have mentioned, in their place, the holy bishops of Gaul, Germany, and Great Britain, whose example preached so loudly against the general corruption of the age. We have spoken of the literary and scientific prodigy of the convent of Gandersheim, the blessed Roswitha, whose writings are as remarkable for pure and elegant diction as for richness and grace of ideas.

6. In fine, to resume in a word our own view of the fourth period of the history of the Church, we look upon it as a period of labor, in which all the elements, religious, political, and intellectual, mingled and blended together, prepared, by their fusion, the splendor and glory of the thirteenth century.

---

* "Sui asperitate, ac boni sterilitate ferreum, mali exudantis deformitate plumboum, inopia scriptorum obscurum."—BARON., *Annales ad ann.* 900, No. 1.

www.ingramcontent.com/pod-product-compliance
Lightning Source LLC
Chambersburg PA
CBHW022123020426
42334CB00015B/737